RAGE FOR FAME

Clare Boothe Brokaw
Pastel by Cecil Beaton, 1933

RAGE FOR FAME

THE ASCENT OF

CLARE BOOTHE LUCE

SYLVIA JUKES MORRIS

RANDOM HOUSE NEW YORK

Library of Congress Cataloging-in-Publication Data

Morris, Sylvia Jukes.
Rage for fame : the ascent of Clare Boothe Luce / Sylvia Jukes Morris.
p.   cm.
Includes bibliographical references and index.
ISBN 0-394-57555-5 (hc)
1.Luce, Clare Boothe, 1903–1987.   2.Ambassadors—United States—Biography.
3.Legislators—United States—Biography.   4.Dramatists, American—20th century—Biography.
5.Journalists—United States—Biography.   I. Title.
E748.L894M67   1997
973.91'092—dc20   96-43084
[B]

Random House website address: http://www.randomhouse.com/
Printed in the United States of America on acid-free paper

24689753

First Edition

For Pauline

You're a great woman . . . Would that I could write
as you do. There's a story properly told that
would become legendary in history.
—DAVID BOOTHE TO HIS SISTER, CLARE, 1945

CONTENTS

PROLOGUE. 3

1   LITTLE DECEPTIONS. 15

2   THE QUEST FOR SOOTHING SHEETS. 29

3   BIG PEARLS AND SMALL HIPS. 43

4   THE MOST CONCEITED GIRL IN THE SCHOOL. 49

5   SOME INNER COMPULSION. 58

6   DAMAGE TO THE BONE. 68

7   AN INDESCRIBABLE LONGING FOR ROMANCE. 74

8   BOILING WATER OF THE HOTTEST. 84

9   CLIMBING HIGH, HIGH. 99

10 A PATH OF WHITE MARBLE. 110

CONTENTS

11 EARTHLY DESIRES. 115

12 UNNOURISHING NETTLES. 126

13 THE LOVELIEST MATRON. 140

14 CUPID'S GRAVEYARD. 154

15 A BIBELOT OF THE MOST ENCHANTING ORDER. 161

16 CHANGING TIMES. 176

17 BARNEY BARUCH'S GIRL. 191

18 A WELL-CONSTRUCTED FAÇADE. 211

19 FAILURE IS IMPOSSIBLE. 222

20 EVERYBODY'S AND YET NOBODY'S. 232

21 COUP DE FOUDRE. 242

22 UPROARIOUS BREASTS. 264

23 MOON-MINDED MAN. 281

24 LUCES THE MAGNIFICENT. 296

25 KISS THE BOYS GOOD-BYE. 313

26 PORTRAIT OF A SUICIDE. 326

27 MARGIN FOR ERROR. 340

28 THE DETERMINING CONDITION. 357

29 PROVEN MATERIAL. 365

30 EUROPE IN THE SPRING. 369

31 THE DAVID PROBLEM. 389

32 RABBLE ROUSER. 393

Contents

33 THE CANDOR KID. 406

34 WINGS OVER CHINA. 413

35 "SIR CHARLES". 421

36 BOMBED INTO GREATNESS. 434

37 THE ROAD TO MANDALAY. 449

38 THE MOST ABLE WOMAN IN THE UNITED STATES. 459

APPENDIX. 475

ACKNOWLEDGMENTS. 479

ILLUSTRATIONS. 485

BIBLIOGRAPHY. 489

NOTES. 493

INDEX. 545

RAGE FOR FAME

Henry Luce and Clare Boothe on Broadway, *1935*

PROLOGUE

W

The theatre is an incredible refuge for an

unhappy child. —Moss Hart

On December 26, 1936, Clare Boothe's three-act satiric comedy *The Women* opened at the Ethel Barrymore Theater on Broadway, before a capacity audience and an astonishing array of some fifty critics and ten talent scouts.

Among the usual contingent of New York society figures was a battery of theatrical and literary élite: the celebrated Miss Barrymore herself, Irving Berlin, Gloria Swanson, Billy Rose and his wife Fanny Brice, Clifton Webb squiring Libby Holman, Max Gordon, the show's producer, the historian Mark Sullivan, and Moss Hart, who, with George S. Kaufman, was rumored to have helped polish the play out of town.[1]

Mysteriously absent from this assemblage of regular first-nighters was the diaphanous blonde wife of *Time* publisher Henry Luce. She was missed in particular because she was the evening's playwright. Having dined with family and friends, Clare Boothe Luce had ascended to—of all places—the top of the Empire State Building, in order to brace herself in solitude and reflect, not only on the performance about to begin thirteen blocks north but on the real-life drama that had brought her to this point.[2]

Just a year before, her play *Abide With Me* had flopped disastrously at the Ritz. It was a melodrama based on her first marriage, at twenty, to George Tuttle Brokaw, an alcoholic millionaire more than twice her age. In words that were burned on her brain, one critic had written, "Its lovely playwright, who must have been crouched in the wings for a sprinter's start as the final curtain mercifully descended, heard a cry of 'author,' which was not audible in my vicinity, and arrived on stage to accept the audience's applause just as the actors . . . were properly lined up." A sheaf of other negative reviews—one even in *Time*—not to mention boos in the audience, had made Clare swear never again to attend her own opening nights.[3]

The evening was unseasonably warm. Fog curling off the Hudson River blotted out lights on the George Washington Bridge and veiled the upper reaches of Manhattan. There, on the fringes of Spanish Harlem, she had been born thirty-three years before, the illegitimate daughter of a traveling salesman and a beautiful twenty-year-old "typewriter."[4]

Friends knew little about Clare's childhood, but memories of its squalor and mendacities were painfully vivid to her, try though she always had to surmount them.[5] As she stood now in her 102nd-floor eyrie, looking out over the glittering metropolis to Forty-seventh Street, where her name was up in lights, it struck her that "none of the ants on the street had ever heard of me."[6] Unless they could be made as sure as she was of her own worth, fame, so ardently sought, might be fleeting.

Clare's ambitious mother had always encouraged her drive and taught her how to dissemble and manipulate men. "Don't talk heavy stuff too much. Let them all tell you how blue the eyes are and golden the hair. But never let them see what makes the wheels go round."[7] Anna Clara Schneider's fantasies of a theatrical career had been dashed after her teenage seduction by William Franklin Boothe. She had then pursued them vicariously, wangling Clare a job as understudy to Mary Pickford, and later a part in an Edison movie.

Pretty as the adolescent girl had been, with her pale gold hair and Bavarian blue eyes, she was not a natural actress. Professionals consistently beat her at auditions. She had shown more talent for stagecraft, mounting an adaptation of *Cinderella* when she was only fifteen. Upon graduation from high school, she had been undecided whether to become an actress or a dramatist. "I simply was certain I'd be one or the other."[8]

Ambitions notwithstanding, she had allowed herself to be distracted by marriage, motherhood, and divorce, then by a brief but heady career in journalism. In just three years, Clare Boothe Brokaw had risen from caption writer at *Vogue* to managing editor of *Vanity Fair*, one of the most beautiful magazines in the world. She had followed these achievements with a syndicated news column. But her congenital hunger for applause had brought her back to writing plays. Not that much applause was forthcoming. *Abide With Me* had closed after only thirty-six performances, and a collaborative script with Paul Gallico remained unproduced.[9]

After marrying Henry Luce she had hoped for a place on the staff of *Life*, her husband's new weekly photojournal. But having suggested both its name and its idea, she found herself barred from participation in its runaway success. Luce's male editors were adamant that they would not accept her in any executive position at Time Inc.[10]

Enraged by their masculine bias, and the gender in which she felt imprisoned, Clare had taken herself off in the spring of 1936 to a West Virginia resort and in three days written a play packed with "the most brutal gossip" she had heard in beauty parlors, exercise studios, and fashion showrooms. She simply gathered together, in her imagination, groups of rich East Side women and Fifth Avenue shopgirls and, as she later put it, "set them to talking, and let it run."[11]

With the help of her former lover Bernard Baruch, who spoke of Clare Boothe as the best female intellect he knew, she had sold *The Women* to Max Gordon. He had immediately shown the script to Moss Hart and George Kaufman. They were impressed enough with the play's potential to invest in it.[12] Clare, having lost money on *Abide With Me*, cautiously refused to back her own work again. Undeterred, Gordon budgeted $70,000 for lavish sets and costumes, and brought in the eminent Robert B. Sinclair to direct an all-female production—the first in Broadway history. More than two thousand actresses had fought over its forty roles. Now *The Women* faced its fate before the most demanding audience in the world.

Clare's worry, just before the curtain rose on the consummation of her two childhood ambitions, was that her play might be perceived as trivial entertainment, rather than as a serious comedy of manners. Would lines composed in the heady mountain air of West Virginia, and recomposed at tryout time in the mists of Philadelphia, sound witty and pungent enough for New York's sophisticated tastes? Should she have included some fashionable leftist political rhetoric? Intellectuals were bound to find *The Women* lightweight, compared with the social reformism of Clifford Odets's *Waiting for Lefty* or Eugene O'Neill's evocations of frustrated desire in *Strange Interlude*.[13]

There was also the question of commercial competition. All the forty-carat diamonds of the American theater seemed to be sparkling that winter night. Within a few blocks John Gielgud was wooing playgoers with his sonorous interpretation of *Hamlet*, Alfred Lunt and Lynn Fontanne were polishing their partnership in Robert Sherwood's *Idiot's Delight*, and Margaret Sullavan was bewitching the Music Box in *Stage Door*, by George Kaufman and Edna Ferber. *You Can't Take It with You*, by Kaufman and Hart, had just opened brilliantly at the Booth. Katharine Cornell was starring in Maxwell Anderson's *The Wingless Victory*, Tallulah Bankhead in George Kelly's comedy *Reflected Glory*, Helen Hayes in Gilbert Miller's presentation of *Victoria Regina*, and Ruth Gordon in Wycherley's *The Country Wife*. A rotating series of short plays by Noel Coward, entitled *Tonight at Eight Thirty*, was filling the National, with the author and Gertrude Lawrence in the leading roles. George Abbott's production of the Rodgers and Hart musical *On Your Toes* featured Ray Bolger, and Beatrice Lillie and Bert Lahr were billed in Vincente Minnelli's revue *The Show Is On*. Crowning all these productions in longevity was Jack Kirkland's adaptation of Erskine Caldwell's *Tobacco Road*, in its third year.[14]

How could a fledgling playwright take wing in such illustrious company?

Backstage at the Barrymore, under glaring work lights, the cast of *The Women* viewed the audience as an enemy to be won over.[15] Dressers made last-minute adjustments to one hundred winter outfits designed by John Hambleton. (Spring, summer, and fall wardrobes would be needed in the event of a long run.) Twenty-seven stage technicians checked twelve scene settings by Jo Mielziner, while the props manager kept tabs on fifteen hundred feminine accessories, from lipsticks to a working bubble bath. The latter was going to require deft operation in Act Three. Four pails of water, mixed with special Swedish soap, would have to be pumped electrically for fifteen minutes in order to sustain foam around a naked actress through six minutes of dialogue.[16]

Out front in the auditorium, the atmosphere was cozy, even clubby. "Angels" in their top-price $4.40 seats looked optimistic. At two minutes to go a final bell summoned stragglers from the lobby and lounge. With twenty seconds left, the houselights dimmed to half power, then darkened.[17]

The curtain rose on a haze of cigarette smoke over four fashionable women playing bridge in a Park Avenue apartment. Ilka Chase, glossily feline as Sylvia, rasped across the footlights, "So I said to Howard, 'What do you expect me to do? Stay home and darn your socks? What do we have money for? Why do we keep servants?'"

"You don't keep them long, God knows," Jane Seymour replied.[18]

Her character, a sharp-tongued writer named Nancy, was, according to backstage rumor, Clare's alter ego. The game proceeded with more tough badinage, punctuated by the snapping of cards.

Men in the audience began to have the uncomfortable feeling they were snooping on a private female ritual—indeed, becoming almost voyeurs when Phyllis Povah, playing an obviously pregnant Edith, rose from the table in nausea.[19] "Morning sickness! I heave the whole darn day. This is positively the last time I go through this lousy business for any man!"

She rushed offstage, only to return a few moments later and disgustedly pick up a sandwich. "Watercress. I'd just as soon eat my way across a front lawn."

The laughter that followed this line was uneasy. Miss Boothe's humor seemed as crude as her observation was surgical.

"I think Mary's gone off terribly this winter," Sylvia said, changing the subject. "Have you noticed those deep lines, here?" She gestured at her mouth.

The women began discussing their hostess, Mrs. Stephen Haines, who had yet to appear. Nancy accused Sylvia of being jealous of a contented woman. "And what are you, pet?" Sylvia wanted to know.

"What nature abhors," Nancy retorted. "I'm—a virgin—a frozen asset."

This was the kind of breathtakingly mordant line that, out of town, had caused both men and women to hiss Clare's dialogue. Provincial audiences were not used to self-mockery.

When Peggy, the fourth cardplayer, acted by Adrienne Marden, wished aloud that she "could make a little money writing," Nancy sniffed, "If you wrote the way I do, that's just what you'd make."

An expensively dressed party from Time Inc. laughed loudly. One woman gushed, "Isn't it wonderful?" Her escort's reply, clearly audible in adjoining rows, was an example of the corporate chauvinism still frustrating Clare. "Well, with the entire staff of *Time*'s rewrite men at her disposal, why shouldn't she write a good play?"[20]

Margalo Gillmore entered as Mary. *A lovely woman in her middle thirties*, the stage directions read. *She is what most of us think our happily married daughters are like.* Her opening lines were deliberately bland. The audience had yet to feel Clare's contempt for Mary as a complacent wife and mother—one who would be humiliated and then toughened beyond recognition by the evening's end.

In a stage whisper, out of Mary's earshot, Sylvia retailed to Edith the latest item of beauty parlor gossip. Stephen Haines was having an affair with "a blonde floosie." Sylvia had it on the best authority: the woman who did her nails.

When Mary placidly remarked that Stephen would be working late that night, Sylvia pounced. "Are you sure it's *work*, darling?" Playing with her prey, she started talking about a "wonderful new manicurist" whose colors Mary should try. She extended her fingertips for all to admire. "Jungle Red."

Nancy quipped, "Looks as if you'd been tearing at somebody's throat." But Mary simply laughed.

"Jungle Red . . . I'll remember that." Cutting the cards, she said, "I feel lucky today."

The Women, original Broadway production
Margalo Gillmore, Jane Seymour, Phyllis Povah, Ilka Chase,
Adrienne Marden

"*Do* you, darling?" Sylvia smirked. "Well, you know what they say, 'Lucky in cards—' " The curtain fell.

A hair dryer hummed at the beginning of the second scene, as Mary kept her recommended appointment. The gossipy manicurist, not knowing who she was, revealed—as Sylvia intended—that Mr. Stephen Haines was keeping a Saks Fifth Avenue perfume salesgirl named Crystal Allen. Stiff with shock, Mary rose from her chair, leaving the Jungle Red unapplied.

A quick scene shift to the Haines apartment showed Mary's mother, in the person of Jessie Busley, advising patience while Stephen's affair ran its course. He was "tired of himself" after twelve years of marriage and needed rejuvenation. "Time comes," she added, in a line of delicious *double entendre*, "when every man's got to feel something new."

There followed a scene of coincidence, as Mary and Crystal, played by the blonde Betty Lawford, stood in neighboring booths of a dress-maker's salon, unaware of each other. Sylvia, vastly enjoying Mary's fall from complacency, barged in to announce that Stephen had taken his small son and daughter to lunch with his mistress. (Crystal, meanwhile, was distracting men in the audience by trying on a negligée.) Then Mary learned from a saleswoman that her rival was next door and rushed out to confront her. "I won't have you touching my children!"

As they shouted at each other, the curvaceous "floosie" made it plain she was determined to steal Stephen for good. "The longer you stay in here, the more confident I get . . . Mrs. Haines, you are a hell of a *dull woman!*"[21]

Clare, alone in her distant observatory, could only estimate the time of the first intermission and imagine the comments of playgoers in the Barrymore lobby. Had she been able to stroll among them, she might have been encouraged, if not flattered, by the general reaction. Women reveled in the bitchy dialogue. Men were titillated by what they had seen, yet disillusioned by what they had heard. Billy Rose snarled half-humorously at Fanny Brice, "I didn't know what I married, and I'm going to kick you right in the teeth."[22]

One tall man in gray remained in his seat, where he had brooded throughout. He was still there when the second act opened, to the sound of tango music in an Elizabeth Arden exercise salon. Bare thighs arched and buttocks rotated on wadded pink satin mats. Between gyra-tions, Edith confessed that she had leaked details of the dressing-room confrontation to a gossip columnist.

"I told her that Mary *smacked* the Allen girl!"

"Edith!"

"Well, that's what Sylvia told me!"

"I didn't!"

"You did, too!"

This was as much as the man in gray could stand. He pushed his way to the aisle and strode toward the exit, saying in a clearly audible voice, "It stinks!"[23]

Richard Lockridge of the *New York Sun*, meditating on his review, felt that Miss Boothe knew altogether "too many sabre-toothed tigresses" and "lived in an atmosphere of rather exaggerated dread." Mark Sullivan had similar thoughts, albeit more personal ones. He knew Clare well and loved her as both a woman and a creative mind. But he had never guessed at the extent of her familiarity with scandal-mongering bitches and shopgirls. She must have had "some hard experiences."[24]

Almost thirty years her senior, Sullivan worried about Clare prostituting her talent with distracting antics such as legs cycling to a Victrola. He must write and remind her that an Ibsen would not compromise important dialogue with visual gimmicks. All the same, Sullivan had to confess that he had never seen "such sustained brilliance" on any stage. "You might like it or not, but you were bound to look at it."[25]

Moss Hart, too, felt ambivalent. His initial reaction to Clare's script had been excitement. He thought it "stood the best chance" of any play he had seen in years. Now for some reason he found himself liking it less. In years to come, when *The Women* was still playing after hundreds of stagings around the world, he would revise his opinion yet again.[26]

Further autobiographical elements were plain toward the end of Act Two, at least to those who knew the story of the author's divorce from George Brokaw. Mary, disregarding her mother's advice, had gone to Reno to get a decree. Also improbably waiting for decrees were Peggy, Sylvia, and an ex-chorine who wanted to marry Sylvia's husband.

There was a hair-pulling, leg-biting catfight onstage between Sylvia and her usurper. In the midst of it, Mary received a call from Stephen. He wanted to confirm that he would be marrying Crystal. Clare's dramatic limitations were apparent as Mary cried out, "Oh, God, why did this happen?" and "It's not ended if your heart doesn't say so." Slowly, the houselights went up.

The final act of *The Women* began with the new Mrs. Haines provocative in a black marble bathtub, bubbles up to her chin, smoking a cigarette. She complained to her maid about having to say good night to

Little Mary, Stephen's daughter, who had come for a visit. "He's tried for two years to cram us down each other's throats."

The telephone rang. Crystal reached out energetically—to the horror of the stage manager, who noticed "there weren't any bubbles left where they should have been."[27] Little Mary (an obvious portrait of Clare's own child by George Brokaw) drifted in, and it soon became apparent to both child and audience that Crystal was hearing from an intimate acquaintance called "Buck." Mark Sullivan, shocked that his angel-faced Clare could portray sexual duplicity so convincingly, once again felt serious moral questions were being overshadowed by extravagant effects.[28]

In the penultimate scene, Mary heard from her returning daughter all about the "lovey-dovey" telephone conversation. At the mention of the name Buck, she deduced that Crystal was sleeping with the husband of one of her own friends. This news, plus Little Mary's "I think Daddy doesn't love her as much as you any more," encouraged her to confront both Crystal and Stephen with evidence of the former's two-timing.

Clare's climactic scene was set in what was, for men, the most revelatory sanctum of all: the ladies' room of a nightclub patronized by all the major characters. Here Crystal, coming in to powder her nose, found herself entrapped by Mary. While she vainly protested her faithfulness to Stephen, Nancy took the opportunity to slip out for a quiet word with someone offstage.

A message came back: "There's a gentleman called Mr. Haines. He says he's been waiting a long time for his wife—" Crystal reached for her wrap, only to be deflected by Mary. "Tell him *I* am coming."

"You are just a cat, like all the rest of us," Crystal snarled.

"Well, I've had two years to sharpen my claws," said Mary, gaily waving a manicured hand. "Jungle Red . . . Good night, ladies!"

The applause that followed the final curtain was too stunned to be overwhelming. Clare had long since descended from her tower, but she felt no need to join the cast backstage, having already sent each actress a bottle of champagne. Since it was Saturday night, there was no point waiting around for reviews: they would not appear until Monday. What mattered, for the next thirty-six hours, was word of mouth. Would the "ants" want to see her play? She could not be sure. So much in her life had turned sour when things seemed to be going well. Her mood, as she returned to her East Side apartment, was something less than optimistic.[29]

Outside the Barrymore, Sidney Whipple of the *World-Telegram* lingered to eavesdrop as patrons departed. He was particularly interested in the comments of Clare's own sex. "So true, so faithful, so delightful!" "Why, I know a woman—you know her, my dear—exactly like—"[30]

"The most amazing thing about it," Whipple would write, "is the cheerful feminine reaction to a comedy that ought actually to blister the ladies in their tenderest regions . . . They applaud the most brazenly cynical utterance. They delight in dissection. They may even take notes for their personal use."[31]

Professional critics had mixed feelings about *The Women*. John Anderson of the *New York Evening Journal* called it "glittering, smart, hard, laughable, fascinating, heartless, and repulsive." Douglas Gilbert of the *World-Telegram* found himself despising "these best-bred hellcats and social filth mongers" with their "ermined smut." The play was "provocative," he had to admit, but "poisonous." Brooks Atkinson approved its portrayals of "unregenerate worldlings" but disliked it overall. Richard Watts of the *New York Herald Tribune* was unsure whether he objected more to its cynicism or its sentimentality. Mary Haines seemed "hardly a person at all" but "merely a kind of symbol representing Miss Boothe's idea of the lost purity of American womanhood." But he left the theater convinced that *The Women* would "make a million dollars."[32]

Other theatregoers headed home. Louis Sobol, a columnist from the *Evening Journal*, told his wife he had seen a play about a classy woman who had lost her husband to "a broad," only to take him back.

"How silly of her," said Mrs. Sobol. "I wouldn't . . . I'd never be sure after that. It's all right to forgive—but don't ever believe a woman can forget."[33]

1

LITTLE DECEPTIONS

We are born into the world, and there is something within us
which, from the instant we live, more and more thirsts
after its likeness. —PERCY BYSSHE SHELLEY

Anna Clara Schneider gave birth to her second illegitimate child in a second-floor apartment at 533 West 124th Street, in an all-white, middle-class neighborhood of New York City, on March 10, 1903.

The birth certificate, signed by George A. Leech, M.D., recorded this date and gave the baby's name as "Ann Boothe." It stated that her father, William Franklin Boothe, a "salesman," was forty-one and, incorrectly, that he had been born in Illinois. Her mother, misidentified as "Anna Clare Boothe" and said to be twenty-five, was, in fact, not William's wife, and was four months short of twenty-one.[1]

These little deceptions, which seemed to have no purpose, unless to conceal bastardy, proliferated as the child grew. She soon became "Ann Clare" and for inscrutable reasons was encouraged to celebrate her subsequent birthdays a month late. This pretense would continue throughout her life. When, at the age of eighty-two, she was asked about it, she furtively explained, "Mother always said I was born on Easter Sunday. Besides, those born under the sign of Aries are always lighthearted and gay." She clung to the myth even when informed that April 10, 1903, was actually Good Friday, and that her true astrological sign was Pisces.[2]

Why did she persist, to the point that the wrong date would be chiseled on her tombstone? Was it just because her mother insisted upon it? Did she really see herself as "lighthearted and gay" when she was often melancholic? Did she ever ponder the coincidence that her father had been born on that date in 1862—and not in Illinois but in Poolesville, Maryland?[3]

Booming sounds of gunfire accompanied William Franklin Boothe's entry into the world, for his place of birth was "debatable land" in the Civil War, an area crossed and recrossed by the armies of both sides. Poolesville was repeatedly shelled, and during these bombardments Sarah Rebecca Deaver Boothe would take her firstborn to the safety of the cellar until the cannonading stopped. Thrown together in a constricted environment, mother and son forged a close bond. She would later attribute her son's tempestuous, unpredictable personality to the turbulence of his early days.[4]

The Reverend John William Thomas Booth (records show that he spelled his name without an *e* at this point) had been assistant pastor at Poolesville Baptist Church since October 1861. His main duty was teaching in the parochial private school, where the curriculum covered all subjects from the three Rs to Neoplatonism. He was a man who lived almost entirely in his mind. After William's birth he wrote in his diary: "Studied Greek for one hour, read Latin for ¾ hour. Read 22 pages of 5th book. Retired at nine."[5]

According to his son Edward, he was a striking figure, "finicky about the cut of his jacket," and a crisp, energetic speaker much in demand as an itinerant preacher at sister churches. In one year he delivered 61 sermons, made 171 visits, distributed 1,050 tracts, and proudly reported "an increasing interest in spiritual concerns" on his circuit. But by 1864 "Brother John" was so war-weary, and in such poor health from his constant travels, that he resigned his pastoral post and moved north to study at the College of Rhode Island.[6]

Meanwhile, William was growing into a handsome, curly-headed boy, with such gracious manners that mothers sought him out as a playmate for their daughters. He charmed adults, his brother Edward later recalled, with his "Yessum to the ladies, no sir to the men, an' when companee is present never pass your plate for pie agin." Sarah Boothe favored William within her growing family (there would eventually be four boys and six girls), indulging his whims and eccentricities. In turn, he loved her without condition.[7]

By the mid-1870s the Boothes had moved to Lafayette, Indiana. Here it was even more apparent that their oldest offspring was no ordinary youth. He was especially gifted in music, languages, and athletics, and his sisters had to admit that he excelled them in crochet. Edward insisted that William was a genius, with "all the concomitants of the type," and compared him with Dryden's

> . . . man so various that he seemed to be
> Not one, but all mankind's epitome!

Yet to his father, William was not faultless. The studious cleric doubted that the multitalented boy would settle into any one discipline. Indeed, there was something restless, even unstable, about his brilliance. In 1876, at fourteen and a half (the usual age was fifteen), he was admitted to Purdue University's preparatory academy for students of superior ability.

He excelled at history and was able to remember and cite all the contrasted characters in Plutarch. With an ease that flabbergasted math teachers, he gave quotients in arithmetic, and was a meticulous scholar in English grammar, Latin, and German. In his first year, he received all A grades, yet he failed to show up for subsequent examinations two years in a row.[8]

William enrolled in the Cincinnati College of Music (later to merge with the Cincinnati Conservatory) shortly after its opening in 1878, and studied violin with the eminent Professor S. E. Jacobsohn. There is, however, no record of his graduation. In the early 1880s he worked for a while in Dakota Territory at Shurtleff's ranch, where he rivaled the wiriest cowboys in "busting out bad range horses without pulling leather" and mastered Brulé Sioux, conversing for hours with White Buffalo men. From out West, he sent lavish gifts of silk stockings, fur coats, hats, and muffs to his family. One cousin remarked that "Billy" had such a generous nature "he could never hold onto his money," and accurately prophesied that he would "die broke."[9]

Though he was reluctant to stay in any place or job for long, there was nothing of the dilettante about William Boothe. When he competed, Edward said, he did so "with professionals." He looked frail as a youth, but he had prodigious muscular strength and was a fearless fighter. Once he boxed to a draw Arthur Chambers, who afterwards fought Dominick McCaffrey, a rival of John L. Sullivan. He became a crack marksman with both revolver and rifle, taking third place in an Adirondack contest against the prize shots Ross Hays and Ezra Bruce. As a powerful long-distance swimmer—he could cover five miles with ease—he entered a race from Wilmington to Penns Grove, New Jersey, and came a close second to the champion, Friday Pearson. He was also an expert yachtsman and navigator.[10]

Outstanding as he was at sports, he cared for none as much as music. Although he could neither dance in step nor hum a tune, he played the piano with verve and skill, and at the age of twenty published two concert études, one of which, in octaves, was frequently performed in its time. But his real gift was for the violin. He made a special trip to Europe to study with Eugène Ysaÿe and returned with a fully developed, professional bow technique. His rendition of Bach's *Air on a G String* reportedly "made the goose flesh come." Yet an innate reticence prevented him from performing in public, and he never realized his own dream of the concert platform.[11]

One possible reason for failing in this ambition was William Boothe's irresistible appeal to women. Outgoing and exceptionally attractive, with a shock of dark hair, bushy brows, broad chin, and sensuous mouth, he made conquests easily. The fact that he was free from personal vanity made women "crazy about him," Edward said. Because he had a loving heart, he could not reject their advances. Only when they discovered he cared more for music than for money did they flee in tears or anger.

In spite, or perhaps because of his inability to handle the opposite sex, William Boothe would acquire no fewer than four wives—three legal and one common-law. In his early twenties, he married Isa Hill, a blue-eyed beauty with hair "yellow as taffy after much pulling." Apparently she had a disturbed personality and passed out of his life "as suddenly as she had entered it—and as stormily."[12]

Soon afterwards William was back East working as a piano salesman for the Philadelphia company of Heppe, Ramsdall and Dearborn, and courting Laura Olivia Brauss, a pretty, ambitious young woman whom he married in New Jersey on November 7, 1886. They settled in Philadelphia, where William opened a piano and organ store at 1416 Chestnut Street.[13]

William Boothe (*top of steps, center*) with Laura Brauss and his family, *1889*

Piano sales had been soaring since the 1850s, and the instrument was now the most desired parlor status symbol—America's "household God," in Charles Dickens's words. To promote his own merchandise in a highly competitive field, William invested in cooperative advertisements of coming attractions at the nearby Opera House and Theater, even brazenly adding his own logo to a silk picture of the actor Edwin

Booth. (The latter was no relation, and his fame was a sore trial to Edward, who was nicknamed after him. Tradition has it that the Reverend John Booth had taken an extra *e* after Lincoln's murder, to disassociate himself from the notorious John Wilkes Booth.)[14]

Sales flourished, and William won recognition as one of the most colorful and innovative figures in the piano world. He adopted new methods of manufacturing as well as distribution, and was a pioneer marketer of the four-foot-ten-inch baby grand. But with his success came a longing for wider horizons. As the Gay Nineties began, he was drawn to New York, the center of his trade and of American social and cultural life. By 1892 he had wound up his Philadelphia enterprise and transferred to the metropolis as a piano salesman. Here, according to Edward, his marriage disintegrated, and he began a documented relationship with the beautiful Teresa Carreño, one of the greatest pianists in history.[15]

During the last decade of the nineteenth century, large piano factories in New York had begun to produce as many as five thousand pianos a year. Added to these were countless others made by "cottage" manufacturers working in lofts. The axis of the retail piano trade was Union Square, with Steinway Hall on Fourteenth Street and Chickering Hall on Eighteenth. Spurred by phenomenal demand, department stores started advertising pianos for "five down and five per month." Wanamaker's sold 265 instruments in a single day, and lured experienced salesmen with lucrative commissions. Impeccably dressed in long-tailed cutaways, these experts gave such gentlemanly imprimatur to the product that even the most reluctant customers were persuaded to buy. Other salesmen took to the road as "piano ambassadors," impressively dressed in bell-crowned silk hats and carrying silver-topped canes.[16]

William Franklin Boothe was at first a beneficiary and then a casualty of this piano fever. In his first six years in New York, he worked for various firms, including the prestigious Sebastian Sohmer. He then organized the Gibson Piano Company for himself, and the Milton Piano Company for his brother Edward.[17] As an entrepreneur with large ambitions, he resumed selling under his own name around the turn of the century. He is listed in a 1901–02 city directory as "Boothe, William F., pianos 207 E. 49th and 503 Fifth Avenue., home 205 W. 56th." In subsequent volumes the listing is dropped, and he appears to have taken a job with a short-lived concern called the American Piano Company, as "President and travelling salesman."[18] From then on his fortunes steadily declined. It is possible, as Edward suggested, that William suffered because his marketing ideas were too advanced for the times. But a more likely reason is that in the spring of 1901 he met his nemesis in Anna Clara Schneider.

The gorgeous eighteen-year-old of German extraction was small and slim, with violet eyes, perfect pearly teeth, a mass of chestnut hair, and great expectations. William was smitten. "When I met your mother," he would write Clare near the end of his life, "I had a big, prosperous factory. She was the sole cause of my losing it . . . her ambition and twenty-five years [sic] difference in age tells the whole story."[19]

The fatal meeting took place "over a wine table," in one of Broadway's popular restaurant-nightclubs frequented by men-about-town and their female counterparts. Thickly painted and powdered chanteuses wearing provocative costumes sauntered from table to table singing risqué songs of the day:

> I can see that you are married
> And you know I'm married too
> And nobody knows that you know me
> And nobody knows that I know you.[20]

Eroticism and alcohol stimulated the natural chemistry between William and the ravishing Anna. By late June she was pregnant—a devastating predicament for an unmarried girl of poor but respectable parents.

John Schneider was the son of Bavarian Lutheran immigrants who, with thousands of his countrymen, had come to America in the mid–nineteenth century to escape famine and revolutionary upheaval in the Old World. Narrowly provincial, these Lutherans settled in close-knit groups on the Lower West Side of Manhattan, clinging to their German-style clothes and German-language newspapers, eating

Anna Clara Schneider, c. 1900

Westphalian ham and sauerkraut, drinking lager in *Biergartens*, and marrying within the faith. The less well-educated often led lives of acute poverty, as they searched for jobs in workshops and warehouses along the waterfront.[21]

Around 1881 John married Louisa Weber (also a second-generation immigrant) and moved into an apartment at 437 West Forty-first Street, in a part of town known as Hell's Kitchen. Their accommodation was a tenement building of five or six stories, housing as many as seven families in tiny rooms with poor light and worse sanitation. Here Anna Clara was born on August 29, 1882.[22]

Her mother was then twenty-two, her father a twenty-year-old butcher destined never to escape his lower-class origins. Before his premature death, John Schneider would also work as a laborer, coachman, driver, and livery-stable foreman. Of his subsequent three children, all would die young.[23]

Anna, the sole survivor, was determined to escape the ghetto before disease threatened her. But that was more easily dreamed than done. In 1900 she was still living with her parents, and working as a letter copyist. The Schneiders had now moved to 353 West Thirty-seventh Street, a short walk to the glitter of Broadway, where Anna could exercise her fantasies of a more privileged life.[24]

"Mother told people that her father was the youngest son of an impoverished Austrian noble," Clare wrote half a century later in "The Double-Bind," an incomplete and patently autobiographical novel. "[She] could spin lies the way a spider spins a web. We were all entangled in them for years."[25]

The stark reality of unmarried pregnancy in 1901 was far removed from Anna's imaginary world of life between silk sheets with a rich, good-looking man. She lay now in a bed of a more mundane kind, from which she might never advance—unless she could rid her womb of its unwanted occupant. That she was indeed so desperate is again suggested in Clare's novel. A mother is talking to her daughter about self-abortion.

> Getting rid of a baby once it starts to grow is a very hard and dangerous thing to do. I tried to get rid of your brother. I stuck a knitting needle up there, trying to poke a hole so he could fall out. I was going to put him in one of your father's cigar boxes and throw him in the garbage can. I stopped, of course, because it hurt so. There's really no safe way, always remember that, except to have a doctor cut it out of you when it's very small.

When the woman's daughter asks, "Did you also try to get rid of me?" she replies, "No, I knew better then. And there wasn't enough money for a doctor."[26]

A witness to Ann's predicament in January 1902 was Walter B. Craighead, a former president of the Milton Piano Company. One night he caught sight of Billy Boothe at Shanley's Restaurant downtown, trying to comfort a distraught female companion.[27]

Craighead went over and was introduced to a now Anglicized "Ann Snyder." She appeared to be about six months pregnant. As the two men talked, drank, and smoked, Craighead noticed that she grew more and more "excited," repeatedly asking what was to become of her after the child was born.

At midnight, William, unable to face Ann's emotional outpourings alone, invited Walter to his apartment in the Criterion Hotel, at the corner of Broadway and Fortieth Street. The suite consisted of a parlor, bedroom, and bathroom. After putting on a wrapper, Ann, still hysterical, lay on a sofa while William tried to calm her. By three o'clock she had exhausted herself, and Craighead, also worn out, left.

Two months later, William Boothe telephoned Craighead from Toronto. He asked him to honor a draft for $100, take it to an apartment at West Eighty-first Street and Columbus Avenue, and give it to a "Mrs. Franklin," saying he would be home in a couple of days. On March 30, Ann Snyder gave birth to a boy, and registered him as "David Franklin."[28]

Shortly after this, the American Piano Company went out of business, and William appears to have quit the music retail trade for good. He quickly found other work, and by the time Clare was born in 1903 (exactly one year after David), William Boothe and Ann Snyder were living in the solidly respectable environs of Upper Manhattan.[29]

"When I came into the world," Clare would recall as an old woman, "it was the horse-and-buggy, wood-and-coal-burning, gas-lit, ice-chest, pump-handle, out-house and tin-bathtub era . . . The prevailing smells were wood smoke, coal dust, gas, horse manure and human waste."[30]

Her father's new job was that of a patent-medicine salesman for the Bromonia Company. Though still married to Laura Brauss, he began introducing Ann as "Mrs. Boothe." This led to bizarre complications. When he was on the road, he had his salesman's paycheck split in half and sent to two Mrs. Boothes, one of whom, a colleague recalled, lived "somewhere up in Harlem."[31]

At three o'clock in the afternoon of March 17, 1906, William was working at his office in the Fuller Building on Broadway when a law clerk representing Laura came in and handed him a divorce summons emblazoned in red ink. The document stated that "between the first day of November 1901, and the first day of March 1906, at the Criterion Hotel . . . and at 533 West 124th Street . . . and at 272 West 127th Street and at divers other places in the city of New York and elsewhere, the defendant committed adultery with divers persons whose real names are unknown to this plaintiff." Confirming that she had not "cohabited with the defendant" since 1901, Laura requested that their marriage be dissolved and the defendant ordered to pay her an allowance, as well as the costs of the action.[32]

At a hearing on August 17, 1906, William Boothe denied all accusations of adultery. Nevertheless, it was established, on the testimony of Walter B. Craighead, that he had indeed "had carnal intercourse and connection" with Ann Snyder at the Criterion Hotel. On December 19, the judge granted Laura her divorce with costs and alimony of fifteen dollars a week. The decree would become absolute in four months, after which the plaintiff, as the wronged party, could remarry. But, in accordance with local law at that time, her former husband would have to remain single in New York State, "until the said Laura O. B. Boothe shall be actually dead."[33]

H. G. Wells, visiting America in 1906, found New York City "lavish of everything . . . full of the sense of spending from an inexhaustible supply." But Ann Snyder had no part of its rich promise that summer. Shunted off to Rockaway Beach in Queens, she felt the ostracism afforded a common-law wife, as well as the stigma of illegitimacy attached to her children. William, beleaguered by his divorce proceedings and the strain of selling patent medicines, joined her whenever he could and, with what energy he had left, threw himself into the task of amusing David and Clare.[34]

"He was devoted to them," Edward Boothe recorded, "but it was a selfish love . . . the desire to possess them, mould them, subject them to his discipline, and stamp into their natures the values which he deemed essential."[35]

To William's chagrin, neither child showed any talent for music. Hoping Clare might at least have inherited his love of swimming, he tossed her one day into the Atlantic.

"Come on, baby," he called out, "you can make it if you try. Daddy's waiting for you." The terrified three-year-old splashed and spluttered her way into his outstretched arms. "A great, pale, emerald wave folded over me," she remembered ever after. "Then I felt my father pluck me from the wave, laughing and comforting me at the same time, and saying, 'Don't be afraid. You can swim all by yourself now.' "[36]

After this harsh initiation, Clare went on to become such an accomplished swimmer that by her early teens she was able to cross Long Island Sound from Greenwich, Connecticut, to the Yacht Club at Sands Point with ease, as well as try out for the 1920 Olympics.[37] In middle age she mastered scuba diving, and in her seventies she still dazzled onlookers with her graceful crawl. Throughout her life the ocean would be a solace during attacks of "the dismals." Two of the compensating delights of her old age were a house on Kahala Beach in Hawaii and a riverview apartment at the Watergate in Washington, D.C.

Yet the experience at Rockaway was so indelibly seared on her consciousness that when, inspired by Winston Churchill in her mid-fifties, she took up painting as a hobby, her first picture was of a child being thrown into the sea by a Herculean man. Meanwhile a small boy sat calmly on a pier and a frantic woman ran helpless along the shore.[38]

For Easter 1907 Clare was given her first pet, a fluffy chick that she called Pip. He lived only a short time, and his demise introduced her to the phenomenon of death. She buried him in a box with one of her mother's fancy collars as a shroud.[39]

A more brutal loss of innocence came from her initiation into adult realities of sex, violation, and homicide. Clare described it long afterwards in "The Double-Bind." The manuscript refers to "a disastrous episode" in the protagonist's childhood, which was "so central, so significant, so full of importance for the understanding of her character—and her fate, that it must be told with considerable elaboration."

Ann Clare Boothe, aged about four

It happened in the summer, when she thinks she might have been four and one-half . . . The Lloyds were living in a slum on 3rd Avenue, confronting the "L." The flat above them, and under the roof, was occupied by a man, who she remembers only wearing a shirt and smelling of sweat and beer . . . She remembers that she and her mother and brother sometimes sat on the stoop, on little straw mats, watching the passerbys [sic], and listening to the "L" overhead . . .

Her mother—it was dark—told her and her brother to go up to bed. Her brother must have got there before her, and

27

gone into the flat, for she met the man upstairs on the land-ing. She tried desperately to remember what he had said to persuade her to go up on the roof with him, but could not re-member, and it is of little importance anyway what reason or excuse he gave for going there. He took her into a walled shadow and sat down, and took her on his lap. She remem-bers feeling frightened when he began to unbutton her pants, and the smell of sweat and beer and heat always evoked in her the feeling of shame and fear. To what extent he molested her, she doesn't know. For the thing she re-members best is her father advancing to the man, with a book in his hand, and that he threw the book which hit her a glancing blow on the head, that she was suddenly dropped as the man rose, and that the man and her father locked in a struggle which carried them to the edge of the parapet over the areaway, that there was the roar of the "L," which may have covered up the man's screams as her father with a blow sent him hurtling to his death seven stories below. She remembers being lifted from the roof in his arms. He ran with her down the stairs, took her into the apartment, stood in the hall and whispered, fiercely, "You are to tell no one, no one, no one,—hear! Not Mickey. Not Mother. No one."

She was crying, of course. "I won't tell, Daddy, I *promise* I won't tell!" "My baby girl! My baby girl, oh, my baby girl." Then he shook her, and buttoned her pants, and made her sit in the little front room, and read a story calmly to her, and when her mother came up, said "The child is tired," and took her to bed, whispering "No one. Tell no one. Tell no one."

The next morning he took her for a walk. "He was a bad man," he said, "a very bad man. He tried to hurt you. Daddy stopped him. But nobody must know that, or they would think Daddy had done wrong. They would hurt Daddy, too."[40]

Whether this trauma happened or not—and the vividness of detail certainly suggests it, or something worse, did—William Boothe and his family left town in the summer of 1907. By the time they reappeared in Memphis, Tennessee, later that year, they were using the name "Murphy."

2

THE QUEST FOR

SOOTHING SHEETS

Childhood is the fiery furnace in which we are melted down
to essentials, and that essential shaped for good.
—KATHERINE ANNE PORTER

The city of Memphis sits on an eastern bluff of the Mississippi River across from the green floodplains of Arkansas. At the turn of the century, eighty-four steamboats routinely plied the great waterway, carrying not only passengers but the biggest supply of lumber and cottonseed products in the world. "John J. Murphy," alias William Boothe, established himself with his "wife" and children in this thriving business climate, hoping to prosper as a salesman and become financially independent, so that he could devote himself exclusively to the study of the violin—again his most consuming passion.[1]

The "Murphys" appear to have settled at 635 Walnut Street, in a neighborhood of small clapboard houses, not far from the railroad tracks. Half of the population of Memphis was black, and the sight of Negroes doing menial work instilled in Clare, at four, "a sharp taste of the bittersweet 'aristocratic' Southern white attitude of superiority." Ann Snyder took advantage of this cheap domestic help, lightening her household responsibilities but increasing her boredom. She longed for the excitement and unpredictability of New York, and whenever the need for brighter vistas grew overwhelming, she would leave the children in a Catholic nursery and disappear for a few days. Clare missed her acutely, and was unconsoled by the lace-edged holy cards the nuns gave her at bedtime. During one of Ann's mysterious absences, Clare had a bloody nightmare. She dreamed of lying under a staircase in a small room whose only light came through a casement of red and purple stained glass. Suddenly, the window opened, and a witch, hovering in a round basket, reached for her, took her to the moon, and cut her throat.[2]

Returning home after such visions of mutilation (she would be tormented by them for the next eighty years), Clare had to endure real-life horrors. Her parents' relationship was deteriorating, and one night she awoke in tears to their loud quarreling. When William picked up his daughter to calm her, Ann snatched her away. He grabbed back, she snatched again. In the ensuing struggle, the little girl crashed to the floor.[3]

"I never drew a happy breath in my entire childhood," Clare later claimed, remembering the insecurity and deprivations of these years. Yet there were tranquil moments. She played under blossoming magnolia trees, whose "pungent sweet fragrance" on the summer air would always fill her with nostalgia. Sitting on her father's knee, she learned to read, using books from the Little Leather Library as primers. At night she enjoyed Ann's telling of the German story "Struwwelpeter," about a cruel boy with endless hair and fingernails. While being tucked into bed, she listened to her mother singing a lullaby, "The sun and the stars and the angels."[4]

Ann Snyder also crooned popular love songs, or melodies from the operettas of Franz Lehár, as she went about her chores. She had a romantic streak and, despite William's modest income, a taste for jewelry and fine clothes. Somehow, even in times of privation, she managed to deck herself with furs and feathers. Clare loved to watch her preening at her dressing table, with its glittering pin tray, nail buffer, and silver-backed brushes.[5]

Ann Snyder "Murphy," *c. 1907*

In 1909 John J. Murphy, who apparently did not profit by Memphis's economic boom, moved his young family to Nashville, in the hills of middle Tennessee. The town was a prosperous capital and port, at the hub of numerous turnpikes bringing produce to the Cumberland River for shipment around the world. Its skyline was dominated by a blue-gray limestone state house—a perfect model of Southern Greek Revival architecture. Commercial development, in contrast, was eroding the impressive houses along Eighth Avenue, Nashville's main thoroughfare, but William managed to rent a holdout at No. 308.[6]

He took a job as manager of a factory making a soft drink with the unappetizing name "Celery-Ade." Its offices at 101 Church Street overlooked the river and the old Fort Nashborough stockade. Simultaneously, he rented a studio nearby to pursue his musical ambitions. Fearing that the name Murphy—or, for that matter, Boothe—was not exotic-sounding enough for a concert artist, he chose the pseudonym "Jord Murfé" and set himself up as a teacher and freelance player. An advertising handbill from this period portrays him heavy browed and distinguished, balancing his instrument above the legend "Violin Virtuoso."[7]

William Boothe, alias "Jord Murfé," *c. 1909*

William's incessant practicing dismayed Ann, who saw her hopes of middle-class security slipping away if Maestro Murfé became a full-time musician. His habit of exercising his fingers on the dining table so annoyed her at breakfast that she threw a saltcellar at him one morning. He began to study Tartini's difficult "Devil's Trill" Sonata, whose screechy scales and sinister twangs disturbed Clare's often feverish sleep.

"The child is ill," Ann complained. "Why don't you stop?"

"She doesn't have to listen," William bellowed, remorselessly fiddling on.[8]

While Clare suffered from the occasional lack of his consideration, Ann felt a constant victim of his neglect. In revenge she discouraged any interest her children might have had in classical music. As a result, David remained forever indifferent to his father's muse, and Clare, though she had rudimentary piano lessons, and even mastered Grieg's Opus 12 *Albumblatt*, grew up unable to carry a tune.[9]

Ann's dislike of William's obsession with music was symptomatic of her growing disillusionment with him. He, in turn, blamed her for rearing both their son and daughter "in an atmosphere clouded with hatred for me." At this early stage, however, he could still enchant them with his breadth of information and omnivorous appetite for life. Time spent with Father, no matter how brief or illicit, was fun. After school they would sneak down to his office and monitor his burgeoning collection of bottle tops decoratively lining the walls, or watch the giant Celery-Ade vats being rinsed out in the adjacent plant. When clean water temptingly filled one, they climbed a ladder and tumbled in for a swim.[10]

Clare underwent a more serious immersion when a group of Negroes "baptised" her in the river. To be thrust, by powerful hands, deep beneath the surface might have frightened a more timid child. But she found that she relished strange, even dangerous experiences.[11]

Soon she was restricted by more rigorous discipline than her parents imposed. Having turned six in the spring of 1909, she registered to attend Ward Seminary that fall as "Clare Murphy." When the dread first day came on September 22, she resisted mightily, screaming and stamping and refusing to go in. "It seemed to me a great indignity, even a cruelty, to be forced to get an education."[12]

Actually she could count herself privileged. Nashville's three-hundred-pupil Ward Seminary (later Ward Belmont College) was one of the best preparatory establishments in the South. William at least saved on uniforms, since Clare was one of its minority of day girls and could wear ordinary clothes. The main campus, located on her street in the heart of town, included a library of over four thousand books and a roof garden with swings and tetherball stands. Twelve nearby acres were set aside for tennis and basketball courts, croquet lawns and hockey fields. There were flower-lined paths for walking and a handsome pergola for reading.[13]

Clare's first day at Ward began at 10:30 A.M. with an address by Dr. Thomas Carter of Vanderbilt University, on a topic that would turn out to be the life strategy of the little girl sitting red-eyed and resentful at his feet. He spoke at length on "The Investment of Power."

By noon the temperature had climbed to eighty-five degrees, and wilting pupils were rewarded with the news that they could stay away the next day to visit the State Fair. For just ten cents' admission, they would be able to watch a vaudeville act, a horse show, an ostrich race, and a band concert. There would also be whistles to blow, balloons to pop, and saddle-pony rides. Finally, at dusk, the whole town could see a fireworks display so spectacular it would make the warm air vibrate.[14]

Once school reconvened after the holiday, Clare adjusted with difficulty to a new world of chapel services, rigid lessons, and organized sport. She was already an avid reader, but routine study seemed to inhibit her. By now she was used to the spontaneities of her semibohemian parents. A class photograph survives of this first year at Ward, showing Clare Murphy cross-legged on the floor, looking small and tentative. Her first report, dated June 1910, recorded an undistinguished string of S's (for Satisfactory) in reading, writing, arithmetic, spelling, and story work. By the following summer, she had mastered the art of success in school, advancing to A's in all subjects, including English grammar and geography. Her second class picture shows her a plumper, taller child, with eyes knowledgeable beyond her eight years. Clare was too intelligent, and had witnessed too much family discord, to survive the loss of innocence unscathed.[15]

William was delighted with her precociousness, not to mention a well-advanced "spirit of humorous analysis." She had unusual powers of retention, and at seven amazed him by reciting a whole chapter of the Book of Genesis. Although not quite a "prodigy" by his severe standards, she had enormous curiosity and was "the best listener of any child who ever lived."[16]

Clare "Murphy" (*above: front row, extreme left; below: second row, with hair bow*) at Ward Seminary, *1910–1911*

Unfortunately, father and daughter never had time to fulfill their potential empathy in Nashville. William distracted himself with yet a third job, merchandising a newfangled product called "G. Washington Refined Soluble Coffee" for the Southern Coffee Company. In this he was fatally ahead of his time, as he had been marketing pianos. Not for thirty years would instant coffee become popular among Americans. The product sat on the shelves, and his commissions dwindled.[17]

Music offered relief but little reward. Telltale signs of restlessness and wanderlust began to appear in William's behavior. After the end of Clare's second school year, in the summer of 1911, the "Murphys" left Nashville abruptly and headed for Chicago, in what Clare later described as "greatly reduced economic circumstances."[18]

At the age of forty-nine, William Boothe (who continued to call himself "Murphy" or "Murfé" for the next several years) seems to have gone north in a last-ditch attempt to pursue a musical career. According to his daughter, he secured "a good job" playing for the Chicago Grand Opera Orchestra, at least during the 1911–12 season. Good or not, the job paid nothing through the long off-season. He had to supplement his income, as in Nashville, with teaching fees and odd sales commissions.[19]

In an attempt to overcome high living costs, William rented a small apartment on the South Side, at Forty-first Street and Indiana Avenue. It stood between the once-elegant mansions of Grand Boulevard and the slaughterhouses, glue factories, and hair works of Packingtown. Periodically drifting from the west came a reek of animal flesh and blood, "rancid, sensual, strong," in Upton Sinclair's words, along with acrid smoke from gigantic chimneys.[20]

Clare's most indelible impression of her new neighborhood was of "a man peeing against the wall" outside her window. David, a streetwise boy, looked back on the South Side as "an obscene and outrageous environment," a breeding ground for prostitutes. Or, as he later phrased it to Clare, "a fit background for an inhabitant of La Belle Fleur Maison."[21] Such euphemisms were their private way of skirting what they both suspected, but dared not say, about their vampish mother—her sudden absences, her budget-defying wardrobe, and her cunning evasions.

At eight, Clare was still too young to guess what David, at nine, precociously knew of the world beyond Indiana Avenue. But she was aware of festering local tensions between Lithuanian, German, and Irish migrants, not to mention an all-pervasive fear and dislike of Negroes, as palpable here as in Tennessee. One evening she and her brother were skating along lower Michigan Avenue when they approached a huge black man in a white sweater. "Oh look," David said, "there's Jack Johnson." Clare stared at the boxer with such fascination that she smacked into a tree and winded herself. Johnson picked her up and began gently slapping her back. A white policeman appeared at once. "Why are you molesting this young lady?" Only David's explanation of what had happened, and his precise identification of Johnson as the owner of a saloon, Café de Champion at 42 West Thirty-first Street, saved the great heavyweight from arrest.[22]

Clare's other childhood recollection of a brush with celebrity was evoked by the remembered sound of Mary Garden's voice filling the Chicago Auditorium, where William played. Clare had the feeling—probably illusory—that her seductive father and the star of *Salomé* were lovers. At all events, he sent her to the Blackstone Hotel with a bunch of long-stemmed American Beauty roses for Miss Garden. Close up, away from the footlights, the soprano looked shockingly unglamorous. She presented a cream-smeared face to be kissed, and Clare noticed that she had "terrible skin." In return for the kiss and the flowers, Garden reached into a cage and gave her young visitor a canary.[23]

In spite of William and Ann's diminishing regard for each other, life on the South Side maintained a semblance of normality. Providing her children with the best education possible remained Ann's priority, and somehow the estranged couple found the means. In the fall of 1911, David entered Racine College, Wisconsin, an Episcopal school with a strong emphasis on military training. Its regimented discipline helped curb his rebellious, roving nature but led to a lasting suppression of his more sensitive qualities, which would have disastrous consequences.[24]

Clare, meanwhile, enrolled in the prestigious Latin School for Girls. It was uptown, on Division Street, yet high-speed cable cars were able to whisk her there quickly from the Thirty-ninth Street stop. Before long she was reciting "*amo, amas, amat*" with children from prosperous North Side homes. She also took classes at the Art Institute and became a compulsive sketcher, producing pastels of its views over train tracks and lake. A painting set of twenty colors gave her endless pleasure, and she showed some signs of artistic talent.[25]

Since so much of William's meager income was spent on schooling, the children could not look forward to many toys that first Christmas in Chicago. Clare coveted an expensive doll she had seen in a department store. "The saleswoman let me hold it. And then I never got it." She also longed "more than life" for a dog but received only a stuffed collie.[26]

David fared better, with a BB gun that aroused envy in his intensely competitive sister. He gloated about his masculine prerogatives, saying he would grow up to be a soldier while she would be always "just a girl." Clare fiercely resented this implication of female inferiority, knowing that she was more than his equal, except in size and strength. Soon he would have to confront the reality not only of her greater poise and social ease but of her creative gifts and extraordinary intelligence. Soon, too, Clare would become aware that the path to recognition and fulfillment might be hampered by her being the "wrong" sex. The only reason she could see why David might consider himself superior was that he had a "dinglebat" and she did not.[27]

Brother and sister declared a temporary truce when the "Murphys" took their 1912 summer vacation at a resort on the shores of Turtle Lake, in northwest Wisconsin. There both children made friends with a lumberjack, who taught them to shoot porcupines and squirrels. Clare kept pace with David, running barefoot through the dense woods, climbing trees, hunting birds, paddling canoes, and fishing the fecund waters. Wearing only a dress, she fearlessly slid down a ramp after some corduroy-clad boys, then spent an embarrassing session with a doctor, having splinters removed from her bottom.

These were her last days of purely careless childhood, and she looked back on them in old age as "the only happy ones I ever knew."[28]

Although a photograph of Ann Snyder at Turtle Lake shows her smiling broadly, over a row of just-caught fish, she was by now completely disenchanted with William Boothe. Clare was of the mature opinion that "lust, rather than love, had brought them together." But there was more to their impending split than waning sexual attraction.[29]

The truth—which for the rest of her life Clare was unable, or unwilling, to face—was that her parents, variously self-styled as "Mr. and Mrs. Franklin," "Mr. and Mrs. William Franklin Boothe," and "Mr. and Mrs. John J. Murphy," were still not husband and wife. Nor would they ever be. Certainly no record of their marrying or divorcing has been found in any of the states they called home. Legal cohabitation was impossible in New York as long as Laura Boothe survived, since William had been the guilty party in court proceedings. His likely reason for taking refuge in the South, under an assumed name, was intent to evade alimony. But lacking valid identification as John J. Murphy, he could not hope to marry Ann in Tennessee or Illinois. In any case, by the time they reached Chicago the liaison had so soured that the question of cementing it was futile.

Ann's most urgent problem, now that David and Clare were approaching puberty, was their illegitimacy. She grew angry, even vengeful, towards the once-debonair man who had wooed her over the wine tables of Broadway. Then, he had been a prosperous executive in his prime, irresistibly handsome and sexy. Now, eleven years later, he was an aging salesman, a vainglorious fiddler, a drinker prone to self-destructive whiskey binges.[30]

Ignoring his protestations, Ann made her plans for flight. She had not risen above the deprivations of Hell's Kitchen to settle for the life of a fallen woman with two bastards in a Midwest slum. She was still only thirty. With her good looks and charm, she felt sure of attracting a richer and more reliable man in the East.

Opportunity presented itself in September 1912, when Ann's father, now living in New Jersey, fell seriously ill. Taking the children, she went to visit him. That she had no intention of coming back was clear, since she simultaneously transferred David from Racine College to Repton Military School in Tarrytown, New York. As time passed and it became obvious to the children that they were not to be reunited with their father, Ann told them that he had absconded with Mary Garden.[31]

She also gradually changed her persona from "wronged wife" to "widow," telling new acquaintances that her husband had died. The children came to believe this too, fiction hardening to fact in their susceptible minds. Sixteen years later, shortly before his actual demise, William would write Clare his version of the "divorce," pretending too, for her sake, that she was legitimate. "Your mother did not love me when she married me." Nor had he forsaken Ann, "unless going on the road to make a living for you children could be construed as desertion. She left me. As long as you children might live, I would never have left."[32]

Ann Snyder—who had a way, which her daughter eventually emulated, of reversing and sentimentalizing unpleasant facts—documented some of her experiences in short stories, composed of equal parts fantasy and harsh reality, and from time to time she described herself as "a writer." Clare's first glimpse into her mother's imaginative world occurred shortly after their arrival in New York. While they were waiting at the Hudson ferry terminal to cross over to Hoboken, Ann went to the ladies' room, leaving on the bench beside her daughter a typed manuscript entitled "The Return." Handwritten on the back was "A. C. Boothe, 1-188 Indiana Avenue Chicago c/o Murphy."[33] Clare began to read.

The piece turned out to be an eight-page story written in overripe style. Its plot was standard woman's magazine melodrama, but the details were significant, at least to Clare. There was an unhappy urban wife, a drunken husband, a secretly planned desertion, a rancorous farewell note, a collecting of jewels, and a parting glance at a silk-covered bed, followed by disappearance into the night. There were also shabby scenes of working-class penury, intermixed with plentiful sobs, sighs, and aching limbs.

Clare puzzled over the manuscript's autobiographical implications. What was her mother's purpose in writing it? The return address suggested it had been a rejected submission to some periodical. Why had she so obviously left it on the seat for her daughter to see? Did she hope it might explain that—whatever difficult times lay ahead—there would be no return to William Boothe?

Ann made no mention of the manuscript when she came back, and Clare, sensing that it sublimated matters "too painful" to discuss, kept her own silence. By tacit agreement, she also kept the story.[34]

Both of them knew that Ann Snyder's lifelong quest for soothing sheets, symbolized by the silk-covered bed of her protagonist, was not to be gratified any time soon. Their immediate destination held, at best, only the prospect of coarse cotton ones.

Clare would make this Hoboken Ferry trip many times over the next few years. She was always entranced by the flotsam and jetsam of the wide river. Its battered, bobbing boxes and crates, irradiated by the sun, reminded her of "whimsical little barks." But cold nights were coming, when the surface would turn black and oily, and heave with shapes that looked to her like "evil deeds in a dark life."[35]

John and Louisa Schneider—who still spelled their surname the German way—lived on the third floor of a house at 107 Sixth Street and Park Avenue in Union City. As Clare walked for the first time into the kitchen, where they spent most of their time, she registered a series of impressions so photographic that they stayed with her forever. She saw her grandfather's blue eyes and bloated face reflected in a cracked shaving mirror propped up against a milk bottle. In one dropsical hand he held a large razor, while with the other he steadied a bowl of water in his lap.

Elsewhere in the little apartment, she noticed a hairy animal's foot, carved out to serve as a plant pot, a picture of Kaiser Wilhelm in a spiked helmet, and two Dresden china figures of a boy and girl. She imagined these last to be David and herself, "as prince and princess." The whole place breathed Bavaria and her Teutonic heritage.[36]

It was clear to Ann, if not yet to Clare, that John Schneider, who was suffering from hepatic cirrhosis and endocarditis, had not long to live. During the next seven months, he filled the long days of invalidism by teaching his granddaughter whist, cribbage, and bezique. Grandmother Louisa taught her German songs.

> *Du, Du liegst mir im Herzen!*
> *Du, Du liegst mir im Sinn,*
> *Du, Du machst mir viel Schmerzen*
> *Weisst nicht, wie gut ich Dir bin.*[37]

In "Onion" City, as local children called it, Clare had a taste of the intense neighborliness of the ethnic poor. She would drop in on the baker's family upstairs, and on warm evenings sit on the steps outside the tenement, reading a newspaper and talking to people as they came home from work. One immigrant with pierced ears, impressed by the nine-year-old's grasp of world affairs, admiringly told the Schneiders, "Your Clara is a frisch kid."[38]

Clare was hypnotically attracted to Saturday night nickelodeon movies. The first play she saw, performed by the Hudson Theatre Stock Company, seemed so real that when the villain stepped up to the footlights, it "scared the bejesus" out of her.[39]

Ann Snyder was struck by Clare's obvious love of drama and noticed that she closely resembled the curly-blonde "child sweetheart" ideal of so many contemporary entertainments. Needing money badly, she somehow secured her nine-year-old daughter a Broadway job, as understudy to none other than Mary Pickford. The play, produced by David Belasco, was a three-act fantasy entitled *A Good Little Devil*. Pickford was cast as a young blind girl, with Ernest Truex as her adolescent lover. Lillian Gish (lured away at twenty-five dollars a week from D. W. Griffith) floated around the stage as a fairy.[40] *Devil* opened at the Republic Theatre on January 8, 1913, to favorable notices, and ran for four months. Unfortunately for Clare, the star's health was robust, so she only got to kiss the delectable Mr. Truex (who was actually twenty-two) in rehearsals.

Throughout that winter and early spring, John Schneider's health worsened. Clare went to see him towards the end of her theatrical stint. On April 14, she heard a strange sound, "like the clapping of horses' hooves," coming from his bedroom. It was the death rattle. He was only fifty-one years old.[41]

Grandmother Louisa prepared to move to other quarters in Weehawken, and Ann set about looking for permanent accommodation of her own in her native city, which she had left, with more promising hopes, six years before.

3

BIG PEARLS AND
SMALL HIPS

*The narcissistic individual is a product of an unhappy family
situation in which the child is seduced into a special
relationship with one parent.* —ALEXANDER LOWEN

Ann Snyder returned to the familiar streets of Manhattan's Upper
West Side, where she had lived as Mrs. Franklin. Now, as Ann
Boothe, she rented dingily wallpapered rooms at 150 West Eighty-
fourth Street and Columbus Avenue. She left David at Repton for the
time being and registered Clare with the Myron T. Scudder School, a
small, private establishment on West Ninety-sixth Street. Every morning she made the girl a breakfast of toast and milk, with an occasional
banana, and packed her a perfunctory boxed lunch. At night she served
her a simple supper. "Mother was strictly a chicken, peas, and rice
cook."[1]

The only playmate in the building near Clare's age was the land-
lady's ten-year-old son, a "monster" who pulled her pigtails and once
even threw a lighted lamp at her. So she befriended a filigree sales-

woman in a neighboring apartment. Clare spent hours looking in her suitcase of glittering samples and listening to her tales of adventures in California and Australia.[2]

Thanks perhaps to this business contact, Ann got a job working behind the counter of M. Tecla, a jewelry store at 398 Fifth Avenue. She touted the company line that artificial pearls were superior to real ones—at least in terms of affordable size. "A woman is fine," she liked to say, "as long as she has big pearls and small hips."[3]

To customers, Ann was a charismatic figure: warm, lighthearted, and witty. The socialite Perle Mesta, who knew her at this time, said that Ann was one of the most beautiful women she had ever met. At thirty, Ann's good looks were still so entirely natural that she needed to spend little time at her toilette. Only her teeth received special care: she was proud of their small, white evenness and smiled often to show them off. David called this enamel flashing "doing the Baroness."[4]

With a salary of ten dollars a week, and a rent approximately half that, Ann had barely enough money to live on. Yet she soon gave up her job. Unaccountably, her income seemed to increase. At first Clare had a child's indifference to her new means of livelihood beyond noting that "the phone seldom rang except at night." After answering it, Ann would put on one of her prettiest dresses and go out, not to reappear until the early hours.[5]

As time went by, various gentlemen began to visit the apartment. Occasionally one of them would ask Clare to join her mother and himself at a restaurant. Instead of the cheap canned peaches and gelatin she was compelled to order when Ann took her out, she would indulge in a sumptuous, twenty-five-cent Charlotte Russe.[6]

Inevitably, both children began to puzzle over Ann's nocturnal disappearances. Where did she go, and where did she get money? Clare asked some pointed questions, but the replies were so evasive that after a while she stopped. "There were so many things we didn't know about Mother. Life with her was always a mystery."[7]

It took many years of denial before Clare could admit to herself that by 1913 Ann Snyder had become "a call girl."[8]

As the weeks passed, and summer heat hung heavy over West Eighty-fourth Street, the odors of boiling cabbage and garbage rotting in the hallway were all-pervasive. Perle Mesta's sister remembered the Boothes' living conditions as so squalid that she could never blame Clare for anything she later did.[9] The child slept fitfully in an airless room off the kitchen, prey to the bites of mice and rats.

Ann's social life dwindled as well-to-do New Yorkers fled to the country and seashore. So did her good humor. She saw no relief from the dusty city and grumbled that, were it not for the burden of her children, she would quit Manhattan too. They had to endure a constant refrain of how much she had sacrificed for them, and how they had ruined her chances "just by being born." When David came home on vacation, seeming more and more a younger edition of William, with a strong jaw and independent spirit, Ann berated him for being "just like his father, a hypocrite, a liar, heartless."[10]

She was cruel to Clare in more sinister ways. Once she lay rigid on her bed, pretending to be dead. When the girl panicked, she sat up and said, "Now that I know you are sorry, I can come back to life." At other times she would hint at suicide, talking of "going away forever" and taking Clare with her. Fluttering her eyes, she would shed tears into the hollows of her cheeks, then brush them away in the manner of a practiced tragedienne.[11]

David, contemptuously dubbing Ann "the waterworks," remained immune to her manipulative appeals for sympathy. He knew that when she called him "dearest," she had "some load of stinking clams to sell." Clare was pained by her mother's attacks on him but tolerant of her general distress. She tried to alleviate it by identifying with Ann's yearnings, to the point that she began to suffer sympathetic ailments: cold sores, earaches, nausea, and excruciating stiffness in the legs. The last symptom suggested rheumatic fever, but Ann diagnosed "growing pains," and treated Clare to prolonged shin baths in hot water and mustard.[12]

As an antidote to the tawdriness of her situation, Ann developed a vicarious interest in rich people. She tracked their movements, avidly read about their mansions and motorcars, and longed for crystal, china, and fine linens for her own table. After studying the rules of etiquette, she impressed on Clare the need to maintain at all times a ladylike decorum. Though pessimistic that her own hopes for wealth and position would ever be realized, she pushed her daughter towards those goals. "I want you," she cajoled in well-modulated but sad tones, "to amount to something."[13]

Clare was made to understand that by failing she would be both delinquent and undutiful. In yielding to this psychological pressure, the girl suffered Ann's most pernicious form of child abuse. She would grow up tainted by distorted values, neglecting her own extraordinary talents and becoming pathologically hungry for adulation, wealth, and power. Not until extreme old age could she admit, "Mother poisoned my life."[14]

Perhaps out of necessity, Ann Snyder's choice of men was eclectic. For a while that year, she had a romantic interest in Homer Rodeheaver, a trombone-playing composer and evangelist. Clare memorized his theme song:

> Brighten the corner where you are,
> There is someone far from harbor
> Who is stuck up on the bar—
> Brighten the corner where you are.[15]

Another of Ann's admirers was Percival K. Frowert, a short, portly, Philadelphia Main Line advertising executive. His wife was in a mental institution, so he needed feminine comforts. Since his apartment was nearby on Riverside Drive, David and Clare became accustomed to it as a second home. There were three Frowert children, under the care of a governess. Clare befriended eight-year-old Dorothy, whose stylish frocks she envied.[16]

Neither of the Boothe children liked "Uncle Percy" very much. Clare thought him pompous, and David called him a "little old half-ass." Even so, his was the first upper-middle-class household they had encountered, and Clare, at least, began to understand her mother's hankering for affluence. She lusted after a bright peacock blue coat with a squirrel collar, but Ann was unforthcoming.[17]

Then, early in the new year of 1914, Ann Snyder met a rich, handsome Canadian named William Higinbotham, who invited her and Clare to accompany him on a trip to Europe.

On Wednesday, February 4, they sailed on the RMS *Carmania*. As Clare entered the ship's paneled and gilt salons, her universe expanded. Aristocrats, millionaires, and diplomats were onboard. To her surprise, she discovered that they not only enjoyed meeting her but seemed entranced by her ethereal gaiety. One distinguished man who taught her to play chess turned out to be the Prime Minister of Hungary. "So," she would later boast, "I had the gift to meet the right contacts early in life." Even the Captain succumbed to her charms, and when she became seasick he sent a sketch of himself weeping, over the message "I am so lonely." On February 11, he gave a dinner in her honor, consisting of oyster-cream soup, sole, filet of beef, mushrooms, rice, and peach Melba, dedicating the menu to "Miss Clarie Booth" [*sic*].[18]

After arriving in Paris (where Mr. Higinbotham grandly checked them all into the Hôtel Bristol), Clare found a marionette park along the Champs-Élysées and enjoyed rolling hoops and spinning tops with French children. Ann saw to it that her days were otherwise filled with reading, language instruction, and museum visits.[19]

They remained in Paris through March 28. Having absorbed the city's harmonious splendors, Clare found their return ship, the *Mauretania*, aesthetically wanting. It was a clashing mixture of styles, with a

Clare and her mother in Paris, *c. February 1914*

Louis XVI library, a Rococo ballroom, and a veranda café modeled after the orangery at Hampton Court.

On April 3, the night before she disembarked in New York, Clare was again the toast of an adult dinner. Mr. Higinbotham gave her an extravagant eleventh "birthday" feast of plovers' eggs, consommé, turbot, chicken, asparagus, vanilla soufflé, and a cake with eleven candles.[20] This, coming on top of six weeks' indulgence in French croissants and hot chocolate, caused her to return home a chubbier girl than the one who had left.

4

THE MOST CONCEITED
GIRL IN THE SCHOOL

You were the most precocious and intelligent child that I
ever encountered. —WILLIAM FRANKLIN BOOTHE

Nine days after getting back from Europe, the pubescent Clare
Boothe resumed her Broadway career. This time, she understudied
Joyce Fair (another Pickford look-alike) in *The Dummy*, a four-act
"crook comedy" based on Harvey J. O'Higgins's detective stories. Her
former costar, Ernest Truex, played the lead. By pretending to be deaf,
dumb, and dimwitted, he rescued Miss Fair from four kidnappers and
won a large reward.[1]

Alexander Woollcott of *The New York Times* found the play "rather
ambling" but "lighted by a shrewd and pleasant humor."[2] Clare substi-
tuted just once for the abducted girl, but this was enough for "Joyce
Fair" to be later attributed to her as a stage name.

During the successful run of *The Dummy*, a drama incalculably
more momentous unfolded in Europe. On June 28, at Sarajevo, the assassination of Austria's Archduke Franz Ferdinand set in motion the
war that would reconfigure world maps. As hostilities spread, and

debate about the United States' alignment intensified, the phrase "German-American" took on ominous undertones. Clare sensed ever more keenly Ann Snyder's desire to transcend her Bavarian roots.

The guns of August were remote from childhood consciousness as Clare and David set off for a dairy-farm vacation in Bulleville, New York. Independent of their emotionally demanding parent a hundred miles away, the children learned about rural working life by participating in it. The elderly farmer paid them fifteen cents a quart for picked berries and two cents a pair for frogs' legs, which his wife would prepare for supper "French style." In the early morning they drove cows to pasture, and they herded them back in the evening. They filled urns for loading onto a milk train that ran through the property, churned butter, collected eggs, and fed chickens. David wrung hens' necks, and Clare stoically plucked their feathers and cleaned out gullets. She also groomed dogs, tended an aviary, maintained an aquarium, and studied a book on how to raise guppies, only to discover that she was "not reading as fast as they were breeding."[3]

David, already a mature-looking adolescent, learned more directly about the facts of life when he lost his virginity to a young local schoolteacher. In keeping with his usual practice, he told Clare about it. She was more upset than shocked. That her brother now loftily regarded himself as a man, while still treating her as a child, created a resentment greater than when he had taunted her about being unable to follow him into the military.[4]

Her own sexual experiences so far, apart from the probably suppressed rooftop incident, were limited to having her bottom pinched on a narrow staircase, romping in a hayfield with a country boy who clutched at her underwear, and being kissed in a hammock. But she was no slower than David in developing physically. Shortly after turning twelve, she began to menstruate.[5]

In later life Clare denied wanting to be an actress of any kind. It was her mother who encouraged her to persist, she said, by arranging a screen test at the Oliver Place Studio in the Bronx early in 1915. Viola Dana (future star of *Naughty Nanette* and *Kosher Kitty Kelley*) joined Clare in the audition. They were asked to express anxiety, fear, and horror. As the cameras rolled, Miss Dana emoted on cue. Her arms held off imagined threat, her lips quivered, and her eyes widened, cascading tears. Clare, awed by such histrionics, forgot to act herself.[6]

In spite of this inauspicious start, she secured a small role in Thomas Alva Edison's single-reel, thirty-three-millimeter picture *The Heart of a Waif*. The lead went to ten-year-old Edith Peters, who, seventy years later, recalled the studio as a cavernous room with four or five sets illuminated by blue-white lights. She and Clare were not allowed to wear rouge or red lipstick because it would "look black" on screen. Between takes, they made rubber-band balls and played with the screenplay's homeless kitten.[7]

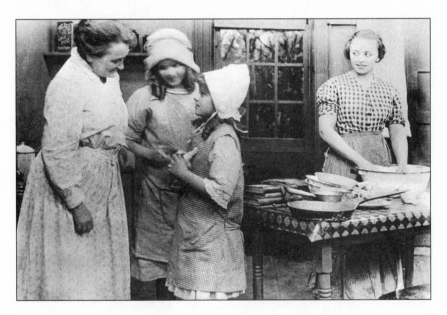

Clare *(second from left)* in *The Heart of a Waif,* 1915

Long before the advent of movie sound, Clare found she was expected to speak lines anyway. Charles Seay, the director, told her to act as if the camera contained a recording cylinder. She was cast as "the Little Girl on the Fence" and required to befriend an orphan child laborer (played by Edith), who thwarted a burglary and won a privileged education. The picture lasted only twelve minutes, and Clare's edited performance amounted to just thirty seconds. In three short scenes, she sat behind Edith in church, visited the heroine at home, and at the end rode off giggling with her in a buggy.[8]

The Heart of a Waif was released on April 24, 1915. Preserved in pristine condition by the Museum of Modern Art, it shows Clare, almost as tall as some of the adult players, acting self-consciously in bonnet and blonde ringlets, unable to resist an amateurish glance into the lens.

Except for one other brief screen appearance as a stand-in rider eight years afterwards, this was the beginning and end of Clare's movie career. But *Waif* did fan her ambition to write for the stage and screen. Even at that early age, she felt she had "the capacity to create."[9]

The sometime actress spent a short vacation with Dorothy Frowert in a boardinghouse on Block Island. When Clare returned to New York City, her mother had a new male friend, richer than Messrs. Frowert and Higinbotham put together, and he was to change their lives.[10]

Joel Jacobs had always been a bachelor, as far as anyone knew. He lived alone in the Hotel Wellington at Seventh Avenue and Fifty-sixth Street, and worked a block away as treasurer of the Keystone Tire & Rubber Company. Forty-eight years old and of German-Jewish descent, he had slicked-down hair, a prominent nose, small, dark eyes, broad, plump cheeks, and, in Clare's phrase, "the shoulders of a man whose ancestors had known the ghetto."[11] With his high, stiff collar, waistcoat, gold chain, and elegant walking stick, he looked every inch a tycoon.

Mr. Jacobs had a vast repertory of Jewish morality tales, which at first entertained Ann's children. But he told the same ones too often, and they began to detect a note of cruelty in them. He liked to tell, for example, of a man who stood his young son on a high brownstone step and asked if he trusted Poppa. The boy said he did. "Then jump, and I'll catch you." As the boy leapt, his father stepped aside, letting him smash his face on the pavement. "I taught you never to trust nobody," scolded the man. "Now you've learned the lesson, you won't be no *schlemiel*."[12]

David listened to such homilies with lowered eyelids and a tight smile, causing Mr. Jacobs to turn pink and angrily jingle the coins in his pockets. Clare did not share her brother's general distaste for Ann's beaux, but she did find this one's accent and religion "strange." Ann reassured her of Joel's good intentions, saying repeatedly that he was "an original." From this the children coined the nickname "Riggie."[13]

His kindness was certainly apparent in gifts of cash, furniture, and jewelry lavished upon the whole family. He took Ann to the races and

Joel Jacobs, *c. 1915*

paid her bets, bought her a player piano that tinkled out "Many a Heart Is Broken," and enhanced her beautiful neck and wrists with gold and diamond necklaces and bracelets. "He liked to feel he owned everybody," said Clare. Soon Mr. Jacobs became indispensable.[14]

Not content with monopolizing them in town, he financed the summer rental of "Kidlodge," a three-bedroom shingle cottage near

Sound Beach (now Old Greenwich), Connecticut. There the Boothes—rapidly adjusting to a life of new bourgeois comforts—would spend four months a year for the next several seasons.

Joel Jacobs had his own room and drove out weekends in a big automobile. He would take them to baseball games in Bridgeport, to dinners at the Pickwick Inn in Greenwich, and on excursions into the countryside. The ensemble began to look more and more like a family. Clare asked her mother why she and Riggie did not marry, and Ann replied without hesitation, "I don't want my children to have a Jewish father."[15]

Whether or not anti-Semitism had impinged on Clare before, she certainly became aware of its subtleties now. A childless Ann Snyder might well have married Joel Jacobs. The two of them had much in common, from mutual distrust of outsiders to a shared belief that wealth compensated for lack of education. Ann's unwillingness to take Jacobs's name was a scruple not uncommon at the time. If David and Clare were to succeed in WASP society, she believed, they should not be hampered by Jewish ties.[16]

This did not, however, prevent her accepting increasing levels of aid from Jacobs, to the point that Clare began to refer to him as "my guardian." Whether Ann ever legally made her children his wards is unknown. But he assumed financial responsibility for them. Only on rare occasions would he mock Ann's social pretensions, sarcastically addressing her as Lady. Clare, whom he adored, was his "Angel."[17]

She liked him well enough. But her deepest affection was for Ann, who celebrated her thirty-third birthday at Kidlodge on August 29, 1915. One of Clare's earliest surviving letters acknowledges the event in exaggerated prose.

> When I grow up—and win for myself a name in the world . . . I shall lead you into a grand home and say—"This, my mother, is yours!" Dearest—I promise you I shall do that . . . And mother, if some times I am petulant, cross and selfish—I am sorry my Boothe temperment [sic] runs away with me . . . but it is the 'me' I am going to overcome . . . I love you. It is a real love that one cannot talk of lightly . . .
> *Ever Your Baby Girl.*[18]

That fall, Ann moved to new winter quarters in the Belleclaire Hotel, at West Seventy-seventh Street and Broadway. David went upriver to the New York Military Academy at Cornwall-on-Hudson, where he had transferred the year before, while Clare, aged twelve and a half, prepared for her first venture into independence. On September 22, she started as a boarding pupil at the Cathedral School of St. Mary, twenty-two miles from Manhattan in Garden City, Long Island.

St. Mary's was considered one of the best girls' schools in the country. The faculty, largely made up of Radcliffe, Columbia, and Smith graduates, offered a formidable curriculum in such subjects as physics, mathematics, Latin, and Greek. Clare understood that if she stayed there for five years, she had an excellent chance to enter college, because the school enjoyed a reputation for placing large numbers of undergraduates.

Autumn leaves had begun to turn when she arrived, weeping with apprehension, beneath St. Mary's turreted, ivy-clad walls. "Don't be a baby," her mother snapped, escorting her in. At the registration desk, Ann effortlessly played the "Baroness," flashing smiles in all directions. She had lied to get Clare accepted by this Episcopal bastion, claiming that her daughter was the grandchild of a bishop.[19]

Clare felt sick after Ann left. The two of them had become preternaturally close, as soul mates and co-conspirators. Parting from Ann was tantamount to losing a limb. After so many years spent with grown-ups, the communal juvenile world of boarding school loomed before her like imprisonment. But she did well enough in her first test for the headmistress, Miss Miriam Bytel, to place her one year ahead of her age-group, in the eighth grade. She was too chic for her class teacher, who found and removed an Erté illustration of a peacock from the lid of the newcomer's desk.[20]

Even though all St. Mary's students wore middy blouses, tunics, and saddle shoes, Clare was afraid the girls would find out that she was poorer than most of them. She hesitated to make friends, but did not try to hide her superior intelligence. In no time she found herself thoroughly disliked.

Her feelings of being relegated to "a dungeon" were intensified by her quarters, a cubicle carved out of a former chapel. She found it a confining and desolate niche. Cherubs were painted on the walls, and two images of kneeling angels flanked her bed. One window looked east across playing fields. The other faced west, towards the Cathedral of the Incarnation, where she was obliged to worship twice every Sunday, and where she would be confirmed at the end of her first year.[21]

St. Mary's school days were structured, from rising bell at 7:00 A.M. to "lights out" at 9:30 P.M. There were six forty-minute lessons before lunch, and games every afternoon: hockey and basketball until Christmas, gymnastics and dancing after the New Year, track and field and tennis in spring. From five to six o'clock was "study hall." The girls then changed into wool or silk dresses for dinner. French and German were spoken exclusively at two tables, and it was compulsory to attend them by rotation. The atmosphere in the dining room was so proper that when one girl retrieved some fallen flatware, Miss Bytel glared. "The fault," she intoned, "was not dropping of the fork. The fault was in picking it up."[22]

After dinner came two hours of "homework," much of which Clare spent drawing "beautiful girls and ladies" around her notebook margins. Seventy years later, the Honorable Clare Boothe Luce would similarly doodle on documents at stuffy Washington political meetings.[23]

Her obvious self-centeredness, plus a lack of girlish frivolity, made Clare an object of increasing scorn. Hurt and lonely, she took refuge one day in the branches of an apple tree on campus. Surprisingly, another girl, dark as she was fair, was also hiding there. Her name was Elisabeth, or "Buff," Cobb, daughter of Irvin S. Cobb, the celebrated humorist.[24]

Buff said that she was homesick, and the two formed an immediate bond, discovering that they both wanted to be writers. To her delighted amazement, Clare found herself meeting Richard Harding Davis and P. G. Wodehouse on a visit to Buff's house. But it was their host who became her first major literary influence. Mr. Cobb was a formidable-looking Kentuckian with a broad, big-lipped face and a 240-pound girth. Cheerfully eccentric, he worked in a study decorated with Indian artifacts, wearing a conch-belted smock and kneesocks. At dinner he betrayed a huge appetite for pickles, relishes, and pigs' knuckles, and expressed himself, between bites, almost entirely in stories and jokes. Despite his gross appearance and avoidance of serious topics of conversation, Clare came to appreciate Cobb's acute intelligence and professionalism.[25]

Clare and "Buff" Cobb at St. Mary's, *c. 1916*

She liked the Cobbs, and they liked her. Buff's mother described Clare as "the most startlingly poised child I ever knew."[26] Visiting often, Clare luxuriated in the kind of close, compatible family warmth she had never had at home, and she was bereft when Buff, ill with bronchitis, did not return to school in the fall of 1916.

Lonelier than ever in her second year, Clare devoured whole sets of Dickens, Thackeray, and Kipling, as well as modern novels. She especially identified with the solitary, clubfooted schoolboy in Somerset Maugham's *Of Human Bondage*.[27]

"What rage for fame," Clare wrote in St. Mary's yearbook, "attends both great and small."[28] Her determination to be eminent did not go unnoticed. Fellow students designated her the most conceited girl in the school. Convinced that she would never be either successful or popular there, she prevailed on her mother to take her away. When she departed Garden City Cathedral precincts in the spring of 1917, America was at war with Germany, and her life was about to take another important turn.

5

SOME
INNER COMPULSION

Je vis en espoir (I live in hope).

—CLARE BOOTHE'S PERSONAL MOTTO AT CASTLE SCHOOL

Ann Snyder was ambivalent about her fourteen-year-old daughter's avid intellectualism. On the one hand, she encouraged her book consumption. On the other, she had compromised Clare's chances of a university education by removing her prematurely from St. Mary's. Her suspicion that advanced study might make the girl an irredeemable "bluestocking" was compounded by fear of keeping her out of the marriage market for several crucial years.[1] Since Ann's chief aim was to find Clare an eligible husband sooner rather than later, she opted for some final polish at a school where parlor arts and graces, and live foreign languages, were considered more desirable accomplishments for an attractive girl than dead languages and college degrees.

The institution Ann chose was the Castle School, a fortresslike granite pile perched on a hill above Tarrytown-on-Hudson. Its prospectus advertised it as "a civic West Point for girls," turning out young

The Castle, Tarrytown-on-Hudson, New York

women "with broad not petty minds, with refined not tawdry tastes, with direct not shifting speech, with strong not nervous bodies"—sensible antidotes to the neurasthenic leanings of the age.[2]

Clare arrived there on September 26, 1917, as a tenth-grade sophomore. She loved the Castle on sight. At her feet stretched "the peaceful Hudson with its hazy border of blue hills, and the tiny village bathed in the warm autumn sunlight." Lacrosse fields, forested walks, and mansarded student residences spread out across spacious grounds. Inside the crenellated main building was a circular drawing room with columns and vaulted ceilings, massive portraits, and a golden harp. At night, after the sun set over the Jersey shore, girls could stand on a broad porch and watch the steady flashings of a distant lighthouse.[3]

Cassity Mason, the Castle's founder and principal, was considered a radical in finishing-school circles. She propelled her students towards professions usually reserved for males. All they needed was self-confidence. "Just ask God, and She will help you." In appearance the headmistress belied her scientific leanings. She was stout, motherly-looking, and monochromatic, with pale-gray, moist eyes and upswept gray hair. In iron gray poplin she was a model of efficiency during the day, while in iron gray satin she appeared a softer presence at the nightly dinner table.[4]

Most of Clare's 111 fellow students came from middle-income families and had already completed high school courses elsewhere. She was assigned quarters with Ruth Balsam, an impressionable Southerner. Their study-bedroom consisted of closely placed cots, two desks with wicker chairs, a dressing table, corner table, geometric carpet, and small chandelier.

Clare, fast approaching her adult height of five feet five, was fashionably plump at 155 pounds (though 30 pounds above her own ideal). To Ruth, she looked like a fairy-tale princess, her hair "golden and soft with polished highlights in the waves," her complexion flawless. It was rumored that Mrs. Boothe bathed her daughter in milk.[5]

Over the next two years, Clare would blossom in mind as well as body, skipping eleventh grade and becoming a senior at age fifteen. The Castle's curriculum placed less emphasis on academic achievement than St. Mary's. Nevertheless, within seven months, Clare achieved an 88 percent average, with 96 for English history, 93 for ethics and sociology, 99 for costume design, and an astonishing 100 for physical training. Her average would soar to 94 by October of 1918. Before she left, her proliferating talents would cause one teacher to recommend that she go on to the Art Students League of New York, and another to prophesy a career in public speaking or journalism. Clare herself was convinced that one day she might produce "the Great American Novel."[6]

Alternatively, after seeing Ethel Barrymore in *Déclassé*, she wrote in her diary, "I'm not flattering myself—but I think with half a chance and some experience I could be every bit as good an actress." She even developed a belated interest in music, and reacted swooningly to a recital by Sergey Rachmaninoff. "My heart aches and aches to play the piano. Or *yes* the violin. Oh, God my father is rising within me."[7]

Her facility in so many fields bewildered her. "For Mother's sake I must make a name for myself . . . What am I supposed to be?"[8]

One of Clare's schoolfriends recalled, "She was always driving herself through some inner compulsion to find out the way of everything. When the rest of us were reading Elinor Glyn, she would be deep in Racine . . . and while she soaked in the tub she'd have Plato propped on the taps in front of her. But she was no goody-goody. If anybody annoyed her, she had a tongue like a black snake whip."[9]

Clare struggled to curb her natural acidity, with mixed results. Having alienated St. Mary's girls by her standoffishness, she took pains to be public-spirited at the Castle. She labored through the night at extracurricular tasks till dark circles appeared beneath her eyes.[10] At different times she was vice president of her class, art editor and business manager of *The Drawbridge* magazine, and chairman of the Current Topics Club.

Other girls were struck by her perfect grooming, vivacity, and enthusiasm. They had no doubt that one day she "would do great things." She always took the honors in weekly speeches on news events. Her poetry was often overwrought and poorly scanned, but they admired it anyway—as they did her prowess on the hockey field. By her own assessment her mind was too quick for her feet in ball games. She preferred, she said, "to sit under a tree . . . with a volume of Rostand or Paillerou."[11]

Maturity was some way off, and in the interim Clare could not conceal all her besetting faults. The bruising judgment of St. Mary's was resurrected when a friend called her "conceited." What Clare longed for most was to be adored. "Wonder what it is about me that no one loves me better than anyone else . . . I'm 'popular'—yes," she confided in her diary, "but I'd rather 'have one person love me paramountly' [*sic*]."[12]

It did not occur to her that her peers might want some affection in return. Indeed, she found it hard to love anyone other than Ann and David. "My whole heart and soul is wrapt up in three things," she wrote, "Mother, Brother and my ambition for success."[13]

Yet she lacked neither affection nor accolades at the Castle. *The Drawbridge*'s final ratings awarded her first place for Most Artistic, Cleverest, and Prettiest, as well as second place for Most Ambitious. "In my heart of hearts," she admitted, "I know I only deserve one—the last."[14]

Clare scored high marks in dancing and deportment (100 percent in the latter) and welcomed the attentions of handsome cadets at Saturday-night balls at the nearby military academy. One purposeful youth

David Boothe at the New York Military
Academy, *c. 1917*

gripped her so tightly as they fox-trotted to "Saxophone Sobs" and "Dark Town Strutters" that she bore the imprint of his uniform buttons on her dress the rest of the evening.[15]

Her first substantial *affaire de coeur* was with an Air Corps lieutenant, Lloyd D. Miller. He held her hand at the movies—"the greatest thrill"— and wrote passionate letters. But then he was posted abroad, and the correspondence ceased. Clare romantically assumed that he was "dead and buried on the fields of Flanders." Her interest in him abated somewhat when she found he was not.[16]

Meanwhile, her appetite for other flirtations continued. Ralph Ingersoll (a future publisher of *Time*) recalled Clare at this period as being "a party girl . . . blonde, good figure . . . would neck, but look out."[17]

The type of man who attracted her sexually resembled William S. Hart, the angular, unsmiling hero of countless silent westerns. "Pretty"

features, like those of Rudolph Valentino, repelled her. When it came
to imagining her ideal husband, she thought not of looks but of practi-
cality. He must be a businessman earning a substantial salary, because
love could not blossom "among greasy pans, soiled linen and smarting
soapsuds." Moreover, he should have "a splendid code of honor" and
worship her "better than God."[18]

Her "dream" man tended to be sensitive looking and unreachable,
like the English poet John Drinkwater, on whose photographic portrait
she yearningly wrote, "*Yours—John.*" Someday, perhaps, an aristocratic
figure like him would enfold her in his manly arms . . .

Her personal bookplate represented a knight on a white charger.
Looking at it in old age, she sighed, "He never came."[19]

Ann Clare Boothe, *c. 1918*

Joel Jacobs provided plenty of pocket money to satisfy Clare's burgeoning needs. On just one day trip to New York, she spent more than twice as much as her mother used to earn at Tecla's in a week. Jacobs paid for her train tickets, taxis, riding lessons, lunches, corsets, combs, and ice creams. He also financed her insatiable entertainment habit. In a year and a half, she recorded seeing approximately sixty plays, movies, musicals, operas, reviews, or vaudeville shows—more than three outings a month. Riggie further indulged her with large baskets of fruit, flowers, and candy dispatched to the Castle, a leather-bound set of the novels of Alexandre Dumas, and sixteen ten-dollar gold pieces for her sixteenth birthday. From time to time he would award her shares in his prospering tire company. On Sundays he often drove out to Tarrytown and treated her to lunch—"Baked Alaska—yum!" Missing his "Angel" in midweek, he would send a chauffeur to collect her for dinners at the Waldorf-Astoria. He jokingly called the great hotel "a joint," but to Clare it was "Life! Life!"[20]

The more lavishly Jacobs spent, the more she enjoyed his company. "Riggie is a wonderful man, and I just adore him," she wrote in her diary. "Jew! Yes. But any white Christian who was ½ as fine as he would be considered a miracle. Riggie thinks very wonderful things of me . . . I shall do my best to make him really proud."[21]

Ann Snyder might have wondered whether Jacobs was becoming more interested in her daughter than in herself. He was furious when the teenager stayed out late with friends at a cheap nightclub, and glowered when other men stared at her, as they invariably did now. Clare suspected, with satisfaction, that his jealousy was a little more than paternal.[22]

Clare's first foray into foreign policy, which was to be the passion of her later years, took place on August 23, 1918, in Sound Beach. Patriotic fervor aroused by the war had spurred her to raise money for the Red Cross by producing and stage-managing a children's performance of *Cinderella* at the town school, for a total profit of seventy-five dollars.

She had no part in the play herself but, clad in a rose-colored gown, made a poised opening speech. "We must have the League of Nations to keep the peace, and America must stay in it . . . Russia must emerge from the war whole and sound. If anything happens to Russia there is sure to be another war."

Next morning a local newspaper reported, "Sound Beach is strong for Miss Boothe today."[23]

On Thursday, November 7, booming West Point guns and downriver sirens signaled—four days prematurely—that Germany had surrendered. Clare and her fellow students, singing "The Star-Spangled Banner," the *Marseillaise*, and "God Save the King," climbed a tower to hoist the American flag. After dark Miss Mason hired four cars to take a group of seniors to New York. Clare caught sight of her mother and Riggie in the traffic and joined them for a ride around Manhattan, through delirious, surging crowds. Caruso was singing "Over There" from a window in the Knickerbocker Hotel, and people stood ankle-deep in newspapers, listening.[24]

Clare gave her own postmortem on the Great War in an eight-page essay written and delivered in French to other Castle students. The title, "*Ce qu'on sème on récolte*" (What one sows one reaps), was apt. She argued learnedly that the recent war had its origins in the failure of Western European nations to prevent Prussia's appropriation of the mines of Lorraine forty-eight years before. Bismarck had seized them in order to build up armaments and, in consequence, encouraged the later megalomania of the Kaiser. This was allowed to go unchecked, and so, she concluded, "1914 est la résultat de 1870."[25]

Focusing more and more on literature as a career, Clare began to write with skill and psychological perceptiveness during her final months at the Castle. In a short story called "The Mephistophelean Curl" and a one-act play, "The Lily Maid," she betrayed a jaundiced view of sexual relations, analyzing respectively the amorous manipulations of a forty-year-old woman and the moral musings of a convent girl torn between purity and profligacy.[26]

Her own experience of sex so far was limited to rather chaste kissing and petting. She wrote rather more convincingly of the Maid's desire to get "boiled, stewed, spiffed and tight." Sex education at the Castle was the province of Miss Lum, a nervous spinster who displayed diagrams of only female organs and was vague about the mechanics of intercourse. "Of course, girls," she would say wistfully, "I have not actually had this experience, but I am told it is very beautiful." The most valuable part of her lecture, as far as the students were concerned, was a list of "tricks" they should *not* practice, lest boys become overfamiliar. They carefully memorized the list for use at the next West Point ball.[27]

Clare graduating, *May 1919*

Clare, cautioned by a teacher's farewell warnings against "egoism" and "coldness," graduated from the Castle on May 27, 1919. To the strains of Mendelssohn's "Priests' March," she entered the gymnasium for the last school day, along with eighteen class members. Her white, georgette-crêpe dress hung straight from the shoulders, a fitting cover for silk and lace underwear that had been made by her mother over many weeks. She carried a bouquet of roses and sweet peas.[28]

"Yes, yes, she is our prodigy and our genius," her classmates were to write in their yearbook.

> Yet, just the same, she is as lovable as she is brilliant. Ann Clare is one of those girls who can do anything. In Art,— well you've seen our class posters. In writing,—just look through the *Drawbridge*. In conversation,—you all know her wit. In fact, she is just a little bit of "all right" from beginning to end. She is very ambitious for a great career, and the Senior Class all wish her the best of luck and feel sure that some day in the future we may say, "Oh, yes, Miss Ann Clare Boothe, the famous author and illustrator? Why I knew her back in 1919 at the Castle School!"[29]

During commencement events, the headmistress was heard to say that Clare Boothe was "a very bright girl who would some day make her mark in the world." Miss Mason had always paid close attention to her smartest pupil, writing her encouraging notes and driving her to town for lunches and matinées. Had Clare not been so self-absorbed, she might have appreciated these special favors. On the contrary, her views of the iron-gray lady grew vitriolic as memories of the Castle faded. "A hard-hearted old cuss," she wrote only three years later, "and very selfish and conceited which is only natural in an unmarried old woman of her age and proclivities."[30]

Clare hoped for more stocks from Riggie as a graduation present. They were not forthcoming, but she was hardly disappointed to receive instead a green Essex roadster and, from Ann, a desk for her own room in a new house.

6

DAMAGE

TO THE BONE

It is better that scandal should arise than that truth
should be deserted. —St. Bernard

Instead of leasing a property for the summer of 1919, Ann Snyder persuaded Joel Jacobs to buy and furnish a two-story, white clapboard house in Sound Beach. She assigned him one of its five bedrooms for his weekend use, and moved in just before her daughter graduated.[1]

"Driftway," named after the sea-level road on which it stood, was a forty-five-minute train ride from New York City and fifteen minutes by trolley from Stamford. With views east across Greenwich Cove and west across Long Island Sound, it was a significant improvement in location as well as size on Ann's former rental in nearby Shorelands. Clare, full of anticipation, turned onto an oval driveway carved out of a well-groomed lawn (already planted with trees and sentinel shrubs by her mother) and entered under the shade of a *porte-cochère*.

Inside she discovered amenities beyond anything she had known at school, or in city apartments. Her love of ease and space was gratified by "closets galore," and three bathrooms with showers and set-in tubs.

"Driftway," Sound Beach, Connecticut

Separate servants' quarters satisfied the snob in her. She moved her desk, leather-bound books, and Maxfield Parrish prints upstairs into a private study-bedroom. As she opened its shutters and looked out over a sheet of still blue water, her life seemed to open up and stabilize in all kinds of agreeable ways.[2]

When the novelty of being a semi-permanent resident of Connecticut, rather than just a summer colonist, wore off, Clare's pleasure in her new surroundings moderated. Sound Beach felt parochial after her sophisticated experiences in New York. The town's year-round population consisted mostly of fishermen, strawberry growers, and onion farmers. Its worst "den of iniquity" was the firehouse, where men reputedly gambled behind closed doors.[3]

It was not a community likely to captivate David Boothe, whom Ann and Clare were expecting for the summer. Over the past six years, he had been shunted off to three military schools, without much thought as to his preferences. Ann felt ambivalent about her son, alternately isolating him and indulging him. She would chastise him when he stayed out late on his rare visits home, then give him too much pocket money. Clare envied the way "he could wind my Mother around his little finger."[4]

The previous fall, just before the start of his fifth year at the New York Military Academy, David had made a dramatic grab for attention by running away to join the Marine Corps. At sixteen, he had been two years short of the legal enlistment age. But through the quirk of having been registered at birth as "David Franklin," he could ingeniously argue that there was no certificate disproving David Boothe was old enough to serve—an early example of the duplicity he had learned at his mother's knee.

By February 1919 he had been shipped to the Dominican Republic with a U.S. Expeditionary Force to help the local government put down native insurgents. Clare could only guess at his experiences in "Bucket of Blood," as David sardonically dubbed Santo Domingo. When he left the USEF with an honorable discharge that spring, some of the fire in him appeared to have died, and he now seemed willing to complete his studies. But first he would come to Sound Beach to relax in the house he had not yet seen.[5]

As it happened, it was not David who first burst in to disturb Clare's newfound tranquillity. Somebody quite unexpected preceded him, to catastrophic effect.

On Thursday, May 29, Clare went shopping in New York. She bought a dresser, some linens to store in it, and a white bulldog puppy whom she named "Lord Kitchener." Back in Connecticut the following morning, she took a fifty-two-mile driving lesson with Riggie's chauffeur, and congratulated herself on doing "rather well" for a beginner.

All of this was recorded routinely in her diary. Then, with no change of pace or tone, the day's entry concluded, "Billy Boothe called up and we had all thought him dead."[6]

This terse announcement of the resurrection of the father who had vanished from her life seven years before was self-deceptively matter-of-fact. His "death" had been Ann's convenient rewriting of the true story of their leaving him in Chicago. Fiction, in time, had become reality, at least in Clare's imaginative mind, and she believed, probably at her mother's urging, that William had allowed the report of his demise "to spread for his own ends." The family now faced the embarrassing prospect of admitting to his existence and accepting him into their lives. "He wants," Clare wrote, "to come up and see me and David."[7]

William Franklin Boothe drove out to Sound Beach on Saturday, May 31, in a shining Packard. Evidently his fortunes had improved. At fifty-seven, lined and gray, he was still handsome and confident. He sat down and seemed straightaway at ease. Without asking a single question about his daughter's recent history, he launched into an account of his own. Since 1916 he had been running a violin school in Los Angeles, as well as working with the Veterans' Bureau on a program of therapeutic rehabilitation for the disabled. He bragged—truthfully, as it turned out—of making a reputation as a teacher of advanced fingerboard exercises, and he said that musicians from around the country were in correspondence with him about his remarkable technique.[8]

As she listened, Clare could see that the stranger who had returned to reacquaint himself with her was far from a contrite prodigal. He brought no gifts, made no apologies "for the shameful manner in which he neglected his family." Nor was he impressed with their spacious new house and possessions. Far from feeling any tenderness towards him, she was ashamed to entertain this living ghost, about whom she had fabricated so many sentimental lies. "I have made him my dead daddy, a character almost ideal . . . a musical genius in fact—a perfect father," she wrote. Unaware of her antagonism, William arranged to see them all again in two days' time.[9]

When Riggie arrived on Sunday, he expressed disdain for the man who had offered Ann "not one cent" in compensation for his long absence. Clare was still enraged that her father had shown no curiosity about her. "I hate, no I just am absolutely indifferent to him."[10]

William Boothe returned to Sound Beach on Monday, June 2, and talked hypnotically, in the same vein as before. Clare was dazzled by his multifaceted intelligence yet simultaneously repulsed by "his colossal gaul [sic] and conceit," despising in him her own most entrenched fault.[11]

Two days after William's second visit, David arrived, looking "badly," Clare thought, and behaving much like the malcontent who had run away nine months before. Now seventeen years old, five foot nine, and heavily muscled, he was more man than boy. Fraternizing with the toughest and most degraded marines in camp and barracks had coarsened his speech, manners, and habits. He grumbled excessively about what he lacked in life, and acted like a hardened misanthrope.[12]

Yet there was something about his swarthy aggressiveness that appealed to Clare and would always make her putty in his hands. "He is remarkably like Billy Boothe," she noted. Next day she was able to compare father and son in the flesh when William came for a third visit. Not only did the two look alike but they shared a "boastful spirit." Disconcertingly, William focused all his attention on her brother. "Do you have any music in you, Davey, any music at all?" he asked, unaware that his son hated the fiddle.[13]

Without realizing they had seen the last of their father, Clare and David sent him recriminatory letters after he went back to California. Nine years would pass before William let Clare know what he felt about their reunion and its aftermath.

> At the time of that visit I was prosperous . . . and received with open arms by you, David and your mother. I wanted *your* affection, I wanted David to admire his Daddy, I was hungry for it, when I left I was happy and I was girded with a new desire to do things—and then I got from you a letter which ended with *vous avez brulez la chandelle tous deux les bouts* [you have burned the candle at both ends], and from David a letter threatening me with bodily injury if I ever again encountered him . . . I knew the motivating cause of those letters . . . the same old propaganda was in working order.[14]

For Ann Snyder, the episode created labyrinthine complications. She had been passing herself off as William Boothe's widow for years. Should his existence now become widely known, she would have to resume the pose of being his wife, or explain their separation. If she ever wanted to "remarry," she must fake a divorce from him. Alternatively, she might acknowledge that their union had never been legalized and that their children were illegitimate. But this admission would destroy her new social status as a homeowner in conservative Greenwich, threaten the stability funded by Joel Jacobs, and hinder her burgeoning affair with yet another lover. Little wonder that she seemed during those late spring weeks to be in neither good spirits nor good health.[15]

As for Clare, she was devastated by her once-beloved father's apparent lack of regret for the lost years and indifference to her future. "He had no eyes or ears for me." Since their parting in 1912, she had maintained the illusion that she had inherited more of Ann's good points than William's bad ones. Now that she had seen so much of her own selfishness in him, she was inconsolable. Her feelings of loss and betrayal would sharpen over the years to sometimes suicidal fears of rejection, of being "unwanted, unloved, *unworthy* of being loved." The damage was to the bone, and irreparable.[16]

7

An Indescribable Longing
for Romance

*Perhaps the most poignant legacy of abandonment is
compulsive wandering from person to person, place
to place.* —Herbert J. Freudenberger

After William Boothe left, Clare concentrated her search for authoritative role models on real people, as distinct from fictional or celluloid ones. Newest and most impressive of these was her mother's latest beau, Dr. Albert Elmer Austin, health officer of Sound Beach and a surgeon at Greenwich Hospital. He and Ann had been friends, if not lovers, since at least the previous summer, when she had consulted him professionally. Soon afterwards he had enlisted in the Army Medical Reserve Corps and been assigned to Camp Custer in Battle Creek, Michigan, to treat repatriated soldiers. Ann had visited him there for a week in February 1919, telling Clare that she was going "to be with Grandma" at the local sanitarium.[1]

Battle Creek seemed a curiously remote place to hospitalize Louisa Snyder. But Ann loved intrigue. Besides, she needed to be discreet. The forty-year-old doctor was married, albeit unhappily, and she dared not risk being cited as co-respondent in another divorce suit. Nor did she dare upset Joel Jacobs, on whom she still depended financially.

The next thing Clare knew, Dr. Austin had appeared at the Belleclaire Hotel for Easter breakfast. Evidently her mother felt free to be seen with him in the city. They had driven and dined out together, to the distress of Percy Frowert, who, "drunk as a dog," had pestered Clare with querulous phone calls.[2]

It remained to be seen what Joel Jacobs would think of his mistress's developing infatuation. Clare wrote in her diary that the doctor was "in love with Mother, altho' he tries very, very hard to conceal it from both of us."[3]

The man with whom Ann Snyder had become involved in the fading days of the war was a tall and large-domed New Englander with an athletic physique, strong features, and pale-gray, bespectacled eyes. He was a snappy dresser and congenial personality who liked to stroll the streets of Sound Beach with his chow, "Rolls," and bulldog, "Royce." They were the nearest he would come, he joked, to the car he coveted. Instead, Dr. Austin settled for a modest Buick, in which he would drive out day or night to any patient who summoned him. Those in straitened circumstances were generally not billed. Sick children called him "Uncle Easy," on account of his gentle persuasiveness. One local girl looked forward to being ill, because he could be relied on to play a riotous game of poker with her on the bedcover. Young beachcombers would dig clams for him, knowing he would pay them fifty cents a bushel.[4]

Throughout the summer of 1919 the doctor continued to court Ann Snyder. He would sit on the upper porch as the sun went down, astonishing Clare with the breadth of his erudition. "He is of the purely mental and spiritual type," she wrote admiringly in her diary, comparing his mind to "the machinery of a tremendous factory."[5]

Elmer Austin, who had been the nation's top medical graduate of his year, was also a classical scholar capable of quoting Cicero in the original and reading the Bible in Greek. He knew the finer points of architecture and music (he was a skilled trombonist and leader of the town band) as well as politics and world affairs. With him, for the first time in her life, Clare was able to experience the cerebral pleasure of

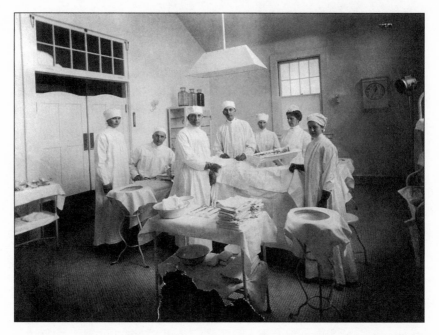

Dr. Austin and his operating team at Greenwich Hospital, *c. 1919*

dialogue at an adult level, and she saw that she could hold her own. "Our conversation," she wrote after one particularly mellow evening, "followed the lines of the moon, being rather roundabout." Yet as the warm weeks went by, she detected a certain constriction in Dr. Austin, a provincial lack of ambition that had kept him from taking a post at one of the great metropolitan hospitals that had once vied for him.[6]

He could not match Joel Jacobs in lavish giving, but he was a similar combination of avuncularity and sentiment. When Clare decided to shed twenty-five pounds, to look svelte in a black satin bathing suit embroidered in red worsted by Ann, he carefully wrote out a diet plan for her. Between its pages, she came upon a pressed four-leaf clover.[7]

Had he entered her life earlier, Dr. Austin might have made a sympathetic father figure. But Clare's personality was already larger than his own. She grew impatient with his pedantry, emotional reserve, and distaste for the glittery city that so enthralled her.

Ann Snyder had no such misgivings. In Dr. Austin's company the thirty-seven-year-old matron became as coquettish as an infatuated

76

teenager. Yet his love went undeclared, even when it transpired that his wife of nine years was having an affair with another man. Ann was strangely relieved by this reticence. She suspected that he idealized as well as idolized her and might be disillusioned if he found out about her murky background. Nor did she want to seem ungracious towards Riggie, who had presented her with $12,000 worth of jewelry that year alone. To give up a millionaire for a man who cared so little about worldly possessions would be foolhardy.[8]

Joel Jacobs was not so preoccupied with Wall Street as to ignore the new presence at Driftway. He showed signs of increasing nervousness and irritability, although he was studiously polite to Dr. Austin, and even deigned to play pinochle with him. Ann, for her part, was tormented at the thought that she might one day (if Elmer divorced) have to choose between them. As always when confused, she distracted herself by concocting fantastic plans for her daughter and exaggerating her accomplishments in public, to the point of lying. "It is the *only* vice or sin of any kind that mars her," Clare wrote, "and one I am afraid I have."[9]

As July began, Clare felt a need for more structured days. Boating with David and perfecting her diving were amusing pastimes but hardly career-enhancing. She decided to apply for acceptance at Columbia University's School of Journalism in the fall, and to that end she enrolled in a shorthand and typing course at Stamford.

Rote learning did not engage her active brain. "I have a marvellous power of conception," she wrote, "and an equally marvellous lack of power to carry out my ideas." Losing interest, she escaped for a weekend with her old friend Ruth on the southern shore of Long Island.[10]

The Balsams' house in Long Beach was a ramshackle, farmlike place not far from an airfield. There, on Sunday, July 13, Clare took her first plane ride, a ten-minute, wildly thrilling mixture of nosedives, tailspins, and loops. "I promptly lost my breakfast, to my immense chagrin . . . but it was well worth while." The aviator, charmed by her, waived his fifteen-dollar fee.[11]

Since early May, when Clare had published a turgid ode called "The New Era" on the front page of *National Magazine*, she had con-

Ann Snyder with her bulldog "Blighty," *c. 1919*

tinued to write verse. One poem, entitled "Contentment," was reminiscent of Rupert Brooke.

> *A few loved books, and fewer friends,*
> *A roomy desk and fresh-nibbed pen,*
> *Lush, ripened fruits, and cream-topped milk*
> *And honied biscuits now and then . . .*[12]

Actually she had little appetite for such simple things, nor for any circumscribed existence, no matter how idyllic. Ann promised her fifty dollars if she could also publish a story, but Clare made no effort to do so. Sound Beach was already "rather boresome," and by late July even her diary entries grew sporadic, as she gave herself up to four months of "pleasure, pain, disappointment, new sensations."[13]

Her first diversion was a fair-mustached Army officer named James Butts, whose stocky frame echoed his name. He proposed too often to be taken seriously, so she began to date Captain Walter Yuill, a young West Point graduate and winner of fourteen bronze stars. "What makes me tremble when I am dancing with him? And what makes my heart sing out when I hear his voice on the phone?" Not, apparently, Walter's financial prospects: he seemed uninterested in making a fortune. Acknowledging that she was, despite her palpitations, more "mercenary" than romantic, Clare showed little concern when the courtship lapsed.[14]

No other men she met that summer satisfied her triple desire for military uniform, intellectual maturity, and wealth. She fell prey to melancholy introspection, and took comfort in her diary. "Although I am twenty mentally [she was still only sixteen] I am such a mere child in physical sensations." Her own personality perplexed her, as she vacillated between being dependent and independent, disciplined and undisciplined, passive and compulsive, prudish and dismissive of ordinary conventions. What would her future hold as a result of these ambiguities: fame, riches, and love, or obscurity, poverty, and lovelessness? She felt confident in challenging any intellect, yet paradoxically sought, as she always would, the approval and encouragement of inferiors. "You do believe in me," she asked Ruth Balsam at this time, "in my power and ability to be a success?" She knew that happiness must be earned and fought for but doubted her courage in making the necessary sacrifices. "I am a coward, I would have a bed of roses and not pluck the thorns."[15]

To men, Miss Boothe seemed strangely constituted, even enigmatic. Though entranced by her incandescent beauty, her quirky sense of humor and probing mind, none could plumb her complexity. "How should they," she concluded, "when I myself marvel at the total composition?"[16]

During this period of heightened sensitivity, mystical stirrings Clare had first experienced in school reasserted themselves. One day, walking along the beach, religious ecstasy enveloped her—a brief but unforgettable moment of exaltation when she knew "all there was to know of life, and death, and the Trinity," and had "the feeling that God had touched my face, and I had touched His." Neither falling in love nor converting later to Catholicism approached this in intensity. She would have to wait forty years for a comparable euphoria induced by LSD, but even that was "not as pure."[17]

As the days shortened, Clare succumbed to her mother's suggestion of a two-week vacation at the Greenbrier Hotel in West Virginia. Before leaving they dined in Manhattan with Riggie and saw Fritz Kreisler's musical comedy *Apple Blossoms*, starring a new brother-and-sister dance duo, Fred and Adele Astaire. Afterwards they went on to a nightspot called the Midnight Frolic. It was, Clare wrote with relish, "foul, sensuous, disgusting."[18]

On Sunday afternoon, November 16, she and Ann set off on their fourteen-and-a-half-hour train journey to White Sulphur Springs. The resort, a complex of elegant white buildings and cottages set in the midst of seven thousand valley acres in the Allegheny Mountains, traditionally attracted an international clientele. Heads of state and rich industrialists, drawn by the beneficial mineral waters, parked their private cars in sidings at the station. But Ann Snyder had motives other than health for choosing this Southern spa.

She had been following newspaper accounts of the North American tour of Edward, Prince of Wales. Now nearing the end of his journey, the exhausted twenty-five-year-old heir apparent had chosen to recuperate at the Greenbrier. By the time Ann and Clare arrived early on the morning of Monday, November 17, he was already into his third and last day of exercise and social activities.

While Clare settled into Room 125, the febrile prince sprinted round the half-mile track and then took a swim. After breakfast he went off to the golf links and stayed there until dusk. Hopes of meeting him that night in the Casino ballroom were dashed when her trunk with evening dresses was not delivered in time. At eight o'clock, after a few fox-trots and two-steps, Edward headed for his private train, and by nine he was speeding to New York.[19]

"The Prince of Wales just left," Clare mourned in her diary, "and I didn't so much as get a peek at him. Poor hounded youth. I feel so sorry for him—and yet—a Prince, you know."[20]

Next day Clare took a ride in mountains whose grandeur made her feel insignificant. She was full of self-disgust at having missed Prince Edward and not having made any friends. Ann accused her of pining for Captain Yuill. "How little she knows me," wrote Clare in exasperation. "There is room in my heart for one great love, and until then I am content with any number of flirtations." But the Greenbrier had a shortage of young men and an abundance of "shiny bald pates." One exception who greatly attracted her was an "adorable, luscious" married man of thrilling *savoir-faire*. Although Clare sensed his corresponding interest, she was unable to manage an introduction. "If someone doesn't talk to me soon, I'll go mad," she scribbled in her diary. "I'm so blame lonesome."[21]

As if in answer to her prayers, another fortyish man made overtures, until Ann banned him because he was "a Jew." All those "who amount to anything," she warned, did the same. Evidently she felt no sense of hypocrisy in indulging selective anti-Semitism while being there on Joel Jacobs's money. Clare had tea with Mr. Straus anyway, but this little rebellion hardly satisfied her craving for excitement.[22]

On Thanksgiving Day, without apparent warning, Dr. Austin appeared. Ann, wrote her daughter, was "in the seventh heaven of delight." He stayed with them for their last three days, during which Clare fought off the advances of hurdling and riding instructors, and went dancing with her attentive Jew. "Gosh, it's great to feel people love and admire you."[23]

The doctor had good reason to agree. On September 23, he had filed for a divorce on grounds of adultery. Since his evidence was unshakable, he expected to be a free man early the next year. Even so, he risked a countersuit in staying under the same hotel roof as Ann Snyder. "Many walking and riding parties were out on the trails today," a special dispatch to the *Baltimore Sun* reported on November 30. "Mrs. A. C. Boothe, Miss Claire [*sic*] Boothe and Dr. A. E. Austin rode to Jericho Draft."

None too soon, the equestrians departed that night on the 11:30 train north.

After their uneventful summer in Sound Beach and luxurious vacation at White Sulphur Springs, Ann and Clare found themselves once again looking for winter quarters in Manhattan. Joel Jacobs would pay the rent, as usual, but he left it to them to choose among the crowded residential hotels of New York's Upper West Side. They tried, and rejected, the Ansonia ("dirty place full of Jews and riff-raff," Clare commented), then the Hamilton on Seventy-third Street ("I wish it were the Plaza") before choosing the Bretton Hall at Eighty-sixth and Broadway.[24]

Clare, frustrated by her lack of qualifications to enter college, felt lethargic and useless. She sought relief in a series of diversions. None satisfied her. At the Turkish baths, she felt shy parading her ample body in front of other women. At Brentano's Book Store, she yearned for a hand-illustrated 1850 edition of *David Copperfield,* but two hundred dollars was beyond her pocket. ("Oh wealth . . . what power is thine . . ."). At Durland's Ring on West Sixty-sixth Street, she took dressage and riding lessons but could only afford a hired cart horse. She was envious of riders with their own thoroughbreds, lean mounts that strutted with hooves high in the air. An indescribable longing for romance and action—almost masculine in its ardor—suffused her. "What a dull prosaic existence we girls of the 20th century who saw no service in the Great War live!"[25]

At dinner with Joel Jacobs one night in mid-December, she saw the "luscious" man she had so admired in West Virginia sitting at the next table. "Oh, I adore him, and I know he does me . . . I am the girl who wants to be a great writer and all I can think of is when my dream man is coming!"[26]

Christmas at the Bretton Hall, with its "horrid red plush furniture," was dismal, despite Riggie's expensive presents. Ann received a gold mesh evening bag with a cabochon sapphire clasp, and Clare a diamond wristwatch. After dining at the Ritz, Clare petulantly told herself that she would have preferred a Dickensian Christmas, with a tree, a turkey, and homemade plum pudding. The day lacked spiritual content and compounded her feelings of futility. David, home on vacation, blamed her discontent on failure to write. "As if I were some sort of 'genius,' " she complained. She doubted she would produce anything of literary value until she had observed and absorbed life in greater variety.[27]

An Indescribable Longing for Romance

To celebrate New Year's Eve, Clare went alone to a party of "drunken, amusing, ill-kept, untidy Bohemians." She found them appealing. One, a classical pianist, obviously returned her attraction, and she congratulated herself on managing to defend her virtue. "I was the most popular girl there and I know it."[28]

On that cadence 1919 came to an end, and the Twenties began.

8

BOILING WATER OF

THE HOTTEST

*The most intimate is at the same time the most
universal.* —THOMAS MANN

Throughout her life, Clare kept in contact with friends and acquaintances whose horizons were narrower than her own. She
needed ego-boosters to support her queenly aspirations, or commiserate
with her when her spirits were low. In March 1920, she visited old
school friends in Illinois and later that spring had others to stay in
Sound Beach, while she tried out, unsuccessfully, for the U.S. Olympic
swimming team.[1] Beguiled by her beauty, brains, and life force, these
acolytes were unaware that, given the opportunity, Clare preferred in-
tellects equal if not superior to her own who could teach her about literature, politics, and world affairs.

Her interest in these subjects was reflected in a sonnet published by
the *Stamford Advocate*, in which the seventeen-year-old Miss Boothe
expressed her dissatisfaction with President Woodrow Wilson for ca-
pitulating on the Fourteen Points.

From quiet cloisters of a scholar's mind
We called you to a world of rapid deeds,
Diplomacies and wars, and foreign greeds,
And politics corrupt. We thought to find
You one to master these, and guide Mankind,
No self-applauding dreamer, babbling creeds,
To all immediate and urgent needs
Of Practical Solutions, wilful-blind.
Well, you had not the steel-strength in your soul,
It was too soft to realize the goal
It dimly saw, and yet could not achieve;
The vision at its best claims our esteem,
The dream as such, is still a splendid dream.
It's for our shattered hopes in you, we grieve.[2]

As a result, or perhaps in spite, of this effort, Clare later claimed she was invited to be spokeswoman for a group of young Washington-bound petitioners urging Wilson not to compromise with Senate opposition to the League of Nations. At the White House, they found the President (who had recently suffered a stroke) sitting at a table with a shawl around his shoulders. He was leaning over a bowl and shaking. Clare stepped forward and made a short speech, ending: "You must go on for the salvation of the world." Wilson neither looked at her nor replied. Mrs. Wilson whispered in her husband's ear, "Say something to this delegation." The invalid mumbled, "There is skin on my milk."[3]

On August 26, the Nineteenth Amendment was ratified in the U.S. Congress, giving votes to women and making them, overnight, 51 percent of the electorate. In November's presidential election, Americans generally proved to be as disillusioned with Democratic leadership as Clare was and elected the Republican Warren G. Harding.

Restless at the onset of winter, Ann Snyder decided to take a long trip to Europe. Clare needed no inducement to act again as her traveling companion. Ever since she was a little girl she had wanted to cry when she saw trains steaming off without her. Wanderlust, she wrote in her diary, "has such complete possession of me I want to scream." She convinced herself that several months overseas would broaden her mind, although she knew that only stay-at-home study would deepen it. "Some of the greatest geniuses have lived and died in little country towns. But think how much greater they would have been if they hadn't kept stationary."[4]

Mother and daughter sailed for England in mid-November. Dr. Austin, already divorced for eleven months, elected to join them a few weeks later in London. From her second-floor room at the Victoria Hotel, Clare finally caught a glimpse of the elusive Prince of Wales, crossing Trafalgar Square in a coach. "Oh what a dear! Little Prince Charming . . ." She also saw Edward's parents one night at the Shaftesbury Theatre. King George V, she thought, looked unhappy and tired, while Queen Mary lit up the royal box with her diamonds.[5]

On another theatrical evening, she became infatuated with the twenty-year-old Noel Coward. He was playing at the Kingsway Theatre in an Elizabethan burlesque, *The Knight of the Burning Pestle*, and made plain his contempt for the genre by strutting, posturing, and speaking his lines in an exaggerated plummy voice. Clare went backstage to meet him, but to her innocent puzzlement, Coward showed no reciprocal interest in her.[6]

Several other Englishmen, however, did. Her chic clothes and high-class demeanor gave them the hopeful impression she might be an heiress. "They file their intentions along with their attentions," she epigrammatically wrote a friend, adding that they misunderstood her straightforward friendliness as a promise of free favors. She claimed to be more engaged by middle-class men in Sinclair Lewis's *Main Street*, which she was currently reading, than by these effete upper-class British boys.[7]

Early in January 1921, the three travelers crossed the English Channel to France in rough seas. Ann and Dr. Austin took refuge below while Clare stayed on deck clinging to a rail. As spray drenched the bow of the steamer, a gust lurched her against the only other person braving the storm. He was a man in his late forties, wearing a British officer's uniform and carrying a swagger stick. Strangely, his tunic bore no insignia. Steadying her with strong arms, he fixed her with steely blue eyes. Beneath an auburn mustache, his mouth was straight as a sword. It gave his face, she thought, "a ferocious, almost cruel aspect."[8]

When he introduced himself, Clare discovered that he was exotically foreign. He spoke a vibrant, Cockney-accented English with Slavic overtones and gave his name as Alexis Aladin, pronouncing it "Aladeen." His destination was Paris, he said, with such a combination of Old World politeness and authority that Clare found herself acqui-

Alexis Aladin in British Army uniform, *c. 1921*

escing as he steered her to a sheltered spot. They sat down between two stanchions, knees almost touching, and began a conversation that lasted for the rest of the voyage.

Puffing on thin cigarettes through yellowed, square teeth, Aladin told her that he was a White Russian who had been imprisoned and decorated for bravery in the doomed resistance to the Bolsheviks. Now as an emissary of General Peter Wrangel, he was raising funds to re-equip and revitalize opposition forces.

Clare was riveted by the quiet tones in which he described his adventures. Aladin loomed, in her young eyes, as a man of heroic magnitude, brave not only on the battlefield but in politics as well. Apparently he had been leader of the Trudoviki Labor Group in the First Russian Duma of 1906. He told her that after this early democratic experiment failed, he had visited her own country to beseech Congress not to lend money to the authoritarian Russian government.[9]

Though Clare knew little about the intricacies of the Bolshevik Revolution, she recalled that when news of the 1918 massacre of Czar Nicholas and his family had reached her, she had sobbed over the grisly fate of the four young Grand Duchesses.[10]

Aladin, though no monarchist, was an advocate of constitutional government. He claimed that nine months after the Ekaterinburg slaughter, he had personally arranged for the Czar's mother, Dowager Empress Marie, to escape from the Crimea and onto a British rescue ship.[11] Perhaps as a reward for this gallantry, Whitehall was now paying his expenses and had granted him the rank of major. His uniform, he explained, was a disguise for avoiding assassination by Red agents.

Rapt by his passionate idealism, Clare forgot about her seasickness, and was startled to hear Dr. Austin saying it was time to go ashore. Alexis Aladin stood, briskly bowed, and moved away, having already arranged to see her on the train to Paris.[12]

Soon after Clare's arrival at the Hôtel Edouard VII, the Russian reappeared. He had checked in there too. Over the next seven days, while Ann and the doctor went sightseeing, the shipboard friends met repeatedly in Aladin's room, No. 419. During these unchaperoned assignations, Clare learned more about Alexis than she knew of any other man, excepting possibly her father. Indeed, his multiplicity of skills and intellectual accomplishments reminded her of William Boothe.

Aladin was the son of a peasant proprietor in the Volga region. He had struggled to educate himself and was now fluent in English, French, German, and Italian. His love of Britain, where he had already spent a third of his life, was apparent. He had read the fiction of Rudyard Kipling and John Buchan, and admired Lord Kitchener and Winston Churchill. At various times he had worked as a journalist, translator, furniture maker, and motorboat builder. In addition, he understood the fine points of microscope manufacture and the dynamics of aeroengineering.[13]

Clare began affectionately calling him "Darling," and "Iron Man." She boasted to an old school chum that he was a "compelling lover." Alexis, enchanted, called her "Kiddie," and promised to dedicate his secret three-year plan to reverse the revolution to her. Candidly, he told a friend that he found himself in "boiling water of the hottest" and that Clare was his "in many senses."[14]

The developing affair was interrupted, but not cooled, by a two-week trip Aladin had to make to London. He wrote, wired, or telephoned Clare daily while she toured the World War I battlefields of northern France and Belgium. On her return she wrote him.

> Barbed wire—miles of it, and the pock-marked fields, the desecrated forests, the crumbling piles of stones that were once prosperous villages, the lonely crosses here and there, the stagnant trenches—! Darling, every man who fought in this war—no matter how rotten he may have been before— was a hero. He had to be to stand the bitter cold in winter, the mud, fleas, dust, flies, heat, stench and all the rest of it thru out the year. Dear God, how they must have suffered. And *why?*

While moved by the ravages of war, Clare philosophized to Alexis that in her view it was "infinitely harder to *live* courageously than . . . to die so."[15]

A few days later, she went to the Cirque de Paris to see her first prizefight. Though not usually squeamish, she told Aladin that the mashed noses, swollen eyes, and "cauliflower ears" made her feel faint. "However," she admitted, "I didn't fail to come away without deriving something of beauty in the whole evening's *mêlée*. Nothing can exaggerate the beauty of the fighters' physiques . . . and the sight of smooth firm muscles playing evenly under glorious pink marble-like flesh. That men can be so beautiful is quite a revelation to me!"[16]

Back together in Paris in early February, Clare and Aladin were dining out one night when a man walked up to their table. He said something in Russian, whereupon Alexis, to Clare's horror, drew a gun and scared him away. Apparently the interloper had repeated a rumor among White Russian émigrés that Aladin was entrapped by an American woman, to the neglect of their cause.[17]

The idea of being a *femme fatale* and having her movements "ascertained" thrilled Clare. But Ann Snyder was thoroughly unnerved by the incident, and decided to remove her daughter from Aladin's influence without delay.[18]

As usual, maternal propaganda was couched in economic terms. On February 17, Clare wrote Aladin with sudden coldness that Ann objected to her having suitors who were "$– instead of $+." Then, on February 18, Dr. Austin set off for America, while the two women, equipped with some "perfectly stunning creations," headed for the Riviera.[19]

Mother and daughter took rooms in Nice, at the Hôtel Negresco on the Promenade des Anglais. Now thirty-eight, Ann was still more beautiful than Clare, her taste in dress more sure, her charm more practiced. Walking along the seafront in a finely tailored suit, with a jaunty hat and a silver-topped cane, she acted as a stylish procurer for them both. The next four weeks in the South of France presented an opportunity to ensnare not only a wealthy son-in-law but also perhaps a man closer than either the doctor or Riggie to those in her exotic dreams.[20]

Clare, rather less selectively, enjoyed dancing in the Negresco's skylit, cupid-decorated ballroom with young men who earned fifty francs a night partnering unescorted girls. She became addicted to baccarat, chemin de fer, and roulette, smoked occasional cigarettes, drank wine with meals and champagne at the gambling tables. The heavy scent of mimosa on the Mediterranean breeze, the moon and dark palms set against midnight skies stimulated the romantic in her. Aladin already seemed far away, and she bragged to him of "sowing wild oats in other men's hearts." Cavalierly she also confessed that she had laid a trap for him in Paris. "Always I take, and never give. To you alone I gave a wee bit of myself and then I stole from you more than I can ever return."[21]

At Nice's annual Battle of the Flowers parade, Mlle. Clare Boothe was adjudged the girl on the prettiest float, an honor she ever afterwards remembered as "winning a beauty contest." The ensuing publicity led to more flirtations. In quick succession she was courted by an

Clare and her mother on the Riviera, *1921*

American Army officer from Koblenz, a one-legged Welsh aristocrat, an Italian count, and an Indian maharaja. Most dashing of all was a tall, dark-eyed man of mystery who was rumored to be "the catch of the season." He was so handsome that Clare, encountering him in the Monte Carlo Casino, felt her blood "course like warm wine" to her cheeks. The occasion was the Great White Ball, where three thousand revelers danced until dawn. The dark man played Pierrot to her

Pierrette, whirling her around the floor and kissing her long and passionately in a garden overlooking the sea.[22]

He turned out to be John J. Tanner, a divorced, "damn clever," forty-seven-year-old photographer from New York. Ann worried that Clare was once again in the clutches of a middle-aged *arriviste*. As she had whisked her daughter away from Aladin, she now removed her from the devilishly attractive Mr. Tanner.[23]

By March 21 they were heading back via Paris to London, where Aladin, though shaken by Clare's rebuff, was optimistic that he could regain her love. He was all gentlemanly attention from the moment of their arrival, escorting them to rooms he had booked at Cox's Hotel, not far from his own quarters at the National Liberal Club in Whitehall.

On March 28 he turned forty-eight and spent the day with Clare. Afterwards, brooding over Ann's objection to his lack of fortune, he sent a friend a newspaper photograph of Clare, to show "against what [a] terrific proposition I am pitched up."[24]

Nine days later, Clare sailed from Southampton on the SS *Olympic*, leaving Alexis to mourn for her. Though she had the capacity to break with anybody or anything that might slow her progress, she later admitted that Aladin could claim "a part of my heart no-one else will ever have." He was inseparable from her passionate love for Paris. "I who so frequently denied you wish now I had given you—oh so much more." On board, she celebrated her eighteenth birthday in the knowledge that numerous relationships awaited renewal in America. Most particularly, she looked forward to seeing Jack Tanner again.[25]

Whatever secret plans Clare had for a romance in Manhattan, she had to postpone them, since her family was spending the summer in Sound Beach. This did not prevent her continuing her fantasies of a rich husband. "Matrimony," she punned, "should be spelled matter o' money." In a letter to a friend she complained that all her relationships with men seemed to flounder, because of either her lack of means or theirs. She pounded out manuscripts on her Underwood, trying to prove that mentally women equaled men. But her thoughts kept drifting away to the male attributes of "virility, adventure, strength, and originality."[26]

She began to show signs of sexual frustration. When thunderstorms broke over Sound Beach, she would put on her bathing suit and swim out into the channel between her house and the mainland. Forty years later Clare remembered what wild excitement drove her. "When I felt the stinging rain on my shoulders, the waves slapping in my teeth, I felt exhilarated, defiant, the master of the storm." Or she would hire a horse from the Greenwich stables and spur him out into the turbulent countryside. "With the nervous beast between my legs, and the wind against my wet eyelashes, I galloped down slippery roads, hoping that the next thunderclap would make the horse shy, so that I could jerk his head up and dig my heels in."[27]

For all this, she confessed at the time, she still wanted "to feel I am delicate, need coddling, petting, idealizing, protecting . . ."[28]

By the second week of June, an even more urgent need propelled her to sudden, extreme action. Early one morning, while her mother was still asleep, Clare slipped out of the house and took a train to New York. Her destination was Jack Tanner's apartment at 135 West Sixty-seventh Street. The full details of what happened there, and to her alone in the weeks immediately following, are not known. Enough fragmentary facts survive to suggest at least the outlines of a core trauma of her life.[29]

Jack's studio apartment belied the $30,000 a year he had claimed to earn in Monte Carlo. A resident teenage amour would severely cramp his style, and he made it clear that Clare was not welcome in that capacity.

Finding herself literally on the street, and for some reason unwilling to go home, Clare took a two-month lease on a room at 244 West Seventy-second Street, under the name "C. J. Tanner." She combed the help wanted columns of city newspapers, poking holes where she saw promising jobs, and succeeded in getting one at Dennison's Manufacturing Company, on lower Fifth Avenue. Registering as "Jacqueline Tanner," she gave her age as twenty-one and negotiated a twenty-five-dollar-a-week salary. A Dennison's sales director recalled afterwards that she must have "mesmerised" someone into agreeing to such a high starting wage.[30]

Clare began work on Thursday, June 23. "I sat out on the assembly line, making bridal mint and nut cups out of frilled paper . . . and dolls from wire and spun green paper, and painted their faces. I got quite good . . . Nobody made contact with me. Nor did anyone mistake me for a prostitute."[31]

The non sequitur—why *should* anyone mistake her thus?—suggests that Clare, in old age, recast her memories of these days to make them less painful. Whatever her co-workers thought of her, the inference is that she felt whorish after her rejection by Tanner, and also lonely and vulnerable.

In the evenings after work, she would sit at her window and gaze across the street at a young man sitting in his. "When you are young, you're full of . . . vague longings . . . every man in the distance is a knight errant in disguise . . . I began to fantasize and fantasize about that boy . . . He was going to save me from all my sorrows." But when they finally met on the sidewalk, she found he was covered with pimples.[32]

During her second week at Dennison's, Clare became acutely ill with what she would always describe as "appendix" trouble. She called her mother to come and get her, and on or about July 5 she underwent surgery at Greenwich Hospital. "They thought I might die," she wrote Alexis Aladin on July 19. "Such pain . . . I'm all wrapped up like a mummy." She described herself as "all eyes and hair and nothing but bones." It would be three weeks before she could walk again, and three months before she could dance or swim.[33]

David Boothe, many years later, said that his sister "had a shock" before her first marriage. He had witnessed its impact, which "affected her for years."[34] Certainly the wounds inflicted by Tanner, whether psychological, physical, or both, were deeply embittering. It may be that Clare did, as she claimed, have appendicitis that summer. But this would not account for some of the stranger aspects of her behavior: the running away from home, the self-abasing walk-up and factory job, the defensiveness about being thought "a prostitute." Indications of a terminated pregnancy are strong, since to women of her generation "appendicitis" was a common euphemism for abortion.

A few years after this episode, Clare described in her diary an operation that had supposedly been performed on an unidentified friend. "I think it an experience . . . almost worthy of the epic character of this journal." But the details and feelings are so intense, and her slip after a few lines into the first-person singular so telling, that it seems unlikely to have happened to anyone other than herself, either in the summer of 1921 or later.

> I heard a story the other day, a pathetic story . . . an intelligent exquisite young thing, pregnant with an illegitimate child, she having given herself in love, in passion, for which every fibre of her nature called out, and so how could she feel herself doing a wicked thing, when so obviously by all the laws of nature it was precisely what she was created to do . . .
>
> This lovely young creature, having been in vulgar parlance "betrayed" found herself two months pregnant . . . a helpful woman friend recommended her to a doctor. Little Miss—— went to him. "Doctor X—— was a big man . . . but at once I trusted him in spite of his brutal physique, his coarse thick features and hard eyes. There was something diabolically clever about him, a Lucifer-like pride too in his dexterity . . . He bargained with me . . . and I at once gave him what he asked! . . . He called me 'little girl,' and said that women should not be 'forced' to have children unless they wanted them . . . He told me to return the next day. Said it wouldn't hurt . . . that it would 'all be over' in a few minutes . . . and there was something cruel and sad about that phrase. I could not sleep all night. I clutched my hips and my loins, and I began passionately to love the growing child within me . . . I wanted my baby, yet knew I must not have it . . . because, because . . . an illegitimate child *must not be* born . . . so the next morning I went . . . he and his nurse lay me on a table . . . Everything was sanitary . . . my legs way up high, the cool impact of the spectrum [*sic*] . . . it's too late to back out now, but if I could . . . I am afraid . . . no . . . it won't hurt he says . . . prick of the needle. Here . . . there . . . another prick . . . 'What is that, doctor?' 'A secret mixture of my own' . . . If . . . *he* could see me now . . . what beasts men are . . . aren't the lights a little blurred . . . oh, God . . . *that* hurts . . . another prick . . . ah, ah, ah don't, don't . . . he is inside . . . he is touching it, taking it . . . tearing it away . . .

NO! NO! that's my heart's soul doctor . . . ah, ah . . . it is gone, I heard something small and wet drop in the pan . . . oh, how inexpressibly evil, how vile . . . this thing is . . . Always I shall remember that moment when you took from me part of my soul . . . the cool douche again. I am ill, a glass of ammonia, nurse . . . I ache so, but I am out of *danger,* and I have paid for a moment's pleasure. I shall never be quite happy again I think . . . I left alone and got in my car and drove home. I told mother I felt ill, a painful period, and there in bed I stayed for two or three days, and always my heart was weeping, weeping, weeping."[35]

Alarmed by her daughter's propensity for improvident older men, Ann Snyder began determinedly to look for a solvent young one. On August 1, at a Greenwich newsagent's, she met Vernon Blunt, a blue-eyed, curly-haired Englishman with an aristocratic profile. He was a Cambridge undergraduate on vacation, staying with his uncle in nearby Cos Cob. Having an eye for clothes, Blunt noticed with approval that Ann's chic black and white dress matched her Ford tonneau. She, in turn, liked his quiet good manners and invited him to tea.[36]

"I had only one outfit to wear," he remembered over sixty years later, "my Trinity Hall Henley Enclosure white woollen trousers with black stripe down the side, a white blazer edged with black satin ribbon, and my black and white check rowing scarf. I rang the bell and suddenly I saw, through the outer fine wire mesh fly screen and the inner glass door, the most beautiful girl I had seen in my life . . . I felt that I had met my fate."[37]

Vernon appealed to Clare's literary Anglophilia. He was a distant relative of the poet Wilfrid Scawen Blunt, had shared a room in college with J. B. Priestley, and was a budding writer himself. They discussed philosophy, Romanticism, and Robert Herrick, whose mistress, Vernon noted slyly, had had the same taste in fabrics as Clare:

> *When as in silks my Julia goes*
> *Then, then (methinks) how sweetly floes*
> *That liquefaction of her clothes.*

She riposted from Browning:

Vernon Blunt at Cambridge, *c. 1921*

A man's reach should exceed his grasp
Or what's a heaven for?

Vernon, encouraged, held her hand but lacked the nerve to kiss her. Their friendship nevertheless flourished. Two or three times a week, Clare picked him up in what she remembered as "the duckiest little five-passenger Hudson touring car."[38] He noticed with alarm that she always had a loaded revolver beside her, and a bulldog on the backseat.

They walked along Tod's Point on the Sound Beach peninsula and around the lake on the Wertheim estate, or went to movies in town.[39]

On September 3, Vernon's twenty-first birthday, Ann gave a party for him. He left for home soon after, consumed with a love that would burn unabated for the rest of his life, and cherishing Clare's promise to see him again in England soon. Inevitably, the time would come when he would be superseded, and would lament in verse more eloquent than any of hers:

> *Had you with all your loveliness been true*
> *With all your understanding yet been sure*
> *Earth had not offered brighter bliss than this*
> *Nor heaven promised more.*[40]

9

CLIMBING HIGH,

HIGH

What a girl I am! I'd bear writing in a book someday,

I think. —CLARE BOOTHE

O n top of all the entanglements and disappointments of the first nine months of 1921, Clare was cast further into gloom by the marriage that fall of Lieutenant Lloyd Miller. He had been her first love, she told Ruth Balsam, and his choice now of a rich, older woman proved that man was "only a sublimated anthropoid ape." That she had long ago lost interest in *him* was irrelevant. From her narcissistic viewpoint, he should have stayed loyal forever. In revenge she vowed to find a husband as soon as possible. "I'll marry for money—lots of it. Damned if I'll be a burden to my family much longer, and doubly damned if I'll ever love any mere man. Money! I need it and the power it brings, and someday you shall hear my name spoken of as—famous."[1]

The question remained as to what kind of career would expose her to the largest possible number of eligible men. At her mother's suggestion, she turned again to the theater, this time opting for professional training at Clare Tree Major's drama school in Manhattan.

To begin with, the freshman student was enthusiastic: "I have already been Henry V and Juliet, besides becoming a past master of the foils," she wrote Major Kerry Skerrett, her latest Army officer, early in the new year. But her thespian ability was no better at nineteen than it had been at nine. She was an unconvincing geisha girl, even with a short black wig pulled over her long fair hair, and her grunting portrayal of a cave man, arms akimbo, elicited more laughter than applause.[2]

Ann begged Clare to persevere, while David mockingly assured her that she would never be an actress. By early May she had quit the school and was back in the "bromidic precincts" of Sound Beach. Yet her training was not entirely wasted. She learned enough about dialogue and production techniques to dash off six single-act plays, one of which was accepted by an amateur dramatic society.[3]

Ann Snyder, meanwhile, had her own future to think about. Dr. Austin, divorced now for over two years, had at last proposed, but she hesitated to accept. Though she liked the security he offered, she hated to give up what Clare called "the roving life she had been used to for so long."[4] Besides, marriage was bound to complicate her already strained relations with Joel Jacobs.

After much vacillation, she set May 17 as her wedding date. The ceremony was performed by a Presbyterian minister from Greenwich, in a hotel in Washington, D.C., far away from anyone who might know of the existence of William Boothe. On the marriage certificate, Ann described herself as a thirty-eight-year-old widow—a triple lie in that she was about to turn forty and had neither lost a husband nor indeed ever had one.[5] To the end of his days, Dr. Austin would remain ignorant of Billy Boothe's reappearance at Sound Beach in the spring of 1919.

Clare and David added an even more bizarre twist to the proceedings by acquiescing, as witnesses, in the fiction that their father was dead. They apparently did not question that he had once been married to and divorced from Ann. But David, his suspicions fueled by the furtiveness of the Washington ceremony, came to wonder, at least, about the divorce part. Some two decades later he would suggest to his sister that their mother's union with Dr. Austin was "bigamously contracted."[6]

In the years that followed the wedding, both children agreed that Ann got a little "cracked," as she struggled to keep track of the multiple stories she had invented. Clare paid lip service to honesty as the greatest virtue while privately worrying that she had inherited Ann's mendacity. "All my life I have been surrounded by lies, subterfuge, petty and gross deceptions," she wrote. "I am completely *trapped* and can never free myself from *all* the traditional lies of my childhood. One lie leads to another necessary to support the first, the lies about me grow in multitude, but one thing I can do. I can tell no more! I can correct what lies now exist to the best of my ability: and in all new relations be truthful with everyone, and firstly *myself*."[7]

Dr. and Mrs. Austin took a two-week honeymoon at the Greenbrier in West Virginia before returning to the house in Sound Beach (still partly owned by Riggie) and the modest life for which Ann had now settled. "She always told me to marry for money," Clare mused, "but she didn't do it herself."[8]

In late fall Greenwich newspapers announced that the doctor would leave his practice for several months to study medical procedures abroad, and that his wife and "daughter" would accompany him. As far as the two last were concerned, the main purpose of the trip was to find a wealthy, perhaps even aristocratic European husband for Clare.

They embarked on the SS *Majestic* in mid-December with over a thousand other passengers. Among them were Pearl White, the silent screen star, and the Irish tenor John McCormack. Miss Boothe's celebrity as former winner of a Riviera "beauty contest" could hardly compare with theirs. Yet she managed to attract the attention of shipboard reporters with a daily exhibition of her young swimsuited body in the Pompeian pool. By the end of the voyage Clare was playing to "a big gallery" of admiring fellow passengers.[9]

The travelers arrived in London on December 22, and Ann promptly set to work on two matrimonial prospects. They were the wealthy identical twins Maurice and Francis Burke-Roche, thirty-seven-year-old sons of the late Lord Fermoy and his divorced American wife, whom Ann had once met in Newport. Maurice, the elder and inheritor of the Fermoy title, was to become the grandfather of Diana, Princess of Wales.[10] He showed no interest in Clare, but "Frank" sent her violets and promised to take her hunting when she returned from the Continent in three months' time. Just before her departure, he presented her with an exquisite lace fan and a red, leather-bound diary. She wrote her first entry on January 1, 1923:

> Had no difficulty whatsoever in landing Frank Roche! He told me right away that he loved me and wanted to marry me. Only the difference in our ages! As if that mattered . . . I shall think it over carefully, *carefully,* find out more, and in the spring perhaps I shall say "yes" and then—well Mrs. Francis Burke-Roche, or perhaps Lady Clare Fermoy. One can never know these things!

Already imagining herself in a tiara, she listed what she wanted to do before she was thirty-five.

1. Own one or several show horses, and show them, winning prizes!
2. Ride to hunt, side-saddle with British aristocracy.
3. Have an ermine evening wrap, and a few fine jewels.
4. Weigh 120 pounds . . . 115 pounds.
5. Have long hair to my waist.
6. Own a yacht.
7. Own a fine roadster.
8. Have a maid.
9. Hear Riggie say he is proud of me, and loves me best in the world.
10. See Brother with a seat on the Exchange.
11. Tour the world on my honeymoon.

Realizing that most of these sounded materialistic, she appended a few "*worth while* things" to achieve by the same deadline:

1. Speak, read and write French, German, Spanish, Italian fluently.
2. Have written a book on the drama.
3. Have written several successful plays and novels, and translated modern French, German, Spanish or Italian ones.

4. Have written political articles and earned $10,000 *on my own!!*[11]

Nearly half of these wishes were to be fulfilled. Through marriage, Clare would indeed acquire ermine, jewels, a yacht, fine automobiles, and many servants. But she would not honeymoon around the globe or become fluent in foreign languages. Independently, she would write Broadway hits (though no work of dramaturgy) and articles without number, earning considerably more than ten thousand dollars over the next fifteen years. She would not win show horse prizes or hunt with the aristocracy. Her weight only once dropped below 120 pounds, and her hair never grew to her waist. David, far from shining on Wall Street, would become a spectacular failure. And her mother, not she, would always be Riggie's chief love.

On January 2, 1923, Clare left England's marrow-chilling damp for Paris and the first-class comforts of the Hôtel Meurice. The multifaceted city kindled her "fires of passion and evil and craving for luxury."[12] But she had little time to indulge them, because Dr. Austin was in a hurry to reach Germany.

In Berlin by the ninth, they took advantage of the Weimar Republic's devalued currency and checked into regal accommodations, first at the Hotel Adlon on the fashionable Unter den Linden, then into a large apartment at 188 Kurfürstendamm.[13]

While Dr. Austin spent his days at the university studying new radiological and plastic-surgery techniques, Ann optimistically began to assemble a trousseau for the future Lady Clare. Her daughter, meanwhile, started riding instruction at the famed Tattersal's stables. She wanted to be able to hunt at Frank's side in March and to be admired one day as the best horsewoman on either side of the Atlantic.[14]

As the short winter days wore on, tensions between Dr. Austin and Clare began to show. Ever curious, she liked to linger over exhibits in museum galleries, while he kept up a steady pace. When he remonstrated, she complained that he was cold and selfish. More seriously, he objected to her eager participation in the libidinous low-life that made Berlin currently the most decadent capital in Europe. By Dr. Austin's small-town New England standards, Clare stayed out too late with too many young men. Ann, in her turn, objected as bouquet after bouquet arrived at the apartment with cards for "*Fräulein* Boothe."

There was a family confrontation, which ended in Clare going to bed "heartsick." She declared in her diary that her mother did nothing for her, spiritually, mentally, or socially. She must look to her own welfare, acknowledging that she was more complicated than most women. "I was endowed with a masculine perception, a half-masculine mentality, and a thoroughly feminine method of living." During bouts of insomnia, she schemed and planned her future success. "I shall make the world and his wife envy me! I shall be rich, loved, beautiful, and talented and have a title, and if with all that I am still unhappy . . . there's no hope for such as I am on earth."[15]

At other times she indulged in depressions and self-doubt. Watching her stepfather's uninhibited clapping at a modern dance performance, Clare judged herself incapable of such direct emotion. Sometimes she feigned enthusiasm and optimism. She felt solitary, even amidst the attentions of countless companions. When a young German offered her presents in exchange for kisses, she reacted indignantly: "I give them. They can't be bought!!!" A rebuffed suitor from the American Embassy told her that it was not right to play with men's souls. Her conduct was "no better than that of a chorus girl who uses a man for a meal ticket!" Again she was outraged, but she admitted to herself that there was "a gleam of truth" in the comparison.[16]

Berlin in 1923 was Europe's most avant-garde showcase of visual arts, opera, music, film, and drama. The sometime understudy to Mary Pickford had her theatrical eyes opened by an expressionistic production of Goethe's *Savonarola* complete with skeleton sets and psychosuggestive costumes. She was further shocked by Frank Wedekind's *Pandora's Box*, in which Jack the Ripper cut out the womb of the prostitute Lulu and carried it across the stage in a basin.[17]

With growing political awareness, Clare saw that the creative fertility of Berlin's artistic élite concealed a virulent new brand of nationalism, festering among ordinary *Volk*. In demonstration after demonstration that winter, huge crowds expressed hateful resentment of the reparations forced upon Germany by the Versailles Treaty signatories, and anger over France's recent occupation of the Ruhr. The collapsing mark fueled a general hysteria. One mob on the steps of the Reichstag got so out of control that Clare was imprisoned in her nearby hotel.

She prophesied accurately that if the Germans ever managed to match their prewar number of men and resources, they would turn them on the French again. But she was less aware of the implications of Jews coming into Berlin "like locusts buying things," and provoking "much feeling of anti-Semitism." Hitler's Munich *putsch* would occur in just eight months. Feverish and frightening though Berlin was, she loved the crisis atmosphere, and found that it suited her cool temperament. Politics was more fun than gambling. "I wouldn't go to the Riviera now," she wrote Kerry.[18]

On March 6, Dr. Austin left Berlin with his wife and stepdaughter for further research at the University of Vienna. As the train sped south, Clare's thoughts drifted northward to Frank Burke-Roche, "my ladder to power, position, all those things."[19] She looked forward to a Paris rendezvous with him in a little over ten days, since he now had an executive position there with Morgan Guaranty. Meanwhile the Austrian capital, with its famous Spanish Riding School of Lippizaner horses, would enable her to continue her equestrian training.

To fill her time profitably, she duly practiced jumping, and found she preferred the graceful, if more dangerous, sidesaddle to riding astride. Invigorated by gravity-defying conquests of fences and hedges, she saw herself "climbing high, high in the world of men." On March 14 she wrote confidently in her diary, "In one week, if things go as I plan them, I shall be Mrs. Francis Burke-Roche."[20]

Next day her mother and the doctor set off for Italy, and Clare, making her first independent excursion as an adult, headed for France. Crossing the Tyrolean Alps, she was intoxicated by the sight of shimmering snow on the mountaintops, and recorded her tearful rapture "when out of the infinite twilight blue gleamed the first evening star." She was rudely brought down to earth in Paris, when the room she had reserved at the Meurice turned out to be the hotel's cheapest and most miserable. "Foolish me to do this silly, expensive, vain thing!!!" More distressing still, she could not find Frank anywhere. Someone told her that he traveled frequently on bank business. Perhaps, as a busy *homme d'affaires*, he had lost interest in her, a girl with neither dowry nor title.

Clare Boothe at about twenty, *1923*

Clare chastised herself for not having thrown her arms around him when he first proposed.[21]

Through a week of mounting suspense, she distracted herself by shopping, sightseeing, and getting "an edge on" with a boozy, young crowd at the Café de Paris. Finally she received a wire from Frank, telling her to come on to London. Confidence restored, she set off at once. "If he doesn't love me, he will be the first man who hasn't . . . in many moons."[22]

Clare checked into Claridges on the night of Monday, March 26, only to discover Frank was once more unavailable. Worried about her rapidly depleting funds, and desperate for reassuring companionship, she contacted Vernon Blunt, her Cambridge beau of two summers ago. He met her for tea at the Royal Air Force Club, and they went on to *The Beggar's Opera*. When Frank finally caught up with her, two nights later, Clare's doubts about him were devastatingly confirmed. "The one man I want will not fall in love with me." They agreed to meet again, but she was not optimistic. "I know him for what he is—a conceited, spoiled, selfish young man, handsome, charming, but very, very stupid!"[23]

On the rebound next day, March 29, she unexpectedly met a heroic figure who was to obsess her romantic imagination and longing for the rest of her life. They saw each other at the Air Force Club, where she had gone again with Vernon. As he stood beside a fireplace in the club's only room open to women, Clare was "smitten" by a combination of height, extraordinary good looks, and quiet presence. He wore an Army officer's uniform with combat ribbons, leather boots, and gleaming belt. His wavy brown hair was parted on one side, and his mustache framed a strong, serious mouth.[24]

He was Julian Hamilton Cassan Simpson, a twenty-nine-year-old captain in Britain's most exclusive regiment, the Grenadier Guards. Although Clare did not know it, he had heard about the scintillating Miss Boothe and asked Vernon to introduce him. Much to Blunt's annoyance, he charmed her over tea and escorted her back to Claridges, on the pretext that it was right next to the Guards Club.

Physically drawn as she was to Julian, Clare's mercenary instincts urged her not to give up entirely on Frank. In fact, Burke-Roche appeared that night at her hotel with a married friend, the Hon. Mary Craig Stopford. They arranged for Clare, who was now practically penniless, to move to the Stopfords' house for Britain's four-day Easter holiday. Frank promptly left again for Paris, and Julian also disappeared, leaving the faithful Blunt to entertain Clare.

For lack of competition Vernon was thus granted a few hours of intimacy, which warmed him still at the age of eighty-five, ailing in a Herefordshire cottage. "Our dalliance was short and sweet . . . Clare did say she had been made love to by Germans, French, Italians and Americans but my efforts were sweetest of all . . . If only I had dared to accept the promise of those lips!"[25]

Frank returned on Thursday, April 5, coincidentally on the same boat as the Austins. Clare was appalled by his indifference the follow-

Captain Julian Simpson, *c. 1923*

ing night when both Roche twins, along with Vernon and Lord Por-chester, dined and danced with her at the 400 Club. Here, at the near pinnacle of London society, she made her move. "I threw myself at his head, and he turned me down with a bang. So that's the end of that, I'm not as clever as I thought I was."[26]

She was saved from total despair by Julian Simpson, who, clearly enraptured, kept her company as the time for departure drew near. On April 11, the day after celebrating her twentieth birthday, he drove her to Southampton. Their relationship had deepened. He talked of visiting her in Sound Beach soon. She rested her head on his shoulder, while he recited the whole of Francis Thompson's long poem "The Hound of Heaven," occasionally kissing her brow.

> *I fled Him down the nights and down the days*
> *I fled Him, down the arches of the years*
> *I fled Him, down the labyrinthine ways*
> *Of my own mind . . .*[27]

The usual gaggle of society and celebrity reporters awaited the docking of the SS *Majestic* in New York on April 17, 1923. "Miss Boothe" tried to convince them of her seriousness by pretending that she planned a career in journalism. Still rankling over Frank's rejection, she was well prepared when pressed on the subject of matrimony. "I don't intend to marry a foreign nobleman, but will probably select a red-blooded American. Even though prices are low in Europe, I can't afford a duke!"[28]

10

A Path of

White Marble

The Twenties in America marked the biggest advances
for women of any decade before or since.
—Paul Johnson

During her trip back across the Atlantic, Clare had met two extraordinary fellow passengers who would influence her life in the
near future. One was Max Reinhardt, the Austrian producer widely regarded as "the first theatre man in the world." He was on his way to
America to raise funds for several plays, including a new production of
The Miracle, a morality spectacular that had been a sensation in Europe. Reinhardt had the reputation of being a practiced seducer of
stage-struck women. When his eyes glowed at them "like a banked
fire," in Josephine Baker's phrase, they melted, in warm anticipation of
a part in one of his productions.[1]

Clare's diary featured Reinhardt's name only once during six days
at sea, and on three of the first ten days ashore. In later life she claimed
that during these encounters Reinhardt had offered her the role of the
Madonna in *The Miracle.* But the part went to Britain's Lady Diana

Cooper, while that of the Nun was given to another of his shipboard conquests, the young, violet-eyed American socialite Rosamond Pinchot. *The Miracle* would run for a total of almost six years on Broadway and across the country.

Clare's other "romance" aboard the *Majestic* was with Alva Belmont. The rich, radical feminist had been in France campaigning for women's rights and was returning to continue the battle in America. At seventy she was a bristling presence, with dyed red hair and pug features. She immediately recognized in the eager Connecticut girl a potential activist, with "brains to go as far as ambition will take her." Mrs. Belmont told a friend she intended to give Clare "a push in the right direction."[2]

The direction she had in mind was south to Washington, D.C., where women were working for passage of the Equal Rights Amendment. Dr. Alice Paul, intellectual soul of the women's movement, had drawn up a bill that was soon to come before Congress. If passed, and ratified by two thirds of the states, it would wipe out all legal distinctions based on sex.

Mrs. Belmont had come into Dr. Paul's orbit by a circuitous route. Alabama-born and Paris-educated, she had acquired vast wealth by marrying, and then daring to divorce, the railroad magnate William Vanderbilt. Liberated by his settlement upon her of $100,000 a year and an $11 million Newport "cottage," she vowed to free other women from marital and financial exploitation. The death of a second millionaire husband, Oliver Belmont, had given her even greater means to fight for complete equality.[3]

Her propaganda shrewdly mixed politics and showmanship. While using her own money to set up the National Woman Suffrage Association, she was not above collaborating with Elsa Maxwell on a fundraising operetta called *Melinda and Her Sisters*, whose libretto contained lines such as "The country has been going to the dogs for quite a while now, why not give it to the cats for a change?"[4]

Mrs. Belmont was now president of the two-year-old National Woman's Party, having donated $146,000 to purchase Washington's Old Brick Capitol as its national headquarters. Ever since 1916 she had been looking for a replacement for Inez Milholland, the Party's emblematic blonde crusader, who had collapsed and died from overwork. Clare resembled Inez in looks and energy, but it remained to be seen if she could reincarnate her zeal and proselytizing skills.

For closer scrutiny, Mrs. Belmont invited the young traveler to stay at "Beacon Towers," her Long Island mansion, for a few days. A secretary there was impressed by the arrival of "a radiantly lovely young woman," who seemed, unlike some militant females, to be both warm and friendly. The house, appropriately, was modeled on a château once associated with Joan of Arc. Sixty years later Clare remembered climbing the staircase to bed on her first night, and seeing on the landing a huge picture of the warrior-girl being burned at the stake. Joan's immolation, and the more recent self-sacrifice of Inez Milholland, gave her pause. She wanted to be famous, "but I didn't want to be a martyr."[5]

In due course, Mrs. Belmont offered her a job with the National Woman's Party at twelve dollars a week. Clare was tempted to accept. She had been interested in women's issues ever since her mother had joined the Women's Political Union, after leaving William Boothe in 1912. She had watched Ann march in its annual parades and listened to her arguments in favor of wage parity, fair alimony, and property rights. Around the age of ten, Clare had written a poem attacking the notion that God, in punishing Eve's "sinful" act in the Garden of Eden, had condemned her and her sex to a rank below Adam's.

> *Thou madest man perfect*
> *Then Thine alone is the blame*
> *If Thou leftest in womankind*
> *The flaw that brought him shame.*[6]

As an adolescent, she had bridled at Nietzsche's line "When thou goest into woman, take a whip!" in *Thus Spake Zarathustra*. "That made me mad! If I had a chance to get even with that kind of guy . . ."[7]

In spite of some misgivings (she was still hoping to be cast by Reinhardt), Clare yielded to Mrs. Belmont's blandishments. The prospect of being groomed and taken up by such a powerful patron could not be refused lightly. With Ann's approval, she traveled to Washington on Friday, April 27, 1923.

From her assigned room in the Old Capitol on First Street, NE, she had an inspiring view of the "new" Capitol's great white dome. But when she sat down to write a letter to Kerry Skerrett (who had seen her off with orchids and enough cash to buy a platinum and eight-diamond ring), she admitted ambivalence about her new job. She could not get "greatly stirred up over the tragedies of the Double Standard," on a salary which was half what she had made in Dennison's paper flower factory. Besides, she had developed a dislike of Mrs. Belmont, even though the old militant was kind to her. And she was already "play hungry" for Broadway. She told Kerry she would happily sell her jade earrings to see Shaw's *Devil's Disciple* and some other current hits.[8]

Nevertheless Clare started work on Sunday morning by delivering tracts to Washington embassies, and that afternoon took a motor trip to Annapolis with Mrs. Belmont on party business. Evidently she had joined up at a dynamic moment in feminist history. On Monday, April 30, *The New York Times* announced that Mrs. Belmont intended to create a third political party made up exclusively of women and to buy another building near the Capitol in which to house it.[9]

Over the next five days Clare found herself dropping off load after load of pamphlets in Congress, urging Senators and Representatives to vote for the ERA. Sore footed in her ankle-strap shoes, she found herself agreeing with Maud Younger. "The path of the lobbyist is a path of white marble."[10]

It was a path, though, that led to some rewards. Chief among these were a few opportunities to work alongside the legendary Alice Paul. Since the 1920 enfranchisement of women, Dr. Paul had been concentrating her energies on writing and producing feminist pageants. She was still only thirty-eight, a small, slender, rather prim figure, with a bundle of black hair anchored at the nape of her neck. Scars from a picketing skirmish were visible on the smooth skin beneath. They had been caused when a sailor, trying to tear off her propagandizing sash, had dragged her thirty feet along the sidewalk outside the White House.[11]

Jailed seventeen times in England and America, Dr. Paul had eaten wormy soup, bathed with syphilitics, slept side by side with psychopaths, and been force-fed through the nose until she bled. Yet her mind, with its solid academic underpinning of a Ph.D. and three law degrees, remained clear and penetrating. Co-workers regarded her with reverence.

Clare could identify with Alice Paul's cerebral and leadership qualities, as well as aspire to Alva Belmont's strength of purpose and wealth. Yet she was unable to match the single-mindedness of either in the championing of women's rights. The monotony of canvassing and fund-raising required more devotion than she could summon. It was not, she told herself, that she lacked ideas or ideals. She felt as free as any man to choose her way in life. That way lay elsewhere, for the moment, than in social activism. "This thing is just beginning to get on my nerves."[12]

Not wanting to decamp too hastily, she spent another week traveling to regional rallies with Mrs. Belmont and Dr. Paul. By Saturday, May 5, she could stand it no longer. "Dashed to N.Y. specially to see Max," she wrote in her diary. Sunday's entry read, "Haystack with Kerry." Before returning to the capital on Monday, she had a final meeting with Reinhardt, who was about to recross the Atlantic. On Friday, May 11, she formally quit.

Clare's sum total of service to the National Woman's Party had been ten working days. She would briefly perform more flamboyant duties that coming summer and fall, and later parlay these into the myth that she was an early and stalwart activist for the cause. But her diary at the time betrayed distaste for some of its "dowdy, dumpy" practitioners. "I don't like older women who get a crush on girls, and several of them around here make entirely too great a fuss over me for it to be comfortable."[13]

11

EARTHLY DESIRES

From a certain point onward, there is no longer any turning back. —FRANZ KAFKA

On Sunday, May 20, 1923, Clare went to hear the famous Baptist Harry Emerson Fosdick preach as a guest at New York's First Presbyterian Church. She was invited by James S. Cushman, a childless philanthropist who had befriended her in London. Ordinarily she cared little for evangelical pieties, but Fosdick was a promoter of ecumenism and liberal race relations, as well as being an inspiring orator.

As the service progressed, she became aware of the persistent gaze of a well-dressed man in the same pew. Afterwards, the Cushmans introduced her to him, and they all went on to lunch.[1]

The stranger was George Tuttle Brokaw, a forty-three-year-old dandy rumored to be New York's most eligible bachelor. As one of four surviving children of Isaac Vale Brokaw, a clothing tycoon of Huguenot descent, he had inherited some $2 million of his father's $12 million fortune and lived with his mother in the family mansion on Fifth Avenue at Seventy-ninth Street. A Princeton graduate and partner in the law firm of Gulick and Brokaw, he was better known as a first-rate golfer, bon vivant, and clubman.

His résumé was probably already known to Ann Austin, an assiduous reader of society columns, if not to Clare. Over lunch Brokaw revealed himself to be well-traveled and versed in European history and art. Clare found his conversation a little dull, but he had an appealingly gentle manner. He was also shy, which did not deter him from driving her all the way back to Connecticut in what she described as a "beautiful yellow locomobile with tubes coming out of it."[2]

Soon after, Brokaw telephoned Ann and asked her, Dr. Austin, and Clare to dine with him at the Pickwick Arms Hotel in Greenwich. He made a favorable impression on both Austins, especially when they saw that he was enthralled with Clare. Somebody may have mentioned that she had tried out locally for the 1920 Olympics, because a few days later he sent her a gift of four Parisian swimming costumes. An enclosed newspaper clipping suggestively labeled them "Kiss of the Waves" (a beribboned, cornflower blue extravagance with pocket for powder and puff), "Trembling Waters," "Preliminary Shower," and "Storm Queen."[3]

Ann objected to his lavish present on the ground of propriety. George promptly wrote to apologize, pleading "an inner desire to be . . . generous." To make amends, he invited Clare to Manhattan for an evening of theater, dinner, and late-night dancing the following Saturday, June 9. "It would be 'awfully' jolly. My mother would only too gladly have you spend the night with us at my house."[4]

This presented Clare with a dilemma. Two days before George's letter, the RMS *Orbita* had brought to New York none other than Captain Julian Simpson, the brooding Guards officer who had so captivated her in London. Julian was already staying in Sound Beach. She suspected he might soon propose, because his visit was only a short one. In fact, he was due to sail home on the day George wanted to take her out.

Not for the first time, she juggled two suitors at once. Ann felt that George was by far the better matrimonial prospect, if only because he was rich. Clare did not disagree, but her romantic inclination was to spend as much time as possible with Julian.

In the process she discovered that he was a deeper, more complicated personality than most people surmised. Instead of being English-born and Oxford-educated, Julian was the Australian son of an English barrister and a Jewish mother. At the start of World War I, he had joined the Australian Expeditionary Force as an infantry sergeant and fought for six months in New Guinea. As hostilities intensified in Europe, he had transferred to the British Army, moving somewhat unusually from infantry to artillery to cavalry before attaining the rank of Captain in the Grenadier Guards. For an erstwhile Australian sergeant to have been admitted as an officer to this élite corps was a rare accomplishment.[5]

Towards the end of the war, Captain Simpson had been wounded twice in a little over a month, winning the prestigious Military Cross and Bar for "conspicuous gallantry and devotion to duty." Lame and bleeding, he had led daylight reconnaissances under heavy machine-gun and shell fire to prepare the Allied advance.[6] After the peace, he returned to England and now lived with his mother in West London. The fact that he was still doing so in his thirtieth year, and had crossed the Atlantic on a cheap mail ship, made it plain to Clare that Julian was far from being a man of means.

During the next three days, he and Clare walked many miles through the woods and along the shore, wrestling with the intractable problem of lack of money. He assured her that when his grandmother died he would be comfortably well off. But Clare suspected that their definitions of "comfortably" were far apart. She seemed genuinely torn, but after many hours of tempestuous argument, Julian realized that Clare was under pressure from Ann to marry a millionaire.

He pleaded, cajoled, and even cried—"not," as he told her years later, "because of what I was to lose, but because of what I believed you were to suffer." Clare bathed his eyes, quarreled with her mother, and prevaricated some more. Brazenly, she suggested they elope: that would save her from George. But Julian, in a sudden, puzzling about-face, said that maybe their families should meet in England near the end of the year before making a final commitment.[7]

Emotionally drained, the frustrated couple traveled to New York on June 8 to spend a last evening at the Biltmore Hotel. Julian asked Clare to sleep with him. She refused but agreed to stay the night, in a separate room. He consoled himself that "the passion which we never satisfied" had made their love stronger.[8]

Early next morning he went downstairs and wrote a sentimental letter to Ann.

> I have never been so happy and contented than when staying in your house . . . All I can ever hope to repay you for your trust, kindness and affection towards me would be to make Clare happy and . . . whether Clare and I marry or do not, I can most sincerely write that my life will be a far finer one for loving Clare—and I have always loved her and must do so—that is how I am made.

As if to emphasize both their chastity and their intimacy, he added, "I am waiting for Clare to descend for breakfast at 8:30 A.M."[9]

When Julian sailed away a few hours later, Clare sensed that he took something with him she would never find again. Asked as an old woman what her heart had really wanted in the spring of 1923, she answered, "For him to have been a little bit bolder, and say 'Come on, let's go, we'll make it somehow.'" She acknowledged that her own will had been flaccid, "because I couldn't connect with anything." Julian was the first and probably the only man she adored. For the rest of her life she regretted not having had at least "two or three years of that kind of young, idyllic married love."[10]

Though Clare would pursue Julian intermittently over the next twenty-five years, a letter she wrote on the day he landed in England rejected him in terms almost cruel. "I would have to completely alter my entire nature to stand any chance of happiness with you." He was altogether too "willful, high-minded, and poor," while she claimed to be romantic and self-indulgent. But her next words chillingly suggested otherwise. "I mistrust love so. It lasts . . . a very little while. There's only one way of keeping it alive: starve it!" In any case, "I do not love you as you love me, or no such obstacles that confront us would deter me from coming to you."[11]

Julian's mother wrote to say that although her son's visit to America had not been "one of unruffled calm," she hoped that when they all met in the autumn he would be "as successful in love as he certainly was in war."[12]

In the meantime, George Brokaw had succeeded in getting Clare to visit his mother before she left town to spend the summer at her country place in New Jersey. An ailing octogenarian, Mrs. Elvira Brokaw wanted to see her son settled with a good wife. Looking closely at her healthy, strong-jawed young visitor, she told him, "Take my advice and marry this nice girl."[13] George, needing no further encouragement, escorted Clare to Cartier to buy her a seventeen-carat, blue-white dia-

Clare with George Brokaw, *c. 1923*

mond solitaire ring. On Friday, July 1, *The New York Times* announced the engagement of Ann Clare Boothe to George Tuttle Brokaw.

By any standards their courtship was rapid. They had been acquainted a little over a month, and Clare took just six more days to persuade her fiancé to add a remarkable codicil to his will.

> Be it known to my mother and other beneficiaries who, between now and the day already set as the day of my marriage to Ann Clare Booth [sic], to wit, August 10, 1923, might take (in the event of my decease before said date) under the provisions of my last will and testament . . . that inasmuch as I love Ann Clare Booth with all my heart and she, on her part, has greatly honored me and given her affections to me in consenting to become my wife, that it is my strong wish and desire that she partake of my estate as if the wedding ceremony had already been performed and the marriage fully consummated.
>
> GEORGE BROKAW
> *Saturday, July 7, 1923*[14]

A few weeks before marrying George, Clare found herself acting unexpectedly in a moving picture. Riding near Stamford one day, she came across Alma Rubens trying to coax a horse over a hedge. The film star was shooting a scene for *Under the Red Robe*, a historical costume piece. Clare volunteered to be her substitute and jumped expertly in a velvet gown and plumed hat as the cameras ground away. She received twenty dollars for this, her second and last cinematic performance.[15]

In another valedictory, she spent eleven days in mid-July working for the National Woman's Party at Seneca Falls, New York. Her assignment was to help prepare and publicize ceremonies marking the seventy-fifth anniversary of the first women's rights conference. George saw Clare off at Grand Central, and would always cherish the memory of her walking down the platform in a "lovely gray frock."[16]

She stayed at the Gould Hotel in Seneca Falls with Mrs. Belmont, Dr. Paul, and several other prominent activists. At 5:00 on the eve of

Clare (*second row, extreme left*) at Seneca Falls with Alva Belmont (*front row, third from right*) and Alice Paul (*front row, extreme right*), July 1923

the opening celebrations, Clare took off from the local fairground in an airplane to drop propaganda leaflets. As usual she attracted news photographers. Next day, Saturday, July 21, she mingled with party delegates and crowds of sightseers to watch a reenactment of the 1848 convention. A chorus of fifty voices led eight hundred banner bearers, dressed in party colors of purple, gold, and white, along the hot banks of the Seneca River. They were followed by seventy-five women impersonating historic feminists such as Amelia Bloomer and Elizabeth Cady Stanton. The pageant raised nine thousand dollars, and in a final tribute to movement pioneers, Alva Belmont headed a Sunday pilgrimage to the Mount Hope Cemetery grave of Susan B. Anthony in nearby Rochester.[17]

George, meanwhile, had gone to Bar Harbor, Maine, for a golfing vacation, and wrote Clare a boyish love letter.

Darling!! You are my ideal, my golden-haired Angel. I love
you with my whole heart. And for once in my life, I can say
I am satisfied mentally, morally and physically. I simply feel
that nature is really smiling on me . . . I can really call you
my "Angel-face"—a face I thought, as a child, I might see
only beyond the Great Divide . . . sweetie, baby mine, I am
yours you bet!!! And I intend to be yours forever.[18]

A few days before her wedding, Clare received another missive from
England. This time Julian's mother sounded angry. She did not refer to
the Boothe-Brokaw engagement, but it was evident that she knew
about it. "As you have never acknowledged three books and three photographs of Julian, which I sent you . . . would you be so good as to return them all to me."[19]

Her disillusionment fell short of Clare's own. In a private prayer
written at this time, the twenty-year-old revealed the aridity of her
spiritual condition.

My one Father. Thy help is grievously needed. The sins of
all the ages seem to crush me and my mind is rolling with
fear and loathing. I have violated the altar of my soul, for I
have raised there a gilded idol to the material. Its false glitter has hid Thy light, and blindness maddens me. Unkind
hands hold me to earth, though I long for a Peaceful
Heaven, and all around burn the hot flames of earthly desires.[20]

In a different vein, Clare went about wooing the well-connected
Brokaw acquaintances whose gifts came pouring in throughout July
and early August. "Mrs. Jones . . . do you remember my table was next
to yours one season at the Negresco and you were the object of my
deepest admiration?" She received copious quantities of rare and fragile chrysanthemum crystal, twenty pieces of which would stay with her
to the end of her life. Ann gave her a silver bowl engraved with the

Boothe family crest. It was an heirloom of her father's, and Clare noted that it was the only thing of his that Ann seemed to care for. "Sheer snobbism, I suppose." Riggie sent her a typically extravagant gift of a diamond pendant. Clare wanted to exchange it for a chest of tableware, but George offered to buy her the silver anyway, so she ended up with both. He also gave her a pearl necklace and eighteen pieces of Vuitton luggage to use on their honeymoon.[21]

From the moment George entered her life, Clare's fantasies about "nebulous Prince Charmings" had ceased. As she lay staring at the ceiling on the morning of her wedding, August 10, 1923, all she could see in her mind's eye was the narrowness of his brow, the thinness of his lips, the prominence of his chin and nose, the puffiness beneath his small glassy eyes, his graying sideburns, and little folds of flesh bulging over his too-tight collar. She knew she was not in love. Her collusion with Ann in capturing a naive millionaire made her feel contaminated.[22]

Nevertheless, by mid-afternoon she had put on her white satin, pearl-embroidered gown, with a cascading *fichu* of lace and cloudy tulle veil. Carrying a bouquet of white roses and lilies of the valley, she went downstairs. Dr. Austin remarked admiringly, "I wish you really were my daughter."[23]

He was not even to have the privilege of giving her away. A little before four o'clock, David Boothe escorted the bride to Christ Episcopal Church in Greenwich. Its precinct was loud with chimes and organ music, and swarming with print and film photographers. Inside, palms, asters, and ribbons bedecked both chancel and altar.[24]

A quartet of bridesmaids assembled behind Clare as she advanced down the nave. She seemed deliberately to have chosen the plainest and most garishly dressed attendants, to set off her own beauty. The maid of honor, Rose Bullard, wore an orchid-colored gown trimmed with pink roses, Dorothy Burns was in corn yellow, Dorothy Frowert in blue, and Marjorie Wolff in apple green. All four wore picture hats of chiffon and wildflowers, and carried roses and delphiniums.[25]

Clare's chief memory of the ensuing ceremony was the smell of alcohol on George's breath as he kissed her. It was not the last time she would notice the aroma of bootleg gin about him and realize his dependence upon a small black portmanteau from which he was seldom parted.[26]

Clare on her wedding day, *August 10, 1923*

The wedding certificate contained not one misstatement of fact (unusual for a document signed by Ann Austin). But the wedding photographs told the real story of that day. Both Clare and her mother seem paralyzed by the camera. For money and social position, a frustrated and disappointed woman has sacrificed her only daughter to a middle-aged alcoholic.[27]

Some key figures from Clare's past were among the 150 guests at the Pickwick Arms Hotel reception afterwards. They included Grandmother Louisa Snyder, who had taught her German songs, William Higinbotham, her host aboard the RMS *Carmania*, Kerry Skerrett and Walter Yuill, her former beaux, plus Joel Jacobs, Alva Belmont, and the darkly seductive John J. Tanner. Conspicuously absent were any senior Boothes or Brokaws. The former family had not been invited, while George's oldest brother, Howard, acting as spokesman for the latter, had sent a stiff note of regret, "owing to mourning for President Harding."[28]

Elsewhere in the upper levels of New York society, scurrilous rumors were already circulating that Clare Boothe had been a "kept woman" and "one of the best known tarts in town," before she married her millionaire.[29]

Mr. and Mrs. George Tuttle Brokaw spent their wedding night in New York City, at the Plaza Hotel. While George prepared for bed, Clare wrote Ann a letter that was meant to sound grateful and reassuring but conveyed a desperate sadness.

> If you think me unhappy, you are wrong. All the things I have ever considered worthy have become mine on this day, and shall I be unhappy—no dearest, it's just my cussedness of spirit . . . I, being of the sort that Riggie says "expected more," am a little disappointed in my mountain-top, and feel that even today I must go scouting around for higher ones. The day itself leaves no fault to be found . . . It is an omen of the new, the wonderful life that opens up before me . . . George is good and sweet. I do not fear him, and am as fond of him as I could be of any man now . . .
>
> Mother dear, you must not cry. What for? . . . After all you haven't "lost" me . . . I belong to myself always! I am always the mistress! I shall do as I please, and it shall please me to see you *often* . . . you know the best and the worst of me don't you darling?[30]

Her poignant use of the word *now* to describe the irreversible compromise she had made revealed a prematurely disillusioned young woman, one who felt an inner emptiness that she feared would never be filled.

12

Unnourishing Nettles

Money cannot bring happiness because happiness is the
fulfillment of infantile wishes, and money is not the
object of infantile wishes. —SIGMUND FREUD

In old age Clare always insisted that she was a virgin when she married George Brokaw. "I wanted to jump out of the Plaza window on my wedding night." She hinted that the marriage was not consummated straightaway. George was drunk most evenings, but when he drank less, he performed better. "He would march into my bedroom with an erection, sidle up, pinch my fanny, and say 'Hello Buttercup!'" Sometimes he chased her around the room, and on occasion his sexual performance could be "fantastic."[1]

The couple sailed for France on August 11, 1923, accompanied by a valet and maid. Their two-bedroom suite on the SS *Majestic* was filled with flowers and fruit. Clare watched the glittering New York skyline slip past the porthole before bathing and dressing for dinner. But her hopes of a sophisticated first night at sea were dashed when she found her husband tipsily asleep with a black silk sock over his eyes.[2]

During the smooth crossing, she cabled Ann that George was "ridiculously happy." She felt she had made a good choice and was walking the decks "as if in a dream." By letter she admitted to being annoyed with him about "certain practices" to which she could not reconcile herself. "I don't think I ever shall."[3]

Whatever these practices were, she soon began to wish for younger, more virile lovers. Julian Simpson and Frank Burke-Roche came immediately to mind. She cabled the former to announce her impending arrival at Cherbourg, airily assuming that he would rush to see her despite everything that had happened. As soon as she and George were ensconced in the Hôtel Majestic in Paris, Clare invited Frank to dinner. Now that she was more in his income bracket, he might reconsider the coldness he had shown her last spring. To her delight, he accepted, and around midnight George was somehow prevailed upon to leave the two of them alone. Through the early morning hours, they indulged the easy pleasures of romantic wistfulness. "If he had only . . . ," she wrote Ann, "if I had only . . ."[4]

Julian replied to Clare's cable, saying vaguely that he might see her in Paris. But after ten days there was no sign of him. The Brokaws proceeded in a chauffeur-driven Rolls-Royce to Biarritz, where George had rented the Villa Thalassa for two months. Long popular with European royalty, the resort now attracted fashionable Americans in such numbers that it had supplanted Deauville as a fall venue. On the calendar were balloon rallies, horse races, flower fêtes, polo, and golf, not to mention bullfights across the Spanish border in San Sebastián. There was the additional allure of two casinos.[5]

From her canopied bed in the villa, Clare could look out across the white-capped Bay of Biscay to the forested Pyrenees. George slept in an adjoining room, but, perhaps because of the invigorating Atlantic breezes, she found it hard to keep him out of hers.[6]

No sooner had she settled into Biarritz life than a letter came from Julian suggesting that *she* should travel to see *him*. And she had better do so "at once," because he was about to go abroad on a dangerous assignment. Fame and fortune, he wrote melodramatically, would follow—"if I survive."[7]

Neither of them made a further move.

As the autumn season wore on, Clare began to notice, with irritation, that her husband never let her out of sight or earshot. Nor was George the only Brokaw to plague her. His younger brother Irving was living in a chalet near the villa, and he now deigned to send her invitations, apparently forgetting that the family had boycotted their wedding. Clare felt his condescension and reciprocated with equal reluctance. She loathed Irving, who talked mainly about duck breeding and made fun of George. She vowed to keep as aloof as possible, to spare her own dignity as well as her husband's.[8]

Although disinclined to act the role of a high-society hostess, Clare ran the Thalassa household with unflustered efficiency, supervising six servants, planning lunch and dinner menus, and entertaining George's friends with copious cocktails. In the morning she went riding and studied Italian. Later in the day she played good enough golf to impress her expert husband, and in the evenings she surprised him even more with her prowess at the gaming tables, winning large sums at baccarat. George was pleased to hear that "the brother of the Czar, or the Grand Duke, or some potentate" had praised Clare as a perfect type of American beauty. He proudly wrote his mother-in-law, "*Mère* dear, I am very much in love."[9]

George would happily have stayed on the links of Biarritz forever. But after six weeks he began to suspect that his young wife was impatient to move on with the fast crowd. "Our plans are indefinite," he told Ann. "What do you advise?" His insipidity was not lost on those at Sound Beach. With undisguised scorn, Joel Jacobs offered to take the newlyweds on a trip to Chicago on their return, if George was "not too busy playing Golf at the office."[10] Clare had always hoped that Riggie would respect the man she married and found this sarcasm discouraging.

Her mind turned again to Julian Simpson, the enduring inhabitant of her dreams. It was insupportable that any man—particularly a soldier!—should give her up without a fight, and refuse to come running as soon as she batted her eyelids. Married or not, she felt he ought to have no other priority but her. Some dire circumstance, or high affair of state, must be keeping him away. His secret mission abroad, as well as his general elusiveness, tantalized her. From recent letters she knew that he worked in British Intelligence, for the Foreign Office Special Branch. Uncontrollably curious, she asked David Boothe to act as her agent in secretly investigating him.

David, now working on Wall Street as a broker, was capable of bizarre behavior himself and accepted his sister's assignment without question. Somehow, from across the Atlantic, he managed to recruit a former Scotland Yard detective inspector and charged him to find out all he could about Julian's background, current activities, and pecuniary circumstances. For eighty-nine dollars the detective produced a two-page report erroneously stating that Captain Simpson had neither served in the regular army nor fought in Europe. Nothing, he said, was ascertainable about Simpson's finances. As to his whereabouts, "it is believed that he is away from the United Kingdom, and that a quantity of personal correspondence delivered [to the Guards Club] during the last two weeks, is still retained there as he left no forwarding address."[11]

Clare declined the sleuth's offer of further services.

In November, *Town Topics* announced Mrs. George Brokaw's return from Europe to "an eminent place in the Haut Monde." She shared her husband's "predilection for society, and will undoubtedly place a puissant finger in the season's social pie."

Clare took up residence in the Brokaw mansion and immediately struck up an affectionate rapport with her mother-in-law. As co-mistresses, they discussed household matters most afternoons over tea. The old lady had a fund of administrative knowledge to share, and by degrees she allowed Clare to assume control of a domestic staff of fourteen servants.[12]

All were needed. Isaac Brokaw had built his three-story granite house and moat, inspired by the Château de Chenonceaux in the Loire Valley, for half a million dollars in 1889. Its interior was morbidly grandiose. Dreary yellow marble and peeling gold-leaf ceilings blighted the entrance hall. Opaque La Farge stained glass windows on the staircase kept out light. Heavy French and Italian Renaissance furniture, faded tapestries, and soiled Japanese screens oppressed the formal rooms. Littered throughout were drab shawls, antimacassars, and hand-painted calendars pinned to damask walls. Innumerable clocks ticked and chimed. Clare marveled that the advantages of money, travel, and association with people of refinement had brought the Brokaws little real luxury or comfort.[13]

The Brokaws returning from Europe, *1923*

She tried to lighten the mansion's gloom with new paint, carpets, fabrics, and fixtures, but it remained obstinately uncouth in proportions and inconvenient in its juxtapositions of bath and sitting rooms, salons and pantries. The awkwardness of her new home was ingrained, and nothing short of demolition would improve it. She began to feel the same about George.[14]

His drinking was worse now that he was back in his old haunts. Clare, indeed, began to realize that she had married "one of the most spectacular drunks in New York." Even when sober, he was evidently more interested in golf scores than in the practice of law. He went to the office occasionally, but his partner did all the work. This lack of professional focus disturbed her, as did the insatiability of his thirst. Fortunately George was so far harmless when intoxicated. "He wouldn't hurt a fly, unless he got so drunk he fell down on it." Most of the time his behavior was merely lewd or sophomoric, as when he pulled off her bedcovers and serenaded her on his banjo with Princeton Glee Club songs.[15]

George was deeply remorseful after a drinking bout and would go "on the wagon" with apparent determination. But abstinence made him so melancholic that Clare, against medical advice, often allowed him back into the liquor cabinet. It occurred to her that he might drink himself to an early death. Ann Austin advised her to sit out the marriage, remarking that it was better to inherit a widow's fortune than have to sue for divorce and alimony.[16]

After a whirl of dinner parties and balls, Clare discovered at the end of December that she was pregnant.

The Brokaw mansion

Distraught about having to withdraw from their intensely social style of living, which she enjoyed, she tried unsuccessfully to abort by taking hot baths. Finally accepting the inevitable, she told George. He was ecstatic, and from an out-of-town golf club wrote his "Angel Chum" that he missed her "lithe and graceful body . . . and 'booful' face." He predicted that their child would be another Buffalo Bill, Sarah Bernhardt, Rudyard Kipling, or Raphael. Saluting his "perfect little 36 Venus" with a kiss, he signed himself "Hubby, Daddy, Mug."[17]

Until she swelled visibly, Clare maintained the fashionable appearance for which newspapers constantly praised her. She hired a press clipping service to keep track of her publicity, and beguiled the powerful gossip columnists Cholly Knickerbocker and Billy Benedik by supporting their favorite charities. They rarely failed to mention her as one of the brightest and best-dressed young women on Fifth Avenue. Slim and blonde in her short-skirted, low-belted frocks and cloche hats, she patronized fashionable restaurants for lunch and gave lavish dinner parties at home.

A typical evening at the Brokaws' began promptly at eight. Men drank iced martinis (Prohibition had not staunched the flow of alcohol in private), while women sipped sherry and smoked cigarettes in long holders. Dinner consisted of seven courses: soup, fish, entrée, game, sorbet, dessert, and savory, all served with appropriate wines, ending with port. Around midnight George would lead the way to some popular speakeasy, where serious drinking began. Clare could not, now or ever, keep pace with tipplers. Although she came to like booze well enough in later life, it quickly went to her head and slurred her speech.

At about three o'clock they might go on to Harlem for dancing and cabaret, taking their own gin in hip flasks. Even George disdained the "bathtub" variety, known as "hootch" or "orange blossoms." It consisted of medicinal alcohol, juniper berries, and citrus juice, and was rumored to induce brain fever.[18]

From time to time Clare reproached herself for devoting herself entirely to pleasure, or what passed as pleasure among George's friends. One night she found herself, her husband, and four others peering through the narrow grill of the Club Mirador "like monkeys waiting for peanuts." George had "pull" there, and for twenty dollars the doorman let them in. Strangers crowded around their small table and spilled illicit liquor on her new ermine and sable coat. The minuscule dance floor was packed with "fat, ugly, vulgar, vulgar people" bumping and grinding to "There She Goes in Her Sunday Clothes." Tired and jostled, Clare wondered why she subjected herself to such tawdry places.[19] Yet she went back to them time and again.

In mid-February of 1924, the increasingly mysterious Julian Simpson passed through New York. He was heading west to Chicago on unspecified business. Clare met him for only an hour and said nothing of the coming baby. He nevertheless sensed something different. "The Clare I knew was not there." It would be six years before they communicated again, and over twenty before they managed to meet.[20]

Clare posed for the Russian portrait painter Savely-Sorine in the seventh month of her pregnancy. He portrayed her in Renaissance style, with a wide braid encircling her forehead and a sweet, quizzical smile. "More like I want my soul to be," she said enigmatically.

In fact the tranquil-seeming sitter sometimes had the venom of a virago. Furious with another of Savely-Sorine's subjects, the heiress Ellin Mackay, for refusing to exchange sitting times, she described her as "willful callous cross-eyed . . . pig-headed Irish."[21]

Savely-Sorine's portrait, exhibited at the Wildenstein Gallery, captured nothing of the acid-tongued future author of *The Women*. Her nightclub companions, however, got an occasional foretaste. When a speakeasy doorman, mistaking her stomach bulge for a bottle, said, "Sorry, you will have to leave that outside," Clare snapped, "Wish the hell I could."[22]

George rented a house for the summer at Port Washington on Long Island but soon saw that his wife was bored there. Thoughtfully, he invited her old school friend Dorothy Burns to keep her company. At the beginning of August, three weeks before her delivery date, Clare moved to the Pickwick Arms Hotel, to be near Ann. On Friday the twenty-second, in Greenwich Hospital, she gave birth to a girl.

The labor was excruciating, but as time went by she forgot most of the pain. "The actual moment of birth was like stars opening and sun rising. I had had a little chloroform, which may have had something to do with it, but I remember it as the most joyful experience, and I wonder if more women don't too."[23]

She named the child Ann Clare after her mother and herself. George celebrated the birth of his daughter by bidding $250,000 for the Fleischman mansion and estate at Sands Point, on the North Shore of Long Island.[24]

Clare Brokaw with her daughter, *1926*

The duties of motherhood absorbed Clare through the fall and most of the winter, bringing a sense of fulfillment. She even felt deepening affection for George. One morning in early February 1925, she woke up in limpid sunshine aware of "the deliciousness of bed" and the "sweet dispassion" of his hand resting in the hollow of her waist. This was the best part of married life, she noted in her diary. Sounding rather like a romance novelist, she continued, "The night of desire is passed, the urge of the body quiet . . . the insistent flesh-call richly satisfied . . . Furtive lovers know not what they miss when they miss the morning kiss of scarcely conscious lips."[25]

Relishing the stillness of the room amidst distant street noises, she contemplated having another baby, a son this time. For *him* she might be willing to brave the nine months' wait and the torment of parturition. If only George had more to pass on in the way of "genius." As it happened, she was already pregnant again. But in the early hours of April 10 (the day on which she would normally celebrate her birthday), Clare miscarried. The fetus was "lost in a Horror of Blood, born away in a dripping basin," while ether numbed her brain. She wept, wondering if it might have been the son she craved. But by the time George came and held her hand, doubt had given way to exhilaration. For the time being the "shuddering agony of childbirth" had been postponed.[26]

As she recuperated, she felt health and relief, common to many miscarrying women, sweep over her. The prospect of bearing and nursing a child every year or so until breasts ached and bled appalled her. How, she asked herself, could wives subject themselves again and again to nausea, ungainliness, and the revulsion of their husbands? Of course they often had no choice. Nature had laid them an unfair trap. Contraception was unaesthetic, and abstinence seemed hardly the answer to Clare, at twenty-two. "What pleasure has my husband of my body unless he may possess it to the fullest gratification of his senses, and what ecstasy ever for me unless he does? But oh, the price is too steep."[27]

On the day of his wife's miscarriage, George Brokaw completed the purchase of the Fleischman estate. A retreat for the Prince of Wales during his North American tour, the colonial-style house stood on six acres of landscaped grounds. It had a polo field and private beach where George could anchor his yacht, *Black Watch*. Alva Belmont's château adjoined the property. The National Woman's Party leader could hardly have anticipated that the "push in the right direction" she had given Clare would catapult her to her own doorstep.

Ann Austin, too, was overwhelmed at how much her daughter had achieved. Touchingly inchoate after visiting Clare in the new house, she jotted in her diary:

> Darling little girl surrounded by books. Books on how to be
> a good mother. Last year before baby came you were painted.
> Then you were already in your mind the ancestral dame
> looking down from the wall on this child's children. You

have your first big country home . . . the Prince of Wales
lived there for days. Here are immaculate maids loaded trays
selected people . . . my child now a great house a loving
husband.[28]

Eighty-four-year-old Elvira Gould Brokaw died that June, and soon afterwards George filed an application in the New York State Supreme
Court to raze 1 East Seventy-ninth Street. He did so with his wife's un-
wavering support. In its place they wanted to build a luxury apartment
block, with a penthouse for themselves. After all, they had the house at
Sands Point for spring and fall, Newport beckoned in the summer, and
every winter they planned to travel abroad. A city apartment would
more than meet their needs for the remaining weeks of the year.
George argued in his petition that the Brokaw mansion was no longer
suitable as a residence, since the character of the neighborhood had
changed and the cost of maintenance was too great.[29]

Clare's energies were overtaxed that December by the demands of
seasonal social rounds, not to mention another stab at being an actress:
the leading role in an Amateur Comedy Club production of Booth
Tarkington's *Tweedles*. Early in the New Year she failed to menstruate.
Panicking, she telephoned a friend, and they went discreetly to an
Upper West Side address. A colored maid let them into a dimly lit
apartment, reeking of Oriental scent. Then a doctor with prominent,
beady eyes and slender hands appeared. He called Clare "honey," examined her, and advocated curretage for $250. But to her surprise he
suggested that she take time to consider it. Clare went home to do just
that, and in the interim "things straightened themselves out."[30]

The false alarm set her thinking again about the biology of women.
At a Castle School reunion on January 17, 1926, she met her former
sex teacher and was intrigued to hear Miss Lum whisper that she had
recently had "all her private innards removed." Wondering why a
maiden lady of irreproachable morality should undergo such surgery,
Clare asked a doctor to explain. He solemnly informed her that sexual
repression could lead to the growth of uterine fibroids. At once she
began to worry about her own considerable desires: "Every time I have
a wandering Romantic thought, or a guilty dream, which I do have, unfortunately . . . I shall be afraid that I am storing up not for myself children on earth . . . but tumors in the future."[31]

The truth was, she confided to her diary, that George Brokaw, now in his forty-seventh year, did not share her "fiery and passionate" nature. She resented spending half the day making herself attractive at the hairdresser and *modiste,* and half the night in a state of sexual hunger. "The Bill of Fare is neither varied nor sufficient."[32]

Feeling in late January that she needed a break, Clare spent a few days at the Ritz-Carlton in Atlantic City. She slept a lot, took brisk walks to fill her lungs with air, and ate little. Even here, Eros pursued her. By extraordinary coincidence, the next room in the hotel was occupied by George's law partner, "saintly Mr. Gulick," having an assignation with a young woman. While vowing not to regard him so reverently in future, she professed sympathy for decent men led astray by wayward girls. "The best of them are the same willing victims of the worst of us."[33]

A fortune-teller on the boardwalk told Clare that she would be widowed in two years' time and remarried to a man not yet divorced. She repented her disloyal marital thoughts. "I would be so miserable to lose my dear darling stupid George. Death is the only thing . . . I would ever permit to separate us. I love him . . . and I pity him so terribly."[34]

The annual and much-anticipated Beaux Arts Architects' Ball took place at the Hotel Astor in New York City on Friday, January 29. Some three thousand people in seventeenth and eighteenth-century costumes circulated through a series of ballrooms illuminated by orange lanterns hanging from a vivid green cloth ceiling. Clare, wearing a low-cut white and silver brocade gown, silky white wig, and emerald and pearl necklace, carried the old rose-point lace fan given to her by Frank Burke-Roche. She had been recruited to play Madame de Montespan in a pageant depicting the birthday celebrations of Louis XIV. To a fanfare of trumpets, she followed the "king" to his throne. A troupe of dancers appeared before them, one, to her consternation, "clad only in a smile."[35]

Clare Boothe Brokaw was at the peak of her young beauty that night. The pale shimmer of her dress and hair emphasized the sky blue of her eyes and translucence of her skin. Among the numerous courtiers to tell her how exquisite she looked was her Pierrot of the spring and summer of 1921, John J. Tanner. She was shocked to see

Clare and George at the Beaux Arts Ball,
January 29, 1926

what dissipation had done to him. "Poor Jack," she wrote afterwards, "he asked me if he did right when he let me go out of his life five years ago . . . when it would have been easier to keep me. Oh yes . . . it was sweet of you . . . Why are you wearing that frowsy clown's costume with its dirty ruche . . . and why do you follow me about with sad, dull eyes . . . Champagne Jack."[36]

The artificiality of the evening, despite the plaudits she had earned, weighed on Clare in retrospect. She had a dawning sense of her life's uselessness. Her women friends collected china and antiques to alleviate their *ennui,* or dabbled in decorating or adultery. None of these diversions appealed to her. By nature she felt she was a bee born to industry, but by accident she found herself trying to be a social butterfly.[37] In reality, she neither worked with bees nor soared with butterflies. Instead, she flitted dizzily from one unnourishing nettle to another.

13

THE LOVELIEST
MATRON

All human evil comes from . . . being unable to sit
still in a room. —BLAISE PASCAL

If the Beaux Arts Ball, with its royalty-aping vanities, privately struck
Clare as decadent, it did not stop her and George from throwing a
costume supper dance five weeks later that regressed through fatuity to
infantilism. On March 2, 1926, they decorated the walls of the Brokaw
mansion with pictures of nursery figures and required party guests to
dress as children. Those in default had ribbons clipped to their hair and
bibs tucked under their chins. Teddy bears were carried and toy trumpets tooted. The hostess appeared as a French doll, with a pink bow attached to her long, golden curls, and the host sported a white blouse
buttoned to little-boy pants.[1]

This mid-Lenten frolic marked the nadir of Clare's career as party
giver and the beginning of the end of her marriage. She would remain
with George three more years and experience pleasures as well as other
fatuities. But from now on she plotted how to escape her gilded prison
with minimum damage and the maximum amount of money. Compli-

cating her strategy were appeals from the two other dominant men in her life—David Boothe, embroiled in financial scandal, and her father, fading in health and almost penniless in Southern California.[2]

At least little Ann (now twenty months old) could be taken care of by a nanny. After a strangely belated baptism of the child by the Reverend Henry Sloane Coffin on April 21, her parents sailed for a short vacation in France.[2]

They stayed in Paris for a few days, which George measured out in morning *porto-flips* at the Hôtel Meurice men's bar. One day he nonplussed a male friend by inviting him to lunch on the Left Bank with Thelma Furness and Gloria Vanderbilt, but not Clare. The friend wondered if George, formerly so uxorious, might be contemplating an affair.[3]

After visiting Biarritz for a few weeks, the Brokaws recrossed the Atlantic in late June to spend the summer at Newport. A gossip columnist took note that they were the only representatives of George's family to have broached this bastion of Old Guard society.

> Clare Brokaw is certain to make a decided impression up here, for in addition to social graces, she is very clever, and writes and draws very well . . . She has the advantage of numbering Mrs. James Stewart Cushman among her intimates, and that lady . . . will see to it that George's pretty, young wife gives the frequently fatal Newport pitfalls a wide berth . . . other Mrs. Brokaws are vert [sic] with envy.[4]

George leased "Beachmound," the Benjamin Thaw villa overlooking Bailey's Beach, for three months. That Mrs. William Vanderbilt II had rented the house the previous season gave it extra cachet. Clare wisely did not offend the *grandes dames* of Bellevue Avenue with new-rich pretensions, and her "unassuming manner and quiet dignity" (to quote Billy Benedik) were generally praised. Only one dowager expressed doubts. "Clare Brokaw is an odd girl. She has a room off her bedroom just filled with books, and she *reads* them." By season's end Clare was so sure of a permanent position in Newport that she persuaded her husband to sell their Sands Point house—at a fifty-thousand-dollar profit—after just twenty months.[5]

Clare Brokaw, *c. 1926*

Back in New York in late September, Clare had noticeably gained social confidence. She was more selective in her choice of acquaintances
and events, and more practiced in handling the press. The satisfying result was seeing her name circled dozens of times in articles sent by her

news-clip service. Reporters at Belmont Park and Carnegie Hall noticed Clare Brokaw smiling at the right people and being conspicuously popular with "stags" at débutante parties. Blonde and exquisite in eye-catching white velvet at the Metropolitan Opera's opening night, she earned one journalist's accolade as the "loveliest matron in the entire 'golden horseshoe.' "[6]

Yet social triumphs did not keep discontent at bay, and Clare enumerated her woes to Ann Austin, who was wintering in Palm Beach. A painful tear in her uterus required stitching, little Ann disturbed her when she was trying to write, it was impossible to find decent dinner guests, and George obstinately refused to cash in all his assets, despite her urging that liquidity would free them both to come and go as they pleased. Instead, he talked in maudlin fashion of dying within ten years. "I should weep now about that?" she wrote her mother.[7]

Actually, George's health was fast deteriorating, exacerbated by his desperate drinking and insecurity about Clare. One day in the Colony restaurant he had a nervous attack when Max Reinhardt ogled her. He seemed afraid she might desert him for the stage. Clare tried to reassure him by joking that, at almost twenty-four, she was already too old to be a showgirl. But she did not mind telling him her real ambition: to write for the theater.[8]

As luck would have it, that spring Clare met a successful European playwright in Bermuda, where she and George had gone on vacation. His name was Seymour Obermer, and she was immediately drawn to his sophistication, as he was to her stock of dramatic ideas.[9]

They decided to collaborate on a three-act comedy called *Entirely Irregular*. The plot, set in a country house twenty miles from New York City, involved a wealthy businessman who, weary of his nagging wife and greedy daughter, feigns a mysterious suicide in order to run away with his secretary. The authors copyrighted the play on April 23, 1927, but it remained unproduced, perhaps because its overtones of melodrama were irreconcilable with its comic satire. One epigram, of the kind that would later characterize *The Women*, echoed Clare's own marital state. "I've always noticed, when a woman is faithful, she takes it out on her husband in other ways."[10]

While the writers worked, George drank. One night, stuttering with shyness, he tried to regale Seymour and Nesta Obermer with his notions of "the g-good, the t-true, and the b-b-b-beautiful." Clare, rescuing him, segued into a haunting ballad she had picked up somewhere, her off-key voice wafting out from their veranda:

> How beautiful they are,
> The lordly ones
> Who dwell in the hills,
> In the hollow hills.
>
> They have faces like flowers,
> And their breath is a wind
> That blows over summer meadows,
> Filled with dewy clover.[11]

Nesta, sensing "a great ocean of loneliness" around her new friend, deduced the underlying cause. Clare had a creative spark, but the "Big Infant" she had married did not.[12]

"It has been many a moon since Newport has seen such a resourceful young hostess as this pretty blonde," *Town Topics* enthused at the start of Clare's second season there. As the summer activities of 1927 got under way, the local press applauded her performance as "Beauty" in a pantomime fund-raiser for the League of Animals, ran pictures of little Ann in her go-cart, and featured George playing golf in the newly fashionable flannels, instead of old-style knickerbockers.[13]

On September 5 the Brokaws trod new cultural ground with a *thé musicale* for 150 people at Beachmound. Clare conceded afterwards it had been "an unsuccessful experiment" wasted on "a group of Philistines, who are living . . . by the sweat of their grandfathers' brows, but who shudder at any mention of the word perspiration."[14]

She continued nevertheless to migrate with the smart crowd, following them in October to the Homestead spa in Hot Springs, Virginia, for two weeks. Riding pine trails alone through the purple-hazed mountains made her feel insignificant yet inexplicably content. She wrote Vernon Blunt that she usually experienced happiness only in social surroundings, "in proportion that I feel myself *impor-tant.*"[15]

The Brokaws returned to Manhattan in time for the opening of the Metropolitan Opera's new season, as well as for a dinner dance and slide show in honor of the transatlantic aviatrix Ruth Elder. Others at the party, hosted by William Randolph Hearst, included New York's flamboyant mayor, Jimmy Walker, Alva Belmont, Jay Gould, Elsie de Wolfe, the designer, and Cole Porter—not yet famous on Broadway but already a conspicuous talent. This gathering marked Clare's formal entry into "café society," Manhattan's charmed circle of Old Guard renegades and new celebrities from the theater, movies, art world, politics, and journalism.[16]

She longed to feel an equal in such cosmopolitan company but often found herself embarrassed by George's drunken behavior. "Don't worry," said Ann Austin, "he'll fall down those marble stairs soon enough." Clare admitted to the same thought, adding that she "often felt like giving him a push."[17]

Her sense of entrapment intensified in December, when George lost his battle to pull down the Brokaw mansion. He had failed to marshal a family majority in favor of demolition.[18] Clare saw no immediate alternative, other than complete redecoration of the fusty old house. When work began in early 1928, she, George, and little Ann moved to temporary quarters on the top floor of the Sherry-Netherland hotel, then sailed to Europe for the spring and summer.

By now Clare felt mentally and emotionally ready to leave her husband, but she was not secure enough financially. Some years before she had set up a surreptitious trust fund, purportedly for Ann Austin, with generous checks that George assumed she was spending on furs and jewelry for herself. David Boothe had grandly promised to double the fund on Wall Street, then lost it all. He had also persuaded her to borrow twenty thousand dollars from his employer, Robert C. Beal of Broad Street, concealing the fact that he had used stocks and bonds of Joel Jacobs as collateral for his own devious purposes.[19]

Mr. Beal soon began to complain that Clare was not paying back her loan fast enough. Reluctantly, she went to George and, without revealing the subterfuge of the "trust fund," got enough money to settle at least part of it. Her aid failed, however, to keep David out of serious trouble. On top of his shady financial dealings, he drank, smoked, womanized, and gambled. To him playing the stock market was akin to betting on cards and horses: the higher the stakes, the greater the thrill. Clare complained that "he couldn't hold onto a dime for more than three seconds." Yet for unexpressed reasons going back to the shared sufferings of their childhood, she was unable to either control or disown him.[20]

Riggie discovered what was going on and threatened to sue. David ran off, re-enlisted in the Marines, and by early spring was in the mosquito-infested jungles of Nicaragua. He wrote Clare that he was fighting Augusto Sandino's guerrillas and hunting down bandits smuggling Communist-supplied weapons across the Honduran border.

Sounding temporarily contrite, he added that he wanted "to do penance and give you and mother a much deserved breathing spell." But he complained about the milkless coffee and hardtack he had to endure, in contrast to his preferred Fifth Avenue diet of oysters and baked Alaska.[21]

When Ann Austin wrote back reminding him that Clare had her problems too, he sent his sister a contrite letter.

> I can understand what you must daily endure and suffer, and I believe that whatever course you take will be the correct one. After all, your life is your own. You've been working for us all long enough, and are entitled to some freedom . . .
>
> Although I've never considered your happiness or your feelings, I would give anything just to be able to die for you. You're the one person I've always looked up to and respected and to me you can never do wrong.[22]

Clare received these effusions in Paris, where the Brokaws had been joined by Ann Austin at the Hôtel Windsor Etoile. Though David might have meant what he penned, he was more likely trying to keep her sweet for further loans.

Weary of George's childlike need for attention and companionship, she invited Vernon Blunt to cross the Channel one day and lunch with

them at Les Ambassadeurs. It was apparent to the still-lovelorn Englishman that if there had ever been tenderness between the Brokaws
none remained. His once gay and ethereal "white narcissus" was married to a shallow, dissolute, and ignorant man, as Vernon saw when the
conversation turned to philosophy. George clearly "knew damn all,"
and it burnt out Vernon's soul to think he had once imagined himself
not good enough for Clare. On the contrary, she was the one with de-
based values, mired now "in the throes of mundane compromise."23

After Ann Austin went home in June, Clare wrote her a series of
dispirited letters. George was staying "comparatively sober," but he had
no pride and was "certainly going crazy." She wondered why *she* had
not taken to drink or become "a babbling idiot." Ann's hope that he
wouldn't "last long" was futile, because he had amazing reserves of
strength. Next winter, after two or three months on East Seventy-
ninth Street, she intended to leave him. "I can't stand it any longer."

She asked Ann to investigate Connecticut divorce laws, because
hearings in New York would be devastating to George. In any case,
adultery was the only ground for divorce there, and Clare was sure that
her husband, whatever his other failings, had never been unfaithful.24

While determined to separate, she did not intend to leave Paris
empty-handed. In addition to acquiring quantities of clothes and jew-
elry, she tried to order some furniture by the Deco master Rhulmann.
But he was too backlogged, and she had to make do with traditional
French pieces, buying enough for all the ground-floor rooms of the
Brokaw mansion.25

In the third week of July, the family went south to Aix-les-Bains,
and checked into the Hôtel Splendide-Royale et Excelsior, situated on
a lake between two Alpine ridges. George, complaining of more or less
permanent tingling in his arms and legs, was warned by a doctor that he
risked paralysis or lunacy if he did not immediately abstain from alcohol. Clare naively hoped he would build up his strength by drinking
milk, because, she wrote Ann Austin, "he's going to get a surprise from
me one of these days." Little Ann was no solace to George. At four
years old, she refused to embrace or even talk to him. Her only diversions in the hot, dull valley were boating and swimming with her
adored mother.26

They all went north on August 6 for three weeks at Le Touquet.
The sea air had its usual effect on George. One night he lasciviously

lunged at his wife, and she pushed him away with such vigor that he fell and cut his head on a radiator—badly enough to require stitches. This behavior was more the result of alcohol than youthful libido. At forty-nine, George showed signs of having aged "terribly"—not enough, apparently, to satisfy Clare. He was by no means in "dying condition," she told her mother, "and I am not going to waste my life waiting for him to get in it."[27]

The Brokaws returned unrefreshed on the *Ile de France* in early September and moved into their newly decorated house. A few weeks later, George decided to resume his convalescence at White Sulphur Springs. Predictably, by the time Clare joined him in early October, he was drinking again. His whole personality was, as she put it to Ann, "so curled up inside of mine" that he was as dependent on her as "an unborn baby." Worse still, he was now beginning to suffer from delirium tremens.[28]

Back in New York, she took drastic action, hiring an authoritative doctor who confined George to his room. The patient was forbidden liquor and all contact with the outside world, including his wife and daughter. Telephone calls and letters were the only means of communication allowed. In a series of pathetic pencil notes to Clare, George tried to enlist her aid in denying his alcohol problem. "I am taking the rest you advise . . . When you see people please say that I had congestion of the lungs or something like that."[29]

On another occasion he wrote, "There is really nothing the matter with me . . . my spirits sink to a low ebb when I cannot even . . . say one word to Sweetie Pie . . . Wish you felt like that towards me." He begged for freedom to attend to some "*most important* stock transactions" and pined for his "library," where Clare had once found gin slopping around in his silver golf cups.[30] The only thing that cheered George during his incarceration was the election of Herbert Hoover to the presidency on November 6.

Clare made formal plans for a Reno divorce. Simultaneously, she was forced to confront another vexing personal problem.

William Franklin Boothe was now abjectly living in a leaky beach cabin just south of Santa Monica. Versa Boothe, the third of his wives—or fourth, if Ann could be counted in common law—had turned against him. He needed five hundred dollars to divorce her and hoped that Ann Austin might provide it. All he wanted from Clare, so far, was the return of a ring he had once given her, presumably so he could pawn or sell it.[31]

Ann's dread was that he might reveal his existence to the still-unsuspecting Dr. Austin and George Brokaw. She had written back warning him not to disturb their daughter's "place." Now, just as Clare was in the throes of divorce, the sixty-six-year-old William contacted her directly.

> Claire. [sic]
> I am writing this from Manhattan Beach, where I have been for some time past ill. Had it not been for John and Charley [his brothers] I would in all probability have had to find friends to help me tide over, for . . . with sight and hearing impaired, and suffering from pernicious anemia as well, it is not so easy to help yourself.

In the four rambling pages that followed, he never specifically asked her for money, for reasons of pride ("*Amour-propre* is . . . strong in me"). He feared, however, that his family was about to ask Clare for financial help on his behalf. "Their attitude is—'Your daughter whom we know is well to do—why does she not come to your assistance?' " Between the badly typed lines, he painted an affecting portrait of a wronged father, sick and down on his luck.

Looking back over their past years of alienation, he recalled that he had once been "one of the biggest piano manufacturers from a standpoint of volume in the world." Somehow or other he had gone "to pieces" and become a salesman to support his family. But he had always been by nature a musician, and music had supported him comfortably until two years ago, when his health broke down. Since then, he had been working on a violin technique treatise—

> A *Gradus ad Parnassum* that will live after I am gone. I am poor—practically destitute, but so have been many very great musicians. I can't teach more because of my hearing— but I hope to hang on to life for a year or two longer in order

149

that I may marshall and array all my notes, progressions, and excerpts.

Despite the querulous tone of the letter, Clare could not fail to be impressed by an enclosed *Los Angeles Sunday Times* profile of her father dated February 27, 1926. Its headline read:

> W. Franklyn Booth's [sic] Bow Wizardry Astounds
> —Left-hand Technique Said Greatest Ever Known—
> Described by Artists as Modern Paganini.

There followed lengthy praise of his digital dexterity, his supple bowing arm, and pyrotechnic feats that not even Jascha Heifetz could match. The writer had witnessed him "flitting up and down a famous Stradivarius. For two hours he kept up a running fire of left hand monstrosities without showing the least fatigue." In superscription William wrote, "This is not an ad. dear it couldn't be bought at any price."[32]

Clare did not reply, but she discussed William's situation with his sister, Ida Boothe Keables, and made it plain she was not disposed to help him. Her father had paid little attention to her for sixteen years and had no call on her now. She claimed to have little money of her own. "I cannot give to others what does not belong to me."[33]

William, sensing reluctance in her silence, wrote again. He did not want to "butt in" on her, he said, certainly not as a physical nuisance. "In fact I have a certain disinclination for the kind of life you are living. I believe," he added, "that material prosperity killed in you a very great woman."[34]

This goaded Clare to write in fury that she had problems too. Her marriage was breaking up, and she was dipping into private resources to assist Ann Austin, Grandmother Snyder, and David. As far as helping him was concerned, she felt "no love towards anyone from whom there has come none."[35]

William's third letter was full of wounded dignity, but he expressed sympathy for her situation, which he had not known about. "It all seems such a pity." He had not meant to beg money from her, nor would he permit his siblings to interpose for him. "I am not a pauper . . . You are the last person in the world to whom in the case of necessity I would make an appeal." What really concerned him, as his life

William Franklin Boothe, c. 1928

approached its end, was the resentment she and David showed towards him, as a result of their mother's endless vilifications. "Now dear," he ended, "don't worry about me, I am recovering. A few months more will, I believe, find me again fit. Getting knocked as I was is simply a part of life."[36]

Clare remained silent. William's last letter, dated December 4, 1928, was typed by a clearly weakened man. "It's six in the morning . . . Rare thing—a storm on the sea, it rained so hard, and my habitation leaks so badly that the combination of the two awakened me." His mood was nostalgic, and he was full of regret for all their lives gone so awry—Ann rusticating with a small-town doctor, David an embezzler, hiding out in Nicaragua, Clare married to a hopeless alcoholic, and he himself dying in poverty, with his great work unfinished. "Far better would it have been for all of you to have struggled along with that which I could have made. There would have been brought from you all that *I know is in you,* and David would at least have had to face the problems of life . . . thinking for himself." For the good of her child, he could only recommend that Clare stay with George, unless another loving provider was in the offing.

He refused to believe what his sister told him, that "you hard heart-edly said nix" to the idea of voluntary help with his medical expenses. Obviously he needed just such help. "My stomach is the despair of my doctors." The Boothes were providing only a fifth of his "bare necessities," and he had been forced to sell everything of value, even his precious violins.

> How am I going to get along? Damned if I know . . . if I can only finish my work, then I am ready to go . . . it seems un-fatherly to crowd upon you my troubles when you yourself are knee deep in woe, but you might as well know . . . I have a presentiment that I won't hear from David. Why I can't say . . . but it just seems that it is not to be my luck. I am dispirited this morning—I should not have written to you in my present mood.

In a shaky hand he signed himself "Your Father."[37]

Eight days later, William Franklin Boothe was admitted to Torrance Hospital in Redondo Beach. He died on Saturday, December 15, of pneumonia and "auto-intoxication"—poisoned by substances generated by his own body. He was buried on December 17 at Roosevelt Memorial Park, with neither of his children nor their mother in attendance.[38]

In January 1929, *Musical Courier* ran a major obituary calling William Franklin Boothe "a many-sided genius" and "a violinist whose virtuosity was widely acknowledged." Versa sent Clare his Boothe-Brokaw scrapbook, and a student, Ruth Paddock, in whose house he had lived for a while, followed up with his locket and some personal items. Among them was a carefully kept article entitled "Sex Hunger Insatiable." Evidently the old roué had retained his libido to the end.[39]

Miss Paddock also wrote that it was her intention to complete William's manuscript and do her best to see his name "among the immortals, as is his right." In December 1931 she placed a copy of the unpublished "Fingered Octaves and Primary Extension Exercises" in the Library of Congress. Reviewing it sixty years later, the eminent violin scholar Josef Gingold confirmed that William Boothe's exercises were impressive, the work of a man who certainly knew his instrument. But he advised fiddlers not to practice them more than fifteen minutes, for fear of developing tendonitis.[40]

Clare claimed to have paid for her father's interment over Ann Austin's objections. But nine years after William's demise, John Boothe sent his niece a news item which alleged that she was turning all royalties from *The Women* over to charity. "If the clipping is true," he wrote bitterly, "your charity might have reached up to one whose funeral expenses were paid by those who could ill afford them."[41]

Perhaps out of guilt, Clare later insisted that little Ann study music. She acquired Bruno Caruso's *Violin Player* and Giacomo Pozzano's *The Violist* for her art collection, entered into a midlife affair with the Mexican composer and conductor Carlos Chavez, commissioned a symphony from him, and in her last years grew dependent on classical recordings, played in the solitude of her room as she fought for sleep.

When George emerged from his weeks of isolation, Clare announced her intent to divorce him. Given that his alcoholism was now a matter of record, he made little protest.

On January 31, 1929, the couple signed a separation agreement in which each undertook not to do or say anything to "annoy, vex, or oppress" the other, and to visit only with mutual consent. George promised to pay his wife $2,500 a month until a $425,000 trust fund was in place for her later that year. Custody of their child was to be shared. Even if Clare remarried, George would continue to pay for Ann's clothing, schooling, and medical treatment. Debts up to $1,500 contracted by Clare before the date of the agreement were also his responsibility.[42]

Clare moved to a hotel for a few days before leaving for Reno in early February. Soon after her departure, Ann Austin went to the Brokaw mansion to see her granddaughter, as she was accustomed to do freely. But she found that her key would no longer fit the door. George had already changed the locks.[43]

14

CUPID'S GRAVEYARD

A woman has to look out for herself.

—PLAUTUS

Though Clare parted amicably from her husband—he sent her farewell orchids—she felt less than sanguine about leaving little Ann with him for the three months she was going to have to spend in Nevada. The best she could do was make sure the child would be in the hands of a competent *mademoiselle*. Dorothy Burns, with whom she visited in Chicago on her way west, could see that she was worried as well as unhappy. "She thought she was marrying George for keeps."[1]

Her train arrived in Reno at 4:30 A.M. on Wednesday, February 6, 1929, in a fierce blizzard. Clare's mood turned as bleak as the weather when she discovered that her reserved apartment at the Riverside Hotel (a red brick building between the Truckee River and the courthouse) was occupied and that she would have to settle for a "cubbyhole" of a room for the first three days.[2]

In a coincidence foreshadowing the Reno scene in *The Women*, Nanny Brokaw, George's aunt by marriage, was also in town for a divorce. Her husband wanted to marry his nurse, and she was insisting on a $5 million settlement. Clare's prospect of less than half a million seemed paltry in comparison. Through the long days ahead, she would have plenty of time to ponder how much more she might have negotiated had George left her.[3]

Forced now to live on $30,000 a year, instead of the $400,000 to which she had been accustomed, Clare braced herself for a severe diminishment in standards as well as style. That applied, first of all, to hotel bills. She began doing her own laundry and mending. For the first time in her adult life she prepared her own breakfasts and lunches of French toast, omelets, salads, and coffee in a tiny kitchen. During her stay her weight would drop temporarily to a svelte 117 pounds.[4]

Back in New York, gossipmongers were saying that Clare Boothe Brokaw would soon make a brilliant match. But she had no such immediate plan. Six years of access to a large fortune had not brought her contentment. Besides, "rich men are notoriously unattractive," she wrote her mother. Having "gone through hell" once with one, she had no intention, at twenty-six, of tying herself down again except for a real love. "I'm not living my life for anybody but myself from now on." George's alimony gave her the freedom to look for both love and money until the age of thirty. After that she might have to marry for money alone.[5]

In most respects, Reno was a typical western town with one stop-go traffic light, a five-and-ten, and several gas stations, movie houses, and speakeasies. Its Chinese and Italian restaurants did a lively take-out business, thanks to the approximately two thousand transients who annually swelled the indigenous population. Some of these women had considerable means. Others worked their way to decrees as cooks, waitresses, chambermaids, and croupiers. Together they contributed $3 million a year to the "City of Broken Vows," otherwise known as "Cupid's Graveyard."[6]

Those who could not afford the casinos spent their evenings playing cards. Clare, while not averse to bridge, tried to improve her receptive mind. She took French and Spanish lessons, and read Lytton Strachey's *Elizabeth and Essex*, L'Abbé Dimnet's *The Art of Thinking*, and Stephen Vincent Benét's verse narrative "John Brown's Body." For exercise she walked and rode. But a strange anemia plagued her. At first she imagined it to be the effect of high altitude, but when her head started spinning and her legs cramped, she saw a doctor, who prescribed injections of iron.[7]

In the beginning Clare saw the barren, colorless Nevada landscape as a reflection of her own physical and emotional dereliction. Then, as the weeks went by, she felt her jaded spirit being soothed by the stark hills, the subtle beiges, tans, and coppers of the terrain, and the blazing blue of the sky. Feeling a return of adventurousness, she rented a car and drove alone over the mountains to Virginia City. The once-prosperous site of the Comstock Lode mines was now a ghost town. Where previously three thousand inhabitants had panned for gold, phantom buildings and skeleton mine shafts were being bleached by the unrelenting sun. Only the Crystal Bar remained open, selling beer, chewing gum, and postcards.[8]

Though geographically distant from George, Clare still felt attached to him as her provider and father of her child. She needed to know whether he was keeping sober, solvent, and faithful. Evidence of drunkenness, profligacy, or adultery would be crucial in any future dispute over money and custody. So she instructed her lawyer to hire detectives to watch him. Word soon came that George was back on the bottle, having difficulties in the stock market, and dating a young woman.[9]

Adamant as she had been about wanting this divorce, Clare now blamed everything on her husband. In the first of a series of self-pitying letters to Ann, she listed her grievances, and hinted at an intriguing arrangement that might have kept them together.

> I married a weak, stupid drunkard with nothing to recommend him beyond a pleasant smile, money, and a fairly equitable disposition. I brought him youth, beauty, intelligence, and a lovely child . . . in the first three months of my marriage, he shattered every illusion I ever had, and made a physical and mental wreck of me. His family tormented and maligned me . . . I entertained his friends, brightened his

life, made him a person of some importance. I stood by him in all his squabbles with his brothers. I was nurse to him, counsellor, housekeeper, mother, wife, and friend. I tried with all my soul in the beginning to make him happy and to be happy myself. He cheated me physically, let me down mentally and spiritually at every turn. He drank, acted disgracefully, made me the object of scorn and pity before his friends. And when the time came for me to leave, treated me like a thief and a gold-digger . . . I lost my health and my looks playing the game. And when I gave my affection to someone else, it was because I cared for that someone else, and not because I wanted to leave him and improve my position. I offered to stay on the most civilized of terms, and he refused to have me. He told me he loved me better than anything in the world and made no effort to keep me . . . and now he sits in his house, with his servants, cars, and more money than he ever had, with the ghost of my five loveliest years about him . . . This is my Nicaragua, and I am paying as David paid for Speculating in Marriage.[10]

The "someone else" Ann evidently knew about was a young stockbroker named Jean, to whom Clare had entrusted "a small amount of money."[11] The inescapable truth seems to be that she wanted to be free to indulge herself sexually while continuing to live with George. Her husband's refusal to tolerate this "civilized" détente was the ultimate cause of the break between them. In marriage, as in other aspects of life, Clare wanted to have everything her own way.

Flowers for his estranged wife notwithstanding, George continued to deny Ann Austin access to his house. She was obliged to see her granddaughter in Central Park or a hotel. "If only that man would die in the next three months," Ann fumed, "things would be easier all around." George was "a quitter, an alibier, a gloater, a sulker, a bum . . . Dumb."[12]

Roused, she went on to castigate her daughter, too. For some time she had been feeling used rather than loved. She noted that "when things were clear sailing," on Fifth Avenue and in Newport, Clare had wanted to see little of her. "You were in my home to visit three times in one year and that was only on your own business." Now, not only was she having to keep an eye on little Ann but she was expected to hunt for an apartment to house Clare in the fall and even sell off her daughter's surplus furs and jewelry for cash.[13]

Ann complained that her personal income of $21,000 a year (most of it contributed by Joel Jacobs) was barely enough to cover expenses. This annoyed Clare, who wrote back to remind her that 90 percent of Americans managed on a lot less, and that her own alimony would amount to little more. Ann countered with further woes. All of Riggie's stocks had dropped in value, his own company had only $80 left in the bank, and he himself was $65,000 "in the hole there." Clare wrote back more sympathetically to say that Ann need never worry about money. Jean had made several thousand for her in investments (so much for her protestations to Ida Keables). If Joel Jacobs lost his fortune and became intolerable, mother could come to daughter. "I'll not annoy you half as much." Or if Dr. Austin should die, they could live together in Sound Beach quite comfortably.[14]

The passing reference to Clare's stepfather shows how completely he was disregarded by both women as a means of support. After years of tolerating Ann's continued intimacy with Riggie, Dr. Austin had become aloof. "Life with 'Doctor,'" said Ann, "is like a curtain on the stage, sometimes he draws it aside and lets me see the show, and then again I never know when that will be."[15] Menopausal resentment of his work and political interests would fester into paranoia in the coming months, damaging their marriage.

David's impending return from Central America added to Ann's troubles. With the help of an influential friend, she had secured his release from the Marines on the ground of ill health. He would have to work for a pittance in the Philadelphia Paymaster's Department while waiting for his official discharge.[16]

After seeing him for the first time in over a year, Ann described him to Clare as thin and haunted-looking. "That boy has suffered." During just one weekend leave in Sound Beach, David had drunk all the liquor in the house. On another occasion she found him on his bed, crying "as if his heart would break."[17]

As usual he claimed to be short of cash. Yet he went to New York for overnight stays whenever he felt inclined. Ann complained that her son had lived off her for most of his twenty-seven years and continued to do so. "I keep him clothed and fed, his laundry and pressing in order, and $20 to $30 each week to help him out," she informed Clare. It was time for him to contribute and help Clare pay back her two-year debt to Robert Beal, $15,000 of which was still outstanding.[18]

David wrote Clare somewhat disingenuously that he would be happy if "mother won't look worried when I offer to pay one of her bills." If he could only refund his sister "what I took, that would out-shine everything." Instead, he suggested moving in with her "for the next three years." He would need only "a few clothes for the necessary 'front' " and would be glad to substitute at dinner or cards whenever she was a man short. Otherwise he would be compelled to look for a wife. "I must have something even if it's only a victrola."[19]

Fathoming what to do about her brother became a preoccupation for Clare as she languished in Reno. "If there hadn't been Riggie's money and mine and George's he wouldn't have been tempted . . . If he had pulled the thing off, he would have been smart, but since he didn't, he's a fool, and a thief, and stupid. So you see, his life and mine have been a vicious circle of troubles, beginning with the desire for money, and ending with the loss of things far more precious."[20]

Clare instituted her divorce action on March 20. Marriage to Mr. Brokaw had affected the plaintiff's health, her lawyer argued, rendering continued cohabitation "unbearable and unsafe to her." Two months later she was granted a decree on the ground of "extreme cruelty."[21]

Neither relieved nor optimistic, Clare returned east on May 24. Faced with a summer of full responsibility for her nearly five-year-old daughter, she took the little girl to Sound Beach. The rooms of Drift-way, which just ten years before had seemed so spacious, now appeared cramped and confining.

Next day Ann Austin sailed to Europe for a six-week vacation as the guest of a friend—her way of saying that she was not a permanent child minder. Clare, lonely after her mother's departure, could hardly turn to Dr. Austin for light relief. Nor did she want to revive her relationship with Jean. She had already distanced herself from him by entrusting the management of her financial affairs to the firm of Louis and Theus Munds. Each month they purchased blue-chip stocks with her $2,500 alimony check. This made her feel more affluent, if not more secure.[22]

Other adjustments were not so easily made. She had no inclination to resume her old life of dress fittings, gargantuan dinners, all-night dances, speakeasies, racing, yachting, and golf. What, she wondered in sudden panic, was to take their place? Sinking rapidly into despair, Clare decided to do the fashionable thing and seek the help of a psychiatrist.

Dr. Dorian Feigenbaum was a middle-aged Viennese therapist on the faculty of the Institute of Neurology at Columbia University. As a Freudian he predictably diagnosed that Clare's problems were rooted in repressed childhood conflicts. From infancy she must have been challenging her mother for her father's love. Failing to win, she had then tried to compete with her brother by behaving like a boy.

Skeptical of these interpretations of her malaise, Clare became alarmed when the therapist suggested that all art was merely sublimated sexual atavism, and that she must transfer her affections to him before he could "cure" her.

After several months of feeling "more vile by the hour" on his couch, she began censoring what she told him. Then she abruptly ended the therapy. "I had not consciously planned to do any such thing," she wrote later. "But one day, right in the middle of a dream I was inventing, having long ago run out of real dreams . . . I jumped up . . . and told him the business was finished."

Dr. Feigenbaum warned her that breaking off now meant carrying "psychic scars" to her grave. But it was clear to her that if neurotic suffering is artistic creation gone wrong, what she really needed was a job.[23]

15

A Bibelot of
the Most Enchanting
Order

The Jazz Age . . . was borrowed time . . . the whole
upper tenth of a nation living with the insouciance of
grand ducs and the casualness of chorus girls.
— F. Scott Fitzgerald

At a dinner party in the early summer of 1929, Clare Boothe Brokaw
met Condé Nast, publisher of *Vogue*, *Vanity Fair*, and *House and
Garden*. Emboldened by his Southern courtesy, she said she was feeling
empty and directionless since her divorce, and asked if he could find
her a position on one of his magazines. Nast had heard this request before from bored society women and usually paid little heed. But Clare's
obvious seriousness, not to mention her beauty, brought an invitation
to visit his headquarters.[1]

Condé Nast Publications Inc. was housed in the Graybar Building
on Lexington Avenue at Forty-fourth Street. The beige and white marble Art Deco structure was then the largest office complex in the world,
with direct access to the train tracks of Grand Central Station. On its
nineteenth floor Clare was interviewed by *Vogue*'s editor, Edna Wool-

man Chase, who had worked on the magazine for thirty-four of her fifty-two years.

Wasting no time, she set the job seeker a test: to write the kind of detailed picture captions for which *Vogue* was noted. Clare's efforts showed promise, and she was told to return in a few days. But by then Mrs. Chase had left for Paris to see the fall collections, saying nothing about Mrs. Brokaw's employability.[2]

Clare had to resign herself to a summer of suspense before the editor returned. Keeping to her Reno resolve to live for herself, she arranged to stay for a few weeks on the breezy shores of Long Island. Since Ann Austin was still in Europe, and little Ann was due to spend August with George, she saw no reason to be marooned with her moody brother in the claustrophobic confines of Sound Beach.[3]

Soon someone sent word that George was "dreadfully lonely," unable to "let up on the gin," and had become an easy prey for "scheming

Clare and Ann at Southampton, Long Island,
July 1929

females."[4] This report confirmed what had for some time been obvious to Clare: she could not permanently tolerate sharing custody of her daughter with a father in such mental and physical disarray.

Bronzed and rested, she moved back to Manhattan in early September, and rented an apartment in the Stanhope Hotel at 995 Fifth Avenue. Only a few doors away stood the mansion she had abandoned just eight months before.

Clare had not heard from Mrs. Chase, but she was still determined to work at *Vogue*. So after Labor Day she put on a gray dress with white collar and cuffs, went back to the Graybar Building, and persuaded an assistant that she was a new employee. She took a seat at an empty desk in the editorial department and waited for some work to arrive. After a while it did. "I kind of oozed on," she recalled. "Nobody knew anything about me, not even the accountant." As a result, almost a month would go by before she received her first thirty-five-dollar weekly paycheck. When Edna Woolman Chase returned and found Clare in place, looking both businesslike and elegant, she assumed Condé had hired her. He, in turn, thought she had.[5]

The newcomer's manner struck Mrs. Chase as being "a little grand." At breakfast, Clare would spread a cloth across her desk and pour coffee from a silver pot. She was accordingly kept busy on a strict diet of captions. There were plenty of them to write, since *Vogue* was then published twice a month. Ambitious to write at greater length, Clare welcomed the eventual opportunity to do an article on the accoutrements of a well-dressed baby. Her manuscript, entitled "Chic for the Newly Arrived," warned that a standard twenty-two-inch christening robe, made of the finest batiste edged with Valenciennes lace, and worn over a slip of *crêpe de chine,* could cost "a great deal more than mother's latest from Chanel." Clare went on in deadpan style to describe other extravagant garments and excesses, such as an appliqué-trimmed crib and a lapin-lined perambulator. She recommended edible toys, because "babies have a passion for playing with their food and eating their playthings."[6]

Far from objecting to her archness, Mrs. Chase spread the piece over five pages, illustrated with pictures of bonnets, bibs, booties, and bassinets. Three years after its publication (without her byline), Clare boasted to an interviewer that her maiden article in *Vogue* was "still pointed to as a classic by merchants of the Wee Garment trade."[7]

In another assignment, covering a new line of lingerie, she flippantly described one filmy pair of drawers as "toothsome" and was horrified to discover that a copy head had sent it to press. Mrs. Chase saw her "pumping down the hall" to rescue the embarrassing phrase.[8]

Notwithstanding her cultivation by Edna Woolman Chase as a young writer of promise, Clare struck up a warmer relationship with Margaret Case, *Vogue*'s society editor. The latter's eye for style was reputedly so unerring that even the fashion editor, Carmel Snow, went to her for advice. "Now what is the story about gloves this season?" Clare heard Miss Snow ask one day. "Leave the buttons open, and wrinkle about the cuff," replied the oracular Miss Case.[9]

"Maggie," as intimates called her, both predicted and influenced dress and decorating trends on both sides of the Atlantic. She showcased Syrie Maugham's all-white room in one issue and a spare but perfectly appointed servantless apartment in another. As the magazine's chronicler of comings and goings, she had real power, and she used it to persuade socially prominent women to pose in glamorous gowns of *Vogue*'s choosing. Yet at thirty-eight she remained a journalist at heart and enjoyed nothing so much as rushing off to Europe with her favorite photographer, Cecil Beaton, to capture a Spanish religious festival or an English royal spectacle.

Clare, whose taste in most things was expensive but unsure, learned much from Maggie Case. The editor believed that "style trickles down" and was generous with advance fashion tips. Surprisingly, her own clothes were staid, even mousy. There was something spinsterishly stiff about her and her way of falling asleep bolt upright. She became the prototype of all the uncompetitive, well-connected women Clare would cultivate and use over the next fifty years.[10]

Just down the corridor from *Vogue* stood the offices of *Vanity Fair*, Condé Nast's prize gift to the *haut monde*. Since its launch in 1913, the periodical's circulation had not advanced beyond 90,000. *Time* disparaged it as a "glossy 'smartchart' " and said that "no magazine prides it-self more on the chic modernity of its readers."[11] These consisted of a small but potent concentration of the more literary and artistic members of society as Black Thursday loomed in the last week of October 1929. To Clare, still scribbling service copy at *Vogue*, the famous monthly was simply the most desirable and sophisticated next step she could imagine, perhaps in the remote future when her byline might mean something.

Between *Vanity Fair's* strikingly original covers were found such stellar short story writers, essayists, poets, and political commentators as Colette, D. H. Lawrence, Noel Coward, F. Scott Fitzgerald, Edna St. Vincent Millay, Robert Benchley, and Walter Lippmann. Among the painters and photographers were Pablo Picasso, Amedeo Modigliani, the Mexican caricaturist Miguel Covarrubias, Man Ray, and Edward Steichen.

Editor for the past fourteen of its sixteen years was Francis Welch Crowninshield, a lean, silver-haired bachelor with the elaborate manners of an Edwardian gentleman. In spite of his Brooks Brothers suits, "Frank" had avant-garde tastes and was a habitué of New York's modern art galleries. Since Condé Nast knew little about this world, he gave his editor carte blanche in making *Vanity Fair* something of a monthly gallery.

Crowninshield's office was as baroque as his personal appearance was austere. Beyond a door decorated with green figures on silver leaf, he sat at a lacquered desk against a background of shimmering Chinese wallpaper. He was assumed to be homosexual, although he vaguely informed Edmund Wilson that he had "a girl who came to see him once a week." No doubt existed of his nose for talent, and he frequently prowled through Edna Chase's adjacent domain, sniffing it out. Earlier in the decade, the scent had led to Dorothy Parker. Now it brought him to the fragrant Clare Boothe Brokaw.[12]

> When first presented to her I thought her the usual Dres-den-china society figure, a shepherdess with pretty teeth, large, round blue eyes, and blonde hair. She had, too, *les at-taches fines*, as her neck, ankles, and wrists were singularly fragile. She was, altogether, a bibelot of the most enchant-

ing order . . . her skin possessed a curious kind of translucence, as if some shining light beneath it were causing the
faint, pearl-like aura which seemed to surround her.[13]

Clare immediately ingratiated herself by offering Crowninshield a hundred article ideas for *Vanity Fair*. Astounded at her speed and facility,
he patronizingly joked that she must keep "a clever young man" under
her bed.[14] She filed the remark in feminine memory and left it to him
to make the next move.

The Wall Street crash of October 29 was still reverberating in the
world's ears when, the next day, a telegraph sent to the Stanhope Hotel
invited Mrs. Brokaw to see *Vanity Fair*'s managing editor, Donald Freeman, the following morning at 11:30.

Clare knew the twenty-five-year-old Freeman by reputation. He
was a Columbia graduate who had studied in Vienna and spoke German and French fluently. For transatlantic promotion of the work of
such writers as André Maurois and Paul Valéry, he had been made a
member of France's Légion d'Honneur. In person he was unprepossess-
ing, with a receding hairline and a shape that revealed a weakness for
sherry-laced soup, beer, and banana splits. Nevertheless, Clare liked his
quiet solidity, and though he was eight months her junior, she recognized Freeman's educational superiority and editorial flair.[15]

He, in turn, had been aware of Mrs. Brokaw's fine looks and candid
gaze from the time of her arrival in the Nast organization. As they
talked he was dazzled by her ready wit, originality, and intellect equal
to his own. More important, he sensed her creative potential and relished the chance to play Pygmalion.

All that remained, after Clare left his office, was for Freeman and
Crowninshield to persuade Edna Woolman Chase to part with her
latest editorial assistant. This did not prove difficult, since Mrs.
Chase, along with millions of other Americans, was currently preoccupied with disastrous personal losses on the stock market.[16] Few anticipated the extent of the debacle in which the United States lost a
staggering $30 billion—in admittedly overheated stock values—
twice the national debt and an amount equal to the entire cost of
World War I.

Clare suffered little, thanks to George Brokaw's canny foresight.
From her $25,000 income, she dropped only $1,200 a year of United

Donald Freeman,
c. 1931

Cigar Store stock, leaving her $425,000 trust fund virtually intact. As the depression set in, she had, at worst, the minor inconvenience and expense of a precipitous descent of hemlines, almost to the ankles.[17]

By December, Clare had moved to *Vanity Fair* as a junior editor, at an annual salary of $1,820. She shared a large, sunny office with the drama critic Margaret Case Morgan (no relation to *Vogue*'s society editor). Freeman worked right next door. Under his tutelage, Clare began proofreading, arranging interviews, and setting up photographic shoots. Keen to learn all aspects of the job, she honed her schoolgirl literary skills on incoming manuscripts. Frank Crowninshield declared a plot she outlined for a blocked author to be "worthy of de Maupassant or Turgenev." With the aid of a French dictionary, she translated short stories by Frédéric Boutet and made what Donald called "a master-piece" of an essay on cats by Paul Morand.[18]

The already captivated Freeman encouraged her to start writing articles of her own. She worked on them in the early morning hours, and utilized Saturday afternoons for library research. What leisure time remained she spent with her mentor. Predictably, his role expanded from that of dinner, movie, and theater escort to that of lover. "As soon as he got me on my feet," Clare later wisecracked, "he wanted me on my back."[19]

Donald shared a weekend cottage in Rhinebeck with his mother and unmarried sister, Gladys. During the week he lived in a book-lined apartment on East Nineteenth Street. From there he would take Clare to evenings with his many publishing acquaintances, including the wits of the Algonquin Round Table. His closest friend was George Jean Nathan, *Vanity Fair*'s theater critic, who suggested that Clare drop "Brokaw" from her professional byline. But she was not yet ready to accept this advice.[20]

So long as it suited her, she concealed an abhorrence for Donald's protuberant belly and grubby fingernails, as she had once hidden her contempt for George's childishness and drinking. Marriage had given her access to money and high society. An affair with her managing editor promised contacts more pertinent to present purposes. Yet she did not see herself in what she humorously called a "jungle" job, "the kind you hang onto with your tail." If it had been, she would not have risked Donald's wrath by flirting with visiting aristocrats such as the Earl of Warwick and Grand Duke Alexander of Russia, who called her his "Dearest Doushka" and boldly kissed her when he submitted a manuscript on world peace.[21]

Vanity Fair published the first of Clare's extracurricular pieces in August 1930. It was a lampoon on upper-crust chat, called "Talking Up—and Thinking Down" and subtitled "How to Be a Success in Society Without Saying a Single Word of Much Importance at Any Time." The opening paragraph heralded its theme:

> Too much has already been written about the dead or dying art of conversation. Drawing-room cynics and critics of so-

ciety assert that the fine art of persiflage and repartee, of making epigrams and *bons mots*, of Pope's "feast of reason and flow of soul," which flourished until Nineteen Hundred in the salons of France and England, received its death blow at the dinner tables of the modern capitals.

Ignoring her own stricture, Clare proceeded to criticize middlebrow talkers for going on at length and without originality about golf, bridge, dogs, racehorses, the stock market, Prohibition, high rents, politicians, absent acquaintances, and sex. She was no less critical of those who affected culture but not too much of it: people who might discuss art, stopping short at Rodin, philosophy only as popularized by George Bernard Shaw or Will Durant, and opera if sung by Jeritza. They might cautiously allow Hemingway a word or two but would not mention Joyce, Proust, Spengler, or Einstein for fear of being thought "highbrow" and jeopardizing their social status.

Clare's long-sentence style was marred by an excess of adverbs, and she petered out of original ideas midway. But "Talking Up" was a creditable début, even though its skeptical tone was stronger than *Vanity Fair*'s customarily cool, urbane "voice."

A literary agency was impressed enough to propose handling foreign publication of all her articles, and any fiction she might write. Donald telegraphed the news, adding that he hoped it would inspire her to "work hard tonight." This exhortation became a refrain in their relationship over the next two years, as he groomed Clare not only for editorial stardom but for a literary career in her own right.[22]

Vanity Fair at the beginning of the Thirties differed little in its basic format from *Vanity Fair* at the start of the Twenties. Unaffected, as yet, by the looming Depression, it still portrayed an America in transition from the age of robber-baron vulgarity to one of more democratic, albeit metropolitan elegance. If its covers in 1930 no longer depicted cloche-hatted young women being wooed against abstract backgrounds of purple pods, or banjo players and Harlem dancers on collages of geometric shapes, its fifty inner pages (routinely preceded by forty of advertising, with forty more at the end) still divided into eight departments that Frank Crowninshield saw no reason to change. They were

"In and About Theatre," "Concerning the Cinema," "The World of Art," "The World of Ideas," "Literary Hors d'Oeuvres," "Poetry and Verse," "Satirical Sketches," and "Miscellaneous"—covering sports, games, music, and fashion for both men and women.

"Ideas" was the only part that allowed for serious discussion of controversial views. An article by Aldous Huxley, published before the crash, had presciently cautioned that the fruits of Western industrialization were a temporary phenomenon. "We are rich, because we are living on our capital. The coal, the oil, the nitre, the phosphates . . . can never be replaced."[23] But on the whole the magazine tried to chronicle the times without excessive economic or political comment. Literary contributions, many of them from Europe, outnumbered current-affairs columns by as much as ten to one when Clare joined the staff. These proportions would alter dramatically in the more prosaic decade ahead, as readers began to look beyond diversion and amusement, and to desire the status of being well informed.

Wall Street's collapse affected *Vanity Fair* first of all in its paying pages. No longer was it possible to fill two thirds of them with advertisements for Cartier jewelry, Guerlain perfume, and $25,000 Mason & Hamlin pianos. Readers were still urged to sleep on the finest linen, dine with the best sterling silver, and cross the Atlantic on the grandest ocean liners. But when Tiffany & Co., long a staple at the front of the book, symbolically gave way to Listerine, circulation would begin to decline.

That day, however, was still some way off in August 1930, when Clare published her first contribution to "We Nominate for the Hall of Fame." This was a regular among *Vanity Fair's* miscellaneous features. The format called for laudatory biographical paragraphs beneath portraits of notable people in the arts, sciences, sports, and business spheres. Clare's assigned subject was Henry Robinson Luce.

She had not yet met the *wunderkind* publisher and knew little about his private life, hobbies, or eccentricities. "Does he save string, or raise fish?" she asked his colleagues and friends. No, they said, Luce did nothing but work. "What a dreary man," she thought as she struggled to write a convincing citation.[24]

> Because he originated the news-magazine idea; because at
> the age of 32 he is the successful editor and publisher of *Time*
> and *Fortune* magazines; because he was born in China; be-
> cause he was once a humble newspaper reporter on the
> *Chicago Daily News*; and lastly because he claims that he has
> no other interests outside of his work, and that this work fills
> his waking hours.

Why being born in China, becoming a reporter, and having no
outside interests qualified Luce for laurels was hard to explain. Clearly,
Clare did not lean towards adulatory prose. She preferred satire, and to
showcase her gift for it, she persuaded a reluctant Frank Crowninshield
to run an antidote to "Hall of Fame." It was called "We Nominate for
Oblivion."

The first casualty of her concept was the tabloid publisher Bernarr
Macfadden, nominated for having America's "raciest stable of cheap
magazines." It was an unfortunate selection, since Macfadden was a
customer of Condé Nast's Connecticut printing plant. He immediately
canceled a $50,000 contract. Nast was furious and insisted on vetting
all future candidates for "Oblivion."[25]

Perhaps as a result, Clare's abrasive feature ran irregularly. The
novelist Elinor Glyn was included for starting "a saccharine and untrue
school of literature," Huey P. Long for spending state money "like an
oriental potentate," Cecil B. DeMille for creating "distorted values of
love, high life and wealth," Queen Marie of Romania for her "devotion
to press-agentry and boosting of cold creams," Aimee Semple McPherson for depending "more on sex appeal than spirituality to bring sinners
into the fold," Al Capone "because he turned out to be a small-time social climber," and Adolf Hitler "because his Jew-baiting campaign is
medieval in its intensity."[26]

"We seldom get orchids . . . from 'Fame' candidates," Clare noted
with glee, "but we do get bunches of lovely scallions from 'Oblivion'
victims." The objection was always the same: they did not mind being
criticized so much as having to keep company with the others.[27]

At an editorial meeting, Crowninshield voiced disapproval of the
creeping harshness—what Paul Gallico called Clare's "guts and tough-
ness"—that he detected in his once-benign magazine. It was bad busi-

ness policy, he felt, to vilify people in print. "Crownie was pretty much of an old lady," Dr. Mehemed Agha, *Vanity Fair*'s art director, remembered years later. "He was terribly afraid of offending anybody . . . or doing anything that wasn't dignified and decorous. Clare on the other hand was a satirical person, with a rather cruel approach to people and things, a debunker." At the time, Agha could only protest, "We shouldn't make everything mild and milk toasty." Crowninshield was not persuaded, and after running ten times in twenty-two months, "Oblivion" was dropped for good.[28]

The name of Clare Boothe Brokaw joined those of Ogden Nash and P. G. Wodehouse on the list of top contributors to *Vanity Fair* in September 1930. Her essay that month, "The Dear Divorced," considered differences between agreeable and disagreeable marital breakups. She had nothing original to say about rancorous splits but wrote approvingly of "good lovers" who, "lacking the energy to become good haters, part in the nick of time, hopeful of becoming good friends." In an age when divorce was considered as mostly destructive, this wry idea of parting in order to salvage a relationship was distinctly new.

A month later Clare published "Ananias Preferred," a tongue-in-cheek paean to the well-told lie. Without deception, she argued, diplomacy might fail, governments fall, and social structures atrophy. "Lying increases the creative faculty" in man, lessens friction, and, effectively done, buttresses the ego. Writing as an unacknowledged expert, she cautioned that successful prevarication requires a faultless memory, in order to keep track of untruths told.

"Your article on Ananias has created quite a furor in the office," Donald Freeman informed Clare. "We all agree that this is the best piece of writing you have ever done. Mr. Crowninshield is more than enthusiastic." Indeed the latter was so impressed that he immediately promoted his twenty-seven-year-old discovery to associate editor.[29]

Clare's November piece, "Bachelors Do Not Marry," was pedestrian by comparison. She seemed to have Julian Simpson in mind as she brusquely condemned men who hover eternally on "the matrimonial brink . . . their eyes gleaming with half-formed resolve." Why, she asked Donald, did she sound so "hard-boiled" in print, when in her heart she felt "compassion and affection for everyone"?[30]

Every Wednesday at *Vanity Fair*, Frank Crowninshield gave a lunch for editorial staff. More often than not, the menu consisted of his favorite eggs Benedict and chocolate éclairs, sent up from the nearby Savarin restaurant. Clare would ostentatiously bring her own spartan snack of melba toast and salad, making other women feel "like harvest hands" and calling male attention to her streamlined figure.[31]

There were always two or three special guests at the table. Out-of-town writers such as Thomas Wolfe and Sherwood Anderson were captivated by Crowninshield, a superb raconteur. He gossiped so entertainingly about dinners at Mrs. Vanderbilt's, or balls at Mrs. Twombley's, that they felt like Park Avenue insiders and agreed to write for lower fees than they might earn elsewhere.[32]

Clare had her own experience of Knickerbocker society, and hit on the idea of writing a series of satiric, interrelated short stories about its stalwarts. Twelve appeared in *Vanity Fair*. With superabundant energy she would complete eleven more, in the hope she might someday collect them in a book.

Each story exposed or mocked the snobbery, affectation, cruelty, bad taste, and carelessness of the old and new rich. Clare's "voice" was in turn melodramatic, sardonic, farcical, and bathetic. Few subjects were deserving of charity, and her distaste for the vacuousness, even malevolence, of the lives described was all-pervasive.

She spiced the bland pomposity of New York and Newport hostesses and their "stuffed shirt" husbands with a variety of seedier characters: a burnt-out painter, a lascivious salon musician, an impoverished nobleman, a venal doctor, a philandering sportsman, a lovelorn stockbroker, an opportunistic flapper, and an assortment of jaded dandies, débutantes, and divorcées.

Easily recognizable real people appeared caricatured or thinly disguised. Mrs. Reginald Towerly in "Life Among the Snobs" was clearly Alva Belmont. Hugo Ashe, the feared theater critic in "Two on the Aisle," amounted to a surprisingly sympathetic portrait of the *New York Times* columnist Alexander Woollcott, and Flora Arbuckle, a fat party

giver in "Exhale Gently" and "The Ritz Racketeer," parodied Elsa
Maxwell. Alfred Clothier, in "The Catch," was a carbon copy of
George Brokaw—a middle-aged heir to a large fortune and a target for
marriage-minded young women.

Season after season for twenty years, Clare wrote, Clothier had
stood "on the stag line of any important coming-out party, his face as
blank as his immaculate shirtfront, his delicate hands alternately thrust
into his pockets or fumbling self-consciously with his pearl and platinum watch chain, as he furtively eyed the more full-blown of the
buds." A solitary patron of speakeasies, he was "as ashamed of his taste
for drink" as he was of his sexual appetites.[33]

Also partly autobiographical was "Ex-Wives' Tale," in which she
recounted the "most fashionable divorce of the season." After six years
of marriage, her *alter ego* protagonist had left a rich, dull husband for
only one reason—boredom. Back from Reno, she moved into a mod-
ernistic apartment, became an interior decorator, and started dating
again. Her hopes of romance, however, were thwarted by men who, in
Clare's coy phrase, were not "as much concerned with her ultimate
happiness as with their own immediate desires." This was especially
true of Bela Dárdás, a laconic pianist whose hands hung "like tired lilies
upon the darker ivories" but who was an Olympian in the bedroom.
After one night of "*grand amour*," he left her "quivering from . . . delicious contact with genius"—and never came back.[34]

Clare usually had free rein in writing what she pleased for *Vanity Fair*,
so she bridled when asked to produce a pair of service articles on
backgammon. She told Donald Freeman that if she wrote like an expert she would be expected to do more, and if she deliberately made
them amateurish, her reputation would suffer. He pointed out that
since the request had come from Crowninshield, it might be good office politics for her to comply. Reluctantly she deferred, but published
both pieces under the pseudonym "Julian Jerome."[35]

Every day Clare felt more confident of her powers. Margaret Case
Morgan came to work one morning and "found that she was employing
my secretary and I was employing hers." Clare had lured the former
away by paying twice the usual salary out of her own pocket. On an-

other occasion Mrs. Morgan left a pair of complimentary first-night tickets on her desk while she went to lunch.

> When I looked for them around five-thirty, they were gone. After a frantic and vain search, I called up the press agent, who agreed to have duplicates for me at the box office that night.
>
> When my date and I walked down the theater aisle with my duplicate tickets, guess who had the real tickets and who was occupying my seats? Right. None other than Clare Boothe and escort. I was so mad that I merely said to her, "Enjoy the play, dear," and stalked back up the aisle. My date and I went to the movies.
>
> Next morning in the office Clare said, "But you left the tickets on your desk, so of course I thought you didn't *want* them!"[36]

It was becoming evident that whatever Clare desired, she simply took, or tried to take. Condé Nast told Mrs. Morgan that she had even offered to buy a controlling interest in his company.[37]

Ironically, only Donald stood between her and the job she now lusted for: that of managing editor.

16

CHANGING TIMES

*And in that town there is a fair called Vanity Fair and in
it are all such merchandise sold as places, honours,
preferments, titles, lusts, pleasures, and
delights of all sorts.* —JOHN BUNYAN

For her summer vacation in 1930, Clare decided to spend two weeks
at a remote, cool spot in the Adirondack Mountains. Loon Lake,
thirty miles from the Canadian border, was an unlikely destination for
one who usually preferred hot sun, sea, and society. But by absenting
herself from both city and ocean distractions, she hoped to start a work
of fiction based on her Reno experiences.

Accompanied by little Ann and a French governess, she arrived at
the resort by overnight train on Tuesday, August 19. A cold morning
mist obscured the higher peaks and hovered above the steel gray water
fronting on a green wooden hotel. Entering, Clare noted xenophobi-
cally that Loon Lake House was full of people with "enormous noses."
In her three-room suite she unpacked in desultory fashion, one item at

a time, and later wrote Donald Freeman that she felt "aristocratically helpless without a maid."[1]

After dining at Fairchild's, a rambling hillside camp with a wide fireplace and red leather chairs, Clare made her way back through a grove of silver birches. The scent of pine reminded her of childhood days in the forests of Wisconsin. How intrepid she had been in comparison with her pampered six-year-old daughter! Ann was afraid to venture barefoot even down well-trodden paths or go near strange animals without asking, "May I? Dare I?"[2]

Finding no spirited fellow guests, Clare went canoeing alone one night. There was little more than a sliver of moon, and the water that she associated with the mysterious drowning in Dreiser's *American Tragedy* gleamed with opalescent tints. The only sounds in the still air were the drip, drip from her paddles and a dog's echoing bark.[3]

Contrary to her usual practice, she went to bed early, slept late, and smoked less. She was exhausted from almost a year of hard work at Condé Nast and doubted that the robust vitality of her youth would ever completely return. A lingering sense of staleness prevented her beginning her novel, and she poured out her frustrations in letters and telephone calls to Donald. In an attempt to ease back into serious writing, she sent him a critique of Somerset Maugham's novel *Of Human Bondage*. The author, she felt, had weakened his story by making the hero a cripple as well as an introvert. The obvious symbolism of a clubfoot was superfluous: any shy person might suffer Philip Carey's social agonies. Donald disagreed. Harshly realistic details, he wrote back, were what made Maugham's work durable, and she should try for a similar vividness.[4]

With his encouragement, Clare completed four chapter outlines in four days, then became mired in technical problems. Her plot lacked suspense, had no central character and no moral point. Convinced she was a mediocre talent at best, she wrote Donald that she may as well settle for a hedonistic life of reading and travel.[5]

While awaiting his reaction, she diverted herself with gambling at Fairchild's and won large sums at backgammon. "Julian Jerome's" articles on the subject had come in useful after all.

Donald took Clare's loss of confidence seriously. He suspected that at twenty-seven she had reached a turning point in her life. On August

25 he wrote a long, impassioned reply. "Yours is a first-rate, most exceptional talent. Not one in a thousand established writers of today can claim as much." Even her letters "could be polished up into essays." Her work for *Vanity Fair* was already getting recognition. "In a few months . . . you will begin to be considered important. You have in one bound skipped over barriers which it takes other authors years to jump."

At this stage, however, everything she wrote needed his "brutal editing." He proudly reminded her that writers of the caliber of Thomas Mann and Sinclair Lewis had submitted their prose to his scrutiny. Clare must not balk at the same treatment. To acquire further discipline and productivity, she needed to spend at least three more years at the magazine perfecting her craft. If she drifted away from journalism and allowed her gifts to atrophy, she would indeed end up wasting herself in "*dolce far niente* places" amidst scenery, gigolos, and vacuous expatriates.

"I do not want a more talented protégée," he assured her, "and as for the more loving sweetheart—well—I have hopes."[6]

Read now, Freeman's letter seems like the exaggerated praise of a lover rather than the sober judgment of a professional. Along with so many other editors, before and since, he saw himself as a writer manqué, forced to earn a living in "the mill of industry." Clare had become his *alter ego*, creating works of the imagination as he thought he could have done.[7] But it was true that she had been noticed, and Freeman was correct in his forecast of imminent success. Critics with minds as fine, if less adoring than his, would soon agree that Clare Boothe Brokaw was headed for a stellar literary career.

By the start of her second week at Loon Lake, Clare had jettisoned her unpromising novel—or rather, put the material aside, to be recast one day as the Reno scene in *The Women*. Instead she worked on a few more of her interconnected high-society tales. She also did several freelance articles, as well as translations of French contributions. These put her three months ahead of her magazine commitments and ensured an extra three or four hundred dollars to supplement her salary.

Donald was pleased to hear of her diligence. If only she would now give up cigarettes, he wrote, his happiness would be complete. "Why do I experience actual pain when you begin to smoke?" Perhaps it was "a sadistic impulse trying to deprive you of something you crave, thwarted heterosexual feelings since you smoke like a man."[8]

Reading this psychologically contorted admission, Clare felt "the imp of the perverse" rise in her. "If I smoke like a man," she wrote back, "you smoke like a woman."[9]

She was even more caustic when they spoke by phone. Realizing she had gone too far, she tried to make amends in a letter.

> Darling:
> Did I distress you this morning . . . ? Then I must admit that my intention was to wound you a little: and with a quite selfish aim. I wanted to see if I could still hurt you, for it is only when we perceive that we still have the power to hurt someone we care for, that we can be certain he cares for us. My experiment, which made you uneasy, made me quite comfortable in my mind, and in the delicious sense of being still loved. However, I suffered instant remorse for my selfish action, when it became apparent that you were really hurt. And so . . . the rhythm of love is developed. All my withdrawals and denials are only veiled pleas that you should ask me to draw near and to affirm my love, and by hurting you, I accomplish this result, without, as it were, moving a step myself. By going away, I achieve the sensation of coming closer, by wounding you, I cause you to need more than ever the solace of my love, and in the remorse I afterwards feel, I need yours. Very pretty, and very Proustian, what?[10]

Clare returned to New York in early September and moved into a $555-a-month penthouse at 444 East Fifty-second Street. From its rooftop terrace she had a magnificent panorama that she described as being especially spectacular at night.

> The East River, sombre as a black velvet ribbon at your feet, shot with phosphorescent slivers that flake away in the wake of river craft. The Queensborough Bridge and Hell Gate, flung like necklaces across the river's dark body . . . the sable silhouettes of the marching skyscrapers, the lance of the Chrysler Building looming near, the flaming

tower of the Radio Building, the golden glow of the New
York Central Building, the red torch of the Empire State
Building, hung high above them all.[11]

She hired four servants, including a personal maid to run her bath
and help her dress. By agreement with the landlord, she paid for a new
mantel, mirrors, and special old wallpaper in the dining room. After
furnishing her living room with an eclectic mix of old and new pieces,
she lined one wall with books, and hung a Foujita sketch of two catlike
nudes on another. Her plans for the bedroom betrayed a compulsive,
not to say precious tidiness, with dresser drawers compartmentalized
even for her stockings.[12]

Proud, if not quite sure of the aesthetic results, she invited *Vanity
Fair's* art director to visit. Dr. Mehemed Fehmy Agha was a brilliant,
thirty-two-year-old Turk in charge of the magazine's latest style update.
Clare admired his taste and hoped that he would favor hers. But Agha
made no comment, and she assumed that his silence signified disapproval.

Stung, she wrote defensively in her diary, "Originality, and 'modernism' means nothing to him." Agha was unable to appreciate her
"somewhat effortless effect of simplicity" and "lack of pretension." It
followed that he must "dislike women."[13]

Donald also moved that fall, one convenient block south of her, to
425 East Fifty-first Street. He coyly dubbed his brownstone apartment
their "love-nest." In the evenings and on weekends Clare made good
use not only of his bed but of a handsome desk and high-powered Underwood, installed mainly for her. The Graybar Building was an easy
ten-minute walk away. After breakfast they would stroll west along
Fifty-first—Clare's favorite street in New York—past a gigantic wisteria vine cascading over the entire front of one four-story brownstone
house. At Lexington Avenue they would turn downtown and take the
same elevator up to their respective offices. There the self-effacing
Donald tended to attract less attention than his blossoming assistant
editor sweeping by in a cloud of expensive perfume.[14]

Frank Crowninshield's secretary recalled half a century later that
Clare had a "translucent glow about her" in those days. She could be
seated at her desk, in a tailored suit with "big horn-rimmed goggles on

her nose, her hair a bit straggly . . . but if a man came into the room an astonishing thing would happen: her hair would gleam; her teeth would shine; her whole person would light up." Clare worked "fantastically hard," and in editorial disputes she usually got her own way. "Then a tiny mischievous look of triumph would appear on her face, and she'd giggle."[15]

She exercised her adamantine will habitually now. Envious stenographers marveled at her discipline, decisiveness, and poise under pressure. Throughout the fall she edited and wrote and tried to be a conscientious mother. These multiple duties affected her sleep and health, and she looked for help to Dr. Austin. He recommended what he called "new-woman-making" pills, plus "Allonal" tablets for insomnia.[16] These, along with tobacco, caffeine, and alcohol, began to fuel in Clare a lifelong dependence on stimulants and depressants.

By November 1930, one year after the Wall Street collapse, *Vanity Fair*'s advertising revenue had fallen 20 percent. Nast was personally unable to handle this decline, and his assets—what was left of a rumored $17 million fortune—were placed in the hands of bankers. A partner of Goldman, Sachs took over as director of the company. Senior staff were forced to take a 33 percent cut in salary. This severely affected Donald Freeman. Clare discovered with incredulity that as well as supporting his mother and sister, he was also financing two Viennese orphans.[17]

Insulated by her alimony and undiminished paychecks, she took advantage of worries and distraction at upper levels to start putting her stamp on *Vanity Fair*. The editor in chief did not object. "Crownie piddling, effusive, charming, ineffectual as usual," she wrote in her diary.[18]

Part of Clare's new job was to see that the magazine reflected changing times and aired the latest philosophies. Crowninshield's belief that it should "cover the things people talk about at parties" was still valid, in her opinion. What he did not realize was that contemporary cocktail conversation had begun to concern itself with economic and social needs rather than fashionable gossip.[19]

With Nast's approval, Clare cultivated writers and artists who best understood this new seriousness. John Franklin Carter, an employee of the State Department, became her Washington source. Writing under the pen name "Jay Franklin," he published an early forecast that "dangerous racial and national animosities" in Europe would lead to war. Clare also encouraged the crankier side of the humorist Corey Ford. Incensed about government interference in personal morality, he campaigned in *Vanity Fair*'s pages for the repeal of Prohibition, formed an Anti-Speakeasy League, and urged his readers to drink "what and when" they liked.[20]

These and other public-affairs articles stimulated such a large response that Crowninshield agreed to print readers' letters on a new page entitled "The Editor's Uneasy Chair." Interspersed were brief topical paragraphs about current contributors. Most of the profiles were written anonymously by Clare, including one (beneath a demure picture) announcing her recent promotion to associate editor. "Mrs. Brokaw," she wrote, liked "swimming, ping pong, backgammon, Persian cats, Proust, and first editions." She also claimed to speak four languages. In fact her only approach to fluency was in French.[21]

Not all staff members and subscribers were enamored of Clare's editorial innovations. Margaret Case Morgan went so far as to protest to Nast about the plethora of political articles now beginning to outnumber others three to one. She mourned *Vanity Fair*'s general loss of "gaiety." The publisher conceded that lighter pieces were still important. But having gone through his own metamorphosis in the crash, he saw a need for weightier input. Mrs. Morgan was not convinced. "Have you ever seen a seesaw with a heavy child on one end and a slim one on the other? The slim child hasn't got a chance."[22]

Clare enjoyed humor and satire too much to downplay it altogether. She maintained some balance by introducing "Who's Zoo?," a feature in which human faces were juxtaposed with look-alike animals and lines of doggerel. One of the best compared Einstein to a gentle canine.

> *This pleasant mild*
> *And wind-blown poodle*
> *Has less than nothing*
> *In his noodle*
> *'Twixt him and Mr. Albert E.*
> *There's thus no relativity.*

Even this menagerie was often invaded by politicians. Mussolini's profile was matched to that of a monkey, and Herbert Hoover was paired with a bulldog.[23]

"I am sure that you and I could be very, very great friends," André Maurois told Clare. The eminent French writer was in town to sign a contract with *Vanity Fair* for four political articles. He said he was familiar with her work, and saw her as a close observer of "words, phrases, and psychologies" but not of "gestures, inflexions and expressions." Maurois asked if he might copy the form of her linked society tales, which had already begun to appear in *Vanity Fair,* for some stories of his own. Clare consented but immediately wondered if she had not been rash, because he might get credit for what she believed to be her own idea.[24] She decided to publish hers in book form as soon as possible.

Before leaving for home, Maurois invited her to visit him in Paris. She found it difficult to reciprocate his obvious warmth. The trouble, she told herself, was that she attached no importance to friendship "either through cynicism, or the fact that in the depths of my soul, I know myself to be alone . . . a friend is the last illusion."[25]

As the last day of 1930 drew to a close, Manhattan was unusually subdued. Clare stayed home working on an article about nightclubs to be published under her "Julian Jerome" pseudonym. On the stroke of twelve, she heard no street revelry except a faint honking of horns. "Probably the saddest New Year's day this country has seen in fifteen years," she recorded in her diary. People seemed more affected by the Depression than they had been by the outbreak of war in 1914.

She was acutely aware of revolutionary sentiments circulating on both sides of the Atlantic. Already some 75,000 Americans were card-carrying Communists.[26] Clare was not herself drawn to socialism, nor was she, as yet, a partisan person. During her marriage to George, she had adopted his Republicanism. Now, halfway through Herbert Hoover's term, she carried no brief for the GOP. While she would not go so far as to publish articles with a Marxian bias, she was not averse to hiring leftist cartoonists.

The work of William Gropper, a young, toothless Yiddish artist who specialized in drawing grotesque and distorted public figures, soon caught her attention. An editor of *New Masses*, he had recently been to Russia as a guest of the Soviet government and spoke at length of Communist achievements, eyes sparkling with fervor.

Crowninshield came in to look at his portfolio of pictures of life under Stalin. "I suppose," he said in what Clare called his "pearl-gray" manner, "they don't have opera boxes in Russia?" Gropper said they did, but plainly dressed workers now sat in the place of aristocrats in evening clothes.

Standing between the two men, lost in irreconcilable worlds, Clare asked Gropper to sketch some prominent capitalists. She suggested assigning Walter Lippmann or Malcolm Cowley to write the captions. More than satisfied, Gropper went off with a contract for several hundred drawings.

That evening, as Clare read *The Wizard of Oz* to Ann, she reflected that the Soviet system of education disallowed such books. "They abolish, I'm told, all fairy tales, all mention of mythology, romance . . . I wonder do they abolish dreams?" Later she dined at Irvin Cobb's, where the talk was again of Communism. No one seemed able to speak with authority about it. She longed to go to Russia and see for herself.[27]

George Brokaw compounded Clare's New Year discontent by sending, unsolicited, a box of family photographs and a poem she had once dedicated to him. His motive became clear on January 10, when a friend telephoned with startling news. George had just married Frances Seymour, a Massachusetts socialite in her early twenties.

Clare's initial shock turned quickly to resentment and then anger. No one, not even gossip columnists, had mentioned that George was about to take on a woman young enough to outlive him. Frances—not to mention their probable children—would inherit part of a fortune that had been slated exclusively for Ann.

Painful memories flooded back and overflowed into Clare's diary. She wished the newlywed couple ill and hoped they would never know "a happy moment."[28]

Happy moments were increasingly few in her relationship with Donald. He could not reconcile the refined, angelic-looking girl of his dreams with a woman who harped on his soiled pocket handkerchiefs and penchant for German beer. As he grew more uncertain of her affection, he exhibited black moodiness, even at the office, and became picky and possessive in turn. Why had she cut her hair? Why did she smoke? Why did she flirt with every man? After dinner he tormented her with sexual demands until she became hysterical. Night after night she fell asleep miserable, his "barrage of insults" ringing in her ears.[29]

As spring turned to summer, things began to improve between them. But she felt a need to get away from Donald for a while. She told him that she mistrusted people who talked as much as he did about feelings. "Real love is often silent."[30]

His response was to write a formal proposal. "My Darling Clare: I have loved you devotedly for a long time now . . . if you would marry me [it] would . . . be the greatest treasure and honor and privilege." He added with astonishing clumsiness that it also made good economic sense. His lease was up for renewal in August, and by moving in with her he would save $4,000 a year.[31]

Clare replied irritably on a scrap of memo paper. "What has [sic] leases got to do with love? I loathe making up my mind more than anything in the world! Because I always make it up wrong."[32]

She wanted to explore other intimate relationships, if only to assert her right to have them. Donald knew of her weakness for rich, good-looking men and her perpetual search for a *grande passion.* But the thought of being deserted cast him into a frenzy of despair. Unable to compete in appearance or wealth, he paraded his vulnerability, accusing her of protecting hers behind an "iron mask." The truth was, he had long since lost the power to hurt her.[33]

The break Clare needed came in early August, when she went to Los Angeles to assist Edward Steichen on a Hollywood celebrity "shoot." Since there was little she could do for the rangy, silver-haired photographer except hold reflectors and arrange backdrops, she decided to gather material about the movie colony for her own purposes. "Steichen feels that I am a bit of a nuisance," she wrote Donald from the

Beverly Wilshire Hotel. To cheer him up, she added that both of them could use his "genius for routing out people facts and places." Neither had his "uncanny sense of direction" nor could they drive as well.

"And as recklessly," she teased.[34]

Time was to imbue this remark, intended as a compliment, with tragic irony. Donald had a passion for fast cars, but he was an expert driver, and Clare never felt any unease with him at the wheel.

She humored him at present, because he was proofreading her completed manuscript of stories. He joshed her in return with a news clip sent on August 10, the eighth anniversary of her marriage. It showed a picture of George's abundantly pregnant new wife. Whereas Clare had produced only one child, Donald pointed out, "the second Mrs. Brokaw gives fair promise of tripling this output."[35]

For the next several weeks Clare and Steichen examined some of the movie colony's largest personalities at close-up range. Josef von Sternberg was one. He lived in an apartment "full of bad examples of good modern painters," as Steichen put it, along with several busts of himself. The director was bombastic and patronizing of Clare, until he discovered that she would be writing the caption for Steichen's portrait, whereupon he became insincerely self-deprecating.[36]

They also went to photograph von Sternberg's protégée, Marlene Dietrich. The actress kept them waiting for twenty-five minutes in a Deco mansion with rainbow-colored geometric designs etched across the walls and painted on velvet drapes. Clare passed the time playing with Dietrich's six-year-old daughter, Maria. She had an unusual ability to understand the fantasies and miseries of children. When Marlene, wearing a purple gown, staged her delayed entrance and interrupted them, the girl screamed with disappointment.

Surprisingly, the scene-stealing star of The Blue Angel, now twenty-nine, proved to be stiff and listless in front of a still camera. Steichen said that "under Sternberg's gaze, she was about as exciting as a wooden cigar-store Indian." Clare reported that she managed only two expressions: "mysterious languor and parched passion."[37]

Fay Wray, future focus of King Kong's celluloid devotion, gave a dinner party for the Easterners and introduced Clare to several matinée idols, including Ronald Colman. On the whole, film actors annoyed Clare with their obsessive worry about the effect of "talkies" on their future careers. She was more concerned with her own, and half-

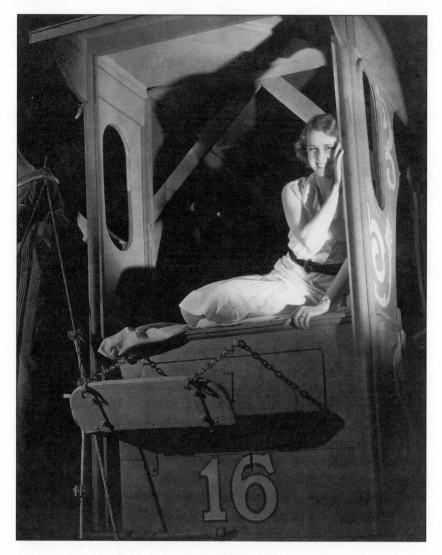

Clare in Hollywood
Photograph by Edward Steichen, August 1931

seriously offered Donald 50 percent if he would come out and help her land a big screenplay contract.[38]

Southern California's balmy air made Clare sleepy and uncharacteristically tender. "If you were here, my angel, I should be very happy to fold up in your arms and sign up for the evening . . . at ten o'clock."[39]

She returned to New York on September 5, excited by the news that Horace Liveright Inc. would publish her book of stories in just two months. At the suggestion of the columnist Arthur Krock, she decided to call it *Stuffed Shirts*. Although the tales previewed in *Vanity Fair* had been illustrated by the Russian artist Constantin Alajálov, the publisher assigned Barbara Shermund to do new art for the collected edition. Clare chose a green binding. She told her editor that it was her lucky color, associated in her mind with money, orchids, and Rolls-Royces.[40]

Stuffed Shirts, priced at $2.50, and dedicated, "for Ann Clare Austin," was published on November 5, 1931. Three days later *The New York Times Book Review* praised it for style, if not originality:

> What we have here is a brilliant series of improvisations upon the not too frightfully unusual idea that the world of expensive fashion is an empty harlequinade after all . . . Parables upon the wages of the smarter forms of sinning are often couched in lovely festoons of epigrams that sparkle with an almost Victorian elegance. What malice there may be in these pages has a felinity that is the purest Angoran.

The monthly periodical *Books* echoed this praise but gave a harsh judgment of Clare's characters:

> All is certainly vanity, according to Mrs. Brokaw, in the plush stratum of New York life . . . No one has a simple capacity for friendship. Every pretext is rooted in some ignoble ambition. Weddings, funerals, balls, concerts and exhibitions hide—beneath the potted palms of their splendor—a lively malevolence.[41]

Other reviews of *Stuffed Shirts* were generally favorable. The *New York Mirror* observed that Clare probed like a psychoanalyst and had the inspiration of one "irked by the sham and hypocrisy of her own social set." *Scribner's* compared the book to Evelyn Waugh's *Vile Bodies*. The

Galveston Tribune bracketed Clare with Edith Wharton, who had also seen tragedy in the decline and replacement of a decadent old society by an inadequate new. But if Mrs. Wharton was wistful at the passing of the former, Mrs. Brokaw seemed to be "humorously resigned."[42]

An unsigned notice in *Vanity Fair*, lauding the book's "kaleidoscopic movement, pattern and colour," turned out to have been written by the author herself.[43]

Donald, understandably, considered *Stuffed Shirts* a work of "genius," and most of Clare's colleagues were lavish in their compliments. Perhaps the most gratifying indication of regard came from P. G. Wodehouse, who wrote from France asking for a copy, saying that he always read her magazine pieces "sedulously."[44]

The ecstatic author lunched with representatives of the International Film Corporation and sent her book to Paramount Pictures, suggesting that any one of its "novelettes" could be developed into a movie. But nothing came of either initiative.[45]

In spite of its favorable reception, *Stuffed Shirts* turned out to be a financial failure. It sold only 2,600 copies in seven months, gaining Clare a mere $600. Half of this had already been advanced to her. By the time she had paid for author's corrections and bought a few copies for her own distribution, she was shocked to find that she owed Horace Liveright $150.[46]

"Now hereafter, Herr Freeman," she wrote disgustedly, "I devote my . . . extra-working hours, not to literature, which pays neither dividends in fame, nor in ducats, but to seeing if I can't bat off an agreeable play."[47]

By the end of the year, Donald felt Clare finally slipping away from him. In an attempt to hold on to at least his role as tutor, he beseeched her, once again, in an eight-page letter, not to abandon literature for society. The party givers and alluring men she had satirized in *Stuffed Shirts* cared nothing for her potential as a writer: they would use her "only as decor." For himself, he now asked for neither marriage nor monetary reward, only the satisfaction of watching her "rise to fame."[48]

Clare's indifference to this self-abnegation reduced him to near wordlessness. Instead of another lengthy plea, he sent her a devastating character analysis in the form of three pictures. The first, labeled "Clare in 1929," was of a flower in a pot, while the second, a caged tiger, stood for "Clare in 1930." The third, representing her current personality, showed the tiger roaring with fangs bared.[49]

17

BARNEY BARUCH'S GIRL

I hope I shall have ambition until the day I die.
—CLARE BOOTHE LUCE

Shortly before six on Friday evening, June 24, 1932, Clare Brokaw passed through departure gate 34 at Grand Central Station and walked along a red and gray carpet emblazoned with the logo of the Twentieth Century Limited. A reserved "roomette" awaited her in a polished steel Pullman, surrounded by clouds of billowing steam. Her destination was Chicago, where delegates from all over the country were gathering for the following week's Democratic presidential convention. She had two reasons for joining them: first to be an observer for *Vanity Fair* and second to work as a lobbyist for the New National Party, a pro-Repeal, anti–special interest organization. This fledgling group, formed earlier that year, hoped to influence both Democratic and Republican platforms and to recruit disaffected idealists, with the eventual aim of becoming a third party.

Clare knew no one onboard and dined alone. At Albany she received an affectionate telegram from Frank Crowninshield. "Can you return at once. I find I am too lonely without you." Before retiring for the night she made a diary comment about her present assignment. "I have a feeling that this will prove something very definite one way or another in my life."[1]

Indeed it promised to be both professionally and romantically significant. Not only would Chicago see the deepening of her political consciousness, but a man awaited her there, by far the most powerful and sophisticated she had yet charmed.

For the last month or so, she had been having an affair with the Wall Street speculator Bernard Baruch. Rumored to be the fourth richest man in America, he was a perennial adviser to presidents and a well-known admirer of intelligent women. Unfortunately for Clare, he was sixty-one years old and married with three children. His alcoholic wife shared neither his Jewish faith nor—Clare assumed—his bed, yet he remained faithful to the ideal if not the practice of conventional family life. Clare therefore had to settle for the belief that he cared for her as much as it was possible for "one of his vintage to care for one of mine."[2]

She was drawn as usual by the triple attributes of money, eminence, and seniority. In looks, intellect, Southern gallantry, and an engaging, naive egotism, Baruch reminded her of her father. Unlike William Boothe, however, he considered himself an effective political operator. Even as Clare's sleeper sped her towards him, he was closeted in the Congress Hotel plotting his role in the upcoming proceedings and trying to figure out who would emerge as the Democratic candidate. He had telephoned her the night before to complain, "All is still confusion."[3]

The train drew into La Salle Street station at nine o'clock next morning, in stiflingly humid weather. Clare had booked a room at the Blackstone Hotel to be near Condé Nast and his young wife, Leslie, but she went first to Baruch's suite.[4]

Though "Bernie" or "Barney," as friends called him, was thirty-two years her senior, he was as vigorously flirtatious as a man half his age. With his six-foot-four-inch impeccably tailored frame, handsome head of copious, centrally parted white hair, and twinkling blue eyes, he was a dominant figure in any assembly. His mother had told him in childhood that "the blood of kings" flowed in his veins, and the majestic confidence this instilled stayed with him.[5]

Bernard Baruch
Photograph by Edward Steichen, 1932

Dazzled by Clare's physical and mental effulgence, he saw her as someone not quite earthly, coming into his life in an aura of light and "dancing on the beams."[6] This morning, since there were other people in the room, he welcomed her affectionately but formally. In a gesture towards her writing talent, he asked her to help his industrial counselor, General Hugh Johnson, compose a statement of policy recommendations for press release. The baggy-eyed veteran was a man of flamboyant high spirits—the result of his steady intake of them, as Clare soon discovered.

While she sat typing, a succession of influential men came by to solicit the opinions of the sage. Among them were William Allen White, vice president of the *Baltimore Sun*, Mark Sullivan, author of the best-selling *Our Times*, a six-volume history of the United States, and Walter Lippmann, star columnist for the *New York Herald Tribune*. Clare already knew Lippmann as an occasional *Vanity Fair* contributor and found him quietly appealing. Frank Crowninshield had noticed that "the impact which she made on men of that type had the effect, approximately, of a queen cobra on a field mouse."[7]

She extracted a promise from Lippmann that he would join the New National Party if—God forbid—the arch-liberal Governor Franklin Delano Roosevelt of New York won the nomination.[8]

Vanity Fair had begun to weigh the year's potential presidential candidates as early as August 1931, in a monthly feature listing their "Credits" and "Debits." The magazine's newfound interest in public affairs had grown to the point that it would print only two nonpolitical covers in 1932. Just two months before it had published a provocative article by its major political writer, John Franklin Carter, entitled "Wanted: A Post-War Party." Carter proposed that this new party should adopt a platform of ten major reforms. These included repeal of Prohibition, repeal of the protective tariff, measures for extra revenue including a liquor tax, and restored relations with the Soviet Union. In tacit support of Carter's program, the editors of *Vanity Fair* invited readers to submit other recommendations and warned that voter inertia could only worsen the current economic paralysis.[9]

Readers had responded so enthusiastically that the indefatigable Carter decided to form the New National Party himself. He assumed the title of president and recruited Clare as unsalaried executive secretary. The New York socialite Mrs. Harrison Williams became the party's chief financial backer and its official representative at the Republican National Convention. Frank Crowninshield was disconcerted when Carter had the temerity to open NNP headquarters a few doors from *Vanity Fair* in the Graybar Building. The prospect of two such ornamental ladies as Mesdames Brokaw and Williams deserting the *haut monde* to go fundraising and "shouting in public" appalled him. If they must swing a political sword, he hoped it would be one "forged by Cartier."[10]

The embryonic organization needed a potent, attention-catching slogan, and John Carter came up with the phrase "A new party for a new deal." Clare acknowledged his authorship at the time in a letter to Donald Freeman, but in later years she gave herself credit for the last three words.[11]

Meanwhile, her education in public affairs had progressed during pillow conversations with Bernard Baruch. She adopted his philosophy that legislators must balance budgets, spend the largest part of revenue on defense, and encourage private enterprise with low taxation. These were typically the views of a conservative Republican, yet Baruch came close to socialism in his simultaneous advocacy of a national health insurance program.

Fortunately for Clare, Baruch's lifelong identity as a Democrat did not preclude a favorable interest in the NNP, and he had asked General Johnson to draw up a prospectus for it. Several of his own strictures about Washington's traditional ways of doing business found their way into the document. Many of them have a familiar ring to modern ears, particularly the accusation that Congress had failed both to cut unnecessary spending and to raise necessary taxes, because of pressure by lobbyists and vocal minorities. If neither major party was going to address such issues in 1932, the prospectus threatened, then the NNP would encourage an independent candidate to enter the race and field one of its own in 1936.[12]

Carter's latest *Vanity Fair* piece, also editorially supported, had the headline "Wanted: A Dictator!" The text envisioned a new President with quasi-wartime powers to rescue America's finances "from the nerveless hands of a lobby-minded Congress." While incendiary, the suggestion was not unprecedented. Senator David A. Reed of Pennsylvania had already cited the need for an American Mussolini to tackle the country's ills.[13]

Well in advance of Monday's convention opening, Baruch had made it clear to Democratic Party officials that if they chose Roosevelt as their presidential nominee, he would not contribute financially or otherwise to the campaign. While conceding that the man from Hyde Park had been a fairly competent state executive, he agreed with H. L. Mencken that Roosevelt was "too feeble and wishy-washy to make a really effective fight" for the White House.[14]

Al Smith, the four-time former New York governor and the party's unsuccessful candidate in 1928, was Baruch's first choice. But Smith seemed reluctant to run again. Other credible aspirants were House Speaker John Nance Garner of Texas, William McAdoo and Newton D. Baker, both Cabinet officers under Woodrow Wilson, and Governor Albert C. Ritchie of Maryland.[15]

A majority of the delegates arriving in Chicago were committed to Governor Roosevelt, but he was still short of the two-thirds margin needed for victory on the first ballot. Aloof from the fray in New York, Carter wrote advising Clare to be general rather than specific about the NNP's aims as she proselytized among disaffected Democrats. He felt that their best chance was to go after Huey Long's machine in Louisiana. "If we can break the Solid South, we will have split the whole system of Party Government in this country at its roots." A grateful nation would someday erect a monument to her, he said, for the important work she was accomplishing.[16]

A storm broke on Sunday night, reducing the temperature by nineteen degrees. Monday's *Chicago Tribune* published the statement Clare had helped prepare, in which Baruch called for an immediate cut of $1 billion in government expenditures to save Americans from becoming "slaves chained to the oar of our economic galley." The metaphor certainly sounded like hers.[17]

For the next four days Clare dutifully "milled around among the delegates." She courted members of Congress and other important Democrats, including former Secretary of the Navy Josephus Daniels, Mayor Jimmy Walker of New York, James Forrestal, and Will Rogers. In addition she lectured a meeting of Junior Democrats, wrote and typed a floor speech for an ambitious young Southern delegate, and reported her doings to Carter. Seeking occasional relief from "politics, endless politics . . . every moment of the day and night," she worked on expanding her social horizons, having lunches, teas, and dinners with Mrs. Woodrow Wilson, Mrs. Marshall Field, Admiral Cary Grayson, Colonel Robert McCormick, and other prominent observers. She enjoyed several evenings with Mark Sullivan, who was fast becoming an avuncular friend. They recognized in each other an ability to "wring the essence from the envisioned moment."[18]

Balloting at the convention began at 3:00 A.M. on Friday, July 1.[19] Over 60 percent of the country's households were able to hear the count by radio. Clare listened in Baruch's suite. As dawn came up over Lake Michigan, Roosevelt, after three tries, was still short of the requisite number of votes. Yet no other aspirant came close.

Clare (*center, rear*) at the Democratic National Convention with Leslie Nast (*on her right*) and Mrs. Woodrow Wilson (*center, front*)

The delegates recessed in exhaustion. Clare returned to the Blackstone and slept all day. Behind the scenes, Joseph P. Kennedy of Massachusetts was persuading William Randolph Hearst of California to move his forty-four delegates from Speaker Garner to Governor Roosevelt. At nine Clare entered the convention hall in time to see the

New Yorker go over the top on the fourth ballot. Garner reluctantly agreed to take the vice-presidential spot.[20]

In his acceptance speech, Roosevelt pledged himself to "a new deal for the American people." Hearing him appropriate the NNP's slogan made Clare feel "a little heartsick." Baruch's face was white and drawn with disappointment. The "S.O.B.," as he called him, had triumphed after all. They consoled each other until the small hours of Saturday morning, pondering the potency of the "political virus that gets in men's hearts and souls."[21]

Aboard the train going east on Saturday night, illicit liquor flowed. Newsmen began lauding Roosevelt as if they had never had any doubts about him. Clare observed that these "jumpers aboard" included Walter Lippmann and Herbert Bayard Swope, former editor of the *New York World*. Baruch, too, had "swallowed his pill," she noted with some disillusionment, "and now he likes it."

She slept in her lover's compartment that night, and circled the page number of her diary as a sign of consummation.[22]

Back in New York on Sunday, July 3, Clare lunched with "Bernie" and told him, to his distress, that she was going to vote the Republican ticket in November. She then motored to Sound Beach to see her daughter. Ann had been sent to George Brokaw at the end of May, but when mumps broke out nearby, she had temporarily left his custody.

Clare noticed at once that the girl was being corrupted by Ann Austin's "incessant chatter about money." So had she been herself in childhood. But there was now a more pronounced note of hysteria in the older woman's materialism. When Clare tried to moderate it, she touched off a torrent of resentment.[23]

Dr. Austin, estranged by such outbursts, spent much of his time now away from home, leaving his wife, David, and Riggie to their own love-hate relations. Without his civilizing influence, Driftway seemed polluted by a spiritual blight. Clare felt it sullying her finer instincts and eroding her ambition. Rain fell on the Fourth, imprisoning her in the house. As often in situations of family claustrophobia, she needed to lash out at someone. She chose Donald Freeman, who was innocently vacationing abroad, and sent him a fourteen-page letter full of unprovoked bile.[24]

After watching damp fireworks, Clare returned to the city and an empty apartment. No message from Baruch awaited her, to her instant desolation. He showed up the following night but was not of much comfort, being distracted by family problems of his own. They spent a self-pitying few hours together, and he left without making love.

Clare burst into tears. Suddenly and with startling clarity, she saw that her life had emotionally "shut down." The fact was that by now she was seriously in love with Baruch—more in love, perhaps, than with anyone in her life. Deep feminine longings demanded that he bind himself to her by impregnating her. But his age, and family preoccupations, made this unlikely. "I will never have another baby," she mourned.

Aside from such primary despair, she saw "so many, many handicaps"—domestic, professional, and psychological—to frustrate what Mark Sullivan called her "lust to function." And so, drunk on brandy, she went unconsoled and inconsolable to bed.[25]

Her spell of morbidity passed, however, as Baruch's stellar connections continued to expose her to the movers and shakers of America. "I prefer being alone with brilliant men," Clare exulted. Those she had met in Chicago had extended her knowledge beyond literature and art, to party politics and economics. She found herself circulating among the foremost practitioners of finance, science, and communications. On July 12, for example, Baruch invited her to his apartment to watch a demonstration of a new broadcasting medium, in company with David Sarnoff. The latter was president of the Radio Corporation of America and personally responsible for the all-electronic beams pulsating from the Empire State Building. They sat watching "a small flickering visual apparatus," she wrote that night in her diary. Television reminded her of "the early days of the movies," except that it had "perfect sound."[26]

Gossip about Clare and her famous multimillionaire grew apace. Even Franklin Roosevelt began referring to her as "Barney Baruch's girl." But then, in late July, Bernie announced that he was going to spend six weeks at a rejuvenating European spa and did not invite her to accompany him. "Oh my beautiful darling," she wrote in anguish, "if you only knew how unhappy I am that you are going." She could hardly trail after him, since she was behind with her rent, owed enormous

sums to dressmakers, and had begun to receive monthly bills of $465
from her mother "to keep Ann." Forced to spend an economical vacation, she leased the summer place of her penthouse neighbor Bill Gaston in a remote spot off the coast of Maine. It was called Crotch
Island.[27]

Never was a place more aptly named, for the summer of 1932 turned
out to be one of sensual and sexual indulgence. It marked the end of
Clare's youth: in eight months she would be thirty. Whatever her fantasies about Baruch, she had to accept that their age difference precluded a long-term affair. Even the younger men she still attracted
(David Sarnoff had tried to force "unwelcome attentions" upon her)
could not be expected to pay court for many more years. Julian Simpson still wrote her the occasional love letter, full of memories of "burning desire" and vague suggestions that they meet, preferably on his
home ground. The devoted Donald Freeman, just back from Europe,
looked "fatter than a pig" and repulsed her with his peeling sunburn
and blistered mouth. He tried to "make" her, but she demurred. On July
29 she escaped on an overnight train to Rockland. From there a yellow
hydroplane sped her in eight minutes to Crotch Island.[28]

Gaston's fifteen-acre property sat in a hillside grove of pines overlooking the harbor and sapphire sea. Lush displays of day lilies, geraniums, snapdragons, poppies, forget-me-nots, veronica, purple
heliotrope, and alyssum bordered a small lawn. Paths of crumbled
seashells led to the door of a two-story log cabin. Inside Clare found
three fireplaces and plenty of comfortable sofas. There was neither
radio nor telephone, only a Victrola with a rusty needle.[29]

A Japanese couple cooked her a delicious lunch of garden vegetables. Then she sunbathed and dozed, as hummingbirds chased bumble-
bees from fragrant delphinium spikes. In late afternoon she took a
launch to the fishing village of Vinalhaven and picked up cables from
Baruch. That evening she read a study of Hamilton and Jefferson, and
was persuaded that despite her recent Republican resolve, "all fine
souls must be Democrats."[30]

Next morning she breakfasted and typed letters on a porch profuse
with rambling roses. Utterly content, she hoped she had not been rash
in inviting three men in succession to share this verdant tranquillity.[31]

The first to arrive, on August 1 for a four-night stay, was William Harlan Hale, a twenty-two-year-old Yale graduate and writer. Clare had met him only five weeks before at Horace Liveright's and been instantly attracted. "He looked like a young eagle coming out of its egg, tall, skinny, a little fuzzy . . . romantic, sensitive, well-bred." After a year in Europe, Hale had just published a two-hundred-page examination of historical and cultural trends called *Challenge to Defeat: Modern Man in Goethe's World and Spengler's Century.* At Clare's request, he was now writing articles for *Vanity Fair.*[32]

William Harlan Hale
Photograph by Clare Brokaw, August 1932

She was not the first older female writer to take an interest in him. Recently in Berlin, Hale had had an affair with Katherine Anne Porter. Though twenty years his senior, the beautiful author had become so enamored she had lent him money from a Guggenheim grant to facilitate his return to New York. Miss Porter had mixed feelings about his current work. *Vanity Fair,* she wrote, exhibited a "deadly sureness of slickness, smartness," which the magazine's airy tone did not quite conceal. "I despise it."[33]

Slick it might be, but Hale felt lucky to have a job of any kind at a time when all his college classmates seemed to be among the nation's 12 million unemployed. As he clambered over the rocks with Clare and caught fish in the cove for lunch, he happily surrendered to her charms. She in turn succumbed to the fertility and amazing maturity of his mind. At night, their suntans glowing in candlelight and firelight, they endlessly discussed literature, exchanged frank anecdotes about their lives, and devised strategies to become famous.

On three nights they made love. Clare reproached herself for being "a terrible little bitch," having sex with a comparative stranger while cables continued to arrive from her adored Baruch. But this young man made her "tremble at the knees."[34]

Before leaving, Hale helped wash and bleach Clare's hair. He bent over the bathtub, and it occurred to him that the chemical fluid in his hand was highly explosive. All at once he was seized by an ecstatic vision of joint immolation with his "porcelain-eyed bundle of sweetness and light."[35]

"It is quiet here," Clare noted after Hale left. As she lay in bed, the sounds of sighing winds, squeaking branches, burbling water in a rain barrel, and lunar moths bumping against the window screen made her feel frightened and alone. In the morning she must begin the writing she had come here to do: some more short stories and a new novel.[36]

She was forestalled by the unexpected arrival of her landlord and two loud couples. Powerless to resist their determination to have a riotous weekend, she allowed herself to be swept into a three-day whirl of speedboat rides, tennis, swimming, and drunken dinners. While young Hale had been eager, idealistic, and virile, Bill Gaston was suave, devastatingly handsome, and sexually dangerous. His marriage to Rosamond Pinchot (Reinhardt's Nun in *The Miracle*) was breaking up, and he had the reputation of a confirmed womanizer. Between him and Clare the air was always heavy, and she tried to avoid his blandishments. She knew that they were the same kind of animal. "The depths of him are like the depths of me, shifting sands, and we each need an anchor, and we could not anchor ourselves to each other."[37]

Resisting Bill now, she told him during a walk in the woods that she disapproved of his rowdy companions. He snapped that in that case it had been a mistake to rent her the cabin. His harshness made her cry, and he tried to kiss away the tears. Her feelings were mixed as she saw him off on the yellow amphibian. Before long she would find herself looking to be comforted by him again.[38]

Clare spent August 10, the ninth anniversary of her marriage to Brokaw, turning the color of a meerschaum pipe. At 137 pounds she was 12 over what she considered her ideal weight but felt proud of her body's firmness and health. She was at the height of her appeal to both sexes. Both Condé and Leslie Nast had made passes at her recently, and the latter, at least, was unsatisfied. She wrote to say that she felt a "sharp pain" of desire for Clare. How hopeless it was. Even when they were in the same city, they had managed only one brief interlude together, because of the demands of others on their time. "Darling . . . why are the forces against us so strong?"[39]

Another sexual conquest, whom Clare unsuccessfully tried to lure to Crotch Island, was Thayer Hobson, a young vice president at the publishing house of William Morrow. For several months he had been assiduously pursuing both her and the autobiographical novel, "This My Hand," she intended to write on vacation. She began to suspect, however, that Hobson preferred the role of fantasy lover to that of real one. "Thayer says 'I adore you' as other men clear their throats."[40] He was thrice married in any case, so she did not press her invitation, content to maintain an affectionate correspondence in the hope of selling him her manuscript.

Perhaps because of her daytime physical exertions, Clare's mind was slow and uninspired when she tried to work after dark. She sent off a few stories to magazines that paid better than her own, such as *The New Yorker* and *The Saturday Evening Post*. None was accepted. Nor did the novel, an austere and biting account of her early days with George, go well. Its portraits of herself as selfish and cynical, and of her mother as a venal social climber, were so searing that she abandoned the manuscript after sending Hobson only five chapters.[41]

She was reduced to "talking the book" when another invited guest arrived. Mark Sullivan, her new friend from the Democratic Convention, was sacrificing the society of his family to be with her. After garrulously summarizing her novel for him, she swung into a marathon description of more recent adventures, including her affair with Baruch. "It's good to share your soul!" she wrote in her diary that night.[42]

At age fifty-eight, Sullivan relished the confidences of a luminously beautiful and intelligent young woman. In Chicago he had seen

Clare's "glittering and brittle" urban façade. Here he found mellowness and "an exceptional . . . sinewy mind." Since he was a close friend of Herbert Hoover, she spent long evenings quizzing him about the making of presidents and the expertise of the men who made them. Inevitably, Sullivan began to display a romantic interest in her towards the end of his five-day stay. But she thought him rather smug, and his shiny red face displeased her aesthetic sensibilities. "So little vanity! And so much conceit!" She was not sorry when the time came for him to go.[43]

For Sullivan, Crotch Island remained a highlight of his late middle age. In gratitude he sent Clare a precious book inscribed to him by Theodore Roosevelt, and reinscribed from him to her.[44]

As August wore on, Clare's feeling of dereliction by Baruch made him all the more desirable. She sent him long, closely typed letters that revealed wistful longings for a future together. He might brood all he

Mark Sullivan
Photograph by Clare Brokaw, August 1932

liked, she wrote, about "the incongruity, the folly, the utter want of logic in our relationship." He might also take "that absurd cure at Vichy" in the hope of cooling his ardor. But she predicted that their affair would continue all the same. "Blood-heat has won more arguments than were ever gained by the white-heat of the brain." Beyond sexual bravado, she felt the need to perform for him.

> I shall work very hard because you want me to succeed, and because when I am not violently loving, I must be violently working . . . One sees so often in life the woman making the man. Now if you will never take your hand from mine, one will see the man making something of a woman. You have taught me beloved to . . . belong to myself, but the lesson has made me eternally your debtor, your dependent.[45]

When she received no comparable replies, she grew maudlin. "I feel incomplete, helpless, uneasy . . . no person, no place, no experience . . . has significance or interest for me, unless I translate them in terms of you." A tear dropped on the red enamel space bar as she tapped this, and she made sure he knew about it. She hoped she would not end up "just a girl who takes a typewriter to bed with her." Her need for him remained intensely physical. "I long to feel myself caught in your arms to put my cheek against yours."[46]

Baruch's cables and notes were circumspect to say the least. Clare could see that he was diffident about putting himself on paper, "afraid so much as to send me a loving word," in case the endearments fell into alien hands. So cautious was he that he frequently began without a salutation, and signed himself with cryptic initials like "P.K." for "Pirate King" or the numbers "1, 4, 3" in lieu of "I Love You."[47]

There was little time, however, for Clare to pine, for men continued to appear at Crotch Island. Kerry Skerrett, her old Hartford beau, came for an overnight stay, and a soused Bill Gaston and friend, back for a second weekend, separately tried to inveigle themselves into her bed.[48]

Meanwhile the relationship with Donald continued to sour. Clare's vitriolic letter from Sound Beach in early July had called him "savage," superficially sophisticated, and lacking in the "refinement of feeling" necessary to make the transition from love to friendship. In turn, he fired off caustic and querulous notes to Maine. "I suppose you are in the throes of illicit love otherwise I would have had a letter from you detailing your bucolic existence . . . I am gradually coming to the realization that all is over between us."[49]

Ever the managing editor, he badgered her for *Vanity Fair* articles, assuming that "excursions into sex and nature haven't dulled the edge of your wit." He sent best wishes to his "successor," and coldly signed himself "Freeman."[50]

Clare left the island on Friday, September 2, a few days earlier than planned, to avoid a third intrusion by Bill Gaston and to see Baruch, who had returned prematurely from Europe.[51]

She arrived next morning in a blistering New York, and stoically submitted to having her hair set under a hot dryer before shopping for fall clothes. That night she dined, made love, and talked politics with Bernie. He had pragmatically decided to recast himself as an adviser to Franklin Roosevelt, whom he now thought could win in November. Clare privately admired the mind, if not the socialist politics, of Norman Thomas and thought that the Democratic candidate was intellectually weak in comparison, a regurgitator of the "pablum of nursery liberalism." But President Hoover's economic record was indefensible. She could no longer in conscience support him and decided to vote for Roosevelt too.[52]

Back at *Vanity Fair* after Labor Day, Clare saw that Bill Hale had settled down and was working conscientiously. She had been thinking of him as a potential assistant editor but now started to have doubts about his all-round caliber. He occasionally seemed gauche, even callow, and she wondered if he had "the imagination, the fire, the inventiveness that I have."[53]

She nevertheless continued to sleep with him as well as Baruch that fall. An intriguing diary entry, made after visiting a doctor, implies that she had possibly suffered a recent miscarriage. "There is . . . no reason why I shouldn't have an infant he says, and was shocked when I told him that I *might* have had one."[54]

If she nurtured any illusion about Bernie leaving his wife and starting a new family with her, she was soon disabused. Baruch told friends that she was just "a poor little kid," who had to be kept happy with gifts. Mark Sullivan reported that the financier had frankly discussed the affair with him and said "his heart was not involved."[55]

Clare deflected this public rejection by blustering, "Perhaps mine is not any longer involved either." Therapeutically, she proceeded to scatter her talents and social energy in as many directions as possible. She posed for a *Vogue* fashion shot by Edward Steichen, had several secret meetings with one of Condé Nast's competitors (declining a $5,000 increase in salary to work for him), considered taking $20,000 to help former Mayor Jimmie Walker write his autobiography, and started collaborating with Paul Gallico on a play. Dashing from work to lunches, teas, cocktails, dinners, theaters, speakeasies, revues, and nightclubs, she often ended her days in one assignation or another.[56]

Donald's jealousy grew to open fury. *Vanity Fair* staff were privy to loud arguments between him and Mrs. Brokaw. Sometimes he would rush out and berate her from a pay phone, so that he, at least, could not be overheard. He hoped that Clare would be embarrassed by a published rumor that Condé Nast intended to divorce his wife and marry her. But she was not, infuriating him further. When she gave a dinner to celebrate the première of *Mädchen in Uniform*, a German film Donald had subtitled, he stayed away in a fit of pique. During a climactic spat on September 24, she accused him of using her talents for his own professional advancement.[57] He remonstrated a few hours later in what would be his final letter to her.

> When I first perceived in you an intelligence which seemed destined to be both creative and flexible, and which you were stifling in an aimless and rather profitless existence, I saw an opportunity to realize by proxy the growth of a career which might make a definite imprint in the contemporary world . . . You had great charm and breeding, a fine but badly trained mind, and a complete independence from financial cares. Thus you seemed to me an ideal person to encourage and to love. If you will recall a conversation at the Stanhope in the first days, I told you that I would only too gladly step aside when my purpose had been served, when you were sure-footed, aware of your own ability and had carved a niche for yourself of sound proportions . . . It is only human nature that I should be discarded—what with . . . men of affairs like

Mr. Baruch sighing for your time . . . It has been only in the past few days that the cloud of my three years love for you has been gradually lifting from the brain of one who has almost been a madman for the whole time. It is not that I found a homeopathic way out for no one will replace you . . . But I am a philosopher and a much worthier man than you seem to think—really incapable of those black actions which I threatened from the depths of my jealousy, and dread of losing you. As you proceed to greater things, it shall be my satisfaction that in the early days we shared many secrets, and my consolation shall be . . . your progress to fame and fortune.[58]

On Friday, September 30, Clare stayed home nursing a cold. That evening, with extraordinary sangfroid, she dined in the company of four individuals who lusted after her—Baruch, Hale, and Condé and Leslie Nast. "We left early," she recorded in her diary, not saying with whom.

She was in bed on Sunday morning when her telephone rang. It was Leslie with bad news. Donald had been seriously injured the night before in an automobile accident upstate and was in a hospital in Mount Kisco. Clare drove north at once to find him unconscious, eyes black and blue under a swathe of bandages. She was told that Mr. Freeman had hit a stanchion en route to his Rhinebeck house for the weekend. Thrown from his car, he had landed on his head and split his skull.[59]

For the rest of the day, Clare sat with Donald's mother and sister, and Frank Crowninshield, listening to Donald breathe. It was evident that he was fading. The thought of his head, which she had so often passed her hand over, "cracking wide open to death" seemed to her a "hideous enormity." Poor Donald, "so young, foolish, clever, tender, tormented, gay, inspired, ugly, mean, generous." He had made her life "so intricate, hard, full, and interesting."[60]

At five o'clock, while she held his hand, he died. He was not quite twenty-nine years old.[61]

Numbly motoring back to town, Clare went with the Nasts and George Jean Nathan to her dead friend's apartment. The sight of his cat, Casanova, upset her but did not prevent her taking Donald's journals. She began reading them as soon as she got home. Apparently she then destroyed the volumes, for they were never returned to his family. All that is known of their contents is what Clare recounted in her own diary. She claimed that he hardly mentioned her name. Only towards the end did he write of her "meteoric" rise. She noted with some annoyance that he had had several other affairs. "I know he loved me best," she presumptuously persuaded herself, adding, "and I loved him more than any of the others."[62]

Though Clare did not say so at the time, she kept two documents that Donald reportedly left for her that fateful Saturday. One bore her initials and a small, rough drawing of a grave with cross and flowers. The other was an unattributed poem.

> There is no virtue in a quantity,
> So many hours, so many days of joy
> Time is no measurement of ecstasy, . . .
> Be happy then that for a moment's space
> You found, together, love and love's delight
> Implicit understanding and bright grace
> About you all the day, and through the night.
> For the gay shining interlude you had,
> And her remembered loveliness, be glad.[63]

In old age Clare insisted that the sketch—which has survived—proved Donald had committed suicide over her. But by delivering it along with the verse, he could have meant merely to symbolize the demise of their relationship. His last letter had stressed that he was incapable of "black actions." Driving into a post, even at high speed, would not have guaranteed death. Deeply disturbed as he was (Nathan confirmed that Donald had been "mad" towards the end), he might have intended not to kill but merely to injure himself, in order to elicit sympathy and perhaps rekindle her love.[64]

On Monday, October 3, Clare went to St. Thomas's Episcopal Church on Fifth Avenue and wept over Donald Freeman's coffin. After dining alone at a hotel, she visited Bill Gaston in his new apartment and stayed until four in the morning, making love. She needed comfort, she told herself, because she was "weary of looking on the face of death, and wanted to feel alive."[65]

209

Next morning at the office, she kept expecting to see her former mentor in the corridors, his underlip thrust out, his stomach held between his hands.[66]

At the funeral on Wednesday, Clare walked up the nave with Donald's mother, as though she were his widow. Thus she appeared to give him in death the commitment she had denied him in life.

18

A WELL-CONSTRUCTED

FAÇADE

*Ah! Vanitas Vanitatum. Which of us is happy in this
world? Which of us has his desire? Or, having it,
is satisfied?* —WILLIAM MAKEPEACE THACKERAY

Clare dined at a speakeasy with Paul Gallico on the night of Donald's
funeral. She felt "a little tight" as she went on to see Bill Hale for
further solace. Alcohol and sex, however, could not resolve the question on both their minds: who was to become managing editor of *Vanity Fair?* For a week Clare had in effect been doing the job, but Condé
Nast seemed reluctant to appoint her officially. Nevertheless she was
determined to tolerate no interlopers. "I am the only one who can do
it . . . they must give it to me."[1]

Over dinner on Friday, October 7, 1932, Nast formally offered her
the position. He had hesitated, he explained, because he was wondering if she would "allow" him at the same time to replace Frank Crowninshield as editor in chief. "With a Lippmann, yes," she replied
guardedly, her confidence bolstered by the publisher's deference. It was
clear to her, too, that Crowninshield was a spent force. *Vanity Fair's* fi-

nancial troubles grew worse each month, and his old-fashioned editorial values were irrelevant to the young, politically aware readers Clare needed to attract. On the other hand, it suited her not to have him replaced: his weakness would give her more control. So she encouraged Nast no further, realizing he would balk at dismissing the man he had worked and socialized with for eighteen of the magazine's nineteen years.[2]

After deflecting the publisher's "usual futile passes," she left to tell Hale her good news.[3]

Clare went to the office the following morning determined to emphasize her authority as Donald Freeman's heir. She placed her jeweled, black enamel cigarette case on his desk, decided to fire his secretary, and displayed a warning motto to all comers:

> Down to Gehenna or up to the Throne
> He travels fastest who travels alone.

Perhaps because it was a Saturday, there were few subordinates around to congratulate her. For a few hours she worked intensively, assisted only by Bill Hale. But she noticed—with a gathering sense of letdown—a subtle change in Bill's attitude towards her. While pleased at her success, he was struggling with chauvinistic resentment that his lover was now his boss.[4]

Clare spent the afternoon in a beauty parlor, scanning other magazines for article ideas. Beyond such new editorial chores, she had long-term problems of publication strategy to worry about. At recent staff meetings Nast had talked seriously of converting *Vanity Fair* to a weekly, in order to compete in topicality and circulation with *Time* and *The New Yorker*. Clare favored the change, although in her heart she suspected it might sink the magazine, "so near are we to going on the rocks."[5]

Most colleagues looked favorably on her appointment in the weeks that followed. Some were outright dazzled by the speed with which she established herself. Crowninshield (whom, as she predicted, Nast kept on) praised her for boldly combining the capacities of "a superfortress, a battleship and a tank." Mehemed Agha delighted in her "advanced

Clare Boothe Brokaw, *1933*

and indecorous" design ideas, and willingness to offend. Nast prized her as his intellectual showpiece, able to impress both contributors and advertising clients.[6]

Cecil Beaton, who photographed for *Vanity Fair* as well as *Vogue*, remarked that Clare's powers of concentration and raw energy were such that she must be "abnormally healthy." Her personal force translated into decisiveness, although she could turn down a manuscript as tactfully as Frank Crowninshield. Responding to a submission from Laura Hobson, wife of her publishing friend Thayer, she wrote, "It is a charming, sensitive, and well-written tale, but unfortunately it is too tenuous and too feminine for a magazine that tries as desperately as we do to be masculine and hard-boiled."[7]

She impartially subjected young and seasoned journalists to line-by-line editing, composing detailed suggestions even for the likes of Drew Pearson.

> Jack the Ripper has always been to my mind the most excit-ing, thrilling, gruesome, spectacular, mysterious and blood-curdling of murderers. Your version, however, of that story seems to leave me strangely disappointed and not the least bit frightened or appalled. I think the reason for this is, for one thing, that you skim entirely over the nature of the rip-per's [sic] crimes. For instance, you say "her murder was in-describable in its savagery," "the operator must have been at least two hours over his hellish job."
>
> Now, what was his hellish job; what did he do to his vic-tims; how did he leave their remains—where were the bod-ies found? These may seem like questions which betray a morbid curiosity on my part, but I promise you that when you write about Jack the Ripper and don't describe his crime, it's like telling a ghost story and, at the last moment, omitting the ghost.
>
> You also refer to "the messages received by the police which contained Americanisms as well as a gruesome form of humour." What were these messages; what did they con-tain? You say they were well-written—what does that mean?
>
> At any rate, all I want you to do is to tell the story again, leaving in everything that is there, but squeezing out of it a good deal of its inherent but, in this case, concealed horror.[8]

In an interview with an NBC correspondent, Clare enumerated the at-tributes of a good editor. He or she must be sensitive to trends, have a "nose for news," a gift for planting the right thoughts in receptive minds, and "a genius for making authors write the thing—not that they may want to write, but which they can write best." Perhaps most important was the ability to discover and the courage to launch new talent, rather than just publish writers of repute.[9]

It soon became apparent that her critical faculties included a sophisticated understanding of color graphics, which served her well when dealing with artists such as Gropper, Alajálov, and Covarrubias. In addition she had a catholic taste in photographic subjects. One visitor to *Vanity Fair*'s reception room was startled to see a circus-like variety of performers awaiting their turns before the camera: a naturalist holding a snake and a porcupine, a sea captain in a sou'wester, and a bullfighter practicing *mariposas* with coat, cane, and chair.[10]

In the sanctum of Clare's inner office, all was contrived calm. Henry Morton Robinson, a fiction writer, recalled that she sometimes received him draped à la Madame Récamier on a *chaise longue*. Every strand of her caramel blonde hair was in place, and the black pennons radiating from the pupils of her blue eyes seemed to see through him. Only a light pink lipstick relieved the pallor of her camellia white skin. While there was nothing pallid about her editorial judgment, the exercise of it appeared to leave her, in his words, "somehow unsmiling and sad." He sensed that "some great sorrow or unresolved decision hung over her." Spiritually, emotionally, intellectually, she was "the embodiment of separateness . . . aloof, detached, with only the bare semblance of cordiality that good editors extended to good writers." Robinson felt that she was already traveling in an orbit far above his own, "towards some destiny that she knew was privately reserved for herself."[11]

Awed though most observers of the new managing editor might be, at least one associate found her professionally and personally wanting. Helen Brown Norden, a dark-haired, adventurous Vassar dropout, had joined the staff of *Vanity Fair* in January 1932. At twenty-five she was already an experienced writer, and an astute judge of character. Four decades hence, as Helen Lawrenson, she would pen the most devastating of all indictments of Clare Boothe Luce. Now, however, her misgivings were tempered with admiration. She saw the managing editor as "alert, industrious, resourceful, brimming with ideas, easy to work for, always serene and cheerful." More important, she was fair in giving creative credit. But Helen suspected that Clare's "trigger-quick" ability to think up titles and captions concealed a mind lacking in profundity. Moreover, her penchant for regaling captive audiences with fact-filled monologues kept intimacy at bay and "made real friendship impossible."[12]

Outside the office on the cocktail circuit, Helen also discovered Clare to be obtuse and manipulative. Although she feigned affection for women, her real interest was in men, and she could be a ruthlessly competitive vamp, telling female guests to dress casually for parties, then wearing something elegant and provocative herself. At one event Helen arrived in a plain linen suit, only to find Clare in long, low-cut, white satin "blazing with diamonds—bracelets galore, necklace, earrings, brooch . . . an altogether breathtaking vision."[13]

Dressed thus, in her thirtieth year, Clare Boothe Brokaw was indeed a spectacular sight. "Her skin was flawless," Helen recalled, "apparently not a pore in it . . . Her eyes were not large, but there was a magical loveliness in her gaze, which was level, disquieting, spellbinding." Cecil Beaton, who drew a pastel portrait of her, denied saying Clare was "drenchingly beautiful," but the phrase stuck. Arnold Genthe spent an hour photographing her and remarked that she had the loveliest face he had seen in years. Only the most perceptive men saw deeper than her looks, intelligence, and wit. Raymond Bret-Koch, a French artist and Clare's occasional escort, felt she was "not real." There was a vacuum in her personality and a lack of warmth in her seductiveness. "It's a beautiful, well-constructed façade," he conceded, "but without central heating."[14]

Clare's headlong advancement in the world of publishing did not satisfy her perpetual hunger for power in yet more spheres. Within weeks of being promoted, she began to cast her eye in a new direction. At a party she gave with Mark Sullivan, she seemed less interested in theater talk with George Gershwin and Laurette Taylor than in hearing political news from Washington. Mark's daughter, Sydney, knew President and Mrs. Hoover and promised to tell them they should invite *Vanity Fair*'s current star to the White House. "If they did," Clare rhapsodized in her diary, "there would be no more worlds to conquer."[15]

Miss Sullivan was true to her word. "I am to lunch with the President on Sunday!" Clare wrote in her diary on Friday, October 28. "Surely," she continued with naive enthusiasm, "I am lucky among women: the editor of a smart and powerful magazine: not too bad to look at, nor too old, rich, or at least not poor, pampered by men, loved by many of them, and knowing, in New York everyone of importance or artistic merit or prestige that there is to know!"[16]

The following evening she arrived in Washington and was met at Union Station by the Sullivans. Impeccably connected in local society, they took her to dine with Supreme Court Justice James McReynolds and Eugene and Agnes Meyer, who were soon to buy *The Washington Post*. The conversation ranged from a weighty discussion of the Hoover campaign to gossip about Alice Roosevelt Longworth and Cissy Patterson. Not many years before, Alice's husband, Nicholas, Speaker of the House, had been surprised *in flagrante delicto* with Cissy on a bathroom floor. Clare was both titillated and challenged by the capital's historic mix of policy and decadence. "What I could do in Washington is without end."[17]

Next morning, as her car drew up at the White House, a black doorkeeper leaped down the steps, coattails flying, to help her out. The First Lady received her with great charm and conducted her on a tour of the state rooms and gardens before they joined the President, the Sullivans, and four U.S. Senators in the dining room.[18]

The national election was just nine days away, and Herbert Hoover showed signs of weary apprehension. He had dark shadows under his eyes and an air of premature defeat. In spite of this, he gallantly regaled them with generalities, praising America's risk-taking spirit and speaking knowledgeably about the collection and preservation of incunabula. The nearest he came to talking politics was a defense of his summer dispersal of Bonus Army protesters. As President, Hoover struck Clare as both proud and dignified. But as a man, he displayed a childlike vulnerability that neither moved nor inspired her—at least not the way the grave-faced Lincoln did in photographs.[19]

When she returned to work next day, the White House conversation was still sounding in her ears. Suddenly, Manhattan chat seemed frivolous, and she felt "horizonless."[20] She began holding forth on political matters to anyone who would listen. An assistant in the copy room at Condé Nast joked, "Maybe *you* will end up in the Senate!" Clare fixed him with a long, cool look and said, unsmiling, "Stranger things could happen."[21]

A huge scheme transfixed her. There seemed little doubt that Franklin Roosevelt was going to be the next President of the United States. In that case, Bernard Baruch, who had been advising the Democratic candidate ("S.O.B." no longer) on economic matters, would surely be offered a Cabinet post—Treasury, perhaps, or even State. But would he agree to serve? Uncertainty always plagued Clare's thoughts about her strong-willed lover.

She set her mind on forcing Baruch to take a place in the next administration, "whether he likes it or not." Fantasy built on fantasy: Bernie could then arrange to make her editor of *The Washington Post*. She would not leave *Vanity Fair* for anything less. Again, Secretary Baruch might influence the President to appoint her to some government office. Relocated in the capital, with Mrs. Baruch remaining in New York, she could privately enjoy full possession of Bernie, while publicly influencing political opinion. "I could make history there."[22]

On November 8, Clare voted the Democratic presidential ticket but exercised her independence by supporting a Republican for governor and a Socialist for mayor. She then went on to one of her regular trysts with Baruch. "The tall Democrat," as she now teasingly called him, was elated that Roosevelt seemed poised to win. Perhaps in consequence, their lovemaking that afternoon was "radiant."[23]

Moments of radiance apart, the aging Baruch was frequently incapacitated by what Clare elliptically described as "his half sex." She realized that she must ultimately look elsewhere for "the sweetness of life." At the moment there was still Bill Hale to make her feel young. But in worldly experience she already felt old, and needed security and wisdom.[24]

She also needed an assistant editor, or so she told Condé Nast. Bill, at twenty-two, was too junior to be of much help. Nast unsympathetically said he thought she could manage alone, and forbade her to write freelance for competitors.[25] Outsmarted, Clare took revenge by applying the ban to journalistic work only, and continued her playwriting collaboration with Paul Gallico.

Working several nights a week for two months in the fall of 1932, they completed a three-act comedy called *The Sacred Cow*. It told the story of a reporter whose "scoop" on an upper-crust scandal was quashed for fear of reprisals by his newspaper's social-climbing advertisers. Gallico, ace sportswriter for the *Daily News*, vouched for the authenticity of his newsroom contributions. Clare asked a friend, Kitty Miller, to show the script to her husband, Gilbert, the international producer. "Crudeness and a certain lusty sincerity are its only virtues," she defensively wrote. Miller was unenthusiastic. As she and Gallico shopped for another producer, Clare began to worry that their play had itself been "scooped" by Hecht and MacArthur's recent hit *The Front Page*. John Golden, Rudolf Kommer (acting for Max Reinhardt), and the Leland Hayward Agency also passed, saying that the plot was "feeble" in parts and too farcical overall.[26]

These repeated rejections prompted Clare to an outburst of snobbish spleen. "It was a mistake for me to go out of my class to write a play," she groused, forgetting that she had sprung from origins much humbler than those of the average newsman.[27]

Her physical stamina began to erode under pressure of work and deteriorating family relationships. David Boothe was out of a job again, and hung around pestering her to fill the voids in his life. Dr. Austin, unable to handle his wife's menopausal moods, had moved into the Pickwick Arms Hotel. Ann Austin, alone at Driftway, had suffered a nervous collapse after being surprised and tied up by burglars. She had to be hospitalized, and upon her release she drove out of state, without saying where she was going. Postcards came from places as far apart as Kansas and Albuquerque, puzzlingly dated the same day. Dr. Austin theorized that she was getting friends to mail them, in some crazed ploy for attention.[28]

Ann soon reappeared in New York and took a room at the Navarro on Central Park South. Clare heard she was in town and ill but made no effort to contact her. The result was a bitter maternal note penned on hotel stationery:

When you are a great success remember it was by being the most selfish human being toward me. Now I'm finished with you too . . . you are a heartless thing and a cold self-interested being . . . someday you may receive the same treatment.[29]

Evidently somebody came to Ann's rescue, for she was soon reunited in Sound Beach with Dr. Austin and the ever-faithful Joel Jacobs. Clare's mind, meanwhile, turned in compensation to her father as the fourth anniversary of his death neared. She recalled William Boothe particularly when his brother Edward came for lunch on December 7. "I cannot begin to describe how odd it seemed to be sitting there next to my *uncle*," she wrote afterwards, "a man whose blood was the same as mine, and whose eyes reminded me of eyes which long ago I had seen and known and yes, loved."[30]

That same week Clare deposited her eight-year-old daughter at Miss Hearst's boarding school in Orange, New Jersey. Ann Brokaw had refused to go back to George after the mumps scare of last spring, and he had initiated legal action to regain custody. In an out-of-court settlement both parents finally agreed to have Miss Hearst look after her during the school year and to share her for six weeks each summer.

This arrangement relieved Clare of the "burden and obligation" of daily mothering. When she thought about it she felt neglectful, but she persuaded herself that little Ann was a vigorous extrovert—unlike the lonely and shy introvert *she* had been at St. Mary's.[31]

As her most extraordinary year so far drew to a close, Clare sank paradoxically into ill health and depression. She suffered from debilitating colds and headaches, plus recurrent bouts of fatigue and nervous colic. "Feel so badly these days," she wrote on December 21, "so discouraged, and seemingly getting 'nowhere.' "[32]

Christmas Day, traditionally a low point for depressives, was rendered even worse by a visit from the Austins and Joel Jacobs. She gave them lunch, but instead of family spirit felt "only a brooding enmity."[33]

On December 26, Clare spent a "charming afternoon" and early evening with Bernie, who was about to leave for his estate in South Carolina. They played backgammon, made love, and seriously discussed ways to balance the budget. Clare was disappointed that Baruch had not been tapped for the Treasury post, and that her dreams of new political connections seemed to be fading. Later that night she saw Bill Hale. "So happy to see me!" she wrote in her diary. "Why oh why cannot I find this blind devotion and passion of youth, and the comforting wisdom and security of age in one man? My heart is heavy, and I *know* I am worthless, shallow, insincere with everyone—and myself."[34]

Two days later she had a spat with Condé Nast. He complained that she had neglected to publish a picture of his latest girlfriend, the singer Grace Moore. Clare reacted sulkily. "As soon as I can find something better I'm going to leave." That same evening, Baruch departed for his winter vacation. So far he had not had a call from President Roosevelt. Wretched weather, overwork, and longing for love plummeted Clare to the depths. "What will be the end of all this for me? Death, suicide?"[35]

She made it up with Nast, and accompanied him to the New Year's Eve Actors Benefit Ball. But she was bored by his conversation, and by the "inept" drinking all around. Even her sumptuous purple velvet gown felt like "scabrous rags."[36]

As 1933 dawned, Clare began to accept that her mature melancholy, different in kind and degree from youthful angst, might be a life-long affliction.

19

FAILURE

IS IMPOSSIBLE

If we must suffer it is better to create the world in which

we suffer. —WILLIAM BUTLER YEATS

A decade had passed since Mrs. Alva Belmont forecast a bright future for Clare Boothe. Following the young woman's progress
since, she could hardly have approved of her quick abandonment of
the National Woman's Party or of her opportunistic marriage. Yet
there was little a feminist could fault in Clare's more recent career.
After all, she had transformed herself in three and a half years from society divorcée to managing editor of one of the nation's most admired
periodicals.

Now, in mid-January 1933, news came that the eighty-year-old
party leader had died in France. The body was shipped home for burial,
and on February 11 Clare joined a crowd of NWP mourners at St.
Thomas's Episcopal Church on Fifth Avenue. Throughout the service
the picketing flag she had seen fluttering over so many equal rights
demonstrations was held aloft in still and reverent homage. She would
always try to live by its legend: Failure Is Impossible.[1]

Soon after the funeral, Bernard Baruch invited her to visit his Southern plantation. She hesitated, for fear of being compromised by the presence of Mrs. Baruch. Mark Sullivan persuaded her to put aside bourgeois scruples in favor of a change of scene. He felt that she was overworked and becoming dependent on cigarettes, coffee, and alcohol. That winter he had noticed her filling, then refilling, her brandy glass after dinner. "You are too fragile for that," he warned. Fewer parties and more country air were what she needed.[2]

Clare arrived in Georgetown, South Carolina, by overnight train. Bernie's estate was six miles to the northeast by car on Pawleys Island, a neck of land twenty miles long and fifteen wide between the Waccamaw River and the Atlantic Ocean. In the late nineteenth century its fertile soil had produced gargantuan crops of rice, but the fields now lay fallow, and the great houses had vanished or decayed. One was no more than a row of skeletal columns.[3]

Baruch had bought up seven of the original ten plantations, totaling some seventeen thousand acres. In 1928 he had built himself a ten-bedroom, antebellum-style mansion and called it "Hobcaw"—a local Indian word for "between the waters." The house made up in remoteness what it lacked in architectural distinction. West of its white-columned portico and sloping lawn flowed the black, slow-moving Waccamaw. Along the reedy waterline, myriad oysters glistened in strong sunlight. Deer, fox, feral pigs, egrets, bald eagles, wild turkeys, and bull alligators populated the surrounding woods and swamps. Cypresses and live oaks festooned with Spanish moss towered over myrtle, yucca, and magnolia trees. Flourishing in the warm, moist air were head-high camellia and oleander bushes, blazing azaleas, blue water hyacinths, yellow jonquils, lilies, and gold jessamine.[4]

This was the most beautiful place in the world to Baruch. Not that he had much aesthetic sense. His "barony" was a banker's idea of a winter retreat, furnished in dull greens and browns, and decorated with golf and hunting prints. But Clare was pleased to find it run like a luxury hotel, with freshly laid fires in every room and bars of French soap replaced daily. There were also plenty of black servants to wash and press her clothes or polish her shoes and riding boots the moment she took them off.[5]

The plantation's languorous, sweet-scented atmosphere evoked memories of her Memphis childhood. "Its allure is that of the senses rather than the spirit," she wrote Mark Sullivan in a letter absent-mindedly dated February 31. She began to sleep nine hours a night and felt her health and spirits reviving. Mischievously she told Paul Gallico that she dreamed of marrying "the Baron," if something would only "happen to his wife." During her waking hours she admitted to a "Napoleon complex" about developing the place and restoring the splendors of its past. The prospect made her feel stronger and more content.[6]

Bernie sought her company infrequently. He was out after quail most of the day and at night had Annie Baruch to consider. Clare managed to ensnare him for the occasional late-afternoon ride, a sunset

Clare and Bernard Baruch at Hobcaw, *1933*

walk along the riverbank, and Sunday service in a tiny Negro church. Seeing her lover for the first time away from the metropolitan North, she fancied she detected an inherent nobility in his character. "His barony becomes him," she informed Mark Sullivan. "He looks like a lord in the saddle with a gun at his shoulder."[7]

Among her fellow guests was Senator Joseph Robinson of Arkansas. As well as being one of Baruch's closest friends, he was, in Clare's own admiring phrase, "a dead shot in a duck-blind." The Senator's exceptional marksmanship was hardly needed around the old rice paddies: wild fowl were so prodigious they obscured the sky. Clare rapidly recaptured the stalking skills she had learned over twenty years before in the Wisconsin woods and became a crack shot too.[8]

Visiting hunters and anglers provided most of the dishes served at Baruch's round dining table—crab, clams, mullet, shad, bass, and partridge, supplemented by baked hams and homemade fruitcake. Replete and mellow with Baruch's fine wines, guests would move after dinner to the sitting room for bridge and backgammon. Between hands they would indulge, to Clare's enjoyment, in "the drone of political chitchat." She asked Senator Robinson to send her copies of the *Congressional Record*, so that she could follow national debates more closely.[9]

All too quickly the country idyll was over. "I shall never be quite happy," she admitted to Mark Sullivan, "until New York becomes a place to which I go often, rather than leave seldom."[10]

On the evening of Friday, March 3, Clare departed with her host for Washington, D.C. The following morning, under overcast skies, they checked into the Carlton Hotel, where Bernie had a permanent suite. After breakfast and a change of clothes, they set off for their next destination, the inauguration of Franklin Delano Roosevelt.[11]

Propriety would not permit Baruch to be seen at the inaugural with a woman not his wife. Clare had to be content to view the swearing in of Vice President Garner in the Senate Chamber. She took a seat in the front row of the gallery, a short way from the President-elect's mother. Beneath them FDR discreetly looked up and smiled, whereupon Mrs. Roosevelt's lips quivered, and a tear splashed onto her purple gown.[12]

Before going south, Clare had asked Miguel Covarrubias to do a cartoon of the event. It appeared somewhat prematurely, in the current issue of *Vanity Fair*. The double-page spread portrayed the new President standing in front of the Capitol, receiving a crown of laurels from Chief Justice Charles Evans Hughes. Immediately behind towered a sulky-looking Eleanor Roosevelt. Elsewhere in the crowd clustered dozens of recognizable figures, among them outgoing Secretary of State Henry Stimson, incoming chief aide Louis Howe, General John Pershing, Walter Lippmann, J. P. Morgan, and, prominent in owlish spectacles, Bernard Baruch. High above, on either side of the dome, hovered two angels blowing trumpets. The face of the one to the left was unmistakably that of Clare Boothe Brokaw.

As a loving token and souvenir of the event, she presented Covarrubias's original (purchased from the reluctant artist for three hundred dollars) to Baruch. Then, while he proceeded to ingratiate himself with the new administration, she looked to other men for companionship. These included Frank Altschul, a Wall Street financier, Sir William Wiseman, a member of British Intelligence, René de Chambrun, a New York lawyer, and Pare Lorentz, *Vanity Fair*'s movie critic. Lorentz, enthralled, wrote her that when he told her he loved her, "it is not in words but in every cell, every nerve."[13]

Clare's most serious affair in 1933 appears to have been with Paul Gallico. It had begun after, rather than during, their playwriting collaboration. She asked why he had not loved her "when I was there for you to take." He said that as a married man of thirty-five he was at a loss to explain the mystery that transforms a professional associate into someone "so beloved that the world suddenly revolves around her."[14]

The huge, bull-necked sportswriter became so obsessed with her that a call canceling just one lunch date was enough to throw him into a rage. Gallico said that he would like to sink his nails into her neck and "shred" her. But then he admitted to being disarmed by the thought of her "soft, lovely mouth . . . so touching, so kindling."[15]

Gallico was not so carried away as to lose his acuity altogether. After an intense few weeks, he wrote to say he had noticed a curious rhythm to their romance. Whenever he professed love for Clare, her sexual feelings became blocked. There was too much masculinity in her and too much femininity in him, he said. It was the male element that prevented her from "surrendering to or enjoying purely emotional moments. You distrust . . . the sweetness."[16]

FAILURE IS IMPOSSIBLE

Like Donald Freeman before him, Gallico discovered that Clare was disdainful of any man who made himself too easily available. Baruch was canny enough to stay somewhat aloof. That was reason enough for Clare to remain devoted. Unrequited love, in her case, was the kind most likely to last.

Clare Brokaw's fourth issue as managing editor carried *Vanity Fair*'s first photoengraved color cover. It anticipated the end of Prohibition nine months hence and, in its exuberant vulgarity, announced the age of the Common Man. Pretzels spelling the magazine's logo floated above a row of foaming beer mugs on a red and white check tablecloth.[17]

"The 'beer' cover," gushed one reader, "has caused more comment and elicited more praise than any . . . I ever heard of." Condé Nast went further, declaring the March number altogether "grand."[18] But its success was immediately followed by a slump in *Vanity Fair*'s advertising, which had dropped to its lowest level since 1919. For the frustrated publisher, this decline in revenue coincided with an impoverishment of his emotional life. Having recently divorced the sapphic Leslie, Nast was now a single man, and he resented Clare's indifference to his sexual overtures. Perhaps as a result, he became less tolerant of her unorthodox work habits and management style. "I do not think you can do your job effectively with such a combined absence and lateness record as the sheets show for you during the past three months," he wrote on March 27, adding drily, "I am not asking you to observe the established nine o'clock arrival hour, but an hour . . . between quarter of ten and ten."[19]

He conceded that she might more effectively develop ideas and edit manuscripts at home. But her job also required teamwork, staff supervision, and consultations with authors and artists—not to mention a fair quotient of material from her own pen.

> In the old days you were not only here regularly in the morning, but much more regularly in the afternoon, and at that time you were a fairly regular contributor of articles . . . For the past three or four months, you have contributed no articles . . . with all your talent, I don't think you can be an editor, write books and become a playwright all at one time. One or another of these will fail.[20]

Irking Nast even more was Clare's unconcealed contempt for his creative opinions and her dislike of taking orders. It was clear to him
that she wanted absolute command of the magazine. He reminded
her that she had only three years' experience in publishing compared
with his thirty. Besides, he had not always found her judgment "on
specific material and broad editorial policies . . . entirely seasoned or
dependable."[21]

Clare confessed to being "impetuous and self-willed" but said that
she was also a perfectionist. Nast should therefore make his objections
before the magazine went to press, rather than afterwards.[22] Another
altercation followed when she revealed summer plans to attend an economic conference in Europe. She would go primarily as a reporter for
Vanity Fair, then spend vacation time traveling and researching articles
for syndication. This meant a combined absence of seven weeks. Nast
forbade it, saying that the magazine's financial position was too precar-
ious. He requested that she take no more than twenty-one days and
stay close to the city, so that he could consult her about the fall issues.[23]

From this moment Clare's commitment to *Vanity Fair* started to
evaporate. As usual when planning a change, she moved to a new
apartment—this time in the Waldorf Towers. Then she rented a vacation cottage on Long Island, sent her daughter to camp at Lake Placid,
and began plotting her future.[24] Bill Hale left the magazine in August
and took a job, as she had wanted to do, at *The Washington Post*.

By September she was ready to inform Nast of her desire for "an independent career." To that end she requested a three-month leave of
absence, beginning in November. She intended to spend most of it at
The Cloister, a new resort at Sea Island, Georgia, where she hoped to
develop her talent for writing plays.[25]

Clare arrived at the hotel in heavy rain on Monday morning, November 6. Her room was disappointingly small, with a damp smell of sea salt
in the bedcovers. At once her depression of the previous winter returned. Feeling lonely and anxious about her forestalled career, she
started to cry. Not until noon, when the sun emerged from rolling fog
to reveal roses, palmettos, butterflies, and a crescent of golden sand, did
her mood improve. Finding no congenial guests at the hotel, she
looked elsewhere for company.[26]

As it happened, Eugene and Carlotta O'Neill lived quite close by, in a large beachfront hacienda called "Casa Genotta." Clare had run a Steichen portrait of the playwright in the October issue of *Vanity Fair* and corresponded with him about it. They shared a mutual friend in George Jean Nathan. With such credits, she felt no compunction in sending word of her arrival at The Cloister. Carlotta's diary entry showed little enthusiasm. "Claire [sic] Boothe Brokaw writes and asks if she can't come to dinner!!? We politely say 'Next Wednesday'!"[27]

Mrs. O'Neill, a fading beauty, was particularly wary of intrusions by attractive, younger women upon her husband's daily regimen of work and exercise. "We are very simple people," she wrote Clare disingenuously. "Wear a comfy frock." Sensing reverse snobbism, Clare determined to "utterly confound them with my simplicity and amiability."[28]

The O'Neills sent their driver to pick her up. She saw at once that building and furnishing their twenty-two-room mansion had left them short of cash. Eugene, dour and inscrutable, looked drained from rewriting, for the seventh time, the script of *Days Without End*, which he hoped would refill his depleted coffers. Clare sensed an "intangible walled inwardness" in the couple. But she took advantage of their reluctant hospitality to gauge the creative intelligence of the three-time Pulitzer Prize winner. Did he have more brains than she, or just greater powers of concentration? Might she at his age—forty-five—be equally successful and famous?[29]

It was encouraging for Clare to hear O'Neill frankly acknowledge that only half of the full-length plays he had shown to producers had been accepted, and quite a few of those optioned had not been staged. Before leaving she exercised her penchant for snooping in other people's closets and found satin ribbons round the linens. Casa Genotta, she decided, was too meticulous an environment for a genius.[30]

For their part, her hosts thought Clare "dull" company. They knew none of the café society names she dropped and were glad to see her go. "She is pretty, well dressed, very New York," Carlotta wrote afterwards, "ambitious, never loses a chance to get further on!"[31]

Back at The Cloister, Clare tried to match what O'Neill had told her of his disciplined workday, but her boundless energy prevented her. Instead of writing dialogue all morning, she scanned newspapers and composed lengthy letters to male admirers. One, to "Willie" Wiseman, invited him to join her for a few days, to see if "by some alchemy of love" he could "co-ordinate my scattered emotions and focus the tangent-flying lines of my mind."[32] In the afternoon, she played golf with the club pro, walked the beach, and swam.

Only after dinner did she bring a tired body and intellect to the creative task in hand. It was a play script called "The Wealth of Nations," from a line by Richard Hovey:

> The wealth of nations is men, not silk and cotton and gold.[33]

Her ambitious intent was to use the lives of an artist, a capitalist, and a worker to illustrate a paradoxical theme: that social progress is achieved more through misunderstandings than by intent to do good. Complete understanding between the classes stultifies action, kills co-operation, and deadens ambition. The idea was promising, but she could not focus enough to execute it. Dissatisfied and bored, she added "The Wealth of Nations" to her growing pile of incomplete manuscripts.[34]

While Hobcaw had whetted Clare's appetite for the South, Sea Island gave her premonitions of being buried there. Exploring, she came upon an old graveyard that so captured her imagination she dreamed of lying in it one day. It was surrounded by a low spike fence and shrunken, silvery bushes. Sloping and fallen tombstones were sheltered by live oaks, whose dripping strands of moss reminded her of "witches' hair." She liked the idea of being memorialized by some such stone rather than ending up on a mausoleum shelf like "a jar of pickled peaches." When she gave advance notice of her interment to the hotel deskman, he said, "Everybody says who sees it, but we ain't had anybody coming back . . . yet."[35]

Towards the end of her stay, Clare arranged an introduction to Sea Island's developer, Howard Coffin. A widower of sixty, he had previously made a fortune in automobiles as well as cotton, and enjoyed entertaining the likes of Herbert Hoover and Charles Lindbergh at his mansion on neighboring Sapelo Island. Coffin was charmed enough to invite her for Christmas and New Year. Seeing, perhaps, yet another opportunity to capture an aging multimillionaire, Clare sought to create an instant family by getting her daughter and brother to join them.

One afternoon David went hunting, and she seized the opportunity to spend time alone with Coffin. Roaming the eleven-mile length of his domain, they passed rice and rye fields, palm and pecan groves, pine barrens, ponds, and herds of black cattle, before reaching the picturesque ruins of Château de Montillet, once home to Bonapartist refugees. Again Clare felt her "Napoleonic" complex surging. Here was another potential kingdom for her queenly hopes. But by nightfall it was clear that Coffin had no more than platonic interest in her.[36]

Clare returned to New York loveless and playless, to find that a new magazine called *Esquire* was seriously challenging *Vanity Fair*. It already had eight times more color pages and was seducing fiction writers with larger fees. She at once tendered her resignation, effective February 15, 1934. Nast was sorry to lose her, in spite of their differences, and asked if she might still be available as an advisory and contributing editor. To humor him she agreed, but in her own mind the break was final.

"I shall always feel about *Vanity Fair* the way a child might feel about an amiable, gifted but somewhat tipsy papa," she wrote Miguel Covarrubias. It was possible to love it, but unwise to follow where it led. She must now apply herself with real dedication to that "independent career."[37]

20

EVERYBODY'S
AND YET NOBODY'S

*All we have been, known and done remains in us, but
most of it has to be evoked.* —OWEN WISTER

lare and a new admirer, Buckminster Fuller, caused a stir on the
night of February 7, 1934, as they drove to Hartford, Connecticut,
in the inventor's three-wheeled Dymaxion car. Bubble-shaped and
streamlined, the vehicle was a marvel of automotive engineering: it
could turn within its own length and allegedly reach 125 mph at 40
miles to the gallon.

Through her work at *Vanity Fair*, Clare had developed a taste for
advanced technology, as well as for modernism in art and design. This
evening she was also to be exposed to avant-garde theater—the world
premiere of Virgil Thomson's opera *Four Saints in Three Acts* at the
Wadsworth Atheneum. Sharing the experience with her and Fuller
were the artist Constantin Alajálov and the sculptor Isamu Noguchi.[1]

Hundreds of other cosmopolitans, resplendent in evening clothes,
converged at the same time by plane, parlor car, and limousine. They
were drawn not only by Thomson's score but by Gertrude Stein's li-

bretto, the sets and costumes of the rococo fantasist Florine Stett-heimer, and the novelty of an all-black cast.

"I haven't seen a crowd more excited since *Sacre du Printemps*," the photographer Carl Van Vechten enthused. "The Negroes are divine."[2]

Clare was stimulated less by the music and lines such as "Pigeons on the grass alas" than by a wealth of theatrical images more brilliant and eccentric than any she had ever seen: a sky of tufted cellophane, trees of feathers and pink muslin, a wall of seashells, and a purple-robed St. Teresa, suffused with an unearthly light.[3]

Her perennial desire to write a successful play resurfaced after she returned to New York. She drew up an experimental list of characters and tried to keep them imaginary, but she constantly reverted to those of her own acquaintance. Long ago she had told Donald Freeman that she wanted to write a book about her life with George Brokaw—"Revenge with a capital R." It occurred to her now that the stage might be a better outlet for her enduring resentment. She began to sketch a melodrama about a young woman, Nan Marsden, living in a gloomy Manhattan mansion with a hypochondriacal and sadistic husband, Henry.[4]

The first draft of what would become *Abide With Me* has Clare's heroine leaving home with her child and seeking solace in the arms of a psychiatrist. During a custody dispute, the rejected father threatens to punish his offspring, whereupon his estranged wife kills him. After conspiring with her sympathetic mother-in-law to make murder look like suicide, she goes off with her lover to live in unpunished bliss. Surprisingly, given the pieties of 1934, Clare's amoral ending was the chief element that would survive through the eventual Broadway production of her play.[5]

As soon as she had a complete typescript, she sent it to John Golden, who had been the least negative of the rejecters of *The Sacred Cow*. Without committing himself, he encouraged Clare to "stick to the work bench," because she might one day write "something important."[6]

Golden's press agent, Jean Dalrymple, read the draft too and was appalled. Even though Clare had tried to disguise its biographical origin, Dalrymple felt that no respectable woman should "expose her tawdry married life to the world that way" and told her so. "What will your child think?" Clare said that little Ann already knew about the plot and characters. This apparent lack of concern persuaded Dalrymple that

Clare had written the play not "to be cathartic, but because she thought it would be a hit."[7]

Taking Golden at his word, Clare worked on her manuscript to the point of exhaustion through the last days of winter and the first of spring. Mark Sullivan feared that she was going to "turn into a tall, pale celery stalk of intellect." He was shocked at how she looked. "To be brutal, your eyes are glassy . . . I suspect from over-use of stimulants to make yourself achieve a false high spirits."[8]

Prescriptions for various uppers and downers were indeed being supplied to Clare by her new physician, Milton Rosenbluth. Like the psychiatrist in her play, he was compliant and amorous. From the moment she first entered his office and threw her hat to one side in an "insouciant, almost impudent manner," Dr. Rosenbluth had been enslaved. She manipulated him by appearing to bestow affection. Married, with two young children, he had to settle for less than he wanted, and in so doing accurately perceived her dichotomous character. "You appear to be everybody's and yet nobody's," he wrote, "wise and yet so childish. Perhaps . . . in these things lies your ineffable charm."[9]

Sullivan's warnings about overwork went unheeded. Far from cutting her load, Clare soon increased it by taking on another journalistic career, that of newspaper columnist. Her contract with the Paul Block syndicate called for three 750-word articles a week, on subjects of her own choosing. But first, in a move that would become a habit before embarking on challenging phases, she decided to make herself over. She took an Easter break at the Greenbrier spa, then, at the end of April, entered the "Private Pavilion" of Mount Sinai Hospital. Afterwards a subtle refinement was discernible in the shape of Mrs. Brokaw's nose.[10]

In late May, Block advertised that Clare's forthcoming column was to be called "This World of Ours." "No one in New York's aristocracy can write more knowingly or entertainingly of society," he proclaimed. "Her articles will be full of humorous, human appeal, as well as piquant revelations of modern smart life."[11]

The initial piece, "Amazon at Night," appeared on June 1. It was an analysis of Clare's own conflicting feelings as a woman of liberated mind, vulnerable body, and feminine instincts. By way of illustration, she gave an account of a midnight walk she had recently taken downtown while waiting for a train.

> Now I was on Broadway, walking very fast towards the bright lights of Times Square, my chin buried in my furs, purse pressed close under my arm . . . A woman who has not four walls about her when she is alone at night, or a man's arm to lean on when she is abroad at night, feels deserted or incomplete or ashamed, or brazen, or . . . inexplicably uneasy. At any rate she feels odd. This goes to show you, that the independence of my sex, when I can be shaken by such a silly and trivial notion, is something that does not go quite to the bone.[12]

The irony was further underlined when, in a subsequent column entitled "Women in War," a tougher-sounding Clare portrayed females as being equal if not superior to men in physical fitness, and therefore just as capable of combat.

> A fighting force of child-bearers would solve several questions: the question of overpopulation that precedes wars and "shortage of men" that follows them. And the question of how to rid war of its romantic implications: there would be far fewer sentimental gold-star mothers of the next war if there had been disillusioned war-veteran mothers of the last. It might even solve the question of war itself. What nation would plunge into a war in which its men fought not for their wives and sweethearts, but with their wives and sweethearts?[13]

In "Love Is a Gift," she castigated the Western illusion that romance is the birthright of every woman. Those raised on the "sentimental pap" that for every Juliet there is a preordained Romeo could only become disgruntled and sour when "malign destiny" cheated them of "a Grand Amour."[14]

She was to publish sixty-one columns in all before her congenital tendency to lose interest brought "This World of Ours" to an end. Yet at least some of these pieces give impressive evidence of Clare's versatility and objectivity as writer and thinker. Her command of the short essay form is evident in arresting first paragraphs, strict adherence to one topic, and logical steps to neatly turned conclusions. She has a born dramatist's flair for dialogue, and two or three of the columns are entirely in script form. Tolerant of all kinds of behavior, she never moralizes, merely observes, casting an unbiased and often sympathetic eye on snobs, panhandlers, cowboys, widows, prizefighters, congressmen, bureaucrats, and judges.[15]

She demonstrates a wide range of interests: European Communism, the economic theories of John Maynard Keynes, Roosevelt's National Recovery Act, the quantity theory of money, Newport manners, body language, the psychology of children, the paradoxical beauty of weapons, animal vivisection, war reparations, boxing, fashion, and voyeurs—a category in which she does not hesitate to include herself.

By way of example, she describes a visit to the penthouse of the cartoonist Ralph Barton, who kept a telescope trained on neighbors. She approvingly quotes his explanation, "A Peeping Tom artist can do no hurt, because the objects of his investigation are unaware of it." As an aspiring playwright, she not only understands this but elaborates on it. "Movement divorced from sound, action without words, pantomime (all you can observe . . . a mile away) distills the inner essence of any scene, defines it as comedy or drama, and reveals character with precision and profundity."[16]

Occasionally she begins a piece well but loses momentum. It is as if the idea itself, fully worked out in her own lightning-quick head, is intellectual satisfaction enough, executing it a chore. Instead she resorts to padding, or lengthy quotations. In one column about ghost mining towns "stirred to new life by the higher price of metal," she fills over half her allotted space by reprinting an anonymous poem she once saw in a Nevada bar.[17]

After the first two months, "This World of Ours" ran with less regularity, and it was destined to peter out by year's end. In the meantime, Clare felt confident she could keep up a rhythm of two pieces a week, even while taking a long summer vacation in Europe.

But first she needed to renew her passport. When the document arrived, it was accompanied by a letter that amused her so much she reproduced it in her column.

> You will note that there is a correction from your recent application in the matter of your age. A review of our 1928 files shows that on your passport of that year you were two years older than you appear to be now. We have taken the liberty of presuming that your earlier version of the date of your birth is the correct one.[18]

Before sailing Clare heard to her joy that *Abide With Me* had been accepted for a week's out-of-town production by the Beechwood Theatre Company of Scarborough-on-Hudson, New York. In further welcome news, her old neighbor and violet-eyed friend Rosamond Pinchot won the female lead, opposite Paul Guilfoyle. Dorothy Hale, an exquisite ingenue, who had ridden with her to Hartford in Bucky Fuller's three-wheeler, was given a supporting role.

Clare was able to catch a few rehearsals in mid-July, but by opening night, July 31, she had already arrived in France. Her brother loyally showed up at the theater, as did Buff Cobb, Condé Nast, Frank Crowninshield, Arthur Krock, James Forrestal, Bill Hale, and Bill Gaston. David sent her a batch of reviews and said some movie scouts were sniffing around. "You're a very, very brilliant young lady . . . it's only a matter of time."[19]

His words were almost exactly echoed in print by Martha Blair of the *Washington Herald*. She said it was unfair for a playwright "to be so bright, so capable, and yet so beautiful." However, Blair seemed unaware that *Abide With Me* was about seriously disturbed people. "It was fun, the whole evening." Other critics liked the play too, and there was talk of a Broadway staging. John Golden sent suggestions to clarify the behavior of the main characters, and the prestigious Leland Hayward Agency asked to represent the work.[20]

August's *Vanity Fair* featured Clare Boothe Brokaw in its "Hall of Fame."

> Because she has written a play . . . because her book, *Stuffed Shirts,* was an authentic and merciless satire on New York

society; because she is now writing a syndicated newspaper column; because she was formerly managing editor of *Vanity Fair*; and because she combines a fragile blondness with a will of steel.

From Europe Clare mailed Paul Block sixteen more columns, covering shipboard life and sightseeing in France, Belgium, Holland, and Majorca. None demonstrated a gift for travel writing, nor much inclination to explore. "I have never opened a Baedeker's," she candidly admitted. Neither was she interested in food, settling for mere lists of foreign dishes, or careless clichés: the soufflé-like ensaimadas of Majorca's Hotel Formentor were "brioche for the gods!" Rather than take the trouble to describe the Valldemosan scenery, she referred her readers to the writings of George Sand.[21]

The Hearst newspapers, whose subscribers cared little for *belles lettres*, canceled Clare's column in mid-August.[22] She felt this rejection acutely, and sought a few days' solace with Bernard Baruch at Chartwell, Winston Churchill's estate twenty-five miles south of London.

Clare arrived at the local station with a suitcase full of Paris underwear still in expensive wrapping. She was met by an extraordinarily handsome man of twenty-three, with pale gray eyes, fair hair, and poetically perfect features. He was Randolph Churchill, her host's only son. Already known for his directness and pugnacity, he was not yet bloated by drink, nor had he reached the stage of being "totally unspoiled by failure," as Noel Coward would later quip. Incurably romantic and flirtatious, he appealed to Clare, who had the same inclinations herself.[23]

The Winston Churchill she saw that evening was by no means the renowned statesman she would one day cultivate. He was merely a fifty-nine-year-old man of letters, paunchy and languishing on Parliament's back benches. After dinner he and Bernie held forth in front of the drawing-room fireplace, showing off their political knowledge. Clare sensed that they were vying for her attention, but she was more interested in charming the young man of the house. Having done so, she excused herself and went to bed. Not yet asleep, she heard someone come in and fall over the coal scuttle. "It was Bernie Baruch," she remembered amusedly, half a century later. "But I was expecting Randolph!"[24]

When the latter subsequently pursued her to Paris for a reunion at the Ritz, he was surprised to find her fully clothed, and wearing a provocative hat. "Now you can take them all off," she purred.[25]

Randolph soon discovered that the warmly affectionate Clare of the evening could present a chilly cheek at daybreak. He wrote her a parting note apologizing for his irritability, which he blamed on frustration and bewilderment at her capriciousness. "Darling . . . you always seem to have a revulsion in the morning!"[26]

In a follow-up letter that reached her after her return to New York, he thanked God for the passions they shared. The Atlantic would not prevent his seeing her at least once a year, so that together they could satisfy "all the longings of my heart you obstinate self-willed little devil!"[27]

In the early fall of 1934, Clare moved yet again, this time taking a one-year lease on a six-room apartment at the Sherry-Netherland. The rent was $500 a month, which she did not begrudge because of the views from her sixteenth-floor windows. At dusk Central Park looked like "a vast meadow of fireflies, rimmed in the distance by the fantastic jewel boxes of the great hotels."[28]

After setting decorators to work, she spent most of October at the Claridge Hotel in Atlantic City. It was not a happy month. Hearst's rejection still stung, and she suspected Block wanted to drop her. In addition she was worried about David, who had contracted one, if not two, venereal diseases. As usual he expected her to help him out by asking Dr. Rosenbluth to arrange a course of treatments. There was no certainty of a cure, and the long-term implications depressed both brother and sister.[29]

By mid-November Clare was established with four servants in her new apartment. From her uncle Edward Boothe, she purchased a small piano to please little Ann, who had inherited her maternal grandfather's love of music. Next she gave a housewarming party. Frank Crowninshield, who could not attend, sent her a jovial note of congratulations. "I am told that your flat is so luxurious that people are beginning to wonder if I have anything to do with its maintenance."[30]

The dining room was especially lavish, with raspberry pink walls, white carpet and drapes, and a long, blue-mirrored table. Attempting to be a brilliant hostess, she marshaled Bernard Baruch, Mark Sullivan,

Sir William Wiseman, Raymond Moley of President Roosevelt's "brain trust," and the playwright Sam Behrman for a housewarming dinner party. The female guests were her actress friend Dorothy Hale, and two writers from Condé Nast days, Laura Hobson and Marya Mannes.

Laura was amazed at the vulgarity of Clare's bathroom. Absurdly spacious, the room boasted a toilet-seat cover of ermine fur, complete with dangling black-brown paws. Clare explained that it was made from a coat her mother-in-law had given her. While the marriage to George had lasted, she had resignedly worn the detested pelt, knowing that one day she would "find a perfect use for it."[31]

Laura Hobson was now thirty-four, a few years younger than her publisher husband, but prematurely graying. The future author of *Gentleman's Agreement* came from a modest Russian-Jewish background. Vivacious and studious, she had worried about Thayer's temporary attraction to Clare in the summer of 1932, but now the two women were becoming close friends.

At a party the Hobsons gave later that month, Clare arrived late and made a dramatic entrance, which Laura never forgot.

> She came through the arch that led from the hall to the living room, and paused, waiting for Thayer or me to come and introduce her. She stood there with her blond head slightly tilted to one side; she was wearing a black evening dress with lovely jewels, but instead of the usual corsage at her shoulder, she was carrying a small nosegay of white flowers in both her hands. As she waited, she seemed to be looking demurely down at them.[32]

After dinner Clare's attention was drawn to a tall, sandy-haired man whose copious eyebrows arched over narrow eyes. She recognized him as the subject of a profile she had written for "Hall of Fame" in *Vanity Fair*—none other than the founder of *Time* magazine, Henry Robinson Luce.

> They stood a little apart from everybody, talking by themselves, she leaning back into the curve of the piano, facing

the room, and Harry . . . turning his back on it, holding forth intensely, and then listening intensely. Clare was too clever to appear impressed with him; she would say something light and laugh, then change moods and seem totally absorbed by what he was saying. Some of our other guests told me she was baiting him about his beloved *Fortune*, tossing out little mots about how bad it was and how easily it could be made better.[33]

Another subject of their rapt discussion was picture periodicals, then popular in Europe. Clare said that she had once proposed making *Vanity Fair* an illustrated weekly, and she described a dummy she had commissioned to show Nast the possibilities. Luce, not to be outdone, said that one of his brightest editors, John Martin, was currently exploring a similar idea. Then he abruptly took out his pocket watch, remarked it was late, and without another word moved away.

Clare was aghast. No one had ever treated her so curtly. He had, in effect, "picked my brains and left me flat." She decided he was the rudest man it had been her misfortune to meet.[34]

21

COUP DE FOUDRE

*There was a natural affinity between them. She drew him
out . . . Of talk they could neither of them ever
have enough.* —VIRGINIA WOOLF

Shortly before midnight on Sunday, December 9, 1934, Clare braved
icy weather to attend a "Turkish Ball" hosted by Elsa Maxwell at the
Waldorf-Astoria Hotel, in celebration of the opening of Cole Porter's
Anything Goes. Several hundred of New York's most prominent people
gathered in the Starlight Roof Garden to eat *couscous* and cake while
star performers paid tribute. Victor Moore sang "Be Like the Bluebird"
from Porter's new musical, and Gladys Swarthout of the Metropolitan
Opera crooned "What Is This Thing Called Love?"[1]

At some point during the entertainment, Clare was sitting alone
on one of the green leather ottomans that rimmed the ballroom, when
a man she knew walked by. It was Henry Luce, who had so brusquely
cut her short at Thayer and Laura Hobson's a few weeks before. He was
en route to a table occupied by his wife, Lila, and Condé Nast, and carrying two sparkling glasses.[2]

Henry Luce
Photograph by Edward Steichen, 1935

On impulse Clare said, "Oh, Mr. Luce, you're no doubt bringing me that champagne." To her surprise, he not only took the hint but sat down and talked quietly in the dark until the music ended. When the lights went up, Clare found him staring at her intently.

"Will you come downstairs with me?" he asked. "I have something important to tell you."

There was nowhere to sit in the Waldorf's crowded lobby, so Clare leaned against the wall near a ticket window, wondering if the publisher of *Time* was going to offer her a job.

"I've read about it happening, I've heard about it happening, now it's just happened to me."

"What?"

"The French call it a *coup de foudre*. I know you are the one woman in my life."

Clare stood in stunned silence. She understood the phrase meant "a stroke of lightning," but she had sent no special bolts in his direction. Could the man be drunk, or deranged? He was neither. Whether or not romance developed between them, Luce said, he had decided to end his marriage of eleven years. For at least the last two, he had felt a need for a different kind of companionship. His wife did not share his interests.

On and on he went. For the first time in Henry Luce's life, passion was taking precedence over reason. He struggled to articulate feelings never before experienced in his thirty-six years. By two o'clock Clare was pacing the lobby floor with him, in increasing bewilderment. She was trying to fathom her own emotions, and make some appropriate response, when Helen Norden, her young colleague from *Vanity Fair*, emerged from an elevator. Seizing this opportunity for relief, if not escape, Clare called out, "Come and talk to us." But Helen, who had a date downtown, dashed for the door.[3]

Luce took out his watch, as on their first meeting. "I'll call on you Thursday afternoon," he said, and went back upstairs.

Later that morning Archibald MacLeish, a writer at *Fortune*, was asked to meet with his boss at the Commodore Hotel. He found a shaken Luce smoking on the mezzanine. "I have fallen in love with a divorcée."[4]

MacLeish scarcely knew how to respond to this startling intimacy. So Luce turned to another *Fortune* employee, managing editor Ralph Ingersoll, and asked him to the Waldorf for a quiet talk in the men's room. Before saying anything, he looked under the stall doors to make sure they were alone. "I'm in love with Clare Brokaw," he said. "*The* Clare Brokaw . . . you can't believe how wonderful she is."[5]

Indeed Ingersoll could not. He had known Clare in her late teens and found her then, as now, "too flashily pretty for her own or anyone else's good." But he dared not say so. As he subsequently explained, Luce the tycoon tended to see things in grandiose terms. It followed that this new romance must be "One of the Great Loves of All Time."[6]

On Thursday, as promised, Luce visited Clare at the Sherry-Netherland, preceded by a basket of red tea roses. It was clear from the gravity of his gaze that he had more than an affair in mind. He had satisfied himself that they were destined for each other, so much so that he treated the matter as a *fait accompli*. Speaking in dry, businesslike tones, he said there were practical matters to arrange before they could be together permanently. They would need a year to become better acquainted. If during those months Clare came to love him as much as he did her, they would marry no later than January 6, 1936. In the meantime, they must conduct their relationship so discreetly that the Luce ménage at 4 East Seventy-second Street—his wife and two sons, aged nine and five—would not be "disturbed" by any public scandal.[7]

For once Clare was rendered speechless. Deep down she knew, "I *did* want to disturb it." Yet she could not see herself presiding over a rival establishment as Ann's mother and Luce's mistress. For her to live even secretly with a man of his eminence would sooner or later attract attention, damaging both her reputation and his. Perhaps she should reject him, as pleasantly as possible, in the hope that he would return with a better offer. The risk was that he might accept her no as final, go back to his family, and forget about her.

As it happened, Clare overrated Luce's domestic loyalties and underrated the speed with which their attraction to each other would develop.[8]

Two days before Christmas, a strange letter arrived from "Harry." It consisted almost entirely of theatrical metaphors, as if he were setting himself up in competition with her as an aspiring playwright. He said that he would like to write an allegory, with two characters symbolizing Clare and himself: an angel and a "tiresome fellow . . . muttering I love you."

Luce rambled on semi-coherently for eight paragraphs, in the strained manner with which the unimaginative try to impress the imaginative. He talked of "mere carpentry of situation stuck together" and "the brightness of the Northern lights." Finally, having had enough of his own "riddles," he said that he returned her to her own authorship, "with what benediction I cannot say. And adoration."[9]

Clare read this effusion sitting at her dressing table. Despite Luce's literary awkwardness, she was surprised and touched by his candor. In her experience, men either fantasized about love when alone or talked about it with others, but they seldom expressed their romantic feelings on paper. She pressed the letter to her cheek and caught a glimpse of herself in the mirror, smiling. Objective even in the midst of emotion, she thought the image would make a good *Saturday Evening Post* illustration. Then she turned to her typewriter.

> You wrote to me without restraint! That was good and sweet and very strange . . . How happy and idiotic and alive I feel because *you*, a generally plain and precise fellow, are so distracted with affection that you are willing to write lovely riddles.

Clare confessed that being loved by such a "young and altogether exciting man" made her "happier and more complacent" than she had ever been. As for her angelic role in his allegory, she promised to play it "up to the hilt." But he must be sure to allow for her "capriciousness, moodiness and . . . well marked perversity of spirit." She would postpone what more she had to say "about the unique excitement" he engendered in her, because she was about to leave for a holiday in Florida with her mother and daughter.

During the flight to Miami, while little Ann played with a toy compass she had brought in case the pilot lost his way, Clare continued her love letter in handwritten, purple prose.

> The fiery clouds have turned the silver wings into sheets of red gold. Still I find it melancholy. You are not *here*. Widowed, my spirit commits suttee in the sky's pyre.

Ruminating on the miraculousness of their attraction, she said she was trying to recapture Harry's "little-boy" laugh, the glint in his narrow eyes, his quick gestures and clipped speech. But the thought of him entrapped in "a solid little household" made her heart feel constricted.

She wrote five pages before a finger-numbing iciness spread through the cabin. While still able to hold her pen, she begged him not to lose his fascination for her. "I cannot do with less, I cannot cope with more."[10]

Clare took an instant dislike to the "tawdry" city of Miami, where Ann Austin and Joel Jacobs were waiting for her at the Columbus Hotel. She greeted them with feigned pleasure. Dr. Austin was nowhere to be seen: Ann still preferred Riggie's free-spending company. As in the past, the prospect of a vacation with her mother was more appealing than the actuality. At least there were flowers in her room from Dr. Rosenbluth—a flattering reminder that Henry Luce was but one of many admirers.[11]

On the twenty-sixth, Harry wrote to thank his "Empress" for the "radiance" of her Christmas missive, in particular the aerial segment. Purple or not, those five pages had seduced his mind and soul. Soon she was able to impress him with more of the same. An invitation arrived from some wealthy friends, Grant and Jane Mason, to visit them in Cuba on December 28. Leaving little Ann with her mother, Clare settled into the velvet seat of a wood-paneled Clipper and again treated "Darling Harry" to her lyrical powers of description. She wrote that she could see the airliner's clearly etched shadow on the sunny banks of clouds below and compared it to the shadow of his love, which "travels with me wherever I go in these new days."[12]

Her hosts lived in Jaimanitas, thirty minutes west of Havana. Grant Mason managed Pan American's Caribbean office, while Jane, at twenty-five, amounted to a younger version of Clare: blonde, classically beautiful, elegant, and athletic. The two women also shared a chronic restlessness and a tendency to promiscuity. Jane's current lover was Ernest Hemingway, so she knew as much as, if not more than, Clare did about the difficulties of intimacy with powerful men.[13]

Harry's next letter displayed his growing concern for secrecy. He asked her to send all future correspondence in care of an old college friend.[14] Clare, complying, began to think seriously about the true extent of their involvement.

In the years since her divorce, she had felt ambivalent about remarriage. Her lifelong desire to capture a perfect mate and bear a perfect son remained. But perfection was elusive—the stuff of myth. Once, in *Vanity Fair*, she had compared Greta Garbo with enchantresses such as Helen of Troy and Cleopatra, and found the star wanting. The reason, she concluded, was the inferiority of Garbo's lovers. "History has never reserved a place for a beautiful woman who did not love, or who was not loved by at least one interesting, powerful, or brilliant man."[15]

Clare herself had despaired of meeting such a triple combination. Had she now, as her thirty-second birthday loomed, found the long-sought ideal?

Just a week after Clare's departure from New York, John Billings, the managing editor of *Time*, noticed a sullen detachment in his employer's demeanor. This puzzled the cultivated Southerner, who usually found Luce congenial. Harry's mood seemed strange, given that he had just been chosen one of America's twelve outstanding men under forty.[16]

On January 2, 1935, as Clare sailed back to Miami on the Masons' yacht, Harry and Lila Luce went to the Metropolitan Opera with Laura and Thayer Hobson. Neither woman yet knew that both husbands wanted a divorce—Thayer had been pursuing someone else for almost a year.[17] Laura, indeed, felt content, having recently been hired to write advertising and other promotional copy for Time Inc. at a substantial salary. This gave her a chance to know Harry professionally as well as socially, and she was able to form a sharp impression of him.

> He had almost none of the social graces that go with success, no urbane good manners, no small talk. At a party, he hadn't the faintest interest in amusing anecdotes or the swapping of jokes, never bothered to make a complimentary remark to a woman about a new dress she was wearing—he didn't even see it—nor to a hostess about the superb dinner he was eating—he never knew what was on the plate before him. He would fire a question at you in . . . almost gruff intensity, usually about one of his political loves or hates, and

if you seemed ill-informed in your reply, or vapid or too casual, he would abruptly turn to somebody else.[18]

What Laura did not sense was Harry's romantic potential. He scarcely knew it himself.

Henry Robinson Luce had been conceived in the United States but was born in Tengchow, China, on April 3, 1898.[19] His father, Henry Winters Luce of Scranton, Pennsylvania, was a phenomenally energetic Yale graduate and Presbyterian missionary. He bequeathed to his son a strong constitution, brains, religious fervor, inflexibility, single-mindedness, and pale red hair. The boy's mother, Elizabeth Middleton Root, gave him curiosity, adventurousness, patriotism, and poor hearing.

Sheltered by the walls of the missionary compound, little Harry only slowly became aware of the animosity with which the vast majority of Chinese regarded foreign churchmen. For all the efforts of his father and like-minded proselytizers over a hundred years, only a fraction of one percent of the native population was converted. The rest resisted Western influences. Blind as his father to this intransigence, Harry never ceased to believe that China would eventually yield to Christ and capitalism.[20]

He was an attractive and precocious boy, with a marked didactic tendency. At five, his younger sister Elisabeth recalled, "he delivered his own sermons—to the neighbor's children, or anyone else who would listen." At six he informed his mother that his globe was always at hand, "to teach the history of George Washington." Already he loved his own country ardently, and he once came to blows with a boy who insulted it.

Harry first saw America when he was eight. At his maternal grandparents' church in Utica, New York, he innocently thought the line "I am the Vine and Ye are the Roots," imprinted on a stained-glass window, referred to his ancestry and related him directly to God. It was a belief his future employees thought he held sincerely. While he was still in the United States, a surgeon, removing his tonsils, allowed him to come out of the anesthetic too soon. Upon recovery Harry was found to have acquired a stutter that afflicted him well into adulthood.

On his return to China he enrolled at Chefoo, a British boarding school in Shantung, where customs of fagging, flogging, and toadying were entrenched. Despite these practices, he benefited from the school's superior instruction and broad curriculum—as did his classmate Thornton Wilder, son of the American Consul General at Shanghai. Harry learned French, Latin, Greek, history, and mathematics. Younger than average, he rose to third in a class of twenty and once scored 100 in algebra. His stammer notwithstanding, he joined the debating society and conquered shyness to become a reporter for the school's weekly journal. An innate journalistic gift soon propelled him to the position of editor in chief. Everything he excelled at as a man was in evidence long before he reached adolescence: preaching, teaching, inquiring, editing, and managing.

At fourteen he went to England for a year at a school north of London, in the hope of being cured of his stutter. Then in the fall of 1913 he won a scholarship to Hotchkiss School in Connecticut. Again he rose to the top of his class, and he edited the school's literary magazine. His closest rival was Briton Hadden, an extroverted sportsman and another aspiring journalist. Their dynamic competitiveness continued into the Ivy League, where they battled for control of the *Yale Daily News*. Hadden became the paper's chairman, while Luce held the post of managing editor. At graduation Harry was voted the most brilliant member of the class of 1920 and "Brit" the most likely to succeed.

During a vacation from postgraduate study at Oxford, the twenty-two-year-old Harry fell in love with Lila Ross Hotz, a tall, well-bred Chicago débutante. Wanting to keep close to her after his return to the States, he took a job on the *Chicago Daily News* as "legman" for Ben Hecht. Briton Hadden soon lured him back east with an arrangement for them both to work at the *Baltimore News*. They stayed there for a spell, then, at the common age of twenty-five, embarked on the publishing venture that changed their lives.

Raising $86,000 from Yale classmates and other investors, they created a weekly newsmagazine called *Facts*. This was immediately changed to *Time*—a name that Harry claimed had come to him while thinking how long it took to travel home every evening. With Stephen Vincent Benét and Archibald MacLeish as part-time writers, and Roy Larsen as circulation manager, they published their first issue on March 3, 1923.

In a year they were confident enough of long-term success to raise their own salaries and issue an optimistic report to stockholders. Luce triumphantly married Lila. A son, Henry Luce III, was born on April 28, 1925, and another, Peter Paul, on May 18, 1929. By then Harry was already a millionaire.

Suddenly and shockingly in February 1929, Hadden died of septicemia. Harry contrived to buy his shares, giving himself sole command of *Time*. Immediately he went ahead with the founding of a business monthly entitled *Fortune*. In 1932 he bought *Architectural Forum*. When he met Clare, he was running all three magazines, exploring the possibility of creating a fourth, and finalizing plans for a major newsreel, *The March of Time*.

Messianic in his editorial zeal, the mature Luce seemed incapable of relaxation. Where lesser men cracked under the pressure of relentless deadlines, he thrived. He found his energetic and intellectual equal in Clare Boothe Brokaw. Unlike Lila, she was ultramodern, tough-minded, organized, and unsentimental. Harry had that last quality too. "Not for one sentimental cause shed one small tear," he had written while still a youth.

He realized at once that Clare's creative imagination was superior to his. Her wit, sense of humor, and powers of repartee left him stammeringly behind. On the other hand, she, insecure and fickle, lacked his cohesive and tightly structured character, his religious beliefs, his stable background of family love and loyalty, and the self-confidence that came from an advanced education. They might embark on a marriage of minds and fusion of bodies, but there were enough fundamental differences between them to portend strains in the long term.

Harry left New York on the night of Friday, January 4, telling Billings that he "felt stupid" and needed a rest. In fact he was heading south for a clandestine meeting with Clare. Simultaneously, Ann Brokaw, accompanied by her mother's maid, was dispatched to Rosemary Hall, her new school in Connecticut. "Was the first one of the little kids to get back," the ten-year-old wrote forlornly in her diary. She wondered why she was there so early, with nobody nearby to mitigate her loneliness. Her grandmother would not return from Miami until the spring, Dr. Austin had the grippe, and Uncle David was in the hospital being treated for something mysterious. All she could do, until the term started, was read her encyclopedias late into the night.[21]

In Miami, meanwhile, Clare surreptitiously moved to the Spanish-style Villa d'Este Hotel facing Biscayne Bay and prepared for Harry's arrival.

Luce acted like a tortured man during the two days and nights they spent there. He kept referring to his pending split from his wife and family as "the problem." Their initial attempts at lovemaking were a dismal failure. In old age Clare painfully recalled Harry's strong hands and long fingers. "If he touched you it was like he was tearing you apart. I suppose today I would have given him a handbook of sex, but in those days women were expected to keep quiet."[22]

Harry admitted being "an awful flop the first few times." His mechanical ineptitude bewildered him. He had seldom experienced impotence with Lila, telling Clare that he "simply did it and then rolled over and thought about *Time*." She consoled herself with the theory that he was temporarily unable to match "erotic fantasies with the actuality of a real live passionate loving woman."[23]

Miami offered few appealing distractions, and Clare did not feel ready to introduce Harry to her mother. So after two days they left for Cuba. One morning in Havana Harry surprised Clare by saying, "Are you *sure* I am what you are looking for?" With that he flew to a business meeting in Palm Beach, while she wrestled with the doubts his question had raised. "I want to feel," she wrote him, "that *you* feel that this is as splendid and right for both of us as things can be."[24]

After four days apart she rejoined him on the mainland and they traveled to Charleston, South Carolina. There they registered as "Mr. and Mrs. Henry R. Lewis" at the Villa Margharita. This small, discreet hotel looked across the Battery towards Fort Sumter and was a popular retreat for politicians and other establishment figures.

Later, having dined in their room, they successfully made love. Ever afterwards Harry would describe the two nights they spent here as their "first honeymoon."[25]

On a cold, damp January 17 the couple arrived at Washington Airport on their way home. Discretion required that they continue north separately. Harry felt the pain of parting enough to record it in another of his attempts at scenario writing:

They tramp across a street, her arm in his, to a bleak cafeteria. They tramp back. He watches her go up the gang-plank into the Douglass [*sic*]—her figure brisk, precise, proud as she is. She looks out of the little window. He stands almost beneath the wing. They signal goodbye. It is a wrench—the worst they have had . . . and yet it was only the goodbye of those who know that they are forever committed. But it was their first and they were strange to the possibility of being separated.[26]

Clare had been back in freezing New York only a week when she told her daughter she would be going south again at the end of January. Just before leaving—this time for Hobcaw—she gave a dinner party at the Sherry-Netherland. Among her usual mix of smart and wealthy guests was Laura Hobson, reeling from Thayer's announcement that he was abandoning her for another woman.[27]

After dessert Clare tapped her glass for attention and said that she had met the man she intended to marry. But with infuriating coyness she refused to name him, saying only that he was "connected with the movies." Speculative names came from around the table. "Clark Gable?" "Robert Taylor?" "Douglas Fairbanks?"

Alone with Laura afterwards, Clare was unable to resist further clue dropping. Her suitor, she said, was powerful, young, and rich, and a friend of both Hobsons. Laura looked blank.

"It's Harry," Clare cried out. "*The March of Time* is connected with the movies, isn't it?"[28]

Lila was philosophical enough to agree to a divorce. She told Harry that she would depart for Reno as soon as their respective lawyers worked out a financial settlement. Without even waiting for that, Harry gave her their recently purchased four-hundred-acre working farm in New Jersey. He hoped that furnishing the Norman-style manor and running the estate with its herd of cattle would be a diversion for her and the boys.[29]

At the Racquet Club, Harry discussed his marital break with Morehead Patterson, the Yale classmate who brought him Clare's letters.

Patterson voiced skepticism about Mrs. Brokaw as a domestic partner. She was too glamorous. Women like her did not "light for long in any one spot."[30]

Harry had no ears for such misgivings. "I am ready to meet you in the fires of sunset and in other fiercer fires," he wrote his lover.[31]

Feeling the burden of marriage lightening, he began thinking of Clare as his responsibility. Though he seldom paid attention to his own health, he found himself worrying about the fast pace at which she lived and the nervous strain imposed, wherever she went, by "shoals of people demanding to sit up with you until the last cigaret is smoked . . . eager to ply you with champagne cocktails."[32]

Clare, meanwhile, arrived at Hobcaw in a turbulent state. Her incomplete resolve about Harry was not helped by a lingering possessiveness towards Bernard Baruch. The unexpected presence of Mrs. Baruch angered her. "Does he welcome this? Is it his planning? And if so, for God's sake why?" She complained to Harry that she foresaw ten days of tension and hypocrisy in company with a woman so "hard on the eye, and fatiguing to the brain . . . I like him less for her."[33]

She desperately needed a confidant and invited Laura Hobson to come down at her expense. Calmed by Laura's acceptance, she began to have daydreams of a "bang-up super-salon" in Manhattan once she and Harry were married. Between weekends with Astors at Rhinebeck or Vanderbilts at Newport, they could be at home to New York's leading politicians, bankers, journalists, and actors. When she communicated this idea to Harry, he reacted negatively, pointing out that salons were operated mainly for the enjoyment of those who came rather than those who held court.[34]

Clare wondered if he and she wanted the same kind of life. Might he, after marrying her, hanker for the "mundane goodies" of home and family he had left behind? "What I could not endure," she wrote him, "would be to have you at some future time reproach me . . . for encouraging you to abandon quiet, conventional, honest fields . . . Please come to me with no regrets for what you lose, and without too much hope of what you will find—or do not come at all."

She warned that in contrast to his methodical and tidy mind, hers was spontaneous and mercurial.

> I have a flair for drama that might be more profitably con-
> fined to the pages of my manuscripts than loosened in my
> daily human relationships. I have fits of morbidity and melan-
> choly that are exhausting to others, but catharsis to me, leave
> my spirit shiny, washed and bouncy. A badly burnt child I am
> so afraid of happiness, that let a perfect moment begin to un-
> fold like a rose in my hands, and I instantly try to crush it.[35]

Harry replied to this poignant, if mixed imagery, with some of his
own.

> Happiness, I thought until recently, had nothing whatever
> to do with my life . . . Now I think otherwise . . . there are
> those who can always hear, beneath the rumble of traffic,
> the stars singing . . . I think that I am to be one of those.[36]

He deluded himself that she, too, had the potential for great happiness, not understanding how much her unstable past and chronic
narcissism precluded this. Nor could he gauge the true extent of her de-
ceitfulness, even when she, with astonishing candor, described it.

As a child, Clare wrote, she had been "extraordinarily truthful,"
but had been "caught up in a web of falsehood" spun by her mother.
Lying became a habit, especially when she discovered that the world in
which she found herself liked being lied to:

> Everybody wanted me to be what they thought I was . . .
> This man, this woman, wanted me to be glamorous: I was
> glamorous. This one (Bernie, let's say) wanted me to be ten-
> der, trustful, baffled, naive, childlike, innocent, and so I was.
> Another wanted a gay, brittle, undependable, whimsical
> Madcap: and oh, what a Madcap was I! . . . Most everyone
> that knew me casually preferred to think of me as a cold, re-
> mote, shrewd, and ambitious woman: I have always con-
> trived to behave so in their company. A few have gone to
> the other extreme; for them I am a sensual, passion-tossed
> Libertine. I never bothered to correct that impression,
> amused by the idea of its collision with the preceding notion
> of frigidity.

Until I met you I never knew anyone who challenged
enough of the real heart and mind of me, to interrupt me in
my emotional juggling . . . I never was *entirely* any of the
things that people think I am; from time to time, I have
been all of them.[37]

For all Clare's bouts of morbid self-analysis, her relationship with
Harry was on the whole good humored, even jovial. She sent him an
arch "Domestic Questionnaire" that sought to determine what she
might get away with in future. "Kindly fill out and return." He did so,
but some of his scribbled answers prove he was no dupe.

Q: Will you leave a party at eleven because you have to
arise early, and allow your mate to remain, if she is enjoying herself?

A: *Yes.*

Q: Do you leave the house in the morning, without waking your wife up to say goodbye?

A: *Yes (but don't guarantee continuance of this admirable
virtue).*

Q: Do you abhor twin beds?

A: *Yes.*

Q: If it turns out that she has a perverted preference for a
particular kind of play, book, or social gathering, will
you permit her a binge (occasionally) in this direction
without taking it as a proof of waning love?

A: *Yes.*

Q: And will you refrain from either converting her or re-
forming her?

A: *Yes.*

Q: And will you insist that she do the same?

A: *No. I perceive that I have spent a good part of my life re-
forming and/or educating others—and I have a passion to
feel how it feels.*

Q: If your lady suddenly takes it into her head to elope
with a belted earl or an Egyptologist, will you pursue
her with a poker and knock her gently on the head,
and nurse her tenderly until she comes to her senses?

A: *Am not quite so dumb as to answer this one—let the lady take her own chance of being left with her goddamned earl.*

Q: Are you prepared to leave your lady a small inviolate section of her life concerning which you must ask no questions and will you be intelligent and foresighted enough to do the same?

A: *Yes—but you help me to this wisdom.*

Q: Are you prepared for the worst?

A: *Yes, Yes, Yes, Yes.*[38]

By the time of Laura Hobson's arrival at Hobcaw on February 3, Clare was alone in the big house. The Baruchs had left temporarily, and she had driven the last of her fellow guests, the novelist Joseph Hergesheimer, to his train. It was a wonder that he allowed her to do so, because she had once visited his library in Dover, Pennsylvania, and, to his stupefaction, taken scissors to the uncut pages of a collection of rare books.[39]

As they drove through Charleston, Hergesheimer sanctimoniously pointed out the Villa Margharita as a place of unimpeachable moral standards. Clare stifled her hilarity, and she later wrote Harry that she had wanted to dash up the steps, bury her face in the pillows of the familiar brass bed, and "not look up until Mr. Lewis put his hand on my hair."[40]

Laura gave her full details about the recent test screening of Harry's newsreel, *The March of Time*. It was his first foray into cinematic journalism, and he had been understandably apprehensive. She said that the première, presented to a black-tie audience at the Capitol Theatre on Broadway, was a disappointment. It consisted of five four-minute, sonorously narrated segments. They included the first sound pictures from the Metropolitan Opera, a report on the "21" Club's speakeasy stash, and coverage of the innovative "Belisha Beacon" pedestrian crossings in London. Considering that America was still gripped by the Depression, and Europe by Fascism, these subjects had struck many viewers as light fare.[41]

Harry acknowledged failure in a letter to Clare, saying he was optimistic that enough initial box-office support would allow him to improve his newsreel. Unsparing, she told him that he had made a mistake in giving tuxedo-clad "super-sophisticates" the impression that they were about to see something unique and substantial, rather than a black-and-white short. Nothing less than an "advance shot, in Technicolor, of Judgement Day" would have satisfied them.[42]

Laura stayed at Hobcaw for a week. She thought that as a hostess Clare was "grand and gracious and wise," as well as entertaining.[43] Every night the author of *Abide With Me* would read aloud from her current work in progress, a Feydeau-style farce entitled "Gaiety of Nations." It was about a French nobleman engaged to marry an American heiress, whose impoverishment in the Crash of 1929 sent him back to his former love—even though she was poorer.[44]

One evening, after dining *à deux*, Clare suddenly asked Laura, who was standing by the sitting-room mantelpiece, to take off her dress. She said she would explain later. Laura was shocked but, detecting no hint of sexual interest, shrugged and dropped her gown to the floor.

> I wore no bra and stood there in my brief silk underpants, my evening dress making a silken circle around my ankles. I was still near the fireplace.
>
> Clare was gazing at me, at my breasts . . . "Would you lie down on the sofa? On your back?"
>
> By now I was thoroughly intrigued . . . What was behind all this? She was scheming something; I could almost feel her mind planning ahead. I lay down on the sofa. For a moment she didn't move.
>
> She knelt down beside me, about three feet away from me, her eyes now on a level with my own. It became clear she was not interested in my entire body, but only in my breasts.
>
> "Put your arms over your head, would you, just for one more minute?"
>
> That I did too . . . As she continued to kneel there on the carpet, motionless and gazing, as if at a portrait in a museum, Clare managed a look of pure approval.
>
> "Thanks a million," she said then, and turned away.

As Laura dressed, Clare explained that after several pregnancies and miscarriages her own breasts were no longer "virgin." She was thinking of having them altered. "I want to be perfect for Harry."[45]

In New York, a recovering David Boothe started to ingratiate himself with Henry Luce over lunch and dinner. The latter found Clare's brother to be charming company, not aware that he was being set up for future jobs and loans. David reported to Clare that her prospective husband appeared to be deeply in love and "anxious to prove it as soon as possible."[46]

She returned to New York on St. Valentine's Day, and on February 22 invited Harry to dine at the Sherry-Netherland apartment to meet her daughter. Little Ann seemed to like "Mr. Luse," as she spelled it in her diary. He subsequently took her to the theater and the Bronx Zoo, promised to buy her something "really Chinese," and at least twice accompanied her back to school after weekends in town.[47]

In early March, Clare went to Washington for a female newspaper correspondents' dinner, and a meeting with Huey Long. Even without a magazine or column of her own, she liked to keep up with personalities and issues of the day. At the same time Luce conveniently arranged an interview with Secretary of the Interior Harold L. Ickes. The lovers met in the afternoons for tea at the Mayflower Hotel, talking endlessly on subjects ranging from housing policy to why Michelangelo's nudes were "roundly female but never feminine." At a dinner attended by Alice Longworth, Joseph Kennedy, and Arthur Krock, they remained interested only in each other. Clare, looking lovely in pale blue, spent most of the evening huddled with Harry.[48]

Lila Luce seemed to bear no ill will and asked Laura Hobson one day what Mrs. Brokaw was like. "She must have been quite unusual to have been managing editor of *Vanity Fair*."

"Yes," Laura replied. "I think she is brilliant."

"That's what I hear," said Lila, laughing.[49]

At first Lila cooperated amicably with Harry over the financial details of their divorce. But when lawyers persuaded her that she should try for a bigger settlement, she postponed her Reno trip. Clare, alarmed, saw this as Lila's ploy to create "an open door" through which Harry might yet retreat.[50] In a countermove, she announced that she was leaving New York indefinitely, not to return for any length of time until all documents terminating the Luce marriage had been signed. She would go to the Greenbrier for ten days, then back to Hobcaw, and finally to Europe. If this meant staying away for a good part of the year, so be it. Instinct told her that absence might make her more desirable.

"Just when it seemed that Harry most needed the woman he loved," observed Ralph Ingersoll, "she packed her bags." The editor recognized Clare's coruscating intelligence yet saw her as a case of "arrested development." In his opinion, she registered life "like a child who observes everything—including her own effect on the people around her—but is unchanged by it, because she is unaffected emotionally."[51]

The same might once have been said of Harry. Before he met Clare he had not been overly sensitive to his own or others' feelings. But having become, under her spell, such an obsessive lover, he felt desolate and trapped without her. A day and night in the company of Lila and the children taught him how much he had changed.

> If ever there was the slightest doubt as to the rightness of my divorce, I can have none now. Not because the last 24 hours were dreadful in any external sense . . . But for no proper reason—except that I do not belong with "my family"—I was bored . . . exasperated to the point where I could no longer endure it . . . I have lived under "strains" before but I have never had to live as I do now through hours and hours which make no damn sense, which are just emptiness.[52]

Clare admitted to missing him too, particularly in her Greenbrier four-poster bed.

> If you were lying there, your white face against the whiter pillow, your slanting blue eyes challenging my heavy ones, your shoulder turned to cushion my cheek, your other hand

on my shoulder, then I might (I would!) tell you all the things I am too tired to put in this letter . . .

Oh, Harry it is a very great pity that a place as lovely as this should not be consecrated by a love as lovely as ours.[53]

Fantasy became reality when Harry came to spend two days with her in White Sulphur Springs. Clare was afraid of being "hopelessly compromised" in such a socially prominent place, but they managed to avoid publicity.[54]

Both now felt hopeful enough about the future to discuss where they would live and vacation as husband and wife. Clare's enthusiasm for the South galvanized Harry to instigate a search for a plantation as their winter retreat. He quizzed John Billings about Dixie customs and instructed his special assistant, Dan Longwell, to help Mrs. Brokaw find properties in South Carolina.[55]

In spite of another influx of houseguests at Hobcaw, Clare finished "Gaiety of Nations" and celebrated an unusually late Easter at the local Methodist church. The structure was little more than a whitewashed box, with green shutters and a tiny steeple. She was the only non-black in the congregation of some twenty people. The women wore gingham and robin's egg blue dresses, and the men were in broad-shouldered suits with bright ties and pocket handkerchiefs. She reported to Harry afterwards that "they shouted and stomped and swayed . . . wailed and brayed their spirituals" until she had to retreat from the mounting heat and noise.[56]

Next day she met Dan Longwell in Georgetown, and they spent two days searching for estates in the neighborhood. Although Dan failed to find Clare a suitable property, he went back to New York bowled over by her. She was "just about the most wonderful example of human personality" he had ever encountered.[57]

When Baruch learned that Luce wanted to buy a South Carolina estate, he half-jokingly offered to sell him Hobcaw for $150,000—about one twentieth of what it had cost—on condition that he put it in Clare's name. She at once assumed this proposal, even if made in jest, proved that her "*père incestueux*" was reconciled to her new attachment.[58]

Missing the sound of Harry's voice, she drove to Georgetown to call him. Their conversations, and almost daily correspondence, soon passed beyond intimacy into fantasy. They discussed the son they hoped to have. "Don't you think Michael Luce is an incredibly good name?" Clare wrote. "It doesn't sound like a president, but it sounds so . . . so irresistible." At times they even addressed each other as "Mike."[59]

On April 25 Cholly Knickerbocker of the *New York American* reported that "the very near future will find Mrs. Claire [*sic*] Brokaw a bride for a second time." He went on to declare that her lover was "sufficiently rich to indulge in any and all extravagant whims the clever and talented Claire may decide to develop . . . He is, in every sense of the word, 'a catch.' " Not to be outdone, Walter Winchell predicted in his nationwide column that Clare would marry "Sir William Wiseman of the British Secret Service" in June.[60]

With exposure imminent, Luce decided to forewarn his father at a breakfast meeting on May 1, steeling himself for a sermon on adultery and family virtues. But the old Presbyterian cleric was surprisingly tolerant. He warned only that since both Harry and Clare were publicly perceived as clever, they risked ridicule if they bungled their second attempts at matrimony.[61]

Clare sailed for Europe on Saturday, May 11. Her family saw her off from the West Side Pier, and she watched them from the rail as the *Conte di Savoia* eased out of its berth. Little Ann, her sharp Brokaw features glowing, looked excited: she knew she would be joining her mother in a few weeks. David was uneasy at the prospect of life without his adored sister. A teary Ann Austin sulked because Clare had elected to take Buff Cobb, and not her, as a traveling companion.[62]

When the liner started towards the harbor, Clare took refuge in the writing room. She dreaded seeing the Chrysler Building as they passed Forty-second Street, knowing that Harry would be at work on the fifty-first floor.[63]

Luce, in turn, was feeling unusually tense and lacking in concentration that morning. Near the hour of Clare's departure, he closed his office door. On hearing the blast of her ship's whistle at 11:45, he left his desk to stand at a sun-filled window. From there he watched the vessel steam down the Hudson, overtake another, and disappear behind the telephone building in lower Manhattan. Seeing the woman he loved slip beyond his ken, he sent her a silent blessing. Then, no longer able to postpone his loneliness, he sat down to face it.[64]

22

UPROARIOUS BREASTS

The emotion of love . . . is not self-sustaining;
it endures only when the lovers love many things
together, and not merely each other.

—WALTER LIPPMANN

Among the flowers and fruit that filled Clare's cabin on the *Conte di
Savoia* was a spray of orchids that made grunting noises. Lifting it
up, she discovered a live white piglet from Dorothy Hale. Whatever
the gift implied, she thought it more suited to a porcine fellow passenger, Elsa Maxwell, and promptly passed it on.[1]

Elsa was one of the few New Yorkers who knew of Clare's secret affair with Henry Luce. As a professional party giver, she already sensed
the "great power" they would wield together in society as well as in
business circles.[2] Indeed it was power, more than mere money, that
Clare now lusted after—not only access to Harry's but power of her
own to shape social, cultural, and political trends.

Two potentially serious obstacles loomed between her and this ambition. Lila Luce could still balk at going to Reno. And there was the

attitude of Harry's Presbyterian relatives, expressed in a letter that reached her before sailing. It was from his younger sister, Elisabeth Luce Moore, and warned of "tragic reactions" in the family if he went through with his divorce. Without actually asking Clare to withdraw, Mrs. Moore hoped that her European sojourn might give her "a better perspective" on the whole affair. If this resulted in a decision not to marry her brother, they would all be spared much grief.[3]

But Clare was leaving so that distance would lend enchantment, not perspective. From the ship she wrote Harry to say that she saw "melodrama" rather than tragedy in his wife's situation. Lila might languish for a while after losing him, but she would hardly die from it. He, however, would be crushed if "Beth" got her way. As for Clare, she had found her world and her life in him.[4]

The Alpes-Maritimes were still covered with snow, and there was a chill in the air when Clare checked into the Hotel Martinez at Cannes on May 19. Her room had a sunny sea view, though, and would be a pleasant place from which to scout the Riviera for a rental property. She intended to make it her base for at least the next four months.

That night, using an introduction from Sir William Wiseman, she dined with Somerset Maugham. The novelist lived with his lover, Gerald Haxton, at the Villa Mauresque, an exquisite eight-acre estate in Cap-Ferrat. Clare was struck by her teenage literary hero's unpleasantly black, glittering eyes. Yet behind them she sensed a sad, kindly man. Years later she was touched to hear that Maugham said his private sorrow was "to have loved, and been loved, but never at the same time."[5]

He showed her his studio, with its desk facing away from the distracting beauty of the Mediterranean. They talked about the discipline that writing requires, and Maugham claimed to rework his sentences as often as fifteen times. Personally, Clare thought he was "far from the smoothest stylist," and his heavy-handed symbolism in *Of Human Bondage* still bothered her. But of all the writers she ever met, he would remain the one she liked best as a person. Though far removed from him in upbringing and education, she shared his philosophy that whatever life's miseries, its pleasures and opportunities should be "grasped."[6]

Spurred by the splendor of the Villa Mauresque, she looked for something similar, if less lavish, nearby. In two days she found a bougainvillea-covered house called "Villa San Gustin" perched high above a cove on Cap-Ferrat. An American couple leased it to her, complete with English cook, French maid, and chauffeur. There was a library of fine leather-bound books, and the bedrooms were so placed that she foresaw no "social problem" when her daughter and Harry came to stay. The nearest neighbors, aside from Maugham, were G. B. Stern, the English literary critic, and Michael Arlen, author of *The Green Hat*. None overlooked her stretch of beach, so she could bathe in the nude whenever she wanted.[7]

On the afternoon of May 28, 1935, George Brokaw died of heart failure in the swimming pool of Connecticut's Hartford Sanitarium. He had been undergoing further treatment for alcoholism and was not yet fifty-six years old. Clare, on a brief trip to North Africa with Buff Cobb, belatedly heard the news from Harry, who wondered if her husband had ever understood he had been "wedded to genius."[8] It was a speculation she let lie, having, no doubt, her own "what if?" thoughts about having divorced George so hastily.

Little Ann was similarly taciturn. David Boothe wrote to say that he had driven the girl to the funeral at Mount Pleasant Cemetery in Newark, New Jersey. Alienated from her father by custody battles, she seemed nervous at the prospect of meeting other Brokaws, so David told her to be natural and cry if she felt like it, because "the only judge of her emotions was herself." After the service he cheered her up with lunch and the movie *Naughty Marietta*, then deposited her with the Austins until she left for France to join Clare.[9]

Not quite eleven years old, Ann was now independently wealthy. Even before George's death, she had $27,000 a year—about $2,000 more than her mother's alimony—from a trust fund set up by her grandfather. Under the terms of her father's will, she would receive some $3,000 annually from rent on the Brokaw mansion. David took pleasure in communicating the figures to his sister, as if being close to money made him rich too.

Clare tolerated his obvious intent to profit from her looming union with Harry because he performed useful services. In exchange for living rent free in her Sherry-Netherland apartment, he took care of her cat, paid bills, handled investments, and engaged a chaperone to accompany Ann across the Atlantic.

As a habitual sponger, he would dearly have liked to make his current arrangement permanent and advised her he would stay put until he saw how she was "situated." He joked that when he entertained his friends in her library, their "respect for my heretofore undisclosed academic background increases plenty." Not content with courting Henry Luce, he cultivated her other intimates, soliciting stock tips from Bernard Baruch, arranging a loan for General Johnson, and using Dr. Rosenbluth to monitor his syphilis and gonorrhea treatments.[10]

For the former, David had to sit regularly in a steam box and take heat-inducing medicines to kill his spirochetes. For the latter, he underwent painful mercury injections into the urethra. Clare was privy to these details. When Rosenbluth mailed her an encouraging report of David's latest laboratory slide tests, she thanked him for helping regenerate "a boy that is dearer to me than any other man I know."[11]

At thirty-three, the "boy" was actually a year her senior. But the fact that she still thought of him as boyish was indicative of their relationship: she the nurturer, he the suckler. Knowing and understanding most things about each other, past and present, they shared a closeness neither found with anyone else. Of all the men in her life, David insisted, "I do love you best."[12]

Harry, missing Clare acutely, spent as much time as possible talking about her, over lunch with David, dinner with Laura Hobson, and cocktails with dozens of her acquaintances at a Condé Nast party. He found them poor substitutes for her luminous presence. They also lacked his ability to give himself up "wholly to worship."[13]

On June 6, the *New York American* finally confirmed the rumors that had been so long circulating. "MRS. BROKAW TO WED LUCE AFTER DIVORCE." Pictures of both Clare and Lila accompanied the column. Harry wrote that he was "almost glad" the story was out. At least now their relationship was "removed from the realm of gossip."[14]

At Time Inc., the news dismayed senior staff. With the intense collegial bonding that executives often feel for their boss, they saw Clare as a threat to evenings when Luce and they rolled up their sleeves over breaking stories and downed company booze while putting the latest issue to bed. "I thought Harry . . . was not really interested in women physically," John Billings remarked. Elsewhere in the office reactions varied from envy and anger to obscene vituperation, as in James Agee's explosion to Dwight MacDonald. "Luce . . . will marry that walking cunt (with stockings by Van Raalte)."[15]

Ann arrived on the Riviera in mid-June, and joined her mother in plunging naked into the water from their private rocks. Soon both were

Clare and Ann at Cap-Ferrat, *1935*

brown from top to toe. It was fun in her thirties, Clare wrote Mark Sullivan, to outswim and outride a healthy eleven-year-old. "No doubt the muscles of my mind have grown a little flaccid . . . but the muscles in my arms and legs are lovely things, and my tummy is as flat as it has been since I was twenty."[16]

Her reference to mental laziness amounted to an apology for not being as interested in Washington politics as Sullivan. She was nevertheless aware in her azure paradise that the President for whom she had voted seemed bent on punitive taxes for the rich. Just as she was building up her physical health with a diet of figs, wild strawberries, and peaches, she cheerfully complained, Franklin Roosevelt "busies himself depleting my fortune."

But she refused to fret. "Let him destroy the American constitution: he can't destroy mine!"[17]

Harry sailed for France on June 19 and arrived at Le Crillon in Paris a week later. Impatient to see him, Clare hustled little Ann off on a sightseeing tour and went north to surprise her lover with a note in his message box:

> There is a really charming woman who longs to make your acquaintance and who will surely provide you with a few pleasant days while you are in Paris—blonde, of a certain age, like yourself—alone. The number of her room is 547 and she will be there any time after 2 o'clock that you care to knock at the door.[18]

He presented himself in a new gray suit and blue tie. For an hour or so after their initial kiss, they felt like strangers. The encounter seemed contrived, unreal, forced. As Clare put it, they knew each other "too well for preliminaries, not enough for ease."[19]

They kept separate quarters in the hotel but stayed mostly in Clare's two-room corner suite. It had a wide terrace with a spectacular panorama across the Place de la Concorde to Les Invalides. Harry teasingly said that they were taking a big risk by standing there "in a manner to announce our love" to every onlooker in the square.[20]

Continuing south, they spent ten days and nights at Cap-Ferrat, "heavy with the sweetness of years to come." They dined with Maugham, got tipsy in San Juan-les-Pins, snuggled in the backs of carriages, and celebrated the Fourth of July with fellow expatriates. Watching the swing of Clare's shoulders on the tennis court, her expert throws of dice at the Salle de Jetté, or the stillness of her sleeping face,

Harry felt more contented than he had ever been. His reawakened libido affected his prose style, to the point of ecstatic incoherence. Clare's laughter, he wrote, "tinkled in her heart . . . and her breasts were uproarious in their unsolemn love."[21]

One dawn as they lay in each other's arms, something miraculous happened. Harry was facing the window and through it saw a phantomlike red and white ship inching slowly along on the misty horizon. When he described it to Clare, they were both astonished to hear that his stutter of twenty-nine years had vanished.[22]

On July 6, the perfection of their time together was shattered by the news that Lila Luce, instead of entraining for Reno, had crossed the Atlantic with both children. She urgently wanted to see her husband in Paris. Harry left at once.

When they met at the Hôtel George V, Lila said that his proposed financial settlement was causing legal problems. Instead of making payments to her over a period of years, he was actually obligated to pay a large cash sum in advance of the divorce. After a half hour's discussion, Harry agreed to cut his vacation short and return home to meet with their respective lawyers. Lila promised that she would leave for Nevada no later than mid-August. Until then she intended to rest for a few weeks in Switzerland.[23]

Harry could snatch only two more days at Cap-Ferrat before sailing from Nice on July 12. He left behind a seriously disturbed Clare. She was so like a child in her sudden insecurities and possessiveness that at times of apparent abandonment she lost her emotional balance. It maddened her that he should be leaving early to take care of another woman's interests. Her old restlessness resurfaced. No sooner had he embarked than she went to a casino and lost eight thousand francs in an all-night session. Then at four in the morning, she packed her bags, boarded a boat from Cannes to Marseilles, and took a Czech plane bound for Salzburg. Little Ann remained behind with her chaperone.[24]

Over Bavaria, Clare's aircraft lost power and had to put down in a cornfield. She found herself in a police station, explaining at wearying length that she was a tourist, not a Prague spy. Finally she was allowed to continue by car across the Austrian border. That night in Salzburg she stayed at the Grand Hôtel de l'Europe. Next morning she set off on a thirty-minute drive to the Alpine spa of Badgastein, where the purpose of her reckless journey became clear: Bernard Baruch was in residence, taking his annual cure.[25]

Clare wanted a sympathetic ear, but Bernie, crippled by gout, had problems of his own. She found him on crutches at the Kaiserhof Hotel, unable to go out except in a wheelchair. To her chagrin, he did not seem jealous when he heard whom she had been entertaining in the south of France, and said with some casualness that he doubted she and Harry would ever marry. This, she persuaded herself, was "wishful thinking on his part."[26]

He stunned Clare again by remarking that Lila Luce, far from being in Switzerland, was staying in a pension directly across the street. Clare's immediate reaction was to drive back to Salzburg. But she promised Bernie that she would return to stay with him, Lila or no Lila, through the end of the month.

Checking out of the Hotel de l'Europe two days later, she handed in a letter to be posted to Mr. Henry Luce, and was startled when the concierge asked her if she knew Mrs. Luce.

"Why?"

"Because I have mail for her, and if you are motoring to Badgastein, you can take it to her, perhaps?"

"You'd better send it," Clare said stiffly.[27]

Lila was nowhere to be seen when she got back to the spa, and Bernie remained incapacitated. "Having nothing better to do," she wrote Harry, "I submitted my beautiful brown carcass to the thorough examination of a Badgastein M.D."[28]

Predictably, the doctor found enough wrong with her to require immediate attention. He told Clare she was anemic and must undergo diathermy "to set certain feminine appurtenances to rights." This involved high-frequency transmission of heat rays to tissues beneath the skin. The treatment, she assured Harry, would facilitate the conception of "Michael."[29]

Within hours of having been probed, Clare started to hemorrhage. The doctor ordered her to lie motionless for ten days and submit to a hypodermic regimen of animal-organ extracts. In the midst of this, Bernie found he had regained his own mobility and must return home to deal with a family emergency. "My last thoughts are of you," he wrote in a farewell note that acknowledged her desolation. "You really have need of me more than anyone else just now."[30]

Clare braced herself for the dread reality of solitude in a foreign hotel room, with July rain pouring down and nothing to do but look out the window in the hope of glimpsing Harry's two boys. To her relief, word of her confinement spread through Badgastein's community of fashionable visitors. Soon her room was full of flowers. Rebecca West came to keep her company. Somerset Maugham and G. B. Stern stopped by regularly, as if they were all still living in Cap-Ferrat.

Harry, seriously concerned about Clare's sickness, offered to recross the Atlantic, but she dissuaded him. In her weakened state, she began skittishly to have doubts about committing herself to him. "I'm scared to get married," she wrote. "That's the real reason I don't want to come back."[31]

Her overall fragility was not helped by a remark Harry innocently reported making about her. Condé Nast had said something critical about the way she worked at *Vanity Fair,* and he had attempted to defend her by protesting she was a "genius without experience." Clare disregarded his hyperbole and heard only his belittlement of her professional credentials. She accused him of betrayal. "Et tu, Brute!" Her competitive spirit surged, fueled by resentment that Harry was "functioning so magnificently" in his publishing empire while she lay stalled in self-imposed exile.[32]

She began to read recent issues of *Time* and *Fortune* from cover to cover and sent him lengthy editorial critiques. His writers, she felt, dealt more effectively with foreign than domestic affairs. They were capable of witty and brilliant imagery, even in business pieces, but "minor poets"—a reference to Archibald MacLeish—were not convincing apologists for the American Dream. Nor did she like the personal slant of many of their pieces. For example, whenever WPA Director Harry Hopkins was mentioned, his dandruff was too. This amounted to "hitting above the collar."[33]

By the end of the month, Clare had had enough of hydrotherapy. She returned to Salzburg and on August 1 met up with little Ann, who had been traveling in Italy with her chaperone. The Festival season was under way, and the town was filling up with international society. Among them she recognized her old friend Rudolf Kommer, the Averell Harrimans, Otto Kahn, William Paley, and Harold Nicolson and his wife, Vita Sackville-West. "She wears large hats with tweed suits and has, definitely, a moustache."[34] Most other female visitors, including herself, affected Austria's native costume of full skirt and vest.

Kommer invited her to visit Max Reinhardt's nearby castle, "Leopoldskron," which was on a lake beneath the Venusberg. She accepted rather than lug her daughter round museums. When the choice came between self-cultivation and the cultivation of the rich, Clare usually opted for the latter. Yet as soon as she yielded, she disliked herself for doing so.

The first person she saw on arrival at Leopoldskron was Kommer, ebullient as always in *lederhosen*, embroidered waistcoat, and feathered cap. He gave her a tour of the castle—a little too baroque for her modern taste in its porcelain stoves, crystal chandeliers, and white and gold paneling—before taking her in to lunch with Princess Hohenlohe, a relative of the Kaiser, and Margot Asquith, widow of the former British prime minister. There was much talk about the upcoming Festival, but since Clare knew little about opera, she quickly became bored.[35]

Back in Salzburg she found it a strain to "play" without Harry. Everything around her seemed "such a footling comedy." Watching a group of socialites pandering to an aged mine owner in Badgastein, she had seen that they cared nothing for him personally, were even contemptuous of his philistinism. Yet they went on "burning the incense of their charm and intelligence at his gilded shrine. Why?"[36] Clare could have asked the same question of herself.

Disenchanted, she saw that the Festival was attended mainly by chic droves who came to Mozart's birthplace not to hear but to be seen hearing. This did not stop her taking her daughter to a five-hour performance of *Don Giovanni*. As their carriage drew up at the opera house, Ann, who had been reading *A Tale of Two Cities*, looked out at some overdressed theatergoers and yelled, "Down with the aristocrats!"[37]

While Clare moralized about the ethics of worshiping at the "gilded shrine," Lila Luce's lawyers were divesting Harry of almost $2 million in cash. This settlement, plus the New Jersey estate he had already sacrificed, reduced his paper assets to $5 million and, he told John Billings, "practically no cash." Even though *Time* and *Fortune* were profitable, *Architectural Forum* and *The March of Time* were still losing money. Harry informed Clare that he must immediately change his domestic base from New York to Connecticut, where there was no state income tax.[38]

Ann Austin, once again Clare's confidante, wrote to commiserate about Lila's delaying tactics and financial demands. She offered practical advice. If Clare could not become Harry's wife straightaway, she should become his mistress. "Don't wait, live and take and give your love. No matter what happens you will have had that."[39]

Feeling diminished in health as well as expectations, Clare was often tearful when she spoke to Harry on the telephone. But she obstinately refused to go home until the Reno divorce was final. That meant at least another month in Europe. She decided to spend a few days at the fashion shows in Paris before returning to the Riviera. As she paid her Salzburg hotel bill, the name Lila Luce leapt at her from the open register. For the past four days the two women in Harry's life had been under the same roof.[40]

Clare reached Villa San Gustin in mid-August to find roses, geraniums, and hydrangeas wilted. The bougainvillea had died. Everywhere she saw traces of Harry: scattered packs of cigarettes, piles of magazines, news clips, a thesaurus, Browning's "Andrea del Sarto," and some Kipling novels. His tennis racquet and eyeshade remained on the hall table. On the terrace was the wicker chair he had sat in at breakfast and the sofa with blue and gold pillows where he had dozed after lunch. His bed—"slept in so little"—lay still undisturbed.[41]

Her mind turned constantly now to their future life together. What would it be like when passion was spent, "in one, two, three years at most . . . Will we be greater friends than we were lovers?" What if they drifted apart even as friends?[42]

In the waning days of the month, she had a disturbing encounter with Maxine Elliott, the once-beautiful actress and lover of J. P. Morgan. Miss Elliott was living in Château L'Horizon at Golfe-Juan. She was now a gross, wrinkled, rouged old harridan with an ever-dangling cigarette. Vanity and purposelessness were written on her face. Clare found it difficult to look at her and not fear a similar fate.[43]

By early September she had shipped little Ann home to school and was ensconced—shades of Lila again—in the Hôtel George V in Paris. Spending money profligately, she began to assemble her trousseau. Harry had said he wanted her to come back as the best-dressed woman in America, and she took him at his word. She went to Vionnet, Lavenal, and Jean Lanvin for dresses, Laura Belin for lingerie, Hermès for scarves, Hertz for jewelry, Vuitton for handbags and luggage, Rose Descat for hats, Caron for perfume, and Elizabeth Arden for makeup.[44]

Her bills mounted to a staggering 127,605.75 francs, far beyond her pocket. Harry, in his current circumstances, could not be expected to pay them, so she placed her hopes on the limitless resources of Bernard Baruch. Her sixty-five-year-old father figure was back in Badgastein and agreed to come to Paris before she sailed.[45]

He wrote to say how much he was looking forward to seeing her. Thanks to the cure, he was now a changed man, with "no tummy, big biceps, full of pep—Oh boy." But he served notice that if she indeed married Henry Luce, their own three-year relationship must end. "The eagle never shares his mate with another." Loving her, he recalled, had not been painless. She had often said or written cruel things, and even accused him of trying to break her spirit. Judging from her recent letters, she had succeeded in breaking it herself.[46]

"I know how you are torn asunder by fears and doubts and misgivings," Baruch wrote. "I would and could comfort you but you hurt me so sometimes . . . that I am diffident." Then, sounding both conciliatory and valedictory, he went on with clumsy eloquence:

> Time and its brother age has [sic] been so cruel to us both. But we have wrested much from them, and there is so much left if but we used our heads. Don't say harsh . . . unfair things to me because I don't want to become bitter . . . I want it to be always a sweet sweet, not memory, but ever re-maining present . . . But Clare Clare Clare I want you to be happy. Will you be? You are now casting the die for both of us. I shall not be too mournful, blue whatever you decide . . .
>
> Get all of your plans and dresses arranged before my arrival. As regards those checks you can wait till I come and we can arrange to meet all your fears my little baby tigress. I

like you better as you came to me first dancing on the beams
and blinded me.[47]

He arrived as promised, paid her bills, and they spent their last few
hours together as eagle and mate. When she embarked on the *Ile de
France* in mid-September, there was a wire waiting. "Million thanks for
blissful days *bon voyage* good luck don't forget."[48]

Clare landed in New York to find Harry about to become a free man,
and she gave Helen Brown Norden the news of her November nuptials
over lunch. But her friend offered no effusive congratulations. "I always
thought you would marry someone old and wise and rich and famous,"
she said. They both knew who fitted that description.[49]

Tears came to Clare's eyes. She would have all the more reason to
cry when she found out that Helen and Bernie, who had met during the
recent "family emergency," were embarking on an affair of their own.

Before her summer in Europe, Clare had received a check for five
hundred dollars from the theatrical manager Al Woods. It represented his advance commitment to stage *Abide With Me* on Broadway.
Now production was under way. Baruch's nephew Donald, in association with a producer named Malcolm Pearson, had raised money,
John Hayden would direct, and P. Dodd Ackerman design the sets.
Clare was promptly corralled for rewrites of a work she had not
touched in a year.

She discussed some technical problems with Clifford Odets and
was gratified when he agreed to attend a rehearsal of her play. The intense, disheveled young Marxist had three hits on Broadway that year,
and critics were hailing him as heir to O'Neill, Chekhov, and Sean
O'Casey. His comments about *Abide With Me* have not survived, but
Clare kept a letter from him that pointed out her main creative problem: a "squirming dissatisfaction" with self. This neurosis, Odets wrote,
made her ambivalent in her attitude to the stage, that great aquarium
that revealed everything:

I have an idea about you: that you can write and that your head and heart are stocked with fine little fish which would look good swimming around in a play.

But! That all has to start with a usage of yourself and your own experience . . . Energy necessary? Sure, but every girl her own fine dynamo once she starts in reference to the real thing. What is wearying in life is never touching the real self . . .

The creator's challenge, he emphasized, was to confront human folly and mendacity. "Listen lady, when you have problems you bust right thru the middle of them, and if you are a writer you write smack thru the trouble instead of around it."[50]

This Clare found hard to do. Reluctant to be totally honest about her experiences, she was at the same time so self-obsessed that she was unable to write well about anyone or anything else. Frank Gilmore, president of the Actors Equity Association, felt she actually feared the more unpleasant aspects of *Abide With Me*: illegitimacy, alcoholism, abuse, infidelity, and murder. If she did not tackle them boldly, the play would fall into the no-man's-land between a comedy of manners and a tragedy.[51]

Clare tried to take both men's advice, changing Henry Marsden to a violent dipsomaniac and having his wife, Nan, become pregnant by the family doctor before asking for a divorce. But no matter how many alterations she made, the characters remained shallow, and the plot became increasingly far-fetched and sank deeper into the melodramatic mire.

To compensate, she tried to lighten the dialogue with epigrams aimed at the eternal male and female conflict. Some were trenchant ("A man's indictment of society is always an indictment of women"), some were cynical ("Of all the ties that bind, money is the last an intelligent woman should cut"). Most sounded like weak Oscar Wilde. "It's easier to marry the man you love, than to love the man you marry."[52]

Though nobody involved was entirely satisfied with the final script, *Abide With Me* opened at the Ritz Theatre on Thursday, November 21,

1935. Barbara Robbins played Nan Marsden opposite Earle Larimore as Henry. Cecilia Loftus was the mother, James Rennie the doctor, and Maria Ouspenskaya the old servant.

As act followed contrived act, Clare mistook the audience's polite clapping for approval. There was certainly no clear sign that her play would be a failure, not even when the old servant improbably undertook to do Nan's job of murdering Henry. Clare was in the wings as the final curtain came down, and she stepped out to take a bow when she believed, or imagined, the audience wanted to see her. To her humiliation the applause fell away and was replaced by booing.[53]

The critics were savage. "Is it ethical to dislike a play, because of the poisonous people who inhabit it?" queried Brooks Atkinson in *The New York Times*. "If not, it is at least human, for Mrs. Brokaw has not given them any dramatic, intellectual or social significance. *Abide With Me* is merely a gratuitous horror play . . . a literal portrait of people who are difficult to get on with in the theatre as well as at home."

Howard Barnes of the *New York Herald Tribune* complained about some "frenetic and rather ridiculous action" in the third act. He said he could forgive a neophyte slips in structure but not "sheer bad writing." The *New York American*'s Gilbert Gabriel was slightly more encouraging. "Her words are neatly strung, her semi-epigrams earnestly scrubbed, her sentiments sweetly perky . . . but an air of foolishness blows in at the open door."[54]

Meanwhile, at *Time*, John Billings agonized over what kind of notice would meet with his employer's approval. He diffidently sent the drama desk's first draft over to Luce, now quartered at the Pierre Hotel. Harry returned it with a note for the critic: "Show isn't that good. Write what you thought."[55]

Billings knew better than to obey this instruction to the letter. "Can we say it is rotten?" He tried to combine some adverse observations with "the proper degree of innocuousness." Rewrites went back and forth between publisher and editor, and final copy was not approved until 8:30 the night *Time* went to press.[56]

The anonymous notice, only two hundred words long, slyly pronounced *Abide With Me* "Manhattan's most gilded opening of the week." It used up as much space as possible recounting the plot, adding that all the characters had good reason to shoot the drunken husband. "In the middle of the last act someone does."[57]

Both Clare and Harry had put enough money into *Abide With Me* to support a week's run. Bernard Baruch was about to, but when told that Luce had come forward, he graciously allowed him "the priority position."[58] Since no other investors volunteered, the play was doomed to close after thirty-six performances.

Clare's future collaborator Alexander King blamed its failure on polite distaste for its subject matter. He believed she had been "damned less for having failed as a playwright than for having used the stage as an arena in which to bludgeon the ghosts of her own past."[59]

Over the years Clare tried to be philosophical about her devastating theatrical début. She said that "loud, derisive whoops and hollers" could be beneficial early in a dramatist's career. After the initial hurt, "no poisoned shaft has ever again any power to penetrate or inflame. It is the quickest way I know to acquire a spiritual elephant hide."[60]

At noon on Saturday, November 23, just two days after the première of *Abide With Me*, Clare Boothe Brokaw and Henry Luce were married at the First Congregational Church in Old Greenwich, Connecticut. The ceremony was private. Only the Austins, David Boothe, and Harry's younger brother Sheldon were present. No photographs were taken. Announcements were not even mailed until February 1936.

Some close friends were informed beforehand. Few wished the couple well. The Baruchs sent a co-signed, insincerely jocular wire: "When you carve the big turkey in the worlds you will conquer . . . save a little wish bone or drumstick for us." Bill Hale responded that he had been away in the country. "That freed you from the menace of a pious telegram." Nothing came from Mark Sullivan. Dr. Austin forwarded bills for flowers, organist, and sexton to Luce, asking for the check to be made out to him.[61]

Harry, whose divorce had gone unmentioned in *Time*, wrote a notice of his remarriage in the magazine's "Milestones" column on December 2. He listed the names of all Luce publications—"obviously to dwarf his wife's onetime connection with pee-wee *Vanity Fair*," remarked John Billings.[62]

The caustic managing editor was not thrilled when his boss invited him to lunch with the new Mrs. Luce. Nevertheless, he painstakingly recorded all the details.

She appeared: yellow hair, slim milky hands, no jewelry and a too-cultivated voice . . . Harry was the jealously attentive bridegroom. At table the talk began with me . . . Then it shifted to *Time*. Did *Time* cover everything? Could a good history be written from *Time*? An hour and a half's chatter that proved nothing—but gave me an uneasy feeling that Mrs. Luce was about to stick her delicate nose into *Time's* affairs.[63]

23

MOON-MINDED MAN

May there never be in my house a woman knowing more
than a woman ought to know. —EURIPIDES

Harry and Clare arrived in Cuba on Monday, December 2, to begin a two-month honeymoon. Grant Mason had offered them his staffed villa at Jaimanitas, so they took along little Ann and one of her friends. The girls would stay until school reopened early in the new year.

Low temperatures and persistent rain kept them indoors for most of the first three weeks. During the day they tried to keep warm by playing table tennis. In the evening they bundled up in the Masons' projection room to watch silent movies or sat reading in the stone-tiled, sunken living room.[1] At least there were plenty of books. Clare worked her way through "heavy stuff"—Cuban and Greek history, as well as Aristotle, Plato, Socrates, Voltaire, and Goethe. Despite the fact that she now had a permanent bedmate, she remained insomniac and wrote to thank Dr. Rosenbluth for his steady supply of "little pills."[2]

As Christmas approached the weather improved. Sunlit palms out-side lent incongruity to a fir tree in the living room, which Clare had hung with imitation snowballs. Feeling a need for exercise, the Luces patronized a nearby golf course, where Harry quickly learned that his wife had not spent five years married to an amateur champion for nothing. She soundly beat him on the links and discovered what his colleagues already knew: Henry Luce hated to lose. "His whole person-ality changed. He became angry." In the interest of domestic harmony, she decided never to swing a club with him again.[3]

Mr. and Mrs. Henry Luce on honeymoon,
Cuba, *1935–1936*

Instead they devoted most of their leisure time to the beach. But even in the sea, Clare's effortless athleticism overshadowed Harry. He soon began to miss his publishing routine and welcomed a visit from Ralph Ingersoll, now Time Inc.'s general manager. Ingersoll was, in Harry's opinion, the one man on the company payroll with "publisher potential," and as such worth only five thousand dollars less than the fifty thousand he paid himself. The two men had more in common than journalism and hair loss: they shared a roving eye. Although

Harry's was temporarily fixed on Clare, Ralph, whose wife had tuberculosis, had recently started an affair with Lillian Hellman.[4]

Ingersoll wanted to discuss a project of momentous import. He said he and Dan Longwell had been exploring the feasibility of a magazine devoted almost entirely to pictures and felt the time had come to produce one.

The proposition was not novel to Harry—even less so to Clare, listening silently as the two men talked. In 1933 Luce had asked a senior *Time* editor, John Martin, to prepare dummies for a heavily illustrated, high-circulation "weekly or fortnightly current events magazine." He explicitly wanted to aim it "at lowbrows." None of Martin's mock-ups had satisfied him, however, and the project was discontinued.[5]

Ingersoll proposed reviving it with himself as developer. He argued that improvements in coated stock had made a mass-market picture periodical commercially viable. He prophesied sales of as many as five million copies in three years.

Clare still said nothing. She was not sure how far she should insinuate her editorial expertise into Harry's affairs. He paced back and forth, characteristically frowning and rubbing an ear in concentration, struggling with his traditional belief that news is copy. Photographs alone were not substantial enough to hold the average reader. "You can't make them tell stories." Ingersoll disagreed, pointing out that illustrations were doing just that in *Fortune*, albeit on a small scale. Finally Luce conceded that Time Inc. was sound enough to risk a *succès d'estime*. Starting something from scratch again "could be fun."[6]

This was just the kind of creative challenge Clare lusted for. She felt she had priority on the idea. Five years before, in the spring of 1931, she had written a long memo to Condé Nast advising him to turn *Vanity Fair* into a picture weekly profuse with candid camera shots, patterned on the Parisian *Vu*. Alternatively, he could buy and adapt the old, ailing humor periodical *Life*.

> It [the new magazine] would . . . contain some of the editorial elements of *Time*, *Fortune*, and even *Vanity Fair*, plus its own special angle, which would be reporting . . . the most interesting and exciting news, in photographs, and interpreting it editorially through accompanying articles by capable writers and journalists . . . For "timely" reasons, of

course, it should remain mainly a picture book, but so edited
as to give the impression that it contained a great deal more
literary matter than it actually would.[7]

Nothing had come of these suggestions. Before her February 1934
departure as managing editor, Clare had submitted a list of "Last
Thoughts," raising the subject again. She tried to convince Nast that
his corporate solvency could best be assured by a "90% pictorial weekly
covering all phases of contemporary American life." She had great
faith "in the photographic formula" and warned that if he did not explore it, "somebody else will."[8]

Her admonition was somewhat disingenuous. She must have
known that John Martin, an occasional lunch companion whom she
once called "the green-eyed boy wonder of the publishing world," was
working on pictorial dummies for Time Inc. Now, as 1935 gave way to
1936, Clare saw the initiative passing to Ingersoll. The most she could
hope was that Harry would allow her to work in some capacity on his
as yet untitled venture. Enviously, she began to hear reports that Ralph
was optioning photographs from picture agencies and news organizations, recruiting star photographers, and predicting a revolution in "the
journalistic machinery of the world."[9]

Towards the end of January, the newlyweds rented a yacht for $2,500
and left Havana on a two-week Caribbean cruise. A storm blew up the
first night out. Clare, unable to think of eating, lay on deck watching
the stars lurch crazily. The cook was seasick too, but Harry, who seemed
to have an iron stomach, insisted on being served a formal, three-
course dinner.[10]

Before sailing, he had stocked up on European picture periodicals.
Clare recovered quickly enough to help clip them and pin experimental layouts to the walls.[11] It soon became obvious that she understood
page design as well as, if not better than, he did. This, coupled with her
superiority at golf and swimming, seems to have threatened his ego and
affected his sexual prowess.

They were making love in calmer seas when he was overcome by
what Clare later called "one of those curious failures of the flesh
which . . . became (*vis-à-vis* me) a permanent condition." Embarrassed

and dismayed, he pointed at the waning, watery moon. "It's a *lousy* moon. Maybe tomorrow night it will be clear, and I'll do better."

Too vain, even twenty-five years later, to accept her own possible share of the responsibility, Clare remembered the conflicted Harry as subject to lunar lapses—"a moon-minded man."[12]

In early February the Luces stopped off in the low country of South Carolina on their way home. They had heard from a real estate agent that there was a large property for sale outside Charleston for $150,000. Clare anticipated something like Howard Coffin's Sapelo, or Bernard Baruch's Hobcaw, lush with semi-tropical flora overlooking water.

During a twenty-five-mile boat voyage along the west branch of the Cooper River, the agent told them it was a former colonial rice and indigo plantation. Henry Laurens, president of the First Provincial Congress, had owned it in the late eighteenth century and named it "Mepkin," a local Indian word for "serene and lovely."[13]

Neither adjective seemed appropriate as they neared the estate in a freak sleet storm. Landing at the foot of a bluff, they climbed to the top and found no house, no garden, no lawn, only a dilapidated shooting lodge. Too cold to explore the rest of the 7,200 acres, Clare was about to leave when she found herself transfixed by clumps of ancient live oaks soaring towards the overcast sky. Girlhood memories of the Deep South came flooding back. "This is it," she said.[14]

On Monday, February 10, Harry returned to the Chrysler Building with forty-eight bottles of Cuban perfume for his female staff. John Billings, who had been in sole charge of *Time* for over two months, would have appreciated a bottle of something himself, but he received no more than a pat on the shoulder. Noting Harry's tan and general good health, he wrote in his diary, "Evidently his new wife agrees with him."[15]

Though the boss was in a carefree mood that first day, he soon annoyed the managing editor by scribbling on what had been considered finished copy. "Things went so pleasantly when Luce was away. Now that he is back, he feels he must complain and criticize." Billings blamed Clare for making Harry "utterly cold and impersonal . . . She's just a yellow-haired bitch who is spending his money like water."[16]

The couple's first Manhattan home could certainly be counted an extravagance at $7,300 a year. It was a fifteen-room duplex in the River House, at 435 East Fifty-second Street, furnished with French, English, and Italian antiques. At most Harry could use it three nights a week, since his tax situation still required that he maintain his principal residence in Greenwich, Connecticut.

Clare and Harry playing croquet
Photograph by Alfred Eisenstaedt, spring 1936

Clare was happy to accompany him out of town, since Greenwich was home territory to her. She was there one day when Harry called to say that Ingersoll and Longwell had invited them both to dinner at Voisin in the city. He suspected their purpose was to suggest offering her a place on the new magazine.

At the restaurant Clare quickly discovered that not only was Harry mistaken but their hosts had no intention of employing her in any capacity. On the contrary, they were determined she not get so much as her narrow foot in the door. Ingersoll made it clear over post-dinner drinks at the River House that something else was bothering him. "Harry, you have got to make up your mind whether you are going to go on being a great editor, or whether you are going to be on a perpetual honeymoon. When you edited *Time* you stayed in the office until ten and eleven o'clock every night. Now you catch the 5:10 back to the country . . . You cannot publish a great magazine with one hand tied behind your back."[17]

Clare, pale and tight-lipped, saw that her husband was struck dumb, and that she must speak for him. "Harry can publish a better magazine with one hand tied behind his back than you can publish with both of yours free." She then fled to her bedroom in tears. By the time Harry joined her, she had recovered her composure and objectivity. It would be better for everyone, she said, if she gave up all ambition for a job at Time Inc. and resumed her own career as a playwright.[18]

A few weeks later Clare left for the Greenbrier, where in three days she wrote the first draft of *The Women*.

If Harry had any remaining doubts about producing a pictorial magazine, they disappeared when he came upon a news photograph of twenty roasted elephants. It had been taken after a circus fire in Saratoga. This proved to his satisfaction that pictures can tell some stories better than words.[19] Inspired, he wrote a prospectus.

> To see life; to see the world, to eyewitness great events, to
> watch the faces of the poor and the gestures of the proud; to
> see strange things—machines, armies, multitudes, shadows
> in the jungle and on the moon; to see man's work—his
> paintings, towers and discoveries, to see things thousands of

miles away, things hidden behind walls and within rooms, things dangerous to come to; the women that men love and many children; to see and to take pleasure in seeing; to see and be amazed; to see and be instructed . . .[20]

On reading it Ingersoll circled Harry's third word and informed him, "That's your name."[21]

Unfortunately the title *Life* still belonged to the old humor magazine that Clare had urged Condé Nast to buy five years earlier. There was no danger of Nast doing so now. His financial problems had multiplied to such an extent that *Vanity Fair* had at last ceased publication and merged with *Vogue*.[22]

Henry Luce accordingly bought *Life's* name and subscription list for $92,000. He put Ingersoll and Longwell in charge of designing a final dummy, authorized Laura Hobson to prepare a promotion campaign, and installed his brother Sheldon as business manager. But he made no immediate move to fill the post of managing editor. Deferential to the sensibilities of his senior staff, Harry could not bring himself to do what he secretly desired: appoint Clare. When Ingersoll and Longwell failed to suggest her name, he deduced their unwillingness to see a third member of his family on the masthead and chose the dependable John Billings.[23]

Sour as ever, Billings was reluctant to move from *Time*. He prided himself on its immense success and resented having to hand it over to hard-drinking John Martin. More disturbing still was Martin's assessment that "the real boss of the new magazine" would be Clare Luce.[24]

As Harry's real-life drama unfolded, Clare polished and repolished her imaginary one. The first idea for *The Women* had come from a conversation she overheard in the ladies' room of the Morocco Club. Familiar voices at the washbasins were "dishing the dirt" about some married friends of hers. At the Greenbrier, venomous new lines took shape in her head. The lines grew into scenes, pouring out with phenomenal speed.[25]

One segment, at least, had a previous incarnation. In the fall of 1931, long before *The Sacred Cow* and *Abide With Me*, she had outlined a play for Gilbert Miller.

> It is a sort of American Grand Hotel—the hotel however
> being the Riverside Hotel at Reno, Nevada, and the charac-
> ters being about as baffled, noisy, worthless and drunken a
> lot as you ever saw disguised as ladies and gentlemen in an
> American play. Considering that it is all supposed to be
> quite tragic beneath the surface and is on top as superficial
> and rowdy as one can very well imagine, you can see that it
> is a topic which wants a great deal of writing.[26]

Clare broadened the scope of the embryonic hotel play and relocated most of the action. She experimented with several titles—"The
Girls," "The Ladies," and "Park Avenue"—before deciding on *The
Women*. In the final version gentlemen were eliminated, and the Reno
episode became merely the last scene in the second act. The need
for twelve sets and numerous costume changes for forty female characters meant that the script, if accepted, would be extremely costly to
stage.

Bernard Baruch persuaded Max Gordon, a producer friend, to take
a look at *The Women*, and Gordon was intrigued enough to ask George
Kaufman for a second opinion. Kaufman expressed enthusiasm, whereupon Gordon cannily suggested a collaboration to Clare. He said he
was going abroad for six weeks and would depend on her to see how far
Kaufman would cooperate. Perhaps sensing her reluctance, he added
that he was "determined to get the play on" after she had revised it.[27]

In June the Luces moved from Greenwich to a leased white clapboard
house on Sky Meadow Drive in Stamford, Connecticut.[28] Much of
Clare's reworking of *The Women* was done in its large garden. She did
not ask Kaufman for help, but on his return Gordon bought the script
anyway and on July 2 he announced plans for a fall production. His
contract with Clare, drawn up by the Leland Hayward Agency, gave
her only a $100 advance ($400 less than she had received for *Abide
With Me*) but guaranteed 5 percent of the first $5,000 of gross weekly
box-office receipts, rising to 10 percent of all grosses in excess of
$7,000. The subsidiary rights clause secured her 60 percent of any mo-
tion picture rights or radio royalties, and 50 percent of amateur performances.[29]

Awareness of the play's worth spread quickly through the Broadway community. An MGM script scout predicted that it would cause "a mad scramble" among picture companies. It was "flashy, hokey material and not too expertly written, but it is an unusually good set-up for the screen . . . The author, a New York society woman, has written of her sex with a knowing and cynical pen."[30]

On July 10 Gordon received a telegram from Moss Hart, saying that he greatly admired Clare's play. Not only that, "I would like to buy a piece of it." He said he had discussed it with Kaufman, who agreed that only slight rewriting would be necessary. As far as he was concerned, it was the most promising Broadway property in years.[31]

Five days later a telegram arrived from Kaufman, asking to see the revised Boothe script. "Much interested."[32]

Her creative urge temporarily satisfied, Clare turned her attention to a physical one. Since miscarrying in her first marriage, she had longed to have a son by a worthy father. At thirty-three she felt it was high time to conceive, but she seemed unable to do so. In early August a salpingogram test revealed that her fallopian tubes were closed—probably the result of a previous infection—and could not be reopened. Dr. Rosenbluth had the unenviable task of confirming that she could never again become pregnant.[33]

She appeared so saddened by this that the doctor suggested adopting a baby and told her how to go about it. Without even consulting Harry, she issued a peremptory order: "Proceed with the adoption business." On hearing the news, however, Harry objected, saying, "We have enough children." Clare gave way but did not put the idea entirely from her mind.[34]

Casting and rehearsals for *The Women* began in early fall. There were the usual frustrations inherent in any major Broadway production. But none seemed to faze Clare, who was generally willing to jettison her old lines for new ones. Soon everyone concerned with the play was in awe of her. She was always perfectly dressed, coiffed, manicured, ready to turn on her charm and show her cleverness. Moss Hart would never forget the sight of her revising her script in the most feminine of boudoirs, sporting a blue ribbon in her hair and an ermine bed jacket fastened with a diamond pin.[35]

Ilka Chase remembered her sweeping in late one night, when the cast, "in varying attitudes of despondency," was sitting on the bare and grubby stage. She was "on her way to a satin soirée . . . gowned by Hattie Carnegie, sabled by Jaeckel, and from her finger flashed one of Flato's larger ice cubes."[36]

The first issue of *Life* appeared on Thursday, November 19, 1936, with Margaret Bourke-White's monumental photograph of Fort Peck Dam on the cover. It was a strangely inert image for a magazine with such a title, but Harry had chosen it himself from the Time Inc. library. Within hours the first run of 466,000 copies sold out, and Billings had to go back to press. The creative staff was ecstatic, but Luce and his accountants turned somber. If future press runs were commensurate with this, production and distribution costs would soar while advertising rates, based on a projected 250,000 circulation, remained locked for a year. Paradoxically, Henry Luce had a financially threatening triumph on his hands.[37]

He later told his wife that *Life* "would not have happened" without the technical advice and inspirational ideas of "Clare-of-Cuba." But Ingersoll saw himself as its prime initiator. Expecting to be treated like a hero, he was mortified when Luce announced that henceforth *Life* was to be the proprietor's own "baby."[38]

By the time out-of-town tryouts of *The Women* began at Philadelphia's Forrest Theater on December 7, Max Gordon had wound himself up into a state of near hysteria over slow box-office sales. "The God-damned show has ruined me; the bastards won't come in."[39]

Tepid initial reviews did not improve his mood. "All the faults of a première were apparent," the *Evening Public Ledger* commented. "The editing was careless, the pace laggard and somewhere some one will have to lose a half hour of exposition." Yet there was "a caustic quality" to much of Clare's dialogue, and the cast was "top-notch." The *Philadel-*

phia Evening Bulletin said the play's fundamental weakness was that it did not create sympathy for any of the wronged women—"so catty, mean, selfish and despicable do they appear."[40]

Harry expressed loyal certainty that *The Women* would be "a smash hit." But Gordon felt there was crucial rewriting to be done. By good fortune Kaufman and Hart were in town with their own new play, *You Can't Take It with You.* Since both had put money into *The Women,* they willingly heeded Gordon's plea for assistance. Hart had seen as long ago as July that Clare had third act trouble—"the worst kind." He and Kaufman recommended changes in curtain lines and thought she should keep an encounter in the Haineses' kitchen that the producer wanted cut.[41]

The scene in question was a contrivance necessitated by Clare's determination not to have any men appear onstage. Her script called for a maid to recount to the Haineses' cook a conversation about divorce that she had overheard between her employers.

Gordon conceded that the scene, though awkward, served a necessary purpose, and it survived. But whispers had begun circulating that Kaufman and Hart were responsible for major adjustments. Margalo Gillmore saw them so frequently in the Philadelphia theater that she believed they were "writing a new last act every night." Clare herself freely admitted that Kaufman and Hart had labored in her suite until two o'clock one morning. "They put on a performance the like of which I've never seen. 'She should do this.' 'No she should do that.' They demonstrated how they wrote a play. Acted it out till I was so confused. Then they said it was fine as it was, and ended up contributing nothing."[42]

Nevertheless, Clare learned much about stagecraft from them and showed herself capable of working under pressure. At noon one day, after a late-night session, a haggard Kaufman was going down in his Philadelphia hotel elevator when Clare got on. Looking fresh in a beige dress and feathered hat, she smiled and waved her revised manuscript. "I'm just taking this to Max."[43]

A typed list of fifteen suggested amendments from Kaufman substantiates Clare's claim that his input was minor. Ten were of little consequence, but he elaborated on those he thought important.

The opening card scene, he wrote, "failed to climax." Moss Hart thought it was the ending itself, but Kaufman found fault in the "content." He suggested restaging it in such a way as to make the voices better heard. In the kitchen scene, he noted, only a couple of sentences needed reworking. And for the last scene he offered to write "a dummy," leaving Clare to "put in the good lines."[44]

The Women opened in New York on December 26 and was playing to capacity by the end of its fourth week. Gossip about it gained momentum in proportion to its success. George Jean Nathan, *Vanity Fair's* former theater critic, hinted in print that certain "Rialto play-fixers" had inserted "several rather shabby Broadway wisecracks" during the tryouts.[45]

After Clare's sale of her screen rights to Max Gordon Plays & Pictures Corporation for $125,000 (a decision she was to regret the rest of her life), skepticism became entrenched. In the fourth month the play broke attendance records for a non-musical Broadway production—over 162,000 seats sold for a take of $350,000. More printed copies of the text were bought than of any other show that season.[46] Audiences and readers alike marveled that a woman so young and relatively inexperienced could have penned such a lucrative hit.

In early March 1937, Harry felt impelled to quash all doubts of his wife's authorship by asking Walter Winchell to publish the facts. His letter to the columnist survives as the most immediate, and probably the most accurate summary of Kaufman and Hart's involvement in *The Women:*

> I was the first to see the first draft of the play . . . within three or four weeks of the time that Clare first outlined it to me . . . The first two acts of the play are substantially (and by substantially I mean almost line for line—and certainly scene for scene) as they were in the first draft. The third act was re-written once or twice before Mr. Kaufman saw any draft. And it was rewritten once or twice thereafter. But no one else ever touched typewriter on it—and the scheme of the last act, as well as all but perhaps *two* lines, were entirely hers. As a matter of fact, in the end, two out of the three scenes of the last act turned out to be substantially as they were in the *first* draft . . .

Hart and Kaufman were useful critics during rehearsals—Hart more than Kaufman I think. Characteristically, they would tell Clare that a certain curtain line was
weak—and a day later she would come up with one that
amused them. The total time they spent on the play outside
of watching two or three rehearsals (and I think Kaufman
only saw *one*) was perhaps four or six hours of general chatter. I do not believe that there are more than three lines in
the whole play that either Hart or Kaufman would even
admit indirect credit for in a court of law . . .

Why Hart and Kaufman don't make more vigorous de-
nials I don't know. Perhaps they think they wouldn't be
believed. But you *will* be believed . . . Ask Hart and Kaufman . . . Ask Bob Sinclair, the director. Ask Max Gordon.
Ask God.

"Obviously people envy Clare," he concluded, "because she's rich and
good looking and—something else besides. Perhaps they dislike her for
reasons good or bad. But it is certainly unfair to take from anyone the
credit for work done."[47]

Before mailing this to Winchell, Harry sent it to Clare. For some
reason she objected and scrawled across the top "never sent." Kaufman
had the last word, saying that if he had written *The Women*, "Why
should I sign it Clare Boothe?"[48]

When *The Women* broke its attendance record, Clare's intimates celebrated in various ways. Condé Nast gave a party at his Park Avenue
penthouse and invited his customary A list of actors, journalists, artists,
and socialites. Bernard Baruch boasted about getting Max Gordon to
produce the play and went to see it at least a dozen times. He bought
scores of tickets to keep up the numbers, giving them away to everyone
from politicians to elevator boys, and pointed out a tiny gold typewriter
on his watch chain that Clare had given him. Ann Austin, an avid the-
atergoer, glowed with maternal pride, and David offered to be his sister's agent.[49]

Controversy about the play's unprincipled characters and brittle
dialogue continued. Eleanor Roosevelt wrote in her syndicated column

"My Day" that she left a performance "longing for a little honest clean talk without any sham or pretense." John Billings reacted predictably. "I thought it was pretty unpleasant . . . Harry, I suspect, is very proud . . . If I were in his place I would be ashamed to have a wife who wrote so autobiographically."[50]

Though Moss Hart was pleased with the play's financial success, he expressed scant praise at the time. Thirteen years later, when *The Women* had become a perennial draw in theaters all over the world, he read it again, and wrote Clare a belated compliment.

> I was filled with an admiration for it that I must confess I didn't have at the time it was produced. It's a first rate job, and to my mind a highly under-rated play. It's a great deal more than just a slick, well-constructed play—it's a highly civilized and biting comment on the social manners and morals of our society, and women's place in it. I had no idea it was so good . . . I don't think you ever got the credit you deserved for it, and I just thought I'd write and tell you so.[51]

24

LUCES

THE MAGNIFICENT

An unsatisfied woman requires luxury.

—ANDRÉ MALRAUX

Tired yet exhilarated by their work on *The Women* and *Life*, both
Luces looked forward to a recuperative first stay at Mepkin in the
new year of 1937. They had completed its purchase the previous April
and hired an up-and-coming architect, Edward Durell Stone, to design
a house and three guest cottages in spare, modern style. These would
replace a mansion of 1906 vintage that they had originally overlooked
because of the dense shield of ancient live oaks surrounding it.

Forty laborers working in shifts had started to demolish the old
house and lay the foundations of the new. After restoring stables and
kennels, they installed power lines and piped in fresh water to replace
that from the pungent artesian wells. Clare, who was always fascinated
by construction sites, had taken some quick trips south to monitor
progress. Fighting off swarms of mosquitoes, she had sat under the trees
and watched haulage trucks struggle through the red mud of summer

rains. At last she was building her own estate and gratifying her "Napoleon complex."[1]

To serve as the main residence, appropriately named "Claremont," Stone built a two-story, whitewashed brick house with a central staircase. An arcade connected it to three air-conditioned guest cottages, eventually to be embellished with clumps of bamboo, pale wisteria, and lush fig vines. They were named "Strawberry," "Tartleberry," and "Washington," after other plantations along that stretch of riverbank. Each consisted of a porch, terrace, two bedrooms, and a sitting room facing the water. From all of them guests would be able to refresh their winter-weary eyes with views of lush swards of bright green ryegrass, herons stalking the old rice marshes, and hundreds of fuchsia azaleas, as well as Clare's favorite white camellias. Diners at Claremont could look out through huge picture windows and see the setting sun, a ball of flame in the dark Cooper River.[2]

Both house and cottages were furnished in the bland contemporary style that Clare preferred: chunky armchairs and couches, mirrored screens, small white desks, block-printed drapes, and wall-to-wall carpeting. Bowls of Cherokee roses perfumed the rooms, and sheets were lavender scented. Gladys Freeman, sister of the dead Donald and now working for a Manhattan interior design firm, helped create some fairly obvious color schemes, such as patriotic red, white, and blue wallpaper and blue linen upholstery with red piping for the Washington cottage. In Tartleberry she made a concession to the past with lace-hung twin four-posters and an antique dressing table.[3]

Mepkin's streamlined architecture displeased local gentry, and they began referring to it as "the Luce Filling Station." Nevertheless, Stone's initial residential design went on to win a silver medal at the 1937 exhibition of the New York Architectural League.[4]

The first of some two hundred names that would appear in Mepkin's guest book over the next decade were those of Harry's sister Elisabeth and her lawyer husband Maurice Moore. Beth had been skeptical of Clare at first. But during their January visit, she came to understand her brother's attraction to a woman who seemed to excel without effort at everything. Aside from Clare's obvious physical appeal, she was a men-

"Claremont," Mepkin Plantation, *late 1930s*

tal match for Harry, challenging his opinions and stimulating him more than his own obsequious employees.[5]

It soon became clear that the Luces did not have enough help to maintain multiple accommodations and 7,200 acres of land. Harry grumbled about local blacks preferring federal handouts to honest jobs. His wife, growing more conservative now that she had so much to conserve, sent a sarcastic wire to President Roosevelt, who had just addressed that same problem in his second inaugural.

Congratulations on your challenge to industry to reduce
budget a billion by taking people off relief rolls. Rushing in
to cooperate. Please tell me how to get seven able bodied
Negroes with families for light farm and house work on
plantation . . . Am willing to pay twenty percent over prevailing wage by yearly contract and provide Negroes with
new living quarters. Have been unable to get any help in
Charleston since purchase of plantation eight months ago
owing to Congress's relief legislation.[6]

Clare established a routine at Mepkin that would vary little over time.
Her breakfast consisted of golden popovers and coffee with thick, yellow cream from the dairy, generally eaten in bed. Afterwards she indulged the habit, begun while working on *The Women,* which was to
remain hers until death: to read and write, surrounded by pillows,
books, and papers, for about three hours before becoming involved in
the events of the day. Harry and her guests, meanwhile, might spend
their morning hunting duck or fishing for bass and trout in the private
lake. Lunch, announced by a gong, tended to be light: salads, shrimp in
curry sauce, and rice dishes. Tea, made by Clare herself, was an exotic,
frothy brew mixed in a blender with cloves and orange and lemon
juice. For visiting children she would concoct chocolate, strawberry,
and pineapple milk shakes.[7]

Later in the afternoon there was riding, or a four-hour buggy trip
around the perimeters of the property. After cocktails, dinner was served
at 7:30. It was a formal affair at a glass-topped table illuminated from
below—unflattering to aging faces. Clare, still smooth-skinned at thirty-
four, glowed impervious opposite Harry. She often dressed as a Southern
belle, in full-skirted, turquoise taffeta, with short, puffed sleeves, pearls or
lapis lazuli jewelry, and velvet bows in her hair. It was as though she saw
Mepkin as a theatrical setting, with herself at center stage.[8]

In fact she was thinking about writing a new play with a Southern
heroine, inspired by an encounter with George Cukor the year before.
The director had been in Charleston scouting talent for the role of
Scarlett O'Hara in *Gone With the Wind.* Clare saw comedy in his quest
and decided to dramatize a similar search for an ingenue to play in the
screen version of a Civil War novel. The idea was promising, but she
would not realize it fully for another eighteen months.[9]

As the predictable result of having a beautiful, talented wife, a thriving publishing empire, and a lavish, peripatetic way of life, Harry was subjected to ridicule by *Time*'s principal competitor. A six-page *New Yorker* profile by Wolcott Gibbs censured him for allowing his latest magazine to feature nude Russian peasants, the mating habits of the black widow spider, and the adulterous gallivantings of Mrs. Wallis Simpson. Behind such "incomprehensible" lapses of taste loomed the "ambitious, gimlet-eyed, Baby Tycoon Henry Robinson Luce."

Gibbs, a master parodist, imitated *Time*'s inverted sentence style, describing Harry as efficient, humorless, and chauvinistic.

> Prone he to wave aside pleasantries . . . To ladies full of gentle misinformation he is brusque, contradictory, hostile; says that his only hobby is "conversing with somebody who knows something," argues still that "names make news," that he would not hesitate to print a scandal involving his best friend . . . Yale standards are still reflected in much of his conduct; in indiscriminate admiration for bustling success, in strong regard for conventional morality, in honest passion for accuracy; physically in conservative, baggy clothes, white shirts with buttoned-down collars, solid-color ties.

The author also noted that although Time Inc. employed highly educated women as fact checkers, its "anti-feminist policy" barred them from editorial advancement. Luce himself, growing ever "colder, more certain, more dignified" in his editorial pronouncements, was openly cultivating "the Great." At thirty-eight he seemed to be already casting "a wistful eye on the White House."[10]

Harry got page proofs of the article before publication. He had cooperated in good faith and was incensed that *Time*'s own bitingly satirical methods had been used against him. He complained to Harold Ross, *The New Yorker*'s editor, but the latter—perhaps because he himself had been unflatteringly profiled by *Fortune*—refused to change a word. Ross wrote to say that Luce periodicals had a reputation for "crassness in description, for cruelty and scandal-mongering and insult." As for Harry, he was generally considered "mean," even "scurrilous" on occasion, and was therefore "in a hell of a position to ask anything."[11]

In early March, Harry, who went back and forth between Mepkin and New York as often as he could, brought his two sons down for a vacation. Henry Luce III, or "Hank," was nearly twelve years old, and Peter Paul almost eight. They were not strangers to Clare, having spent two weeks cruising the New England coast with her the previous summer. Hank, intelligent and sensitive, found his stepmother "poised," in contrast to his somewhat absentminded mother. He registered the "regal" way in which Clare told the maid to unpack his suitcase and how she liked monogrammed towels.[12]

Clare arranged so many activities at the plantation that both boys fell in love with it. They spent happy hours riding or hiking in longleaf pine groves and woods rich with cypress, magnolia, dogwood, and scarlet holly. In the afternoons, armed with .22 rifles, they hunted quail, dove, and wild turkey. At night they played monopoly or mah-jongg.[13]

Hank saw his father infrequently now and found him "stern and forbidding." Yet he yearned to know him better.

> I had a vague feeling of disappointment that Dad didn't seem to be more in my life. I admired his enormous abilities, his judgments about world affairs, his anecdotes about meeting Presidents . . . I longed to please him, but when I'd report my little accomplishments it was very hard for him to compliment. He didn't understand that things that were easy for him were a whole lot more difficult for others.[14]

His stepmother, selfish and manipulative as she could be with adults, had a sympathetic understanding of the fantasies of children and generously shared her time with them. They admired her inventiveness, curiosity, knowledge of unusual subjects, and wizardry at cards and jigsaw puzzles. Hank left Mepkin feeling that he had not one but two awe-inspiring parents, and diffidently signed the guest book "Henry Luce, Poor 3rd."[15]

Having entertained Harry's family, Clare prepared for a late March visit from Ann Austin, who for the past four months had been in Miami as usual with Joel Jacobs. Mother and daughter had not fully recaptured their old intimacy after Ann's midlife difficulties. Perhaps to compensate, Ann kept in touch by writing gossipy accounts of her resort life. Clare was therefore aware of her masquerade as a Northern lady of means, energetically working the Florida gambling and party circuit. "No one here knows me . . . Or I them," her mother confided. "So it's all even."[16]

Ann's letters were like herself: disconnected, charming, and frank. She wrote with sensuous delight of putting on soft silks and pearls and sallying forth to dine in "smart diggins." Invariably she outshone "the other old dowager buzzards . . . I fall over a Widner [sic], a Whitney or Vanderbilt on every hand." Yet with fatalistic cheerfulness she acknowledged, "I may look young but each day . . . I move a day closer to the rendezvous with death."[17]

She was unabashed about leaving her sedate husband in Connecticut while spending a third of the year in the sun with the easygoing Riggie. Except at the races, she saw little of Jacobs during the day. "At night I take people to dinner and he pays. Nice arrangement."[18]

Though the months in Florida satisfied her obsession to be accepted socially, Ann envied her daughter's intellectual life compared with her own mindless one. "The thing I resent is I made such bad use of youth. To Hell with muscle oil on the eyes wish I could get some for the brain."[19]

Their reunion at the plantation was affectionate. ("Felt cared for . . . as if I had come home," Ann recorded in her diary.) Inexplicably, however, she left after only two days. By the time Clare stopped off in Sound Beach to pick up little Ann a few weeks later, all daughterly warmth had vanished. "Oh God to think I would live to have one I've loved so dearly treat me like a stranger and walk out without the offer of help, or a kind word."[20]

Back in town for the spring season, Mr. and Mrs. Henry Luce settled into a new apartment at the Waldorf Towers. Clare, as restless married as single, had wanted to leave the River House within months of renting it, and preparations for this latest move had been under way since January.

Ann Austin with her granddaughter, *c. 1936*

The thirty-sixth-floor suite had a drawing room as large and sumptuous in its Art Deco appointments as any contemporary movie set.
Mirror and glass flashed on walls and cocktail tables, and thick, pale carpets covered the floors. Heavy crystal ornaments, silver lighters, and expensive backgammon sets lay scattered about, and there were enough
cut flowers to stock a small florist's shop.[21]

Harry, left to his own choice, would have been content with something more modest, so long as it was near Rockefeller Center, where
Time Inc. was soon to move. "Just like things convenient and sensible,"
he had told Wolcott Gibbs. But he now had another person's taste to

consider. "Whatever furniture and houses we buy in the future will be my wife's buying, not mine."[22]

There was neither resentment nor reproof in this remark. Harry let Clare know he was willing to live wherever she chose, so long as each place pleased "your eyes and your fingers when you touch it." But he reminded her that they had agreed not to give themselves social airs as "Luces the Magnificent." No matter how wealthy they became, he wrote, "I take it we have decided we will not play any such role—certainly not in New York." Surely all they needed was "an utterly charming pied-à-terre for a lady of great chique(?) and her husband," coupled with a large Connecticut house and Mepkin as a winter retreat. So far as dignity was concerned, "we have all we can grow up to in our live-oaks." The less they tried to impress "with foyers and footmen," the better.[23]

But Clare, ever more enamored of luxury, intended to live like the movie star she had fantasized about becoming at age twelve. In the first three years of her marriage to Henry Luce, she would occupy no fewer than four apartments and five houses.

Her acute need to be perceived as stylish extended beyond herself and her surroundings to Harry. Gibbs's derogatory statements in *The New Yorker* rankled. She suspected that her husband affected a sloppy appearance, despite the services of a valet. His trousers were often wrinkled, his shirts yellowing and frayed, his fedora battered, and his panama wilted. Sometimes he left for work in odd socks, or one black and one brown shoe. He would walk along the street, hat pulled low over his brow, staring at the pavement.[24]

Clare gave him a sleek platinum watch, but Harry ignored it in favor of an old-fashioned one of his father's. The only other jewelry he wore, on the little finger of his right hand, was her wedding gift: a sapphire ring carved with the Luce family crest, already cracked from emphatic fist-pounding. She decided to take him sartorially in hand and steered him towards an exclusive tailor. Harry's ill-cut suits gave way to elegant double-breasteds, which so enhanced his tall, lean frame that he was soon named one of the best-dressed men in America.[25] Ironically, Clare had to wait a while longer to achieve similar distinction.

Having conquered Broadway with *The Women*, she now yielded to the blandishments of Hollywood. Norman Krasna, the writer-producer, asked her if she would like to adapt his story "Turnover" for Metro-Goldwyn-Mayer, at a salary of two thousand dollars a week. Clare replied that she would be crossing the country in May, en route to a Hawaii vacation, and would stop off in Los Angeles for consultations.[26]

Traveling in advance of Harry, she arrived in Southern California with little Ann on May 17, 1937. Almost immediately after checking into the Beverly Wilshire Hotel, she discovered that the movie industry was as interested in her looks as in her talent. Darryl Zanuck, vice

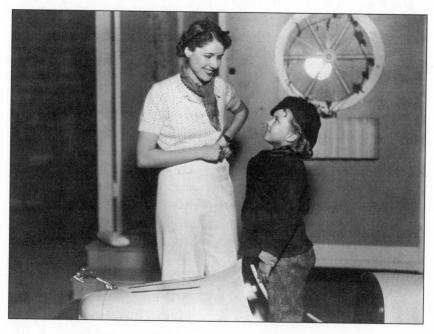

Clare in Hollywood with Shirley Temple, *1937*

president of Twentieth Century–Fox, invited her to take a screen test. This opened such intoxicating new vistas of fame and possible stardom that she felt she had to get Harry's approval. He proudly wired her: "You are unforgettable . . . be afraid of nothing."[27]

Even though he had agreed to spend six weeks in Hawaii, Luce volunteered to stay with her in California for a further three if she won a movie role. This gesture of self-exile from his beloved magazines showed how starved he was for her company after the long Mepkin months. Should she now become a bicoastal creature of stage and screen, Harry must compromise his own career or see even less of her. In a post-departure letter, Clare had spoken ominously though vaguely of "renunciation" and "something having to go." He wired back begging her to remember how blessed they already were and how careful they must be of their privileges. "Oh darling, we have got it—the chance to ride to glory."[28]

Brooding and perplexed, Harry stopped over in Chicago for a dinner with local Time Inc. employees at the Blackstone Hotel. Ralph Ingersoll joined him in his room for a nightcap.

"I brought you here to tell you that when I go away tomorrow I may never be back," Harry began in an almost angry voice. He said that love for his wife meant more to him than the company he had founded. "If I have to choose between them, I will choose Clare."

After this outburst, he talked most of the night. Ingersoll sensed a tortured need to confess. There was "an unrealized component" in his marriage, Luce said, that had to be taken care of. Since Clare was all any man could desire, shortcomings in their relationship could only be blamed on him. His commitment to her was "imperfect and must be purified" or his life would amount to nothing. He should dedicate himself to "breaking through to total oneness" with her.

Harry admitted to previous failures in religion and creativity. His spiritual odyssey had been diverted towards a place in the pantheon of the powerful, and he had long since given up an ambition to write, realizing he would never be able "to make words sing." Now he had found a new challenge in love. "I do not know how I am going to fulfill it, but only know that I have to . . . and to hell with Time Incorporated!"[29]

Like a priest searching for self-abnegation in God, he wanted to forge a holy bond with Clare.

In spite of Harry's encouragement, and the efforts of the studio makeup department, Clare did no better in front of a movie camera now than she had in *Heart of a Waif* twenty-two years before. Nor did her story conferences with Norman Krasna go well. She had no sympathy for his female protagonist, who, trapped in a dead marriage, timidly asked for separation rather than divorce.[30] After three days she lost interest and set sail on the SS *Malola* for Hawaii.

She had, however, so captivated Krasna that follow-up entreaties from him tracked her across the Pacific. He cabled a mock threat to kill himself over his inability to persuade her to do the script.[31]

To satisfy his wife's need for sun and sea, as well as real estate, Harry undertook to find her a "little palace by the waters of Hawaii" that they could use for future vacations. While he went looking, she hired a handsome surfing instructor. No sooner had she mastered, with her usual quickness, the difficult art of manipulating a board in high seas, than she set herself to riding Waikiki's notorious Queen breakers. "It's a dangerous business," she acknowledged. "If you miss the wave, you are likely to be 'boiled' in the surf, and dragged under." Three or four people died each year in the attempt, but she did it twice. Afterwards she wondered why. "No one expected it of me, nothing was proved by it. But it was what I wanted to do."[32]

Harry found no suitable Hawaiian "palace" on Oahu. Nor would he try again for another thirty years—by then, sadly, too late for him. In the meantime, the "total oneness" he sought with Clare failed to mate-

Clare with surfing instructor, Waikiki, *June 1937*

rialize. Apparently their airing of the "renunciation" question was inconclusive. Brought to the test, neither was prepared to give up anything. Both wanted to explore and experience all their own lives offered. Clare was alarmed by Harry's expressed need to save his soul in her. She realized he had placed her on an impossibly high pedestal and now wanted to deify her. If she became a Madonna in his eyes, she feared with good reason that his Calvinistic conscience might put her sexually out of bounds.

Intimates sensed their sudden unhappiness across thousands of miles. Bernard Baruch was struck by how "disconsolate" Clare sounded during a long-distance call, and David Boothe warned her of the erosive effects of marital fights. When they returned to New York in late July, Ralph Ingersoll looked carefully for signs of change in Harry—"some little hint that he had fulfilled himself"—but saw nothing. The Chicago soul-searching might never have happened. Clare was "briskly anecdotal" over dinner, saying that Harry had "almost mastered" the art of surfing, and that she was glad to be back in Manhattan after the insularity of Hawaii. In their suntanned complacency, the Luces seemed to Ingersoll "almost middle-aged."[33]

In September 1937, *The Women*, still a Broadway hit, began a cross-country tour that would last a year and earn Clare an extra fortune. This was encouragement enough for her to start work on her satire of a Hollywood talent search. But first she had to see Ann settled at Foxcroft School in Middleburg, Virginia. Academically the girl was well prepared for the switch from Rosemary Hall, but emotionally it required painful adjustments. She would no longer be near her beloved grandmother and "Grumpy" Austin, not to mention "Uncle David" and the Manhattan movie jaunts they both enjoyed. Moreover, she must now associate and compete with girls from the most prominent families in the country.

At thirteen Ann Brokaw was over five feet, six inches tall and weighed about 120 pounds. She had a plain, angular face, fine skin, deep blue eyes, and thick chestnut hair. With adolescent sensitivity, she lamented her big nose and braced teeth, and contrasted her large-knuckled hands with Clare's long, slender ones. Shy and melancholic, Ann knew she had "none of mother's versatility or brains."[34]

Having deposited her daughter at Foxcroft, Clare looked forward to a quiet literary sojourn at Mepkin. She was traveling there in mid-November when a special-delivery letter from Harry pursued her. He had written it on the second anniversary of their marriage but touchingly and cryptically dated it "Anno IV." This signified that for him their real intimacy had begun at the Starlight Roof on December 9, 1934. There was no mention of their recent difficulties.

> I am so excited about you that I am willing to forget these last 1,000 days—ready to lock them carefully in a great diamond-studded vault, to be brought out again and blissfully remembered only when the future comes to a dead stop and all my treasure is this great store of glittering days . . . Darling, darling, I love you. No woman who ever wore silk stockings pulled taut by strange devices to a girdle was ever so immaculate *and* such delicious flesh. And no matter how often I may observe your face, I shall never catch the lightning trick by which it shifts from brilliant theatrical beauty to the heart-shattering beauty of tender and companionable affection . . . Sure I love you for yourself—but that's just the trouble, I don't just happen to know it, that self of yours—I love it. It causes me infinite amusement, for example, but then, half the time, instead of just having a good laugh, my only desire is to throw my arms around you, to pick you off the floor, squeeze you and tell you you're the sweetest bundle of baby God ever sent into a nursery. Or, perversely, in a great gathering of people, that same self of yours will make me bow inwardly with admiration.[35]

Little Ann came down to Mepkin for her Christmas vacation. Then, on New Year's Day, 1938, Clare received a devastating message from her stepfather. Ann Austin, wintering as usual in Florida, had just been killed in a train-auto crash outside Miami. Joel Jacobs was comatose in Jackson Memorial Hospital with a fractured skull.[36]

Clare and Harry flew to Florida that night and met David Boothe there next morning. Police informed them that Ann had been driving her Buick sedan along South Dixie Highway at 6:45 P.M., on her way back to the Columbus Hotel from Tropical Park racetrack. At the Seventeenth Avenue railroad crossing, she appeared to have accelerated past several stationary vehicles, straight into the path of an oncoming train. Her action seemed almost deliberate, given that the whistling locomotive, traveling at about forty miles an hour, was in unobstructed view.

Both motorists had been thrown clear of the wreckage and lay immobile. A Catholic passerby knelt beside Ann and prayed for her, but by the time medical help came she had died from a broken back and internal ruptures. She was fifty-five years old.

Her left foot, severed at the ankle, was found some distance away. An onlooker recalled seeing an unidentified man pick up her purse and run off—in understandable haste, since the bag contained $27,000 worth of jewelry—two diamond and sapphire bracelets, a diamond and sapphire ring, and a diamond brooch. Ann had worn them the night before to a party and would have returned them to the hotel safe but for the absence of a clerk. Neither jewels nor thief were ever traced.

Joel Jacobs died on Monday evening, January 3. He was nearly seventy. By then Clare had arrived in New York with her mother's body. Three days later family and friends gathered at Campbell Funeral Chapel on Broadway at Sixty-sixth Street. The service was conducted by the same clergyman who had married the Austins almost sixteen years before. Afterwards Ann's body was cremated and her ashes taken to Strawberry Cemetery, not far from Mepkin.[37]

Clare and David were publicly quiet about their bereavement (the latter, enraged by Ann's vampishness, had once expressed a private wish to "piss on Mother's grave"). To one bystander Dr. Austin looked "like a soul in torment." Ann Brokaw was inconsolable. She had probably spent more time with her namesake than with Clare, her father, her stepfather, her stepmother, and her half sister combined. "Dear Granny" had chosen her clothes, seen that she got a pretty haircut, housed and amused her on weekends away from school. "How I loved her," she mourned in her diary. "I hope I shall grow to be much like she was."[38]

Clare's chief emotion over her mother's premature death was guilt. She felt she had "let her down" during periods of illness and unhappiness. Since her divorce from George Brokaw, and her vow not to live "for anybody but myself from now on," she had gradually—and now permanently—lost touch with the only person who could forgive whatever she might say or do.

"When one's mother dies," she wrote many years later, "one suddenly ceases to be a *child*. The structure of childhood . . . collapses, and in that hour adulthood, with all its responsibilities really begins."[39]

Ann died intestate, leaving a $17,000 mortgage and only $2,250 in cash after inheritance taxes. Evidently the $500 a month that Joel Ja-

Ann Clare Austin
1882–1938

cobs allowed her, supplemented in the last year by a further $200 from Clare, had not been enough to satisfy her extravagant habits and gambling debts.[40]

Jacobs, in death, took unexpected revenge on his companion of twenty-three years, who had refused to marry him because of his race and religion. He had always led Ann and Dr. Austin to believe that he intended to bequeath them the bulk of his $5 million fortune. But in a will only two years old, he settled everything on immediate relatives, an attorney, and various Jewish philanthropies.[41]

One Connecticut obituary further upset the grieving doctor by stating that Ann had been "divorced" from her first husband. He placed a correction in the *Greenwich Times*, pointing out that the deceased was in fact "the widow of Mr. Boothe." Thus he unwittingly perpetuated his wife's most long-standing lie about her past.[42]

Ann Clare Austin's diaries and letters reveal a romantic, spunky, but ultimately sad woman. In William Franklin Boothe she had found a sensual lover whose cerebral preoccupations, musical pursuits, and financial difficulties had driven her away after twelve years of wavering loyalty. In Dr. Austin she had married a fine, professional, but undemonstrative man, who cared nothing for the material things that mattered so much to her and who was aloof to the point of neglect.

Aging, she had come to see her dual existence with him in the North and Jacobs in the South as the only game available, and she had played it to the end. A few weeks before her death, she claimed to have found at last, in Miami, the freedom to be herself. And that self was, for all her flirtations with high society, fundamentally simple and joyous.

> The social register never did anything for me but put my name on a lot of mailing lists. I've bobbed my hair—nothing more to let down—I've painted my toe nails a bright hue, burned my body a gorgeous tan, and am now enjoying the last gasp . . . I know just what I want out of life . . . my pearls large and my hips small.[43]

25

KISS THE BOYS GOOD-BYE

The only thing necessary for the triumph of evil is that
good men do nothing. —EDMUND BURKE

In the days immediately after Ann Austin's funeral, Clare revised her own will. She also wrote an overwrought letter addressed to Harry and instructed her lawyer to deliver it within twelve hours should she die first.

"How many million times have I told you I love you?" she rhetorically asked. "Let me tell you again . . . I love you, love you, love you, beyond the gates of death itself. If there is another life, I am in it now, still adoring, worshiping, idolizing my little China Boy . . . Having you, and belonging to you, the joy of your arms . . . the honor of your name were my great fortune. You were my first true love and you are my last."[1]

This effusion seems more an indulgence in literary theatrics than real emotion. Clare was again casting herself at the center of an imagined drama, perhaps as a stimulus to begin her long-delayed new play. At last she had a title, *Kiss the Boys Good-bye*, a phrase that had caught her fancy in some recent discussion of U.S. military involvement overseas.[2] It would also do double duty, in her plot, as the name of both the Civil War novel and screenplay in search of a star.

Clare conceived as her leading character a Georgia senator's daughter, Cindy Lou Bethany, whose initials were an anagram of her own. The first act called for Cindy Lou to journey north to a fashionable Connecticut house party, in which unlikely surroundings she would audition for the movie role of "Velvet O'Toole." There Clare's parody of the hunt for Scarlett O'Hara became more elaborate. Cindy Lou turned out to be a Southern reactionary, and more than a match for the big-city liberals who wanted to hire and publicize her. These featured a duplicitous movie director, a philandering producer, a columnist with socialist proclivities, and a polo-playing WASP "born with a silver bit in his teeth."[3]

Clare grandiosely told *The New York Times* that *Kiss the Boys Goodbye* was meant to be a political allegory about the South's "highly-matured form of Fascism with which America has lived more or less peacefully for seventy-five years." Not content with developing this promising theme, she set out to satirize Cindy Lou's snobbish antagonists, torn between commercial interest and dismay. They were the so-called Smart Set she knew so well, the "cocktail sages" who had bored her at parties over the years with their *arriviste* sophistication. As such they could not prevail against a Southern belle whose spunky self-assurance came from her privileged, parochial background.[4]

For all Clare's ambitions, her draft lacked political weight and was more farce than allegory. Although it was destined to be her second Broadway success, it would always be seen as derivative of the casting crisis for *Gone With the Wind*. Nevertheless, she created a shrewd and lively ingenue. Whereas Mary Haines in *The Women* had been saccharine and sanctimonious, Cindy Lou was capable of butting media men in the stomach and shooting sexual predators with her own small pistol. But at the end, in an excess of bourgeois sentimentality, Clare had her turn down a seven-year Hollywood contract in favor of marriage to the polo player and a chance to be "the mother of famous sons."[5]

Elsewhere the dialogue and stage directions of *Kiss the Boys Goodbye* display some sly humor. Clare included in her cast a pompous publisher who kept a Southern plantation just for duck hunting, as well as thinly veiled caricatures of the columnist Heywood Broun and the millionaire John Hay Whitney. There were flashes too of her own spoken wit, as when the womanizing producer claimed his movie would "lay the ghost of the Civil War" and a female character cracked, "That's the only thing in skirts *you* haven't tried."[6]

The first visitors to interrupt Clare's creative seclusion at Mepkin were Helen Brown Norden and Irwin Shaw. Clare had first met the twenty-three-year-old Shaw in 1936, just after publication of his acclaimed antiwar play *Bury the Dead*. Envious of Helen's affair with him, she had made advances herself, ostentatiously studying a copy of his script and grilling him about his work and aims. But Shaw, having heard of her earlier reputation for "playing the field," had not responded, and he warned Helen that she was not to be trusted.[7]

This scruple did not prevent either of them from enjoying her Southern hospitality in 1938. They arrived on January 17 with what they thought was momentous news, having heard over breakfast on the train that Bernard Baruch's wife had just died. Clare, however, already knew.

She received them in the sitting room, her back to the picture window. Without even a greeting, she stared at Helen and said, "Why don't *you* marry him, Brownie?"[8] There was sadness as well as irony in her voice. Baruch was finally available, and she was not. Timing, as well as age disparity, had combined to thwart them.

After this icy start, the rest of the week passed pleasantly. Shaw was impressed in spite of himself by Clare's wit and intelligence, as well as by her tomboyish enthusiasm for masculine sports. On the range she displayed unerring marksmanship, and *sang-froid* in wringing birds' necks. He observed that she "ran" Harry and that, for all her delicate beauty, Clare Boothe Luce was "feminine as a meat axe."[9]

Clare could certainly be as cutting in speech as in her written dialogue. Harry, who lacked humor, often felt the sting of her sarcasm without the balm of being able to laugh at himself. He would try to articulate his feelings on paper, as when he wrote querulously that he hoped their marriage would be "happier" than the Baruchs' had been. So far he had no complaints—"except sometimes when you have been really too cruel!"[10]

Harry did not elaborate on the nature of Clare's cruelty. But while she luxuriated in Mepkin's sociable warmth all winter, he had to endure bachelor weeknights in New York and silent weekends in Con-

Clare shooting at Mepkin

necticut. "Being mostly alone all day always has a slightly strange effect on me," he confessed. "I think you are way ahead of me both in the art of companionship and of solitude . . . being alone makes me a little frightened."[11]

This fear drove him to make frequent, tiring journeys south to spend a mere forty-eight hours in his wife's company. When he arrived, he usually found her surrounded by guests. The queen had to have her court, whether the king was in residence or not.

In early May, Luce and his staff took over the top seven floors of Rocke-feller Center's newest skyscraper, just off Fifth Avenue on West Forty-ninth Street. The rent, in what at once became known as the Time-Life Building, was an astronomical $220,000 a year. Harry moved into a du-plex at the summit, overlooking the skating rink and the Hudson River. John Billings called it a suite "fit for Il Duce" and theorized that success had spoiled "the shy simple fellow I first knew."[12]

Perhaps in compensation, Harry downgraded his title from presi-dent to editorial director before moving in. He said he was tired of both corporate politics and worrying over sales figures. "I have had so damned much of it . . . From now on I intend to be a journalist."[13]

Luce was sincere in protesting that he did not really care for total administrative and budgetary control. Nor was he luxury loving. Hav-ing spent a couple of years trying to enjoy the baronial lifestyle his ac-quisitive wife preferred, he was reverting to evangelistic type. His main quest, as Hedley Donovan later remarked, was "discovering everything he could about everything that mattered, and sharing it with the widest possible audiences." It was as a reporter, therefore, that on May 11 he sailed with Clare for a fact-gathering tour of Europe. In his baggage on the *Queen Mary* was a copy of Adolf Hitler's *Mein Kampf*.[14]

Eight weeks had passed since the Führer had annexed Austria, and Czechoslovakia was now apprehensively mobilizing to protect itself. Always more curious than his fellow press lords, Harry wanted to learn at first hand how European statesmen, diplomats, and intellectuals in-tended to deal with Nazi imperialism. Among those on his schedule of contacts in Britain were the publishers Brendan Bracken and Lord Beaverbrook, Harold Nicolson, M.P., and the new American ambas-sador, Joseph P. Kennedy.[15]

Clare had her own, less political agenda in joining him. Max Gor-don had opened negotiations with London promoters to stage *The Women* in the West End, but there were fears that her risqué script might run afoul of the British censor. She hoped to persuade the Lord Chamberlain's Office to permit its production with only token cuts. That done, she would spend the remaining weeks cultivating as wide a European acquaintance as possible.

During the crossing she found no one "with any claim to fame" to talk to except Alexander Kerensky, Russia's pre-Bolshevik prime minister. But her luck was soon to change. On May 17, the day after arriving at Claridges Hotel, she accompanied Harry to Rose Kennedy's first official dinner. During the course of the evening she not only won the libidinous interest of the Ambassador but captivated Lord Halifax, the British Foreign Secretary, Oliver Stanley, President of the Board of Trade, and Count Dino Grandi, Benito Mussolini's envoy to London.[16]

With the same guile that had prompted her to send herself ostentatious deliveries of flowers at *Vanity Fair*, she arranged an attention-getting device at the embassy to establish her professional separateness from Henry Luce. A cable from Max Gordon arrived, addressed to her "c/o Joseph Kennedy," saying that he had arranged with Jack Buchanan to produce *The Women* "subject to censors."[17]

Three days later, she heard directly from the Lord Chamberlain. He found particularly objectionable the hospital scene in Act II where Edith drops cigarette ash on her newborn child while nursing. Unless it was cut, *The Women* would be refused a license.[18]

Clare fought back in the British press. She told the *News-Chronicle* that what really offended His Lordship was her refusal to romanticize maternity. "The woman treats childbirth neither as a tragedy nor as a blessing, but just as one long bore." Edith felt so indifferent about breast feeding that she whiled away the time smoking. Like the other thirty-nine characters in the play, "she is a portrait from contemporary Manhattan life." If most of them came across as "touchy, spineless and self-centered," that was typical. *The Women* was "inspired by a definite moral conviction," she stated, without elaboration. What was more, it had already been produced in Stockholm, Budapest, Prague, and Vienna.[19]

In addition to trumpeting the censorship issue—a sure way of stimulating audience interest—Clare used Beaverbrook's *Daily Express* to publicize the gossipy and voyeuristic aspects of her play. Looking like "sugar and spice" in a frilly veil tied over a scarlet hat, and speaking in a soft, husky voice, she remarked that its catty characters destroyed each other with "poison tongues." This was a feminine trait not only in New York but throughout the world. "Whenever a woman walks out of a roomful of other women, she expects uncomplimentary comments to follow her."[20]

Finally, Clare agreed to do what milord wanted, clearing the way for *The Women* to be mounted during the 1938–39 season.

Fleet Street was struck by Harry's dynamism, and by his wife's beauty and clarity of mind. The *Daily Mirror* and the *Bystander* speculated that he was being fawned over by peers and statesmen as a future presidential possibility. The BBC's embryonic television network tried to interview them both on fatuous topics such as "Are British women smart?" and "What is happening in the United States that Britain doesn't know about?" They declined, choosing instead to leave for Paris and a dinner on May 28 in honor of the Duke and Duchess of Windsor.[21]

The Duke, an admirer of the Third Reich's domestic policies, had recently ruffled British and American opinion by visiting Hitler. Harry had no plans to meet the Führer but on the basis of present evidence was no more disposed than Edward to condemn National Socialism outright.

Clare was competitively interested in meeting the middle-aged divorcée who, in addition to seducing a king from his throne, had become *Time*'s first Woman of the Year (in 1936). Wallis Warfield Simpson was clearly not hampered by being American, and unusually plain. Her capture of the Prince was no less improbable than Ann Austin's long-ago fantasy at the Greenbrier that Clare might have done the same. In any case, the two women liked each other well enough to strike up a friendship that would endure over the years.

The Luces next flew to Berlin. Clare found the Hotel Adlon much changed since the inflationary period of the Weimar Republic, when, as a twenty-year-old, she had spent far-stretching dollars on its luxurious rooms and restaurants. Now the menus were limited, the bathroom taps stiff, the water cloudy, and the toilet paper primitive. Germany's resources were evidently devoted to other things.[22]

Over tea at the British Embassy, the tweed-suited Ambassador, Sir Nevile Henderson, told the Luces that the Reich was in the grip of a disturbed personality. During several recent audiences, Hitler had "flown into a violent temper" with him. This had not prevented the Embassy from registering a formal protest at the current massing of German troops along the Czech border.

During the next few days Harry, looking around him with characteristic American positivism, saw little evidence of tyranny. There were few uniforms in the streets, he noted in a six-thousand-word account of his travels. If Berlin's citizens were enslaved, "their chains are not visible." Every German seemed to own a motorcycle and was at liberty to go where he chose.

A more direct encounter with Nazism came at Bayreuth, when he read a newspaper, published by the notorious Julius Streicher, "entirely devoted to attacking Jews." Discussing it with his chauffeur, Harry found that the man, although not a party member, "accepted anti-Semitism as, at least, a necessary evil in the rebuilding of Germany under the Third Reich." At Nuremberg he and Clare saw the vast Zeppelin Field, used for annual spectacular Nazi rallies, and in Munich several monumental structures designed for Hitler's glorification. Harry was more impressed by the city's fifteen thriving theaters. "Any idea that the Nazis have put the kibosh on culture is ridiculous."

Other aspects of Fascism struck him as commendable. Hitler had "suspended the class system." The average German was free to "grumble into his beer about local bureaucrats," and there had been no state attempt to "soak the rich." Two successful Berlin businessmen half-convinced Harry that National Socialism "works mightily for the masses, however distasteful it may be to them personally in many ways."

Clare, with her greater perceptiveness and pessimism, was more disturbed by what she saw and heard. She began to develop a theory, later expounded in the introduction to *Kiss the Boys Good-bye*, that Nazism owed something to the American experience. Hitler's Brown Shirts had their precedents in the White Shirts of the Ku Klux Klan:

> The carpet-bagger-inspired Communism of the Negro was ruthlessly and passionately stamped out [after Reconstruction] even as the "Jew-inspired" Communism of the laborer in Germany has been. Indeed the swastika never burns more brightly or savagely in the Schwarzwald than the Fiery Cross of the Klan once burned in the bayous and cypress swamps of Dixie. To be sure, practically all of the more spectacular outward, and most of the more vicious inward, manifestations of this pyrotechnic night-shift *Kultur* have long since

passed overseas, where it is not for me to prophesy, but merely to hope, they will stay.[23]

The Luces drove south from Munich on June 5, along the same *autobahn* German troops had taken in the *Anschluss*. They made one detour to see Hitler's mountain retreat at Berchtesgaden before crossing into Austria. While in Vienna, Clare tried without success to retrieve some hundreds of dollars in royalties owed her by the local producer of *The Women*. But because of Nazi currency restrictions, she had to settle for a Contax camera instead. "Germany intends to take all and give nothing," Harry concluded as they flew on to Czechoslovakia.

The stolid, hardworking citizenry of Central Europe's only liberal democracy reinforced this impression on a massive scale. Czech military defenses were strong, even formidable. Unfortunately Hitler's attraction to the German-speaking Sudetenland, as an easterly base from which to push toward Russia, might prove even stronger.

Harry and Clare had two conversations about this grim possibility in Prague with the Czech president, Eduard Beneš. Ensconced in the splendor and security of his white palace, Beneš thought war could be avoided. He wildly speculated that the totalitarian Reich was "already broke." As for Russia, he was sure that fellow Slavs there would come to Czechoslovakia's aid in the event of any Nazi attack.

Traveling on to Paris by deluxe train, Harry and Clare dined with William Bullitt, the American Ambassador to France, on June 14. Clare's old friend from *Vanity Fair* days André Maurois was there. But she had little opportunity for literary talk because Harry, his head still full of Beneš's apocalyptics, asked characteristically direct questions of another guest, the publisher Léon Bailby. He had heard that *Le Jour*, which Bailby owned, had received money from Mussolini to promote pro-Fascist interests in France. What were the "morals" of a national newspaper that could be bought for political purposes by foreign dictators? Bullitt managed to change the subject by saying he personally feared a Communist-Fascist showdown in Europe. He distracted Harry with the information that France already had seventy-two "Red" senators and deputies. Whole suburbs of Paris were in thrall to the party organization.

On June 15 the Luces sailed for New York on the *Queen Mary*. Ambassador Kennedy traveled with them. Clare made no secret of reveling in "Joe's" company. Harry enjoyed it less.

A photograph taken before disembarking survives in marked contrast to Alfred Eisenstaedt's shots of the couple as happy newlyweds. It shows Harry looking unhappy and overweight. His smile is weak, his jacket tight, his once-sharp jawline ill defined. Clare, standing beside him at the rail, reveals none of her usual desire to beguile the camera. Wearing a dowdy dress and unbecoming straw hat, she presents a tense, expressionless face.

Clare and Harry returning from Europe, *June 1938*

After three and a half years as lovers, they had lost their romantic bloom. But Clare would not confront the reasons for more than a year.

On July 9, *The Women* closed on Broadway, having run for seventy-eight weeks and 657 performances. By then Clare had sold *Kiss the Boys Good-bye* to Brock Pemberton for a $1,400 advance, plus 10 percent of the box-office receipts. Pemberton chose the gifted Antoinette Perry as director and scheduled the play for early fall.[24]

After a two-week trip to Bermuda, Clare spent the summer in the same Stamford rental as the year before. Harry meanwhile asked *Fortune*'s research chief, Allen Grover, to look for a large, comfortable, but inexpensive house he could buy for his restless wife. It must not be "a show place," he said. "We have got that in South Carolina."[25]

Grover discovered a dour, Georgian-style mansion on King Street in Greenwich, with thirty rooms and views of the Connecticut Hills. It was the first of several strangely unattractive houses that the Luces would own over the years. They called it, simply, "The House." In September they put down $34,500 of the $181,000 asking price and took a mortgage on the rest. Harry allowed Clare $35,000 for repairs, improvements, and decorating. She hired Gladys Freeman to help with alterations and furnishing of the public rooms, while retaining the ultra-exclusive Dorothy Draper to do her own bedroom.[26]

Heedless of budgetary restraints, and careless of the house's classical architecture, Clare replaced the original staircase with a hanging glass spiral. She also converted several outbuildings to guest cottages. It would be months before Harry learned that she had run up $100,000 in outstanding bills, and that irate contractors were threatening liens.[27]

Kiss the Boys Good-bye began previews in Princeton, New Jersey, on Friday, September 16. A talented radio actress, Helen Clair, starred as Cindy Lou, along with Benay Venuta, Sheldon Leonard, Millard Mitchell, John Alexander, and Hugh Marlowe. John Root designed some much-admired train and house sets. After three days the production moved to Washington, D.C., where Clare stayed up until the small hours, polishing dialogue. Her secretary, Isabel Hill, first in a long line of adoring assistants, was amazed by how efficiently her mind worked, "no matter how tired she gets."[28]

Rumor reached New York that Miss Boothe's latest work was the funniest thing ever seen along the Potomac, "except Congress." Fans with fond memories of *The Women* eagerly anticipated the September 28 opening at the Henry Miller Theatre.[29]

Its first-night audience, the *Daily News* reported, "was as happy as any that season." Walter Winchell of the *New York Mirror* correctly forecast that *Kiss the Boys Good-bye* would fill seats for many months to come. The *World-Telegram* called it a fast-paced, ribald, and irreverent play for sophisticates. Clare's satire bit viciously into "the follies and foibles, the mannerisms and affectations, the grosser appetites and the carnal sins of the society she knows so much about." John Mason Brown in the *New York Post* said that her muse must drink nothing but carbolic acid.[30]

Richard Watts of the *New York Herald Tribune* remarked on Clare's "capacity for malice," which was "the most interesting feature of her peculiar talent." In *Kiss the Boys Good-bye* he felt she had fully demonstrated her contempt for mankind. He wished only that she had provided more explicit reasons for not liking most of the people she wrote about.[31]

In contrast, *The New York Times*'s influential Brooks Atkinson found her characters dull and her script labored. Then he contradicted himself by saying that every line of the dialogue was "equally bright and devastating." *Time* discreetly printed more of a plot summary than a review. Its only adverse criticism was "Playwright Boothe's wisecracking cutthroats are dramatically flat." *Life* covered the production with no fewer than twenty-four pictures, all with favorable captions, spread over four pages.[32]

Kiss the Boys Good-bye went on to run for 286 performances and was included on at least one critic's list of the best ten plays of 1938–39.[33] It would eventually be made into a movie musical scored by Frank Loesser and starring Mary Martin, Don Ameche, and Oscar Levant. But the work would never have the appeal or longevity of *The Women*, which after sixty years was still able to fill theaters around the world.[34]

A few hours before Clare's new play opened, the British Prime Minister, Neville Chamberlain, was handed a Foreign Office note while addressing the House of Commons. As he read it, his clouded countenance lightened. Hitler, he announced, had agreed to postpone his imminent attack on Czechoslovakia for twenty-four hours. At the suggestion of Signor Mussolini, the Führer would meet immediately with the leaders of Great Britain, France, and Italy at Munich.[35]

The conference was no sooner under way on September 29 than Henry Luce and his senior staff discussed *Time*'s editorial policy towards its possible outcome. Harry was for appeasement, and made what

Billings called "a 30 minute stump speech" in favor of a cover story on Chamberlain as hero. The Prime Minister had "lured Germany back to Law and Peace," and Munich had "staved off war" for the foreseeable future. Only Roy Larsen and Dan Longwell were skeptical of Hitler's good faith, and Luce's optimism. As far as they were concerned, "fighting has already started."[36]

Early next morning, Chamberlain, Edouard Daladier, and Mussolini effectively ceded to Germany the Sudetenland and all its formidable military installations. The Czechs, unrepresented at the conference, capitulated. Harry had to swallow his belief of the previous June that they would do battle for their democracy.

Bernard Baruch, who had spent his customary summer in Europe and witnessed the worsening situation at first hand, returned to New York with a prophecy by his friend Winston Churchill. "War is coming very soon," the backbencher had told him. "We will be in it and you will be in it."[37]

Baruch was sufficiently concerned to visit the White House on October 12 and warn President Roosevelt that German military spending had reached some 105 billion marks. He also conveyed a quietly ominous trade fact: Japan was shopping for enormous quantities of copper. For its own security, the United States should start producing warplanes without delay—at least 50,000 of them. "The nation is not ready," Roosevelt said.[38]

Clare's own reactions to recent events in Europe were equivocal. She seems to have been outwardly content to let Harry formulate his editorial ideas, drawing her own conclusions about what she saw and felt but keeping no diary, writing no articles, and confining her public statements to matters concerning the theater. The first indication of her true emotions came after the *Kristallnacht* riots in Germany on November 9. She appeared at Baruch's apartment, extremely agitated, saying that the Nazi purges were crimes not against Jews alone but against all civilization. What, she asked him, was the United States prepared to do?[39]

26

PORTRAIT OF A

SUICIDE

There is no greater cause of melancholy than idleness.
—ROBERT BURTON

Improbably, in the fall of 1938, a smashed body on a Manhattan side-walk caused Clare to confront the true nature of artistic genius. On Friday, October 21, she learned that Dorothy Hale, a close friend and a star in the Scarborough production of *Abide With Me*, had committed suicide at thirty-three, following an aborted love affair with WPA Ad-ministrator Harry Hopkins. Dorothy had left three letters, disposing of her few personal possessions and giving instructions for her burial. In none did she say why she was taking her own life, but intimates knew she had been depressed about her lack of success as an actress as well as her failed romance. Clare told the press that Mrs. Hale had recently been taking a lot of "sleeping powders."[1]

By grim coincidence, Dorothy's death came only a few months after the suicide of their mutual friend and *Abide With Me* alumna Rosamond Pinchot. Clare was so disturbed by this second bereavement that friends saw an element of self-identification with it. Both Dorothy and Rosamond were beautiful and talented, yet plagued by an inner emptiness.[2]

In her twenties Dorothy Donovan, a convent-educated girl from Pittsburgh, had been a stage and screen ingenue of modest talent and extraordinary beauty. Having first married and divorced a millionaire broker, Gaillard Thomas, she became the wife, then the widow of the muralist Gardner Hale. Before his death in a California car accident in 1931, she was moving in circles that included Diego Rivera, Frida Kahlo, Miguel Covarrubias, and Isamu Noguchi. When it became clear she would never get far in movies, she moved to New York, hoping to find theater work. "What a horrible place Hollywood is," Clare remembered her saying over lunch at "21."[3]

Though Dorothy pleaded poverty, she soon began entertaining lavishly in an East Side town house. Clare suspected that a rich lover was financing her—which was indeed the case—and felt a vicarious thrill in observing a life that well might have been her own had she not made fortunate marriages.[4] She felt in some way responsible for this adventurous alter ego who lived so close to the edge.

How close had become apparent the previous winter, when the exquisite brunette sent Clare a telegram begging for $1,000, repayable in six months: "I find myself in a desperate financial jam." Clare, whose policy was to treat all urgent demands as exaggerated, had prudently obliged with $500.[5]

Shortly afterwards, in a scene that might have come straight out of *The Women*, Clare was at Bergdorf Goodman looking at a prohibitively expensive model dress when she learned from a saleslady it had just been ordered by Mrs. Hale. Her angry assumption that Dorothy had borrowed money for that purpose was replaced by more complex feelings when she discovered that the gown was paid for by Bernard Baruch.[6]

Even so, it was Hopkins, a recent widower of forty-eight, and not Bernie that Dorothy had fallen in love with. Telling friends and gossip columnists that she was engaged to President Roosevelt's chief aide, she had moved into a small apartment at the Hampshire House on Central Park South and started buying her trousseau. Clare thought the match "brilliant," and Buff Cobb excitedly looked forward to watching the effect of their flamboyant friend on austere New Dealers.[7] Hopkins, they soon discovered, was having second thoughts—not least about the consequences of passion on his fragile physique. Rather than risk finding out, he had ended the romance.

"It was quite clear that she was jilted," said Clare. It was also clear that Dorothy was trying to recover when she announced she was holding a cocktail party at her home on October 20. Clare declined her invitation but recommended that Dorothy wear a black velvet gown with cleavage.[8]

After the party, Dorothy had gone to the theater and arrived home alone at 1:15 A.M. Four hours later, still sheathed in black velvet, with a yellow rose from Noguchi pinned to her bodice, Dorothy's corpse was discovered sixteen floors below her window.[9]

When Clare next met Harry Hopkins, she took no pains to conceal her fury over his cavalier treatment of Dorothy Hale.

"You don't like me, do you?" he said.

"No, and I think you know the reason."

"Well, I don't care whether you like me or not. It is not of the slightest bit of importance; there is nothing you can ever do for me, or against me."[10]

On November 1, eleven days after Dorothy's death, Clare went to a reception celebrating the first New York exhibition of Frida Kahlo's paintings. It was held at the Julian Levy Gallery on East Fifty-seventh Street. She was looking for modern art to cover the many walls of her new Connecticut house.[11]

The Mexican artist's twenty-five paintings—mostly colorful oils on copper—were startlingly different from any Clare had seen. She could compare them only with the surrealist work of Salvador Dalí. Kahlo, however, expressed surprise when told her art resembled his. "I simply paint because I need to paint and without any other consideration."[12]

Intensely personal, her art was not for the squeamish. Her husband, Diego Rivera, described it as "acid and tender, hard as steel . . . profound and cruel."[13] One painting at Levy's, entitled *My Birth*, showed Frida's head emerging from her mother's vagina in unsparing close-up. Two others depicted Frida suckling a massive black-faced figure and floating in a bathtub, displaying trophic ulcers on her feet (a manifestation of her congenital spina bifida). The most startling of all had Frida prone on a blood-stained bed, recovering from a miscarriage or abortion. Above her, in an incongruous blue sky, looking like a tranquil Buddha, hovered the baby, still attached to a bright red umbilical cord.

The New York Times, commenting on Kahlo's fascination with mutilated body parts and gory medical procedures, said her work was "more obstetric than aesthetic." Time quoted the French poet André Breton as saying her art was "like a ribbon around a bomb."[14]

This last simile uncannily resembled one soon to be applied to Clare, that her effect on people was like being "dynamited by angel cake."[15] Both she and Kahlo had burned and been burnt, and performed most dramatically when documenting their own fiery experiences. The fundamental difference between them was that Frida exposed herself unflinchingly on canvas as she confronted physical and psychological horrors with the honesty of genius. Clare, on the other hand, diluted pain in her prose by resorting to jokes, even slapstick. She seemed always to write with her sentimental mother in mind. Had she been a genuine artist like Kahlo, rather than a modestly gifted entertainer always calculating effect, she might have divined a Dorothy Hale among the vapid socialites of The Women and had her plunge to desperate death in the final scene. What Frida Kahlo could have done with the symbolism of "Jungle Red" was easy to imagine if not to emulate, because Clare was by nature unable, or unwilling, to explore metaphor to its artistic limit. Her own life had amply furnished her with the stuff of pure comedy and tragedy, but she could draw from it only farce, satire, and melodrama.

Several of Kahlo's exhibited paintings were already owned by collectors.[16] The one Clare bought for six hundred dollars was a self-portrait Vogue had reproduced to illustrate a piece on Kahlo by Bertram Wolfe. It was called Between the Curtains and showed Frida in a pink and white, full-skirted Spanish colonial skirt, wine-colored blouse, and ocher stole, with a red ribbon in her jet black, plaited hair. She was standing against a green background, between two tasseled drapes, a small bouquet cradled in her arms. In her hands, facing outward, she held a piece of paper that testified to her ardent Communism. On it was written, "For Leon Trotsky with all love I dedicate this painting on the 7th of November, 1937. Frida Kahlo in San Angel, Mexico."[17]

Standing in the gallery in her long-skirted Tehuana costume, thick brows meeting over dark eyes, a hint of a mustache above flaming red lips, Frida Kahlo was as colorful and arresting as any of her pictures. Clare, accustomed to being the center of attention in any gathering, looked like a pallid nymph by comparison. Though short in stature, Frida at thirty-one had a personality so vibrant, and sexual allure so potent, that crowds gathered wherever she went, and children followed her as though she were a female pied piper.[18]

She talked to Clare about the recent death of their mutual friend Dorothy Hale. "I would like to paint a *recuerdo* of her," Frida said. "Her life must not be forgotten." Clare, understanding *recuerdo* to mean an idealized memorial portrait, commissioned one on the spot for four hundred dollars.[19]

Rivera, hearing about the encounter, urged his wife to paint Clare herself, even without a fee. "You will get a chance to speak with her. Read her plays . . . it may be that they will suggest to you a composition for her portrait." Knowing about Clare from Covarrubias, he added, "Her life . . . is extremely curious; it would interest you." But Frida was not drawn to Clare, finding her "cold, brittle and impenetrably defensive."[20]

When the Dorothy Hale memorial was almost finished in late spring 1939, Kahlo asked an intermediary, the photographer Nikolas Muray, to find out the exact day of Dorothy's suicide. She wanted to inscribe it on the painting. "I can't send the picture until I know that damn date," she wrote in her blunt English. "And it is urgent that this wench of Claire [*sic*] Luce has the painting in order to get from her the bucks."[21]

The completed oil arrived in August. Clare opened the package, expecting to see Dorothy's face in all its perfection. Instead she was so shocked that she "almost passed out." What confronted her was not a memorializing *recuerdo* but a graphic, narrative *retablo* detailing every step of her friend's suicide.[22]

The uppermost part depicted the sloping roof of Hampshire House against a pale violet sky. The rest of the building was partly hidden by swirling clouds. Near the top, an upright, black-robed female figure had just stepped birdlike out of one of the windows. In the center, the woman was falling upside down through billowing clouds. Her classic oval face, with staring eyes, was clearly that of Dorothy Hale. At the bottom, her shoeless, inert body lay, not on hard flagstones but on soft brown earth. Noguchi's yellow corsage remained pinned to the right breast. Her face was unmarked, but blood trickled from mouth, nose, and ear onto her right cheek and outstretched left arm. From there it ran over the frame, as if to bring the horror directly into any room in which the painting came to rest. Immediately beneath the dead woman's foot, Frida had handwritten a legend in red, with the names of subject, artist, and patron in capital letters.

> En la ciudad de Nueva York el día 21 del mes OCTUBRE de 1938, a las seis de la mañana, se suicidó la señora DOROTHY HALE tirándose desde una ventana muy alta de edificio Hampshire House. En su recuerdo, la señora CLARE BOOTHE LUCE encargó este retablo, habiéndolo ejecutado FRIDA KAHLO
>
> (In the city of New York on the twenty-first day of OCTO-BER, 1938, at six [sic] in the morning Mrs. DOROTHY HALE committed suicide by throwing herself out of a very high window of the Hampshire House building. In her memory Mrs. CLARE BOOTHE LUCE commissioned this narrative painting, having executed it FRIDA KAHLO.)[23]

Such a terrifying scene could not have been more remote from the gentle memento Clare had envisaged.[24] Not knowing quite what to do with the offending picture, she asked Frank Crowninshield, a benefactor of the Museum of Modern Art, if he would store it with others he intended to bequeath. He obligingly agreed, and on August 18 Clare wrote Muray:

> I intend to have Noguchi, a great friend of both Dorothy Hale and Frida Rivera, paint out the legend—that is to say the actual name of the unfortunate girl and my name.
>
> I hope Frida Rivera will understand why I have taken this liberty.
>
> The painting will then be put in storage for a number of years, after which I will send it to some museum.

The Suicide of Dorothy Hale, oil by Frida Kahlo, *1939*

> . . . May I please ask you . . . not to speak of the inci-
> dent to anyone.[25]

Frida, who had doubtless heard of the *retablo*'s reception from Muray,
smoothly wrote to thank Clare for full payment of the four hundred dollars. She had done her best and hoped the picture pleased Señora Luce.[26]

PORTRAIT OF A SUICIDE

To ensure that *Kiss the Boys Good-bye* continued filling seats at the Henry Miller, Clare stepped up her efforts to garner publicity for both her play and herself. In the November 1938 *Vogue*—the same issue as the Kahlo article—she appeared in five poses shot by five different photographers, under the headline "Changing Face." The portraitist Bassiano sat her sideways in a high-necked dress, her jaw out-thrust and her expression dour. A specialist in Broadway stills made her look theatrically feminine, with bare shoulders, fluffy hair, and glossy mouth. An anonymous Hollywood cameraman showed her languidly recumbent, with false eyelashes and cheeks highlighted like Dietrich's. Alfred Eisenstaedt caught her in a bathrobe, laughing with her hair damp. Horst, the consummate fashion artist, posed her leaning against a giant balloon in a low-cut evening dress with plumed hat and fan, jewels blazing at throat and wrists.

Simultaneously, Clare published in *Stage* an article entitled "Confessions of a Trojan Horse." It addressed the accusation that she had infiltrated New York and Newport society by marriage, then betrayed its members with satire. The piece was full of sarcasm and mock self-deprecation.

> It *did* hurt me way, way *down* to be told I'm looked upon as a traitor to all the *dear* people—those nymphomaniacs, dipsomaniacs, egomaniacs, and schizophrenic lice—I've so long felt were part of my ineluctable class structure. But if that's the way they *do* feel, it's *awful*, but one just has to face things, doesn't one? I learned facing things in the depression when I had to give up my chauffeur for three months. Although I was going to fire him *anyway*. He was a perfectly revolting fellow who *absolutely* refused to wait outside a nightclub after 4:00 A.M.

She was pained to hear that Social Registerites felt "pouty" about her work.

> But what *would* I have written about, if not the Social Register, I ask. After all, *think* of my life, a life of seclusion and

333

grace and luxury, in which one is *never* exposed to the world of brutal fact, of bitterness, of moral or intellectual strife . . . of war, and Fascism, and Socialized Medicine, and the C.I.O. and the A.I.F., and the increasing insanity rate, and HOUSING, and Mr. Corcoran and Mr. Cohen, and other absolutely tear-making topics. But I just haven't had much *dynamic* contact with all that. Though, when I do make out my income tax checks, I *dimly* suspect that the size of them *does* bear *some* relation to these problems.

Flighty though she might be considered, she seemed somehow to have chosen a "hobby" that made reporters devote whole columns to her. In the Twenties she had been lucky to get a mention by Cholly Knickerbocker. Now there were long discussions by critics of her "art."

And sometimes in this connection they *do* say very *nice* things. Then I *purr* until the cream slops over in wide concentric circles. But when they say *horrid* things (those are the days when even the kitchen maid, whom I've never laid eyes on, feels the repercussions and trembles) I do feel inclined to go right [*sic*] and scratch their eyes out . . . But Mr. Watts and Mr. Anderson and Mr. Atkinson just don't seem to get around to "21" and the Colony, or even Elsa's parties. And I mean, I just can't *bring* myself to go slumming way over to Sardi's . . . Oh, on the whole, I do just *love* reading them. They can say *anything*, just so long as they don't ignore me.[27]

Carl Van Vechten thought the piece "brilliant . . . sensational in its implications, and bitter in its irony." He compared her style to that of Swift and Congreve.[28]

Harry's reaction was more mixed. He did not mind his wife seeking publicity for work accomplished, but he resented it when she invited scrutiny of their private life. "This made me mad," he wrote, sending her a news clip in which she was quoted as complaining she could not work at Mepkin because of entertaining "too many house guests."[29] The complaint was disingenuous. Far from seeking creative solitude, Clare welcomed the distraction of admirers. In her heart she knew that she would never be a star in the pure sense of being the best at her craft—on a level, say, with Eugene O'Neill, Thornton Wilder, and Robert Sherwood. But she had an insatiable need to be perceived as clever.[30] Having already passed her peak, she was perilously close to settling for stardom's poor relation, celebrity.

Among the eighty-one Republicans who won House seats in the midterm fall elections was Dr. Albert Austin of Fairfield County, Connecticut. Clare's stepfather had considered running in 1936 while Ann Austin was alive, but he chose to wait until he had completed twenty years as Greenwich health officer.

He and Clare had drifted apart during recent years, following a stepfatherly criticism of her published grammar. He had written to say what a shock it had been for him, who had always regarded her as "a pure diamond," to find any "flaw" of expression. If she did it again, he added morbidly, his life would have been spent "to no purpose."[31]

Clare, seldom willing to take the blame for her own mistakes, had petulantly replied, "The fault may be yours. You might have devoted a little more time to those English lessons in my early youth, and a little less time to the Masons."[32]

Pressed, she had contributed a thousand dollars to his election campaign, explaining she could not afford more because of the cost of furnishing her Greenwich mansion. In October, when Dr. Austin seemed sure to win, Harry had also given a thousand. It would take another four years before both Luces realized the true extent of their investment.

The "too many" people Clare entertained at Mepkin that winter included Condé Nast, Sir William Wiseman, Countess Clarita de Forceville, and her old colleague from *Vogue* Margaret Case. They wrote obsequiously in the guest book as well as in thank-you notes— "You pour comfort and luxury over your friends, and sit up and give so much of your own spirit and electrifying charms." Helen Brown Norden, arriving pale from New York in early December, humorously assailed Clare for looking so "dewy" and unlined. "My God, how do you expect women to like you?!"[33]

By Christmas Harry's extended family, including eight children, was in residence. Coincidentally, Clare began to suffer pain in her lower back. It was diagnosed as inflammation of the sacroiliac joint, suggesting that long hours at her desk, running three homes, and entertaining copious visitors were all taking their toll.

Nevertheless, she managed to finish a new script, loosely based on *Romeo and Juliet*, called "The Wedding Day." Max Gordon was sufficiently impressed to send it to Rodgers and Hart for possible adaptation as a musical. But they declined, and hopes for its production died.[34]

Early in the new year of 1939, Clare sent a *cri de coeur* of sorts to Eleanor Roosevelt. The First Lady had seen *Kiss the Boys Good-bye* and predicted, in her newspaper column, that Miss Boothe would become a first-class playwright "when the bitterness of the experiences which she has evidently had are completely out of her system." Clare wrote to say it was possible she might one day "make the world a sweeter place," but she rather doubted it.

> One lives swinging so violently between cold anger at the stupidity, the cruelty, the *tragic impudence* of men, and a pity too deep for tears, that one seldom comes to rest on the good ground of "the human love of human people." It is only in such a mood, "seeing life steadyly [sic] and seeing it whole"—that great plays are written. But if ever I do come within curtain-rise of a great play—I shall have come *that* much closer to it precisely because you believed privately— and said so publicly—that I *could* . . . !

She was cheered by a flattering response from Mrs. Roosevelt.

> I am quite sure you will write a really great play some day. Of course it takes great cleansing of spirit, and I will agree with you that swinging from rage to pity is pretty hard to get away from.
>
> Some day perhaps when you have time you will stop off here to see me for a talk. I think it would be pleasant for both of us.[35]

Already bored at Mepkin by mid-February, Clare returned to New York to give a ten o'clock, Sunday-night party for three hundred at El Morocco. She said she wanted to honor the three female leads in *Kiss the Boys Good-bye*, but the event was really a showcase for herself. Burgess Meredith, Ilka Chase, and George Kaufman were among the guests. Clare had an argument with the last about Fascism and tried to make light of it afterwards. "Hot words make warm friends," she explained to a reporter, "and I wouldn't have a friend I couldn't row with."[36]

Another journalist studied Clare's method as she systematically worked the room. "I don't believe there was a table at which she failed to pay a visit or a guest of whom she failed to make a personal enquiry." The sculptor Russell Aitken was similarly impressed and concluded that she would be a diplomat one day. "I watched you, a vision of loveliness float around from table to table, greeting and sitting with every one of your guests so that each felt the party was given especially for himself or herself." After a lifetime of fabulous wealth and party going, he would assure her, "I've known a passel of wonderful hostesses in my time—but that evening stands out in my book as the ultimate."[37]

Aitken, a champion marksman who enjoyed the duck blinds at Mepkin, did not fail to notice a typographical error in a *New York News* profile of Clare published later that month. "Her real hobbies," the paper commented, "are surf-board riding, shooting cats and (surprise!) needle-point." The mispunctuation was picked up by *The New Yorker*, and thence by a scion of the du Ponts of Delaware. Clare was convulsed when he contacted her to say that he, too, liked shooting cats, particularly when they were on a rooftop during a full moon, silhouetted against the sky. He would be delighted to have her join him one night in the hunt.[38]

Along with publicizing herself, Clare seemed anxious to record her thirty-six-year-old beauty before it faded. That year was to see three formal portraits. First she sat in a rural setting for Paul Lewis Clemens but was not happy with the result, even after the artist had given her realistic hands with bones instead of "the usual fashionable tendrils." Clemens showed the oil to a clergyman friend who rhetorically asked, "Who is she that looketh forth as the morning, fair as the moon, clear as the sun, and terrible as an army with banners?"[39]

A charcoal sketch by Doris Lupas made Clare look distinctly middle-aged, so she asked the eminent Jo Davidson to sculpt terra-cotta likenesses of herself and Harry. The results illustrated Davidson's belief in the importance of "*rapport* between the artist and the sitter." Harry evidently had no trouble giving himself, and Clare liked the way Davidson captured his smile of amused detachment. Her own head, however, was devoid of expression, with a vulgarizing polychrome finish that accentuated blue eyes and pink lips and cheeks.[40]

She much preferred a cool marble bust in the sophisticated modernist style that Isamu Noguchi had carved of her almost six years earlier. But since then she had changed the size and shape of her nose, and the difference was now embarrassingly apparent. So she prevailed upon Noguchi to come to her apartment, armed with chisels, for some discreet cosmetic adjustments. While he was about it, he could bring brushes and paints to doctor the Frida Kahlo *retablo*.[41]

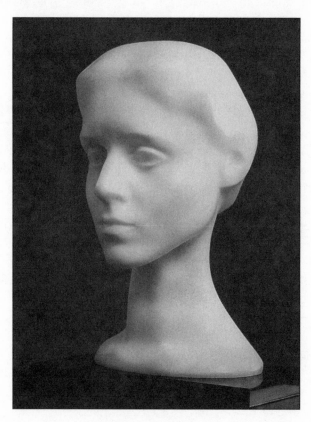

Clare Boothe Luce
Marble bust by Isamu Noguchi, 1933

Ann Brokaw recorded his arrival in her diary.

> Noguchi . . . came to finish a marble head of Mother . . .
> then covered the place with Ma's name and Dorothy Hale's
> name on it in the corner of the picture of Mrs. Hale—
> suicide which Mother nearly destroyed because it is so grue-
> some. She is going to give it to a museum or something.[42]

Many years later Noguchi denied altering the bust. He claimed that he
had taken a handful of marble dust to the apartment and pretended to
chip away while Clare posed, letting the dust trickle between his fingers to the floor.[43] But the nose in the final bust was considerably
smaller than Clare's original one. Noguchi also denied tampering with
the *retablo*. Dorothy Hale remains prominently named in Kahlo's legend, but there is a wide, painted-out space where the words "la señora,
CLARE BOOTHE LUCE encargó" are missing.

As if to haunt her, the *retablo* found its way back after Frank
Crowninshield's death in 1948. Although she had come to acknowledge by then that "of its sort, it was a rather beautiful thing," she still
could not bear to keep it in her house.[44] Instead, she decided to store it
before lending it to the Phoenix Art Museum, with the request that she
remain anonymous.

Despite her caution and insistence on secrecy, a museum catalog
later identified her as owner. It also revealed that she had commissioned the painting in memory of Dorothy Hale. Thus Clare got, as she
often did in life, what she most ardently resisted.

27

MARGIN FOR ERROR

Writing is the willful interruption of other interruptions.
—JOHN MASON BROWN

The late spring eastbound crossing of the SS *Normandie* was usually its second busiest. But on May 30, 1939, only thirty-two passengers were aboard the massive liner—a grim sign that war in Europe was now considered certain. Clare, traveling alone, was among the intrepid few. The mysterious chill permeating her marital relations had not warmed. Ostensibly she was going to publicize the London production of *The Women*, which had just opened to generally favorable reviews ("the wittiest play in ten years"). But she also wanted to measure how much she would be missed at home, while using every independent moment, until Harry joined her in four weeks' time, to consolidate and expand her list of professional and social contacts.[1]

A few days before leaving she had cabled Ambassador Joseph P. Kennedy. "Save me lunch and or dinner chat alone love Clare." He not only agreed to this and more but gallantly offered to meet her at Southampton and drive her to London.[2]

Some sample entries from Clare's diary, beginning with a weekend at Lord Beaverbrook's country house, show how assiduously she pursued her multiple objectives:

Sat. June 17	3.30: Beaverbrook's
Sun. June 18	Beaverbrook 8: De Rochemont, Embassy movie.
Mon. June 19	11.30: Rehearse cast of *The Women* 1: Vernon Blunt 3: Miss Lane 4: Billy Boisservaine 5.30: Charlotte [Nast] 8: Joe [Kennedy] 12: Cast party
Tue. June 20	1.15: Carlton–Oliver Stanley. 5: Augustus John 6: Joe 8: Castlerose–Oliver 12: [Thornton] Wilder, [Sybil] Colefax–Savoy[3]

Kennedy's name appears more frequently than any other. As well as entertaining her *à deux,* "Joe" squired her to the Ascot races and an evening performance of *The Women.* But he was not Clare's only ardent escort that June. Randolph Churchill took her off for another country weekend, and Oliver Stanley, seeking to advance on the previous year's acquaintance, lunged at her randily during a night on the town. "He nearly broke my front teeth," she complained.[4]

She also spent three days sailing on the yacht of Ambassador Norman H. Davis, American delegate to the Nine-Power Conference at Brussels, accompanied by envoys from Japan, Greece, Yugoslavia, Egypt, and Iran. Afterwards she sent a list of her new friends to Time Inc. editors, with a self-satisfied covering note. "If anybody wants to ask me about any of them—I know all."[5]

Clare's most thrilling encounter, however, was with her literary hero George Bernard Shaw. She thought *St. Joan* was "the greatest and tenderest" of his works, and the one of all modern plays she would most like to have written. In response to Clare's request for a meeting, Shaw agreed to see her at 11:30 A.M. on Friday, June 16, at his flat.[6]

At the appointed hour she was received by a stiff secretary and shown into the playwright's study. He sat with his back to her and wheeled around welcomingly. "Come in, come in."

The Nobel Prize winner, now eighty-three, had lost none of the flirtatious charm and wit for which he was renowned. Clare found herself telling him of her early ambition to be a dramatist, and how she kept his photograph beside her bed for inspiration. His example must have borne fruit, she said, since she was in London to promote her second Broadway and first West End play. "If it weren't for you, I wouldn't be here!"

Shaw smiled impishly. "Let me see. What was your dear mother's name?"[7]

Before leaving, Clare asked him whom else he thought she should see. "That is an unnecessary question," he joked. "You have already met incomparably the greatest figure in this land."[8]

Later that day he sent her a wry postcard. Shaw wrote that in the thrill of meeting Clare he had neglected to offer his help to her "or to Mr. Boothe," but she had only to say the word and he would be happy to do so.[9]

Back in New York "Mr. Boothe" was already pining for his wife. "This is all so much like 1935," he wrote her at Claridges. "Particularly remarkable are those thump-thumps in the heart at odd moments and the tenseness in the stomach all the time." Insecure as well as lonely, Harry grumbled about not hearing often enough from her and summoned David for familial sympathy. He showed him Clare's first cable, signed "love and kisses," and said he wouldn't exchange its sentiments "for all of Time Inc."[10]

She, meanwhile, was again giving the kind of self-revealing interviews that appalled Luce but delighted the London press. She announced that she had once been a chain smoker and that her husband was now paying her five thousand dollars a year to abstain. Lack of nicotine had not improved her sleep or palate. "All that happens is that I eat more . . . so I weigh an extra 10 lb., which I don't like."

"Well," said one reporter encouragingly, "it must have improved your wind, at least."

"Maybe, but I've nowhere to run to."[11]

The growing celebrity of Clare Boothe Luce had its downside in that it brought her quantities of tiresome mail from strangers and forgotten acquaintances. A Tennessee woman who had known her briefly as a child accused her of becoming a snob and received a tart reply.

> When one becomes even such a minor public character as
> myself, one is beset on all sides by people who want to get at
> one for this, that, or the other thing. One must adopt a
> "high hat" [or] a "Ladyship" air as a mere matter of personal
> protection, or simply be nibbled away at like a piece of
> cheese by hundreds of hungry little mice who feed on one's
> poor (cheesy) little fame . . . In the course of an ordinary
> lifetime . . . one gets to know some 50,000 people. When
> one has written a play or a book, it is surprising how it seems
> that 49,999 of them make demands on one's time.[12]

A certain name from the past retained its power to evoke old longings,
even if it came at second hand. Julian Simpson's mother wrote to say
that her son was on duty in Palestine but would otherwise certainly
want to see her. Both of them had read *The Women*. She hoped to entertain Clare for lunch, tea, or dinner, so that "I may meet you at last."[13]
Clare did not accept, though she privately determined to pursue Julian
again if the chance arose.

Harry and Ann Brokaw arrived at the Gare du Nord in Paris on June
28. Gladys Freeman, who was to be Ann's chaperone in Europe, traveled with them, as did the writer John Gunther, Harry's shipboard dining companion. He was impressed by the sight of Clare standing on the
platform in "a cloud of gold, tissue, fur."[14]

Ann, two months shy of fifteen, was more interested in four gen-
darmes waiting nearby. She was told they were there to protect Harry,
who was being sued by a syndicate of French newspapers for repeating,
in *Time*, his belief that the national press took bribes from Fascists.[15]

Clare's platform splendor was not surprising, for she had spent several days being fitted at Vionnet, Balenciaga, Mainbocher, and Schiaparelli, as well as shopping for luxury items at Vuitton, Porthault,
Cartier, and Van Cleef & Arpels. She had dined at the American Embassy, at Maxim's, and at *châteaux* out of town, not to mention the
Palace of Versailles, where she had attended a party for the designer
Elsie de Wolfe.[16]

On July 4, having sent Ann and Gladys off on a continental tour,
Harry and Clare quit the Ritz for five days in Geneva. From there they

went to the Hôtel Splendide-Royale et Excelsior in Aix-les-Bains to take a "cure." Clare had not forgotten being miserable there eleven years earlier, nursing a sick George Brokaw. But now she herself, as well as her husband, needed the discipline of supervised diet and exercise.

After a few thermal treatments, they used an introduction from Harry's old classmate Thornton Wilder to arrange a meeting with Gertrude Stein. The expatriate writer and her lover, Alice B. Toklas, were renting a small hillside *château* in nearby Bilignin for the summer. Wilder told the Luces that Gertrude had strong and original views on politics and the coming war, so Harry hoped to recruit her to write some pieces for his magazines. Clare saw a chance to add another name to her personal roster of geniuses.[17]

Stein told a friend that a couple of overambitious New Yorkers were "here giving us the 'rush.' " But as a freelance writer she could hardly pass up the chance to meet Henry Luce, and was intrigued by what Wilder said about Clare's "granite" personality. She invited them to lunch on July 12.[18]

Driving up to the iron gates of the *château*, they could see the peak of Mont Blanc looming behind it. Clare's first impression of Stein, awaiting them in the rose garden, was of a short, masculine woman whose stocky torso, square head, and cropped hair were almost as rugged as the mountain. Yet she also found the author of *Tender Buttons* curiously feminine in a pink brocade vest and yellow shirt.[19]

After a tour of the house, Stein led them to her *salon*. She sat down in one battered rocking chair and offered Harry another. Clare took an upright, and while they waited for lunch demurely worked at needlepoint, a new hobby to occupy her hands now that she had given up smoking.[20]

The meal, consisting of simple fish and potatoes, was prepared by Miss Toklas, who welcomed them in a pleasantly modulated voice. Clare looked askance at her red sack dress tied in the middle, two ropes of carnelian beads, a prominent mustache, and severe black, bobbed hair with long bangs.

Neither host attempted to conceal the nature of their relationship. Alice was "Pussy," and Gertrude was "Lovey" throughout the conversation, which was dominated by American politics. In Stein's robust opinion, only Republicans were natural rulers. She made plain that she despised Franklin Roosevelt and said that under him the

Harry and Clare with Gertrude Stein, Bilignin, *July 1939*

United States was heading towards bankruptcy. The country had lost its moral fiber and needed an external challenge, such as making China democratic.[21]

Harry, enraptured, asked her why most intellectuals who supported Roosevelt seemed to be "leftist." She said they had to be revolutionary in their public attitudes because, unlike artists, they were incapable of revolutionary work. It saddened her that her friend Picasso was such a socialist. True artists were, or should be, "always conservative."

Clare was amazed by Stein's concentrated force, and the ease with which the "swift-flowing river" of her mind slipped from one subject to another. She and Harry enjoyed the conversation so much they stayed until six. Before leaving they invited their new friends to join them on Bastille Day for a gala lunch at the Splendide-Royale.[22]

Chronic self-absorption prevented Clare from imagining that Stein and Toklas might be less captivated with her than she had been with them. Though she did not know it, they were already making fun of her and Harry. Samuel Steward, a young American writer, happened to be staying at Bilignin, and he recorded their arch conversation in his diary.

ALICE   Henry Luce and his wife are taking the cure at Aix-les-Bains. It seems they have both been eating and drinking too much on this trip to Europe.

GERTRUDE   Tell Sammy what they do during the cure, Pussy, do tell him.

ALICE   Well, at one point they have to be separated, male from female, while they get massaged, and each time before they do, they give each other a thought to think about. And when they come out from being broiled and whacked they exchange their conclusions about the thought.

STEWARD   (*laughing*) Not a wasted moment—an executive's combination of business and benefits.

GERTRUDE   You'd think an ordinary person would just want to relax and be thumped. That was a bitchy play she wrote about women. But I liked it, at least I liked it a little. Now she's taken up knitting or crocheting or something like that.[23]

When a horn on the fourteenth announced that the Luces had arrived to pick up their lunch guests, Steward tagged along. He noticed that Stein seemed oddly nervous about this second encounter, and wondered if she was unsettled by the couple's combination of brains, worldliness, and good looks. Harry emerged from the limousine, "tall, craggy, Ciceronian," and his face "held a great deal of power." Clare, in a festive white suit and tricolor blouse, was so "willowy, blond, and beautiful" that Steward surprised himself by saying so, as he bent to kiss her hand.

On their ride to town, he sensed an "unaccountable tension" in the car. It was obvious that Toklas felt resentful of the glamorous Mrs. Luce, who was wooing Stein. In contrast, Clare treated Toklas like a domestic, patronizingly pulling out a piece of blue crochet and forcing her to demonstrate a French knot in the cramped backseat. Harry, oblivious to the subtle power play, asked Stein one of his mind-paralyzing questions. "What do you think of Hitler?"

"Hitler is an Austrian," she replied, more than ready. Her implication was that the Führer disliked Northern Teutons and was subconsciously bent on ruining Germany.[24]

When Harry proposed Stein do some articles for *Life*, she said that at sixty-five she wrote hardly anything. He persisted. "You're a brave man," she said, without committing herself.

Over lunch they talked about the inevitability of war, and Stein said how tragic it would be if the French peasant who saw combat in 1914 should have to fight again, this time alongside his son. In the distance they could hear celebratory cannon fire, and faint strains of *La Marseillaise*. Parachutes hovered over Lac Bourget, carrying small French flags.

On the way home, Stein mischievously took the Luces to meet a friend, the Baronne Pierlot, who was known to be one of the most acerbic women in Haute-Savoie. Clare at once made the mistake of complaining to the Baronne about being seasick on the Atlantic. "It's a great price to pay to come to France."

"We are sorry that our country has unwittingly put you to such great trouble," the Baronne replied. Then, turning away, "Perhaps it would be wiser to stay at home next time."

Clare, stunned, could only whisper to Steward, "The French are beyond me."

Telling Harry she had a headache, she made a move to go. "A minor indisposition," she explained to the others, expressionless. By the time they reached Bilignin, she had recovered sufficiently to remind Stein of a private rendezvous. "Dear Gertrude—would ten be too early for you tomorrow?"

Toklas and Steward looked at each other as the limousine pulled away. "Well, I told you she was giving us the rush," said Stein, embarrassed. "You don't mind do you now, Pussy?"

She and Clare did not get back from their exploration of the Ain Valley until two o'clock the following afternoon. "We talked a lot," said Stein, "and then I read her palm and she tried to read mine but she was all wrong. And do you know what, Pussy, she has a whore's hand."

As Toklas and Steward absorbed this, Stein continued conspiratorially, "I'll tell you something else she doesn't want known . . . Henry is thinking of wanting to be President, not this election but maybe the next one."

"Oh my God," said Toklas.

"Her maybe yes," remarked Stein. "But him no . . . not him, not ever!"[25]

The regimen of swimming, tennis, Scotch douches, and massages Clare submitted to in Aix did not undo the effects of rich French sauces and desserts. She was distressed to find her belt as tight as ever, and her ideal weight of 125 pounds still elusive. "All my life has been a struggle against fat," she lamented. "Not really fat, but fat enough so that no one will call me slim."[26]

Harry, who had turned forty in April, also needed to lose a few more inches. But when the American Ambassador to Warsaw, Anthony Biddle, invited him to visit, he terminated his spa routine without regret. The word on the diplomatic circuit was that the Poles were frantically arming against Hitler. It sounded like a story for *Time*.

Instinct told Luce he should be better prepared than he had been on his foray into Central Europe the previous year. Knowing that the British were treaty-bound to defend Poland in the event of invasion, he decided to fly first to London for high-level briefings. In three days he saw twenty-one public men, including Winston Churchill, Anthony Eden, and Lord Beaverbrook. His notes of these interviews are strangely superficial, even naive. Of the last named he wrote, "My God, what a man, in his huge London Palace-Prison, in his terrifying and fantastically expensive discomfort—Power, Power, Power."[27]

Clare, who accompanied him, jotted down her own observations of Europe on the brink of war for an article she would later publish in *For-*

tune. She could see the British were scared. They realized that neither the desperate appeasements of Neville Chamberlain nor the resources of their vast empire could stop a determined Hitler. Londoners had begun to prepare for the worst. She noticed gas masks everywhere—on the mantelpieces of paneled libraries, on kitchen shelves next to teapots, even in baby carriages. During blackout practices at night, "motor sirens shriek through the dark streets, so nobody can sleep or play cards." There were dugouts in back gardens, and "earth-red trenches in the green parks." Yet cricketers continued to play in the swatches of lawn between. "People can be brave and frightened at once," she marveled.

The same upper-class Englishmen who the year before had struck her as condescending were now querulous about whether the United States would come to their aid in an emergency. At first Clare said yes, but as she thought more deeply about it, her native republicanism asserted itself. She began to doubt the morality of sacrificing American lives to preserve aristocratic titles, protect ancestral mansions, and defend colonial "loot."[28]

Ann Brokaw was also in London that last week of July—unhappily ensconced in a cheaper hotel than that of her parents. Having completed her tour with Gladys Freeman, she was homesick for Connecticut and singing and tennis lessons. Instead she was shunted off on excursions to a Birmingham chocolate factory, a Norman castle in Dudley, Worcestershire, and the Glyndebourne Festival, while Harry and Clare socialized with the most interesting people in town.

She vented her spleen in her diary. "Gawd I wish I'd never come on this damn trip!! I've met no one really notable . . . except, maybe tedious old Mr. Gunther . . . Here's hoping the end will come soon." Clare was not "being a good mother at all," Ann added resentfully. "She gives me everything that money can buy but money just won't do the trick."[29]

When Clare, to Ann's surprise, said she would be allowed to sail for New York sooner than planned, the girl was contrite. "I of course instantly loved her, and realized I hadn't meant any of those horrid things I'd said about hating her. I love her so and want to be like her although I never shall be for I've so many faults."[30]

Clare let her daughter go early because she wanted to be free to join Harry in Poland, sensing that, if war came, "that's where it was all going to happen."[31]

At a welcoming dinner in Warsaw on July 31, Polish officials assured Harry that their military could hold off any Nazi attack. Clare was not so sure. She saw that the Poles were by no means ethnically united and noted, with heavy irony, that they had "quite a Jewish Problem."

> None of the Poles are Jewish of course, but there are 3,000,000 Jews in Poland, whom the Poles are now calling Polish. The Poles like their Jews just now. The Jews also don't want Poland partitioned, because they wouldn't be treated like Poles, which would be bad enough, but like Jews, which would be very much worse.[32]

Visiting the richly fertile Polish Ukraine, a day's ride from Warsaw, she saw how easy and tempting it would be for Hitler to march across and harvest wheat for Germany. This was territory that Stalin surely coveted too. Communism, indeed, seemed a closer prospect than Fascism. Parcel by parcel, local aristocrats were already giving land back to the peasants, out of obvious fear of the future.[33]

Rumania struck her as even more ripe for conquest. "It's so lush and plump and green . . . it could grow anything." In Bucharest the Foreign Minister showed the same empty bravado as Eduard Beneš had the previous year. "Everywhere in Poland and the Balkans they've got too many guns," Clare wrote Gertrude Stein, "and now nobody can think what to do with them but shoot them off."[34]

Clare disembarked from the *Normandie* in New York on August 14 and went straight to Connecticut. She told Ann, "There'll definitely be war next year." Harry, meanwhile, headed for Rockefeller Center to brief his staff optimistically, as he had the summer before. "He thinks the Poles will fight for sovereignty," Billings wrote. "We laughed to ourselves and kissed the Poles goodbye."[35]

Nine days later in Moscow, the foreign ministers of Germany and the Soviet Union clandestinely agreed to divide Poland. They also arranged for German control of Lithuania, while the USSR could appropriate land along the Rumanian border and occupy the Baltic States. The free world was told only that Hitler and Stalin had concluded a "Non-Aggression Pact."

Clare had her own name for it: "the CommuNazi Alliance." It proved, she said, that Europeans were "not really interested in ideologies now." Unlike Americans, who really cared "about saving democracy or civilization," totalitarians "each want to save their own shirts."[36]

Keen to stay abreast of developments, she called Oliver Stanley in London on the morning of August 29. He told her he had just left a cabinet meeting and felt depressed. There was "absolutely no way out" of Britain's pledge to defend Poland if Germany invaded.[37]

Harry, realizing that he had wrongly assessed the European situation, was in a sour mood when news came early on Friday, September 1, that German battleships and bombers had simultaneously attacked Danzig, in northern Poland. Associated Press bulletins through the day detailed the advance of fifty-three Wehrmacht divisions across the border.[38]

A million copies of next week's *Time* cover had already been printed, with a ludicrously inappropriate portrait of Jack Benny. Luce ordered them scrapped. The obvious substitute was Prime Minister Neville Chamberlain, who was at that moment preparing a Sunday-morning ultimatum of war to Hitler. (Only nine months earlier, the latter had been *Time*'s Man of the Year.)[39] But Harry, with improved foresight, chose instead to feature Winston Churchill.

With incredible energy and timing, Clare had spent the last two weeks writing her next Broadway production, a two-act "satirical melodrama" about Nazi perfidy called *Margin for Error*. She took its title from a twice-spoken line of dialogue—"the Third Reich allows no margin for error." Her plot was partly inspired by Police Commissioner Theodore Roosevelt's provocative assignment of Jewish policemen to protect an anti-Semitic German speaker in 1896.[40]

Since Broadway had seen at least eight anti-Fascist plays, including one by Clifford Odets, flop in the last two years, Clare felt she had to temper the seriousness of her themes of corruption and subversion with humor. In her first scene she had the consul's secretary, Max, tell a would-be American Führer, Otto Horst, that he should tone down his rhetoric:

> MAX   You harp too much on the race issue . . . what about the unequal distribution of wealth—?
>
> HORST   Oh, the New Deal has that argument patented. Besides, nobody starves here. At least very few people—
>
> MAX   You should make an issue of those exceptions—
>
> HORST   Then how different would I sound from a Communist? No, Baron, my best bet is to create conflict among creeds and colors; then step in when they're exhausted, and take the country over—Bang! Next week I attack the Catholics, Masons, Negroes, and Café Society.
>
> MAX   [Rises] Perhaps you'd better just purge Elsa Maxwell, and leave the rest to Hitler.[41]

By thus frivolously referring to a professional party giver in the midst of a discussion of serious anarchic intent, Clare showed early that she would be unable to resist diluting her play with cheap wisecracks.

The first act of *Margin for Error* is dominated by the consul, Karl Baumer. Bald and monocled, he is a sadist, traitor, embezzler, blackmailer, and double-crosser, taking money from American Jews on the pretext that he can rescue their relatives from concentration camps. He also affects support for Horst, knowing that he is little more than a midwestern National Socialist stooge.[42]

Clare's policeman, Moe Finkelstein, resents having to protect Baumer from physical harm. But as the consul ominously reminds him, if he is derelict in his guard duty, "international Jewry will be held responsible." Uniquely situated to observe all the comings and goings at the residence, Officer Finkelstein senses gathering tensions not entirely explained by the approach of war. It seems that at least five people, including Baumer's wife and her American journalist lover, have separate and serious reasons for hating the consul. Finkelstein is therefore not too surprised when, under cover of a deafening Hitler radio speech, Baumer is surreptitiously shot dead. While investigating this apparent murder, he discovers that the consul was not only shot but stabbed. Even more improbably, neither attack seems to have been the cause of death. It transpires that Baumer, terrified that an aide was going to reveal his theft of government funds to Berlin, had prepared poisoned whiskey for him and mistakenly drunk it himself.

> MOE   Well, Captain Mulrooney, it seems the Con-
>   sul was shot, stabbed, and poisoned.
> MULROONEY Well, the son-of-a-bitch! Did it kill him?[43]

Though ingenious for long stretches, and thought-provoking overall, Clare's script shows signs of haste and creative ambivalence. Its two acts could almost have been written by different playwrights. The first explores such fundamental moral issues as the dilemma of a Nazi who begins to divine that he is not entirely Aryan.

> CONSUL One might suspect that there's something you are
>   frightened of about yourself—
> MAX   What's in that letter?
> CONSUL Can't you guess, Max?
> MAX   Look here, Schroeder can't know anything about
>   my English grandmother. I've already tried to find
>   out myself. I—
> CONSUL Ja. One's blood begins to ask questions—
> MAX   There's no answer in my blood that says I do not
>   belong to Germany, that Germany does not be-
>   long to me.
> CONSUL Isn't there?
> MAX   For God's sake, Sir—you know I love Germany.
>   [Points to Hitler bust.] I love all he has done for it.
>   He gave us back our honor, our belief in the
>   beauty of our own traditions—
> CONSUL Please, Max, this is not a Nuremberg rally.[44]

There are sharp epigrams throughout, equal to those in *The Women*. One was especially resonant in light of Munich and the invasion of Poland, revealing Consul Baumer to be shrewd as well as evil. "Peace is a static state of misunderstanding. When nations understand each other clearly, war is inevitable." Another, uttered by Horst, is an astute dig at Rooseveltian patronage. "In America the protection of the discontented amounts to a political monopoly."[45]

The second act quickly degenerates into little more than an Agatha Christie–style whodunit. Clare's strained attempts to make fun of anti-Semitism, purportedly showing her own understanding of bigotry, instead raise questions of her sensitivity to the feelings of Jews. Blithely unaware that words like *Anschluss* and *Blitzkrieg* cannot be used lightly, and confident that she had written in defense of America and its liberties, she sent her script to George Kaufman.

She received a biting response. To him the persecution and annihilation of his ancestral people was not the stuff of comedy. In fact, he objected to the play's subliminal patronizing tone. "Jews don't want to be saved," he wrote. They ought to be left alone to find their own path to oblivion, or damnation, or whatever fate they chose. He suspected other professionals might feel similarly.[46]

Max Gordon, Clare's first choice as producer, certainly did. He said that having read the play, he was "scared stiff" of the material. "I really don't want to do it."[47]

But Richard Aldrich and Richard Myers saw potential in the play's topicality and moved to capitalize on it. They engaged Otto Preminger, an Austrian protegé of Max Reinhardt, as both director and consul. Sam Levene, a well-known New York character actor, won the plum role of Finkelstein. Donald Oenslager designed a swastika-hung library set, with prominent photographs of Hitler.[48]

On October 14, a mere six weeks after delivery of the script, *Margin for Error* began tryouts in Princeton. Both Albert Einstein and Thomas Mann were in the capacity first-night audience.[49] The show then moved to Washington, where some of its wittiest lines raised political hackles:

> MAX   What would Hitler say if he found out his mother was
>   Jewish?
> MOE   He'd say he was Jesus.[50]

Someone in the auditorium was heard complaining, "Jew propaganda." The German Embassy registered a protest to Secretary of State Cordell

Clare with Albert Einstein *(second from left)* and Thomas Mann *(right)* at the
Princeton opening of *Margin for Error, October 14, 1939*

Hull that the play was "derogatory" to the Reich.[51] Undeterred, Aldrich and Myers moved the production to Broadway and opened it at
the Plymouth Theatre on November 3.

Clare, as usual, stayed home. She was pleasantly surprised to receive a between-acts call at the Waldorf from her fellow playwright
Alexander King. He said that the audience was "laughing and responding" in an atmosphere of "electric" participation. She need not worry,
the play was "surely a hit."[52]

Next morning she awoke to find a plethora of favorable reviews.
Most ecstatic was one headlined "Heil Clare Boothe!!!" by Walter
Winchell, in his nationally syndicated *Mirror* column. "Clare Boothe,
who convulsed playgoers with *The Women*, and hilariously entertained
them with *Kiss the Boys Good-bye*, is back again with another hit." The
Herald Tribune's Richard Watts, previously her severest critic, said that
in the Nazi consul she had at last found a foe worthy of her "fine capacity for malice."[53]

Sidney Whipple of the *World Telegram* wrote that "she treated the
entire ideology of the Reich government as something which, when

the world's sense of humor is restored, will be laughed to death." A dissenting voice, as usual, was that of Brooks Atkinson in *The New York Times*. He liked *Margin for Error* no more than he had Clare's other plays, and called it "a curious and unsatisfactory mixture of political unmasking and detective story, relieved only by the witty lines written for Sam Levene."[54]

George Jean Nathan, by then at *Newsweek*, detailed some faults in plot and staging. Clare's murder mystery was arbitrarily complicated, he thought, by the revolver shot seen yet not heard. The onstage reporter would have immediately telephoned news of the consul's death to his office. Confusion of drinks, crucial to the dénouement, failed to take account of the dissimilar glasses in which whiskey and brandy are usually served. Most serious of all, the police officer ultimately made an arrest without a warrant.[55]

Alexander King had professional as well as personal reasons for his intermission call to Clare. She had asked for his help with the script, and though "full of misgivings" about the material, he had agreed to give it. Years later King was still amazed by the play's lengthy run. "At its best, it was just a mediocre after-dinner anecdote, with some dubious murder-mystery overtones," he wrote. "Some of the smartest people in show business, who came down to see the preview in Washington, assured me confidentially that our little disaster didn't have a chance in the world."

Alone, he said, he could never have "put over Clare's childishly contrived dramatic absurdity," because he did not have faith in it. But she certainly did. He theorized that her theatrical drive came from an unfulfilled ambition to be an actress, and her success from a stagestruck devotion to her work. In addition, she displayed "a wild talent for purposeful acquisitiveness and a fantastic gift for merchandizing [sic] her accomplishments." Most admirable of all was that, in spite of many handicaps and limitations, "she believes implicitly in her own perfectibility."[56]

28

THE DETERMINING
CONDITION

Sex is basic to security. If you think you fail in that,
nothing else can compensate. —LOUISE BROOKS

Shortly after finishing the script of *Margin for Error*, Clare surprised
John Billings by walking into his office and asking to be sent abroad
as a war correspondent for *Life*. The editor assumed that Henry Luce
had already sanctioned this extraordinary request and felt obliged to
say yes. "Her stuff should be good," he wrote in his diary.[1]

Whether or not Harry did approve, he appeared in Washington on
September 12, 1939, to apply for a special passport in his wife's name,
because new federal restrictions permitted only bona fide reporters to
visit the battlefronts of Europe.[2] Actually, he feared for his wife's safety,
and ached at the thought of a long separation. But Clare insisted that
time apart was essential, to examine and try to deal with the rift between them, which had been widening for two years.

Its most serious physical manifestation was Harry's chronic lack of
libido. Their first assumption had been that he was suffering mental and
physical fatigue. The previous summer they had hoped to cure it with

rest, exercise, and copious pummeling at Aix-les-Bains, but the trip to Poland had forestalled any benefits. Back home, with the problem unresolved, Clare had started waking up with "vicious" headaches—a possible symptom of sexual frustration. She was bewildered by the impotence of a husband who swore, "I shall love you till I die," and at last wondered if she might be its cause.[3]

Dr. Rosenbluth somewhat naively assured her that the problem was Harry's. Any "normal" man left alone at night with a willing, attractive female would want to sleep with her, unless he was in love with another woman, "and even then, if he hasn't 'had it' for a spell." The problem surely lay in Luce's mind rather than his body. "He is crippled by some erotic neurosis . . . and you had best leave him."[4]

Clare, unprepared for such a drastic step, confronted Harry and asked if his "blockage" specifically related to her. Denied a satisfactory answer, let alone a solution for herself, she began seeing a psychiatrist. But the sessions came to an abrupt end when Clare, with a distinct sense of *déjà vu*, heard the analyst offer to cure her of "inhibition" physically rather than psychologically.[5]

Still miserable, but prevented by the success of her new play from leaving for Europe, at least until the New Year, she reverted to the "infinitely understanding" Rosenbluth. He put her on a diet, prescribed sleeping pills, and gave her injections to mitigate depression.[6] Far from rejuvenated, she sought solace at Mepkin in mid-November. Harry followed at the end of the month for a two-week vacation.

To Clare the plantation, with its servants and copious guests, had come to symbolize the aristocratic privilege she had dreamed of as a girl in the Deep South. She had written two successful plays there and was contemplating a third script before she went abroad. Harry saw Mepkin rather as a place to recuperate from the demands of publishing. They both hoped that the tranquil spot on the Cooper River, which had seen romantic moments early in their marriage, might work its magic again in the Christmas season of 1939.

It was not to be. Harry, nervous about being too much alone with his wife, invited two of his executives, Roy Larsen and Dan Longwell, down for shoptalk (Russia had just invaded Finland), leavened with a little hunting. He seemed tired and disconsolate, carped endlessly at tiny household hitches, and resented Clare's preoccupation with writing. When they were all together, he behaved irritably, even boorishly.

Larsen and Longwell returned to the office after a few days, complaining of Luce's "bad manners."[7]

Clare let her own irritation show by cruelly berating Harry about his loss of looks and virility. After he too sought sanctuary back in New York, she sent him a frank letter. For reasons obscure to her, she wrote, he had made her feel that she and "this pleasant place" had failed him. He could not excuse himself on the grounds of a "deep psychic maladjustment"—at least none that she was aware of. Nor had he any right to complain about their life in general. "To conjure up some dominant discontent or misery out of such good fortune as ours is positively wanton." If their marriage was to founder, it should do so for serious reasons, such as ill health, financial calamity, or falling out of love.

> There are times when a man or woman does better to act with sense than to react with sensibility. This seems to me to be one of them. You are a pretty complicated person—you are also intelligent enough to see that after a certain point complications in one's mind or heart become destructive forces, *not* to be endured. I would like to show more sympathy to you in this matter, but . . . if I did, I should not be acting with as much love as I feel for you. You see, I not only love you . . . but I like you, and admire you far more than you think. Indeed, you always seem to be afraid that if I didn't love you blindly, I would dislike you openly. That is not the case. You know, I've seen you in some pretty tight places, I've judged you often, in relation to your fellow-men . . . Never have I seen you fall below the level of an extraordinary generosity and decency . . . That is why, perhaps, it surprises me all the more to have you behave—well, *childishly,* with me . . .
>
> Am I scolding you? I most certainly am. Indeed, if *I* were as strong as you, I'd dispense with words, and give you, what you have, with a rather salutary effect, given *me* once or twice—a hell of a spanking . . .
>
> Now darling, to bed. I do not like to go to bed without you. But somehow, lately, even when I'm with you, I seem to go to bed without you.[8]

Harry's reply to this well-reasoned lecture shows a man alarmed by midlife mental burnout, physical deterioration, and waning sexual appeal. "I have the feeling I am racing against something which may vaguely be called Time," he began, with an involuntary pun.

> It is really myself that I am racing against I suppose. But in any case I feel a little panicky—and it will perhaps serve some purpose in trying to face it.
>
> Others find me in excellent health and spirits. Only to you does it matter that my hair is falling out, that my teeth are decaying and that the chances of my ever becoming a moderately respectable example of Nordic strength are rapidly vanishing. As to my spirits—it is of course you, who besides myself, have most cause to find me "difficult," to see me lacking in guts, and in general resembling nothing so much as a spoiled pup.
>
> Though it is possible that you know me better than I do myself . . . nevertheless I do think I have some data in regard to myself which it is worthwhile to put on the record . . .
>
> I do believe that relatively to most men, and relatively also to whatever superiority should be expected of me, I have been living through rather long periods of nervous strain. (With one year out at Oxford and a few other shorter interludes it may be described as about 30 years in duration.) And it is the cumulative result of that of which I am afraid.
>
> My feeling of the race against Time is of a race toward the time when, not overnight but gradually the nerve-tensions may have a chance to ease and a balance of work and leisure and generosity restored.

Having unburdened himself to this unusual degree, Harry stressed that there was only "one possible event that terrorizes me . . . that I should damage, more than I have, our love . . . lose because I had no right to stay."[9]

The new play Clare had in mind was only partly her own. Alexander King, who had helped her with *Margin for Error*, needed aid himself on an unfinished comedy entitled *The Yohimbe Tree*. Set on a Caribbean island, it dealt—ironically for poor Harry—with the miraculous effects on a group of uptight Americans of an aphrodisiac made from sacred bark.[10]

Clare had known the multitalented and eccentric King (who habitually wore green suits and pink ties) for over a decade. In her editorial days, she had admired his contributions to *The New Yorker*, his artwork for H. L. Mencken's *Smart Set*, and his splendid illustrations for Horace Liveright's special editions of classic novels. A year or so after her marriage to Luce, she had recommended Alex for a job at *Life*, where his talents and wide knowledge of foreign cultures soon made him a valued editor, and "picture gatherer without peer."[11]

With his painter's eye and playwright's sharp sensibility, King described Harry as "a timber-wolf kind of man," with "a great deal of dangerous integrity." Yet he saw that in the corridors of Time Inc. it was Clare who was perceived as the "potent ogre." In fact, at the mere mention of her name, the staff "practically crossed themselves."[12]

King had doubts about compromising the originality of his play by taking on the formidable Clare Boothe as co-author. She struck him as a woman of "relentless ambition" who was embittered by having been "snubbed plenty" in her youth. As a result, she never felt sorry for anyone else. What concerned him most was her shallow-mindedness and what he—surprisingly, in view of her reputation for wisecracks—considered a lack of native wit.[13] Yet he could not dismiss the value of Clare's analytic powers, or her Broadway contacts.

King arrived at Mepkin in the new year of 1940 and found several other guests in residence. They included Rudolf Kommer, Iris Tree, the English poet, and some "undistinguished recent arrivals from Europe." He wondered if he was expected to be "obligingly multilingual" in exchange for Clare's help. When Harry came down on the weekend of January 13, nine people assembled for dinner. King at once sensed tension, as Harry, carving a wild duck at one end of the table, and Clare, passing vegetables at the other, carried on a heated debate about the Hollywood star system. As their contention grew more personal and acrimonious, everyone else fell silent. Finally, Harry rested his knife and fork, leaned forward, and icily addressed his wife.

"You're sure you're right, aren't you?"

"Yes, I'm absolutely sure!"

"Well, if you're really so certain . . . are you willing to bet a million dollars on it?"

King noticed the blood draining from Clare's face. She was about to take up the challenge when the enormity of the wager, as well as the sight of her astonished and embarrassed guests, gave her pause. Somebody changed the subject.[14]

During his solitary journey back to New York, Harry asked himself what he, a missionary's son, was doing owning a plantation with horses and game when all he wanted was to publish magazines. There was ambivalence in his heart now about the place where he had once been happy, and which every other member of his family loved. "Mepkin has not been very good to me this year," he wrote his wife. "But someday . . . the gods may permit me to come there as one who does not intrude on Paradise."[15]

King went north at the end of the month with two acts of *The Yohimbe Tree* completed. Not long after he submitted an article to *Vogue* mischievously called "Clare Doesn't Care." It did not run, perhaps because he had to pull his punches in describing his employer's wife. But the manuscript has a few telling observations about her disciplined professionalism as a playwright. Clare Boothe exemplified, he wrote, "the process of refrigeration which turns a warm impulse into a cold resolution." Her mind had the "tenacity of a beaver trap" as she labored over lines, gags, and dramatic devices. She acted out each part until she achieved the "quality of seeming casualness" that is an essential ingredient of fine dialogue.

He also tackled the subject of her social personality. While she could be gushingly friendly, she suffered from the most "astonishing unpopularity." One reason might be envy. King quoted a nameless acquaintance as saying, "She wants to be Franklin Roosevelt, Sinclair Lewis, Bernard Shaw, Mme. Curie, and Greta Garbo." His own theory was that Clare was disliked for conveying the sense she "could do tranquilly, beautifully, and endlessly" without anyone.[16]

Harry realized the truth of this as far as he was concerned. Clare seemed content at Mepkin whether he came or not. She was at ease in foreign palaces with or without him, thrived among the theater and Hollywood people who made him uncomfortable, and, most perplexing of all, enjoyed creative solitude, whereas he could hardly bear being alone, even after a hard day at the office.

Admiring though he was of her independence, he was troubled by what he considered her most serious flaw. They quarreled about it frequently and violently. "What's all the shooting about?" he wrote after one altercation. "The shooting is about consistency."[17]

Clare's quixotic changes of mind about the kind of work she preferred confused Harry to the point of incoherence. When they met she had been a journalist and author of a book of stories. Then she had told him, "I want to write plays." Yet she had continued publishing articles, done radio broadcasts, tried her hand at movie scripts, and even taken a screen test. Now she wanted to be a war correspondent.[18]

In early February some symbolic mishaps at Mepkin conspired to persuade Clare that it was time to carry out her plan to visit Europe. First, an unexpected snowstorm killed her beloved camellias. Then, a house party, which she had arranged in order to seduce Gilbert Miller into producing *The Yohimbe Tree*, was catastrophically cut short when the plantation's power plant burned down, denying all buildings light, heat, water, and plumbing for the rest of the season.[19] Her dramatist's instinct called for at least a change of scene. It might conveniently, she thought, be expanded into a prolonged intermission.

On the tenth Clare made her formal announcement, saying that her traveling papers were in order and that she was ready to set off, "to find out whether this war is our business or not." In New York six days later, she met with three of Harry's senior editors. Over a lunch of tomato juice and hot baked apple, she asked their views on "the phony war" and said she was determined to find out how long the statesmen of England, France, and Italy were prepared to tolerate it. Billings, impressed in spite of himself, said that one way *Life* might publish her material was in the form of letters from the "front."[20]

That weekend Clare bade farewell to Ann at Foxcroft. She would not be back for Easter, she said, and recommended her daughter spend it with "Uncle David." Preparing Harry for her departure was not so easy. He knew that the trip would be dangerous and lengthy. They quarreled loudly, and for the first time talked of divorce.[21]

In a calmer moment Harry diagnosed their marriage as lacking cohesiveness, "or what I might more poetically call an inner relationship of everything." On the romantic level, they enjoyed many superficial things together, such as holding hands at the cinema. Fundamentally, though, their stars were taking them along different trajectories. They had not yet fixed on "the determining condition" of their shared life. Harry believed that it was simply love, but asked, "love how lived?"[22]

Clare had no answer to such a philosophical question. She did not even know what she ultimately wanted for herself. Mark Sullivan had once told her, "Writing is the thing your nature longs for . . . writing out of you what is in you."[23] By returning to journalism, she would be recording the exterior tragedy wrought by foreign squabbles instead of creating fictional works from her interior thoughts and feelings. In putting aside, or postponing, her theater ambitions, she tacitly acknowledged that Harry was justified in accusing her of "inconsistency."

Unwilling or unable to alter her quixotic nature, yet sure that she was doing the right thing to save her marriage, Clare embarked on the SS *Manhattan* on February 24. Margaret Case was ostensibly her traveling companion, but the passenger list also included Ambassador Joseph Kennedy.

As she said good-bye to Harry, Clare told him not to "come chasing" after her.[24] He promised not to, and spent his first wifeless weekend in agony over her absence. "You have taken the immediate destiny of our love, our forever-love, completely into your beautiful hands," he wrote. "Of vast destinies you are the privileged observer, but of that little private destiny, so unimportant in the cosmos, you are now the keeper."[25]

29

PROVEN MATERIAL

A satirist is too often a sadist . . . thinly disguised.

—MAX GORDON

When "Mrs. Henry R. Luce" had last crossed the Atlantic, she had been moderately famous, at least in the United States, as a successful playwright. Now, in late February 1940, the name Clare Boothe was internationally known because a star-studded movie version of *The Women* had been showing for some six months in thousands of cinemas around the world. Directed by George Cukor, the picture featured Norma Shearer, Joan Crawford, Rosalind Russell, Joan Fontaine, Paulette Goddard, and no fewer than 130 other actresses and female extras.[1]

Almost two years had passed since Metro-Goldwyn-Mayer had acquired the rights to Clare's Broadway hit. As a measure of the property's box-office potential, the producer, Hunt Stromberg, had hired F. Scott Fitzgerald to adapt it for the screen. Buff Cobb wrote Clare to say that Fitzgerald had told her how much he admired the author of *The Women*.[2] As it turned out, the final shooting script was not his. But he had written several versions, and his painstaking summaries of Mary Haines's early history—as he imagined it—survive as evidence of his need as a novelist to understand what shaped and motivated Clare's bland heroine. As the educated daughter of a presumably religious mother, Mary would not, in his view, be comfortable with Park Avenue socialites who operated entirely according to their temptations. He therefore chose to make her "active, intelligent, and courageous," rather than "passive, simple, and easily influenced."[3]

Stromberg was afraid these alterations might intellectualize Miss Boothe's hugely successful comedy, so he reassigned the script to Jane Murfin. Cukor approved the move because he believed you should not "muck around much with proven material." Fitzgerald could not summon up much regret over the lost opportunity. The work had been, he told his daughter, "the last tired effort of a man who once did something finer and better."[4]

Miss Murfin's interpretation was as pedestrian as Fitzgerald's was inventive. So Anita Loos, author of *Gentlemen Prefer Blondes*, became Murfin's accredited collaborator. Loos's most challenging task was to insert "clean" jokes where some eighty of Clare's more risqué lines had been cut by the Hays Office.[5]

Cukor loved working with women to such an extent that he had been removed from *Gone With the Wind* for favoring Vivien Leigh over Clark Gable. Here he had the luxury of a project that would exclude men from every frame. He fanatically adhered to Clare's conceit that all the sets—designed with exceptional flamboyance by Cedric Gibbons—were to be feminine domain: ladies' rooms, couture departments, boudoirs, mud and bubble baths, cosmetics counters, and kitchens. Grips built a vast, circular, twenty-four-unit beauty and exercise salon sporting the most up-to-date equipment. Cukor also ordered an exact replica of a Reno dude ranch as a hostelry for would-be divorcées and carpeted it with Navajo rugs. For authenticity he trucked in fifty loads of desert sand, as well as fragile glass furniture for Mary Haines's Deco apartment. All the prop paintings, photographs, and figurines were female. Every book captured by the lens was by an "authoress," and not one had a male name in its title. Yet nine tenths of the dialogue was about men, leading one reviewer to call them "the absent presence."[6]

The director's gender obsession even extended to on-screen fauna. His opening credits symbolically dissolved the faces of animals into those of leading characters: a gentle doe became Shearer's Mary Haines, a fierce black cat Crawford's Crystal Allen, a predatory leopard Russell's Sylvia Fowler, and a lynx Goddard's Miriam Aarons. Thanks to the insertion of a zoo scene, no fewer than twenty-five species—feline, canine, equine, simian, and avian—populated the production.[7]

Joan Crawford as Crystal in the movie version of
The Women, 1939

The animal motif was continued throughout the action proper. Cukor began his 132-minute movie on a suitably bitchy note with two leashed dogs snapping at each other. He then segued not to Clare's bridge game but to a beauty parlor scene, in a rapid montage of shrill-voiced women pampered by manicurists and masseuses.

Gilbert A. Adrian, MGM's top costume designer, created 237 outfits and co-directed a five-minute fashion show in color that interrupted the black-and-white footage halfway through.[8] The result was decidedly bizarre. For the first time in couture history, thirty-five models were required to act as well as strut, forsaking the runway for scenes of "real," albeit monosexual, life. A beach belle removed a robe that was held between her breasts by a life-size *papier-mâché* hand. First-nighters in elaborate gowns arose from an all-female auditorium and undulated to the bar to buy their own drinks. Zoo visitors tossed peanuts at caged chimpanzees dressed, like themselves, in *haute couture* suits and hats.

Most audiences found the color segment intrusive, but the picture as a whole was a commercial and critical success. In a compliment as much to Anita Loos as to Clare, *The New Republic* praised *The Women* for having "more wicked wit than Hollywood has been allowed since *The Front Page*." Frank Nugent of *The New York Times* said every studio should make at least one "thoroughly nasty picture" like it every year. He included it on his annual list of the ten best movies, as did *Film Daily* and the newspaper film critics of America.[9]

As Clare's ship steamed towards Europe, Motion Picture Academy members were casting their Oscar votes. *The Women* was not nominated in any category. Competition was formidable that spring. Candidates for best picture were *Dark Victory*, *Wuthering Heights*, *Of Mice and Men*, *The Wizard of Oz*, *Mr. Smith Goes to Washington*, *Love Affair*, *Goodbye, Mr. Chips*, *Ninotchka*, *Stagecoach*, and the eventual multiprize winner, *Gone With the Wind*. Still, Clare had her first screen credit as progenitor of a major picture, and two more were looming for *Kiss the Boys Good-bye* and *Margin for Error*.[10] Hundreds of thousands, if not millions, of moviegoers now knew who she was, and Hollywood producers would soon be offering her the chance to write original screenplays.

But for the time being she was headed east, not west, in the hope that dispatches from the European front would further burnish the name and fame of Clare Boothe.

30

EUROPE

IN THE SPRING

God is always on the side of the big battalions.

— VOLTAIRE

Arriving in Rome on March 4, 1940, Clare found the Hotel Excelsior crowded with Fascist Congress delegates and Army officers wearing "musical-comedy uniforms, which all looked a little too big for them." Good rooms were scarce, so she bribed her way into a marble suite just vacated by President Roosevelt's roving envoy, Sumner Welles. It was still full of welcoming flowers. She convinced herself that, as *Life*'s newest war correspondent, she too was on "a fact-finding commission . . . for the benefit of the American people."[1]

Clare intended to stay in the capital for five days, trying to find out from ordinary Italians the chances of Benito Mussolini taking Hitler's side against France and Britain. Il Duce had not yet committed himself, but his bellicose proclivities were obvious. Everywhere she went on her initial sightseeing tour, she noticed signs of his addiction to the archaeology of Ancient Rome. Max Thornburg, a Texan she had flirted with on the way over, wisecracked, "Unable to build an empire, he's had to excavate one."[2]

For all her populist intentions, Clare soon reverted to the kind of company she found most congenial. Maggie Case's connections enabled her to dine with local aristocrats, pay court to the English scholar and aesthete Harold Acton, and secure, if not an interview, at least a group audience with Pope Pius XII. At a party on March 7 in Donna Cora Caetani's fashionable apartment, Clare had her first, frustrating lesson in the wiles of European salon diplomacy. Her instructor was Mussolini's foreign minister and son-in-law, Count Galeazzo Ciano, a suavely handsome man with an aquiline profile and athletic build.

At first Clare thought she would be able to handle him as easily as she handled socialites back in New York—providing she could steer the Count away from his wife, whom she sensed was "cruel and strong." To her delight, he was placed next to her at dinner and spoke fluent English.[3]

The conversation at table mainly concerned Italy's coal crisis, about which Clare knew nothing. After dessert, waiters cleared the tables and brought out cards and chips. "I don't like gambling," Ciano said. "Come talk to me." He escorted her to an empty room. She was pleased at the prospect of a *tête-à-tête* with a member of Mussolini's innermost circle. But she told him frankly she was afraid to speak her mind in totalitarian Rome. Ciano, showing off his command of American idioms, encouraged her to "shoot the works."

"I'd like to say that the Germans are double-crossing so-and-sos," Clare began.

Ciano, toying with her, remarked, "All right, say it."

She repeated her little speech. "And I think Italy will make the mistake of its history to go in with them."

"Now, you see," said the Count, still teasing, "nothing has happened to you!"

Not to be put off, she said she needed a quotable "reaction" from him.

"Demanding a reaction to what you say is supposed to be rather more Fascist than democratic, don't you think?"

Unctuously changing the subject, Ciano asked why a successful playwright should be so interested "in the ugly world of politics." For the rest of the evening he evaded all her attempts to get a hint of Italy's war plans. Instead he expounded on his admiration for the United States, his thwarted literary ambitions, his love of music, art, and modern sculpture. When Edda Ciano appeared and signaled it was time to go, the Count stood up. Clare asked sarcastically, "May I quote you on all these vital matters?"

"Oh, by all means," Ciano answered, flashing two rows of perfect teeth.[4]

Three days later it became excruciatingly clear to her that she had failed to get a historic scoop from the one Italian besides Mussolini who "really knew what was going to happen." Just as her train to Paris pulled out on March 10, that of Hitler's foreign minister, Joachim von Ribbentrop, pulled in at a neighboring platform. There, waiting to meet him, was Count Ciano.[5] The purpose of their meeting, she later discovered, was to arrange the climactic conference between the Führer and Il Duce at the Brenner Pass on March 18. It would bring Italy into the war, and seal the fate of France.

Alighting at the Gare de Lyon in Paris, Clare began to sense the city's vulnerability. The windows of the station had been painted out and reinforced against bomb blasts with strips of gummed paper. Yet at the Ritz the usual comings and goings of perfumed, fur-clad women created an unreal aura of normalcy.

She was guiltily aware that she had spent too much time in Rome fraternizing with high society. Making amends here, she began using her schoolgirl French on *citoyens* in public parks and small cafés. They assured her that Hitler could not have the three-to-one superiority in troops and weapons needed to overrun France or he would have done so after securing Poland. It was in any case naval supremacy that decided the fate of nations—and France and Britain had that. Clare tried to challenge their complacency, with little success. Her interviewees were reluctant to accept what she had learned from Bernard Baruch and others—that in eight months of "phony war" the Führer had hugely increased his armaments.[6]

Despite France's shortages of food, heat, and light, its entertainment and luxury industries continued to thrive. Maurice Chevalier packed the Casino de Paris nightly, couturiers held their spring shows, vintners shipped new wines, and factories exported tons of silk—unaware that some German industrialists were buying it for parachutes.[7]

Clare made a quick flying visit to England for the Easter weekend. Joe Kennedy was alone at his country place near Windsor, having shipped Rose and the children home to Massachusetts, out of harm's way. The usually ebullient ambassador was glum because he had failed to convince President Roosevelt of the enormous economic consequences of being drawn into another European war. He predicted it would cost the United States "a hundred percent" more than the last one.[8] Clare found herself sympathizing less and less with Kennedy's isolationism, even as she comforted his solitude.

Back in Paris, she received a passionate letter from Harry, who was pining for her early return to New York. Many mornings he saw dawn before having any sleep. "It takes practically nothing—your scrawled initials on a memo pad—to explode well-ordered emotions into a flame of recollection and hope." Just before leaving, she had disingenuously warned him that he would "be risking a great deal" if he ever let her stay away more than a month. That length of time had now passed, and she was by no means ready to come home. She insisted that she loved him. "Forgive the fact that I don't prove it by living with you more." Meanwhile she had an appointment at Balenciaga and intimate plans to entertain her diplomatic admirer from across the Channel. "JPK in bedroom all morning," she wrote in her diary on April 2.[9]

Most important of all, she wanted to be the first female to see France's famed Maginot Line. Everybody assured her this chain of concrete fortifications along the German border was impregnable. To smooth her way, Clare volunteered to become the *marraine*, or sponsor, of one of the forts and sent "her" soldiers champagne and cigarettes—not to mention a flag with the motto *"Ils ne passeront pas."* Mustering her considerable charm, she persuaded the French supreme commander, General Maurice Gamelin, to grant her request.[10] Then she cabled Harry as tactfully as possible:

DARLING IF YOU WOULDN'T BE TOO DISAPPOINTED FEEL VERY
IMPORTANT I SHOULD STAY . . . GOVERNMENT OFFERS MAR-

EUROPE IN THE SPRING

On April 5 she received a note from the officer assigned as her escort
to the front. "Dear Miss Boothe: Be ready please for morning . . . You
will visit your Maginot Fort . . . All the safe conducts are signed."[12]

At dawn next day, a captain named Charles Brousse picked her up
in a General Headquarters staff car. As they set off eastward towards *la
zone des armées*, he cautioned that possible danger lay ahead. "The war
in the Ritz is one thing, the war out there is quite another!" As Clare
subsequently discovered, he exaggerated. German forces behind the
Siegfried Line were under orders not to fire until fired upon.

By noon the travelers were at Châlons-sur-Marne, a small town
well within the zone. Liaison personnel welcomed them to its only
hotel and presented a lunch of *hors d'oeuvres*, salmon, Bresse chicken,
mushrooms, artichokes, cheese, fruit, and *champagne rosé*. "No matter
what happens to France," Brousse remarked, "her officers will always
dine like kings."

Moving on across the fertile meadows of Lorraine in pale sunshine,
Clare noticed snouts of field guns protruding from haystacks. It was one
of the gross juxtapositions of war:

> Half-built cottages everywhere housed machine-gun nests.
> And on the little green brows of hundreds of tender hills nes-
> tled a vast nasty brood of camouflaged cement pill-boxes.
> Plains bristled like porcupines with thick-growing, short vi-
> cious iron quills to repel tanks. Wide, deep-dug holes pocking
> the valleys yawned for them. And far-flung across the uplands
> lay wide, unbroken lines of barbed wire . . . fakir's beds of
> shining nails, defying Nazi mystics to immolate themselves
> upon them painlessly.

In the surrounding forests—though she could not see them—were
thousands of armed men. "It looks peaceful," said Brousse, "but let one
German division move over the Siegfried, and it will all turn into an
inferno."[13]

Near sunset they arrived at the Hôtel Royal in Metz. Here Clare was
reunited with her old friend from *Vanity Fair* days Count René de

Chambrun. He was now a public relations lieutenant in the French Army and had spent much of the past eight months showing the Line to distinguished visitors, including King George VI of England.[14] Clare decided René was just the kind of diplomatic contact she needed to help her reportage. As a great-great grandson of the Marquis de Lafayette, he was an honorary American citizen, and as the son-in-law of France's former premier Pierre Laval, he had contacts at high levels. He told her that Laval was poised to reassume power, with two old warriors, Marshal Philippe Pétain and General Maxime Weygand, at his side should events conspire to topple the current administration of Edouard Daladier.

At dinner René learnedly expounded upon the strategic differences between 1914 and 1940. The Kaiser, he said, had been obliged to fight fifty powers on five fronts. But Hitler, with the acquiescence of Mussolini and Stalin, could concentrate most of his aggression on one. It was to defend this vulnerable two-thousand-kilometer border that eleven years ago France had begun building the $500 million Maginot.

Clare, curious about things military since her adolescent tour of the Great War battlefields, asked why German forces, given the probable odds against penetration, would choose to attack the Line.

"They always have," replied René. Since the days of Attila the Hun, they had invaded by way of Alsace and Lorraine no fewer than thirty-two times. Catching himself, he conceded, "The last time they did come through Belgium."[15]

Next morning Clare, Brousse, and de Chambrun made the final hour's drive from Metz to her adopted fort, "Le Mont des Welsches." The commandant met her at the security gate and took her up the hill. As they crested the top, she saw an immense row of cement redoubts. Their green, mushroom-shaped domes lifted a few inches to salute her, revealing the muzzles of antitank and machine guns. "Madame," said the commandant, tapping the ground with his stick, "it is beneath us, here, at a depth of four hundred feet, that your six hundred boys live day and night."

"Let's go down and see them," Clare said.[16]

Soon she was descending through multi-storied chambers, protected by fireproof sliding doors, and booby-trapped to drop invaders into fifty-foot pits. An astonishing amount of weaponry was crammed on the upper level. Below were control, chart, and supply rooms storing machinery, oil, tanks, electric gadgets, ammunition, medicine, and food. Subterranean rail tracks connected the fort to others along the line. The commandant assured Clare that sabotage of any kind was impossible because of triplication of every mechanism. In any case, only trustworthy troops of the finest quality manned the installations. Some had been there six years.[17]

Her visit ended in a steel-lined artillery turret that housed two great green-barreled guns, poised on a greased axis. A sergeant shouted, *"Garde à vous!"* As his voice echoed down the staircase, soldiers sprang to their positions, and the two-hundred-ton assembly rotated and rose.

To Clare the whole construction seemed to combine both myth and science fiction. It was a "Trojan city of sinister Martian ingenuity." Strangely stirred, yet skeptical of male posturing at work around her, she again asked, "Why should the Germans try to come this way?"

"Oh, *madame*," the commandant replied, "what have we got our two great armies for, except sooner or later to hurl them at one another?"

"But can't they get into France some other way?"

He and the other officers laughed at her feminine naiveté. Belgium had its own smaller version of the Maginot Line, they explained, while Holland could seriously hamper any invader by opening its dikes to flood the land. Surely the Nazis would not want to take on 3 million Lowlanders, on top of 6 million French.[18]

When Clare emerged into the sunlight, she was greeted by a white-faced *poilu* who presented her with a bunch of wilted carnations. He had walked twenty miles to buy them. As she drove away, and glanced back at the fort in farewell, de Chambrun noticed her blue eyes fill with tears.[19]

On April 7 Clare was enjoying a lunch of oysters, sardines, and a glass of red wine with officers of the Seventh Division of the Third Army when her host, the commanding general, received a message. He read it with his face twitching and called for quiet. German troopships, he announced, were sailing through the Kattegat, bound for Norway. The phony war was over.

"This is the affair of England," he said to his stunned audience. "They have the navy." Handing the note to Clare as a souvenir, he reached for more oysters.[20]

In Paris by the ninth, Clare sent a cable to *Life*. The earliest of her dispatches to survive in Time Inc.'s archives, it shows her conscientiously performing as a foreign correspondent, submitting raw, unpolished material to John Billings's editorial department. She was unable to recount her visit to the Line because of stringent French censorship and so had to confine herself to political observations.

> The likeliest new member of the new Supercabinet is Laval . . . Another figure to be closely watched is Jean Mistler whereon it were wise to check the morgue to see whether there is a good biopersonality in hand . . .
>
> The French regard the [Sumner] Welles trip with almost unanimous suspicion and distrust, deeming its outcome at best a fiasco, at worst stooging for a future Hitler peace offer based on the Allies letting him get away with Poland which is unacceptable to the French because they're unwilling to have to mobilize every six months and want to settle Europe once and for all . . .
>
> One fact emerges clearly that whatever happens the little neutrals are going to get screwed—as anachronisms they've just got to go.[21]

The following afternoon she austerely celebrated her thirty-seventh birthday. It was a "sugarless" day at the Ritz (field kitchens had priority on basic foodstuffs), so guests were not able to celebrate with cake. Writing to Ann, Clare reported that France had lost 1.4 million potential fathers in the Great War and hence had a critical scarcity of able-bodied men. Women were running farms and businesses as well as their own households. "What twists your heart is that they bear it with so much fortitude and cheerfulness."[22]

By now, contrary to René's predictions, the leadership of the Third Republic had been taken over by Paul Reynaud. He and his cabinet welcomed the invasion of Norway as establishing at least another, non-French front. Clare decided that London would be the best place to learn what preparations were under way to liberate Oslo. Before going there she cabled Harry again and said it was crucially important for him to see "this twilight world," the better to describe it for his magazines.[23]

Her language avoided any hint of personal need, but Luce required no urging. He sailed on April 13, telling his staff he was going not "for love" but because important friends had "high-pressured" him.[24]

Clare, meanwhile, attended a crash course on the status of the war from the U.S. military attaché in Paris, Colonel Horace Fuller. He explained why Norway was such a huge prize for Hitler. Not only did the Führer now have vital submarine and air bases but he had sandwiched Sweden's rich supplies of iron ore, nickel, and chromium between his own occupying forces and those of his ally, Joseph Stalin. In Norway he had also a vast capacity to produce cellulose for explosives, as well as copious quantities of cobalt and nitrogen. Considering Germany's further access to the arms, coal, and oil of Poland, Austria, Czechoslovakia, and Rumania, plus the abundant food of Italy, it was plain that Britain and France faced almost insuperable odds.

Colonel Fuller's tactical pointers and precise facts and figures hypnotized Clare. Here at last was someone talking not politics but war. A passion for military language and maneuvers dawned in her, and she was more exhilarated than distressed when Fuller said that the target of the next Nazi offensive was indicated by movement of crack Panzer divisions to the borders of the Low Countries. This had been, at the Maginot, her deduction exactly.

The American Embassy's air attaché, Lieutenant Colonel George Kenny, joined them. He said he was about to go home on a crucial mission to U.S. aircraft manufacturers. If the one thousand fighter planes a month President Roosevelt had promised the Allies were to have any chance against more sophisticated German models, it was essential to update both their design and their technology. This would probably slow production—a depressing prospect.

"We'll get them in plenty of time," Clare said, tentatively optimistic.

Kenny quoted Confucius in reply. "He who follows is always *behind*!"

She turned to Colonel Fuller. "Is there really no hope?"

"The British never know they're licked," he replied. "On, on into the jaws of death, no matter if it is a lousy piece of strategy."[25]

Together again professionally, if not as reconciled lovers, Harry and Clare reached London on April 25 in glorious weather. The city's spring flowers were blossoming, and silver barrage balloons hovered in cloudless skies. But on the ground aging sandbags had split and leaked their contents into the gutters. Some were sprouting greenery: profiteers, evidently, had stuffed them with cheap soil. The seeping bags seemed symbolic of the false sense of security Chamberlain's inept government had fostered over the last eight months.[26]

For the next two weeks the Luces monitored Britain's reaction to the Nazi move into the North Sea. Harry pumped politicians all day with unanswerable questions, while Clare tried to seduce them into indiscretions over the dinner table. She recognized that Parliament was in a state of paralysis. But it was not until May 1, when Britain's hastily trained Expeditionary Force began to withdraw in defeat from the Norwegian fjords, that she noted "the first faint fissure in the wall of British conceit and complacency." Even die-hard Tories like J. L. Garvin, editor of the London *Observer*, began to talk of bringing back seventy-seven-year-old David Lloyd George, the former Liberal prime minister, because, unlike Chamberlain, *he* knew how to delegate authority. Blue bloods, such as those she met at Cliveden, Nancy Astor's country house, sought to deny the importance of the retreat: "England always loses every battle but the last."[27]

Harry and Clare were more interested in the upcoming confrontation, which seemed increasingly certain to be in the Netherlands. Leaving the House of Commons to debate Britain's failed campaign, they flew to Amsterdam, then took a train to The Hague. Field after field of late-blooming white and scarlet tulips stood tall as they traversed the *polderland*. That evening Clare found herself the dinner partner of Holland's Permanent Secretary General for Foreign Affairs, Snouck Hurgronje. He confirmed what Colonel Fuller had told her: the Germans were making troop movements right along Holland's border. When he added that his government had been forewarned of the assault on Norway, she was aghast. Had they not passed this intelligence on to the British and French?

"Why should we? They're not our allies."

After trying to absorb this, Clare pressed him to tell her why, if Hitler was poised to strike, the Dutch failed to join the Allies.

Hurgronje said that, being American, she did not understand. "While we don't want to be 'protected' like Poland and Norway, still we are in no hurry to be 'assisted' in the way the Allies assisted them."[28]

If nothing else, this exchange taught the future U.S. ambassador to Italy two vital elements in Old World diplomacy: its clubby myopia on the one hand, and its obsession with saving face on the other.

On May 9 the Luces moved on to Belgium, where Harry had an appointment with King Leopold III. Arriving near midnight at the American Embassy in Brussels, they went straight to bed in a fourth-floor room overlooking a small park. At dawn Clare was aroused from deep sleep by an excited maid shouting, "Wake up, the Germans are coming!"

She rushed to a wide window. The sun was rising behind a clump of black trees across the square, and overhead she caught sight of about twenty airplanes flying in formation, undersides shining in the first light. As she watched mesmerized, there was a sudden, prolonged whistle, followed by a loud "*bam!*" A three-storied house opposite shattered, hurling glass, wood, and stone into the square. Hitler's long-dreaded *blitzkrieg* had begun.[29]

Through initiative, drive, and uncanny timing, Clare was experiencing something unimaginable to others of her generation, as they luxuriated in the security of the United States: the reality and occasional beauty of war. She was understandably changed by it. For the rest of her life she would be not only in awe of military men but fascinated by their disciplines of tactics, ballistics, and espionage.

Dressing quickly, she went down to the kitchen for coffee and met Ambassador John Cudahy. He told her he had heard at 12:30 A.M. that the Germans were on their way and had telephoned the news to President Roosevelt. Sounding exactly like Ambassador Bullitt, he added that perhaps now the Administration would realize how desperately Europe needed American warplanes. For another hour or so they both stayed below, listening to the deafening noise of antiaircraft guns. At last came the wail of an all-clear siren. Cudahy left for the Foreign Office, and Clare ventured forth to see the wrecked house. Its front, bellied out, reminded her of a yacht in full sail. A postman passed by. Adjusting his pack, he said sardonically, "This is what we call civilization?"[30]

She continued to the center of town. There she watched frantic Belgians buying newspapers, and heard them curse the superior airpower of "the Boche," as they compared the relative merits of Spitfires, Hurricanes, Wellingtons, Messerschmitts, Faireys, and Heinkels. At lunchtime she returned to the embassy, where Cudahy defiantly served his best wine. In the garden afterwards, a secretary showed her a low tin tunnel covered with a few inches of earth, saying it was probably the only air-raid shelter in Brussels.[31]

During what remained of daylight, Clare listened to the radio and finished an elegiac cable report for *Life* describing "this first day of the big show." It reveals her succumbing to the temptation to write rather than merely report.

> The long afternoon is almost gone. In the green square where the glass from the bombed house lies like jagged hail, a child is playing. I hope he will play there again tomorrow. Two children were killed in that early morning raid . . . in this brave new world of Hitler's the sun often sets at dawn.[32]

John Billings liked the account and decided to use it in his next lead. When a subordinate cynically consoled him for "having to run it," the managing editor said he was glad to publish "such simple emotional writing."[33]

At seven o'clock that evening Clare asked if she should dress for dinner. "Why not, *madame?*" a maid replied coolly. "The Germans have not yet arrived."

Ten other people, all in evening clothes, joined her and Harry. Bombs were still dropping around the city. As they dined, a crystal chandelier over the table shook gently with distant reverberations. Only once, when planes droned overhead, was the formality of the meal interrupted. A country gentleman, who might have stepped out of Jean Renoir's *La Règle du Jeu*, told them he was lucky to be there at all. Just that morning he had emerged from a hunting blind to recover a woodcock, only to be surprised by a volley of gunfire from an advance patrol of Germans.[34]

The following day the radio announced that Winston Churchill had succeeded Neville Chamberlain as prime minister of Great Britain. Since Belgium was about to be overrun, Harry had no hope of interviewing King Leopold. The Luces therefore opted for a car ride to Paris with the wife of a Hoover Polish Relief Commission official. Along the Ghent road, Clare stared at the passing figures of displaced people carrying or pushing bundles of possessions. There were also huge camouflaged trucks, "guns mounted on tractors and goggle-eyed motorcycle corps." Beyond Courtrai she watched British troops marching towards her "up the wide glistening road." The soldiers were smiling and singing, *"Roll out the barrel, We'll have a barrel of fun . . ."*[35]

Reaching Paris on the afternoon of May 12, Harry and Clare found the Ritz as busy as ever. That night they attended a dinner party in Versailles. On the way back they were caught on the Boulevard Suchet by an *alerte*. Searchlights crisscrossed the sky, shells burst, and guns blasted all around. A *gendarme* stopped their limousine and directed them to shelter in a nearby apartment-house basement. "This is not a life for *ordinary* people to lead," an irritated housewife said to Clare. "Why can't the Germans let our soldiers fight this war?"[36]

Meanwhile, Winston Churchill was telling the British, in the first of his inspirational radio broadcasts, that he had nothing to offer them "but blood, toil, tears and sweat." Next day the Nazis crossed the River Meuse at Sedan and Dinant, sweeping French tanks out of their path. On May 15 General Gamelin warned that he could not guarantee the safety of Paris for more than another twenty-four hours. Prime Minister Reynaud made plans to move the seat of government to Tours.

At this point Clare realized that the enemy's war of movement, involving indiscriminate destruction of men, women, children, houses, churches, trees, and fields, as well as soldiers and weaponry, was the result of a new tactical phenomenon.

> Before the invasion nearly everybody in France who was really thinking about war, was thinking about it in terms of firm battle lines and forts and trenches and "fronts." Now they knew that the real front in France was the entire blue sky over it, and that the Germans were already bombing that front from the coast to the Maginot and back, and from

the Belgian border to Versailles. They were dropping parachutists with thermite bombs, with flaming torches, in villages defended and undefended. They were sending tanks, like clever gigantic cockroaches scurrying across a kitchen shelf, through all the French lines and back to the dark holes they came from. They were driving civilian populations here and there with bombers, cluttering the roads and machine-gunning them and the troop columns coming up, and ambulance trains, with equal ferocity.[37]

As increasing numbers of blistered and bleeding casualties of this total war poured into the city from the north, Clare saw Harry off on a train to Lisbon, where he had a seat reserved on the Pan Am Clipper.[38] Since she was his correspondent, he could not argue with her decision to stay behind. The curtain was rising on what she saw as Act Two of an immense and gruesome tragedy. She had missed Act One in Poland by only a week. Now, with General Rommel's Seventh Panzer Division less than a hundred miles away, she found herself with what she had always coveted in the theater of life—a place in the front row.

A White Russian traveling in Harry's compartment noticed Clare on the platform and said she looked "distinguished." Luce agreed. What he saw as his locomotive pulled out was not only a beautiful woman but a fearlessly independent one, fast becoming aware of her own powers and importance. From the Hotel Biarritz in San Sebastián, he addressed a letter to his "Dearest Goddess, shining-helmeted in the battle," and told her "for the 10,000th time" that she was "completely adorable."[39]

Two days after Harry's departure, Reynaud made Marshal Pétain his deputy. General Weygand, recalled from Syria, became supreme commander in place of Gamelin. Both appointments were ill-fated. At eighty-four, Pétain had energy for organizing little more than orderly retreats. Weygand, though only eleven years younger, believed in unremitting attack. Strategically they would cancel each other out.

Clare, still gathering information for her articles, went to the Gare du Nord and mingled with the latest trainloads of refugees. An old Red Cross nurse feeding soup to hungry children tugged at her sleeve. "Who has betrayed us?" she asked bitterly. "We have the Maginot—we sacrificed so much for it—and *they* promised the Germans could not pass!"[40]

In the hours and days to come, Clare would hear the word *trahi*—betrayed—many times. "At first it was no more than a whisper. And then the whisper became a great wail that swept through France."

In sparkling sunlight, she made her way home to the Ritz and found it a scene of frantic activity. Vuitton trunks were piled high on the pavement, and the revolving doors spun giddily with departing guests.[41]

Clare's penultimate cable to Billings, dated May 23, 1940, contained a playwright's perception of how the capital of a great nation gradually accepts that it is doomed.

> Paris gets its information about what France has been doing all day, all night, the way a woman gets hers about what her husband has been up to . . . All the smiles or frowns on the politicians' faces when they leave their offices, the way military mustaches droop or bristle at midnight, the inflections of well known voices saying nothing on the radio, on the telephones, the way important people walk in the street, the way ministry doors are slammed, by the significant silences of a great race of talkers, by a thousand little downward percolating uncensorable gestures and indications, the contagious climate of a mood spreads from the top of Paris to the bottom, from clerk to doorman, to domestic, to waiter, to policeman, to taxi drivers . . . so that the people of Paris know from hour to hour how the fate of France is going. Love may be blind to the faults, but is seldom blind to the physical condition of the beloved.[42]

Harry frantically cabled his wife on May 25 to leave Europe by whatever means of transport possible. "Grab anything you can get." But Clare was having far too stimulating a time to think of escape. She stayed another six days, while the Ritz rapidly emptied. On May 30 the concierge told her, "You too must pack, *madame*. The Germans are coming."

Clare asked how he knew for sure.

"Because they have reservations."[43]

Unable to catch a plane that day, she resolved to leave for Le Bourget Airport early the following morning. With the afternoon free, she decided to fulfill a long-standing desire: to see the famous Sphinx brothel, which for years had been one of the capital's more titillating attractions. A friend, Count de Poligny, offered to escort her.

No sooner had they arrived at the *bordel de luxe* than to her consternation de Poligny selected a whip from the wall and disappeared with a large-breasted *poule*. "I'll only be ten minutes," he called out over his shoulder.

The matron of the establishment, wearing black satin and a cross around her neck, offered to give Clare a tour of the unoccupied *chambres à coucher*. Each was uniquely designed to satisfy the most bizarre of sexual fantasies. One was a simulated train compartment that rocked gently, as if on rails. Another, resembling a medieval torture dungeon, featured branding irons and a rack. Next came a mock gynecologist's office equipped with stirrups and instruments. Elsewhere, distant foghorns sounded through the portholes of a captain's cabin down the corridor, while in a nearby hayloft a *papier-mâché* cow mooed, and a rooster sang "cock-a-doodle-do."

A petite young whore, who seemed to think Clare was from Hollywood, invited her into a room with mirrored walls. She pointed to a leather couch and said, "It is here that I always entertain Marlene."[44]

Clare spent her last evening in Paris dining with Otto von Habsburg, the twenty-seven-year-old son of Austria's last emperor. "It was incredibly macabre," von Habsburg recalled half a century later. "The city was two-thirds surrounded by German troops, the sky was lit up with artillery fire, and there, at the Ritz, everything was as it had always been: waiters in tails, the food, the wine."[45]

The hotel proprietor asked them to sign his distinguished guest book. Little did they know that the name beneath theirs would be that of an aide to General Erwin Rommel.[46]

By now the Belgian Army, unable to resist the German onslaught, had surrendered. Some 200,000 British soldiers fighting alongside in Flanders found themselves with no country to defend. They were instructed to abandon all arms and equipment and head for the beaches of Dunkirk. Luftwaffe bombers swooped overhead as flotillas of fishing boats and paddle steamers joined troop carriers in ferrying the men across the English Channel. One in four of the escapees was hit, leaving the survivors to fight another day.

Clare had managed to secure a Clipper reservation out of Lisbon on June 10, but Spanish and Portuguese red tape prevented her connecting from Paris. She decided to try her luck from London and went at 7:00 A.M. to the airport in the hope of transferring there. Flights were scarce and dangerous, since a furious air battle was developing over the Channel. During the next eleven hours, as she waited, the RAF would shoot down thirty-eight Nazi aircraft and lose twenty-eight of its own.[47]

A calm little Frenchman in gray suede gloves and spats said to her, "*Il n'y a pas de situations désespérées, il y a seulement des hommes désespérés.*"[48]

At 6:30 she left on a British plane to Heston. The sun was setting as she flew there via a western route that kept well clear of the fighting to the east.

In London on June 1 she found everybody illogically proud of the Dunkirk rescue. *The Times* lauded it as "one of the most magnificent Naval and Military feats of all time." In fact, coming just over a month after the withdrawal from Norway, it was another retreat.[49]

At Claridges, Clare encountered survivors of the Belgian rout. They had come straight from Dover. Their uniforms were saltwater damp, and flecks of Flanders mud still clung to their whiskers. "Just like old times," she heard one officer remark. "In the last war I used to sleep at the Ritz in Paris every night, and barge out to the front right after breakfast. Queer though, I should now be coming back from the front to Claridges."[50]

With several days to spare before her connection, Clare continued to ferret out what information she could. The British head of Military Intelligence told her that pillow talk was seriously jeopardizing Allied operations. Top officials "who should know better" were revealing secrets to their lovers that were "innocently blabbed by rosebud mouths all over London."[51] If Oliver Stanley, now Secretary of War, told Clare anything of a classified nature, she was responsible enough not to include it in her cabled reports to Time Inc. The most Stanley would say on the record was that Hitler's planned invasion of Britain would be the "final struggle between the principle of law and the principle of violence." Whether England won or lost it meant for him, and his fellow blue bloods, "the end of everything we stand for."[52]

To Clare, a more immediate consequence of Germany's threat was that her play *Margin for Error*, due to open in the West End that week, had to be postponed. As she drily wired Harry, "The kind of audiences expected in June will not like it."[53]

On the eighth she left for Lisbon. Max Thornburg, her former shipboard companion, took her to the airport. She told him she was in despair about England's unpreparedness. "I don't understand the British at all . . . It just makes me so ill and so mad! Don't they, for God's sake, know what they're in for?"

"Do you think they'll take it when it comes?"

"Why yes, of course," she replied impatiently.

"I mean *really* take it, from John o'Groat's to Land's End, until there's hardly an English home standing or an Englishman left alive."

"You know I think they will."

"Then you've found out the only fact worth knowing here."[54]

In Lisbon Clare stayed with an old Newport friend, Herbert Pell, Minister at the American Legation. By one of the strange coincidences characteristic of wartime, René de Chambrun was also in town. He had been waiting almost a week for an unreserved place on the Clipper. "There's something wrong with democracy when I have to give priority to zipper-salesmen and throneless royalty," he grumbled, "and me with a message to the President in my pocket!"[55]

He indeed carried desperate top-level notes from Ambassador Bullitt and General Weygand. France's need was now so acute that the commander was reduced to begging, not for parts, as in the recent past, but for finished guns and aircraft. Clare believed that the requests were already too late. Even as they spoke Germans had reached the Seine, and Reynaud was appealing to the United States for direct intervention.

Her plane came in from New York on the evening of June 10, a day behind schedule. Noel Coward, Madeleine Carroll, and the English painter Simon Elwes were among the passengers. At midnight Clare met all three in a café.[56] They drank red wine and talked about the precipitous spread of the conflict. Just that day Mussolini had come in on Hitler's side, over Count Ciano's objections. "It's really frightening," Coward said. "America is so smug and complacent, in a way, and everybody says: 'Oh, we have plenty of time!' "

"Nobody has time," she responded.

"So you really believe the French are going to surrender!"

"Yes, they are."

"England," he insisted, white faced, "will never, never surrender!"

He began to make a grandiose speech. Clare found she was less moved by his words than their companions.

> They were so fine and so heartfelt and so really and grimly determined that Madeleine Carroll wept copiously, and her beautiful face looked smeary and pulled apart and honest, not at all like the neat, dishonest, glycerine-teared face she uses to cry with in the movies. Even Simon Elwes, who is not an actor . . . looked very wretched and said some emotional and patriotic things, though of course he didn't say them as beautifully as Noel.
>
> Finally Noel said, very embarrassed, "I'm afraid that everything I say sounds rather like lines from *Cavalcade*, doesn't it?"
>
> And I answered: "Yes, a little."

As they cheered themselves up with more red wine, Clare waxed oratorical herself, and ended up declaiming Shakespeare's "Once more unto the breach" exhortation from *Henry V*.

"How can we fail?" she asked as they parted in the small hours.

"Darling," Coward replied, "I can't possibly imagine."[57]

At 9:20 the following morning, war correspondent Clare Boothe took off from the Tagus, landing a little over twenty-four hours later at La Guardia Marine Terminal. Harry and Ann were waiting. The latter, soon to be sixteen, luxuriated in her spectacularly well-informed mother's "gobs and gobs of news."[58]

On June 14 the Wehrmacht entered Paris. With possible unconscious irony, John Billings and five other senior Time-Life executives entertained Clare to lunch that day in New York's Louis XIV restaurant. They wanted to hear more details of her foreign adventures, given that her cables had been partly censored. Billings, even so, thought some of the earlier ones "absolute perfection."[59]

Clare, businesslike in a dark blue dress with matching gloves and hat, launched into one of the lengthy monologues that were becoming her habit. "Some was good and some was tiresome," the managing editor wrote in his diary.[60] Sensing, perhaps, that Harry's staff resented her "platform" manner, she decided to write no more articles about her recent experiences.

The copious material she had spent almost four months gathering might make a timely book, if produced fast enough. She would call it *Europe in the Spring,* and dedicate it cryptically to her husband:

> For H.R.L.
> WHO UNDERSTOOD WHY
> I WANTED TO GO

31

THE DAVID PROBLEM

He who has no position . . . cannot even get a dog to
bark at him. —NICCOLÒ MACHIAVELLI

"Mother never comes to anything but supper anymore," Ann
Brokaw wrote on July 7, 1940. "She is trying to finish her
book."[1]

Clare's work on *Europe in the Spring* was not without distraction.
What Harry delicately referred to as "the David problem" had come to
a head some nine days before, when her brother had been seen drinking heavily in a Philadelphia hotel room during the Republican National Convention. Nobody had any idea where he went afterwards,
but Clare had received a bill for a rented Cadillac.[2]

David Franklin Boothe at age thirty-eight was more than ever his
sister's physical and social opposite. Street-smart, swarthy, muscled like
a wrestler, he was attractive to women in a bruising sort of way, yet always somehow a loner. Whereas she was calm, disciplined, and a clever
survivor, he was fiery, uncontrolled, intellectually mediocre, and self-
destructive. Yet in spite of their differences they had many attributes in

common: duplicity, manipulativeness, personal extravagance, stinginess with others, and charm. Perhaps because of these shared characteristics—or guilt arising from some deep childhood secret—Clare indulged her brother almost as much as she did herself.

One year before, while the Luces were abroad, David had unexpectedly wed a Bonwit Teller "hostess." Her name was Nora Dawes, and she came from Montreal. He had written Clare a casual letter after the fact.

> So—I got married. Yes sir. The gal comes from a swell family, educated Canada and abroad. Age 24. Fortunately considerably above that mentally . . . excepting that she didn't know about men, only from the book. That one had me scared plenty . . . I'm related to all the social and financial oligarchy in Canada. The young lady has been given the once over by Drs. Austin and Rosenbluth. The first told me he'd punch my nose if I didn't take advantage of such a nice girl. The second lad was really delighted.[3]

At least one of these physicians knew that David Boothe had frequently been treated for venereal disease.[4]

Though far from beautiful, Nora satisfied his social aspirations if not his financial ones. He discovered with some chagrin that there would be no dowry from her father, who owned racehorses and was head of Canadian National Breweries. Yet David had extravagantly hired Gladys Freeman to decorate an apartment on Park Avenue and paid her with an overdrawn check. "If the bank says balance is n.g., please give it to Harry."[5]

Luce had indulgently honored it and other Boothe debts, knowing there was no hope of reimbursement. Encouraged, the couple began sending him trivial domestic bills, including laundry receipts. These, too, were honored, because Harry and Clare felt that Nora had become by extension their responsibility. After about four months of their marriage, Ann had innocently asked when she and David were going to have children. "Not for a long time," Nora had said evasively. The truth was that she had contracted her husband's gonorrhea, leaving her no choice but to have a hysterectomy.[6]

David and Nora Boothe, *1939*

Harry now found that David, as an aspiring broker, had been systematically embezzling from his sister. An audit revealed that Clare, despite all her freelance earnings in the past five years, was personally poorer than when she met Harry. David had been entrusted with her signature to buy and sell stocks, and he must have stolen or mismanaged $250,000—over half her Brokaw settlement.[7] Rather than confront Clare and other creditors, some of whom were calling for his imprisonment, he had evidently run away.

"Maybe that's the best solution," Harry ruminated. "I don't know . . . he's an awful hard fellow to help . . . But he is so darn likeable!"[8]

In mid-July Clare, still rushing to finish her book, received a letter from David postmarked Elizabeth City, North Carolina.[9] It was a suicide threat. She had received similar notes before, but this time the situation was serious enough to merit her active intervention. At all costs David must be committed to safekeeping, so she decided to try tricking him into a psychological examination that might give grounds, alcoholic or otherwise, for confined treatment. With Harry's approval, Clare hired a private investigator to locate her brother, cautioning that he was a strong man and could be dangerous if provoked.

The detective found him almost at once on the streets of Elizabeth City and contrived to have him arrested for nonpayment of a bill for his luxury hotel room overlooking the bay. (He had rented it under an assumed name.) On the seventeenth Dr. Rosenbluth flew south to inform the local sheriff that Mr. Boothe was a heavy drinker, "a constitutionally inferior personality," and should be taken into custody "to protect him from himself." But a jail doctor found no grounds to incarcerate him.[10]

At this point Nora, distraught, telephoned and offered $15,000 "in cash" if her husband would return to her. Where the money would come from she did not say. David politely declined. "She is a good kid," he told the detective, whom he had already beguiled into being his confidant. But Nora was the main reason he had left New York. He loved another woman and wanted a divorce.[11]

Clare read the investigative report and decided there was little more she could do. David must come back of his own accord, in his own good time.

32

RABBLE ROUSER

The love of power is the love of ourselves.

—WILLIAM HAZLITT

Clare finished the manuscript of *Europe in the Spring* on July 24, 1940, after just six weeks of intensive work.[1] The following afternoon, she and Harry flew to Washington for a private White House screening of a *March of Time* feature, "The Ramparts We Watch." It made a case for war preparedness that they hoped would not be lost on the President. They were to dine with Roosevelt before the movie and spend the night in the Executive Mansion.[2]

An usher in a summery, sky blue suit took them up to the Rose Bedroom overlooking Lafayette Square. Britain's Queen Elizabeth had slept there the year before, but Clare found it less than regal, "without an iota of charm or dignity." Pink carpets and matching drapes installed at the turn of the century by Mrs. Theodore Roosevelt had faded, and the ill-matched furniture included Andrew Jackson's four-poster and Abraham Lincoln's desk. The most welcome fixture, since the weather was stiflingly humid, was a large, modern air-cooler. Beside the bed were a few copies of *Ladies' Home Journal*, with articles by Eleanor Roosevelt.

The First Lady herself was not at home. When Clare and Harry went along to the President's study for drinks at seven, they were greeted by his secretary "Missy" LeHand, in rose chiffon with silver sash. Their only fellow dinner guest, apart from a small party of Time Inc. executives, was the man for whom Dorothy Hale had jumped out of a window, Harry Hopkins, now Roosevelt's live-in Secretary of Commerce.

The President, wearing a white linen suit, sat behind a desk vigorously shaking cocktails. He thrust out his chin, in a way Clare recognized from photographs, and beckoned her over. She noticed that his hands were "gnarled and old and spotted." At rest, they "trembled apoplectically." Roosevelt grinned at her, but she saw no smile in his china-blue eyes. Obviously used to getting his way, he insisted she try one of his strong martinis and loudly addressed Harry as Henry. Clare, irritated, thought that people who affected first names should make a point of knowing what a man was usually called.

Roosevelt asked about her trip to Europe. "I worried terribly about you when you were over there." She wondered how many returning travelers he had said that to. The air, thick with cigarette smoke, grew hotter, and she longed to sit down. But there were not enough chairs, so everyone stood before the Chief Executive "like schoolchildren, feeling rather foolish because we'd left our big red apples at home." Dinner was announced. While guests respectfully stepped aside, the crippled President was transferred to a wheelchair, trundled to the elevator, and whisked downstairs.

Throughout dinner Roosevelt concentrated his attention on Clare. She found him an amiable and easy talker, with one galling fault that she had to admit was also hers: he liked to monopolize the conversation. Another defect they shared was the need to command attention before starting an anecdote. "Hey, listen, Henry . . . I want you to hear this one, too."

Afterwards they gathered in the windowless second-floor corridor, where a screen had been erected before rows of chairs. Despite the almost unendurable heat, Clare was instantly absorbed by flickering images of Belgian refugees trudging along a country road. The scene was an eerie duplicate of what she had witnessed on her trip from Brussels to Paris in May.

The footage, shot during the Great War twenty-six years before, moved her to tears. History was repeating itself for lack of policy. Just as the United States had delayed going to the aid of the beleaguered Belgians in the last war, it was delaying now. Clare turned to Roosevelt and said that the issue in 1940 was the same as it had been in 1914: whether or not to defend freedom of the seas. He said that he agreed with her "utterly" and blamed current isolationist sentiments on William Randolph Hearst's yellow press, which for twenty years had "robbed the American nation of any ability to recognize its own vital interests."[3]

At the end of the screening, Roosevelt took Harry back to his study for a man-to-man talk. Clare knew that her husband would urge the President to heed Churchill's request that America lend fifty "older destroyers" to protect Allied shipping, even though the Neutrality Act forbade it. He might also make the same argument for military spending she had just done in the final chapter of *Europe in the Spring*: "What England and France have been and were until the invasion of the Low Countries, America is. We are on the same road they took to disaster."[4]

Frustrated at being excluded, she took refuge from the heat with Harry Hopkins and Missy LeHand in the former's air-conditioned bedroom. Even here she felt shut out, because Hopkins drank several large glasses of whiskey and soda, reclined on a sofa, and was soon gently snoring.

> I looked at him lying there with his wraith-like face, his sleeping, caved-in chest and the little belly that protruded like a small watermelon below his belt line. He looked so inexpressibly common; sleep robbed him of that rather ferocious and intense quality which, when awake, rather redeemed him.[5]

Something she and Missy said on the subject of youth brought Hopkins out of his slumber. Inexplicably, he began to rant about the nation's current crop of "spineless" undergraduates. He did not say what kind of courage they should display. Then in a vague shift to Roosevelt as Hitler's undeclared enemy, he exploded, "The reason I want my man for a third term is because I believe him to be the only man in America who . . . can lick this fellow economically."

Clare was tempted to ask if Roosevelt, reelected, would be a candidate also in 1944, when the world crisis might be worse. "And if he won't run for a fourth term . . . why should he run for one now?" But Hopkins started to tell a self-serving story of how he had once bullied the Mayor of New York into restoring a lawbreaking saloonkeeper's license, simply because the man was down on his luck. She was repelled by the "phony" sentimentality of New Dealers. To them, lack of money made even the venal deserving. In disgust she asked herself, "What is there in this twisted humanitarian that holds such power over the President?"

Three days after the Luces returned from Washington, David appeared in Connecticut. His ostensible purpose was to meet with Nora and confirm that he wanted a divorce. Even in his present abject state, he still had a roving eye. Ann Brokaw, about to turn sixteen, proudly recorded in her diary that her uncle had noticed she was "filling out." But the reunion left nobody else satisfied, and Clare, exasperated, said that she wished David would start a new life as far away as possible.[6]

Europe in the Spring was published by Knopf on September 6. With no illustrations in its 324 pages, the book relied on hard, clear prose for its force. Walter Lippmann confirmed on the jacket that Clare's account of the buildup to war was "devastatingly and absolutely truthful."

Eminent reviewers added their voices, giving Clare the most substantial praise of her literary career. Janet Flanner, in the *New York Herald Tribune*, said, "Miss Boothe writes with spotted brilliance, coins phrases that really clink with talent, sums up all and something new in a single line." Katherine Woods in *The New York Times* found "glimpses of nobility" in the prose, and lauded Clare's admonition "to save what remains of the civilization that is our heritage from England and France." André Maurois, writing for *Saturday Review*, cited *Europe in the Spring* as an important work and said some passages had "the impressionistic charm of a Colette." Even the Marxist *New Masses* conceded that Clare had proved herself to be more than a "champ diner-outer in the midst of Peril."[7]

It was left to Dorothy Parker to produce in *PM* what was, predictably, the wittiest notice of *Europe in the Spring*. She called her piece "All Clare on the Western Front." Feigning admiration for Miss Boothe's account of the bombing of Brussels, she added tartly that "while it is never said that the teller is the bravest of all those present, it comes through."[8]

In a few weeks the book reached number 2 on *The New York Times* best-seller list, and by early November it had sold 22,500 copies. Anti-Fascist as it was, it brought Clare the approval of intellectuals for the first and only time in her life.[9] Requests poured in for her to lecture and participate in broadcast forums. The alacrity with which she accepted these new challenges would lead to another change of career. But before embarking on it, she had much to learn.

Refreshed by a two-week vacation at Averell Harriman's house in Sun Valley, Idaho, Clare resumed her collaboration with Alexander King on *The Yohimbe Tree*. She hoped to persuade Gilbert Miller to produce it, and Alfred Lunt and Lynn Fontanne to play leading roles. But the work did not go well, mainly because her penchant for light drama was giving way to an infatuation with current affairs. This intensified after Labor Day, when the 1940 presidential campaign moved into high gear, and she found herself irresistibly drawn to Roosevelt's challenger, Wendell Lewis Willkie. The Republican nominee, only forty-eight years old, was a burly, rumpled, chain-smoking utilities executive from Elwood, Indiana. He had never held elective office, but he appealed to the disenchanted middle class and was closing on Roosevelt fast.

Listening to Willkie's radio speeches, Clare was impressed by his no-nonsense recital of what seemed to her obvious facts.

> As a nation of producers we have become stagnant. Much of our industrial machinery is obsolete . . . The national standard of living has declined . . . the New Deal has failed in its program of economic rehabilitation. And the victims . . . are the very persons whose cause it professes to champion.[10]

She wrote Joe Kennedy that Willkie was hampered by his flat midwestern voice. "The world is terribly crooner conscious, which still leaves FDR the Number One American Glamor Boy." On the other hand, she knew from recent experience that the President no longer looked as good as he sounded. Willkie should capitalize on his boyish handsomeness. Presciently recognizing the importance of media image in modern politics, she wrote that November's election would be "a toss up between the power of photography and the radio . . . Mr. Willkie's wild Byronic fetlock [sic] appeals enormously to the public in pictures; Mr. Roosevelt still has the golden voice."[11]

In a letter to Herbert Pell, Clare shrewdly pinpointed the Republican's disadvantages compared with FDR's. "It is a bad break for Willkie that the real issue between them—New Deal economy—has been blitzkrieged by events. Therefore the only question remaining is—who can get the country armed faster? . . . The real accusation against Willkie seems to be that he has had no experience to date as President."[12] This last sentence preceded by some weeks a repudiation of Willkie, on the same grounds, by one of his most influential backers. On October 9 the wordy Republican columnist Dorothy Thompson, in her syndicated *New York Herald Tribune* feature, "On the Record," had stunned millions of readers by endorsing Roosevelt.

Miss Thompson confessed to having initially leaned towards the President while visiting the Maginot shortly after Clare. "Roosevelt must stay in office and see this thing through," she had decided, because he knew the world "better than any other living democratic head of state."

Clare was appalled. She knew the statuesque, silver-haired writer personally, and admired her vehement anti-Fascism as well as her anti-Communist stance. Several times Clare had attended soirées in the New York apartment Thompson shared with her novelist husband, Sinclair Lewis, and listened to her hold forth about repressive ideologies.

As women they had much in common. Both had worked for the suffrage movement, had married alcoholics, and had been endowed with prodigious physical and mental energy. Accused of thinking like men, they were also romantics (a date with Dorothy, someone said, meant "a walk in the moonlight and a talk about Hegel"). Nevertheless, Clare shied away from intimate friendship. Thompson struck her as overwrought, and "something of a masochist" for her tolerance of the heavy-drinking Lewis.[13]

Dorothy in turn thought highly of Clare, who was nine years her junior. She publicly placed her on a par with Noel Coward as party material and rated her number one on her 1939 list of ideal female guests, above Alice Roosevelt Longworth, Beatrice Lillie, Helen Hayes, and Katharine Hepburn.

> She is very beautiful. She is exquisitely dressed. She is really adult. She is interested in nearly everything and knows something—even a great deal—about nearly everything. She can discuss politics, letters, fashion, the stage and sports with equal vivacity and knowledgeability. She knows all the gossip . . . but is sufficiently discreet and seldom really malicious. She is a delightful conversationalist, quick to pick up an idea, give it a new twist and toss it back to the sender. She never holds forth. If she has convictions, she keeps them to herself.[14]

But the Clare of 1940 was no longer diffident in airing her opinions. Some instinct suggested that now was the time for her to become a Republican spokeswoman, and that Dorothy Thompson was meat for "Jungle Red" treatment.

She accordingly volunteered to speak at a "Work with Willkie" rally downtown on October 15. Since it was to be her first political address, she asked Bernard Baruch to draft some remarks. When the text failed to materialize, she fired off a nervously jocular wire: "So where's that speech you promised me before Monday. No speechie no likee."[15]

At the appointed hour, she put on a simple suit with soft white ruffles at the neck and cuff, and appeared before an audience of several thousand people in the Manhattan Center on West Thirty-fourth Street.[16] Within minutes it was plain that Clare Boothe Luce needed rhetorical help from nobody.

There was only one possible explanation, she said, for Dorothy Thompson's last-minute embrace of Roosevelt as Commander in Chief: "acute fear." Brutally hinting at a menopausal lapse, she continued:

> Fear is an *emotional* and not an intellectual reaction to a problem. Fear distills adrenalin into the blood, the victim sweats, her breath comes fast, her nostrils dilate, her pulse races, her breast heaves . . . and she begins to babble incoherently. But worst of all the blood leaves her head, and her brain ceases to function normally.

Clare reminded her listeners that she, not Thompson, had been the first woman to see the Maginot Line, and made sure they understood who had stayed longer at the battlefront, quitting it mere days before the surrender. Then she swung suddenly to attack the President.

> I want to put on my record now that one of the main reasons France folded was that the French people did not change their leadership in time, and that the leadership of France had strangely resembled our present leadership in these respects: it seldom told the truth to the people, it was not prepared, and it was tolerant of incompetent men and intolerant of competent ones.

She was interrupted repeatedly with applause and laughter, and sat down to cheers.

Dorothy Thompson, not amused, broadcast a response in kind, claiming that snobs and "advertisers" had taken over the Willkie cause.

> Miss Boothe . . . has torn herself loose from the Stork Club to serve her country in this serious hour. She has everything—everything to pull in the orders. The Powers-model face that you see on the magazines; the recommendations of Lady Whosis . . .
>
> I have met you before, Clare, in various costumes and under various hats. I have met your type in London, in the Cliveden set, and in Paris salons. I have met the ladies of Café society, who save nations in their time of crisis, and I have visited the nations they have "saved."[17]

The press highlighted these exchanges with pictures of the "two blonde Valkyries" that contrasted a stern Dorothy with a smiling Clare.

PM recorded that CBS had received many calls voicing resentment of Miss Thompson's attack on Mrs. Luce. Clare triumphantly invited her rival to an hourlong debate, and got a wired refusal. "Congratulations on your wonderful performance in *The Women* and your offer of a part in the cast. I fear however that the role does not suit my type."[18]

Support for Thompson's "honest and courageous stand" came from an unexpected source—Mrs. Henry Winters Luce, Clare's mother-in-law. The columnist replied, saying how hurt she was to have been attacked by one whom she "liked, admired and consistently defended against her catty women 'friends.' "[19]

Elsa Maxwell followed the titillating clash with relish. "Dorothy is at the opposite end of the thermometer from Clare," she reported in her gossip column. "Where Clare is calm and icy, Dot is heated and argumentative. She gets red in the face . . . She is smart enough to realize that ice can conquer fire in speech-making, and wisely refused Clare's challenge to debate."[20]

The staunchly Republican *Tribune* punished Thompson's endorsement of Roosevelt by not renewing her contract. Clare, on contrite reflection, vowed not to engage in a slanging match with a member of her own sex again. "The time has not yet come," she wrote, "when two women can safely debate politics (or any other subject) in public. Differences of opinion between women are always treated by the press as inspired by personal dislike and are used as evidence that every woman, at bottom, fears and hates every other woman for reasons of sexual jealousy."[21]

Clare soon began to sound like a seasoned campaigner, with hard-hitting speeches for Willkie at Carnegie Hall, Town Hall, and the Ritz Theatre, where six years before she had been soundly booed as the author of *Abide With Me*. She chastised the President for being "the No. 1 bottleneck of production" and blamed his Administration for "forming an unholy alliance . . . with city managers and corrupt politicians."[22]

Stunned by the vitality of Willkie's supporters, Roosevelt scuttled his plan to campaign only from the sanctuary of the White House. He joined his opponent on the speechmaking circuit and echoed him in calling for national conscription and an increase in armament produc-

Clare campaigning for Wendell Willkie, *c. October 1940*

tion. As he did so, daily headlines recounted the relentless progression of the London blitz, which more and more looked like the precursor of a land invasion of the British Isles. This inevitably swung the national debate away from domestic to foreign affairs and put the President at a decided advantage. Not even a surprise endorsement of Willkie by the liberal *New York Times* could arrest Roosevelt's late surge.

With the election less than two weeks away, Clare appeared at the prestigious New York Herald Tribune Forum, held in the Waldorf-Astoria. The theme for the three-day event was "America's Second Fight for Freedom." Among the seventeen other speakers were Eleanor Roosevelt, Walter Lippmann, Secretary of the Navy Frank Knox, Mayor La Guardia of New York, Wendell Willkie, and, on the final afternoon, the President himself. Daily audiences approximated three thousand, and millions of radio listeners worldwide usually tuned in.[23]

Mrs. Roosevelt opened the proceedings on a militant note. She said no nation was invincible whose people did not believe its philosophy of government was worth dying for. Secretary Knox followed with a statement that alarmed more than a few, probably for different reasons. "By March 1942," he predicted, "we shall have an Army fit to meet any challenge."[24]

When Clare's turn came later in the day, she took care to project her low, measured voice to the most distant seats. She began with a provocative supposition, drawing on her special experience of Europe on the brink of war: that France's collapse could be attributed to a general loss of faith in democratic institutions, which she equated with moral cowardice.

> How often Frenchmen said to me, "If a great country like yours, so strong geographically and rich in man power and material, has millions on relief . . . a budget too colossal perhaps ever to be balanced—if democracy can't work in America, what chance have we?"
>
> Too many Americans are frightened of this now. I do not like to think . . . how many of us will this year cast [our] votes not in faith but in fear. Fear that the machinery is forever out of kilter, that until Socialism or Communism or Fascism or some system still undreamed and unnamed, absorbs our present system, there will never again be jobs, security, peace, prosperity in this land. This fundamental fear breeds a Pandora's box of fears: fear that we won't get into the war in time, fear that we will get in too soon, fear that we will get in at all, class fears and racial fears . . . Fear admitted to the counsels of a government, or behind the curtains of a polling booth, is treason's other name.[25]

The climax of Wendell Willkie's candidacy came in New York on the night of Saturday, November 2. It was an occasion that strained superlatives. Over 22,000 people gathered inside Madison Square Garden to see him, and some 50,000 stood outside listening to the proceedings over a loudspeaker. He had just completed the longest and most strenuous campaign tour ever undertaken, and now he faced the greatest demonstration in the history of the Garden.

Clare spoke shortly before Willkie's 10:15 P.M. arrival. She wore a plain black dress, and as she stepped forward on the platform, a powerful spotlight beamed down from distant rafters onto her glossy blonde hair. The crowd responded with wild enthusiasm even before she opened her mouth.[26] None of her experiences on a movie set or theater stage had equaled this moment. It was the giant arena she had sought since adolescence.

H. L. Mencken, the crusty sage of the *Baltimore Sun*, reported:

> La Boothe presented a really tremendous contrast, both in manner and appearance, to the average female politico, and the crowd was quick to see it. Slim, beautiful and charming . . . with no ornaments save two immense pearl earrings, she outshined even La [Joan] Crawford, and when she began to unload her speech, it appeared at once that she was also a fluent and effective talker.
>
> In large part, her remarks were aimed at Dorothy Thompson, with whom she has been carrying on an oratorical hairpulling match for several weeks past.
>
> "New Deal policies," she said, "make some very strange bedbugs. Dorothy will have plenty of time to scratch herself after election day."
>
> This somewhat sassy *bon mot* delighted the crowd, and the rest of the lady's remarks were liberally sandwitched [sic] with applause. When she concluded there was so long and hearty a roar that many persons thought that Willkie was coming into the hall.[27]

Allene Talmey described Clare in *Vogue* as "a powerful rabble rouser" whose "glow, intense conviction, and crusading zeal" infected all who heard her.[28] When Willkie finally did step onto the platform, he was unable to stem the uproar for ten minutes of expensive radio time.

On November 5, some 49 million Americans went to the polls, the largest turnout ever. Early evening returns ran in Willkie's favor, and he went to bed exhausted at two o'clock without knowing the result. The final count, however, was 27,244,160 popular votes for Roosevelt and 22,305,198 for Willkie. Although the loser had succeeded in halving his opponent's last margin of victory, he failed ultimately to alter popular perception of Roosevelt as protector of the working man.

"Well the champs are still the champs," Clare, magnanimous in defeat, telegraphed Dorothy Thompson. "No one more earnestly hopes that you and the voice of the people have spoken well and truly than I do . . . against you I had no personal bitterness nor ever shall have any. I also did what I thought right. Yours for a great country. Clare Boothe Luce."[29]

33

THE CANDOR KID

A foolish consistency is the hobgoblin of little minds.
—RALPH WALDO EMERSON

Another Republican casualty of the 1940 election was Clare's stepfather, who lost his House seat by 1,100 votes. She speculated that
the Democrats had won "by voting all the tombstones in the Catholic
cemeteries" of Fairfield County.[1] True or not, she was less surprised by
Dr. Austin's defeat than she had been by his marriage—twenty months
after her mother's death—to a private nurse exactly half his age.

Their union was to be short-lived. During the campaign an aide
had noticed that the hitherto robust candidate appeared to be ill. "He
was always taking his temperature, and drinking from a little bottle of
whiskey." One day, while he was making a speech at the Pickwick
Arms, the doctor's voice failed completely. It turned out he had cancer
of the throat.[2]

Clare, meanwhile, continued to emerge as a political orator. In December, when President Roosevelt announced his Lend-Lease arrange-

ment with Churchill, she returned to the lecture platform, sounding again her Willkie campaign theme that aid to Europe now might obviate the need for American troops later. She felt that she and Harry had been influential in the destroyer deal, and that the United States had acquired a strategic advantage by gaining in exchange bases in Newfoundland, Bermuda, and the Caribbean.

As isolationists like Charles Lindbergh continued to insist that the Nazis were exclusively Europe's problem, those who preached intervention began warning that America itself might be an eventual target of the Third Reich. Clare stated this case forcefully when she said that the world was being swept to disaster by "the corrupting evils of pride-bloated state sovereignty, of hog-wild nationalism."[3]

In acknowledgment of Clare Boothe Luce's outspokenness and growing celebrity, *The New Yorker* published a two-part profile of her in January 1941 entitled "The Candor Kid." It was written by Margaret Case Harriman—the same veteran journalist who, as Margaret Case Morgan, once complained that Clare Brokaw was politicizing *Vanity Fair*. Whether out of envy or revenge, Mrs. Harriman downplayed Clare's current role as Cassandra, treating her mainly as a theatrical and social phenomenon.

The profile began with a satiric, Hans Christian Andersen–style account of Clare's entry into the world.

> Once upon a time, in a far country called Riverside Drive, a miracle child was born and her name was Clare Boothe. Over her cradle hovered so many good fairy godmothers that an SRO sign was soon put up at the foot of the crib and a couple of witches who had drifted along just for the hell of it had to fly away and come back for the Wednesday matinée. To the infant Clare, the first good fairy gave Beauty, the second Wealth, the third Talent, the fourth Industriousness, and the fifth Success.[4]

All were bestowed in triplicate so that the child was "more shiningly endowed than any other infant in the land." But two curses pronounced by the witches complicated the baby's long-term prospects. "I will give her Unpopularity, the distrust of her fellow men and women," said one. "I have already given her Candor," said the other, "which amounts to the same thing."

Having interviewed a number of Clare's friends and enemies, Mrs. Harriman felt qualified to comment on her objective way of looking at things.

> People who know Clare Boothe well realize that the clear beauty of her face, the straight regard of her limpid eyes, and the light, high laughter with which she punctuates her conversation conceal nothing sinister. She is exactly what she seems to be—an amused, tolerant, unusually good-looking woman who has, perhaps, a blind spot in her perceptions. She writes vitriolic plays about vicious people not from any conviction that vice is wrong but because she honestly sees most people as bitches, two-timers, and phonies.

An unnamed source was quoted as remarking, "Most of us are used to the fact that a lot of people are louses, but Clare never fails to get a kick out of it." Another repeated Dorothy Parker's crack when Clare was said to be kind to her inferiors. "And where does she find them?"

For the most part Mrs. Harriman's profile was a fairly accurate account of Clare's life. What facts she had wrong were due mainly to her subject's tendency to reinvent herself in interviews.[5]

Any pleasure Clare had from "The Candor Kid" was marred by a federal warrant claiming seven thousand dollars in back taxes from her brother. Having failed on Wall Street, then as manager of a cinema chain, and finally as an executive with Canadian Colonial Airways, David had now taken up flying. Thanks to Harry's generosity, he had gone to the Ryan School of Aeronautics in Southern California, claiming to be thirty-six rather than almost thirty-nine. After training he hoped to become a pilot in any air force that would take him.

David had gone west swearing temperance, and Harry's secretary warned him not to abuse his monthly seventy-five-dollar allowance. She understood that he was "on the wagon," but even if he was not he must pay for drinks from his own cash, rather than add them to bills being paid by Mr. Luce.[6]

From San Diego, David wrote Harry ominously that "every other door is a saloon, gin mill or Palace de Joie." He saw no harm in celebrating his first solo flight with "a little debauching." Clare had not helped matters by giving him a car, and extra money for Christmas. In

Clare visiting her brother at the Ryan School of Aeronautics, *April 1941*

return he sent her the small span of gold wings he had just earned. "If you manage to outlive me," he wrote, anxious to repossess the gift in death, "place said wings on my coffin."[7]

On January 22, Clare made a "Union Now" radio broadcast urging the English-speaking democracies to unite in the face of a common peril.

> Morally, we are at war now . . . American planes are already bringing down German planes. American shells are landing on German objectives. All talk of non-belligerency, of technical neutrality, of loan-leasing, is just so much congressional persiflage . . . we have done, or are doing everything that becomes a great nation on the brink of war, except the one truly important thing: we have *not* stated our war aims.[8]

A few weeks later she spoke at the National Republican Club with Wendell Willkie, still the hope of the party. On a recent trip to London he had been treated like a movie star. This made Clare want to return to Europe again herself. Vague desire soon mutated into a daring plan to interview Hitler for *Life*. Telling John Billings only that she wanted to write about Germany, she applied for a visa.[9]

Harry, not to be overshadowed as an oracle, in the meantime adapted three of his speeches for a *Life* article entitled "The American Century"—a phrase that would be remembered long after the body text was forgotten.[10] His essay, calling for the United States to assume its rightful place as a world force, was a plethora of platitudes, abstract nouns, and clichés, in spite of the best efforts of Billings and other editors. Luce asserted that Americans were unable to adapt "spiritually and practically" to the duty of world leadership. Their neglect of this duty brought dire global consequences. The remedy, as he saw it, was "to accept wholeheartedly our duty and our opportunity as the most powerful and vital nation in the world and in consequence to exert upon the world the full impact of our influence, for such purposes as we see fit and by such means as we see fit."

Luce made only general suggestions as to how his grand design was to be implemented. America should begin by officially entering a war in which the Roosevelt Administration had already taken sides. Next it would be her duty, as the wealthiest participant, to guarantee universal freedom of the seas, to feed the destitute, and to share technical expertise. At the same time she should promote ideals of justice, equal opportunity, and self-reliance around the world.

Conservatives on the whole applauded "The American Century" when it appeared on February 17, 1941. But socialists and communists, looking to the postwar age for the liberation of the working man, felt it promoted "political tyranny and economic monopoly." *The Nation* condemned Luce's ideas as "lacking in a decent regard for the susceptibilities of the rest of mankind" and accused him of Anglo-Saxon imperialistic tendencies.[11]

On February 8, the German Embassy in Washington, smarting still from Clare's barbs in *Margin for Error,* turned down her visa application.[12] A few weeks later she sounded depressed in a speech billed as "Credo" and delivered at Pierson College, Yale.

"I believe," she began, "that life is essentially tragic, but I believe this immemorial essential tragedy has a meaning. I believe that this tragedy can be endured by sane men, and that the meaning can be felt, comprehended, understood only in terms of religion . . . I believe that the status quo and the ante–status quo are both doomed."

A strongly religious country, she went on, had the best chance of survival against such odds. Even so, its moral choices in an amoral world were "never between the desirable and the undesirable, but between the more or less undesirable." Assuming the United States entered the war and helped defeat Hitler, victory would precipitate its own problems. "I believe that the horrors of the peace to come may be worse than the horrors of war, if we do not face the fact that the winning of a brave new world will be quite as hard and heartbreaking."

Twenty years ahead of a young future president, she ended by eloquently cautioning that America's political and economic systems were in danger of becoming corrupt. "I believe that our whole democratic conception of what the country owes the individual, of his rights and privileges, ceased to be valid when the last physical frontier was won, and that we will be forced by the iron veracities of events to put our emphasis more and more on what the individual owes society."[13]

Clare had recovered her good humor when Orson Welles invited her and Harry to a private preview of his new movie, *Citizen Kane*. The director was nervously intrigued to see how Luce, the news tycoon, would react to the stinging portrait of his Hearst-like protagonist. Not only that but the picture began with an obvious parody of *The March of Time*. He need not have worried: his audience of two roared with laughter, if not quite in tandem. Welles recalled that Clare saw it as a joke, "and he had to because she did."[14]

With her German trip aborted, Clare agreed to join Harry on a tour of the war-torn country in which he was born. Few Americans realized that millions of lives were being lost in an invasion half a world away from the nearer conflict in Europe. Harry's idea was to write a report for *Life* while Clare took photographs. But she also saw the trip as a chance to collect material for a book to complement her last one. She might even call it "China in the Spring."[15]

34

WINGS OVER CHINA

The only way for America to save itself is for America
to save China. —GERTRUDE STEIN

"Today, my first in Chungking," Clare noted on May 9, 1941, "we saw two things we had travelled eight thousand miles to see."

She and Harry were staying at the residence of a government minister in China's wartime capital. That morning she had sat writing by a window overlooking a small walled garden and cliffs that dropped to the yellow Yangtze River. "The air was hot and heavy with dust, and the smell of China. A distant rhythmic beating of drums drifted up on the wind." Every now and then the rhythm was broken by blasting noises that shook walls and rattled lamps. Workers, Clare had been told, were tunneling into the hillside to give all 400,000 of Chungking's citizens cover from daily Japanese bombing raids.[1]

At eleven-thirty a servant came in and said apologetically, "The red ball has gone up." This meant that enemy planes were only half an hour away. Mr. and Mrs. Luce must go at once to the American Embassy across the river, where they would be safe.[2]

No sooner had they arrived on the other side than the launch that brought them rushed back and returned with an entourage accompanying a slim, lithe man in a black uniform and white helmet. As he tipped it in greeting, the Luces recognized Chiang Kai-shek, leader of the Chinese Nationalists and Generalissimo of the armed forces. They were due to take tea with him the following afternoon. Chiang did not stop, and a limousine whisked him away.[3]

Within minutes of arriving at the Embassy, Clare found herself in an eerie repeat of her Belgian experience exactly one year before. She stood on the terrace and counted no fewer than forty-two Japanese planes approaching the city. Whereas in Brussels there had been only one bomb shelter, here she watched "orderly riverlets of people" moving into caves hewn from slopes of solid rock. In seconds the whole sky was ablaze, and a pall of smoke a mile long curled slowly upward. Then, skimming the riverbank, where junks and sampans were moored, the planes dumped incendiaries and high explosives that burnt gold-red in the sunlight, before returning whence they came.[4]

Playwright Boothe could not have invented a more dramatic start to her stay in the Orient. She had hoped to see both the Generalissimo and the war up close but hardly expected to do so straight away. Hostilities provoked by Japan's expansionism in Manchuria, and along the eastern seaboard, had been raging for four years, so violently that Chiang and his Kuomintang government had been forced to withdraw from Shanghai to this remote city in Szechwan. The Japanese, unable to pursue with heavy artillery along China's narrow, unpaved interior roads, had resorted to air assaults on Chungking. Already their planes had dropped ten times as many bombs per acre as the Germans had on London. At first casualties had run as high as five thousand daily, but now, thanks to the industrious shelter builders, they were down to as few as a hundred. In other provinces, she had been told, over 3 million Chinese had been killed or wounded, 2 million orphaned, 50 million left homeless, and 300,000 raped. Unaware, as was most of the world, of the magnitude of Stalin's purges in the Ukraine, Clare reckoned this was the greatest suffering mankind had ever known.[5]

At the appointed hour the next day, Harry, full of scarcely hidden joy at being back in China, escorted Clare to the residence of Chiang Kai-shek and his wife, Mei-ling Soong. The latter received them first, in a large, dimly lit living room. Elegant and forceful, yet visibly drained by the bombing, she conversed for an hour in fluent, Wellesley-accented English. Clare, recognizing an intelligence comparable to her own, was content to listen. Luce, who was captivated as much by Madame's charm as by her cleverness, hardly noticed when Chiang slipped quietly into their midst.

The Generalissimo, a taciturn man who expressed himself largely in grunts, thanked them for coming so far to see his people. Gifts were exchanged: a jade ornament and silk pajamas for the visitors, cigarettes and an album of photographs for the hosts. Getting to the prime purpose at hand, Harry told Chiang that he wanted more than anything to see the battlefront along the Yellow River. As he spoke, and Mei-ling translated, he had the feeling that Chiang's "pinhead black eyes" were burning into him. To his surprise, he and Clare were granted permission. Not only that, they were offered the use of a small plane.[6]

Clare and Harry with Madame Chiang and Chinese orphans,
Chungking, *May 1941*

Afterwards Harry wrote up the encounter for *Life*, in his customary awestruck style. He said that Chiang's presence outshone every other, while Madame was "an even more exciting personality than all the glamorous descriptions of her." Together they would be remembered "for centuries and centuries."[7]

On the afternoon of May 13, the Luces took off in a tiny Beechcraft from Chungking's "airport"—a sliver of dry riverbed on the lip of the Yangtze—and flew north towards the front. Clare, sitting beside the pilot, was immediately struck by the absence of anything like a modern highway in the terrain below. It seemed to her that the country Harry hoped to see transformed by Western industrial ways was not so much exploitable as exhausted.

> Was this land so precious that men dare not even sacrifice an inch to run roads across it? . . . Even in "good years" the overburdened soil must be weary of the plow, the harrow, the thousands of water buffalo feet, the billions of human ones that dig and dredge and prod and poke about in it end-lessly. It must want to be left alone, to be just mud, quiet pri-mordial slime. Like an old mother, it must be infinitely tired of bearing, hungry to be fed, sick of feeding.[8]

Night-stopping in Chengtu, they met with the head of a military academy and the presidents of four colleges. Hearing her husband pro-mote republican democracy, Clare saw the full extent of his missionary zeal. "Harry always trying to find out how many people understand the principles of Sun Yat-sen," she scribbled on tissue-thin notepaper.[9]

The following morning they flew over the snow-topped Tsingling Mountains towards Hanchung. As the Great Wall of China came into view, "writhing and coiling" like a dragon, all the reading Clare had done for the trip came back to fertilize her imagination. She vented her thoughts in the literary form she found most natural, a dialogue with herself:

> "It was built, thousands of years ago, to stem the hordes of Huns, Tartars, Mongols, Manchus, and later the Turks,

Arabs, Tibetans, Barbarians, who beat against China in cruel, never-ending waves, seeking to pillage the fruits of the fat years, to loot the looters, the Princes and Lords of China, to enslave the enslaved still further."

"But China always absorbed them! The way they will absorb those disgusting Japs."

"You just can't wait to get to the Japs. You are like everybody else, infatuated with ephemeral headlines."

"Now, I'm on China's side. I want her to win, even though you make China sound so dismal—and hopeless."

"But we *can't* help China today, until we know China's yesterday."

In her mind's eye Clare saw the European colonizers who had come in between, imposing tariffs and forcing the buying of opium, the bloody Boxer Rebellion, the Manchu dynasty toppling, and the coolie cutting off his pigtail, "that ignominious symbol of servitude, that convenient rope for swinging pates from poles."

As yet Clare seemed less aware of another momentous change in China, which the conflict with Japan obscured. It was a decade-long civil war, temporarily abandoned, between the Communist forces of Mao Tse-tung and Chiang's Nationalists—nothing less than a struggle for China's political soul that would resume after the common enemy had been vanquished. But for the time being, the indigenous antagonists were joining forces along the Yellow River to discourage the Japanese from crossing.[10]

The ancient city of Sian marked the farthest point that the Luces were to travel by air. At the headquarters of the northern armies nearby, they saw a map of defensive positions, stretching a hundred miles east. That night they boarded a slow train going in the same direction. Just before dawn they transferred to a car. It was chilly and the moon was still shining as they proceeded across the Shensi plain. Skirting the beautiful Flower Mountain, they arrived at a village where a group of cavalry was waiting to accompany them on the final stage of their journey.[11]

Mounted on Mongolian ponies, Harry and Clare rode six miles in oppressive heat to the heavily shelled city of Tungkwan. Close now to the ultimate outpost, they walked through twisting lines of trenches, gun nests, and thickets of trees. Clare could conceive no greater contrast to the bare, streamlined fortifications of the Maginot Line. All at once the famous "bend" of the Yellow River opened out ahead. Aiming binoculars at the opposite cliffs, she spotted Japanese emplacements, a sentry, and the flag of Nippon.[12]

Back in Chungking, the couple dined with the Communist general Chou En-lai, and continued to record their separate impressions for publication. Though Harry had some knowledge of the language, and in a moment of vanity had once said he could think of nobody with a better intellect than his, he offered no analysis of the country's history, culture, or current plight.[13] On the contrary, his reportage consisted mainly of facts and figures, assembled like a field report.

> We went into the caves—each cave bedding about 15 soldiers. In each cave a writing table and a bookcase—in all about 100 books. In front of one of the caves 50 soldiers sat in a circle listening to a lecture on political science.[14]

Clare gamely snapped pictures to illustrate his article—observing such details as a colonel's flower garden made out of bomb rubble—while continuing to scribble notes for her book. Some of the finished prose would end up in *Life*, and it was among the best she ever wrote. Making brilliant use of the overview air travel had given her, she described the rice paddies of Kwangtung as "silver, brown, tender green geometrical patterns . . . shaped like cockleshells, half-moons, shining slivers of quarters, interlocked endlessly." Villages and towns were "all alike in color and structure: gray clusters of roof tops, cellular growths like wasps' nests." She wrote of "cities lying like black spiders" or "like muddy hubs in the brassy wheels within wheels of the wheatlands."[15]

Where Harry nostalgically saw only a China of "intricate and fairy-like beauty," Clare both saw and understood the physical and metaphysical relationship of the Chinese peasant to the land he cultivated.

> The toiling son of Han endlessly plows his lovingly hoarded thin excrement back into the weakening soil. The rice, the

millet, the soybean, even the peaches and persimmons he
eats become compound of him, he of them most intimately.
The man eats his farm. His farm eats him—so man himself
becomes the greatest crop, the animate crop of the soil of
China. Sometimes when the man-crop grows too large, and
the soil too weak to bear it, a drought . . . touches off a long
disaster of famine. Sometimes the floods partially retrieve
the disaster of the droughts. Rising convulsively, the rivers
drive the ravenous and surplus crop-man from it, or trap him
under turgid waters by thousands, plowing him under, to fertilize the good and weary earth, with rich silt and slime, and
with flesh and bones built of rice and peaches.[16]

The misery and homelessness that pestilential disasters wrought drove
rural survivors to disease-ridden, urban slums.

> The cripples and dwarfs and lepers who infest the cities, the
> ulcerated blind beggars, cracking the lice from their own
> mangy beards in their yellow teeth, the blood-spitting chil-
> dren, eyesore and snot-nosed, verminous and scabrous, the
> white-eyed, sunken-eared women, all the fang-toothed id-
> iots were born of the floods and the famines, are the spawn
> of the catastrophe called China . . . Chinese cities smell of
> dung, tears, sweat and corpses. In Shanghai today, the au-
> thorities do not count the bodies. They report, "so many
> *tons* of human matter gathered up this morning."[17]

Her last sentence touched on the country's real tragedy: its ingrained tolerance of centuries of despotism, which would soon enough
mutate into Communist enslavement.

One rainy night Clare satisfied her abiding fascination for the drama by
taking a rickshaw to the theater district. Protected by an awning pulled
down to her eyebrows, and an odorous canvas drawn up to her chin,
she set off down a muddy side street. After ascending numerous flights
of steps that streaked the flanks of the town "like hundreds of frozen es-
calators," she transferred to a litter. In the fading light she noticed that

the shoulders of her coolies had callused dents from supporting the bamboo poles.

Over the course of the next several hours she saw part of a modern romantic play, a patriotic-epic movie, and a classical drama. The last was performed in a brightly lit auditorium full of soldiers, women, and children laughing, eating, reading, and calling out to friends. On a bare stage, seemingly oblivious to the confusion, creatures in bearded masks, towering headdresses, and flapping sleeves "went through stylized motions, to the desultory and arbitrary clanging of cymbals, and the strange, reedy wailing of alien stringed instruments."

Her guide noted some inattentiveness among spectators and said it was a sure sign that the old drama was dying. Modern plays and movies had heroes and heroines more relevant to a China at war. No matter how fanciful the plot, their message was always the same: "Defeat the Japs!"[18]

The Luces left China on May 21. Airborne again, Clare mulled over what she had seen and heard in the last two weeks. She especially remembered something a Chinese diplomat had said to her: "You have taunted Europe with its Munich, and for four long years have failed to recognize your own." He was referring specifically to Japan's onslaught on China. Why, he wanted to know, was the Roosevelt Administration still trading with the imperial aggressors?

"If Japan really gets tough we'll stop," she had weakly replied.

"Japan is tough," he went on, "thanks to your scrap and oil." If Americans really cared about what was happening to the Chinese, they would end Japanese exports. But then, he said, "you will *have* to go to war."[19]

Clare saw now, even more clearly than she had in Europe in 1940, a fundamental fact of modern geopolitics: "There are no hemispheres in an air world." When the Japanese, land-hungry and bristling with fighters, bombers, and aircraft carriers, realized that Singapore and the Dutch East Indies could be conquered more easily than China, they would cast their expansionist gaze to a more distant horizon: the resource-rich Philippines, five hundred miles away. From there Hawaii, and even the American mainland, might seem obtainable goals.

The time had come for Americans literally to "reorient" themselves, to modify their preoccupation with Europe, and to look to the Pacific, where "the bloodstained Sun of Japan was rising fast."[20]

35

"Sir Charles"

One's real life is so often the life that one does not lead.
—Oscar Wilde

During a stopover in Manila on her way home, Clare met "the one man . . . that I could have run away with." He was Lieutenant Colonel Charles Andrew Willoughby, intelligence chief to General Douglas MacArthur. Over six feet tall and still handsome at forty-nine, Willoughby had a somewhat intimidating hauteur. Fellow officers associated this with his professed aristocratic ancestry and behind his back called him "Sir Charles." In fact the colonel was of humble German birth, spoke with a pronounced accent, and more closely resembled a member of the Prussian Guard than an English knight.[1]

Rumor had it that his cask-like chest and erect deportment came from wearing corsets, and that his lacquered, dark hair was dyed. But at first sight Clare was struck mainly by his immaculate grooming and the panache with which he tucked a handkerchief sprinkled with eau de cologne in his uniform sleeve.[2] He was clearly a worldly man, though somewhat world-weary. This paradox, coupled with his carefully culti-

Colonel Charles Willoughby, Manila, *1941*

vated air of mystery, reminded her of Julian Simpson, the English major she had fallen in love with eighteen years before. Like Julian, Willoughby was supremely well versed in espionage matters, which had always interested her. Indeed, she felt so attuned to him mentally, as well as physically, that he began to dominate her fantasies.

Clare got no further with her book on China that summer than three incomplete chapters and a few notes. The subject was too esoteric, and her experience of it too brief, for her to produce anything comparable to *Europe in the Spring*. Feeling frustrated and snappish, she put the manuscript aside.[3]

One reason for her short temper was that she had not heard as promised from Charles Willoughby. When several weeks elapsed without a word, she reached him with a costly hemispheric telephone call. He sounded astonished but pleased, if slightly strange to her. "I had forgotten your voice," she later wrote.[4]

At last, near the end of July, a batch of Clipper-delayed letters arrived from Manila. Despite having weekend guests, Clare sat down at once to pen a flirtatious reply. "For one reason or another (none of them good, I'm afraid) I think of you rather often." She asked Charles to tell her more about himself. "I would like for instance to know how French and German came to be your 'childhood tongues,' and why you never married." She did not believe his description of himself as an "elderly lemonade claret drinking man" who went to concerts or shopped rather than carouse with younger colleagues. "I strongly suspect that the 'bricabrac' you've collected for your apartment had very pretty ankles."

At such a distance there was nothing she could do about female rivals. But knowing Willoughby to be a snob, she did try to impress him with her military connections. "I am dining next week with General Marshall," she wrote. "It's going to be a long war, and I want to keep track of the army."[5]

Rather than abandon all the material she had collected for her book, Clare recast much of it as "Wings over China," for which *Life* paid her a princely $1,500. Next she proposed doing a profile of General Douglas MacArthur, newly appointed commander of USAFFE—the United States Armed Forces in the Far East. Needless to say, this would necessitate another, more extended visit to the Philippines. She was already in correspondence with the general, who wrote to say that President Roosevelt's recently imposed oil embargo gave the Japanese an excuse for a retaliatory attack on the Philippines.

"Its geographical position," MacArthur wrote of the archipelago, "makes it perhaps not the door to the mastery of the Pacific, nor even the lock to the door, but certainly it is the key that turns the lock that opens the door."[6]

John Billings was more concerned over the exclusion of American reporters from Roosevelt's Atlantic meeting with Churchill than he was with another article on the Far East. Since the trip would also be expensive, he thought it prudent to leave the decision to his boss. "Luce is hollering for big names," he wrote, "and Clare Boothe is such a name."[7]

Obviously, Clare had more than one reason for going to Manila again so soon. As her Waldorf neighbor Irene Selznick said, it was "a long way to go for a slap and tickle," but she was intent upon exploring her new friendship with Charles. They had, in his phrase, a "marvellously thin thread" binding them, and she was keen to strengthen it.[8]

After the unsuspecting Harry approved the assignment, she became guiltily agitated. Billings found her in a cubbyhole office at Rockefeller Center on the eve of her departure, working frantically on illustrations for the China piece. Her hair was "all frizzed," and she looked "scrawny and unpretty."[9]

That night, August 23, the Luces exchanged letters assessing the state of their union, as they often seemed to do before a long parting. In his otherwise loving note, Harry mentioned six years of marital "ups and downs." Clare, even as she contemplated betraying him, blamed whatever difficulties they had on his not "really" loving her. She nevertheless followed this with a plea that he never desert her.

> I am content, and willing, forever to have you love me as little or as much as you choose, providing you will always love me just enough to want to stay married to me. So that you will not want to share your life or your thoughts with anyone more than you want to share them with me; so that you recognize that ours is a "royal marriage."
>
> . . . I know my true home is whatever place I have in your thoughts, in your heart, Harry. I think for all the fierce pride I have, I would sicken and die if I had no home there.[10]

Clare's Philippine-bound Clipper was full of military personnel and diplomats. Among the latter was the Englishman Alfred Duff Cooper, on his way to Singapore to coordinate British empire defenses. Accompanying him was his wife, Diana, still, at forty-nine, as delicately pink-cheeked and classically lovely as she had been in *The Miracle* almost two decades before. At that time Clare was merely one of millions of her admirers. Now, celebrated herself, she attracted the attention of her fellow passenger, and during the first leg of the flight to Honolulu, the two were drawn together.

Diana Cooper thought Clare Luce "a great beauty, alarmingly intelligent." It was easy, she wrote their mutual friend Rudolf Kommer, to see why this combination of looks and brains might arouse envy.

> I think I am the only woman in England and one of a very very few in America who like Clare. The bother is that it's impossible not to be jealous of her. She has too much, and much, much too much confidence—which is what I am jealous of . . . No one likes it—if she concealed it, she'd be loved.[11]

On a purely feminine level, Diana was impressed by Clare's ability to look smart throughout the fourteen-hour journey. After the sun went down, she simply added gold jewelry and "a correct bag" to her sand-colored slacks, jacket, and turban. Yet she was quick as any mechanic to notice one of the Clipper's engines misfiring. Completely unconcerned, she told the nervous Diana about it with a "*tsee-tsee* silvery laugh."[12]

When they reached Honolulu the captain announced they would have to wait three days for a substitute plane. This gave Clare and the Coopers time to enjoy the palatial comforts of Doris Duke's estate near Diamond Head. Aptly named "Shangri-La," the mansion had lush seafront gardens bright with caged parrots and macaws. Monkeys swung freely from the trees, and tropical fish darted in tiled fountains. The azure swimming pool's diving platforms were retractable, so as not to spoil the view from the terrace. With a warm breeze blowing, and the moon shining on a tranquil ocean, descriptions by Duff Cooper of "the hell over London" sounded unreal. After dinner their hostess performed an expert hula, with "sweetly serpentine arms and mellifluous hips." Clare, beguiled in spite of her consciousness of carnage in the real world, once again toyed with the idea of a Hawaiian "pleasure dome" someday.[13]

After transferring to the Anzac Clipper, they continued on via Midway—already busy with military preparations—to Wake Island. "Not even a coconut palm!" Clare wrote in her *Life* account of the trip. "Just those great red dredges and cranes and tractors . . . remind one even out here in the middle of the Pacific of—war!"

After a vigorous game of tennis on a cement court, she took a cooling dip with Duff's assistant. It yielded her an unforgettable image.

> I swim out to the end of the pier where the Clipper lies alongside and tread water under the angle formed by its seawing. On the underside of the great wing, just above my head, they have painted a great American flag. It casts its reflection on the clear water. The clear water casts its reflection on the flag, making it seem to wave silkily. The young secretary paddles out into this Star-Spangled grotto. He looks up at the banner that covers him. He makes no comment. Is one required?[14]

With a day lost crossing the international date line, it was not until September 8 that Clare completed her seven-thousand-mile journey to Manila. Emerging from the seaplane at Cavite harbor, she at once felt the omnipresence of the United States. There were American ships and uniforms everywhere. As she drove into town along Dewey Boulevard, she saw American cars, taxis, soda parlors, and small Filipino boys wearing American sneakers as they snapped photographs with American Kodaks. It struck her as ironic that the city was so Americanized, while back home people thought Manila was "something you take when you don't want chocolate."[15]

It was Luzon's hot and rainy season, and by the time she checked into the air-conditioned Manila Hotel she felt "like a boiled potato dropped into an Arctic ice floe."[16] Unfortunately for her, the fifth-floor penthouse, with pool, was occupied by General MacArthur. Admiral Thomas Hart, Commander of the Far East fleet, lived in a Tudor-style suite one floor below. She wanted to interview him as well. Colonel Willoughby had less lavish quarters on del Pilar Street. He was fortuitously assigned to be Clare's guide and mentor during her monthlong stay, but for the first few days her need to establish professional contacts, and his duty to maintain official decorum, would preclude much intimacy.

Leaving the hotel that evening, Clare now felt "like a frosted fish popping from the Frigidaire into the fire." She was invited to the house of the American High Commissioner, Francis Sayre, for a party in honor of the Duff Coopers. Over two hundred people were there, and she quickly discovered that many of them were disillusioned with President Manuel Quezon. He was spending lavish sums on a city named after himself instead of buying equipment to defend his country. Many of the guests expressed dread of independence, now only five years off. Even Filipinos among them doubted the national government's military capability should Japan invade soon.[17]

Later, when Clare secured an interview with Quezon at Malacañan Palace, she relayed some of the concerns she had heard. The president, who had fought tirelessly against American imperial rule forty years before (surrendering his sword to the father of General MacArthur), was now weary and ill with tuberculosis. "There will be no war," he told her. "Washington will protect us."[18]

Nothing she heard in the weeks that followed was said with such conviction. But Clare saw Quezon was falling into the same trap as most of her countrymen in mistaking American prestige for power. Moving from island to island, and talking to civilians as well as military personnel, she understood more and more the menace confronting this "rich and splendid necklace across the throat of all the China seas."[19] In spite of some 150,000 Filipinos now officially serving under American colors, only about a third were fully trained. Nor did MacArthur have sufficient planes and ships to protect his command, let alone retaliate, should Tokyo bomb Manila.

Clare voiced this concern directly to Admiral Hart. After a tour of the Navy base on his yacht, she had formed a high regard for the flinty, four-star veteran. At sixty-four he outranked MacArthur by age and seniority and was the greatest living expert on the Pacific waters stretching from Australia up to Hong Kong and across to Hawaii. For this reason, if no other, Roosevelt had broken a precedent by letting him continue beyond retirement age.

Short, lean, and febrile, the admiral personified naval courtliness. But he spoke bluntly about the inadequacy of his Asiatic squadron, with its mere handful of submarines, cruisers, and overage destroyers. In six months' time he expected to have improved harbor facilities, subtenders, torpedoes, and planes for his carriers. "But until then I have the biggest blank check for them you ever saw."[20]

As things stood, Japan had the power to force his ships back to Hawaii, unless British forces in the region continued to provide backing. Yet he believed that any immediate Japanese victory would be temporary. They must lose the war in the end, Hart said, because their arms replacement production could not compete with America's. And, he volunteered with a wry smile, "They know it."[21]

Clare went ashore at Corregidor, a three-mile-long island fortress in the mouth of Manila Bay. It had its own airfield and was honeycombed with underground defenses cut from rock. In the event of an invasion of Luzon, these shelters were ready to host important evacuees. But with the skies above so scantily protected, she saw no point in such an elaborate hideout.[22]

Douglas MacArthur had been associated with the Philippines in one capacity or another much of his life. After graduating at the top of his West Point class, he had gone to the islands where his father had once been Military Governor. From then on his rise had been rapid, and in the Great War he had repeatedly been decorated for bravery. At age fifty he had become one of the youngest four-star generals in the nation's history, as well as its most junior Chief of Staff. After retiring from the latter post in 1935, he had for two years served as Quezon's director of defense.

Although MacArthur's credentials did not intimidate Clare, she was impressed on her first and subsequent meetings by the sheer force of his presence. Despite narrow, sloping shoulders, thin black hair combed across the top of his head, and small, nervously moving hands, he gave, at sixty-one, the impression of being tougher in body and spirit than most men ten years younger. His pallid face looked more intellectual and aesthetic than martial. At an informal dinner at Willoughby's apartment, and during an interview in the general's own book-lined penthouse, Clare found him disappointingly circumspect.

Nevertheless, it was instantly apparent to her why MacArthur had won accolades as the most effective spokesman for the army. His knowledge of military history, coupled with dramatic flair and speed of delivery, impressed Clare as "positively pyrotechnic." While his speeches could be overly baroque, his ideas made "shattering sense," and in her profile she gave him credit for all he had accomplished in the Philippines.

MacArthur's language is sometimes rhetorical but his behavior is usually realistic. From the day that he landed in the Islands to organize their defense, he had in fact proceeded as though he had seen in a crystal ball the Japanese landing . . . The problem that faced him was technically complex: it was to build in a peaceful agricultural nation of 16,000,000 people an effective modern military machine, to create, literally from scratch, a respectable army . . . which could be called swiftly into being at the threat of attack.[23]

Clare with General MacArthur, Manila,
September 1941

The commander was doggedly taciturn, if not outright evasive, on specifics. He took refuge in proclamations, telling Clare, "We stand on the eve of a great battle." When she pressed him to say how long this "eve" would last, he surprised her with the terse declaration, "Six months."

Apart from this one hard fact, she was obliged to pad her piece with biographical material and general opinions. Some detractors, she wrote, found MacArthur an aggressive, obstinate, dictatorial swaggerer. They saw his plum-colored ties, Corona cigars, and the rakish tilt of his brassed hat as attention-getting affectations. Others chastised him for promoting only his acolytes, and Filipino wits sneeringly referred to men like Willoughby as "the Knights of MacArthur's Round Table."[24]

Since Clare believed that in wartime it was important to instill confidence in leaders, she chose to play down MacArthur's vanity and flamboyance, and not to mention his early affair with a vaudeville star, his failed marriage, or his lucrative Philippine investments. As far as she was concerned, the general was "a hell of a good soldier," with more savvy and vision than any other man President Roosevelt could have chosen at such a crucial time.[25]

Clare continued her education in tactics and strategy during a dinner at USAFFE headquarters. It was built on top of Fort Santiago, and as rain drummed down on the tin roof she asked Willoughby where the Japanese might strike if they invaded the Philippines. He drew a map on the tablecloth and pointed to Luzon's Lingayen Gulf in the west and Polillo Bight in the east.

"Ye old pincer movement," he said.

"You're not giving away military secrets?"

Charles laughed. "No, just quoting military gospel—according to Homer Lea."

Clare had never heard the name. Willoughby explained that Lea, who had died in 1912 at the age of thirty-six, had been a Colorado-born hunchback with a passion for all things military. Too crippled to enter the U.S. Army, he had studied the maneuvers of the great commanders from Hannibal to Napoleon. Then, moving to China, he had become strategic adviser to Sun Yat-sen, leader of the revolution that overthrew the Manchu monarchy. In two brilliant books, *The Valor of Ignorance*

(1909) and *Day of the Saxon* (1912), he had predicted not only the rise of Japan and Germany but the exact methods both powers would employ to attack the British and American empires. Long before the construction of the Maginot, he had warned of the vulnerability of permanent fortifications, describing them as nothing more than "dream castles" of a nation's vanity.[26] When Clare discovered that Hitler himself had read Lea on the supreme value of mobility in warfare, she was captivated. This smart cripple was worth a biography, and she resolved to find out more about him.

One night, with Charles as her escort, Clare went to Manila's Santa Anna dance hall—the largest in the world—to watch lofty American sailors doing the "shag" with four-foot Filipinas. It was a scene of mass abandon, in which a need to relieve prewar tensions was as palpable as plain sexual energy. Clare noticed that the sight of men throwing tiny partners over their shoulders and between their legs only increased Willoughby's customary reserve. In his opinion, the average seaman danced that way because he lived mostly in claustrophobic or unsteady spaces. "Imagine if he did that in his narrow bunk, or on a heaving deck."[27]

It was not in the cavernous hall, but after a Saturday night ball at the Manila Polo Club on September 13, that the spark of passion between Clare and Charles ignited. Strolling to her hotel in the moonlight, they stopped by a small Spanish church. Candles flickered in the dark interior, and a pungent fragrance of incense wafted on the humid air. Willoughby turned suddenly and said he loved her.

Clare was sometimes surprised at the speed and ease of her conquests, and she did not know how to respond to the intensity of the feelings she engendered. To her, seduction was usually more satisfying than consummation. She tended to grow cold as lovers became hot. This did not prevent her from indulging sexual appetites unsatisfied by her marriage, but sooner or later men sensed that she withheld the deepest part of her real self from them.[28]

It is unlikely that she gave herself to Willoughby there and then. But she later admitted that he was the only man since Bill Hale who made her weak at the knees. A letter Charles wrote her recalling the evening of the ball, suggests frustration on his part. He never forgot the

fierce blaze of his feelings, and how after leaving her he had paced endlessly up and down, "in a nightmarish, fantastic hour of anguish" that
had "left its mark."[29]

During the remaining weeks of her stay, Clare learned as much
about the colonel's background as he let anyone know. He had been
born in Heidelberg, Germany, and said that his father was Baron T. von
Tscheppe-Weidenbach. (Later research in the city register suggested
otherwise.) Charles joked that he would "have hung on" to his title had
he realized "the American penchant for Coronets."[30]

He had emigrated to the United States at the age of eighteen and
attended Gettysburg College. Then, Americanizing his name, he had
taken a commission in the Army and served in France and South
America. Accepting a post as lecturer in military history at Fort Leav-
enworth, he had met Douglas MacArthur, a man he came to revere to
the point of idolatry. MacArthur, in turn, respected Willoughby's erudition and eventually included him in his circle of advisers.[31]

While in the mess and at Manila cocktail parties the colonel could
be witty and irreverent, he was often distant and cold at work. Colleagues noted certain fascistic tendencies. He would inordinately praise
Spain's Generalissimo Francisco Franco, and had a paranoid inclination to "find a spy under the table." But to Clare he revealed a romantic side. "I like candlelight, and gleaming silver, and a bowl of roses," he
told her, while admitting to slight interest in food itself. As she came to
know Charles better, she discovered that beneath the chivalrous exterior his emotions were volatile. In seconds he might switch from high
spirits to the depths of gloom, and fly into a rage if anyone crossed him.
These extremes disturbed her. She was prone to depression herself and
knew how debilitating it could be.[32]

As the end of her visit drew close, Clare was touched by the acute-
ness of Willoughby's need for her. She was drawn to him too. However,
vague desires at long distance were not enough. Propinquity was of the
essence.

As they said good-bye, Clare promised to return to the Philippines
in the near future. Or, if war did not break out, they could meet in New
York. But two interminable years would pass before they managed to
see each other again.

She planned to spend her last evening in Manila, as she had her first, at the High Commissioner's. A car was sent to the hotel to collect both her and Sir Henry Brooke-Popham, commander of British air forces in the Far East. Their driver recorded what transpired when Clare (who shared Evelyn Waugh's belief that punctuality was a virtue of the bored) kept her fellow passenger waiting. Sir Henry, the party's guest of honor, spoke sharply to her about being late. But Clare came back at him so much faster than he could "dish it out" that the chauffeur feared they might "come to blows."[33]

Clare carried two highly symbolic visual images back home with her. One was a silhouetted view from the Sayres' terrace of Mariveles, the mountain that some Filipinos said resembled a young warrior fallen in battle, one arm thrown over sightless eyes. The other struck her during her Honolulu stopover. She was driving close to Pearl Harbor in light rain, and as her car rounded a bend she caught sight of America's gray fleet at anchor on blue water. Spread over the ships was a rainbow with bands of color as bright as she had ever seen. If only the scene could be reproduced, she thought, it would be "the greatest recruiting poster in the world."

Then she remembered another rainbow over a vessel that had survived the worst disaster in history, and some words of Genesis came back to her. "And it shall come to pass," God had said to Noah, "when I bring a cloud over the earth, that the rainbow shall be seen in the cloud."[34]

36

BOMBED

INTO GREATNESS

It is undefended riches which provoke war.
—GENERAL DOUGLAS MACARTHUR

Clare hardly recognized the young woman who flung herself into her arms when she landed in San Francisco from Hawaii on October 15, 1941. Ann Brokaw had grown from gawky schoolgirl to seventeen-year-old college student with amazing speed. Now in her first semester at Stanford, she was a slim five feet, seven inches tall, with wavy, reddish brown hair, large teeth, and a prominent freckled nose. Yet she was attractive enough to have featured recently in both *Vogue* and *Harper's Bazaar*. A Pan Am engineer named Walton Wickett, who liked to watch seaplanes land at Treasure Island, noticed how warmly the two women greeted each other. He decided to try to meet the younger one.[1]

After answering press questions, Clare checked into the Mark Hopkins hotel and took her daughter to dinner in a Chinese restaurant. "Mummy was her usual beautiful, inspired and radiant self," Ann

Ann Clare Brokaw, *1941*

wrote after hearing about her adventures, including her new friendship with a mysterious "German Baron."[2]

Ann always missed Clare but never realized how much she loved her until they reunited. "I don't know what I should ever do without her." The girl's dependence was understandable, since her mother was everything she was not: sexually appealing, gregarious, witty, and creative. About all they had in common was an analytical power—though here again Clare's intellect was superior—a passion for reading, and gift for self-expression.[3] These traits were apparent in Ann at Foxcroft, where she had won several writing prizes and, in her final year, the prestigious editorship of *Tally-ho* magazine. But she excelled in music, to which Clare remained tone-deaf. Like her Grandfather Boothe, Ann played both piano and violin. She also sang soprano arias in a clear, natural voice of remarkable range.[4]

Clare had persuaded her to forgo a conventional début. Modern girls, she explained, were no longer "cloistered" and already enjoyed so much freedom that a formal presentation to society was unnecessary. No one ever took a débutante seriously if she wanted "to establish herself in a business or art." Unspoken were more pertinent objections: a traditional début was enormously expensive as well as time consuming, and Clare had no inclination to spend vast sums on a celebration not centering on herself. She suggested that Ann just hold a few small dinner and theater parties.[5]

One of the young men Clare tried to pair Ann with was John Fitzgerald Kennedy, son of her own old flame Joe. But when the future President appeared to collect his date, he showed more interest in mother than in daughter. This happened so often when Ann brought boys home that she would grimace at any mention of Clare's attractions and talents.[6]

Even though Ann was more or less grown up, Clare saw no reason to discontinue her thrifty habit of going through her clothes closets and handing down cast-off outfits. She asked her secretary, Isabel Hill, to ship an old mink to "a cheap furrier," to dye and recut for Ann "so she could have it by Christmas."[7]

Clare submitted her sprawling, seventy-three-page MacArthur manuscript to John Billings as soon as she reached New York. It was not well received. The editor felt, accurately, that she had "gushed" over her subject without revealing much about his character or his accomplishments, at least not in Manila. "Just a jumble of words . . . a mess!" She conceded that the piece was not "a peephole on the General"—given MacArthur's evasiveness, it could hardly be that—but more like a political history of the country he was defending. "I have made an awful flop of this," she wrote Harry. "Please help me."[8]

Billings realized that his boss was "in a box between Clare's ambitions at home and our criticisms at the office," and suggested a solution. He would run another piece by Clare, about island hopping across the Pacific, in the next issue, under the title "Destiny Crosses the Dateline." Meanwhile, Noel Busch, one of *Life*'s best editors, could make order out of the chaos of her profile for later publication.[9]

It was becoming apparent to professional eyes that Clare was turning into a facile, self-obsessed writer, too restless to amass the hard facts and ask the probing questions that journalism entails. Her playwright's eye and ear were quick to pick out or invent colorful details, but being primarily imaginative and self-dramatizing, she did not care much if what she wrote about others was less than truthful.

Someone who was willing to point this out was her occasional Waldorf Towers neighbor David O. Selznick. That fall the producer dealt blows to her creative esteem much more devastating than those of her *Life* editors. Making full use of his powerful influence in Hollywood, she had already sold two stories to Paramount and was floating an idea for a screenplay about the Soong Sisters. Harry had also persuaded Selznick to be West Coast fund-raiser for his pet cause, China Relief.

Clare's latest proposal was to rework an introductory chapter to "China in the Spring" into an article about the movie colony. She blithely assumed "David" would like it, since it mentioned his charity work, to the disparagement of other producers, whom she accused of making "escapist" pictures while ignoring the reality of war in Europe and the Orient.

Selznick responded to her draft manuscript with vituperative outrage. "The story is filled with inaccuracies and untruths," he wrote. "I think this is false, malicious, insincere, and ungrateful." He was especially incensed by her setting him up as a "stooge" to her "superior discernment.

> I don't like the portrait of myself straight out of an old fashioned burlesque as having breakfast at one, without some explanation that I have been working the whole night previously. I don't like a distortion and misquotation of my opinions, that were ventured in large part half seriously when we were both drunk. I don't like the rather sad and disillusioning revelation that my guest had a reporter's pencil and notebook, with the notes, incidentally, not being used until months later when the filling in was dependent upon memory of conversations over champagne.[10]

Selznick reminded her that he and his colleagues "have done a monumental job . . . in raising money for China Relief" and noted that she was now advertising herself as a platform speaker for the same cause. "Are you contributing everything you make on your lecture tour to China, or are you lecturing on China in order to make money that you personally pocket?" As for the adjective "escapist," her own comedies hardly deserved anything better. If she cared so much about politically conscious scripts, why had she not written one of the caliber of *All Quiet on the Western Front*, or *What Price Glory*, instead of *The Women* and *Kiss the Boys Good-bye*?

Beyond his criticism of her article about Hollywood, Selznick unsparingly pointed out an aspect of Clare's literary personality that he felt bordered on the pathological.

> Forgive me if I say that seemingly you have some irresistible impulse to tear things down. I am fond enough of you, Clare, to wish that you could get some help, from friends if not from psychoanalysts in curing you of this habit. Believe me, it is going to boomerang on you increasingly . . . unless you will reduce the extent to which you persist in glorifying yourself at the expense of others.

He signed off after seven tightly typed pages, "With affection—which is certainly sometimes put to a very sore trial, David."[11]

Nobody since Donald Freeman had so penetrated her amour propre. Mortified, she withdrew the piece and postponed her lecture tour. She sent Selznick a weak protest, saying that he could have given her a simple rap on the knuckles. He stingingly replied, "It is a bit inconsistent for the executioner to hate the axe."[12]

Professional struggles and global uncertainty wore Clare down as winter approached. She complained of a recurring tropical fever and became contemptuous of the popular ambivalence regarding America's world responsibilities. On Saturday, December 6, she assessed the country's mood. "Nobody would be the slightest bit surprised if we went to war with Japan tomorrow, *but* if we did . . . *everybody* would fall flat on his face with astonishment."[13]

Sunday dawned cold and crisp in Connecticut, yet by noon the sun was so warm it felt like Indian summer. As lunch guests began to arrive, a wind sprang up, whirling clouds across a lowering sky. Clare had invited a large party of diplomats and newsmen, as well as the Chinese philosopher Dr. Lin Yutang. In spite of her efforts to direct the table conversation towards Pacific affairs, it stubbornly focused on the European war.

During dessert a message was brought to Harry. He read it out. At about eight o'clock that morning, Honolulu time, Japanese bombers had attacked Hawaii and severely damaged the American fleet anchored at Pearl Harbor. Everybody jumped up and headed for telephones and the radio. Only Dr. Lin calmly finished his pudding. To him the Second World War had begun over four years before, when the Japanese attacked China.[14]

Harry left at once for New York. His *Life* staff had less than two hours to pull some morgue photographs of Honolulu, make new layouts, rewrite a seven-page lead, and rush the new issue to press in Chicago. Billings kept Clare's cover story, "MacArthur of the Far East," giving her one of the scoops of the century. Evidently she celebrated, because when she spoke that night as a guest on Jimmy Sheean's weekly radio program, she struck at least one listener, the novelist Josephine Herbst, as being "slightly under the influence of liquor." She gave "a mixed batter," Herbst wrote in her diary, "of what everyone knows with the air of a spy returning from the front line, and as if the Japs had held off a day or so on purpose to reward her with this Hour of Hours."[15]

Even as Clare drawled her Japanese conspiracy theories, diners in Manhattan restaurants looked quite serene, and skaters seemed blissfully unconcerned while careening around the ice rink in Rockefeller Center.[16] But with the morning newspapers, the full horror of the surprise raid began to permeate America's consciousness. The Honolulu casualty figures were staggering: over 2,000 servicemen killed outright or missing, and almost 1,200 wounded. Eighteen ships, including eight obsolete battleships, were in varying states of wreckage—only the *Arizona* had been irretrievably sunk—and 347 Navy planes lay destroyed or damaged. Luckily, two American carriers out to sea had escaped, along with dry docks and fuel dumps crucial to supplying the Far East theater.

Clare was distressed to hear that Japan had also hit Cavite harbor in the Philippines. Most of the newly imported B-17 bombers and P-40 fighter planes she had seen lined up at Clark Field had been obliterated. She worried particularly about Willoughby. Was he safe with MacArthur on Corregidor? Had his spies told him the raid was coming? Could the Islands be protected from infantry invasion if Admiral Hart carried out his hinted willingness to withdraw the Asiatic Squadron to safer waters? She longed to be back in Manila to ask these and other questions. But with the enemy already moving on Guam, Wake, Midway, and possibly the Aleutians, Clare knew she had little hope of crossing the Pacific as long as the war lasted.

What she did hope for was an opportunity, at this time of crisis, to capitalize on her own many talents. She was not sure yet what the best of them were, and of what use they might be. But she felt with rising spirits that both she and her country were coming into their own. Over thirty years later, speaking in Honolulu, she would nostalgically reminisce about this decisive moment in history. "No nation has ever been born great," she said. "Greatness was thrust upon the United States by the Japanese attack on Pearl Harbor. We were literally bombed into greatness."[17]

The brazen suddenness of the Japanese assault, and the realization that the American mainland was now vulnerable, changed popular complacency overnight. Even Charles Lindbergh renounced isolationism on December 11, when Germany, honoring a pact with Japan, declared war on the United States. Clare's own immediate reaction was to make herself an oracle of the master strategist Homer Lea.

Inspired by her talks with Willoughby about the tiny, forgotten hunchback, she spent several weeks in the New York Public Library researching Lea's life and completed a thirty-page outline by the end of the year. She then invited Noel Busch to Mepkin to look it over. Billings rightly surmised that Busch would be expected to "pay" for her hospitality by recommending she submit the fruits of her scholarship to *Life*. When Clare telephoned to offer a two-part profile "at her usual rates," the editor rejected it, saying Lea was merely "a footnote to history."[18]

He should have known that Clare was a force not to be deterred. She sold the piece to *Life*'s nearest rival in circulation, *The Saturday Evening Post*. The hundred-dollar fee did not matter, she told Ann, since scholarly work gave her more pleasure than the most lucrative Hollywood scripts.[19]

Lavishly illustrated, "Ever Hear of Homer Lea?" appeared in two separate issues later that winter.[20] With perfect timing, Clare simultaneously published an introduction to a reissue of Lea's *The Valor of Ignorance*, elevating him to the rank of prophet.

> Here was the prediction that Manila would be forced to surrender in three weeks. It was occupied by the Japs twenty-six days after the opening of hostilities. Here was the very picture of the convergent attack at right angles—the pincer movement—from Lingayen Gulf and Polillo Bight before which MacArthur's troops fell back to entrench themselves on Bataan Peninsula . . . Here, above all, was a solemn warning against putting undue faith in "impregnable forts" in Manila Harbor (Corregidor, Il Caballo, El Fraile), unless they formed the base of a great fleet, equal to Japan's, or were defended by a great mobile army.[21]

Not even this quadruple coup quelled Clare's biographical ardor. She tried to interest both Irene Selznick's father, Louis B. Mayer, and her husband in adapting Lea's life to the screen, but without success.[22]

Stimulated by her work on Lea, and her recent exposure to the extreme right-wing views of Charles Willoughby, Clare spent New Year's Day 1942 composing an extraordinary, twenty-nine-page, closely typed memorandum to Harry entitled "A Luce Forecast for a Luce Lifetime." While much of the document showed her perspicacity and grasp of *Realpolitik,* it degenerated into paranoia, and worse. She began on a personal note.

> We have had so many arguments about the war in the past three or four years. They have been a strain on our nervous systems and often on our affections. But once we were in the war we should have stopped them. Since the stake is America itself, we ought to have agreed on everything at last. But we didn't and we don't. Bitter arguments still flourish like an evil tangleweed in the otherwise happy garden of our affection, common admiration and respect. What makes these debilitating arguments so fruitless is that we argue most, not about past or current events upon which some decision might be found in books, but about The Shape of Things to come.

The word *bitter* had become habitual in her speeches and articles since their marriage underwent its great change. She was to use it six times in this polemic.

"I hope that we will both live to the year 1970: a quarter of a century more," she wrote. "All I am going to do is to try to define a *trend* in political forces, based on geographical, political and racial *facts*, which, if not reversed in the next ten years, will lead inevitably to destruction of the U.S.A." Given that the American Army had as recently as 1938 ranked nineteenth in numbers (below even Portugal), she considered it vital that the country now become and remain the world's dominant force. This meant transforming its economic, spiritual, intellectual, and political wealth into overwhelming physical might, with an amply equipped, standing military—George Washington's recommendation. The United States could no longer afford a foreign policy calculated to bring about defeat "at the hands of our enemies."

Throughout the century, Clare observed, the most threatening nations had been those that had expanded territorially—Germany, Japan, and Russia—while the British and American empires had been declining in both size and "white" birthrates. The United States had consistently ignored this phenomenon, choosing its allies for ideological and commercial, rather than military or geographical, reasons. At the same time it had ignored evidence that the expansionist powers were arming themselves and annexing neighbors. In Europe, Americans had elected to support the weak consortium of Britain, France, Belgium, Poland, Czechoslovakia, and Holland, "which resulted in Lend-Lease and the emasculation of the Neutrality Act." In Asia the Roosevelt administration had illogically chosen China as an ally, while at the same time strengthening Japan with trade.

> There are no words existent, nor will there be in history, for
> the sublime folly of choosing a country for your sentimental
> ally and at the same time supplying its immediate geograph-
> ical and military enemy and yours with the essential ma-
> teriel of warfare. This piece of gigantic stupidity will stand
> unchallenged in the annals of Democratic Foreign Policy.

As a result, Clare continued, disaster now loomed. A government "which leads a 'great' nation . . . into a two-ocean multiple front war, with a one-ocean navy and no armies to put in the field is a monstrosity, which if not traitorous, is surely imbecile."

She felt that there was only "a fifty-fifty chance" of victory. If the Anglo-Saxon powers were defeated, then the future was too awful to contemplate. Even if they won, it would hardly be a triumph for democracy. The Allies might, with luck, negotiate peace in Europe "about 1945," but it was likely to be on German terms. As for the Far East, she accurately predicted that Singapore, key to British defenses, would be lost to Nippon by March. The Dutch East Indies would fall soon after, and it would take "six years" to liberate the empire Japan had so defiantly acquired.

Win or lose, Germany, Japan, and China would continue to grow through the Fifties and Sixties, and beyond, because growth was "in their racial genes." Weaker, darker nations, hitherto subject to domination, would simultaneously feel "stirrings of racial solidarity" and demand independence. "The day a 'subject' people becomes 'free,' the next day it allies itself with its former master's enemies." Hence, "we are doomed . . . to *police the world*."

Clare's peroration moved beyond reason to demagoguery. After expressing mock horror at "bloodthirsty" social theoreticians who suggested that the only way to restrict Nazi genes in future would be "to emasculate or slaughter all the males," she found the idea tolerable herself. And not only in Germany, "for there is no other *certain* way to keep the Japs and the Russians *down*." Ranting on, she wrote, "If we raze their towns and factories and manage to slaughter greater numbers of *them* than they do of us, we will have put a crimp for a number of years in their racial style."

There remained the question of what to do about America's biggest and most unpredictable ally. Lucid again, she set out an amazingly prescient scenario for the next two decades. After the war the United States would "sit down at a democratic peace table with the Russians," only to endure "ten years of the 'phoniest' peace . . . we have ever known." While Anglo-Saxons proceeded to consolidate their fragile commonwealths, "Demo-Russo Revolutions" would engulf Eastern Europe, and by the late 1950s "the Russian Century will have dawned."

Her language was a deliberate jab at Harry's notion of an American Century based on butter and Bibles. Clare's own considerably less benign plan of action was, she frankly admitted, "totalitarian." It was also fantastical, suggesting the corrosion of a personality denied the power that she felt born, if not qualified, to exercise. Abroad, the English-speaking peoples must combine, she insisted, into one super race. Germany, to contain Russia, should be granted Poland and "a hunk of the Ukraine," not to mention control of the Danube basin and a few African colonies. Italy would get back Ethiopia. Scandinavia, in turn, would be cordoned off from Germany, and France restored to her pre-war continental strength, keeping only Algeria overseas. Indochina would be given to the Chinese in exchange for U.S. naval bases. Last, "we send all immigrant Jews of the world . . . someplace . . . You pick where."

Meanwhile she was quite prepared to abrogate the Four Freedoms at home.

I believe *any* means justify the patriotic end of helping our country to survive . . . If it should prove necessary in our lifetime and our children's to scrap 'our American way of life,' our free enterprise system, our two-party system of government, and our constitution, to get it, I am for that, if only for the simple and logical reason that if we *don't* get it, and if our enemies do, these things will be scrapped anyway.

She saw no other choice. "So I am a Fascist, I suppose."[23]

One night at the plantation that winter, Clare had put on a green plaid housecoat, smothered cold cream on her face, and was ready for bed when a servant came in to announce the arrival of two young visitors from the Charleston Navy Yard. One of them was Ann's escort of last summer, Ensign John Kennedy. "He looked very handsome," Clare wrote Ann, "and he's such a bright clever boy." She passed on Jack's news that a friend of his had thought her "swell" and "pretty." Although Jack did not echo these opinions, Clare hinted that it might be worth cultivating his younger sister, Eunice, who had just gone to Stanford. "Do what you can to see that her first weeks are not too lonesome."[24]

But Ann's attentions were otherwise engaged. Walton Wickett, the young engineer who had been attracted to her at the Pan Am terminal, had succeeded in tracking her down. As luck would have it, he lived in Palo Alto, near the university, and soon contrived to meet her over hot chocolate at the Stanford Union. At twenty-seven Walton was ten years older, but he found Ann a mature match. He rated her at the top on his intelligence scale, admiring her extensive vocabulary and musical abilities, as well as her "lovely laugh."[25]

Clare encouraged the friendship, so long as it made Ann happy. She did not know that Walton found Ann unusually introspective and not "a real part of the college." This appealed to his sense of protectiveness, and he saw that she "liked being with somebody who was a little older." Soon he had taken her home for supper with his parents. Afterwards, Mrs. Wickett remarked that Ann was a girl "with great outer poise, but great inner turmoil."[26]

Rejuvenated as always by her stay at Mepkin, Clare was ready to fulfill an outstanding professional obligation to the Columbia Lecture Bureau. Her decision to postpone platform appearances after David Selznick's onslaught had lost money for the agency. Fifteen speeches had been advertised in various cities, and Columbia wanted to recoup promotional expenses as well as 25 percent of an estimated $12,400 in fees.[27] She now agreed to reschedule at least some of the engagements, and delivered the first lecture, "America Reorients Itself," to an audience of 3,500 on January 9, at Constitution Hall in Washington, D.C.

According to one attendee, who wrote an account of the event, many listeners had difficulty concentrating on Clare's words, so effulgent was her stage personality. They were distracted by her svelte black dress, the American Beauty rose on her left breast, and her "golden halo of pompadoured soft waves." Until Mrs. Luce reached fifty, the writer felt, people would probably pay more attention to her beauty than her brains, in spite of an oratorical "flair for the poetic-dramatic." One of her most theatrical warnings, that Japan could well capture twenty-five American generals in the Philippines—"the biggest bag of brass hats in the history of any civilized nation"—had elicited a collective gasp.[28]

By now Clare was an expert self-promoter. Coinciding with her resumed lecture schedule, she published an article in *Vogue* entitled "What Price the Philippines?" In February the magazine would feature her in a glamorous portrait by Horst. She posed in the living room of The House on a sumptuous couch, wearing a black satin gown by Valentina, long black gloves, and jewelry by Verdura.[29] Backed by mirrors, and surrounded by Art Deco ornaments, she gave off waves of elegance that were somewhat at odds with her role as global strategist.

Shortly after, it was announced that Clare Boothe was about to leave for the Middle and Far East on a two-month *Life* assignment. The peripatetic war correspondent had yet again orchestrated maximum publicity in advance of her reports from the danger zones.

Amid all the preoccupations of her luxurious and literary life, Clare found herself obsessing that same month over a yellow pottery fruit

Clare Boothe Luce
Photograph by Horst, 1941

bowl. She noticed that it was missing from a shipment of furnishings and *objets d'art* sent to her by Dr. Austin, voiceless now from throat cancer and failing rapidly. Feigning ignorance of his true condition—she had not seen him for several years—she wished him well in recovering his "amazing energy and bounce."[30]

Most of the items from Driftway were emblems of Ann Austin's social aspirations: an ornate tea service, a champagne cooler, crystal candlesticks, bejeweled evening bags, a thirteen-volume set of *Little Journeys to the Homes of the Great,* and a collection of silver toilette brushes that had always sat on the master bedroom dressing table. Clare was especially grateful for the last. She remembered Ann using them as far back as Memphis days. But she also wanted the yellow bowl, which she had bought for her mother as a girl, and she asked the doctor to look for it. "I will never forget how long it took me to save up the $12."[31]

On January 26, Albert Elmer Austin died at the age of sixty-four. His stepdaughter, to whom he had brought respectability if not security, did not go to his funeral. She sent a fifty-dollar wreath and told the doctor's former political aide, Al Morano, that although a snowstorm and sickness had kept her away, she had said a prayer at St. Bartholomew's on Park Avenue.[32]

Morano was disappointed. He had been impressed by her speeches for Willkie and looked forward to telling her so. There was to be a congressional election in Fairfield County that year, and he had been optimistic, until Dr. Austin fell ill, that his former boss might recapture the seat for the Republican Party. "After the burial it hit me—I didn't have a candidate."

An idea occurred to him: why not approach Clare Luce?[33]

37

THE ROAD TO

MANDALAY

When the mist was on the rice-fields an' the sun was droppin' slow
She'd git 'er little banjo an' she'd sing Kulla-lo-lo!
— RUDYARD KIPLING

The situation in North Africa and Indochina was so critical by February 1942 that Clare undertook a three-month assignment to cover both theaters for *Life*. She had scant hope of reporting directly from the front, but at least she could round out her self-education in global affairs.

Arriving at La Guardia Marine Terminal on the eleventh, she found herself the only woman among a planeload of military and diplomatic personnel en route to the Middle and Far East. As luck had it, the officer she most wanted to interview was traveling with her. He was Lieutenant General Joseph Stilwell, Chiang Kai-shek's newly appointed Chief of Staff, not to mention Commander of all American forces in the CBI (China-Burma-India) theater. In his fifty-ninth year, "Vinegar Joe" was a wiry, bespectacled figure with a peppery directness and a well-known dislike of publicity. Warily, he noted in his diary for the day, "Clare Boothe gets to ride the plane."[1]

Stilwell's intelligence aide, Colonel Frank Roberts, caught sight of her in the crowd and was instantly beguiled. "Watch yourself," he thought with a married man's conscience, "you're up against something very big."[2]

Outside, Clare saw a familiar shape bobbing on the waters of the basin. It was the Clipper beneath whose star-spangled wings she had swum off Wake Island six months before. But the formerly sleek, silver flying boat had been transformed into a bulkier-looking warbird, camouflaged with wavy whites and grays. She understood that, once airborne, it would resemble "a giant scudding cloud."[3]

In its sameness yet fundamental difference, the great plane seemed to symbolize the metamorphosis that Clare herself had undergone since her first sight of bombs dropping on Brussels. During the coming weeks she would gain some knowledge of desert and jungle warfare, and of the frustrations of a fractured Allied command. But not all of her experiences would be novel enough to translate into inspired writing, or to keep boredom at bay.

On March 30 *Life* ran Clare's first dispatch, headlined BY CLIPPER TO AFRICAN FRONT. The subhead, over a photograph of a pensive author that showed the tranquil beauty of her eyes, read, "LIFE's War Correspondent Crosses South Atlantic with Vanguard of U.S. Reinforcements." But the text amounted to little more than a dogged travelogue of hops and delays. It was enlivened only by her brief description of standing "submarine watch" at the pilot's request, searching the ocean beneath "for the long dark shapes that are prowling wolfishly in our territorial waters."

Six other pieces were to appear at sporadic intervals through midsummer: "U.S. General Stilwell Commands Chinese on Burma Front," "Brereton," a portrait of the head of the Tenth U.S. Air Force in India, "Burma Mission" (in two parts), "The Battle for Egypt," and "The A.V.G. Ends Its Famous Career."[4] The first two were workaday profiles, while the last were rendered dry by censorship and lack of cooperation from the American Volunteer Group's fanatically daring leader, Colonel Claire Chennault. Only Burma, in its colonial death throes as the Japanese closed in, afforded Correspondent Boothe the kind of dramatic personal experience that excited her imagination.

A chance encounter at Stilwell's Lashio headquarters led to the one big scoop of her trip. Going up a lamplit staircase on the evening of April 5, she met the general coming down. They had not seen each other since their shared crossing of the South Atlantic. He was smoking a cigarette in a long black holder and energetically chewing gum at the same time.

"Hello, hello," he said brusquely. "Burma is no place for a woman."

Despite Stilwell's manner, there was no hostility in his voice. Clare had dutifully avoided mentioning him in her Clipper article for reasons of security. She started to protest, but he was already halfway down the stairs. At the bottom he turned. "Tomorrow I'm driving to Maymyo. If you can get up that early you can join me—on the Road to Mandalay."[5]

Shortly before dawn the next morning, they set off together in a rattly old Ford for the five-hour drive to Burma's summer capital. The sun came up as they careened along a dusty, curving road, fringed with tamarisk, bamboo, and banyan trees. Through a hot mist its dim rays revealed the gray outlines of needle-spired pagodas. As the day brightened, they turned from pink to rose to gold and finally chalk white.

An aide entertained them most of the way with stories of contretemps among the three Allies at the Toungoo front, causing Clare to ask herself, if not Stilwell, "Why is an American general leading Chinese armies in Burma?" And why was Chiang Kai-shek relinquishing command of his own troops to a foreigner—albeit one who spoke their language? She soon found out the answers. Chiang wanted American muscle to help him free China, while President Roosevelt's prime aim in sending Stilwell to the CBI was to keep the Japanese out of India.

By mid-morning the party reached their destination in the Shan hills, where the air was soft and balmy with the scent of petals. "Florally, at least," Clare noted, "East and West meet in Maymyo." Poinsettias and roses, eucalyptus and larkspur, frangipani and honeysuckle grew side by side. Purple bougainvillea covered an old red-brick mission that served as U.S. Army headquarters.

In the mess she had lunch with Stilwell and some thirty other senior staff. Among them was Colonel Roberts, already infatuated after having escorted her in Brazil, Cairo, and Calcutta. Their conversation did not yield much hard military information. Somebody noticed that the strawberry shortcake was made with stewed fruit and asked, "What the hell goes on here?"

Roberts explained that bombed-out refugees from Mandalay were streaming into town, bringing cholera with them.

"You boys have eaten your last fresh food," said a medic.

After lunch Stilwell, ignoring Clare, left to meet with Chiang and Britain's General Sir Harold Alexander. He wanted to sell them his idea for entrapping the Japanese at Pyinmana. Frustrated, Clare rounded up a photographer and continued forty miles south to Mandalay. From a considerable distance she could see thick curls of smoke, and as the jeep drew closer, a smell of seared and rotting flesh assaulted her nostrils.

The legendary city was a scene of utter desolation. Monasteries, houses, and bazaars had been leveled to a mass of charred timbers and twisted roofs. Thebaw's Palace survived, along with parts of the fort that had served as Government House. In its moat lotus pads floated on hot, green scum. As she walked about the perimeter, Clare saw the most chilling sight of all: babies' bottoms "bobbing about like unripe apples . . . gray naked breasts of women . . . and the bellies of men—all with their limbs trailing like green stems beneath the stagnant water."

Buzzards and carrion crows wheeled overhead. She learned that most of Mandalay's 150,000 inhabitants were dead or had fled, except for several thousand entrapped in rubble. "Here and there lay a charred and blackened form swaddled in bloody rags, all its human lineaments grotesquely fore-shortened by that terrible etcher—fire." Fewer than thirty live people were visible in the smoldering streets: a group of Burma Rifles, some native cyclists, and a flock of Buddhist priests in orange silk robes, carrying tattered black umbrellas.[6]

Back in Maymyo for dinner, Clare asked Stilwell if he had managed to sell his entrapment plan. "Yep," he replied, "everybody took it right out of the spoon."

"That's nice, but—will it *last?*"

Roberts kicked her ankle beneath the table.

"Nope," the general went on. "It won't last long." All they could do was play for time, and wait for RAF and AVG reinforcements to buttress their Indian and Chinese flanks, while Brereton's Flying Fortresses

Clare with General Stilwell and the Chiangs, Maymyo, *April 1942*

bombarded the Japanese in Rangoon. Burma was the key to the whole Pacific war, Vinegar Joe insisted. Then he laughed. "But every general thinks the front he is on is the most vital."

Clare sat up late in the liquor-free mission lounge eating peanuts with Frank Roberts before the fire. Huge, silent mosquitoes circled the room, waiting to pounce after lights-out. The mild-mannered colonel, professorial behind thick glasses, talked of imperial Burma, and the irony that Kipling had written "The Road to Mandalay" without having seen it. He said that whole lines of the poem, about a soldier's yearning for a beautiful girl he was obliged to part from, kept coming back to him, "pregnant with new, unhappy meaning."

Later, just as Clare was climbing into bed, she heard Frank call out to her from the landing. "The Japs have attacked Ceylon, and bombed some places in India."[7]

Two days later she was typing notes in her room when a siren summoned everyone at Maymyo headquarters into slit trenches in a nearby grove.

Clare in a Burma trench with Frank Roberts, *April 8, 1942*

As she took shelter, Clare heard the steady hum of aircraft engines approaching, and in a patch of blue sky between the trees she saw what looked like twenty-eight "little white birds" flying in perfect formation. "They're right overhead now," Frank Roberts shouted. "Here it comes!"

More terrified than she had ever been, Clare burrowed animal-like against the muddy sides of the pit.

> There was a long, long whine like the whistle of an onrushing train in an interminable tunnel. I closed my eyes and dug my chin into my breast, hunching my shoulders about my ears, as shuddering blast after blast tore the earth and air and woods all about us. And then the *thrum, thrum, thrum* faded and there was an awful silence.
>
> My insides had not stopped quivering, but my hands had when we came out of the trench on the all-clear . . . Until you've heard death scream in shell or bomb through the insensible air, impersonally seeking you out personally, you never quite believe that you are mortal.

Right across from the mission several houses were in flames. A five-hundred-pounder had landed in the road, making a crater thirty feet deep.[8]

That afternoon Clare went to see General Alexander in his Victorian-style house on a hill outside town. She was greeted by a turbaned servant who showed her to a terrace overlooking immaculate gardens. There she found the veteran of Flanders and Libya sipping pink gin. He was dressed in a robin's egg blue, Indian-style flannel bush jacket that matched the color of his eyes.[9]

He referred with Harrovian casualness to the morning's assault—"Everything all right your way?" Then he escorted her to lunch at a table set with silver and exquisitely arranged flowers, and talked with utmost candor of his plans. "We will hold Burma as long as we can."

Unlike Stilwell, Alexander was ready to admit that the country was strategically doomed. What was important was saving India. He said he would fight as hard a delaying action as "your MacArthur" had in the Philippines, destroying Burma's oil fields if necessary, scorching the earth behind him and retreating to the western mountains to fight a guerrilla war. Tanks were useless in this terrain. "I'm getting my units into native transportation as rapidly as possible." And he was as willing as Hannibal to use elephants, if he could get them.

Clare asked, "How are we then going to lick the Japs in this part of the world?"

"You always forget," Alexander replied, "people who are not militarists always forget, that Japs have their troubles too." The enemy's lines were already overextended. They did not have the capacity to replace lost planes quickly, and would soon have to cope with the monsoon.

Clare pointed out that flood rains affected the Allies as well.

Alexander's eyes blazed, but he was thinking of the war elsewhere. "What happens out here is only secondarily important . . . We've got to beat the Hun first. He's the real enemy. Never forget that." Only when Germany was crushed could America concentrate wholly on the Pacific theater. The Allies would help by sending "everything we have from the Near East. Russia will then be free to attack from Siberia."

In her account of the interview Clare wrote, "I thought: 'Where a soldier's heart is, there is his battlefront also.' Alexander's heart, bitter with the vengeance he had brought off Dunkirk, lay not in the Burmese jungle fronts of Empire but on the White Cliffs of Dover."[10]

Her piece on Stilwell was unrewarding by comparison. This was due as much to her growing reportorial laziness as to his unquotable Anglophobia and horror of news cameras. "You'll never get a picture of me at any front drinking any cup of tea." Had she been a Martha Gellhorn or a Margaret Bourke-White, Clare would have pestered him until he gave her something worth publishing. But the truth was that her interest in war was not so much journalistic as voyeuristic, even envious. She felt more at home with men in the field than with her own sex. Her thirty-ninth birthday, moreover, evoked telltale signs of melancholy. She turned down an invitation to spend an afternoon with Madame Chiang, pleading, "I'm tired," and a chance to visit the Burma front lines—"I'd get fatigued."[11]

Returning home via North Africa, Clare wrote at length about critical distances between water holes and oil dumps, maintenance of sand-choked machinery, and comparative equipping of British and German bivouacs. Perhaps realizing her prose was dry, she tried to liven it with dropped names, such as those of Sir Stafford Cripps, Special Envoy to the

Indian independence movement, General Sir Claude Auchinleck, and Sir Arthur Tedder, RAF commander in Egypt, not to mention Cecil Beaton, now a war photographer, and the Cairo socialites Sir John and "Momo" Marriott.[12] Her chronic propensity to settle for dinner-table chat, rather than do necessary legwork, led her to fill columns with inconsequential anecdotes and potted military history. Almost cynically, she fell back on long passages of overwriting, as in this description of the Sahara.

> Its vast, blind, dry demonic face, pocked with scabrous holes, pimpled with jagged rocks, wrinkled with barren wadies, bearded like the jowls of a lunatic with dirty tufts of scrub or camels'-thorn, or here and there smooth and glistening cheekbones of a skull, seems . . . more real and terrible than the iron snouts of tanks. It is gluttonous alike of men and machines, insatiable alike of bone and iron, blood and oil . . . The tired, thirsty soldier cannot throw himself down and suckle at its breast, for its breast is dry and withered as an old crone's.[13]

Such literary padding represented "War Correspondent Clare Boothe" at her garrulous worst. Confident that through Harry she could jockey for any amount of space in his magazines, she indulged a fatal facility with words, at the expense of her real gift, epigrammatic terseness. Asked at Lashio airport what the story of U.S. involvement in Burma was, she cracked, "*Veni, Vidi, Evacui* . . . We came, we saw, we got the hell out."[14]

Though the trip failed to enhance Clare's reputation as a reporter, it increased her store of military and foreign policy knowledge. It also enhanced her list of power players around the world. These last may not have told her all they could, but they were taken with her by now perfected combination of feminine wiles and intelligence. "Charming and lovely women are nature's autocrats," Jawaharlal Nehru wrote after his first meeting with her in New Delhi.

Clare in turn thought that the coming man of Indian politics had the greatest mind, along with that of Buckminster Fuller, she had yet encountered. She admitted finding Nehru "beautiful" and said she had fallen "a bit in love" with him. They were to develop an epistolary friendship over the next few years.[15]

457

At Trinidad, her penultimate stop before returning to New York, she found herself the subject of a mini-crisis in Anglo-American relations. British colonial authorities, inspecting her briefcase when she deplaned for the night, found that she had broken the official censor's seal placed on her notes before she left Cairo. Since much of what she had scribbled was either classified or disparaging of the British Army, the papers were confiscated and sent to His Majesty's Ambassador in Washington, Lord Halifax.[16]

Clare's material, on closer scrutiny, was more mocking than subversive. She wrote of effeteness and lack of offensive spirit in the British command in Egypt, of General Ritchie sending his laundry from the front to Cairo, and of General Auchinleck living far from the battlegrounds on a Nile houseboat (unlike Rommel, whom she said the average Tommy admired for staying close to his troops). As for the vaunted pilots of the RAF, she disdainfully referred to them as "flying fairies."[17]

On May 1, Clare was permitted to proceed to New York. Coincidentally or not, General Ritchie would be relieved as commander of the Eighth Army a few weeks later, thus clearing the way for the eventual succession of General Bernard Montgomery.

38

THE MOST
ABLE WOMAN IN THE
UNITED STATES

The whole dream of democracy is to raise the proletariat
to the level of the bourgeoisie. —GUSTAVE FLAUBERT

lbert P. Morano may have been the first, but he was by no means the
only Connecticut Republican operative to have the idea of Clare
Boothe Luce for Congress in 1942. Even before she left for Burma, a
high-level request that she consider the nomination had come her way.
She characteristically took it to be tantamount to election in November
and wrote Ann.

> I've said no, even tho they insist they won't take no for an
> answer. "The Halls of the House" are, to be sure, a fine plat-
> form for someone who has something to say, and a good way
> to serve one's country, and my going there would make
> something of a sensation even in Washington, but I don't
> really think that I want to do it. I'm not sure that as a politi-
> cian I would be a great success: I find it too hard to tell the
> lies that are necessary, it seems, in politics, and if I couldn't

say honestly what I thought, and vote as my conscience instead of my constituents dictated, I'd be miserable, and only
wind up making a terrible lot of trouble for everybody. And
besides, a writer is what I really am, and really want to be,
and it's only that this war has sidetracked and cannalized
[sic] my actions and words into things that seem political.[1]

Party leaders indeed refused to accept Clare's refusal. Shortly after
she returned from the Far East, Republican National Committeeman
Samuel F. Pryor raised her name at a dinner party in Wendell Willkie's
New York apartment. Pryor, who had been at Yale with Henry Luce,
was a vice president of Pan American Airways and a tireless lobbyist for
the company in Washington. "She is the most able woman in the
United States," he told the Greenwich Times, "and I only hope and pray
she consents to make the race."[2]

The paper's chief editorial writer was skeptical, but after hearing
Clare speak publicly on foreign policy, he admitted being "completely
sold" on her representing Fairfield County. She had "much of the same
magnetism and appeal that makes Franklin Roosevelt a stand-out
leader."[3]

An anonymous voice at The New Yorker, professing weariness of
her journalism, agreed that it would be a good idea to "bring Clare
Boothe back from the war front and keep her home." Over at Life, John
Billings echoed the sentiment. "On all sides I hear we are running too
much 'Clare Boothe,' and her pieces are becoming a general joke."[4]

Aware that she had not distinguished herself lately as a roving correspondent, and flattered by continued overtures from the state Republican organization, Clare agreed at least to consider a run for the
Fairfield County nomination. An incentive was that if she won it she
would be able to take on Congressman Leroy Downs, the Democrat
who had defeated Dr. Austin in 1940. Yet when her grassroots champion Al Morano came to discuss possible tactics with her at The House
on Sunday morning, May 24, she did not want to seem too eager. She
sent him coffee and cognac and kept him waiting for an hour.[5]

Morano was far from the kind of visitor Clare usually entertained.
He was a swarthy, thirty-four-year-old factory hand of Italian descent
who loved politics and had found working in Washington with her
stepfather more fun and more profitable than being on a Bridgeport

production line. Nothing would make him happier than to return to the nation's capital with the illustrious Clare Boothe Luce. Years before, when she had dropped by the doctor's office, he had sensed that she was "100 percent a politician, with all the instincts and wiles."

Now, in the contrasting luxury of her mansion, Morano was intimidated. A maid at last showed him into an upstairs boudoir, where he was surprised to find Clare still not dressed. She had long ago adopted the technique of receiving men *en levée*, to discomfort as well as vamp. Calmed by the brandy, Morano presented his reasons why she could win back Dr. Austin's seat. Clare listened noncommittally, then called for Harry and told him to take Morano into the garden for further discussion.

The two men ambled about the estate while Luce asked innumerable questions. Since none of them touched on campaign finances, Morano realized that "he didn't know the first thing about how a congressional race was run." Finally Harry said, "It's all up to her."[6]

Clare made no decision that day, nor for the next nine weeks, but Morano had the impression that she would run. He tried to persuade local newspapers to tout her as the best potential Republican nominee. Not all were convinced. She was, after all, famously elitist and controversial. Her combination of feminine allure and masculine drive was thought likely to offend some voters. The *Bridgeport Herald* reported a certain amount of dissension among local GOP leaders about her, "despite the fact they need somebody who can pitch lots of green hay into the party's loft."[7]

She remained unsure, for reasons even she could not articulate. Throughout June, Morano quietly lobbied delegates to the state convention. Harry, meanwhile, polled a select group of Time-Life executives. All but one favored her candidacy, although Luce never suspected they might simply want her out of the corporate offices. Bernard Baruch, now seventy-two but still loyal to Clare, also voiced support.[8]

On July 17 the Greenwich Council of Women endorsed her, followed four days later by the Negro Republican League of Fairfield County, which announced, on the strength of her articles and speeches about the Far East, that Mrs. Luce understood "the problems of minority groups the world over."[9]

Nevertheless, opposition to Clare strengthened as no fewer than five male candidates declared their interest in the Republican nomination. But her most vocal challenger was Vivien Kellems, a petite, forty-five-year-old Westport industrialist whose plant made cable grips for the military. Miss Kellems seemed to be the most likely nominee to draw vital labor backing from Congressman Downs. Clare dreaded, or pretended to dread, a repetition of the Dorothy Thompson episode. She wrote Frank Roberts, now at a desk job in Washington, that she felt personally torn. On the one hand she liked the prospect of being "in a spot where what I say and do can count." On the other she feared seeing news pictures of herself "with my mouth wide open, yammering."[10]

Under increasing pressure from all sides to make up her mind, Clare grappled with demons that had haunted her since childhood: fear that her amateurish inadequacies would be exposed by professionals, fear of looking foolish, fear of outright failure, and terror of rejection. She confessed as much to Frank, saying she "did not want to be in the humiliating position of seeking something and being turned down."[11]

On August 4 she again summoned Morano to the House, and again kept him waiting downstairs. Finally a secretary appeared and handed him a draft letter addressed to State Republican Chairman J. Kenneth Bradley. He was to read it before Mrs. Luce joined him.[12]

Clare's text was wordy and amounted to an apology for having to say no. She explained that although she had been a resident of Fairfield County since girlhood, she had spent most of the past fifteen years either in New York City or traveling. As a result, she felt out of touch with local desires and concerns.

> The more I reflected on the quality of my own qualifications for Congress, the clearer it became to me that a Congressman's job is two-fold. First, he must represent his constituents in the service of the nation. But secondly, he must represent his constituents by attending to their particular needs . . . in seeking the answers to America's problems abroad, I have, I am sorry to say, not been able to keep in close touch with my own neighbors here.

She had therefore made "an irrevocable decision not to seek the nomination."[13]

Morano obstinately marshaled his arguments. But when Clare, as he later put it, "floated" down the great spiral staircase, he found himself weakening before the force of her exquisite presence. He managed, however, to persuade her to withdraw the word "irrevocable." Buoyed by this concession, he urged George Waldo, owner of the *Bridgeport Post*, to publish an editorial countering the scruples expressed in Clare's letter. Waldo did so, pointing out that her candor in admitting ignorance of domestic issues was refreshing, and that her knowledge of world events more than compensated. Chairman Bradley, not entirely sure Clare was the right choice, nevertheless requested that she take time to reconsider.[14]

Clare chose to do so in Abingdon, Virginia, where she and Ann arrived by train on August 11. The little town's colonial Barter Theatre, second oldest in America, was rehearsing a play called *Love Is a Verb*, by one "Karl Weidenbach."[15] This was in fact a revision by Clare herself of *The Yohimbe Tree*, begun in collaboration with Alexander King. Their working relationship had soured in disagreement over changes she had tried to make in the original plot.

Whatever her reasons for wanting total script control, Clare had taken shrewd advantage of King's personal difficulties. He had been fired from *Life* for exacting bribes from would-be contributors and was about to be tried and imprisoned for perjury. Clare bought him out for $5,000. "I thought you would prefer a good straight business deal between us, rather than all the headaches and heartaches and worries of loans."[16]

Unsure of the revised play's merit, she went back to her *Vanity Fair* practice of sometimes using the names of men as pseudonyms and impishly adopted the name on Charles Willoughby's birth certificate. Later she would assert she disguised her authorship of *Love Is a Verb* because a woman running for Congress in 1942 could hardly take credit for a play about aphrodisiacs.[17]

In the midst of the familiar, absorbing routine of rehearsals and rewrites, Clare was surprised to hear via long-distance telephone that she had been attacked on the front page of the *New York World-Telegram*. Vivien Kellems—unconvinced by her withdrawal letter—was quoted as saying that "Clare Boothe's sex appeal," coupled with "Luce millions" and "the power of the Time-Life-Fortune Axis," would steamroll the following month's Connecticut convention.[18]

Clare responded with a dignified yet ambiguous statement, expressing the hope that Fairfield County's "several strong Congressional candidates" would fight for nomination on the one issue that really mattered—"successful conduct of the war." But she spoiled the effect by asking a reporter, "What's the matter with that wild-eyed little woman? . . . She is getting herself into the newspapers on the strength of my name."[19]

These responses revived Clare's candidacy, whether or not she intended them to. On August 15 she flew north for consultations, leaving Ann behind at the Martha Washington Inn. The girl was eager to stay on in Abingdon, having developed a crush on a thirty-four-year-old Hungarian actor. But no sooner had she put her mother on the plane than she felt "how helpless I am in equalling her conversational ability, her wit, her charm . . . I am ever so much inferior." When the Hungarian, too, temporarily left town, Ann became deeply depressed. "It is a terrible thing how often the idea of suicide occurs to me," she wrote in her diary. "I long to know the beyond—to see Granny again."[20]

Life became "vital and interesting and stimulating" once more when Clare rejoined her daughter after five days to attend the world premiere of *Love Is a Verb*. The play's heroine is an attractive widow whose search for grand passion in the Caribbean is consummated when she and a fellow hotel guest, a handsome psychiatrist, sample a love potion made from the *yohimbe* tree. Audiences enjoyed the mix of romance and comedy, and the producer extended the run from three to eleven performances.[21]

Back in Connecticut, politics again claimed Clare's attention, while her lovelorn daughter fell into renewed despair. Ann was unconsoled on August 22, her eighteenth birthday, by a gift of twenty pearls—probably because it came not from one of her own few beaux but from one of her mother's many—Max Thornburg, the oil engineer. "It has been a sad day," she recorded. "How little spark and zest for life there is in me—how few my accomplishments are, how ugly I am, how slowly I learn, how fast I forget."[22]

"You can do anything in this world if you're prepared to take the consequences, and consequences depend on character," Clare wrote Bernard Baruch a few days later. She was archly quoting the epigrammatic statement made to the heroine of Somerset Maugham's *The Circle* by a wise, silver-haired man, and added that it sounded "like the words of my favorite adviser." Turning serious, she said, "I am facing certain consequences dependent on my character which I am not particularly enjoying."[23]

Clare was apparently hinting at her tendency to seek a new arena for her talents, only to find that she had no relish for grubby work behind the scenes. And political work, she knew, could be grubby indeed. As she continued to wrestle with indecision, delegates to the state convention, just two weeks away, were growing impatient. The time had come, they told reporters, for Clare Luce "to stop playing hide-and-seek, take off her Lily Dache hat and throw it into the political ring." On August 31 she sent a letter to the Clare Boothe Luce for Congress Committee, retracting her decision not to run.[24] Connecticut's Republican leaders promptly invited her to be keynote speaker at the convention—the first woman in state history to be so honored.

All five of her male opponents now dropped out, leaving only Miss Kellems.

On September 10, Clare arrived at Bushnell Memorial Hall in Hartford for the GOP State Convention, suffering from a cold. She was unaccompanied by her husband. The press noted without comment that Henry Luce had gone to Washington and would not be back in time to hear his wife speak.[25]

No newspaper had yet guessed at the strains in the Luce marriage, but Ann, at least, saw that things were deteriorating. She had heard her mother burst untypically into tears after one recent row and noted that her stepfather was "close to a nervous breakdown." This was probably the result of overwork, since Harry was now functioning as both publisher and co–managing editor of *Time*. He had not had a real rest for months and was irritable with his staff.[26] In addition he had to adjust to yet another extreme career move by his headline-hugging wife. There was no further talk of elective office for him. Even his own magazines reserved the honor for her.

Shortly before nine o'clock that Thursday evening, after dining with Governor Raymond Baldwin and Chairman Bradley, Clare climbed onto the stage and faced a battery of microphones. She looked fragile but glamorous in a black silk dress embellished with a gold pin, her hair styled in a "feather cut." Tucked under her left arm was a stout red pocketbook housing her speech, and in her right hand she carried a stopwatch. Since her seventeen-page script was printed in large type, she was able to make graceful gestures with a pair of blue-rimmed, "harlequin" spectacles, clearly to show she was just as businesslike as Vivien Kellems. "She can even wear glasses!" murmured one spectator.[27]

As lights blazed blindingly down, Clare began by saying that it was "the darkest hour" in the country's history. "With every tick of the clock," people all over the world were dying, and looking to America to save them. "Our argument tonight is this: we want the war well conducted . . . If we permit another year of bungling and muddling we will be a very long and bloody time winning it." Although the President and his men "talked a tough war," they had so far fought a soft one.

She addressed herself to the broadest possible spectrum of Republican opinion, sounding at times more like a European socialist than the self-styled "fascist" who ranted to Harry. Blacks and other minorities, she said, were entitled to serve in the U.S. military with equal dignity alongside whites. After the war all Americans should be guaranteed "an adequate standard of living," which meant decent housing and basic medical care, as well as educational services. Every citizen deserved a minimum wage, a minimum diet, and—Clare was unable to resist one of her wisecracks—"a minimum set of teeth to eat it with."[28]

Vivien Kellems, looking small and subdued, failed to join the repeated applause. But Ann, sitting on the platform in the press section, felt both proud and awed. "Was that glorious woman really my mother?" A reporter nearby was equally dazzled and pulled out all his alliterative stops to describe how the "blonde, beautiful and brilliant" Mrs. Luce outshone all "bald, baggy and bumbling" politicos.[29]

Four days later Clare became Fairfield County's GOP nominee by 84 to 2 on the first ballot. She celebrated at her hotel until 4:00 A.M. After she dragged herself upstairs to bed, ecstatic supporters continued drinking and carousing for what remained of the night.[30]

Next morning Clare found herself the subject of a laudatory editorial in the influential *New York Herald Tribune*. Few campaigns that year,

Ann with her mother, *fall 1942*

the newspaper remarked, had aroused greater interest than that of Mrs. Luce. Her election in November was desirable, because she was "fearless, clear-minded and hard-hitting," and not beholden to any individual or group. Not only that, but her personal tours of at least five war fronts had given her an understanding of the international situation.

These factors, coupled with her gift for forceful speech, assure her a position in the spotlight if she is elected. She can be a force for clarification and constructive action in Congress. That very quality of unyielding pursuit of her objectives, which her enemies have resented, can be a valuable weapon in her skilled hands.[31]

Clare's congressional campaign got under way in the third week of September. She showed instant political acumen and requisite ruthlessness in choosing William H. Brennan as her campaign manager rather than the less experienced Al Morano. "Bill" Brennan was a 225-pound Irish Catholic with huge teeth and a face like a boxer. As an eighteen-year veteran of Connecticut politics, and a methodical organizer, he knew how best to tap the state's ethnic vote.[32] He was also merciless in pushing his candidate to the limit—as she soon discovered.

Shortly after sunrise, disregarding Clare's lifelong need to sleep late, he would drive her to a factory to shake hands with employees arriving for the first shift. From there he would whisk her to bleak school auditoriums, hospitals, firehouses, or hotel ballrooms, for as many as seven speeches a day. Given time, they grabbed a hamburger in a diner. While he gulped coffee and dragged on Pall Malls, she puffed Parliaments and tried to soothe her raw throat with hot milk.[33]

Clare contributed $1,739.91 of her own money to the campaign, slightly less than a fifth of the total $9,267.00 eventually spent. Harry came through with $1,897.00 and delegated Wesley Bailey, a Time Inc. staffer, to handle her advertising and printing, while keeping him on the company payroll. Other donors were less generous. David Selznick sent $250.00 and Max Gordon $100.00.[34]

Brennan, who habitually wore buttoned-up shirts without ties, lectured Clare on the need for "dressing down" if she wanted to win the hearts of upstate apple growers and Danbury hatmakers. But instinct told her that voters were not fooled by Mrs. Henry Luce pretending to be a person of modest means. She continued wearing her preferred outfit, an elegant dark blue suit, with a red rose in a tiny crystal vase pinned to the lapel. Eyes jaded by wartime drab, she reasoned, would rest with pleasure on a woman willing to indulge her own femininity. Before long Brennan admitted she was right. "If only all the voters could just *see* her," he said admiringly.[35]

From the start Clare was sure of two groups: the so-called "horsey" and "ritz" sets—landed gentry with old money, and New York commuters with new. But winning a working-class majority in larger towns beholden to the Democratic Party would not be easy. She gamely directed some of her 116 speeches specifically at blue-collar Bridgeporters and their union leaders. But her fundamental lack of interest in the underprivileged showed itself in tired platform clichés about labor's vital role in the economy and its right "to bargain collectively."[36]

She was more at home discussing geopolitical issues. Wireless, airplanes, and strategic alliances had shrunk the world, she stressed, bringing the peoples of Europe, Africa, Asia, and other far-flung places as close as the family next door. Americans must consequently develop their gift for good-neighborliness and end global conflicts once and for all. "Win the War" became her major theme. Reminding voters of her familiarity with distant battlefronts, she said she had been privileged "to witness such horrors of war as few [American] women have." She had seen mothers "buried with babies in their arms, under the ruins of their own homes," and whole populations living "sunken-eyed, bare-boned, rickety, easy prey to pestilence."[37]

Careful to avoid denigrating Leroy Downs, Clare assured her listeners that he was "just as anxious to win the war as I am." The difference between them was that she knew better "how to do it. I have had more experience. And I know what the shooting is about!" As for the Congressman's domestic record, he was "just another rubber stamp" for the New Deal. More rashly, she also described him as one of the men in Washington without faces.[38]

This was a gross gaffe. As Clare soon found out, Downs had been scorched by a gas bomb during the Great War and undergone facial plastic surgery.[39] But her political losses were slight, because she refused publicly to acknowledge the indiscretion and thus minimized it. "Never apologize, never explain" had long been her motto.

Accusations of being overly "ambitious" continued to hound Clare. She looked up the origin of the word and learned it came from the Latin *ambitio*, appropriately meaning "the going about of office seekers." This

amused and consoled her, as did the warm reception she received in ethnic neighborhoods. Italian women in particular liked both her confidence and her looks, calling her La Ricciulella—"the girl with curly
hair." One signorina, the daughter of a dentist, promised to vote for her
because she had "such beautiful teeth."[40]

Even Dorothy Thompson magnanimously endorsed Clare in a
signed newspaper advertisement. "Mrs. Luce isn't running for Congress
in order to . . . further her personal career, but in order to put what she
has at the service of the American people." Wendell Willkie, just back
from his world tour as presidential envoy, appeared at a Luce rally to
praise her as "a person of complete integrity," with "a liberal approach
to our questions."[41]

Congressman Downs, fully cognizant of the threat Clare posed to
his incumbency, was careful not to attack her in any way that might
make him seem ungentlemanly. But he adroitly managed to keep the
bulk of his core supporters together, and the race remained close
through the final suspenseful days of October. By then the *Greenwich
Times* was asserting that Mrs. Luce had "waged as active a campaign as

Clare with her campaign team: Wesley Bailey (*third from left*),
Bill Brennan (*center*), and Al Morano (*third from right*), *November 1942*

had ever been put on in the county." True or not, she was exhausted, and so pessimistic about her chances that she began calling Morano late at night for reassurance. "You can't miss," he would say. "Get some sleep."[42]

Just before 9:00 A.M. on Tuesday, November 3, Clare put on a fur-collared coat and drove with Harry to vote at the Greenwich Armory. Heedless of light rain, they then went on a tour to monitor the turnout in all twenty-three Fairfield voting districts. After lunch in Danbury, they returned home in sunshine. That evening Clare changed into a black dress, relieved only by white ruffles. After dinner Harry escorted her to campaign headquarters.[43]

Early returns from metropolitan voting machines had Leroy Downs ahead. But paper ballots in outlying areas of the county showed Clare gradually overtaking him. The "horsey" set were delivering as expected. Although she seemed outwardly calm, her eyes were glistening, and she confessed to "bursting inside." At 10:45 P.M. Brennan said she had the plurality. She let out a joyful shriek and hugged him. Downs sent a telegram at 11:00 P.M. conceding defeat, and near midnight the count was confirmed. Clare had 63,657 votes to the Congressman's 56,912. Her victory margin was a narrow 6,745, approximately 5 percent of the total vote of 134,855. Had a Socialist candidate not been on the ballot to cream off 14,286 votes—which would almost certainly have gone to Downs—Clare could not have won.[44]

Reporters clustered around for a victory statement. "The people of Fairfield County," she grandiloquently vowed, "may expect all that is possible to expect from one Congresswoman." With that she reached for a secretly written "defeat" speech, hidden in her left pocket throughout the evening, and gave it to Brennan as a souvenir. She rewarded Al Morano with a formal invitation to become her administrative aide in Washington.[45]

Then, taking Harry's arm, Congresswoman-elect Clare Boothe Luce climbed into a large car at the head of a motorcade and set off behind a triumphantly blaring sound truck along the Post Road to radio station WSSR in Stamford. Here she broadcast thanks to those of her constituents who were still awake, promising to go to Washington "to win the war first, and then to build a better world."[46]

Congresswoman Clare Boothe Luce with her Frida Kahlo painting
Photograph by Karsh

THE MOST ABLE WOMAN IN THE UNITED STATES

In her long letter to Ann, musing on the pros and cons of returning to the "white marble paths" of the Capitol that she had first trodden at age twenty, Clare had concluded that her real talent was for writing, not politics. Now she was not so sure. She might be forgiven for indulging once more the thoughts she shared with her daughter. "Would it amuse you to have your ma run for Congress and one day get to be a Cabinet minister, or maybe the first lady Vice-President?"[47]

Appendix

The Perfect Panhandler

by Clare Boothe Brokaw

[Undated news clip from "This World of Ours," no. 12, 1934]

The red light flashed; and my taxi stopped on the corner of Park Avenue and Fiftieth Street. A young man's face appeared in the window of the taxi. The face was thin, white, unshaven, but not a very sad face, because there was a pleasant enough smile upon it. Then a hand slipped over the top of the door, palm up, empty. It was a thin hand but not very dirty.

"Spare a fellow something for a cup of coffee?" this thin, unshaven man said to me, looking at me with gray, level eyes.

I do not like panhandlers. I mistrust them. The reason I mistrust them is that I read so many stories in papers how panhandlers are very well off, some even having bank accounts and cars and daughters in fine foreign convents, and most of them working their begging racket with the connivance of the police. "Go away, go away," I said to the young man, very crossly. His smile widened and I saw that he had even white teeth.

"Please, lady, I'm out of a job, and—"

Now all panhandlers say this. I am told that they are out of work because they find it more profitable to beg, that if you offered them jobs they wouldn't take them. Charitable organizations also warn you about this, sending you little books of tickets in the mail to give to panhandlers who accost you. They can exchange the tickets for work and soup if they are telling the truth about being jobless. "You probably wouldn't work if the chance were given to you," I said, and looked hard out of the other window of the taxi, wishing that the lights would change.

"Are you giving me the chance?" the young man said. "Have you a job waiting for me?"

That put it up to me, and I began to feel very silly and mean, so I began to fish in my purse for a quarter. After all, no matter how much he had, the chances were I still had more than he!

"What can you do?" I said, on the defensive.

"That's just it," the young man said. "I can't do anything. I am a college graduate. Oh, I was not very bright, but I got a B.A. degree. I know a good bit about biology, astronomy, English poetry, early American history and I know a prodigious lot of Greek and Latin. What kind of a job do you suggest I look for on the basis of that?"

"A librarian," I said, baffled.

"It should be obvious," the young man said simply, "that that was the job I lost."

"You could be a plumber, or a ditch digger, or a shipping clerk, or a waiter, if you were not too proud to use your muscles," I said, handing him the quarter.

"I could, but I am a consumptive," the young man said, pocketing the coin. "Thank you." He coughed politely.

"Why don't you go to a hospital?"

"Hospitalization?" the young man said sweetly. "At my age hospitalization? Oh, no!"

"But begging on the streets is so destructive to the ego. You lose your self-esteem," I said.

"Not if you look at it in the right way," the young man said. "Not if you look at it as art. It takes judgment, imagination and good feeling for human nature to be a successful panhandler. Why, you've got to know in a flash which people are naturally hard-hearted and will waste your time, which have guilty consciences about having money and will give if you persist, and which can be touched by the right kind of a story. You've got to know what kind of a story to tell them."

"Don't you always tell the same story?" I asked.

"Of course not," he said. "I told you I've made something of an art of this. Usually I tell the young ones I have just lost my job and have a young wife, and a two-month-old baby. I tell the old ones I have an aged mother and a dying father dependent on me. I tell mild old ladies that I am just out of Sing Sing but there's no place in society for a man who is trying to go straight. I tell gay-looking young ones my gay young wife left me when I lost my job. Sometimes when I spot a student I curse Capitalism for my troubles. And sometimes when men look rich and Republican I am the rugged individualist, done in by the Democrats and the brains trust."

"But the story you told me?—"

"Is the true one. That is a luxury I sometimes allow myself. But I seldom get anything, at best only a quarter for it! There are very few people who will sob about the tragedy of a good college education. My other stories are more human, and the way I tell them they are 50-cent and dollar stories." I gave him a dollar.

"Listen to me, young man," I said pulling out my gold pencil and a scrap of paper. "Write your name and address here. I will really try to get you a job."

He took the paper and pencil, hesitated, leaned up against the side of the taxi where I couldn't for a moment see him, and wrote hastily. The lights changed for the third time. The young man folded the paper, passed it to me, laughed in a mocking sort of way, and disappeared in the traffic. My taxi driver, listening all the while, shook his head, shrugged his shoulders in disapproval, and drove on.

APPENDIX

I unfolded the paper. The young man had written, in quite a nice hand, "Artful James. Panhandler by Circumstances and Preference— "*Et mihi res, non me rebus, subjungere conor . . .*"

This, I found out, meant, "And I endeavor to subdue circumstances to myself, and not myself to circumstances."

That is a gallant approach, I thought, and after all, why should panhandling, alone of the rackets, be below gallantry or art?

ACKNOWLEDGMENTS

Above all, I wish to thank the late Clare Boothe Luce for cooperating with me on this biography during the last six years of her life. From the age of fifteen, as if conscious of her destiny, she had kept letters, diaries, scrapbooks, and masses of other documents, all of which she courageously allowed me to see. She also submitted to countless hours of interviews and let me stay and work with her in her Washington apartments, her Honolulu house, and a rented mansion one summer in Newport. We spent time together in New York City, her birthplace, in Connecticut, her main residence for most of her life, and at Mepkin Abbey, the former Luce plantation in South Carolina, where she would be buried. We traveled to Canada and London for semicentennial productions of *The Women*, and to Rome to see the villa and embassy where she had lived and worked as United States Ambassador to Italy. The fruits of that last research, as well as details of our complex personal relationship, will appear in the second volume of this biography.

My next greatest debt is to Dr. Daniel J. Boorstin, the former Librarian of Congress, and his wife, Ruth. As friends of Mrs. Luce, they organized a dinner for the express purpose of overcoming her initial reluctance to authorize any biography. If it had not been for Dr. Boorstin's passionate eloquence on this occasion, she might never have

ACKNOWLEDGMENTS

said yes to me. Later, Dr. Boorstin persuaded her to add her vast private archive to the mainly public Clare Boothe Luce Papers already on deposit at the Library of Congress.

I am also indebted to Selwa ("Lucky") Roosevelt for initially arranging for me to meet my subject at a party in her Georgetown house. She then steered me towards potential interviewees and invited me to stay with her during early days of research, when I was not yet established in Washington. As a former journalist, and Chief of Protocol in the Reagan Administration, Ambassador Roosevelt understood the value of my seeing something of the capital's political, diplomatic, and social worlds while Mrs. Luce was still alive.

Henry Luce's elder son, Henry ("Hank") Luce III, granted me access to family papers, art and photographs, as well as many hours of thoughtful interviews. He and his wife, Leila—a fellow writer—have been immensely hospitable to me and a constant source of fresh information.

Hundreds of other people have helped over the years. Many will be acknowledged more appropriately at the conclusion of my next volume. Here I must particularly mention Wesley Bailey for sharing memories and photographs of Mrs. Luce's 1942 Congressional campaign; Vernon Blunt for letters, poetry, and taped recollections of his love for the young Clare; Ann Charnley for reminiscenses and access to some psychologically revealing paintings by CBL; Dr. Reginald F. Christian for alerting me to the correspondence of Alexis Aladin, and for selflessly sharing his own scholarly researches into that enigmatic character; Frances Brokaw Corrias for family genealogy, anecdotes, and photographs; Timothy Dickinson for a brilliant critique of my manuscript, enriched by his universal knowledge and his special understanding of CBL; Dr. Frederic H. Dippel for showing me around St. Mary's School in Garden City, L.I., and help in tracking down alumni; Margaret Emerson for painstakingly writing out her impressions of Dr. Austin; Dorothy Farmer, CBL's assistant for almost forty years, for stories and source leads; Joseph Kanon for reading a late draft of my manuscript; Dr. Michael Rosenbluth for sharing CBL's correspondence with his father, Dr. Milton Rosenbluth, and for guidance on medical matters; Fr. Wilfrid Thibodeau for giving me letters from CBL; Walton Wickett for his detailed written and verbal recollections of Ann Brokaw, as well as for letting me stay at his house while doing research

ACKNOWLEDGMENTS

in Stanford, California; and Althya Clark Youngman for her biographical essay and recollections of CBL's teenage years.

I have received other special favors from Margaret Bates, Buffy and William Cafritz, the Hon. William P. Clark, Richard and Shirley Clurman, Richard Cohen, Alfred Eisenstaedt, Dr. John Gable, Josef Gingold, Dr. Ivan Jacobson, Mr. and Mrs. Yousef Karsh, Commander Edward Koszack, the Hon. Theodore Kupferman, John Lawler, James and Marie Marlas, Anthony Mason, Norman Ross, Raymond E. Scheller, Irene Selznick, Dr. David Sibulkin, Anthony Summers, and W. A. Swanberg.

In the publishing world I owe thanks to my agent, Georges Borchardt, and my editor, Robert Loomis, for their patience and perspicacity, as well as to Robert Bernstein, Tina Brown, Graydon Carter, Harold Evans, Howard Kaminsky, Susan Mercandetti, and Nan A. Talese.

Among Library of Congress personnel I single out Nan Ernst above all for her exceptional diligence in sorting and cataloguing the 460,000-item Clare Boothe Luce Papers. Dr. David Wigdor and John Kominski smoothed out bureaucratic and legal difficulties for me, and John Haynes facilitated my access to stored materials, as did Stephen Ostrow in the Library's Prints & Photographs Division. Elsewhere the following archivists, curators, librarians and registrars also conscientiously aided me: Ann Alley and Florence Greenwood of the Tennessee State Library; Mary Angelotti, Collection of American Literature, Beinecke Library, Yale University; Brother Luke Armour, OCSO, Mepkin Abbey Archives; Eleanor Au, Special Collections, Hamilton Library, University of Hawaii; Dr. Robert L. Beare and Mary Boccaccio, McKeldin Library, University of Maryland; M. S. Brown, History Committee, Baptist Convention of Maryland and Delaware; Janet Carruthers, Department of Rare Books, Olin Library, Cornell University; Cynthia Cathcart, Lorraine Meade, and Charles Scheips, Condé Nast Archives; Ned Comstock, Department of Special Collections, Doheny Library, University of Southern California; Dr. Robert S. Conte, historian of the Greenbrier Hotel, White Sulphur Springs, West Virginia; Elaine Fleischer and Bill Hooper, Time-Life Archive, New York City; Eugene R. Gaddis, Austin House, Hartford, Connecticut; Cathy Henderson, Humanities Research Center, University of Texas; Lois E. Hughes, University of Cincinnati Library; John N. Jacob, George C. Marshall Foundation; Rachel D. Kelly, Sea Island Company, Georgia;

ACKNOWLEDGMENTS

David Lashmet, Manuscripts Library, University of Florida; Kenneth A. Lohf, Rare Books and Manuscripts Department, Butler Library, Columbia University; Linda McCurdy, Public Services Department, Duke University; Janice McNeill, Chicago Historical Society; Mildred Mather, Herbert Hoover Library; Vernon W. Newton, Franklin D. Roosevelt Library; Richard H. Richardson, Maryland State Archives; Susan Richardson, Historical Society of the Town of Greenwich; David E. Schoonover, Collection of American Literature, Beinecke Library, Yale University; John J. Slonaker, Historical Reference Branch, US Army Military History Institute; Jane C. Sween, Montgomery County Historical Society; Thomas W. Tamblyn, Second Baptist Church, Mount Holyoke, New York; John Verso, Oral History Research Office, Columbia University; Larry A. Viskochil, Chicago Historical Society; Dr. Albert W. Wardin, Belmont College, Nashville, Tennessee; Sabrina L. Weiss, Dickinson Music Library, Vassar College; and June E. Williamson, Purdue University, Indiana.

For research assistance I am especially indebted to Michael Teague for tracking down elusive documents and illustrations and other tasks too numerous to mention; also Marion Elizabeth Rodgers for a year of extraordinary industry, including Spanish translations, and an invaluable quotation derived from her own more recent work in the papers of H. L. Mencken. I thank five young interns: Karen (now Dr.) Chapel and Kathy McLane for careful transcripts of tape recordings, Sienna Craig and Amanda Deaver for library work, and Anthony Davidowitz for fact-checking and computer scanning. Harlyn S. Blum, Susan Hannah, Sharon Harris, Clare McMillan, Miles Richards, Kathy Smith, Steven D. Taylor, and Laurie Thompson assisted me in individual ways that I gratefully remember.

So many other people have contributed so variously to this biography that I can only list their names in alphabetical order, with thanks to all. They are: Louisa Ackerman, James L. Baughman, Laurence Bergreen, Michael Beschloss, Faubion Bowers, Benjamin Bradlee, Henry Brandon, Bobby Brown, J. Bryan III, Christopher Buckley, Dr. Hayes Caldwell, Fr. Christian Carr and the monks of Mepkin Abbey, Kathleen Carr, Frances Miller Cole, Gen. Theodore J. Conway, Sybil Cooper, Kate Ludlum Cort, Allerton Cushman, Loyal Davis, Osmonde De Kay, Arthur Dodge, James Dodge, David M. Doll, Katherine H. Doyle, Amanda and Philip Dunne, Amintore Fanfani, Ed Feulner,

ACKNOWLEDGMENTS

Anne Ford, William S. Forshaw, Arlene Francis, Pie Friendly, Clayton and Polly Fritchey, Rosalie Noland Gambrill, Jane Lank Garrison, Katharine Graham, Thomas Griffith, Otto von Habsburg, Pamela Harriman, Jones Harris, Kitty Carlisle Hart, Mrs. John Hill, Michael Z. Hobson, Gordon Hyatt, Ivan Ivanovich, Dottie Jensen, Walter Judd, Phyllis Kaminsky, Dorothy Reid Kittell, Marjorie Wolff Kittleman, Helen Simpson Kooi, Commander Edward Koszack, Nancy Lanham, Edith Peters Lank, Helen Lawrenson, John Leader, Mary Leader, Joseph K. Levene, Kenneth S. Lynn, Senator Giovanni Malagodi, Robert Manning, Mary McGrory, Barrett McGurn, Hank Meijer, Gerald Miller, Elisabeth Luce Moore, John J. Moore, Lillian Moore, Alma Morales, Eleanor Nangle, George Nash, Steve Neal, Nesta Obermer, Ambassador Egidio Ortona, Sen. Claiborne Pell, Ann and Spud Pierce, Curtis B. Prendergast, Ambassador and Mrs. Maxwell Rabb, Mabel Reid, Daphne Root, Oren Root, Diane Scharf, Stephen Shadegg, Philip Simpson, Sen. Alan Simpson, Sally Bedell Smith, Wells Stabler, Michael Stern, Mae Talley, Jeanne Thayer, Lucien Truscott III, R. Emmett Tyrrell, Eugene Woods, Helen Worth, Marjory Wright, Mrs. Paul Zarnowsky, and Arthur M. Zipser.

Finally I wish to thank my husband, Edmund Morris, for whipping me, figuratively speaking, whenever I got overwhelmed, discouraged, or just plain tired during the many years I have spent on this project.

ILLUSTRATIONS

Clare Boothe Brokaw. Pastel by Cecil Beaton, 1933.
   Henry Luce III Collection . . . . Frontispiece

Henry Luce and Clare Boothe on Broadway, 1935. UPI/Bettmann Newsphotos 2
The Women, original Broadway production. Library of Congress 9
William Boothe with Laura Brauss and his family, 1889. Author's collection 19
Anna Clara Schneider, c. 1900. Author's collection 22
Ann Clare Boothe, aged about four. Author's collection 27
Ann Snyder "Murphy," c. 1907. Author's collection 31
William Boothe, alias "Jord Murfé," c. 1909. Author's collection 32
Clare "Murphy" at Ward Seminary, Nashville, 1910–1911.
   Tennessee State Archives 35
Clare and her mother in Paris, c. February 1914. Author's collection 47
Clare in The Heart of a Waif, 1915. Museum of Modern Art Film Stills 51
Joel Jacobs, c. 1915. Author's collection 53
Clare and "Buff" Cobb at St. Mary's, c. 1916. Author's collection 57
The Castle, Tarrytown-on-Hudson, N.Y. Author's collection 59
David Boothe at the New York Military Academy, c. 1917. Author's collection 62
Ann Clare Boothe, c. 1918. Author's collection 63
Clare graduating, May 1919. Author's collection 66
"Driftway," Sound Beach, Connecticut. Author's collection 69
Dr. Austin and his operating team, c. 1919.
   Historical Society of the Town of Greenwich 76
Ann Snyder with her bulldog, c. 1919.
   Historical Society of the Town of Greenwich 78

ILLUSTRATIONS

Alexis Aladin in British Army uniform, c. 1921. Author's collection 87

Clare and her mother on the Riviera, 1921. Library of Congress 91

Vernon Blunt at Cambridge, c. 1921. Author's collection 97

Clare Boothe at about twenty, 1923. Author's collection 106

Captain Julian Simpson, c. 1923. Author's collection 108

Clare with George Brokaw, c. 1923. Author's collection 119

Clare at Seneca Falls with Alva Belmont and Alice Paul, 1923.
Library of Congress 121

Clare on her wedding day, August 10, 1923. Author's collection 124

The Brokaws returning from Europe, 1923. UPI/Bettmann Newsphotos 130

The Brokaw mansion. Frances Brokaw Corrias Collection 131

Clare Brokaw with her daughter, 1926. Author's collection 134

Clare and George at the Beaux Arts Ball, January 29, 1926. Author's collection . . 138

Clare Brokaw, c. 1926. Author's collection 142

William Franklin Boothe, c. 1928. Author's collection 151

Clare and Ann at Southampton, Long Island, July 1929.
UPI/Bettmann Newsphotos. 162

Donald Freeman, c. 1931. Author's collection 167

Clare in Hollywood. Photograph by Edward Steichen, 1931.
Courtesy Vogue/Condé Nast Archives. © 1931 Condé Nast Publications 187

Bernard Baruch. Photograph by Edward Steichen, 1932.
Courtesy Vogue/Condé Nast Archives. © 1932 Condé Nast Publications 193

Clare at the Democratic Convention. Library of Congress 197

William Harlan Hale, August 1932. Author's collection 201

Mark Sullivan, August 1932. Author's collection 204

Clare Boothe Brokaw, 1933. Library of Congress 213

Clare and Bernard Baruch at Hobcaw, 1933. Author's collection 224

Henry Luce. Photograph by Edward Steichen, 1935.
Courtesy Vogue/Condé Nast Archives. © 1935 Condé Nast Publications 243

Clare and Ann at Cap-Ferrat, 1935. Library of Congress 268

Mr. and Mrs. Henry Luce on honeymoon, Cuba, 1935–1936.
Author's collection 282

Clare and Harry. Photograph by Alfred Eisenstaedt, 1936.
Alfred Eisenstaedt, *Life* magazine © Time Inc. 286

"Claremont," Mepkin Plantation, late 1930s. Library of Congress 298

Ann Austin with her granddaughter, c. 1936. Author's collection 303

Clare in Hollywood with Shirley Temple, 1937. Library of Congress 305

Clare with surfing instructor, Waikiki, June 1937. Author's collection 307

Ann Clare Austin, 1882–1938. Author's collection 311

Clare shooting at Mepkin. Author's collection 316

Clare and Harry returning from Europe, June 1938.
UPI/Bettmann Newsphotos 322

The Suicide of Dorothy Hale. Oil painting by Frida Kahlo, 1939.
Phoenix Art Museum 332

Clare Boothe Luce. Sculpture by Isamu Noguchi, 1933.
The Henry Luce Foundation 338

Harry and Clare with Gertrude Stein, Bilignin, July 1939. Author's collection 345

ILLUSTRATIONS

Clare with Albert Einstein and Thomas Mann, October 14, 1939.
  George Karger, *Life* magazine © Time Inc. 355
Joan Crawford in the movie version of *The Women,* 1939.
  UPI/Bettmann Newsphotos 367
David and Nora Boothe, 1939. Author's collection 391
Clare campaigning for Wendell Willkie, c. October 1940. Author's collection 402
Clare visiting her brother at the Ryan School, April 1941. Author's collection 409
Clare and Harry with Madame Chiang, Chungking, May 1941.
  AP/World Wide Photos 415
Colonel Charles Willoughby, Manila, 1941. Author's collection 422
Clare with General MacArthur, Manila, 1941. Author's collection 429
Ann Clare Brokaw, 1941. Author's collection 435
Clare Boothe Luce. Photograph by Horst, 1941.
  Courtesy Vogue/Condé Nast Archives. © 1941 Condé Nast Publications 447
Clare with General Stilwell and the Chiangs, April 1942.
  George Rodger, *Life* magazine © Time Inc. 453
Clare in a Burma trench with Frank Roberts, April 1942.
  George Rodger, *Life* magazine © Time Inc. 454
Ann with her mother, fall 1942. UPI/Bettmann Newsphotos 467
Clare with her campaign team, November 1942. Author's collection 470
Congresswoman Clare Boothe Luce. Photograph by Karsh.
  © Yousuf Karsh/Woodfin Camp & Associates, Inc. 472

BIBLIOGRAPHY

PRIMARY SOURCES

Abbreviations in capitals will be used in the notes section.

Collections

AAP — Alexis Aladin Papers, University of St. Andrews, Scotland.

AEAP — Albert Elmer Austin Papers, Greenwich Historical Society, Greenwich, Conn.

AHP — Alden Hatch Papers, Rare Books and Manuscripts Division, University of Florida, Gainesville, Fla.

BCA — Belmont College Archives, Nashville, Tenn.

BRTC — Billy Rose Theater Collection, Library of the Performing Arts, New York Public Library, New York, N.Y.

CBLP — Clare Boothe Luce Papers, Library of Congress Manuscript Division, Washington, D.C. Before her death, CBL granted the author exclusive access to this enormous archive (c. 460,000 items, 312 linear feet). It is still partially closed to the general public. The collection features, as well as Boothe and Luce family papers and business and correspondence files, a literary file (65 boxes) containing the bulk of CBL's published and unpublished writings, mostly in manuscript or typescript form: articles, essays, reviews, commentaries, journals, notebooks, memoir fragments, proposals, novels and short stories, plays, screenplays, poetry, notes, and fragments. It also contains CBL's Congressional files, plus scrapbooks, clippings, motion picture films, and photographs.

Bibliography

CVVP   Carl Van Vechten Papers, Beinecke Rare Book and Manuscript Library, Yale University, New Haven, Conn.
DLP   Dan Longwell Papers, Butler Library, Columbia University, New York, N.Y.
DRP   David Russell Papers, John Rylands Library, Manchester University, England.
DTP   Dorothy Thompson Papers, George Arents Research Library, Syracuse University, Syracuse, N.Y.
ERP   Eleanor Roosevelt Papers, Franklin Delano Roosevelt Papers, Hyde Park, N.Y.
HHP   Herbert Hoover Papers, Herbert Hoover Presidential Library, West Branch, Iowa.
JAP   James Agee Papers, Beinecke Rare Book and Manuscript Library, Yale University, New Haven, Conn.
JBP   John Shaw Billings Papers, South Caroliniana Library, University of South Carolina, Columbia, S.C.
KAPP   Katherine Anne Porter Papers, University of Maryland, College Park, Md.
LZHP   Laura Z. Hobson Papers, Butler Library, Columbia University, New York, N.Y.
MGM   Metro-Goldwyn-Mayer Collection, Cinema-Television Library, University of Southern California, Los Angeles, Calif.
SJMP   Author's Papers, Washington, D.C.
TIA   Time Inc. Archives, New York, N.Y.
YCAL   Yale Collection of American Literature, Beinecke Rare Book and Manuscript Library, Yale University, New Haven, Conn.

Manuscripts, Diaries, Dissertations, and Scrapbooks

Austin, Ann Clare   Diaries, CBLP.
Billings, John Shaw   Diaries, JBP.
Brokaw, Ann Clare   Diaries, CBLP.
Burt, Sarah L.   "*L'Automne du Monde:* The Last Eight Years of *Vanity Fair.*" Ph.D. dissertation, University of Kansas, 1984.
Luce, Clare Boothe.   "The Double-Bind," five chapters of an autobiographical novel, c. 1962, CBLP. In this 100-page ts., written c. 1962, the author's youthful alter ego is named "Anne Cranston." CBL's own given-name initials as a girl were "A.C."
———. "Love Is a Verb," play ts. in CBLP.
———. "My School Days," picture album/diary, CBLP.
———. "This My Hand," fragment of an autobiographical novel, 1932, CBLP.
———. "This World of Ours," scrapbook of clips from CBL's syndicated column, 1934, SJMP.
———. Scrapbooks in CBLP, variously compiled and microfilmed.
———, [with Alexander King]. "The Yohimbe Tree," play ts. in CBLP.
Luce, Henry Robinson.   Publisher's memos to Time-Life editors, TIA.

Interviews

Clare Luce Abbey, Julian Bach, Letitia Baldrige, Alice Austin Basim, Betty Beale, Simon Michael Bessie, Vernon Blunt, Kay Brown, Ruth Buchanan, William F. Buck-

BIBLIOGRAPHY

ley, Jr., Jeanne Campbell, Dr. Patricia Carter, Dr. Reginald F. Christian, Shirley Clurman, Frances de Villers Brokaw Corrias, Fleur Cowles, Jean Dalrymple, Peter Finley Dunne, Elbridge Durbrow, Alfred Eisenstaedt, Olive Evans, Gladys Freeman, Laura Z. Hobson, Yousef Karsh, Cynthia Lasker, Malcolm Lovell, Clare Boothe Luce, Henry Luce III, Leila Luce, Nancy Bryan Luce, Elisabeth Luce Moore, John J. Moore, Lillian Moore, Albert P. Morano, Elizabeth Navarro, Ann Pierce, Eleanor Wood Prince, Alan Pryce-Jones, Whitelaw Reid, John Richardson, Jack Shea, Evelyn Stansky, Stan Swinton, Dr. Edward Teller, Jeanne Thayer, Marylois Purdy Vega, Rose Waldeck, Gen. Vernon Walters, Walton Wickett, Jeanne Ballot Winham.

PUBLISHED SOURCES

The following is a partial list of items used in researching this book. Other secondary sources are cited in full in the notes.

Books

[Works by CBL are listed by the name she used professionally at the time of publication.]

Boothe, Clare. *Europe in the Spring*. New York, 1940.
———. *Kiss the Boys Good-bye*. New York, 1939.
———. *Margin for Error*. New York, 1939.
———. *The Women*. New York, 1937.
Brokaw, Clare Boothe. *Stuffed Shirts*. New York, 1931.
Busch, Noel F. *Briton Hadden: A Biography of the Co-Founder of Time*. New York, 1949.
Chase, Edna Woolman, and Ilka Chase. *Always in Vogue*. New York, 1954.
Chase, Ilka. *Past Imperfect*. New York, 1942.
Coit, Margaret L. *Mr. Baruch*. Cambridge, Mass., 1957.
Elson, Robert T. *Time Inc: The Intimate History of a Publishing Enterprise, 1923–1941*. New York, 1968.
———. *The World of Time Inc: The Intimate History of a Publishing Enterprise, Vol. II: 1941–1960*. New York, 1973.
Fearnow, Mark. *Clare Boothe Luce: A Research and Production Sourcebook*. Westport, Conn., 1995.
Hart, Moss. *Act One*. New York, 1959.
Hatch, Alden. *Ambassador Extraordinary: Clare Boothe Luce*. New York, 1955.
Henle, Faye. *Au Clare de Luce: Portrait of a Luminous Lady*. New York, 1943.
Hobson, Laura Z. *Laura Z: A Life*. New York, 1983.
Hoopes, Roy. *Ralph Ingersoll*. New York, 1985.
Jessup, John. *The Ideas of Henry Luce*. New York, 1969.
King, Alexander. *Mine Enemy Grows Older*. New York, 1958.
Lawrenson, Helen. *Stranger at the Party: A Memoir*. New York, 1975.
Schwartz, Jordan A. *The Speculator: Bernard M. Baruch in Washington, 1917–1965*. Chapel Hill, N.C., 1981.
Seebohm, Caroline. *The Man Who Was Vogue: The Life and Times of Condé Nast*. New York, 1982.

Bibliography

Shadegg, Stephen. *Clare Boothe Luce*. New York, 1970.
Sheed, Wilfrid. *Clare Boothe Luce*. New York, 1982.
Swanberg, W. A. *Luce and His Empire*. New York, 1972.

Articles

Harriman, Margaret Case. "The Candor Kid," I and II. *The New Yorker,* Jan. 4 and 11, 1941.
Lawrenson, Helen. "The Woman." *Esquire*, Aug. 1974. [Reprinted in slightly different form as Ch. 7 of Lawrenson, *Stranger at the Party*, above.]
MacKaye, Milton. "Clare Boothe," *Scribner's Magazine*, Mar. 1939.

Miscellaneous

Luce, Clare Boothe. Interview on *The Dick Cavett Show*, January 20, 1981.

Notes

For consistency, the name of the subject of this book is abbreviated throughout the notes as CBL, even though at earlier stages of her life she carried the initials ACB, CB, and CBB. Other names cited frequently will be abbreviated as follows:

ACA   Ann Clare (Schneider/Snyder/Franklin/Murphy/Boothe) Austin
ACB   Ann Clare Brokaw
AEA   Albert Elmer Austin
BMB   Bernard Mannes Baruch
DFB   David Franklin Boothe
HRL   Henry Robinson Luce
WFB   William Franklin Boothe

Additional abbreviations are "int." (interviewed by), "qu." (quoting or quoted by), "ts." (typescript).

Prologue

1. *New York Sun, New York Evening Journal,* Dec. 28, 1936. Hart and Kaufman's few contributions to *The Women* are discussed in *New York Herald Tribune,* Oct. 25, 1936, and *New York Times,* Dec. 26, 1936. See also Ch. 23.
2. CBL int. SJM, Jan. 10, 1982; Wilfrid Sheed, *Clare Boothe Luce* (New York, 1982), 128.
3. Richard Watts, *New York Herald Tribune,* Nov. 24, 1935; CBL int. Richard Watts, *New York Herald Tribune,* Oct. 6, 1940; Margaret Case Harriman, "The Candor Kid II," *New Yorker,* Jan. 11, 1941.

4. *New York Evening Journal*, Dec. 28, 1936; CBL birth certificate, CBLP (see Ch. 1); U.S. Census, 1900.

5. "The truth is, my private life [has] been sad, unhappy, and sometimes tragic." CBL to SJM from Hawaii, Mar. 9, 1981; CBL at Daniel and Ruth Boorstin dinner, May 5, 1981.

6. CBL qu. Sheed, *CBL*, 128.

7. ACA to CBL, n.d. Apr. 1935, CBLP.

8. CBL qu. *New York Times Book Review*, Oct. 13, 1940.

9. "The Sacred Cow," ts. in CBLP. See Ch. 18.

10. See Ch. 23.

11. CBL at Tarrytown Conference Center, N.Y., *San Francisco Chronicle*, Oct. 21, 1971; CBL qu. *New York Times Book Review*, Oct. 13, 1940.

12. See Ch. 23.

13. CBL had warned an *Esquire* reporter, "There isn't a line in it about Communism." Doris Kinney to CBL, n.d. Mar. 1964, CBLP. But see n. 18.

14. *New York Daily News* listings, Dec. 28, 1936.

15. *New York Times*, Dec. 27, 1936.

16. *New York Daily News*, "Betty's Bath," Feb. 28, 1937; *New York Sun*, Jan. 28, 1938; *New York World-Telegram*, Sept. 30, 1939; *New York Sunday News* clip, n.d., Museum of the City of New York Theater Collection.

17. Brooks Atkinson in *New York Times*, Dec. 27, 1936.

18. All quotations from the director's working script of *The Women* (1936), BRTC. CBL revised the published text of her play several times to make it more topical. For example, wisecracks about "Commyanists" and "Townsendites" appear in the 1937 Random House edition, p. 198. This was dedicated to her school friend, Buff Cobb.

19. John Mason Brown wrote in the *New York Post*, December 27, 1936, "It is doubtful if a nastier group of women has ever been assembled on one stage. They may wrap themselves in sables, but, with one or two exceptions, they are skunks."

20. *Cleveland Press*, n.d., c. Dec. 1936, qu. Doris Kinney to CBL, Mar. 1964, CBLP.

21. Working script, *The Women*.

22. CBL int. SJM, Aug. 3, 1985.

23. Richard Lockridge, "Defense of Women," *New York Sun*, Jan. 2, 1937.

24. Ibid.; Mark Sullivan to CBL, Dec. 28, 1936, CBLP.

25. Ibid.

26. Moss Hart to Max Gordon, July 10, 1936, and to CBL, n.d. 1949, CBLP. Also see Ch. 23.

27. *New York Daily News*, Feb. 28, 1937. When fatuously asked by an English reporter why she had not written an all-male play, CBL replied, "Because I doubt that anybody would want to look at even Noel Coward in a bathtub." Qu. Lucius Beebe in *New York Herald Tribune*, c. Apr. 1937, CBL Scrapbooks, CBLP.

28. Mark Sullivan to CBL, Dec. 28, 1936.

29. CBL int. SJM, Jan. 10, 1982; Margalo Gillmore in *Playbill*, Dec. 1966.

30. *New York World-Telegram*, Dec. 28, 1936.

31. Ibid.

32. All datelines Dec. 28, 1936.

33. Qu. Louis Sobol in *New York Evening Journal*, Dec. 29, 1936.

Notes

1. Little Deceptions

1. WFB actually turned forty-one four days after the certificate was signed on April 6, 1903. CBLP.
2. CBL int. SJM, Jan. 8, 1982. CBL remained so sensitive on the subject of her birth date, not to mention her illegitimacy, that the author was never able to get a satisfactory reason for the subterfuge.
3. Boothe family Bible, CBLP.
4. Maryland Baptist Union Association, *Minutes of the Twenty-sixth and Twenty-seventh Meetings of the M.B.U.* (Baltimore, Md., 1861, 1862), *passim;* Edward Milton Boothe to CBL, n.d., c. Jan. 1931, CBLP.
5. Ibid.; John W. T. Boothe Diary, Apr. 10, 1862, CBLP.
6. E. M. Boothe, "Memorabilia of W.F.B.," ts., n.d. c. 1932, in CBLP; *Minutes of the Twenty-seventh Meeting of the M.B.U.,* 7.
7. E. M. Boothe to CBL, c. January 1931; "Memorabilia of W.F.B." Except where otherwise stated, the following information about WFB comes from one or other of these documents, written by his brother to CBL when she was gathering information about her ancestry.
8. *Purdue University Catalogue,* 1876–77, 5–6; June E. Williamson to SJM, Nov. 27, 1990, SJMP.
9. E. M. Boothe to CBL, c. Jan. 1931; Grace Quinn to CBL, Oct. 23, 1974, CBLP.
10. E. M. Boothe to CBL, c. Oct. 1930 and c. Jan. 1931, CBLP.
11. W. F. Boothe, *Two Concert Etudes, No. 1: Octaves, No. 2, Sixths,* Philadelphia: Wm. H. Boner & Co., 1881; copy in Music Division, Library of Congress, Washington, D.C.; E. M. Boothe, "Memorabilia of W.F.B."; E. M. Boothe to CBL, c. Oct. 1932, CBLP. WFB claimed to have written the octave étude during an orchestral concert, to win a bet that he could compose while listening to other music. Ruth Paddock, WFB pupil, to CBL, Jan. 15, 1929, CBLP.
12. E. M. Boothe, "Memorabilia of W.F.B."
13. Marriage certificate of WFB and Laura O. Brauss, State of New Jersey, Nov. 7, 1886 (the couple's subsequent divorce papers in the New York State Supreme Court, New York, N.Y., erroneously state that they were married in 1888); Philadelphia City Directory, 1889. William and Laura lived at 310 North Thirty-third Street.
14. Philip K. Eberly, "A Classic in American Culture," *Washington Post,* Nov. 22, 1990; advertisements in CBLP; Margaret Case Harriman, "The Candor Kid II," *New Yorker,* Jan. 11, 1941. E. M. Boothe denied the legend in a letter to CBL, Jan. 12, 1941, CBLP.
15. E. M. Boothe to CBL, Feb. 13, 1941, CBLP. According to Edward, Carreño's biographer Marta Melinowski wanted to use "correspondence between my brother Will and Carreño, 1890–1891," for a second edition of her book. "But I may kill it: I know he would want me to, I know." Efforts by the author to trace the Melinowski papers have proved unsuccessful. For a descriptive portrait of Carreño, see Harold Schonberg, *The Great Pianists* (New York, 1963), 328–332.
16. Eberly, "Classic."
17. Charles Boothe to CBL, May 9, 1949, CBLP.
18. Ibid. Not to be confused with the giant American Piano Company (Ampico), which flourished from 1907.

19. WFB to CBL, n.d. Oct. 1928, CBLP. Anna's father was the same age as WFB.

20. Ibid.; Michael and Ariane Batterberry, *On the Town in New York* (New York, 1973), 22.

21. Robert Ernst, *Immigrant Life in New York City, 1825–1863* (New York, 1949), 63–65, 77–78, 112–184.

22. New York City directory, 1882; ACA birth certificate, SJMP. Before escaping to New Jersey at the turn of the century, the Schneiders would live in at least five such places. Ibid. and Weehawken City directories, 1883–1913.

23. Charles of pulmonary tuberculosis, Louisa of pneumonia and pleurisy, and Arthur of traumatic meningitis. Schneider family death certificates, SJMP.

24. U.S. Census, 1900.

25. CBL, "The Double-Bind," 60, 66. See bibliography.

26. Ibid., 72. ˙

27. The following account is based on evidence in the divorce papers of William and Laura Boothe.

28. DFB birth certificate, copy in SJMP. WFB's name is given as "William Franklin," ACA's as "Anna C. Franklin," *née* "Anna C. Smith." WFB's birthplace is "Chicago," and ACA's "Savannah, Ga." Her age is listed as "18," although she was nearly twenty. See also Ch. 6.

29. New York City directory, 1903.

30. CBL address to Foothill Community College, Los Altos Hills, Calif., Oct. 12, 1984.

31. Boothe divorce papers.

32. Ibid.

33. Ibid. Laura went on to become a successful writer for the *New York Sunday World*.

34. H. G. Wells, *The Future in America: A Search After Realities* (New York, 1906, 1969), 41. Boothe divorce papers.

35. E. M. Boothe, "Memorabilia of W.F.B."

36. CBL, qu. *Bridgeport Post*, Nov. 21, 1950. "Her face had scratched against the sand, the green water had rushed into her mouth, and there was a great ringing of bells under the green waters." CBL, "This My Hand," CBLP. See bibliography.

37. Harriman, "Candor Kid II."

38. Private collection Ann Charnley, ACP.

39. CBL, "Without Portfolio," *McCall's*, June 1963.

40. CBL, "The Double-Bind," 78–81. A possible interpretation, of course, is that CBL may have been romanticizing the even worse trauma of being molested by WFB. Earlier in the same ms. (69–70) she wrote: "Her earliest memory of anything which a Freudian would call sexual was being in bed with her father . . . at the age of four . . . I remember I felt happy. Warm. Safe, I suppose." Elsewhere in the ts. (81–82), there is this passage: "When he [her father] took her to the toilet, he said, pointing to her little sex: 'Never, never let a man touch you there. Never, never touch yourself there, so long as you are a little girl. It is wicked, very wicked.'"

2. The Quest for Soothing Sheets

1. CBL int. SJM, Jan. 23, 1985.

2. CBL pamphlet, "Saving the White Man's Soul," 1949, CBLP; CBL int. SJM, Oct. 14, 1986; "Dreams and Nightmares," memoir file, CBLP.

Notes

3. CBL, "The Double-Bind," 61, CBLP.

4. Ibid., 91; CBL int. SJM, Feb. 12, 1985.

5. CBL to AEA, Jan. 20, 1942, CBLP.

6. Nashville city scrapbook, Tennessee State Archive, Nashville, Tenn. The house no longer stands, but 101 Church St., where CBL also lived, survives.

7. CBL int. SJM, Jan. 23, 1985; WFB advertising handbill in CBLP.

8. CBL int. SJM, Oct. 11, 1985, Jan. 9, 1982.

9. CBL int. SJM, Feb. 12, 1985. WFB to CBL, c. Oct. 1928, CBLP, says that Ann Snyder told his sister, Ida Keables, that she "hated the very sight of a fiddle . . . that you wouldn't listen to a Kreisler—that because of me musics [sic] world of pleasure was entirely taboo with you."

10. WFB to CBL, c. mid-Nov. 1928, CBLP; CBL int. SJM, Feb. 12, 1985.

11. CBL int. SJM, Feb. 12, 1985.

12. CBL int. Nashville Tennessean, Dec. 24, 1937, coincident with the local opening of The Women.

13. Ivar Lou Myhr Duncan, A History of Belmont College, Belmont College booklet (Nashville, Tenn., 1974), 3; Forty-sixth Annual Announcement of Ward Seminary, 1910–1911, SJMP.

14. Nashville Banner, Sept. 23, 1909; Nashville Tennessean, Sept. 24, 1909.

15. CBL school reports, BCA.

16. WFB to CBL, Nov. 7, 1928. CBLP.

17. CBL int. SJM, Feb. 12, 1985. Instant coffee became popular when U.S. soldiers acquired a taste for it during World War II.

18. CBL, "Saving the White Man's Soul."

19. CBL int. SJM, Feb. 12, 1985.

20. Upton Sinclair, The Jungle (Champaign, Ill., 1988), 25.

21. CBL int. SJM, Feb. 12, 1985; DFB to CBL, June 20, 1944, CBLP.

22. CBL int. SJM, Jan. 8, 1982.

23. CBL int. SJM, Jan. 8, 20, 1982. Mary Garden admits, in her memoirs, to an affair with a "rich" Chicago businessman at this time. The adjective would appear to disqualify WFB. Mary Garden's Story (New York, 1951), 194–208.

24. DFB was confirmed at Racine in 1912.

25. CBL int. SJM, June 14, 1982, Jan. 23, Feb. 12, 1985.

26. CBL int. SJM, Feb. 12, 1985.

27. CBL to Dr. Sidney Cohen, n.d. 1962, CBLP.

28. CBL int. SJM, Mar. 31, 1985; Look, Jan. 25, 1934; CBL to Donald Freeman, Aug. 20, 1930, CBLP.

29. CBL, "Double-Bind," 60–61.

30. Whether Ann thought him a certifiable alcoholic or not, her lawyers would later allege that he had "for fifteen years drunk a gallon of whiskey daily." WFB vehemently denied this improbable accusation, saying, "Any doctor or intelligent layman knows that such could not be true." WFB to CBL, c. Oct. 1928, CBLP.

31. CBL int. SJM, June 23, 1982.

32. WFB to CBL, Dec. 4, 1928, CBLP.

33. Ts. CBLP.

34. CBL int. SJM, June 23, 1984; "The Return" ms., CBLP.

35. CBL to Rev. W. Thibodeau, Feb. 16, 1949, SJMP.

36. CBL int. SJM, June 12, 1982, and Apr. 2, 1982.

NOTES

37. "You, you remain in my heart, / You, you remain in my mind, / You, you make me so sad, / You don't know how good I am to you!" Ibid.
38. Louise Dreher to CBL, Aug. 6, 1945, CBLP; CBL int. SJM, July 11, 1987.
39. CBL int. SJM, Apr. 2, 1982.
40. Richard Schickel, *D. W. Griffith: An American Life* (New York, 1984), 137.
41. CBL int. SJM, June 11, 1982; John Schneider death certificate, Apr. 14, 1913, SJMP.

3.   BIG PEARLS AND SMALL HIPS

1. CBL int. SJM, June 11, 1982; CBL, "The Double-Bind," 76; CBL int. SJM, Feb. 20, 1985.
2. CBL int. SJM, Jan. 8, 1982.
3. CBL int. SJM, June 20, 1985.
4. Perle Mesta to CBL, Dec. 20, 1953, CBLP; CBL, "Double-Bind," 100, CBLP.
5. Ibid.
6. CBL int. SJM, Feb. 20, 1985.
7. CBL, "Double-Bind," 87.
8. CBL, "Double-Bind," 76, CBLP. In old age CBL had nightmares of her mother falling down, her breasts exposed. "Memoirs" folder, CBLP. An enigmatic passage in Helen Lawrenson, "The Woman," *Esquire,* Aug. 1974, refers to a wealthy Manhattan party-giver named Yves de Villers, who met Ann Snyder in "circumstances . . . [that] must remain vague." Apparently at some later stage in their relationship, Ann "woke him in the middle of the night and asked him to marry Clare because she was worried about her." When Lawrenson asked the middle-aged CBL about de Villers, she "looked me straight in the eye and said calmly, 'Do you feel like going for a swim?' " The author, asking a similar question in the 1980s, received a similar response.
9. Marguerite Tyson qu. Helen Lawrenson to SJM, Mar. 3, 1982.
10. CBL int. SJM, June 12, 1982; CBL, "Double-Bind," 64, CBLP.
11. CBL int. SJM, Feb. 20, 1985, June 23, 1984; CBL, "Double-Bind," 64–65, CBLP.
12. CBL, "Double-Bind," 95, CBLP; CBL int. SJM, July 16, 1985.
13. CBL, "Double-Bind," 59, 84.
14. CBL int. SJM, Nov. 19, 1986.
15. CBL int. SJM, June 23, 1984.
16. CBL int. SJM, Feb. 20, 1985.
17. CBL, "Double-Bind," 87. CBL int. SJM, June 6, 1982.
18. CBL int. SJM, Jan. 8, 1982. In the spring of 1921 CBL wrote, "I have cultivated the chess habit, and am getting to be quite a shark." CBL to Alexis Aladin, c. May 16, 1921, AAP. Captain's letter and menu, CBLP.
19. CBL int. SJM, June 23, 1985.
20. CBL int. SJM, Jan. 8, 1982, CBLP. Ship's menu, CBLP.

4.   THE MOST CONCEITED GIRL IN THE SCHOOL

1. *New York Times,* Apr. 14, 1914.
2. Ibid.
3. CBL, "Without Portfolio," *McCall's,* Aug. 1960, June 1964.

4. CBL int. SJM, June 13, 1982.

5. CBL, "The Double-Bind," 64, CBLP. On p. 74 CBL's *alter ego* narrator writes: "She never remembers masturbating."

6. Margaret Case Harriman, "Candor Kid I," *The New Yorker*, Jan. 4, 1941.

7. Edith P. Lank to CBL, Dec. 12, 1979, CBLP, and to SJM, Apr. 21, 1985, SJMP.

8. Ibid.

9. CBL, "Double-Bind," 94.

10. CBL int. SJM, Mar. 31, 1985.

11. CBL, "Double-Bind," 88.

12. Ibid., 89.

13. Ibid., 90; CBL int. SJM, June 12, 1982.

14. CBL int. SJM, June 23, 1984.

15. CBL int. SJM, June 12, 1982.

16. CBL int. SJM, Jan. 8, 1982.

17. CBL to Alexis Aladin, Feb. 3, 1921, AAP; CBL int. SJM, Jan. 8, 1982.

18. CBLP.

19. CBL, "Double Bind," 96–99; CBL int. SJM, June 12, 1982.

20. Ibid.

21. CBL int. SJM, June 12, 1982.

22. Dorothy Reid Kittell to SJM, June 1984, SJMP.

23. Kate Ludlum Cort to SJM, June 28, 1984, SJMP; CBL, President's Foreign Intelligence Advisory Board Papers, CBLP.

24. Alden Hatch, *Ambassador Extraordinary: Clare Boothe Luce* (New York, 1955), 36.

25. Anita Lawson, *Irvin S. Cobb* (Bowling Green, Ohio, 1984), *passim*.

26. Hatch, *Ambassador*, 38.

27. CBL to Donald Freeman, Aug. 19, 1930, CBLP.

28. *Cathedral School of St. Mary Yearbook*, 1915–16, CBLP. CBL is quoting the English satirist John Wolcot, alias "Peter Pindar" (1738–1819), *"What rage for fame attends both great and small! /Better be d—n'd than not be nam'd at all!"* (From *The Works of Peter Pindar, Esqur.* [London, 1974], Vol. I, "Lyric Odes to the Royal Academicians for 1783," Ode IX, p. 76.)

5. Some Inner Compulsion

1. CBL, "Without Portfolio," *McCall's*, Oct. 1964.

2. Castle School prospectus, qu. *New York Times* obituary of Miss Mason, Aug. 25, 1933. CBL's annual tuition, paid by the ever-generous Joel Jacobs, was a steep $1,500. Dorothy Burns Holloran, CBL Castle School classmate, int. Alden Hatch, n.d. c. 1954, AHP.

3. CBL, "Lights on the Jersey Shore," *The Drawbridge 1919*, Castle School Yearbook, CBLP.

4. CBL address to Princeton senior class, May 6, 1958; CBL Commencement Address, Briarcliff, June 7, 1964, CBLP.

5. Ruth Balsam Morton memo, Oct. 1941, CBLP; Althya Clark Youngman to SJM, Oct. 11, 1984, SJMP.

6. CBL Castle School Reports, 1917–1919; CBL Diary, Jan. 17 and Aug. 23, 1919, CBLP. Clare's lowest mark in her first year was 80 for science and physics. See "College Memorabilia Book," CBLP.

7. CBL Diary, Dec. 17, Jan. 29, May 9, 1919.

8. Ibid., Feb. 2, 1919.

9. Dorothy Burns Holloran, qu. Alden Hatch, *Ambassador Extraordinary: Clare Boothe Luce* (New York, 1955), 42.

10. CBL Diary, Feb. 5, 1919.

11. Lorna Simpson Kooi to SJM, June 1, 1989, SJMP; CBL Diary, Apr. 8, 1919.

12. CBL Diary, Apr. 29, Feb. 14 and 6, 1919.

13. CBL Diary, Feb. 6, 1919.

14. CBL Diary, Mar. 4, 1919. Ambition sometimes ran counter to religious aspirations. After months of chapel attendance, Clare confessed in her diary that she could not "make Christ seem real." She wanted Him as her "companion" but was scared that if she submitted her soul completely, He might monopolize her time and prevent her being "a world success." Apr. 13, 1919.

15. CBL Castle School Scrapbook, CBLP.

16. Morton memo, Oct. 1941; CBL, "My School Days," 66–67, CBLP.

17. Ray Hoopes, *Ralph Ingersoll* (New York, 1985), 28.

18. CBL int. SJM, Apr. 16, 1982; CBL Diary, Sept. 11, 1919.

19. CBL int. SJM, Aug. 19, 1982.

20. CBL Diary, Feb. 19, Mar. 14, 1919, and *passim*.

21. Ibid., Mar. 11, 1919.

22. Ibid., Dec. 20, 1919.

23. Althya Clark Youngman essay, "In the Dazzle of Her Brilliance," SJMC; *Greenwich Times,* June 25, 1942; CBL scrapbook no. 123, CBLP.

24. CBL Diary, Nov. 7, 1918; Stanley Weintraub, *A Stillness Heard Round the World: The End of the Great War, November 1918* (New York, 1985), 29.

25. CBL, "My School Days," 61 [*sic*]. Alsace-Lorraine was actually annexed by Bismarck's Germany in 1871. One of CBL's lifelong intellectual quirks was to be cavalier about dates.

26. Mss. in CBLP.

27. Marjory Wolff to SJM, n.d. Dec. 1983, SJMP.

28. CBL, "My School Days," 130.

29. *The Drawbridge 1919,* CBLP.

30. Ellide D. Rea to CBL, May 8, 1970; CBL to Ruth B. Morton, Mar. 16, 1922, CBLP. A clergyman urged the Class of 1919 to "go to the heart of a few things" rather than "skim the surface of many." Miss Mason added that they must "cultivate sleepless energy" as they went through life. CBL was receptive to at least the latter advice. CBL, "My School Days," 130.

6. Damage to the Bone

1. CBL Diary, Mar. 2, 1919. The asking price for Driftway was $27,000, but DFB to CBL, n.d. c. 1935 says that Jacobs paid $22,000. ACA later took a $17,000 mortgage to make improvements, paying monthly interest only. CBLP.

2. CBL Diary, May 29, 1919.

3. Ibid., June 1919.

4. CBL int. SJM, Jan. 8, 1982.

5. CBL Diary, Feb. 6, Mar. 22, 1919.

6. CBL Diary, May 30, 1919.

7. Ibid.
8. *Los Angeles Times*, Feb. 7, 1926; *Musical Courier,* Jan. 3., 1929, obituary of WFB.
9. CBL Diary, May 31, 1919.
10. Ibid., June 1, 1919. The word *hate* is lightly crossed out.
11. Ibid., June 2, 1919.
12. Ibid., June 4, 1919.
13. Ibid.; WFB to CBL, c. Oct. 1928, CBLP.
14. WFB to CBL, c. Oct. 1928, CBLP. A persistent story, recounted in various biographies and articles, has CBL meeting WFB in a commuter train between Connecticut and New York. It lacks validation. Although the story seems to have originated with herself, CBL was always evasive when questioned about it by interviewers. See, e.g., *The Dick Cavett Show*, PBS, Jan. 20, 1981. Since her diary for 1919 details the most trivial occurrences yet mentions no such meeting, we can only conclude that the story is a romantic invention, typical of abandoned children in later life. For some of the legal complications arising out of WFB's return to his family, see Ch. 9.
15. CBL Diary, May 1919, *passim.*
16. Ibid., June 5, 1919; CBL to HRL, Feb. 29, 1960, CBLP.

7. An Indescribable Longing for Romance

1. *Stamford Advocate*, Jan. 27, 1942, obituary of AEA, CBLP.
2. CBL Diary, Apr. 20, 1919.
3. Ibid.
4. Information about AEA comes from the following sources: Margaret Emerson memo, "Dr. Austin," n.d., c. 1992, SJMP; John and Lillian Moore to SJM, n.d., May 1984, SJMP; Harry Mortimer oral history int., April 14, 1976, Old Greenwich Library, Greenwich, Conn.; AEA scrapbooks and photographs, AEAP; Albert P. Morano int. SJM, October 6, 1981; CBL int. SJM, January 8, 1982.
5. CBL Diary, June 12, Aug. 5, 1919, CBLP.
6. Ibid., June 13, 1919, CBLP.
7. Ibid.
8. CBL Diary, Jan. 4, 1919. On the other hand, ACA found the street-smart Joel Jacobs boring, with his constant talk of stocks and shares, compared to the dignified, well-read doctor. Ibid., Jan. 5, June 8, 1919. CBL wrote that Firestone Tire and Rubber Company's capital would amount to $1 million "in the next few years. Riggie will be a multimillionaire. Oh God! What will Mother do? If only she would make up her mind and carry it out." Ibid., Jan. 19, 1919.
9. Ibid., July 6, 8, 15, 19, June 12, July 6, 1919.
10. Ibid., July 9, 1919.
11. Ibid., July 13, 1919.
12. Ibid. See also Ann Clare Booth [sic], "The New Era: On Seeing Miss Mary Mason's Statue," frontispiece to *National Magazine*, May 1919. Also see "To Marshal Foch" and "Up Stamford Way," two poems of the same period published in the *Greenwich Times* and signed "D.I.A." (David Ivor Austin, first of CBL's several male *noms de plume*). News clips, n.d., CBLP.
13. CBL Diary, July 17 and Nov. 11, 1919.
14. CBL Diary, year-end summary, 1919.

15. Ibid.; CBL to Ruth B. Morton, n.d. 1919, CBLP.
16. CBL Diary, Sept. 2, 1919.
17. CBL int. SJM, Jan. 9, 1982.
18. CBL Diary, Nov. 15, 1919.
19. CBL int. SJM, Apr. 15, 1984.
20. CBL Diary, Nov. 17, 1919.
21. Ibid., Nov. 20 and 21, 1919.
22. Ibid., Nov. 25 and 23, 1919.
23. Ibid., Nov. 27 and 28, 1919.
24. Ibid., Dec. 3 and 4, 1919.
25. Ibid., Dec. 2 and 9, 1919.
26. Ibid., Dec. 13, 1919.
27. Ibid., Dec. 14 and 26, 1919.
28. Ibid., Dec. 31, 1919.

8. Boiling Water of the Hottest

1. Stephen Shadegg, *Clare Boothe Luce* (New York, 1970), 23.
2. CBL poetry, CBLP.
3. CBL address, Woodrow Wilson International Center for Scholars, Washington, D.C., Feb. 28, 1983. Author's notes, SJMP.
4. CBL Diary, Feb. 16, 1919, CBLP.
5. CBL to Mildred Price, c. Nov. 1920, CBLP.
6. Noel Coward, *Present Indicative* (New York, 1937), 110–111, 118. Coward said, "I played that poor apprentice with a stubborn Mayfair distinction, which threw the whole thing out of key." Lesley Cole, *Remembered Laughter* (New York, 1976), 47; CBL int. SJM, Apr. 29, 1986.
7. CBL to Florence Martin, c. Dec. 1920, CBLP. Clare told Florence that *Main Street* was, in her opinion, the best novel of the year. Indeed, it won the Pulitzer Prize for fiction.
8. CBL to Mildred Price, Feb. 17, 1921, CBLP. Aladin was a major, but Clare called him "Colonel." In Mayfair circles he allowed himself to be addressed as "General."
9. CBL int. SJM, Dec. 18, 1986; R. F. Christian, "Alexis Aladin, Trudovik Leader in the First Russian Duma, Part I, 1873–1920," *Oxford Slavonic Papers*, Vol. XXI (1988), 141; CBL, "Without Portfolio," *McCall's*, June 1960; see also *New York Times*, Mar. 6, 1907. Aladin's Russian name was Alexsey Fedorovich Alad'n.
10. CBL int. SJM, Feb. 5, 1982.
11. Alexis Aladin wire to Hugh Fisel, c. Nov. 1919, Public Record Office, London. "See Sir William and ask him to assure Lady Plymouth that personally I supervised the measures taken in the savety [sic] of our Dowager Empress." Sir William Tyrell thought Aladin "disreputable," according to a PRO document.
12. CBL, "Without Portfolio," *McCall's*, June 1960.
13. Christian, "Alexis Aladin," *passim*.
14. CBL to Mildred Price, Feb. 17, 1921; Alexis Aladin to CBL, May 16, 1921, AAP; Alexis Aladin to Sir David Russell, Feb. 18, April 9, 1921, DRP.
15. CBL to Alexis Aladin, Jan. 17, 1921, AAP.
16. CBL to Alexis Aladin, Jan. 22, 1921, AAP. She swore never to go to another

boxing match, but subsequently became an avid fight fan, attending the great Dempsey, Carpentier, and Tunney championship bouts, and becoming friends with Tunney.

17. CBL to Mildred Price, Feb. 17, 1921, CBLP.
18. Ibid.
19. Ibid.
20. Ibid. CBL wrote Aladin on Feb. 21, 1921, "All my beautiful frocks and hats are here . . . and such a *robe ravissante!* . . . cut low, but not too low . . . 'Show all you can, and what you can't—suggest!' " AAP.
21. SJM notes on visit to Negresco Hotel, Nice, May 1985; Jean Negulesco, *Things I Did . . . and Things I Think I Did* (New York, 1984), 64; CBL to Alexis Aladin, Feb. 25, 1921. "Gambling blood runs strong in my veins," she wrote Aladin on Feb. 21, "and has been carefully nurtured by circumstances since childhood." AAP.
22. CBL int. SJM, Jan. 8, 1982; CBL to Ruth B. Morton, Mar. 21, 1921.
23. Ibid.
24. Alexis Aladin to David Russell, Mar. 28, 1921, DRP. For Aladin's later career, see Christian, "Alexis Aladin."
25. CBL to Alexis Aladin, Apr. 29, 1921, AAP.
26. CBL to Mildred Price, c. May 1921, CBLP.
27. CBL to Dr. Thompkins, Mar. 17, 1961, CBLP. Sensing the girl's unrest, Joel Jacobs gave her a new Hudson roadster. CBL to Alexis Aladin, May 16, 1921, AAP.
28. CBL to "Middie Lamb," c. May 1921, CBLP.
29. CBL to Alexis Aladin, June 21, 1921, AAP.
30. CBL int. SJM, Jan. 8, 1982; Schuyler Van Ness to CBL, Jan. 9, 1941, CBLP. On June 21 CBL wrote to Alexis Aladin from New York, "I have my books, my work and my ambitions, but I'm a wee bit lonesome." The position she applied for was that of "traveling saleswoman," on the understanding that a preliminary period of training would be necessary. "They want me to open a branch office . . . in *Paris!!*" she wrote excitedly. AAP.
31. CBL int. SJM, Jan. 8, 1982, June 23, 1984.
32. CBL int. SJM, Jan. 8, 1982.
33. CBL int. SJM, Jan. 8, 1982; CBL to Alexis Aladin, July 19, 1921, AAP.
34. DFB to Isabel Hill, c. 1944, CBLP.
35. CBL Diary, c. Jan. 1926. Dr. Ivan Jacobson int. SJM, Aug. 13, 1992, stated that the abortion details seem to reflect firsthand experience.
36. Vernon Blunt memo, 1983, SJMP; CBL int. SJM, Feb. 18, 1985.
37. Vernon Blunt audiotape memo to SJM, 1983.
38. CBL to "Middie Lamb," c. May 1921, CBLP.
39. Vernon Blunt memo, 1983, SJMP.
40. Poem by Vernon Blunt, ms., n.d., SJMP.

9. Climbing High, High

1. CBL to Ruth B. Morton, Nov. 18, 1921, CBLP.
2. CBL to Kerry Skerrett, Jan. 3, 1922, CBLP; Margaret Case Harriman, "The Candor Kid I" *New Yorker*, Jan. 4, 1941.
3. CBL to Ruth B. Morton, c. Apr. 1922, CBLP.

4. CBL to Ruth B. Morton, Mar. 16, 1922, CBLP.
5. ACA-AEA marriage certificate, Marriage Records Bureau, Washington, D.C.
6. DFB to CBL, n.d. Apr. 1938, CBLP. Among the welter of half facts and nonfacts that complicate the issue of CBL's and DFB's parentage, the following stand clear: (1) Both children discovered in late May 1919 that WFB was alive. (2) Both children knowingly colluded in a lie to the contrary when ACA married AEA. By doing so they thought they were sparing her the embarrassment of telling her groom that she was not, after all, a widow. However, this played directly to her bluff, because she was thereby saved from having to produce divorce papers as an alternative ticket to matrimony. The irony was that ACA was perfectly free to marry anyone she chose, except this would disclose the illegitimacy of her children. (3) WFB went to his grave pretending, for their sake, that they were legitimate. (4) DFB remained convinced as late as April 1938 that his father and mother had been married at some point, or he would not have used the word *bigamous* in describing the Austin alliance. (5) Although proof is lacking, CBL seems to have shared this belief in her parents' marriage until late in her life. In an undated letter to HRL in 1960 she said that she was "probably illegitimate." CBLP.
7. CBL Diary, Feb. 2, 1923, CBLP.
8. CBL int. SJM, Feb. 20, 1985.
9. CBL Scrapbook, 1923, CBLP.
10. Ibid. Fermoy's daughter, Frances, married Earl Spencer, father of Princess Diana. They were divorced in 1969.
11. CBL Diary, 1923, back page.
12. Ibid., Jan. 3, 1923.
13. CBL to Florence Martin, Jan. 14, 1923, CBLP.
14. CBL Diary, Feb. 17, 25, 1923.
15. Ibid., Mar. 14, 12, 1, 1923.
16. Ibid., Jan. 24, 25, Feb. 19, Mar. 5, 1923.
17. Ibid., Jan. 23, 1923; CBL int. SJM, Feb. 12, 1985.
18. CBL to Kerry Skerrett, Jan. 22, 1923, CBLP.
19. CBL Diary, Mar. 7, 1923.
20. Ibid., Mar. 9, 10, 13, 14, 1923.
21. Ibid., Mar. 16, 1923.
22. Ibid., Mar. 23, 25, 1923.
23. Ibid., Mar. 28, 29, 1923.
24. CBL int. SJM, Jan. 23, 1982; Vernon Blunt audiotape memo, 1983, SJMP.
25. Vernon Blunt to SJM, June 11, 1983, SJMP.
26. CBL Diary, Apr. 6, 1923.
27. "The Hound of Heaven" was CBL's "favorite poem in the English language." CBL to Eugene J. Woods, May 7, 1945, CBLP; CBL int. SJM, Feb. 12, 1985.
28. Unidentified news clip, n.d., AEA Scrapbook, AEAP.

10. A PATH OF WHITE MARBLE

1. Gottfried Reinhardt, *The Genius: A Memoir of Max Reinhardt* (New York, 1979), 17; Josephine Baker in "Chasing the Rainbow," PBS TV documentary, Jan. 17, 1990.
2. Elsa Maxwell, *RSVP: Elsa Maxwell's Own Story* (Boston, 1954), 106.

3. Frederick Platt, "I Am the Woman of the Future," *L'Officiel/USA*, Fall 1977; CBL int. SJM, Jan. 20, 1982; CBL, "Without Portfolio," *McCall's*, Apr. 1961.
4. *L'Officiel/USA*, Fall 1977.
5. Phyllis Forbes to CBL, Apr. 29, 1976, CBL to Amelia Fry, Nov. 1, 1979, CBLP; CBL int. SJM, Jan. 21, 1982.
6. CBL address, "Friend or Foe of Women?" Fort Lauderdale, Fla., Nov. 11, 1981, CBLP.
7. CBL int. SJM, Jan. 20, 1982.
8. CBL to Kerry Skerrett, Apr. 28, 1923, CBLP.
9. The Sewall-Belmont House, at Constitution Ave. and Second St., NE, is now a museum of the National Woman's Party.
10. Inez Haynes Irwin, *The Story of Alice Paul and the National Woman's Party* (Fairfax, Va., 1964), 11.
11. CBL to Fry, Nov. 1, 1979; Irwin, *Alice Paul*, 239.
12. CBL Diary, May 11, 1923, CBLP.
13. Ibid.

11. Earthly Desires

1. Stephen Shadegg, *Clare Boothe Luce* (New York, 1970), 38; CBL int. SJM, Feb. 12, 1985. According to George Brokaw's daughter Frances de Villers Brokaw Corrias, the family fortune derived from government contracts for military uniforms, awarded during the Civil War. The proceeds were invested in real estate. Int. SJM, May 7, 1996.
2. CBL, "This My Hand," 24, CBLP; CBL int. SJM, Dec. 10, 1981.
3. Unidentified news clip, n.d., CBLP.
4. George Brokaw to CBL, June 6, 1923, CBLP.
5. His maternal grandfather, Sir Julian Salomons, had briefly been Chief Justice of New South Wales. *Who Is* [sic] *Who in Australasia; Australian Dictionary of Biography*, Vol. 6, 1851–1890.
6. *London Gazette*, Jan. 11, 1919, 643; Clare McMillan to SJM, July 18, 1990, SJMP.
7. Julian Simpson to CBL, July 22, 1930, CBLP; CBL int. SJM, June 28, 1982.
8. Julian Simpson to CBL, July 22, 1930, CBLP.
9. Julian Simpson to ACA, June 9, 1923, CBLP.
10. Julian Simpson to CBL, July 22, 1930; CBL int. SJM, June 28, 1982, Dec. 8, 1981, May 3, 1982.
11. CBL to Julian Simpson, June 18, 1923, CBLP.
12. Simpson's mother, Lilian Thompson, to ACA, June 21, 1923, CBLP.
13. CBL, "This My Hand," 7.
14. CBLP.
15. CBL int. SJM, Apr. 29, 1986.
16. George Brokaw to CBL, July 20, 1923, CBLP.
17. *New York Times*, July 22, 1923.
18. George Brokaw to CBL, n.d. July 1923, CBLP.
19. Lilian Thompson to CBL, July 29, 1923, CBLP.
20. Ms., n.d. summer 1923, CBLP.
21. CBL to Mrs. Jones, July 30, 1923, CBLP; CBL int. SJM, June 14, 1982, June 23, 1985; CBL to ACA, Apr. 3, 1929, CBLP.

22. CBL, "This My Hand," 53.
23. Marjorie Wolff Kittleman to SJM, June 1983, SJMP.
24. *New York Times* and *Greenwich News*, Aug. 11 and 13, 1923.
25. *Greenwich News*, Aug. 13, 1923.
26. CBL, "This My Hand," 57, 69, 73.
27. CBLP.
28. Howard Brokaw to ACA, Aug. 8, 1923, CBLP.
29. CBL int. SJM, Feb. 12, 1985, June 23, 1987.
30. CBL to ACA, Aug. 10, 1923, CBLP.

1 2 . Unnourishing Nettles

1. CBL int. SJM, Feb. 12, 1985; CBL, qu. Shirley Clurman int. SJM, Feb. 10, 1988; CBL int. SJM, Apr. 11, 1982.
2. CBL, "This My Hand," 74–79, CBLP.
3. CBL to ACA, Aug. 13, 17, 22, 1923, CBLP.
4. CBL to ACA, Aug. 22, 1923.
5. CBL to ACA, Aug. 26, 29, 1923, CBLP. Biarritz Sept.–Oct. 1923 calendar, CBLP.
6. CBL to ACA, Aug. 29, 1923.
7. Julian Simpson to CBL, Sept. 13, 1923, CBLP.
8. CBL to ACA, Sept. 10, 1923, CBLP.
9. Ibid.; George Brokaw to ACA, Sept. 5, 1923, CBLP.
10. Ibid.; Joel Jacobs to CBL, Aug. 24, 1923, CBLP.
11. Joseph Madigan to DFB, Oct. 30, 1923, CBLP.
12. CBL int. SJM, June 20, 1982.
13. CBL to Donald Freeman, Aug. 21, 1930, CBLP; Charles Frederick Rose, *Era of Elegance* (New York, 1947), 92–103; David Selznick, "The Wreck of the Brokaw Mansions," *New York Herald Tribune*, Apr. 11, 1965.
14. CBL to Freeman, Aug. 21, 1930, CBLP.
15. CBL int. SJM, Dec. 10, 1981, and Apr. 26, 1982.
16. Clurman int. SJM, Feb. 10, 1988; CBL int. SJM, Dec. 15, 1981, Apr. 26, 1982.
17. CBL int. SJM, July 16, 1985; George Brokaw to CBL, c. Feb. 1924, CBLP.
18. CBL scrapbooks, CBLP; CBL int. SJM, Sept. 26, 1984.
19. CBL Diary, Feb. 27, 1925, CBLP.
20. Julian Simpson to CBL, May 9, 1930, CBLP.
21. CBL Diary summary, Jan. 1926, CBLP. When Miss Mackay later married Irving Berlin, Clare mocked him as a Jewish "King of Jazz and son of the gutter." She also gloated over the Catholic Clarence MacKay disinheriting his daughter.
22. Malcolm Lovell, qu. his parents (friends of the Brokaws), int. SJM, May 18, 1988. Customers in speakeasies were urged to talk softly so as not to attract police—hence the name.
23. CBL int. SJM, Jan. 21, 1982.
24. *New York Post*, Apr. 9, 1925.
25. CBL Diary, Feb. 8, 1925.
26. Ibid., Feb. 8, Apr. 10, 1925.
27. Ibid.
28. ACA Diary fragment, 1925, CBLP.

29. George Brokaw petition, *New York Times*, Dec. 6, 1925.
30. *New York Sun*, Dec. 4, 1925, reported that CBL's "merits . . . on the amateur stage have been demonstrated." CBL Diary, Jan. 5, 1926.
31. CBL Diary, Jan. 17, 1926.
32. Ibid.
33. Ibid., Jan. 24, 1926.
34. Ibid., Jan. 25, 1926.
35. Ibid., Jan. 29, 1926.
36. Ibid., Jan. 31, 1926.
37. Ibid., Feb. 15, 1926.

13. The Loveliest Matron

1. *Town Topics*, Mar. 11, 1926.
2. Baptism announcement, unidentified newsclip, CBLP.
3. Ernest H. Rice to CBL, June 8, 1976, CBLP.
4. *New York American*, June 19, 1926.
5. CBL scrapbooks, CBLP; Bea Grover to Alden Hatch, Oct. 29, 1954, AHP; Sands Point house sold for $300,000, *New York Herald Tribune*, Dec. 30, 1926.
6. CBL scrapbooks, CBLP; *Town Topics*, Dec., Nov. 1926.
7. CBL to ACA, n.d. 1927, CBLP.
8. Ibid.
9. Nesta Obermer to SJM, Apr. 25, 1984, SJMP.
10. Ts. CBLP.
11. "Fiona Macleod" (William Sharp), "The Lordly Ones," reprinted in Ethel Fowler, *The Second Daffodil Poetry Book* (London, 1931), 29.
12. Nesta Obermer to CBL, Dec. 6, c. Mar. 1929, CBLP; Nesta Obermer to SJM, Apr. 25, 1984, SJMP.
13. *Town Topics*, Sept. 1927; CBL Scrapbooks, CBLP.
14. CBL, *Stuffed Shirts* (New York, 1931), 268.
15. CBL to Vernon Blunt, Oct. 14, 1927, CBLP.
16. *Town Topics*, Nov. 1927, CBL scrapbook, CBLP.
17. CBL int. SJM, July 11, 1987.
18. New York Appellate Court ruling, *New York Times*, Feb. 5, 1927.
19. CBL int. SJM, June 13, 1982: "He managed to rob poor old Riggie of about $15,000 . . . He borrowed some stocks and bonds without mentioning it and put them up as collateral and he bought out margins when the depression hit."
20. CBL int. SJM, Jan. 8, 1982.
21. DFB to CBL, Mar. 28, Apr. 29, 1928, CBLP.
22. DFB to CBL, Apr. 28, 1928, CBLP.
23. Vernon Blunt int. SJM, June 10, 1985; Vernon Blunt to SJM, Aug. 26, 1985, SJMP. Blunt was on the verge of bankruptcy at this time, and seems to have come to Paris hoping that CBL would lend him money. It is evident from her letter inviting him that she really wanted to hear the latest news about Julian Simpson. CBL to Vernon Blunt, Sept. 12, 1927, CBLP.
24. CBL to ACA, June 26, 1928, CBLP.
25. Ibid. CBL was unsure of her taste. "If only me little goil friend were here," she wrote. "I should have so much more confidence in what I bought."

26. CBL to ACA, July 19, 22, 27, 1928, CBLP. Long letters from Jean, a young New York investor with whom CBL had become mildly enamored a year or two back, were all that kept her buoyant. "His only crime, the poor lamb, is being poor," she wrote Ann Austin on July 27, 1928.
27. CBL int. SJM, Apr. 26, 1982; CBL to ACA, c. August 7, 1928, CBLP.
28. CBL to ACA, Oct. 28, 1929; DFB to CBL, Mar. 26, 1929, CBLP.
29. George Brokaw to CBL, Nov. 1928, CBLP.
30. Ibid. CBL int. SJM, Dec 10, 1981.
31. ACA to CBL, c. Oct. 1927, CBLP.
32. Letter and enclosed news clip, WFB to CBL, c. Oct. 1928, CBLP.
33. WFB qu. CBL to CBL, c. Nov. 1928, CBLP.
34. WFB to CBL, Nov. 7, 1928, CBLP.
35. WFB qu. CBL to CBL, c. Nov. 1928, CBLP.
36. WFB to CBL, c. Nov. 1928, CBLP. WFB said he carried miniatures of both children in his watch fob, and had kept scrapbooks about Clare's life as a Brokaw.
37. Ibid., Dec. 4, 1928, CBLP.
38. WFB death certificate, State of California, copy in SJMP.
39. Anniversary Boothe to CBL, Jan. 23, 1929; Ruth Paddock to CBL, Jan. 15, 1929, CBLP.
40. Ruth Paddock to CBL, Dec. 19, 1928, Jan. 15, 1929, CBLP; W. Franklyn Boothe [sic], "Fingered Octaves and Primary Extension Exercises," edited by Ruth Paddock, unpublished ms., Music Division, Library of Congress; Josef Gingold to SJM, Mar 13, 1991, SJMP. "As to Mr. Boothe's playing fingered tenths, I have my doubts, because had he done it, he would not have lived to a ripe old age, nor during his lifetime had any tendons in working order."
41. John Boothe to CBL, Apr. 2, 1937, CBLP.
42. Copy in CBLP.
43. CBL to ACA, Feb. 7, 1929. "They put new locks on the front door because they know you have a key."

14. CUPID'S GRAVEYARD

1. CBL legal memo, June 1931, CBLP; Dorothy Burns Holloran int. Alden Hatch, n.d., AHP.
2. CBL to ACA, Feb. 7, 1929, CBLP. Some incidental details for this chapter come from CBL, "Reno," an unfinished autobiographical ts. in CBLP.
3. CBL to ACA, Feb. 7, 1929.
4. CBL to ACA, Feb. 13, 1929, CBLP.
5. Ibid.
6. State laws required potential divorcées to stay in Reno for ninety consecutive days. But a local airline had a discreet arrangement with the District Judge that women who wanted to take short breaks in Las Vegas, Los Angeles, or San Francisco would not have time counted against them. Roscoe Turner to CBL, Apr. 23, 1957, CBLP.
7. CBL to ACA, Feb. 7 and c. 20, 1929, CBLP.
8. "Julian Jerome" (CBL pseudonym), "Where Bonds Are Broken," Vanity Fair, Jan. 1931; CBL, "This World of Ours," 31, SJMP.
9. A Miss Minerva Sherman. CBL to ACA, c. Mar. 7, 1929, CBLP.

10. CBL to ACA, Feb. 7, 1929. On Feb. 13 CBL wrote ACA vowing not to accept a proposal from Jean "unless he has the right to ask." That "right" meant success in his profession. CBLP.
11. CBL to ACA, n.d. "Wednesday, 3," 1929, from Reno, CBLP.
12. ACA to CBL, Mar. 29, 1929, CBLP.
13. ACA to CBL, n.d., c. Mar. 1929, CBLP.
14. CBL to ACA, "Wednesday, 3," 1929; ACA to CBL, Feb. 17, 1929; CBL to ACA, c. Mar. 7, 1929, CBLP.
15. ACA to CBL, Mar. 23, 1929, CBLP.
16. ACA to CBL, Mar. 11, 1929, CBLP.
17. ACA to CBL, Mar. 18, 1929, DFB to Margaret Beamish, Apr. 7, 1929, ACA to CBL c. Apr 7, 1929, CBLP.
18. ACA to CBL, c. Mar. 1929, CBLP.
19. DFB to CBL, Mar. 26, 1929, Feb. 26, Apr. 23, 1929, CBLP.
20. CBL to ACA, Feb. 7, 1929, CBLP.
21. Findings and Decree of Divorce, May 20, 1929, CBLP.
22. CBL to ACA, "Wednesday, 3," 1929, CBLP.
23. CBL, "The Real Reason," *McCall's*, Feb., Mar., Apr., 1947; CBL qu. *Liberty*, June 14, 1941.

15. A Bibelot of the Most Enchanting Order

1. CBL int. SJM, June 11, 1982.
2. CBL int. Margaret Altschul, n.d. 1938, CBL scrapbooks, CBLP.
3. David resented her absence and fired off a letter complaining that she had left household bills in arrears, even though their mother had given her a large sum of cash to pay them. He sarcastically hoped that she would at any rate "go to plenty of parties" and have many proposals of marriage. DFB to CBL, n.d. summer 1929, CBLP.
4. Sumner Gerard to CBL, Aug. 28, 1929, CBLP.
5. CBL qu. Edna Woolman Chase and Ilka Chase, *Always in Vogue* (New York, 1954), 230; CBL int. Altschul.
6. Jeanne B. Winham to CBL, Jan. 29, 1959, CBLP; Chase, *Always*, 231; CBL, "Chic for the Newly Arrived," *Vogue*, February 1, 1930.
7. CBL int. W. W. Lundell, May 17, 1933, NBC transcript in CBLP.
8. Chase, *Always*, 231.
9. CBL int. SJM, Sept. 26, 1984.
10. CBL int. SJM, Sept. 26, 1984, July 18, 1985; Chase, *Always*, 226–228; Irene Selznick int. SJM, Feb. 8, 1988; Jean Dalrymple int. SJM, Feb. 5, 1988.
11. *Time*, Mar. 3, 1930.
12. Sarah L. Burt, "L'Automne du Monde: The Last Eight Years of *Vanity Fair*," Ph.D. diss., Univ. of Kansas, 1984; Jeanne B. Winham, "Very Innocent Bystander," *Vanity Fair*, Dec. 1983; Edmund Wilson, *The Twenties: From Notebooks and Diaries of the Period*, ed. Leon Edel (New York, 1975), 39.
13. Frank Crowninshield, "In the Cubs' Den III," *Vogue*, Mar. 15, 1945.
14. CBL int. *Christian Science Monitor*, Dec. 9, 1980.
15. Donald Freeman to CBL, Oct. 30, 1929, CBLP; Gladys Freeman int. SJM, Nov. 10, 1982; Jeanne B. Winham to CBL, Jan. 29, 1959, CBLP.

16. Dr. Mehemed Agha, *Vanity Fair's* art director, said many years later that Mrs. Chase was happy to let CBL go because she lacked fashion sense. "From the *Vogue* viewpoint, she was an unbeliever. The same thing happened to Dorothy Parker." Int. Hubert Kay, Oct. 7, 1958, CBLP.

17. Condé Nast, Inc., felt the chill of changing times acutely. Its stock plummeted from $93.00 a share to $4.50 when banks drew on company holdings to cover a personal loan Nast had taken to invest in Goldman, Sachs. In the long term, this was a catastrophe from which *Vanity Fair* would not recover. For details of Nast's finances, see Caroline Seebohm, *The Man Who Was Vogue* (New York, 1982), 305–317.

18. Margaret Case Harriman, *Blessed Are the Debonair* (New York, 1956), 158; Donald Freeman to CBL, Mar. 10, Feb. 25, 1930, CBLP. He would pay her $120, the equivalent of about $1,200 today, for editing a short piece in French and writing an article on divorce.

19. CBL int. SJM, June 24, 1982.

20. Donald Freeman to CBL, c. Aug. 21, 1930, CBLP.

21. CBL qu. Helen Lawrenson, *Whistling Girl* (New York, 1978), 62; Grand Duke Alexander to CBL, Feb. 15, 1930, CBLP.

22. Donald Freeman to CBL, July 24, 1930, CBLP. About this time, CBL became involved in a mysterious adventure possibly involving illicit drugs, abduction, and medical malpractice. The known facts are too sketchy to be completely reconstructed, but they may be cited here. It appears that in 1930 she struck up a friendship with the notorious George Gordon Moore, a wealthy, Indian-looking Midwesterner who haunted prizefights and society parties on both sides of the Atlantic. (Some fifteen years before, in London, Moore had been an unlikely escort-about-town to Lady Diana Manners, the future Diana Cooper, who was both fascinated and repelled by him, and may possibly have acquired her wartime morphine habit in his company.) It is not certain when CBL began to suspect, or indeed know, that Moore was a drug dealer, but in old age she would hint that she had nearly become one of his customers.

    She said (CBL int. SJM, June 13, 1982) that they were attending a prizefight together when she suddenly developed such a sharp abdominal pain, "I thought I was going to die." The next thing she knew, she had been injected with a sedative and transferred to a private clinic at 591 Park Avenue. It was run by Dr. Edward Cowles, a specialist in nervous disorders and drug addiction who was much patronized by show business people. CBL was vaguely puzzled by the clinic's lack of admission formalities but soon fell into a deep sleep.

    On waking some hours later, she found herself in a fourth-floor room overlooking a garden. The agonizing stabs had gone, and she assumed she had passed a kidney stone. A nurse came in with needle poised, but CBL, growing suspicious, sent her away. Then a woman wearing a kimono sauntered in and remarked that the film star Jeanne Eagels, a frequently hospitalized heroin and morphine abuser, occupied the room below and was "in a bad way."

    Scared, CBL looked around for her clothes. Two "doctors" arrived, forestalling her escape, prodded her, and diagnosed an "inflamed ovary." They prescribed another shot. CBL insisted on calling her stepfather. When Dr. Austin heard where she was, he reportedly said, "Oh my God, I'll be right over."

    Eagels died some time later in the clinic, after going into drug-induced convulsions. That, and a mysterious suicide there, prompted New York State authorities to begin an investigation into Dr. Cowles's practice. He was suspected, but never indicted, of prescribing excessive narcotics for routine ailments. As for George Moore, he continued to be seen around talented and attractive young people.

CBL's story is lent partial credence by a letter from Donald Freeman to her, Aug. 21, 1930, CBLP: "Dr. Cowles is in pretty deep . . . Dr. Evan Evans and his other consultants will have to go before the grand jury to explain the connection . . . If I were you . . . I would not mention your visit there as, along with his other patients, you will be suspected of being a dope, as all the tabloids openly accuse him of catering to wealthy addicts." For the Moore/Cooper relationship, see Diana Cooper, *The Rainbow Comes and Goes* (Boston, 1958), 91, 141–142, *Trumpets from the Steep* (Boston, 1960), 17, and Philip Ziegler, *Diana Cooper* (London, 1981), 55, 62–63.

23. Aldous Huxley, "Progress—How the Achievements of Civilization Will Eventually Bankrupt the Entire World," *Vanity Fair*, Jan. 1928.
24. CBL qu. "Only Human," syndicated column by "Candide," n.d. CBL scrapbooks, CBLP.
25. Seebohm, *The Man*, 320. Harriman, *Debonair*, 158, says it was her idea to feature Macfadden. "That picture cost me exactly fifty thousand dollars," Nast complained. Ibid.
26. *Vanity Fair*, Oct. 1930, Feb. 1931, Sept. 1931, June 1932.
27. CBL int. Lundell.
28. Qu. Crowninshield, "In the Cubs' Den III." Gallico cited "We Nominate for Oblivion" as "perhaps the most venomous and courageous feature ever published by a magazine." Ibid. *Vanity Fair* office memo, Oct. 11, 1933, CBLP; Mehemed Agha int. Hubert Kay, Oct. 7, 1958, CBLP; *Vanity Fair* editorial meeting minutes, June 18, 1934, CBLP.
29. Donald Freeman to CBL, Aug. 25, 1930, CBLP.
30. CBL to Donald Freeman, Aug. 27, 1930, CBLP.
31. Milton MacKaye, "Clare Boothe," *Scribner's Magazine*, Mar. 1939.
32. In 1945 Paul Gallico said of *Vanity Fair* that "it paid off in the lowest fees and the highest prestige of any periodical ever published." Qu. Crowninshield, "In the Cubs' Den III."
33. CBL, *Stuffed Shirts* (New York, 1931), *passim*, and 111, 120.
34. Ibid., 75–83. In one version of *The Women* Clare has Mary Haines return from Reno and become an interior decorator.
35. CBL to Donald Freeman, Aug. 27, 28, 1930, CBLP; Julian Jerome, "The Perfect Backgammoner," *Vanity Fair*, Nov. 1930, and "The Official Laws of Backgammon," ibid., Dec. 1930.
36. Harriman, *Debonair*, 158–159.
37. Ibid., 159.

16. CHANGING TIMES

1. CBL to Donald Freeman, Aug. 19, 1930, CBLP.
2. Ibid.
3. CBL to Donald Freeman, Aug. 28, 1930, CBLP. A month earlier CBL had written Julian Simpson, asking if he would be glad to see her again. He replied that he certainly would. Again, neither of them made a move. Julian Simpson to CBL, July 22, 1930, CBLP.

4. CBL to Donald Freeman, Aug. 21, 1930, CBLP.
5. CBL to Donald Freeman, Aug. 22, 1930, CBLP.
6. Donald Freeman to CBL, Aug. 25, 1930, CBLP.
7. Ibid.
8. Donald Freeman to CBL, Aug. 28, 1930, CBLP.
9. CBL to Freeman, Aug. 29, 1930, CBLP.
10. CBL to Donald Freeman, Oct. 29, 1930, CBLP.
11. CBL, "The Hanging Gardens of Gotham," in "This World of Ours," 32, SJMP.
12. Helen Lawrenson, "The Woman," Esquire, Aug. 1974; CBL int. "Modern Women Need Masters," Seattle Sunday Times, Jan. 24, 1932; Althya Clark Youngman to SJM, Oct. 11, 1984, SJMP.
13. CBL Diary, January 2, 1931, CBLP. Agha's first impression of CBL, recalled years later, bore out her suspicions. "Nice shoes and a mink coat." But of her abilities as an editor he grudgingly admitted, "She displayed amazing brilliance in a woman, a real gift for Swiftian phrases and ideas." Mehemed Agha int. Hubert Kay, Oct. 7, 1958, CBLP.
14. Donald Freeman to CBL, Aug. 28, 1930, CBLP; CBL, "This World of Ours," 25; Lawrenson, "Woman."
15. Jeanne B. Winham, "Bystander," Vanity Fair, Dec. 1983.
16. Margaret Case Harriman, "The Candor Kid II," New Yorker, Jan. 11, 1941; AEA to CBL, Dec. 13, 1932, CBLP.
17. Donald Freeman to CBL, Sept. 13, 1932. For Nast's finances, see Caroline Seebohm, The Man Who Was Vogue (New York, 1982), 305–317.
18. CBL Diary, Jan. 3, 1931.
19. Helen Lawrenson, "A Farewell to Yesterday, When You Couldn't Care Less," Esquire, July 1961.
20. Jay Franklin, "The Next War," Vanity Fair, Nov. 1930; Corey Ford qu. Vanity Fair, May 1930.
21. Vanity Fair, Oct. 1930.
22. Margaret Case Harriman, Blessed Are the Debonair (New York, 1956). Mrs. Harriman, in 1930, was the Margaret Case Morgan referred to in the text (her father was Frank Case, owner of the Algonquin Hotel). She left Vanity Fair for The New Yorker in 1931, and later wrote the two-part profile of CBL cited in the Bibliography. For examples of the kind of serious political articles Harriman objected to, see two pieces by Maurice Hindus, "Red Bread" (Stalin's oppression of the kulaks) and "Red Love" (emancipation of women in the USSR), Vanity Fair, Apr., Oct. 1931. By August 1933 an internal Vanity Fair memo pointed out that the first seven issues that year had 59 articles and pictures on politics and economics. In June alone there were 6 such articles prominently placed, while fiction and humor had been relegated way back.
23. Reproduced in Cleveland Amory and Frederic Bradley, Cavalcade of the 1920s and 1930s: Selections from America's Most Memorable Magazine: "Vanity Fair" (London, 1960), 190. CBL was also a frequent contributor to Vanity Fair's popular feature "Impossible Interview," featuring imaginary confrontations between, for example, John D. Rockefeller and Josef Stalin, or Calvin Coolidge and Greta Garbo.
24. CBL Diary, Jan. 2, 1931. The form of interrelated short stories had actually been pioneered by Sherwood Anderson in Winesburg, Ohio (1919).

25. CBL Diary, Jan. 2, 1931.
26. Gus Hall qu. John Chamberlain, *A Life with the Printed Word* (Chicago, 1982), 52. According to Hall, there were ten "state-of-mind" Communists for every CPUSA card carrier in the 1930s.
27. CBL Diary, Jan. 5, 1931.
28. CBL Diary, Jan. 10, 1931.
29. CBL to Donald Freeman, Aug. 10, 1931, June 24, 1932, CBLP; CBL Diary, Jan. 2 and 3, 1931; Donald Freeman to CBL, n.d. c. summer 1930, CBLP.
30. CBL to Donald Freeman, n.d., c. summer 1931, CBLP.
31. Donald Freeman to CBL, n.d., c. summer 1931, CBLP.
32. CBL to Donald Freeman, n.d., c. summer 1931, CBLP.
33. Donald Freeman to CBL, n.d., c. summer 1931, CBLP.
34. CBL to Donald Freeman, Aug., 10, 1931, CBLP.
35. Donald Freeman to CBL, Aug., 10, 1931, CBLP.
36. Ibid.
37. Edward Steichen, *Steichen* (New York, 1963), Ch. 8, "The Theater"; CBL to Donald Freeman, Aug. 11, 1931, CBLP.
38. Ibid.
39. CBL to Donald Freeman, Aug. 10, 1931.
40. CBL to Arthur Krock, July 7, 1931, CBLP; CBL to Tom Smith of H. Liveright, Inc., July 16, 1931, CBLP.
41. *Books,* Mar. 20, 1932.
42. *New York Mirror,* n.d. c. Nov. 1931, news clip in CBLP; Milton MacKaye, "Clare Boothe," *Scribner's Magazine,* Mar. 1939; *Galveston Tribune,* Nov. 21, 1931.
43. *Vanity Fair,* Nov. 1931.
44. Donald Freeman to CBL, Aug. 13, 1931; P. G. Wodehouse to CBL, Feb. 8, 1932. CBLP.
45. CBL to Merritt Hulburd, Dec. 1, 1931, CBLP; CBL Diary, Oct. 21, 1932, SJMP. According to the novelist Dawn Powell, CBL enlisted a young publicist, Selma Robinson, to promote her book. Miss Robinson was flattered to be lunched and treated as an equal by the dazzling Mrs. Brokaw, and was particularly beguiled by what seemed to be CBL's healthy contempt for social snobbery. CBL suggested they go together to a party for "that old bitch" Grand Duchess Marie of Romania, then flabbergasted the young woman by curtsying to the guest of honor along with everybody else. *The Diaries of Dawn Powell, 1931–1965,* ed. Tim Page (South Royalton, Vt., 1995), 175.
46. CBL to Donald Freeman, June 24, 1932, CBLP; CBL Diary, June 23, 1932, SJMP. Forty-six years later *Stuffed Shirts* was reprinted, but it brought CBL only about another $100. CBL to Nesta Obermer, Aug. 10, 1977, CBLP.
47. CBL to Donald Freeman, June 24, 1932, CBLP.
48. Donald Freeman to CBL, n.d. "Tuesday," 1931, CBLP.
49. Montage in CBLP.

1 7. BARNEY BARUCH'S GIRL

1. CBL to Donald Freeman, June 24, 1932, CBLP; CBL Diary, June 24, 1932, SJMP; CBL, "For Release On Receipt," ts., June 25, 1948, CBLP.

Notes

2. John Billings Diary, May 13, 1933, JBP; CBL Diary, June 17, 1932, SJMP. CBL had met BMB earlier in the year when they were dinner-table companions at Condé Nast's apartment. He had invited her to lunch the next day and gallantly driven her home afterwards. CBL int. SJM, June 11, 1985. She first mentions him in her diary on May 25, 1932, SJMP.
3. CBL Diary, June 23, 1932.
4. Ibid., June 25, 1932.
5. Ibid., July 15, 1932.
6. BMB to CBL, Aug. 29, 1935, CBLP, recalling his first impression of her.
7. Frank Crowninshield, "In the Cubs' Den III," *Vogue*, Mar. 15, 1945.
8. CBL Diary, June 25, 1932.
9. *Vanity Fair*, Apr. 1932.
10. Margaret Case Harriman, *Blessed Are the Debonair* (New York, 1956), 163–64.
11. CBL to Donald Freeman, June 24, 1932, CBLP; CBL, "Without Portfolio," *McCall's*, July 1964.
12. NNP Prospectus, CBLP.
13. *Vanity Fair*, June 1932.
14. Jordan A. Schwartz, *The Speculator: Bernard M. Baruch in Washington, 1917–1965* (Chapel Hill, N.C., 1981), 267; Michael Barone, *Our Country: The Shaping of America from Roosevelt to Reagan* (New York, 1990), 54.
15. Schwartz, *Speculator*, 267.
16. John F. Carter to CBL, June 30, 1932, CBLP.
17. *Chicago Tribune*, June 27, 1932.
18. CBL Diary, June 25–29, 1932; CBL to Mark Sullivan, July 6, 1932, CBLP.
19. Ibid., July 1, 1932 [sic]. Arthur M. Schlesinger, Jr., and Fred I. Israel, *History of American Presidential Elections, 1789–1968* (New York, 1971), III, 2723, puts the start-ballot time at 4:28 A.M.
20. CBL Diary, July 1, 1932; Samuel Eliot Morison, *The Oxford History of the American People* (New York, 1965), 948.
21. CBL Diary, July 1 and 19, 1932.
22. Ibid., July 2, 1932.
23. Ibid., July 3, 4, 26, 1932.
24. CBL to Donald Freeman, July 4, 1932, CBLP.
25. Mark Sullivan qu. CBL Diary, July 5, 1932.
26. Ibid., July 12, 1932. The first successful test of RCA's new Empire State Building television mast had occurred on May 17, 1932. *New York Times*, May 18, 1932.
27. CBL Diary, July 13, 1932; Schwartz, *Speculator*, 172; CBL to BMB, c. July 27, 1932, CBLP; CBL Diary, June 17 and July 26, 1932.
28. CBL Diary, July 12, 1932; Julian Simpson to CBL, Sept. 29, 1930, CBLP; CBL Diary, July 29, 1932.
29. CBL to BMB, Aug. 2, 1932, CBLP; CBL Diary, July 30, Aug. 8, 1932; CBL to BMB, late July and Aug. 6, 1932, CBLP.
30. CBL Diary, July 31, 1932.
31. Ibid., July 30–31, 1932; CBL to Mark Sullivan, Aug. 1, 1932, CBLP.
32. CBL int. SJM, June 13, 1982.
33. William Harlan Hale to Katherine Anne Porter, May 25, 1932, KAPP; Porter to Hale, Sept. 13, 1932, KAPP.
34. CBL Diary, Aug. 2, 1932; CBL int. SJM, June 13, 1982.

35. William Harlan Hale to CBL, July 3, 1962, CBLP, recalled the hair-dyeing incident. William Harlan Hale to Hubert Kay, Oct. 23, 1958, CBLP.
36. CBL Diary, Aug. 5, 1932.
37. CBL Diary, Aug. 6–9, 1932.
38. Ibid.
39. Leslie F. Nast to CBL, n.d. 1931, CBLP. CBL, int. SJM, Dec. 10, 1981, recalled that around this time, at a Long Island house party, Leslie Nast came into her bedroom and made direct sexual overtures. At first CBL submitted (whether out of desire or curiosity, she did not say), but she soon found out that their intimacies were rendered painful by Leslie's "very long nails." She was reminded, she said, "of Wedekind's play about the man who discovered his wife's lesbianism and took her viscera to the lover."
40. CBL Diary, July 26, 1832.37. Ms. in CBLP. The A. D. Peters literary agency rejected "This My Hand" for serialization, saying that it was "in its very essence subjective, a little inclined to morbidity." Carol Hill to Thayer Hobson, Aug. 19, 1932, CBLP.
41. Ms. in CBLP.
42. CBL Diary, Aug. 14, 1932.
43. Mark Sullivan to CBL, c. May 1933, CBLP; CBL Diary, August 18, 1932, SJMP. Despite CBL's protestations, some sexual intimacy does seem to have existed between them. Eight months later Sullivan would write: "If you say again that I 'have a unique place in your cosmos,' I'll do one of two things . . . either beat you up, or reduce you to physical exhaustion the other way." Mark Sullivan to CBL, c. Apr. 1933, CBLP.
44. In SJMP.
45. CBL to BMB, c. July 27, 1932.
46. CBL Diary, July 28, 1932; CBL to BMB, Aug. 2, 1932, CBLP.
47. CBL Diary, July 22, 1932; BMB to CBL, passim, CBLP.
48. CBL Diary, Aug. 24, 25, 27, 1932.
49. CBL to Donald Freeman, July 4, 1932, CBLP; Freeman to CBL, Aug. 11, 1932, CBLP.
50. Donald Freeman to CBL, Aug. 29, 30, 1932, CBLP.
51. CBL Diary, Sept. 2, 1932.
52. CBL to BMB, Aug. 6, 1932, CBLP.
53. CBL Diary, Sept. 10 and Oct. 9, 1932.
54. Ibid., Sept. 8, 1932.
55. Helen Lawrenson, "The Woman," Esquire, August 1974; CBL Diary, Sept. 14, 1932, SJMP. According to Lawrenson, BMB used to bring back from Europe antique gold snuffboxes for his women friends. CBL had first choice. "She wants them all," he said. "Poor little kid, it's hard to refuse her anything." She ended up with about two dozen.
56. CBL to Mark Sullivan, Sept. 17, 1932, CBLP; CBL Diary, Sept. 20, 23, Oct. 10, Sept. 22, 1932.
57. Lawrenson, "Woman"; CBL Diary, Sept. 21, 1932. Two months before, Nast had told CBL that he and Leslie were divorcing and that he wanted to marry her. "But that doesn't interest me, my dear!" she wrote. Ibid., July 25, 1932.
58. Donald Freeman to CBL, n.d., c. Sept. 24, 1932, CBLP.
59. CBL Diary, Oct. 1, 1932.

60. Ibid. CBL to Paul [Gallico?], n.d. Nov. 1933, CBLP.

61. CBL Diary, Oct. 1, 1932.

62. CBL Diary, Oct. 16 and 2, 1932. A legal memorandum, "Re: Estate Donald Freeman deceased," Dec. 30, 1933, reveals that Freeman was in an extreme financial crisis at the time of his death, with $9,833 in debts and only $599 in assets. Copy in CBLP. He had borrowed $500 from CBL only a few days before his death. CBL Diary, Sept. 26, 1932.

63. CBLP.

64. CBL Diary, Oct. 22, 1932, qu. George Jean Nathan.

65. CBL Diary, Oct. 3, 1932.

66. CBL Diary, Oct. 4, 1932.

18. A WELL-CONSTRUCTED FAÇADE

1. CBL Diary, Oct. 4 and 5, 1932, SJMP.

2. Ibid., Oct. 7. For a time, between Nast's marriages, the two men had shared an apartment.

3. Ibid.

4. Helen Lawrenson, "The Woman," *Esquire,* Aug. 1974; CBL Diary, Oct. 8, 1932.

5. Ibid., Sept. 26 and 28, Nov. 18, 1932.

6. Frank Crowninshield, "In the Cubs' Den III," *Vogue,* Mar. 15, 1945; Mehemed Agha to Hubert Kay, Oct. 7, 1958, CBLP. Crowninshield also wrote that in "fifty troubled years of editing, I have never encountered a Managing Editor so able, so daring, or so resourceful."

7. Hugo Vickers, *Cecil Beaton: The Authorized Biography* (London, 1985), 206; CBL to literary agent Carol Hill, July 11, 1932, CBLP.

8. CBL to Drew Pearson, Feb. 6, 1933, CBLP.

9. CBL int. W. W. Lundell, May 17, 1933, NBC transcript in CBLP.

10. *New York World-Telegram,* Feb. 6, 1933.

11. Henry Morton Robinson to Hubert Kay, Nov. 1, 1958, CBLP.

12. Helen Lawrenson, "Woman"; Lawrenson to SJM, Mar. 10, 1982, SJMP.

13. Lawrenson, "Woman."

14. Ibid.; CBL Diary, Nov. 30, 1932, records Genthe's comment.

15. Ibid., Oct. 26, 1932.

16. Ibid., Oct. 28, 1932.

17. Ibid., Oct. 29, 1932.

18. Ibid., Oct. 30, 1932.

19. Ibid.; CBL to Mark Sullivan, Nov. 6, 1932, CBLP.

20. CBL Diary, Oct. 31, 1932.

21. Crowninshield, "Cubs' Den III."

22. CBL Diary, Oct. 16, Nov. 28, Oct. 23, 1932.

23. CBL to Mark Sullivan, Aug. 23, 1932, CBLP; Diary, Nov. 8, 1932.

24. Ibid., Dec. 2, Nov. 1, 1932. In old age CBL complained, "Bernie spent more time in bed with the gout than with me." CBL int. SJM, June 13, 1982.

25. CBL Diary, Oct. 14, 1932.

26. CBL Diary, *passim;* CBL to Kitty Miller, Dec. 15, 1932, CBLP; John Golden to CBL, Nov. 6, 1933; Leland Hayward Agency to CBL, relinquishing play, having

submitted it to 33 producers, Mar. 3, 1934, CBLP; CBL Diary, Dec. 17, 1932, qu. Rudolf Kommer ("too farcical").

27. CBL Diary, Dec. 13, 1932.
28. *Greenwich News*, c. Mar. 16, 1932, AEAP; CBL to Donald Freeman, Aug. 27, 1932; AEA to CBL, n.d. c. 1932, CBLP.
29. ACA to CBL, "Friday a.m." 1932, CBLP.
30. CBL Diary, Dec. 7, 1932.
31. Ibid., Dec. 4, 1932.
32. Ibid., Dec. 21, 1932.
33. Ibid., Dec. 25, 1932.
34. Ibid., Dec. 26, 1932.
35. Ibid., Dec. 28, 30, 1932.
36. Ibid., Dec. 31, 1932.

19. Failure Is Impossible

1. *New York Times*, Feb. 12, 1933. Alva Belmont is buried in St. Hubert's Chapel, Woodlawn Cemetery.
2. Mark Sullivan to CBL, n.d. c. Jan. 1933, CBLP.
3. Margaret L. Coit, *Mr. Baruch* (Cambridge, Mass., 1957), 316.
4. SJM notes from 1984 visit, SJMP; CBL to Paul Gallico, Feb. 31 [*sic*], 1933, CBLP.
5. Coit, *Mr. Baruch*, 317; Laura Z. Hobson, *Laura Z: A Life* (New York, 1983), 150.
6. CBL to Sullivan and Paul Gallico, both letters dated Feb. 31 [*sic*], 1933, CBLP.
7. CBL to Sullivan, Feb. 31 [*sic*], 1933, CBLP.
8. *Vanity Fair*, Mar. 1933; Lawrenson, "Woman." In 1941 *The New Yorker* reported that CBL baited wildfowl blinds in South Carolina, and a friend, Daniel Longwell, wrote a letter to the editor in her defense. "She doesn't have to bait game to hold her own. I have seen her knock down her limit of doves neatly, and . . . have applauded a half-dozen of her shots that brought high, fast-flying ducks down dead . . . She [once] shot her limit of ten ducks within an hour, using only thirty-odd shells." Gratefully replying, CBL admitted to Longwell that she had just shot two turkeys almost simultaneously, with alternate barrels. "I had indeed broken the law . . . but I pulled that second barrel automatically." Longwell to *New Yorker*, Jan. 15, 1941, CBL to Longwell, Feb. 7, 1941, DLP.
9. CBL to Sullivan, Feb. 31 [*sic*], 1933; CBL to Joseph Robinson, Apr. 14, 1933, CBLP.
10. CBL to Sullivan, Feb. 31 [*sic*], 1933.
11. Ibid.
12. CBL, "The President's Widow," n.d. 1934, "This World of Ours," 40.
13. CBL Diary, Dec. 21, 1932, SJMP; Pare Lorentz to CBL, Apr. 27, 1934, CBLP.
14. CBL qu. Paul Gallico to CBL, n.d. 1933, CBLP.
15. Ibid.
16. Paul Gallico to CBL, Aug. 27, 1933, CBLP.
17. *Vanity Fair*, Mar. 1933. *Vogue*'s first color cover was almost a year earlier, in Apr. 1932. Garetto's cover of Adolf Hitler as a swastika in November 1932 had also caused a stir.
18. Letter qu. *Vanity Fair*, May 1933; Condé Nast to CBL, Feb. 19, 1933, CBLP.

19. Advertising revenue in May 1933 was $210,213. Sarah L. Burt, "L'Automne du Monde: The Last Eight Years of *Vanity Fair*," Ph.D. diss., Univ. of Kansas, 1984, 154; Nast to CBL, Mar. 27, 1933, CBLP.

20. Nast to CBL, Mar. 27, 1933. CBL's last article (Dec. 1932) had been on Al Smith. Her next would be in June 1933.

21. Nast to CBL, Mar. 27, 1933. Nast's criticisms notwithstanding, John Franklin Carter said a quarter of a century later that CBL was "the best magazine editor to deal with I've ever known." Int. Hubert Kay, Oct. 1958, CBLP.

22. CBL to Condé Nast, Mar. 27, 1933, CBLP.

23. Condé Nast to CBL, May 22, 1933, CBLP. Mark Sullivan told CBL that Nast's picking at her was the result of "his being in love with you—whether he knows it or not, You have a strong conquering streak in you, and you are determined to run *V.F.* even if your way of running it is contrary to the owner's way. It's merely a case of you instinctively following the law of your nature." To CBL, c. Apr. 1933, CBLP.

24. CBL rented *Time* employee John Martin's house, "Fox Hollow," in Brookville for $501 a month. She seems to have been unaccountably short of cash, because she deducted $54 from her last payment for "*objets domestiques*," telling Martin not to cash her check before October 17. To sweeten the pill, she sent him a watercolor of his house. CBL to John Martin, Oct. 16, 1933, CBLP.

25. CBL to "Paul," Nov. 7, 1933; to Frank Altschul, Nov. 9, 1933; to William Wiseman, Nov. 12, 1933, CBLP. It would appear that politics figured, if only briefly, in CBL's plans for her future that fall. BMB's friend Gen. Hugh Johnson had been appointed head of the National Recovery Administration to revitalize industry. Through his influence, in Oct. 1933, CBL was given seats on the Legitimate Theater and Motion Picture Code Authorities. Her mandate was to persuade industry executives to adopt and then abide by codes of business practice consistent with New Deal policies. Her initial enthusiasm for the assignment waned when she realized that the NRA had more in common with the right-wing socialism of Mussolini's Italy than its purported model, the World War I War Industries Board. She decided that government control of free markets and free expression could only be done "with bayonets," and resigned her position after eight months or so. In 1934 she began a play about government interference in labor relations called "O, Pyramids!" She was still tinkering with it in 1937, but the play was never produced. CBL int. SJM, Jan. 8, 1982; Stephen Shadegg, *Clare Boothe Luce* (New York, 1970), 69; CBL to Sol A. Rosenblatt of the NRA, July 1, 1934, CBLP; CBL qu. *New York Times Magazine*, Apr. 22, 1973; Mark Fearnow, *Clare Boothe Luce: A Research and Production Sourcebook* (Westport, Conn., 1995).

26. CBL to "Paul," Nov. 7, 1933, CBLP; CBL to Frank Altschul, Nov. 9, 1933, CBLP; CBL to William Wiseman, Nov. 12, 1933, CBLP.

27. Carlotta O'Neill Diary, Nov. 6, 1933, YCAL.

28. Carlotta O'Neill to CBL, Nov. 6, 1933, CBLP; CBL to "Paul," Nov. 7, 1933, CBLP.

29. CBL int. SJM, Sept. 9, 1986; CBL to Wiseman, Nov. 12, 1933; CBL to BMB, Nov. 7, 1933, CBLP.

30. CBL to DFB, Nov. 9, 1933, CBLP; CBL to Frank Altschul, Nov. 9, 1933.

31. Carlotta O'Neill Diary, Nov. 8, 1933. Notwithstanding the O'Neills' distaste for CBL, she managed to arrange a second invitation to "Casa Genotta." O'Neill

recorded only "C. Brokaw to dine," without further comment. Eugene O'Neill Diary, Nov. 10, 1933, YCAL.

32. CBL to William Wiseman, Nov. 12, 1933.
33. Hovey quotation (1892), unidentified, *Macmillan Book of Business and Economic Quotations* (New York, 1984), 117.
34. CBL to "Paul," Nov. 7, 1933, CBLP.
35. CBL to Frank Altschul, Nov. 17, 1933, CBLP.
36. Ibid., Jan. 1, 1934, CBLP; Howard Coffin's guest book, Cloister Hotel archives, Sea Island, Ga. Howard Earle Coffin, an Ohio farm boy, founded the Detroit Hudson Motor Company. During World War I he served on the Aircraft Production Board. In the 1920s he moved south and became a leading textile manufacturer. His first wife died in 1931. He married Miss Gladys Baker of New York in June 1937, and died the following November—the eve of hunting season—from an accidental or suicidal gunshot wound. *New York Times,* Nov. 23, 1937.
37. CBL to Miguel Covarrubias, Feb. 5, 1934, CBLP. She gave another reason for leaving. "I am very ambitious, and like to work very much—but for myself." Ibid.

20. EVERYBODY'S AND YET NOBODY'S

1. CBL to Eugene R. Gaddis, Nov. 18, 1985, CBLP.
2. Virgil Thomson, *An Autobiography* (New York, 1966), 232–242; James Mellow, *Charmed Circle: Gertrude Stein and Company* (Boston, 1974), 368–369.
3. Elisabeth Sussman and Barbara J. Bloemik, *Florine Stettheimer: Manhattan Fantastica,* Whitney Museum of American Art catalogue (New York, 1995), 52–55.
4. CBL to Donald Freeman, Aug. 21, 1930, CBLP.
5. Ts. in CBLP.
6. John Golden to CBL, June 6, 1934, CBLP.
7. Jean Dalrymple int. SJM, Feb. 5, 1988, SJMP.
8. Mark Sullivan to CBL, n.d. 1934, CBLP.
9. Milton Rosenbluth to CBL, n.d. c. 1934, CBLP.
10. Jeanne B. Winham int. SJM, Nov. 13, 1984, SJMP.
11. Unidentified news clip in "This World of Ours," SJMP.
12. "This World of Ours," 1, SJMP.
13. Ibid., 24.
14. Ibid., 28.
15. The complete text of one of CBL's best columns, "The Perfect Panhandler," is reprinted in the appendix. It not only demonstrates her newspaper prose at its best, but offers documentary proof that New York's begging techniques have changed little over the years.
16. CBL, "Man with a Telescope," in "This World of Ours," 19.
17. CBL, "Bonanza Lament," in "This World of Ours," 31.
18. CBL, "Bureaucrats Are Beasts," in "This World of Ours," 33.
19. DFB to CBL, Aug. 1934, CBLP.
20. *Washington Herald,* Aug. 31, 1934; John Golden to CBL, n.d. c. Aug. 1934, BRTC; Miriam Howell to CBL, Aug. 7, 1934, CBLP.
21. CBL, "Brussels Again," in "This World of Ours," 52; "A Balearic Breakfast," ibid. 57; "A Lovers' Retreat," ibid. 53, SJMP.

22. Mae McGinnis of the Block agency informed CBL of the cancellation on Aug. 9, 1943. CBLP.
23. Pamela Harriman to SJM, Apr. 16, 1983; Noel Coward qu. Wilfrid Sheed, *Clare Boothe Luce* (New York, 1982), 23.
24. CBL int. SJM, June 13, 1982. Winston Churchill was impressed with CBL, telling Baruch, "She's the tops." Helen Lawrenson, "The Woman," *Esquire,* Aug. 1974.
25. Jeanne Campbell int. SJM, Apr. 13, 1982.
26. Randolph Churchill to CBL, Aug. 17, 1934, CBLP.
27. Randolph Churchill to CBL, Oct. 11, 1934, CBLP.
28. CBL, "Hanging Gardens of Gotham," in "This World of Ours," 93, SJMP. A few months later she wrote, "I see a vista of lofty towers and skyscrapers that shatter the winter sun into splendid splinters of shadow and light. Anyone who lives in New York City and does *not* continue to live high up misses the greatest sight that modern life has to offer." Ms. fragment, "As Manhattan goes so goes the nation," c. 1935, CBLP.
29. CBL to Dr. Milton Rosenbluth, Dec. 27, 1934, CBLP.
30. Lawrenson, "Woman"; Frank Crowninshield to CBL, Nov. 30, 1934, CBLP.
31. Laura Z. Hobson, *Laura Z: A Life* (New York, 1983), 138–139.
32. Ibid., 137.
33. Ibid. CBL's first impression of HRL was that he was "nice-looking . . . but not handsome. He had seemed strangely ill at ease, and his humorlessness had made him look dull, and his eyes which peeped out from under his lashes had seemed hard." CBL memo on HRL, 1960, CBLP.
34. CBL int. SJM, June 13, 1982.

21. COUP DE FOUDRE

1. *New York Sun,* Dec. 10, 1934; *Reading Times* (Pa.), Aug. 1, 1942.
2. The following account is primarily based on CBL int. SJM, June 13, 1982, SJMP. Supplementary details from Elsa Maxwell int. Alden Hatch, c. 1954, AHP; Robert T. Elson notes, TIA; and Helen Lawrenson, *Stranger at the Party: A Memoir* (New York, 1975), 115.
3. Lawrenson, *Stranger,* 115.
4. W. A. Swanberg, *Luce and His Empire* (New York, 1972), 114.
5. Roy Hoopes, *Ralph Ingersoll* (New York, 1985), 120.
6. Ibid., 120–121.
7. CBL int. SJM, Oct. 30, 1981, and June 13, 1982; CBL to HRL, Apr. 2, 1935, CBLP.
8. Ibid.
9. HRL to CBL, Dec. 22, 1934, CBLP.
10. CBL to HRL, Dec. 23, 1934, CBLP.
11. CBL to Milton Rosenbluth, Dec. 27, 1934, CBLP.
12. HRL to CBL, Dec. 26, 1934, CBLP; CBL to HRL, Dec. 28, 1934, CBLP.
13. CBL int. SJM, June 12, 1982; Paul Johnson, "Portrait of the Artist as an Intellectual," *Commentary,* Feb. 1989.
14. HRL to CBL, Dec. 28, 1934, CBLP.
15. CBL to Dorothy B. Holloran, Dec. 15, 1931, CBLP; CBL, "The Great Garbo," *Vanity Fair,* Feb. 1932.

16. John Billings Diary, Dec. 31, 1934, JBP.

17. Laura Z. Hobson int. SJM, Oct. 19, 1983. See Hobson's *Laura Z: A Life* (New York, 1983), 131–156, for an account of her divorce and relationship with the Luces.

18. Laura Z. Hobson Diary, Jan. 2, 1935, LZHP.

19. The following biographical portrait is based on SJM interviews with Henry Luce III and Elisabeth Luce Moore, plus accounts of HRL's life in Swanberg, *Luce,* and Robert T. Elson, *Time Inc.: The Intimate History of a Publishing Enterprise, 1923–1941* (New York, 1968). References to HRL's relationship with Briton Hadden are taken from Noel F. Busch, *Briton Hadden: A Biography of the Co-Founder of Time* (New York, 1949).

20. A century later, however, China's Christian population is growing.

21. John Billings Diary, Jan. 4, 1935; Ann Brokaw Diary, Jan. 11, 1935, CBLP.

22. Elson notes, Oct. 9, 1967, TIA; CBL int. SJM, June 20, 1982, SJMP.

23. CBL int. SJM, Oct. 15, 1982, SJMP. She added, "Why couldn't he be like that with me?"

24. CBL qu. HRL in a letter to him, Jan. 10, 1935, CBLP. In old age CBL would tell an interviewer, "His love was like a sunburst. Mine was based on slow acceptance." Qu. Marian Christy, *Port Chester Daily Item* (N.Y.), July 25, 1972.

25. Hotel bill in CBLP; HRL to CBL, Mar. 7, 1935, CBLP.

26. HRL ms., Mar. 7, 1935, CBLP.

27. Ann Brokaw Diary, Jan. 20, 1935, CBLP; Hobson, *A Life,* 148.

28. Hobson, *A Life,* 148.

29. HRL to CBL, Jan. 27, 1935, CBLP.

30. HRL to CBL, Jan. 29, 1935, CBLP.

31. HRL to CBL, Jan. 30, 1935, CBLP.

32. HRL to CBL, Jan. 27, 1935.

33. CBL to HRL, c. Jan. 27, 1935, CBLP.

34. CBL to HRL, Jan. 28, 1935 (misdated "Feb. 1"); HRL to CBL, Feb. 5, 1935, CBLP.

35. CBL to HRL, Jan. 30, 1935, CBLP.

36. HRL to CBL, Feb. 7, 1935, CBLP.

37. CBL to HRL, Feb. 4, 1935, CBLP.

38. Questionnaire, c. Feb. 1935, CBLP.

39. Margaret Case Harriman, *Blessed Are the Debonair* (New York, 1956), 160–162.

40. CBL to HRL, Feb. 2, 1935, CBLP.

41. CBL to HRL, Feb. 4, 1935, qu. Laura Hobson and giving her own opinions.

42. HRL to CBL, Feb. 2, 1935; CBL to HRL, Feb. 4, 1935, CBLP.

43. Laura Z. Hobson to CBL, Feb. 11, 1935.

44. Ms. in CBLP. See Mark Fearnow, *Clare Boothe Luce: A Research and Production Sourcebook* (Westport, Conn., 1995), for alternative summaries of this and all other CBL plays, produced and unproduced.

45. Hobson, *A Life,* 150–152. On Jan. 30, 1935, CBL wrote Dr. Milton Rosenbluth: "My Pygmalion, I expect you, while I am away, to make great research into the matter of how I may yet become a beautiful woman. (Wouldn't it be odd if I were to become a beautiful woman in my thirty-second year?)" CBLP. Honeymoon snapshots, however, show CBL with droopy breasts.

46. DFB to CBL, Feb. 13, 1935, CBLP.

47. Ann Brokaw Diary, Feb. 22, Mar. 1, 3, 24, 1935.
48. HRL to CBL, Mar. 7, 1935, CBLP.
49. Laura Hobson to CBL, Feb. 16, 1935, CBLP.
50. CBL to HRL, Jan. 30, 1935, CBLP.
51. Hoopes, *Ingersoll*, 121.
52. HRL to CBL, Apr. 21, 1935, CBLP.
53. CBL to HRL, Mar. 29, 1935, CBLP. While at the Greenbrier, CBL also wrote HRL, "Only a love like yours can redeem the sorrows and sins of all my other days." Apr. 3, 1935, CBLP.
54. CBL to HRL, Apr. 2, 1935, CBLP.
55. John Billings Diary, Apr. 22, 1935, JBP.
56. CBL to HRL, Apr. 22, 1935, CBLP.
57. HRL to CBL, Apr. 23, 1935, CBLP, repeating Longwell. CBL in turn repeated to HRL what Longwell told her: that everyone at Time Inc. considered Henry Luce to be "the most impossible, the most brilliant, the most tireless, and the most lovable of men." He further said that he had always known his boss to be unhappy, and wondered if Harry would ever discover it himself. CBL to HRL, Apr. 23, 1935, CBLP.
58. CBL to HRL, Apr. 27, 1935, CBLP.
59. CBL to HRL, 1935, CBLP.
60. *New York Daily Mirror*, Apr. 29, 1935, CBL scrapbooks, CBLP.
61. HRL to CBL, May 1, 1935, CBLP.
62. CBL to HRL, May 12, 1935, CBLP. Helen Lawrenson wrote that Pare Lorentz, hearing that CLB was thinking of marrying Luce and would sail that day to Europe, "was so upset that he wanted to rush to the boat and stop her. I had all I could do to dissuade him." Helen Lawrenson, "The Woman," *Esquire*, Aug. 1974.
63. CBL to HRL, May 12, 1935, CBLP.
64. HRL to CBL, May 14, 1935, CBLP.

22. UPROARIOUS BREASTS

1. CBL to Milton Rosenbluth, May 13, 1935, CBLP; Elsa Maxwell, "Party Line," *New York Post*, Sept. 8, 1942. Maxwell took the piglet to her farm in Provence, "where it grew up to be a huge, ferocious boar." The animal had to be destroyed when it began killing poultry. CBL got her friend to admit that it had "probably" ended up as pork, and subsequently punned, "It was the only time I have ever known Elsa to have a bore for dinner." Elsa Maxwell int. Alden Hatch, AHP.
2. CBL to HRL, May 12, 1935, CBLP, qu. Maxwell.
3. CBL to HRL, May 12, 1935, CBLP, qu. Mrs. Moore.
4. CBL to HRL, May 12, 1935.
5. CBL in "Remembering Mr. Maugham," Univ. of Southern California broadcast, Apr. 18, 1966, transcript in CBLP.
6. Ibid.; CBL int. Gary Lautens, unidentified Canadian news clip, 1971, CBLP.
7. CBL to HRL, May 22, 1935, CBLP.
8. HRL to CBL, May 30, 1935, CBLP.
9. DFB to CBL, early June 1935, CBLP.
10. DFB to CBL, c. late June 1935; CBL to Milton Rosenbluth, July 28, 1935, CBLP.
11. Ibid., Dec. 27, 1934, CBLP; Dr. Michael Rosenbluth int. SJM, May 7, 1984, SJMP.

12. DFB to CBL, n.d. early June 1935, CBLP. CBL told Alexis Aladin that she "loved her brother more deeply and truly than I thought it possible to love any human being," and felt "such sympathy and peace" in his presence. Letter, c. May 16, 1921, AAP.

13. HRL to CBL, c. May 18, 1935, CBLP.

14. HRL to CBL, June 6, 1935, CBLP, anticipating the news break.

15. John Billings to H. J. Hammond, June 11, 1935, JBP; John Billings Diary, June 6, 1935, JBP; James Agee to Dwight MacDonald, July 1, 1935, JAP.

16. CBL to Mark Sullivan, July 10, 1935, CBLP.

17. Ibid.

18. CBL to HRL, c. June 26, 1935, CBLP.

19. CBL to HRL, July 26, 1935, CBLP.

20. HRL to CBL, July 7, 1935, CBLP; CBL to George Freulinghuysen, Nov. 7, 1983, CBLP.

21. HRL to CBL, July 7, 1935.

22. Recalled by CBL to HRL, May 10, 1960, CBLP.

23. HRL to CBL, July 7, 1935, CBL, "Aide-Memoire," July 9, 1935, CBLP.

24. CBL to HRL, July 15, 1935, CBLP. CBL was particularly insensitive in abandoning ACB just after the death of George Brokaw. The girl was having to adjust not only to the recent loss of her father but also to her mother's transferral of affections to a new lover. A letter received by CBL later that year from the owner of San Gustin reported some apparently pathological destruction of books in the villa library. Many leather-bound volumes had been mutilated or lost. Six backs had been ripped from a set of Dickens, and a valuable history was found coverless "on the rocks." Lillian Broadhurst to CBL, Oct. 18, 1935, CBLP.

25. CBL to HRL, July 15, 1935, CBLP; ACB to HRL, July 22, 1935, CBLP.

26. CBL int. SJM, Oct. 30, 1981; CBL to HRL, July 15, 1935, CBLP.

27. Ibid.

28. CBL to HRL, July 29, 1935, CBLP.

29. Ibid.

30. BMB to CBL, July 26, 1935, CBLP.

31. CBL to HRL, July 27, Aug. 1, 3, 1935, CBLP.

32. HRL to CBL, July 25, 1935, CBLP; CBL to HRL, Aug. 5, 1935, CBLP.

33. Ibid. CBL was a critic of pictures as well as text, telling HRL, e.g., that an industrial article illustrated with overdramatic photographs looked like "unpalatable spinach." Ibid.

34. CBL to HRL, Aug. 1, 1935.

35. Ibid.

36. Ibid.; CBL to HRL, Aug. 5, 1935.

37. CBL to HRL, Aug. 1, 1935.

38. John Billings Diary, July 22, 1935; HRL to CBL, July 22, 1935, CBLP.

39. ACA to CBL, July 15, 1935, CBLP.

40. CBL to HRL, Aug. 16, 1935, CBLP.

41. CBL to HRL, Aug. 15, 1935, CBLP.

42. CBL to HRL, Aug. 30, 1935, CBLP.

43. CBL to HRL, Aug. 29, 1935, CBLP.

44. Receipts, Sept. 1935, in CBLP.

45. CBL telephoned Randolph Churchill and asked if he, too, would consider coming to Paris. She apparently had to be sure of at least one last fling, in case Baruch failed to show. Thrilled at the sound of her voice, Churchill waited to be summoned—in vain. Randolph Churchill to CBL, Sept. 8, 1935, CBLP.
46. BMB to CBL, Aug. 29, 1935, CBLP; CBL to BMB, July 21, 1934, CBLP.
47. BMB to CBL, Aug. 29, CBLP.
48. BMB to CBL, Sept. 11, 1935, CBLP.
49. Helen Lawrenson, "The Woman," *Esquire,* Aug. 1974. HRL's divorce became final on Oct. 5, 1935.
50. Clifford Odets to CBL, Nov. 12, 1935, CBLP.
51. Frank Gilmore to CBL, June 27, 1934, CBLP.
52. CBL, *Abide With Me,* ms., CBLP.
53. Carol Hyatt and Linda Gottlieb, *When Smart People Fail* (New York, 1987), 43; CBL int. Richard Watts, *New York Herald Tribune,* Oct. 6, 1940; Margaret Case Harriman, "The Candor Kid II," *New Yorker,* Jan. 11, 1941.
54. All newspapers Nov. 22, 1935.
55. John Billings Diary, Nov. 24, 25, 1935, JBP.
56. Ibid.
57. *Time,* Nov. 25, 1935.
58. DFB to CBL, Dec. 21, 1935, CBLP.
59. Alexander King, "Clare Doesn't Care," unpublished essay for *Vogue,* 1940, CBLP.
60. CBL int. Watts, Oct. 6, 1940. See also CBL, *Europe in the Spring* (New York, 1940), 57.
61. Bernard and Annie Baruch to CBL, Nov. 28, 1935, CBLP; William Hale to CBL, n.d., CBLP; AEA to HRL, Nov. 26, 1935, CBLP. "I did feel hurt," CBL wrote Sullivan, "that you were so very silent during an event that had some importance to me." CBL to Mark Sullivan, c. Dec. 26, 1935, CBLP.
62. John Billings Diary, Nov. 25, 1935.
63. Ibid., Nov. 29, 1935.

23. MOON-MINDED MAN

1. Anthony Mason int. SJM assistant, Mar. 30, 1994.
2. CBL to Milton Rosenbluth, Dec. 26, 1935, CBLP.
3. Ibid.; CBL int. SJM, Dec. 20, 1981.
4. Roy Hoopes, *Ralph Ingersoll* (New York, 1985), 128, 130, 127. Asked by one of his young editors why he paid such high salaries, HRL replied, "I was poor once and I didn't like it. Why should you?"; John Kobler, *Luce, His Time, Life and Fortune* (New York, 1968), 188.
5. HRL to John Billings, Nov. 1, 1933, JBP; John Billings Diary, Nov. 11, 1933, JBP; Hoopes, *Ingersoll,* 134–135.
6. Hoopes, *Ingersoll,* 140–141.
7. CBL to Condé Nast, May 9, 1931, CBLP.
8. CBL memo to Donald Freeman, Dec. 9, 1931; CBL to Condé Nast, Jan. 10, 1934, CBLP. In her memo to Freeman, CBL anticipated by some four decades the highly visual, celebrity-oriented, minimal-text format that would characterize American popular media in the television age. She advocated, for example, a subjective lead article written in "short paragraphs of pungent comment,"

a no-carry-over policy, and "two portfolios of pictures . . . like those of Marlene Dietrich and Clark Gable," or other current celebrities. The cost of such extra artwork would be offset by savings of "some thousands of dollars in manuscripts."

At least two of these documents were resurrected in the summer of 1942, when HRL was sued by two artists claiming that he had appropriated their "new, novel, original and unique plan" for a picture magazine similar to *Life*. The judge, finding against the plaintiffs, cited CBL's memos, plus her own "uncontradicted testimony," as proof that she had preempted their ideas by at least a year. Judgment, June 26, 1946, in *Corcoran, et al. v. Time, Inc.*, 1445–1466, copy in CBLP.

9.   CBL to John Martin, Feb. 20, 1933, CBLP; Roy Hoopes, "The Agony of Ecstasy," *Regardie's Magazine*, Oct. 1985.
10. John Billings to H. J. Hammond, Jan. 28, 1936, JBP; CBL int. SJM, Dec. 20, 1981.
11. Kobler, *Luce*, 99.
12. CBL to Dr. Thompkins, Mar. 17, 1961, CBLP.
13. "Mepkin," visitor's leaflet, Mepkin Abbey, S.C.
14. CBL int. SJM at Mepkin, May 18, 1984.
15. John Billings Diary, Feb. 15 and 10, 1936, JBP.
16. Ibid., Feb. 20, 14, June 26, 1936, JBP.
17. Laura Z. Hobson, *Laura Z: A Life* (New York, 1983), 233; Robert T. Elson, *Time Inc.: The Intimate History of a Publishing Enterprise, 1923–1941* (New York, 1968), 289–290; Elson notes, TIA.
18. Elson, *Time*, 289–290; Elson notes, TIA.
19. Mehemed Agha to Hubert Kay, Oct. 7, 1958, CBLP.
20. June 8, 1936, copy in TIA.
21. Hoopes, *Ingersoll*, 144, and Hoopes in *Regardie's*.
22. Sarah L. Burt, "*L'Automne du Monde:* The Last Eight Years of *Vanity Fair*," Ph.D. diss., Univ. of Kansas, 1984, 173–174.
23. John Billings Diary, Oct. 23, 1936, JBP. By December HRL was leaving the editorship increasingly to Billings. Ibid., Dec. 8, 1936.
24. Elson, *Time*, 291; John Billings Diary, Aug. 24, 1936.
25. CBL at Tarrytown Conference Center, *San Francisco Chronicle*, Oct. 21, 1971.
26. CBL to Gilbert Miller, Jan. 18, 1932, CBLP.
27. Max Gordon to CBL, May 12, 1936, CBLP; Max Gordon, *Max Gordon Presents* (New York, 1963), 205.
28. The house belonged to the Untermeyers.
29. Contract for *The Women*, July 2, 1936, CBLP.
30. *The Women* production file, MGM.
31. Moss Hart to Max Gordon, July 10, 1936, copy in CBLP.
32. George Kaufman to Max Gordon, July 15, 1936, copy in CBLP.
33. The salpingogram was performed c. August 10, 1936. Dr. Michael Rosenbluth (son of Milton) int. SJM, May 7, 1984. CBL said that she had three miscarriages while married to George Brokaw. CBL to ACA, Feb. 27, 1929, CBLP.
34. CBL to Milton Rosenbluth, "Monday," c. late Aug. 1936; CBLP; CBL int. SJM, Mar. 19, 1985.
35. Kitty Carlisle Hart telephone int. SJM, May 6, 1984.
36. Ilka Chase, *Past Imperfect* (New York, 1941), 185.

37. John Billings Diary, Nov. 6, 1936; Hoopes, *Ingersoll*, 152; Billings Diary, May 11, 1938.
38. Ingersoll was instead given the tough task of raising *Time*'s circulation to subsidize the printing of 2 million copies of the new magazine each week—the minimum required for solvency. Hoopes, *Ingersoll*, 152. He subsequently left to start *P.M.* newspaper.
39. Chase, *Past Imperfect*, 188.
40. Both reviews Dec. 8, 1936.
41. HRL to CBL, Dec. 8, 1936, CBLP; Moss Hart, *Act One* (New York, 1959), 389.
42. Gillmore qu. Malcolm Goldstein, *George S. Kaufman* (New York, 1979), 279; CBL int. SJM, Feb. 10, 1985.
43. Margaret Case Harriman, "The Candor Kid II," *New Yorker*, Jan. 11, 1941.
44. George Kaufman memo to CBL, n.d., CBLP.
45. *Midweek Pictorial*, n.d., CBL scrapbook, CBLP. *Time* printed a 500-word review, glowingly rewritten by HRL. "*The Women* is calculated to give The Men two of the most shockingly informative hours of their lives and is so clever that few women would willingly miss it." *Life* gave the play a three-page feature, illustrated in color. W. A. Swanberg, *Luce and His Empire* (New York, 1972), 135.
46. *New York Times*, Jan. 28, 1937; *Hollywood Reporter*, Apr. 26, 1937. The *Times-Union*, Apr. 29, 1937, reported that the published script of *The Women* had sold more copies than any other play in "the last ten years."
47. HRL to Walter Winchell, Mar. 6, 1937, CBLP.
48. George Kaufman qu. *Time* researcher Doris Kinney, memo to CBL, n.d. Feb. 1964, CBLP.
49. Nast's party was held Apr. 27, 1937. Helen Lawrenson, *Stranger at the Party* (New York, 1975), 137. ACA Diary, Apr. 13, 1937, CBLP; DFB to CBL, Dec. 17, 1935, CBLP.
50. *New York World-Telegram*, May 13, 1937; John Billings Diary, Jan. 26, 1937.
51. Moss Hart to CBL, n.d. 1949, CBLP.

24. Luces the Magnificent

1. CBL int. SJM at Mepkin, May 18, 1984; Isabel Hill to CBL, Dec. 28, 1949, CBLP.
2. CBL, "The Victorious South," *Vogue*, June 1, 1937; *Charleston* (S.C.) *News & Courier*, Apr. 12, 1936; *New York Sun*, Jan. 9, 1940; Noland Gumbrill to CBL, Aug. 7, 1987.
3. *New York Sun*, Jan. 9, 1940; *Charleston* (S.C.) *News & Courier*, Apr. 12, 1936; Gretta Palmer, "The New Clare Luce," *Look*, Apr. 15, 1947, for colored pictures of Mepkin.
4. John Chamberlain memo, c. Jan. 1946, TIA; Milton MacKaye, "Clare Boothe," *Scribner's Magazine*, Mar. 1939, *New York Post*, May 2, 1937.
5. Mepkin Guest Book, CBLP; Elisabeth Moore int. SJM, Nov. 22, 1983. Mrs. Moore said, "There were so many people around who were frightened of him, that didn't dare speak up."
6. John Billings Diary, Jan. 10, 1937, JBP; CBL to FDR, Jan. 9, 1937, CBLP.
7. Martha Blair, "These Charming People," unidentified clipping; *Republic*, 1939, unidentified clipping, CBLP.

8. Palmer, "The New"; "Only Human," syndicated column by "Candide," n.d. CBL scrapbooks, CBLP.

9. CBL int. *Charleston* (W. Va.) *Gazette*, Jan. 22, 1942; CBL to George Abbot, Nov. 17, 1939, CBLP.

10. Wolcott Gibbs, *"Time . . . Fortune . . . Life . . . Luce,"* *New Yorker*, Nov. 28, 1936.

11. Qu. Robert T. Elson, *Time Inc.: The Intimate History of a Publishing Enterprise, 1923–1941* (New York, 1968), 266; Elson notes, TIA.

12. Henry Luce III int. SJM, March 1, 1989.

13. Ibid. Mah-jongg is a complicated Chinese game played with 136 or 144 domino-like "tiles."

14. Ibid.

15. Henry Luce III int. SJM, Mar. 1, 1989; Mepkin Guest Book.

16. ACA to CBL from Miami, n.d., c. Mar. 1935, CBLP.

17. ACA to CBL from Miami, n.d., c. Mar. 1936, CBLP.

18. ACA to CBL, n.d. c. Apr. 1936, CBLP.

19. Ibid.

20. ACA Diary, Mar. 22 and Apr. 17, 1937, CBLP.

21. *Nashville Tennessean*, Dec. 24, 1937; John Billings Diary, Jan. 10, 1937; Lucius Beebe, "Stage Asides," *New York Herald Tribune*, Apr. 25, 1937.

22. Qu. Gibbs, *"Time . . . Fortune."*

23. HRL to CBL, Nov. 23, 1937, CBLP.

24. Henry Luce III int. SJM, July 24, 1984. "If you didn't know who he was," Hank Luce said of his father, "you would say 'That is a pretty withdrawn man.' " One of HRL's employees described his "plodding-through-snowdrifts gait." Eric Hodgins, *A Trolley to the Moon* (New York, 1973), 339.

25. W. A. Swanberg, *Luce and His Empire* (New York, 1972), 133. CBL, whose departure from *Vogue* in 1930 was unopposed because of her lack of fashion sense (see Ch. 15), was, in the words of *Vanity Fair* art director Mehemed Agha, "never a clothes-horse . . . To meet important people she used to think that she had to dress like a Southern belle—beige, rose, organdie—things that really weren't in character for her." Int. Hubert Kay, Oct. 7, 1958, CBLP.

26. *New York Evening Post*, May 8, 1937; *Brooklyn Times*, May 19, 1937; *New York American*, May 14, 1937; CBL to Norman Krasna, Apr. 27, 1937, CBLP.

27. CBL int. *Nashville Tennessean*, Dec. 24, 1937; HRL to CBL, May 20, 1937, CBLP.

28. HRL to CBL, May 18, 1937; CBL qu. HRL to CBL, May 17, 1937; HRL to CBL, May 17, 1937, CBLP.

29. Qu. Roy Hoopes, *Ralph Ingersoll* (New York, 1985), 159–161.

30. CBL to Norman Krasna, May 22, 1937, CBLP.

31. Norman Krasna to CBL, May 24, 1937, CBLP.

32. HRL to CBL, Jan. 27, 1935, CBLP; CBL to Max Beaverbrook, June 7, 1949, Max Beaverbrook Papers, House of Lords Record Office, London.

33. DFB to CBL (also quoting BMB), n.d. summer 1937, CBLP; Hoopes, *Ingersoll*, 166. Having failed to find his total salvation in Clare, Harry was no longer satisfied with routine work. John Billings found him at the office in early August, trying to assemble a new spread for *Life* called "People." This idea would eventually prove to be the seed of one of his company's most successful future ventures, but it failed to germinate then. After "tossing everything up in the air like a juggler,"

he left the hapless Billings "to catch the pieces as they came down." John Billings Diary, Aug. 6, 11, 1937.

34. Ann Brokaw Diary, Jan. 17, 1940, and May 27, 1942, CBLP.
35. HRL to CBL, Nov. 22, 1937, CBLP.
36. The following account of ACA's death is based on Sarah B. Kurtz to CBL, July 7, 1951, CBLP, supplemented by *Greenwich Times*, Jan. 1–7, 1938; *Miami Herald*, Jan. 2–3, 1938; *New York Herald Tribune*, Jan. 2, 1938; *Boston Post*, Jan. 3, 1938.
37. Miscellaneous clippings, AEAP.
38. CBL int. SJM, July 11, 1987; Margaret Beamish to CBL, Jan. 19, 1938, CBLP; Ann Brokaw Diary, Jan. 22, 1939.
39. CBL int. SJM, June 23, 1984; CBL to ACA, c. Feb. 1929, CBLP; CBL to Ann Charnley, Mar. 5, 1985, Ann Charnley private collection, Washington, D.C.
40. William Hirschberg (lawyer) to Alexander Hehmeyer (*Time* employee), Mar. 5, 1942; ACA to CBL, Nov. 6, 1937; CBLP.
41. Joel Jacobs Will, May 7, 1936, New York Surrogate Court, New York, N.Y., copy in SJMP.
42. *Greenwich Times*, Jan. 4–5, 1938.
43. ACA int. an unidentified Miami newspaper, n.d., CBLP.

25. Kiss the Boys Good-bye

1. CBL to HRL, c. Jan. 7, 1938, CBLP.
2. CBL qu. *Charleston Gazette* (W.Va.), Jan. 22, 1942.
3. CBL, *Kiss the Boys Good-bye* (New York, 1939), 13.
4. CBL int. *New York Times*, Jan. 27, 1939; CBL int. *Brooklyn Eagle*, Nov. 27, 1938.
5. CBL, *Kiss*, 247.
6. Ibid., 57. The critic Heywood Broun had disliked *The Women*, but wrote a flattering preface to *Kiss the Boys Good-bye*.
7. Qu. Helen Lawrenson, "The Woman," *Esquire*, Aug. 1974. Clare apparently warned Shaw that Helen was "an old man's darling." He, in turn, told Helen that Clare was "no friend of yours." Ibid.
8. Ibid.
9. Wilfrid Sheed, *Clare Boothe Luce* (New York, 1982), 108; Lawrenson, "Woman."
10. HRL to CBL, Jan. 17, 1938, CBLP.
11. HRL to CBL, "Thanksgiving" 1938, CBLP.
12. John Billings Diary, Dec. 4, 1937, and May 11, 1938, JBP.
13. John Jessup, *The Ideas of Henry Luce* (New York, 1969), 24–25.
14. Donovan qu. Jessup, *Ideas*, 29; CBL to Dan Longwell, c. May 12, 1938, DLP.
15. List in TIA.
16. CBL to Longwell, c. May 12, 1938, DLP; London *Daily Telegraph*, May 17, 1938.
17. Lawrenson, "Woman"; Max Gordon to CBL, May 17, 1938, CBLP.
18. CBL int. *Daily News-Chronicle* (U.K.), May 21, 1938.
19. Ibid.
20. CBL int. *Daily Express* (U.K.), May 21, 1938.
21. W. A. Swanberg, *Luce and His Empire* (New York, 1972), 154; Richard de Rochemont memo to HRL, May 20, 1938, CBLP.
22. Except where otherwise cited, the following account of HRL's 1938 European trip quotes from his official memo to his editors, June 22, 1938, TIA.

23. CBL, Introduction to *Kiss*, xi.
24. CBL offered the script to Max Gordon first. When he did not respond as promptly as she now expected, she turned to Pemberton.
25. HRL to Allen Grover, Aug. 3, 1939, CBLP.
26. CBL to ACB, n.d., c. Oct. 1938; "The House of a Distinguished Couple," *Vogue*, Feb. 15, 1942; *House & Garden*, June 1940.
27. HRL to Allen Grover, Feb. 12, 1940, and to CBL, Aug. 7, 1941, CBLP.
28. Isabel Hill to Corinne Thrasher (HRL's secretary), Sept. 21, 1938, CBLP. Brock Pemberton was as impressed as Mrs. Hill. He knew of few writers, he said, who were as willing and able to make last-minute changes. Pemberton qu. *Philadelphia Bulletin*, Oct. 24, 1949.
29. John Anderson in *New York Evening Journal*, Sept. 29, 1938.
30. All newspapers, Sept. 29, 1938.
31. Oct. 9, 1938.
32. *New York Times*, Sept. 29, 1938; *Time*, Oct. 10, 1938; *Life*, Oct. 28, 1938.
33. By January 1939, three companies would be playing *Kiss the Boys Good-Bye* simultaneously nationwide, and five *The Women*. CBL to ACB, c. Jan. 18, 1939, CBLP.
34. Except in Paris, where the play opened in November 1938 at the Pigalle Theater before a glittering audience including Marlene Dietrich, Schiaparelli, and Baron Henri de Rothschild. "In many instances," according to *The New York Times*, Nov. 5, 1938, "the intensely American humor failed to carry."
35. Harold Nicolson, *Diaries, 1930–1939* (New York, 1966), 370.
36. John Billings Diary, Sept. 29, 1938, JBP.
37. Margaret L. Coit, *Mr. Baruch* (Cambridge, Mass., 1957), 467.
38. Ibid., 467–468. Nevertheless, Roosevelt would call for exactly that number of aircraft nineteen months later, when America's need to rearm could no longer be denied.
39. Ibid., 469.

26. Portrait of a Suicide

1. *Pittsburgh Press*, Oct. 22, 1938. Dorothy was not related to William Harlan Hale.
2. Rosamond Pinchot killed herself with carbon monoxide fumes on Jan. 24, 1938, after an unhappy love affair with the producer Jed Harris. New York *Daily News*, Jan. 25, 1938; Martin Gottfried, *Jed Harris: The Curse of Genius* (Boston, 1984), 166. William Harlan Hale said the two suicides "seemed to have everything. And yet there was some horrible interior gap that made them want to die." Int. Hubert Kay, Oct. 23, 1958, CBLP.
3. *Pittsburgh Press*, Oct. 22, 1938; CBL Diary, Sept. 24, 1932, SJMP.
4. "She is a clever woman to keep it so dark," CBL wrote of Dorothy's secret lover (probably George Blumenthal) on Nov. 11, 1932. CBL Diary.
5. Dorothy Hale to CBL, Dec. 14, 1937; Isabel Hill to Dorothy Hale, Dec. 15, 1937, CBLP.
6. BMB had given Dorothy a thousand dollars and told her to buy a dress glamorous enough to capture a husband. CBL int. SJM, June 20, 1982.
7. CBL to James Harithas, Curator, Corcoran Galley of Art, Oct. 24, 1966, CBLP; Hayden Herrera, *Frida: A Biography of Frida Kahlo* (New York, 1983), 290–293,

qu. CBL on Dorothy Hale's death. Elisabeth Cobb Rogers to CBL, n.d. 1938, CBLP.

8. CBL to James Harithas, Oct. 24, 1966, CBLP; Herrera, *Frida*, 678.

9. *Pittsburgh Press*, Oct. 22, 1938. Ann Brokaw Diary, Sept. 12, 1939, quotes CBL to the effect that Noguchi was a lover of Dorothy Hale.

10. CBL ts. "White House," July 1940, CBLP.

11. At another gallery a few days before, she had lost a Dufy to Diana Vreeland and hoped to find a substitute. CBL to Carl Van Vechten, Nov. 3, 1938, CVVP.

12. Qu. Bertram Wolfe, "Rise of Another Rivera," *Vogue*, Nov. 1938.

13. Herrera, *Frida*, 229.

14. *New York Times*, Nov. 6, 1938; Herrera, *Frida*, 231.

15. Allene Talmey, "Clare Boothe . . . in a Velvet Glove," *Vogue*, Dec. 15, 1940.

16. Four of them belonged to the actor Edward G. Robinson.

17. The picture (now in the National Museum of Women in the Arts, Washington, D.C.) may be seen in the background of Karsh's portrait of CBL, reproduced at the end of Chapter 38. Soon after Trotsky had arrived in Mexico in January 1937, he and Frida, an ardent Communist, had become lovers. That fall, in celebration of the twentieth anniversary of the Russian Revolution, she had done the portrait, framed it in pink and green velvet, and hung it in Trotsky's studio, where it was admired by André Breton. Herrera, *Frida*, 213–214.

18. Ibid., 234.

19. CBL to Harithas, Oct. 24, 1966; Herrera, *Frida*, 229, 226. CBL paid twice as much as Edward G. Robinson had paid for his Kahlo paintings. Ibid.

20. Qu. Herrera, *Frida*, 229; Diego Rivera, *My Art, My Life* (New York, 1960), 223–224.

21. Frida Kahlo to Nikolas Muray, June 13, 1939, qu. Hayden Herrera to CBL, Feb. 11, 1981, CBLP.

22. CBL qu. Herrera, *Frida*, 292–293.

23. Now in the Phoenix Art Museum ("gift of an anonymous donor"). Reproduced in Martha Zamora, *Frida Kahlo: The Brush of Anguish* (San Francisco, 1990), 60.

24. Like all Kahlo's art, the work had its ultimate inspiration in her own life and feelings. Sickly and conscious of mortality, Frida had also been depressed, while painting the retablo, over Diego Rivera's blatant marital infidelities. In fact, soon after its completion their nine-year marriage ended in a divorce that was to last two years. The surreal symbolic interpretation of Hale's suicide therefore reflected not only the artist's apprehension of death but also her trauma of loss and abandonment.

25. CBL to Nikolas Muray, Aug. 18, 1939, CBLP.

26. Frida Kahlo to CBL, Sept. 5, 1938, CBLP.

27. *Stage*, Nov. 1938.

28. Carl Van Vechten to CBL, Nov. 8, 1938, CBLP.

29. George Ross, "So This Is Broadway," unidentified news clip in HRL to CBL, Dec. 1, 1938, CBLP.

30. In her unfinished autobiographical novel "This My Hand," CBL tellingly describes the protagonist as being "shy and cold and infinitely fastidious . . . she knew that she could not sing or write. If she could, she supposed she would have felt within her that glow of genius which burns like a little, uncomfortable, unextinguishable spirit lamp in the breast of the true creative artist." CBLP.

31. AEA to CBL, Aug. 24, 1933, CBLP. The piece with grammatical faults was "The Birthday of Barge, the Banker," published in *Vanity Fair*, Sept. 1933. Mark Sullivan thought it "in most respects the best thing of yours I have ever read." Sullivan to CBL, Aug. 18, 1933, CBLP.
32. CBL to AEA, Aug. 30, 1933, CBLP.
33. Mepkin Guest Book, CBLP; Helen Lawrenson to CBL, c. Mar. 1939, CBLP.
34. *New York Times*, Apr. 20, 1939, reported that Rodgers and Hart were conferring with CBL about "The Wedding Day." The ms. is in CBLP.
35. Eleanor Roosevelt in "My Day," *Washington Daily News*, Dec. 21, 1938; CBL to Eleanor Roosevelt, Jan. 10, 1939, ERP; Eleanor Roosevelt to CBL, Jan. 19, 1939, CBLP. The two women had met some time before at a fair in Rhinebeck, N.Y., and had together bought the President a cake.
36. CBL int. *New York Daily News*, Feb. 14, 1939.
37. Harry Evans in *Family Circle*, Apr. 21, 1939; Russell Aitken to CBL, Apr. 10, 1953, CBLP.
38. Julia McCarthy in New York *Daily News*, Feb. 14, 1939; CBL int. *Dick Cavett Show*, PBS, Jan. 20, 1981; CBL int. SJM, June 20, 1982.
39. Paul Lewis Clemens to CBL, Jan. 24, 1939, CBLP.
40. Jo Davidson, *Between Sittings* (New York, 1951), 117; CBL to Elisabeth Moore, Apr. 9, 1964, CBLP. The Davidson busts are now in the National Portrait Gallery, Washington, D.C. In 1933 Miguel Covarrubias had done two caricatures of CBL. They were sold at auction after her death. In 1942 Gerald Brockhurst, a British Royal Academician, would paint an oil portrait of her wearing a green silk Chinese tunic. She, or HRL, paid an extravagant $5,000 (c. $50,000 in current values). The picture is now in the Phoenix Art Museum.
41. Nancy Grove, *Isamu Noguchi: Portrait Sculpture* (Washington, D.C., 1989), 80–81. Bust now in Henry Luce Foundation, New York, N.Y.
42. Ann Brokaw Diary, Sept. 12, 1939, CBLP.
43. Grove, *Noguchi*, 80.
44. CBL to Hayden Herrera, Feb. 11, 1981, CBLP.

27. Margin for Error

1. *Sunday Times* (U.K.), Apr. 23, 1939.
2. CBL to Joseph P. Kennedy, May 26, 1939; CBL to HRL, June 3, 1939, CBLP.
3. CBLP.
4. CBL Diary, June 25, June 14, 1939; CBL int. SJM, Apr. 29, 1986.
5. CBL memo, Aug. 15, 1939, TIA.
6. CBL to ACB, Oct. 11, 1940, CBLP; Blanche Patch (GBS secretary) to CBL, June 10, 1939, CBLP.
7. CBL int. SJM, Aug. 2, 1985.
8. CBL qu. *Evening Standard* (U.K.), June 20, 1939.
9. George Bernard Shaw to CBL, June 16, 1939, CBLP.
10. HRL to CBL, June 2, 1939, CBLP; DFB to CBL, July 21, 1939, CBLP.
11. CBL int. Charles Graves, *Daily Mail* (U.K.), June 22, 1939. CBL had smoked what she hoped was "my last cigarette for a year" on Nov. 22, 1938. CBL to HRL, Nov. 22, 1939, CBLP. Whether or not she kept this resolve is unknown, but soon she began smoking again, and continued to do so off and on into her seventies.

Notes

12. CBL to Kate Bergeda, Apr. 25, 1939, CBLP.
13. Lilian Thompson to CBL, Apr. 23, 1939, CBLP.
14. John Gunther to CBL, Mar. 10, 1967, CBLP.
15. Ann Brokaw Diary, July 28, 1939, CBLP; *Washington Times-Herald*, Sept. 11, 1939.
16. CBL Diary, *passim*.
17. According to Gilbert A. Harrison, *The Enthusiast: A Life of Thornton Wilder* (New York, 1983), 140, Wilder believed Stein and Freud to be the world's two greatest living human beings.
18. Samuel Steward, ed., *Dear Sammy: Letters from Gertrude Stein and Alice B. Toklas* (New York, 1977), 32.
19. Except where otherwise stated, the following account is based on a CBL Diary fragment, July 12–14, 1939.
20. Alice B. Toklas qu. *New York Post*, Apr. 14, 1963.
21. Harrison, *Enthusiast*, 178; CBL address, Woodrow Wilson International Center for Scholars, Washington, D.C., Feb. 28, 1983, author's notes, SJMP.
22. For the following account of CBL's relations with Stein, the author is indebted to Mr. Steward's excellent firsthand narrative.
23. Steward, *Dear Sammy*, 31–32.
24. Ibid., 37, 39.
25. Ibid., 39–46.
26. CBL Diary, July 14, 1939.
27. HRL European trip memo to Time-Life staff, 1939, TIA.
28. CBL (signed "A.C.B."), "An American Letter—Europe," *Fortune*, Oct. 1939.
29. Ann Brokaw Diary, July 23, 10, 16, 1939.
30. Ibid., July 24, 1939.
31. CBL, "American Letter."
32. Ibid. In 1939, Poland was the fifth-greatest military power in the world, capable of mobilizing an army larger than that of France. British forces were small in comparison. Tom Shachtman, *The Phony War, 1939–1940* (New York, 1982), 25.
33. CBL to Gertrude Stein, Aug. 16, 1939, YCAL.
34. Ibid.
35. Ann Brokaw Diary, Aug. 14, 1939, CBLP; John Billings Diary, Aug. 14, 1939, JBP.
36. CBL, "American Letter."
37. Ann Brokaw Diary, Aug. 29, 1939, CBLP.
38. John Billings Diary, Aug. 28, 29, 30, 1939, JBP.
39. Robert T. Elson, *Time Inc.: The Intimate History of a Publishing Enterprise, 1923–1941* (New York, 1968), 408.
40. CBL, *Margin for Error* (New York, 1940), 28, 31. In an unpublished introduction to the play, CBL cited TR as inspiration. Ts., n.d., c. 1939, CBLP.
41. CBL, *Margin for Error*, 4.
42. Horst P. Horst, the photographer, objected to CBL's use of his name for "a nasty Nazi." Horst to CBL, Oct. 4., 1939, CBLP.
43. CBL, *Margin for Error*, 24, 91.
44. Ibid., 31.
45. Ibid., 33.
46. George Kaufman to CBL, n.d., CBLP.

47. Max Gordon to CBL, n.d., CBLP.
48. The program stated that "no actual person, living or dead" was depicted in the play.
49. Photograph in CBLP. The *Princeton Packet* reported that *Margin for Error* "breaks all theatrical records for speed of production." Richard Aldrich and Richard Myers had accepted it the day they read it. Contracts were signed at 10 A.M. the following morning, casting took place in a matter of hours, and rehearsals began four days later. *Packet*, Oct. 5, 1939. For a local rave review, see *Daily Princetonian*, Oct. 16, 1939.
50. CBL, *Margin*, 84.
51. Isabel Hill to CBL, n.d. 1939, CBLP; *Time*, Nov. 13, 1939.
52. Alexander King, *Mine Enemy Grows Older* (New York, 1958), 318.
53. Both newspapers, Nov. 4, 1939.
54. Ibid.
55. *Newsweek*, Nov. 20, 1939. Perhaps the most surprising criticism of *Margin for Error* was that of Henry Luce. He agreed to write, or put his name to, a shrewd thirteen-page introduction to the official text published by Random House in 1940. The piece begins by challenging a syndicated article which claimed that "next to the British blockade . . . the cause of the Nazi Reich has not sustained as great a disaster as Clare Boothe's new play . . . launched at the Plymouth Theater to the huzzahs and plaudits of a highly enthusiastic initial audience." *Margin for Error* was indeed wittily satiric of National Socialism, HRL conceded, but it had two serious flaws: a villain deficient in Fascist ferocity, and a press protagonist who was too flabby-minded and platitudinous to be freedom's champion. "The defense of democracy ought not to be left to the unsupported efforts of one Jewish policeman." No other contemporary playwright had produced an entirely successful anti-Nazi work. Even Broadway's liberal conscience, Clifford Odets, offered no effective counter to brutality in his *Till the Day I Die*. "There were no Christs on his barricades . . . no redemption in the blood he spilled." What the stage urgently needed was a writer capable of creating an Average Man "without any particular ax to grind," who could speak out fearlessly on behalf of truth and justice. "That dramatist," HRL regretted to say, "is not, at the moment, my dear wife, Miss Boothe." The fact that CBL countenanced this extraordinarily candid essay speaks volumes for her shrewd sense of publicity. The style is less that of HRL than of a Time-Life wordsmith (probably Noel Busch) rephrasing his boss's views. A few of the sentences read like CBL herself.
56. King, *Mine Enemy*, 318, 319.

28. THE DETERMINING CONDITION

1. John Billings Diary, Sept. 6, 1939, JBP.
2. *Washington Evening Times-Herald*, Sept. 11, 1939.
3. CBL to HRL, qu. him, May 10, 1960, CBLP.
4. Ibid., qu. Dr. Milton Rosenbluth.
5. Ibid.; CBL to Dr. Thompkins, Mar. 17, 1961 (unmailed?), CBLP.
6. CBL to Dr. Rosenbluth, Oct. 20, 1939, CBLP.
7. John Billings Diary, Dec. 11, 1939.
8. CBL to HRL, Dec. 13, 1939, CBLP.

9. HRL to CBL, n.d. c. Dec. 18, 1939, SJMP.
10. CBL and Alexander King, "The Yohimbe Tree," ts. in CBLP.
11. Dan Longwell to CBL, Feb. 3, 1938, CBLP.
12. Alexander King, *Mine Enemy Grows Older* (New York, 1958), 196, 267.
13. King qu. John Billings Diary, Dec. 29, 1939.
14. King, *Mine Enemy*, 268, 267–269.
15. CBL int. SJM, Jan. 6, 1982; HRL to CBL, c. Jan. 1940, CBLP.
16. King ts. in CBLP.
17. HRL to CBL, n.d. c. Feb. 1940, CBLP.
18. CBL to HRL, fragment, n.d. c. Feb. 1935, CBLP.
19. Ann Brokaw Diary, Feb. 4, 1940.
20. John Billings Diary, Feb. 16, 1940.
21. Ann Brokaw Diary, Feb. 18, 1940, CBLP; Walton Wickett to SJM, Nov. 15, 1983, SJMP; John Billings Diary, Mar. 29, 1941, qu. C. D. Jackson's memory of the previous year.
22. HRL to CBL, n.d. c. Feb. 1940.
23. Mark Sullivan to CBL, May 30, 1934, CBLP.
24. HRL to CBL, qu. her, c. mid-Apr. 1940, CBLP.
25. Ibid.

29. Proven Material

1. After *The Women* opened in Los Angeles on Aug. 31, 1939, the careers of Crawford, Fontaine, Goddard, Russell, and Main experienced an upsurge.
2. Rogers wrote CBL that while lunching with Scott Fitzgerald she had noticed three copies of *The Women* on his desk. When she asked him why he had "this collector's mania" for Clare's plays, he replied, "I love her." Elisabeth Cobb Rogers to CBL, n.d. 1938, CBLP.
3. F. Scott Fitzgerald, working notes for his screen adaptation of *The Women,* June 17 and July 2, 1938, MGM. In his first outline Fitzgerald said, "The biggest triumph is not of Mary over Chrystal [sic], but of the home over the more predatory and destructive habits of the female." FSF Notes, 28–29.
4. Gary Carey, *Anita Loos* (New York, 1988), 184. Cukor said, "If the weak scenes got by on stage, they'll get by on screen. And if you try to improve on them, you may unravel everything." Fitzgerald qu. Andrew Turnbull, *The Letters of F. Scott Fitzgerald* (New York, 1963), 33.
5. Anita Loos, *Cast of Thousands* (New York, 1977), 225. Loos wrote that Cukor was ready to start directing when he was "balked by a Board of Censors that removed the best jokes from Clare Luce's script, so George and I had to concoct each scene right there on the set before the cameras started to grind."
6. Production file for *The Women*, MGM. One scene called for $50,000 worth of jewelry. Clifton Fadiman wrote, perhaps with tongue in cheek, "*The Women* is the most convincing argument for homosexuality I have ever encountered." *The Stage*, March 1937; U.K. undated 1986 review by Helen McNeil, SJMP.
7. Ibid. Feminine rivalry became so intense on the set that Cukor warned his cast that anyone caught scene-stealing would be edited out of the final print. This did not deter Rosalind Russell from twice biting and drawing blood from Paulette

Goddard's leg during their knock-down Reno fight. Unidentified London newspaper, CBLP.

8. Twenty-four of Adrian's outfits were for Norma Shearer alone.

9. *New Republic*, Sept. 6, 1939; *New York Times*, Sept. 22, Dec. 31, 1939, Jan. 13, Feb. 28, 1940.

10. *Kiss*, Oct. 1941; *Margin*, Feb. 1943.

30. EUROPE IN THE SPRING

1. CBL Diary, Mar. 4–5, 1940, CBLP; CBL, *Europe in the Spring* (New York, 1940), 34–35. CBL had spent time after docking in Naples touring with Ambassador Joseph P. Kennedy.

2. CBL, *Europe*, 38.

3. Ibid., 52. CBL sketched a vivid cameo of Edda Mussolini Ciano. "She was very pale and emaciated, and her red-gold hair and heavy-lidded eyes slipped by my direct eager glance, like a green wave from the prow of a ship, impersonal, indifferent, curiously cruel and strong. You felt right away that Edda Ciano 'met' nobody. In the course of events you came into contact with her, and then moved on, and she was there, sullen and ambiguous as a March sea, and you were gone." Ibid.

4. Ibid., 54–58. Ciano's diary entry for Mar. 7, 1940, eschews any mention of CBL in favor of the *carbonara* [coal] shortage that had dominated the dinner conversation. Galeazzo Ciano, *The Ciano Diaries, 1939–1943* (New York, 1947), 21.

5. CBL, *Europe*, 59–61.

6. Ibid., 87.

7. Ibid.

8. CBL Diary, Mar. 23–25, 1940, reads "Country Joe." CBLP; Michael Beschloss, *Kennedy and Roosevelt: The Uneasy Alliance* (New York, 1980), 192.

9. HRL to CBL, Mar. 18, 1940; CBL to HRL, Apr. 11, 1940, CBLP; CBL Diary, Apr. 2, 1940. CBLP.

10. CBL, *Europe*, 148–150.

11. Cablegram, Mar. 31, 1940, CBLP.

12. CBL, *Europe*, 150.

13. Ibid., 150–152.

14. CBL met de Chambrun on Long Island in the summer of 1933. As a lawyer in Paris, he had successfully defended Harry in the suit brought by French newspapers against Time Inc.

15. CBL, *Europe*, 152–153, 180, 154.

16. Ibid., 156; René de Chambrun, *I Saw France Fall* (New York, 1940), 102–104; and *Mission and Betrayal, 1940–1945* (Stanford, Calif., 1993), 30.

17. CBL, *Europe*, 157.

18. Ibid., 156–157.

19. Ibid., 159–160; de Chambrun, *I Saw*, 104.

20. CBL, *Europe*, 161–167.

21. CBL cable report to Time-Life editors, Apr. 9, 1940, TIA.

22. CBL to ACB, Apr. 12, 1940, CBLP.

23. Ibid.

24. John Billings Diary, Apr. 11, 1940, JBP.
25. CBL, *Europe*, 172–176.
26. Ibid., 186–187.
27. Ibid., 205, 207.
28. Ibid., 214–215.
29. Ibid., 223–224.
30. Ibid., 225.
31. Ibid., 229.
32. CBL cable report to Time-Life editors, May 11, 1940, TIA.
33. John Billings Diary, May 5, 1940.
34. CBL, *Europe*, 233–234.
35. Ibid., 239–241.
36. Ibid., 245.
37. Ibid., 255.
38. HRL to CBL, May 17, 1940, CBLP.
39. Ibid.
40. CBL, *Europe*, 250.
41. Ibid., 250–251.
42. CBL to John Billings, May 23, 1940, TIA. Also see CBL, *Europe*, 253.
43. CBL int. SJM, Apr. 3, 1987.
44. Ibid.
45. Ibid.; Otto von Habsburg qu. *Time*, Sept. 4, 1989, and to SJM, Sept. 7, 1989, SJMP.
46. CBL int. SJM, Apr. 3, 1987; Otto von Habsburg to SJM, Sept. 7, 1989, SJMP.
47. CBL, *Europe*, 269.
48. "There are no hopeless situations, there are only men who have grown hopeless about them." CBL, *Europe*, 271.
49. Ibid.
50. Ibid., 284–285.
51. Ibid., 33.
52. Harold Nicolson, *Diaries, 1930–1939* (New York, 1966), 359. Oliver Stanley was the son of an earl.
53. CBL to HRL, June 3, 1940, CBLP.
54. CBL, *Europe*, 291.
55. Ibid., 301.
56. The following account is taken from ibid., 302–304.
57. Ibid., 302–304. CBL had come to know Coward well during her years at *Vanity Fair*, and had never quite gotten over her teenage crush on him. But she had long realized that their friendship could not progress beyond mutual admiration. At a business lunch on December 2, 1932, he had thrilled her with the brilliance of his repartee, and complimented her on her editorial expertise. "What a pity he is a fairy," she wrote in her diary that night. SJMP.
58. Ann Brokaw Diary, June 12, 1940, CBLP.
59. HRL to CBL, qu. Billings, cablegram, May 23, 1940, CBLP. Billings praised CBL, in some embarrassment, after having rejected an article by Harry because of its excessive partisanship. John Billings Diary, May 25, 1940.
60. John Billings Diary, June 14, 1940.

NOTES

31. THE DAVID PROBLEM

1. Ann Brokaw Diary, July 7, 1940, CBLP.
2. HRL to CBL, cable, n.d. June 1940, CBLP; Al Morano int. SJM, Oct. 6, 1981; Corinne Thrasher to CBL, June 28, 1940, CBLP.
3. DFB to CBL, July 21, 1939, CBLP.
4. See Ch. 22.
5. DFB to Gladys Freeman, May 28, 1940, CBLP. The bill was for $1,050, in today's terms over ten times as much.
6. Nora Boothe to HRL, enclosing seven invoices, c. July 14, 1940, CBLP; CBL int. SJM, June 24, 1982.
7. HRL to CBL, Mar. 8, 1940, CBLP; Ann Brokaw Diary, June 20, 1940; DFB to CBL (confirming he got $250,000 in four years), Jan. 28, 1940, CBLP. DFB had also taken money from Joel Jacobs.
8. HRL to CBL, Apr. 3, 1940, CBLP.
9. DFB to CBL, July 15, 1940, CBLP.
10. Daniel A. Doran's report to the Luces, July 19, 1940, CBLP.
11. Ibid.

32. RABBLE ROUSER

1. Ann Brokaw Diary, July 24, 1940, CBLP.
2. The following account is based on CBL, "The White House," ts. memorandum, July 25, 1940, CBLP.
3. CBL, *Europe in the Spring* (New York, 1940), 23–24; CBL, "White House."
4. CBL, "White House"; *Europe*, 307.
5. CBL, "The White House."
6. Ann Brokaw Diary, July 29 and 26, 1940.
7. *New York Herald Tribune*, Sept. 29, 1940; *New York Times*, Sept. 22, 1940; *Saturday Review*, Sept. 14, 1940; qu. Allene Talmey, "Clare Boothe . . . in a Velvet Glove," *Vogue*, Dec. 15, 1940.
8. *PM*, Oct. 13, 1940.
9. Helen Lawrenson, "The Woman," *Esquire*, Aug. 1974; CBL int. Marc Pachter, Historian National Portrait Gallery, Mar. 21, 1983.
10. *New York Times*, Aug. 26, 1940, CBLP.
11. CBL to Joseph P. Kennedy, Aug. 26, 1940, CBLP.
12. CBL to Herbert Pell, Sept. 3, 1940, CBLP.
13. Peter Kurth, *American Cassandra: The Life of Dorothy Thompson* (Boston, 1990), 35; CBL int. SJM, June 13, 1982.
14. Dorothy Thompson, "Off the Record," *New York Herald Tribune*, Mar. 29, 1939.
15. CBL to BMB, Oct. 11, 1940, CBLP.
16. The following account is based on a report in the *New York Herald Tribune*, Oct. 16, 1940.
17. Kurth, *American Cassandra*, 325.
18. Luce, Clare Boothe, *Current Biography*, 1942.
19. Dorothy Thompson to Mrs. Henry Winters Luce, n.d. c. Oct. 1940, DTP.
20. *New York Post*, July 22, 1943.

Notes

21. CBL to John S. Mayfield, July 15, 1963, CBLP.
22. *New York Times*, Oct. 20, 1940.
23. *New York Herald Tribune*, Oct. 23, 1940.
24. Ibid.
25. Ibid.
26. CBL scrapbooks, CBLP; Talmey, "Clare Boothe."
27. *Baltimore Sun*, Nov. 3, 1940.
28. *Vogue*, Dec. 15, 1940.
29. CBL to Dorothy Thompson, cablegram, Nov. 6, 1940, CBLP.

33.   THE CANDOR KID

1. CBL to Wilfrid Sheed, May 30, 1973, CBLP.
2. Albert P. Morano int. SJM, Oct. 6, 1981.
3. Unidentified news clip, c. Oct. 20, 1940, CBLP.
4. Margaret Case Harriman, "The Candor Kid I," *New Yorker*, Jan. 4, 1941. In fact Clare was born nearer to Spanish Harlem than Riverside Drive.
5. See also Harriman, "Candor Kid II," *New Yorker*, Jan. 11, 1941.
6. Corinne Thrasher to DFB, Oct. 29, 1940, CBLP.
7. DFB to HRL, Nov. 11, 1940, CBLP; DFB to CBL and HRL, Dec. 23, 1940, CBLP.
8. Transcript in CBLP.
9. Diana Cooper, *Trumpets from the Steep* (Boston, 1960), 68; John Billings Diary, Feb. 27, 1941, JBP; Ann Brokaw Diary, Mar. 12, 1941, CBLP.
10. Henry Luce, "The American Century," *Life*, Feb. 17, 1941.
11. Qu. W. A. Swanberg, *Luce and His Empire* (New York, 1972), 182. The accusation shocked HRL, who considered himself an opponent of colonialism. Billings coined the title and he and Noel Busch worked on "The American Century." HRL complained that his editors had "cut all his transitions, which he admitted were weak, but which he wanted replaced with better stuff." John Billings Diary, Feb. 6, 1941.
12. John Billings Diary, Feb. 8, 1941. CBL went to Washington herself on March 12 and spent the day trying to get a visa, without success. She saw her daughter, who wrote, "Mother told me her big secret . . . why she must go to Germany." ACB Diary, Mar. 12, 1941.
13. Ts. dated Mar. 9, 1941, in CBLP.
14. Peter Bogdanovich, *This Is Orson Welles* (New York, 1992), 74.
15. *New York Times*, May 6, 1941.

34.   WINGS OVER CHINA

1. CBL, "Mr. and Mrs. God," notes for a planned book, "China in the Spring," CBLP.
2. Ibid.
3. HRL, "China to the Mountains," *Life*, June 30, 1941.
4. CBL Diary fragment, n.d. 1941, CBLP.
5. Ibid.; CBL, qu. "Chungking's Broadway," *Vogue*, Sept. 1, 1941.
6. HRL, "China to the Mountains."

NOTES

7. Ibid. Theodore White, *Time*'s correspondent in Chungking, wrote that no visitor he had seen in China, not even Nehru, was received with the deference given the Luces. White, *In Search of History* (New York, 1978), 126.
8. CBL, "Wings over China," *Life*, Sept. 8, 1941.
9. CBL Diary fragment, n.d. 1941.
10. CBL, "Wings over China."
11. CBL Diary fragment, n.d. 1941.
12. HRL, "China to the Mountains," and CBL, "Wings over China."
13. "A friend of the Luces . . . says that one of the few quarrels that ever took place in their home life occurred one evening when Luce remarked that he could not think of anyone who was mentally his superior. His wife felt that this was extreme, and argued with him hotly and in vain, bringing in the names of Einstein (who, Luce objected, is a specialist), and John Kiernan (a freak, said Luce). After five years of marriage Luce has finally convinced his wife that he invariably means what he says." Margaret Case Harriman, "The Candor Kid I," *New Yorker*, Jan. 4, 1941. James Gould Cozzens, who worked briefly at Time Inc. in 1938, corroborated HRL's opinion. "Though in vanity and self-assertion I yield to no man . . . at heart I knew . . . that I was not in his class . . . He was a more considerable person, with a better brain." Qu. Matthew J. Bruccoli, *James Gould Cozzens: A Life Apart* (New York, 1983), 139–140.
14. HRL, "China to the Mountains." According to Steve Neal, *Dark Horse: A Biography of Wendell Willkie* (New York, 1984), 258, the Luces were duped by Chiang's exhibitions of military prowess. In fact over half his soldiers were starving, and peasants were forced to the front tied together by ropes.
15. CBL, "Wings over China."
16. HRL, "China to the Mountains," and CBL, "Wings over China."
17. CBL, "Wings over China."
18. CBL, qu. "Chungking's Broadway."
19. CBL, "America Reorients Itself," address to the Junior League of New York, Jan. 13, 1942, CBLP.
20. Ibid.

35. "SIR CHARLES"

1. CBL int. SJM, June 21, 1982; D. Clayton James, *The Years of MacArthur* (Boston, 1970–1985), II. 79.
2. Faubion Bowers int. SJM, May 1, 1995; Edward Larrabee, *Commander in Chief: Franklin Delano Roosevelt, His Lieutenants, and Their War* (New York, 1987), 333–334.
3. Ann Brokaw Diary, July 7, 1941, CBLP.
4. CBL to CAW, July 25, 1941, CBLP.
5. Ibid.
6. Douglas MacArthur to CBL, Aug. 4, 1941, CBLP.
7. John Billings Diary, Aug. 5, 1941, JBP. Tex McCrary to CBL, n.d. Nov. 1941, re: her *Life* articles: "You still aren't the best editor, but you are easily the best reporter in the racket now." CBLP.
8. Irene Selznick int. SJM, Feb. 4, 1988; CBL qu. Willoughby in her letter to him, July 25, 1941.

9. John Billings Diary, Aug. 23, 1941.

10. CBLP.

11. Diana Cooper, *Trumpets from the Steep* (Boston, 1960), 97; Diana Cooper to Rudolf Kommer, Mar. 26, 1941, copy in CBLP.

12. Cooper, *Trumpets*, 99.

13. CBL, "Destiny Crosses the Dateline," *Life*, Nov. 3, 1941.

14. Ibid.

15. CBL, "The Filipino Nut," unpublished chapter of "China in the Spring," CBLP; CBL debating on "Philippines: Asset or Liability," Univ. of Chicago Round Table broadcast, Nov. 16, 1941, ts. CBLP.

16. CBL, "What Price the Philippines?" *Vogue*, Jan. 2, 1942.

17. Ibid.; CBL, "Filipino Nut." Diana Cooper left Manila on September 9 for Singapore. She wrote CBL from the Manila Hotel. "Goodbye—be happy. I've always had faith in you—tho' shy and inarticulate I felt happy with you this morning. . . . Come and stay with us at Sing Sing." CBLP.

18. CBL, "America Reorients Itself," address to the Junior League of New York, Jan. 13, 1942, CBLP.

19. Ibid.

20. Hart qu. CBL notes, Manila, Oct. 1941, TIA.

21. CBL, "America Reorients."

22. Ibid.

23. CBL, "MacArthur of the Far East," *Life*, Dec. 7, 1941; CBL to Noel Busch, Oct. 17, 1941, CBLP.

24. Ibid.

25. Ibid. At a dinner in Willoughby's apartment with MacArthur towards the end of her stay, CBL became "gloomily prophetic" as she "envisaged an America at war, growing daily more totalitarian." Later that night she told Charles that the United States needed a great military leader and that "MacArthur would either never be heard of again, or he would one day return to the U.S.A. while the whole American people yelled, 'Hail MacArthur.' " CBL reminding Willoughby of the evening in a letter dated "Bastille Day" 1942. CBLP.

26. CBL, "Ever Hear of Homer Lea?" *Saturday Evening Post*, Mar. 7, 14, 1942.

27. CBL, "What Price the Philippines?"

28. CBL int. SJM, June 21, 1982; Charles Willoughby to CBL, May 28, 1945, CBLP; CBL to Willoughby, Jan. 5, 1946, CBLP.

29. CBL int. SJM, June 13, 1982; Charles Willoughby to CBL, Feb. 15, 1945, CBLP.

30. Charles Willoughby to CBL, Aug. 20, 1944, CBLP. The Heidelberg city register showed only the birth of one Adolf August Weidenbach in 1892, to a rope maker of that name. Eric Larrabee, *Commander in Chief* (New York, 1987), 334 qu. *Der Spiegel*, 1951. Willoughby confessed to CBL that he "squirmed" when reporters "probed and dug" for his genealogy. He also said that American citizenship was more valuable to him than a title.

31. News clips in CBLP.

32. Faubion Bowers int. SJM, May 1, 1995; Charles Willoughby to CBL, May 4, 1944, CBLP.

33. Capt. Parker [CBL's Manila driver] diary excerpt, Oct. 5, 1941, ts. CBLP. Influenced by HRL, CBL later became unfailingly punctual in keeping appointments.

34. CBL, "America Reorients."

NOTES

36. Bombed into Greatness

1. *Vogue*, Sept. 1, 1941; *Harper's Bazaar*, Aug. 1941; Walton Wickett int. SJM, Nov. 15, 1983.
2. Ann Brokaw Diary, Oct. 15, 1941, CBLP.
3. ACB to Dorothy B. Holloran, Oct. 17, 1941, CBLP; CBL to Mrs. Reece, Apr. 29, 1937, CBLP. Clare had earlier written of eight-year-old Ann: "Since she is no 'brain' I must make an athlete of her." CBL Diary, Sept. 5, 1932, SJMP.
4. Unless otherwise attributed, the descriptions of ACB here and elsewhere in this book are based on her school reports, diaries, and correspondence in CBLP, supplemented by the author's conversations with CBL, Walton Wickett, Norman Ross, Daphne Root, Evelyn Stansky, and other contemporaries who knew her.
5. CBL to ACB, Nov. 20, 1938, CBLP.
6. Evelyn Stansky int. SJM, Apr. 5, 1988; Malcolm Lovell int. SJM, May 18, 1988.
7. CBL to Isabel Hill, Sept. 2, 1941, CBLP.
8. John Billings Diary, Oct. 18, 1941, JBP; CBL to HRL, Nov. 15, 1941, CBLP.
9. John Billings Diary, Oct. 17–18, 1941.
10. David O. Selznick to CBL, Nov. 21, 1941, CBLP.
11. Ibid.
12. David O. Selznick to CBL, Nov. 29, 1941, CBLP.
13. CBL to Elizabeth Sayre, qu. Stephen Shadegg, *Clare Boothe Luce* (New York, 1970), 132.
14. Gladys Freeman int. SJM, Nov. 10, 1982. CBL, interviewed by Stephen Shadegg in the 1960s, characteristically remembered the butler giving the message to her rather than Harry, whereupon she announced the bombing to their guests. Shadegg, *CBL*, 132. Gladys Freeman was at the Dec. 7 lunch, and recalled it vividly.
15. Elinor Langer, *Josephine Herbst* (Boston, 1983), 245–246. That night, HRL called his father to ask what he thought the outcome of Pearl Harbor might be. The old missionary said that China and America could only be drawn closer. A few hours later Henry Winters Luce, aged seventy-three, died in his sleep. W. A. Swanberg, *Luce and His Empire*, (New York, 1971), 189.
16. John Billings Diary, Dec. 7, 1941.
17. CBL, "A Reappraisal of U.S. Foreign Policy," address to Association of the U.S. Army, Hawaii, June 18, 1975, ts. CBLP.
18. CBL, "Ever Hear of Homer Lea?" *Saturday Evening Post*, Mar. 7, 1942, John Billings Diary, Dec. 31, 1941, Jan. 3, 6, 1942.
19. CBL to ACB, Feb. 5, 1942, CBLP.
20. *Saturday Evening Post*, Mar. 7, 14, 1942.
21. CBL, "The Valor of Homer Lea," introduction to Homer Lea, *The Valor of Ignorance* (New York, 1942), 4.
22. CBL to Irene Selznick, Feb. 2, 1942, Irene Selznick private collection, New York, N.Y.
23. Ts. in CBLP.
24. CBL to ACB, Feb. 5, 1942, CBLP.
25. Walton Wickett int. SJM, Nov. 15, 1983.
26. Ibid.
27. Alexander Hehmeyer to CBL, Oct. 16, 1941, CBLP.

28. "Maggie" to "Felix," unidentified letter forwarded to HRL, Jan. 12, 1942, CBLP.
29. The Horst shoot took place in November 1941. Margaret Case borrowed the dress and gems on behalf of *Vogue*. She gave the costume details to CBL in a letter dated November 12, 1941, CBLP. The portrait illustrating this chapter is different from the one used in the article "The House of a Distinguished Couple," *Vogue*, Feb. 15, 1942.
30. CBL to AEA, Jan. 20, 1942, CBLP.
31. Ibid.
32. Clare told Ann she stayed away from Dr. Austin's funeral because "there were too many people there I didn't want to face again and get all mixed up with after so many years." CBL to ACB, Feb. 5, 1942, CBLP; Albert P. Morano int. SJM, Oct. 6, 1981.
33. Morano int., Oct. 6, 1981.

37. THE ROAD TO MANDALAY

1. Qu. Theodore H. White, *The Stilwell Papers* (New York, 1991), 35.
2. Recalled by Frank Roberts to CBL, Dec. 9, 1942, CBLP.
3. CBL, "By Clipper to African Front," *Life*, Mar. 30, 1942. See Ch. 35.
4. *Life*, Apr. 27, June 1, June 15, June 22, July 13, July 20, 1942.
5. CBL, "Burma Mission I," *Life*, June 15, 1942.
6. Ibid.
7. Ibid.
8. CBL, "Burma Mission II," *Life*, June 22, 1942.
9. Ibid.
10. Ibid.
11. CBL Diary fragment, "On the Road to Mandalay," Apr. 5–8, 1942, CBLP; CBL, "Burma Mission II," *Life*, June 22, 1942.
12. CBL, "The Battle for Egypt," *Life*, July 13, 1942.
13. Ibid.
14. CBL, "Burma Mission II."
15. Jawarharlal Nehru to CBL, Apr. 1, 1942, CBLP; CBL Diary fragment, Apr. 1, 1942; CBL to Frank Roberts, June 28, 1942, CBLP. CBL was not overly impressed with India's military capability, writing that the Allies would find it "risky to turn over vital matters of defense to a bunch of people who have for hundreds of years wrangled and fought as to whether you should kiss a cow or kill it." CBL to David Hulburd, c. Apr. 12, 1942, CBLP.
16. CBL Diary fragment, May 1–5, 1942; CBL int. SJM, June 28, 1982.
17. CBL int. SJM, June 28, 1982; Hugo Vickers, *Cecil Beaton: The Authorized Biography* (London, 1985), 262.

38. THE MOST ABLE WOMAN IN THE UNITED STATES

1. CBL to ACB, Feb. 5, 1942, CBLP.
2. Marilyn Bender and Selig Altschul, *Pan Am, Juan Trippe: The Rise and Fall of an American Entrepreneur* (New York, 1982), 375; CBL int. SJM, June 16, 1982; *Greenwich Times*, June 8, 1942.

3. *Greenwich Times*, June 26, 1942.

4. John Billings Diary, July 1, 1942, JBP.

5. Albert P. Morano int. SJM, Oct. 6, 1981. All subsequent Morano quotes are from this interview.

6. Ibid. Eric Hodgins, a Time-Life senior editor, once said, "Harry just plain disliked giving orders. He would prefer to discuss, to soliloquize, debate and do everything else imaginable in preference." Qu. Robert T. Elson, *The World of Time Inc.: The Intimate History of a Publishing Enterprise, Volume 2: 1941–1960* (New York, 1973), 61.

7. News clip, n.d., CBLP.

8. John Kobler, *Luce, His Time, Life, and Fortune* (New York, 1968), 124–125.

9. Stephen Shadegg, *Clare Boothe Luce* (New York, 1970), 159; *Greenwich Times*, July 22, 1942.

10. CBL to Frank Roberts, July 31, 19, June 28, 1942, CBLP.

11. Ibid., July 31, 1942, CBLP.

12. Shadegg, *CBL*, 159.

13. *Greenwich Press*, Aug. 5, 1942.

14. Morano int., Oct. 6, 1981; Shadegg, *CBL*, 160; *Bridgeport Post* editorial Aug. 5, 1942; *Greenwich Press*, Aug. 5, 1942. CBL met George Waldo on June 16 and made such an impression that he never forgot the date.

15. Ann Brokaw Diary, Aug. 11, 1942, CBLP; theater program, CBLP.

16. John Billings Diary, Oct. 29, 1942; CBL to Alexander King, Mar. 7, 1941, CBLP.

17. The Barter Theatre playbill for the Tenth Annual Drama Festival advertises the play as a new one by "Karl Weidenbach." At school CBL had written under the name of "David Boothe." As a teenage runaway she had called herself "Jacqueline Tanner" (see Ch. 8), and as a teenage poet she had signed three odes with the name "David Ivor Austin." At *Vanity Fair* she used the nom de plume of "Julian Jerome." A draft of her unpublished play "O, Pyramids" (1935) is credited to "John Grace." CBL int. *The Dick Cavett Show*, PBS, Jan. 20, 1981.

18. *New York World-Telegram*, Aug. 14, 1942.

19. *Bridgeport Herald*, c. Aug. 17, 1942, news clip in CBLP.

20. Ann Brokaw Diary, Aug. 15 and 19, 1942. Ann's boyfriend was named Geza Corvin. He was playing the lead in a concurrent production of *There's Always Juliet*. Ibid.

21. Ibid., Aug. 20, 1942.

22. Ibid., Aug. 22, 1942.

23. CBL to BMB, Aug. 27, 1942, CBLP.

24. John Crosson in unidentified Bridgeport newspaper article, Aug. 28, 1942, CBLP; CBL to Cecilia Murray, Aug. 31, 1942, CBLP. "I am aware of the responsibility," she wrote. "It is now my decision to run for Congress and to fight with you for the election."

25. Perhaps sensing HRL's feelings of being neglected, CBL went out of her way to cable affectionately from Port Chester: "Good night my darling and wonderful husband. I know so much of what goes on in your secret heart but what can I do. Always Wiff." Oct. 17, 1942, CBLP.

26. Ann Brokaw Diary, July 5, 1942; John Billings Diary, Sept. 3, 1942. Billings said that Harry was working as managing editor of *Time* "two weeks on, one week off" and was "short-tempered and unreasonable."

27. *Hartford Courant*, Sept. 11, 1942; *New York Daily News*, Sept. 11, 1942; Faye Henle, *Au Clare de Luce: Portrait of a Luminous Lady* (New York, 1943), 150. *Time* reported on her spectacles and the reaction to them in its Sept. 21, 1942, issue.

28. CBL address, ts. in CBLP.

29. When State Chairman Bradley informed Kellems that he was supporting CBL, she accused him and Committeeman Pryor of "dictating Mrs. Luce's nomination in order to . . . repay Henry Luce for the thousands he poured into Mr. Willkie's campaign." *New York Sun*, Sept. 4, 1942; Ann Brokaw Diary, Sept. 10, 1942; *Time*, Sept. 18, 1942.

30. Ann Brokaw Diary, Sept. 10, 1942. Former President Herbert Hoover sent her a congratulatory telegram: "You will be a most valuable addition to the government of this country." Sept. 15, 1942, HHP.

31. *New York Herald Tribune*, Sept. 15, 1942.

32. Morano int., Oct. 6, 1981.

33. Shadegg, *CBL*, 163.

34. Memorandum, n.d., CBLP. Congressman Downs incurred only $3,302 in expenses.

35. Henle, *Au Clare*, 150, 153.

36. Ibid., 146.

37. Ibid., 148, 144.

38. Ibid., 142; *Waterbury Republican*, Sept. 19, 1942; *Greenwich Times*, Oct. 2, 1942.

39. Ibid., quoting a broadcast speech of Gov. Robert T. Hurley.

40. Wesley Bailey Campaign Diary, Oct. 31, 1942, CBLP; *Current Biography*, 1942.

41. Henle, *Au Clare*, 154. Miss Thompson further said, over WSSR radio: "I am for Clare Boothe Luce for the same basic reason I was for the President [in 1940]—I believe that she knows more about world affairs than the other candidate." News clip, CBL scrapbooks, CBLP; Henle, *Au Clare*, 153.

42. *Greenwich Times*, Nov. 2, 1942; Morano int., Oct. 6, 1981.

43. *New York Daily News*, Nov. 11, 1942; Bailey Campaign Diary, Nov. 3, 1942. CBL was accompanied at dinner and to campaign headquarters by HRL, Elisabeth Moore and her husband, Maurice, John Gunther, and ACB's boyfriend Geza Corvin. ACB had returned to Stanford University.

44. *Long Island Star Journal* and *Bridgeport Telegram*, Nov. 4, 1942. Downs, haggard and unshaven, conceded: "I guess I just haven't got glamor." Shadegg, *CBL*, 165. An Independent polled 250. *New York World-Telegram*, Nov. 4, 1942. *Sunday Worker*, Aug. 13, 1944, noted that CBL's 1942 win was made possible by the Socialist candidate's 15,573 votes.

45. *Bridgeport Telegram*, Nov. 4, 1942; Bailey Campaign Diary, Nov. 3, 1942. Later she would give Morano a watch engraved with the legend "You can't miss." Morano int., Oct. 6, 1981.

46. Bailey Campaign Diary, Nov. 3, 1942; Henle, *Au Clare*, 156.

47. CBL to ACB, Feb. 5, 1942, CBLP. In the ts. CBL actually wrote, "First lady Vice-President."

INDEX

Abbott, George, 6
Abide With Me (Luce), 4, 5, 233–34, 237,
    276–79, 289, 326
Ackerman, P. Dodd, 276
Acton, Harold, 370
Adrian, Gilbert A., 367
Agee, James, 268
Agha, Mehemed Fehmy, 172, 180, 212–13,
    510n, 512n, 527n
Aitken, Russell, 337
Aix-les-Bains, 147, 344, 346, 348, 358
Aladin, Alexis, 86–90, 87, 502n, 523n
    CBL's correspondence with, 89, 90, 92, 94,
    503n
Alajálov, Constantin, 188, 215, 232
Aldrich, Richard, 354, 355, 533n
Alexander, Grand Duke of Russia, 168
Alexander, John, 323
Alexander, Sir Harold, 452, 455–56
"All Clare on the Western Front" (Parker),
    397
Altschul, Frank, 226
"Amazon at Night" (Luce), 234–35
Ameche, Don, 324
"American Century, The" (H. R. Luce),
    410–11, 538n
American Piano Company, 21, 24, 495n
American Tragedy, An (Dreiser), 177
"America Reorients Itself" (Luce), 446
"Ananias Preferred" (Luce), 172
Anderson, John, 13
Anderson, Maxwell, 6
Anderson, Sherwood, 173, 512n
Anthony, Susan B., 121
Apple Blossoms (Kreisler), 80
Architectural Forum, 251, 274
Arlen, Michael, 266
Astor, Nancy, 378
Atkinson, Brooks, 13, 278, 324, 356
Atlantic City, N.J., 137, 239
Auchinleck, Sir Claude, 457, 458

Austin, Albert Elmer, 74–77, 76, 116, 149,
    220, 247, 279, 302, 390, 406
    Ann Clare's death and, 309, 310, 312
    CBL's relationship with, 74, 75–76, 103–4,
    159, 181, 335, 510n
    death of, 448, 542n
    divorce of, 77, 81, 86, 100
    European travels of, 86, 88, 90, 101, 103–5,
    107
    health problems of, 251, 406, 448
    marital problems of, 158, 198, 219, 312
    in politics, 335, 406, 460, 461
    second marriage of, 100–101, 312, 504n
Austin, Ann Clare (Schneider/Snyder/
        Franklin/Murphy/Boothe; mother),
    21–30, 33–47, 55, 67–82, 90, 99–101,
    116, 151, 255, 266, 294, 302, 310,
    447–48
    ambition of, 4, 21, 39, 42, 45
    beauty of, 21, 39, 44, 90
    Brokaw and, 116, 124, 125, 128, 131, 145,
    153, 157
    CBL influenced by, 4, 16, 33, 45–46, 50,
    58, 90, 92, 96, 99, 101, 116, 117, 131,
    198, 255
    CBL's beaux and, 90, 92, 96, 98, 99, 101,
    103, 104, 116, 117, 118
    CBL's correspondence with, 54, 125, 127,
    143, 147, 155–58, 200, 219–20, 274, 302,
    508n, 509n
    CBL's marriages and, 122–25, 124, 279
    CBL's pregnancies and, 133, 134
    CBL's relationship with, 45, 54, 55, 57, 61,
    81, 94, 104, 117, 123, 124, 125, 150,
    157–60, 219–20, 262, 274, 302, 498n
    in CBL's writing, 203
    charm of, 39, 44, 55, 90, 302
    creative writing of, 40
    cruelty of, 45–46
    David's relationship with, 45, 69–70, 146,
    158–59, 310

Austin, Ann Clare *(cont'd)*:
  death of, 302, 309–13, 464
  diary of, 135–36, 302, 312, 464
  "divorce" of, 39–40, 72, 312
  European travels of, 46–47, 47, 85–86, 88,
    90, 101, 103–5, 107, 146, 147, 159, 162
  family background of, 21–23, 50
  feminism of, 112
  in Florida, 143, 246, 247, 251, 252, 302,
    309–10, 312
  granddaughter and, 158, 159, 198, 200,
    247, 266, 302, 303, 308, 310, 464
  at Greenbrier, 80–81, 100, 319
  health problems of, 219
  jewelry store job of, 44, 64
  male companions of, 44, 46–48, 52–54, 53,
    64, 65, 72–77, 100; *see also* Jacobs, Joel
  marital problems of, 158, 198, 219, 312
  marriage of, 100–101, 312, 504n
  mysterious disappearances of, 30, 36, 44,
    219
  photographs of, 22, 31, 47, 78, 124, 124,
    303, 311
  pregnancies and childbirths of, 4, 15, 21,
    23–24
  in Sound Beach, 54, 68–80, 82, 92, 93, 158,
    198, 302
  William's death and, 153
  William's deteriorating relationship with,
    30, 33, 34, 38–40
Austin, Mrs. (Albert's first wife), 77
Austria, 105, 270–73, 317, 321, 377
"A.V.G. Ends Its Famous Career, The" (Luce),
    450

"Bachelors Do Not Marry" (Luce), 172–73
Bailby, Léon, 321
Bailey, Wesley, 468, 470
Baker, Josephine, 110
Baker, Newton D., 196
Baldwin, Raymond, 465
Balsam, Ruth, 60, 77, 79, 99
Baltimore Sun, 81, 194, 404
Bankhead, Tallulah, 6
Barnes, Howard, 278
Barrymore, Ethel, 3, 60
Barton, Ralph, 236
Baruch, Annie, 192, 218, 223, 224, 225, 254,
    257, 279, 315
Baruch, Bernard, 192–200, 193, 223–27, 238,
    239–40, 257, 261, 285, 308, 399, 514n
  CBL's affair with, 192–93, 195, 198, 199,
    200, 202–8, 218, 220–21, 223–25, 227,
    254, 255, 275–76, 315, 524n
  CBL's campaign with, 461, 464–65
  CBL's correspondence with, 199, 202,
    204–5, 272, 275–76, 464–65
  CBL's plays and, 5, 279, 289, 294
  gift giving of, 207, 275–76, 327, 515n, 529n
  at spas, 199, 202, 204–5, 271–72, 275
  World War II and, 325, 371
Baruch, Donald, 276

"Battle for Egypt, The" (Luce), 450, 456–57,
    458
Beachmound, 141, 144
Beal, Robert C., 145, 159
Beaton, Cecil, iv, 164, 213–14, 216, 457
Beaux Arts Architects' Ball, 137, 138, 139,
    140
Beaverbrook, Maxwell Aitken, Lord, 317,
    318, 341, 348
Behrman, S. N. "Sam," 240
Belasco, David, 42
Belgium, 89, 375, 379–81, 384–85, 394–95,
    414, 443
Belmont, Alva, 111–14, 120–21, 121, 124,
    135, 145, 173, 222, 517n
Belmont, Oliver, 111
Benchley, Robert, 165
Benedik, Billy, 132, 141
Beneš, Eduard, 321, 350
Benét, Stephen Vincent, 155, 250
Benny, Jack, 351
Berlin, 103–5, 201, 319–21
Berlin, Irving, 3, 506n
Bermuda, 143, 323, 407
Between the Curtains (Kahlo), 329, 472, 530n
Biarritz, 127–28, 141
Biddle, Anthony, 348
Bilignin, 344–48, 345
Billings, John, 249, 251, 261, 268, 278, 294,
    325, 410, 441, 527n–28n, 536n, 538n
  diary of, 279–80, 285, 317, 388, 543n
  Life and, 288, 291, 357, 363, 376, 380, 383,
    387, 423, 424, 436–37, 439, 460, 525n
"Birthday of Barge, the Banker, The" (Luce),
    531n
Bismarck, Otto von, 65, 500n
blacks, 37, 233, 320, 461
  in South, 29–30, 33, 223, 261, 298–99
Black Watch (yacht), 135
Blair, Martha, 237
Bloomer, Amelia, 121
Blumenthal, George, 529n
Blunt, Vernon, 96–98, 97, 107, 108, 144–47,
    507n
Blunt, Wilfrid Scawen, 96
Booth, Edwin, 19–20
Booth, John Wilkes, 20
Boothe, Anne Clare, *see* Luce, Clare Boothe
Boothe, Charles (uncle), 149
Boothe, David (brother), ix, 44, 69–72, 230,
    237, 279, 308, 363, 391
  birth of, 24, 70, 496n
  CBL compared with, 389–90
  CBL's ambition for, 102, 103
  CBL's correspondence with, 146, 159, 266,
    390, 410, 509n
  CBL's relationship with, 37–38, 50, 61, 72,
    82, 100, 145–46, 150, 159, 160, 219, 262,
    266–67, 294, 389–90, 392, 409–10,
    509n, 523n
  childhood of, 25–26, 29, 30, 33, 36–40,
    43–46

divorce of, 392, 396
education of, 37, 39, 43, 62, 69, 70, 497n
in financial scandals, 141, 145–46, 151, 159, 391–92
health problems of, 158, 239, 251–52, 267, 390
HRL's relationship with, 259, 389–92, 408–10
in Marines, 70, 72, 146, 158
marriage of, 390
mother's beaux and, 46, 52, 54
mother's death and, 309, 310
mother's marriage and, 100–101, 504n
mother's relationship with, 45, 69–70, 146, 158–59, 310
at Ryan School of Aeronautics, 408–10, 409
sexuality of, 50, 389
Simpson investigation of, 128–29
in Sound Beach, 54, 69, 71–72, 77, 158, 162, 198
Boothe, Edward (uncle), 16, 20, 220, 239
on William, 17, 18, 21, 25–26, 495n
Boothe, Ida, see Keables, Ida Boothe
Boothe, Isa Hill (William's first wife), 19
Boothe, John (uncle), 149, 153
Boothe (Booth), John William Thomas (grandfather), 16–17, 20
Boothe, Laura Brauss (William's second wife), 19, 19, 20, 24–25, 39, 495n, 496n
Boothe, Nora Dawes (sister-in-law), 390, 391, 392, 396
Boothe, Sarah Rebecca Deaver (grandmother), 16, 17
Boothe, Versa (William's third wife), 148–49, 152
Boothe, William Franklin (father), 4, 15–21, 19, 24–40, 49, 112, 123, 149–53, 312, 497n
ambition of, 18, 20, 29, 32
CBL's correspondence with, 21, 40, 72, 149–52
CBL's lovers compared with, 88, 192
CBL's relationship with, 25–26, 30, 33, 34–35, 40, 71–73, 148–52, 166, 496n
David compared with, 45, 72
death of, 18, 40, 70, 100, 152–53, 220, 312
divorces of, 19, 25, 39, 100, 149, 495n
family background of, 16–17
financial problems of, 30, 31, 36, 141, 148–52
health problems of, 141, 149, 152
marriages of, 18–19, 20, 24–25, 148–49
physical appearance of, 18, 19, 32, 39, 71
pseudonyms of, 28–40, 32
reappearance of, 70–74, 100, 501n
as salesman, 15, 19–21, 24–25, 29, 36, 149
violin playing and musicianship of, 17, 18, 29, 32–33, 32, 71, 149–50, 151, 152–53, 436, 497n
Bourke-White, Margaret, 291
Boutet, Frédéric, 168
Bracken, Brendan, 317

Bradley, J. Kenneth, 462, 465, 544n
Brauss, Laura Olivia, see Boothe, Laura Brauss
Brennan, William H., 468–69, 470, 471
"Brereton" (Luce), 450
Bret-Koch, Raymond, 216
Breton, André, 329, 530n
Brice, Fanny, 3, 10
Brockhurst, Gerald, 531n
Brokaw, Ann Clare (daughter), 228, 230, 246, 259, 281, 305, 387
appearance of, 308, 434
baptism of, 141
birth of, 133–34
CBL compared with, 177, 308, 436, 464
CBL's correspondence with, 445, 459–60, 473
CBL's plays and, 12, 234
CBL's relationship with, 143, 147, 220, 245, 349, 363, 434, 436, 466, 523n, 541n
dating of, 436, 445, 464, 543n
diary of, 251–52, 259, 310, 339, 349, 389, 396, 434, 436, 465, 538n
education of, 220, 251–52, 275, 308–9, 363, 434, 436, 445
European travels of, 262, 266–70, 268, 272–73, 343, 349–50, 410–12
father's relationship with, 147, 157, 220, 266
grandmother and, 158, 159, 198, 200, 247, 266, 302, 303, 308, 310, 464
health problems of, 198, 220
inheritance of, 184, 266
inner turmoil of, 445, 465, 523n
loneliness of, 251–52, 445
music studies of, 153, 239, 436
parents' divorce and, 153, 154, 156, 162–63, 220, 266
photographs of, 134, 144, 162, 268, 303, 435, 467
Brokaw, Clare Boothe, see Luce, Clare Boothe
Brokaw, Elvira Gould (mother-in-law), 115, 116, 119, 129, 136, 240
Brokaw, Frances Seymour (George's second wife), 184, 186
Brokaw, George Tuttle (first husband), 115–17, 119–41, 143–49, 166
alcoholism of, 4, 123, 124, 126, 130–32, 143, 144, 145, 147, 148, 151, 153, 156, 157, 162, 168, 266
background of, 115–16
CBL's correspondence with, 116, 122
CBL's courtship with, 116, 119–20
CBL's divorce from, 5, 11, 140–41, 147, 148, 149, 153–57, 266, 310
CBL's engagement to, 120–21
CBL's first meeting with, 115–16
CBL's investigation of, 156
CBL's marriage to, 122–25, 124, 222, 240
CBL's plotting of escape from, 140–41, 145, 147, 148, 149

Brokaw, George Tuttle (cont'd):
  CBL's problems with, 127, 130–31, 137,
    144, 145, 147–48, 168
  CBL's writing and, 4, 11, 12, 174, 203, 233
  death of, 266, 523n
  European travels of, 126–28, 130, 141,
    145–48, 344
  health problems of, 143, 147, 344
  last will and testament of, 120, 266
  mansions of, 115, 129–30, 131, 134, 135,
    140, 145, 147, 153, 266
  photographs of, 119, 130, 138
  Republicanism of, 148, 183
  second marriage of, 184, 186
  sexuality of, 126, 137, 147–48, 152
  wealth of, 4, 115, 143, 266, 505n
Brokaw, Howard (brother-in-law), 124
Brokaw, Irving (brother-in-law), 128
Brokaw, Isaac Vale (father-in-law), 115, 129
Brokaw, Nanny (George's aunt), 154–55
Bromonia Company, 24–25
Brooke, Rupert, 78
Brooke-Popham, Sir Henry, 433
Broun, Heywood, 314
Brousse, Charles, 373, 374
Brown, John Mason, 324, 340, 494n
Bruce, Ezra, 18
Brussels, 379–81, 397, 414
Buchan, John, 89
Buchanan, Jack, 318
Bullard, Rose, 123
Bullitt, William, 321, 379, 386
Burke-Roche, Francis (Frank), 101–2, 103,
    105–9, 127, 137
Burke-Roche, Maurice, 101
Burma, 450–52, 453, 454
"Burma Mission" (Luce), 450–56
Burns, Dorothy, 123, 133, 154
Busch, Noel, 437, 441, 533n, 538n
Butts, James, 79
Bystander (London), 319
Bytel, Miriam, 55, 56

Caetani, Donna Cora, 370
Caldwell, Erskine, 6
"Candor Kid, The" (Harriman), 407–8
Cap-Ferrat, 265–66, 268–70, 268
Capone, Al, 171
Carmania, RMS, 46–47
Carreño, Teresa, 20, 495n
Carroll, Madeleine, 386–87
Carter, John Franklin, 181–82, 194–95, 196,
    518n
Carter, Thomas, 34
Caruso, Bruno, 153
Caruso, Enrico, 65
Casa Genotta, 229, 518n–19n
Case, Frank, 512n
Case, Margaret, 164, 335, 364, 370, 542n
Castle School, 58–61, 59, 64–67, 66, 136,
    499n–500n
"Catch, The" (Luce), 174

Cathedral School of St. Mary, 55–58, 60, 61,
    499n
Catholics, Catholic Church, 30, 80, 406
Celery-Ade, 32, 33
"Ce qu'on sème on récolte" (What one sows
    one reaps) (Luce), 65
Challenge to Defeat (Hale), 201
Chamberlain, Neville, 324–25, 349, 351, 378,
    381
Chambers, Arthur, 18
Chartwell, 238–39
Chase, Edna Woolman, 161–66, 510n
Chase, Ilka, 7, 9, 291, 337
Chavez, Carlos, 153
Chennault, Claire, 450
Chevalier, Maurice, 371–72
Chiang Kai-shek, 414–16, 449, 451, 452, 453,
    539n
Chicago, Ill., 36–39, 70, 128, 154, 203–4, 306
  Democratic convention in (1932), 191–92,
    194–98, 197
"Chic for the Newly Arrived" (Luce), 163–64
China, 171, 249, 345, 412–20, 415, 422, 423,
    438, 439, 443–44, 539n, 541n
Chou En-lai, 418
Chungking, 413–16, 415, 418–20
Churchill, Randolph, 238–39, 341, 524n
Churchill, Winston, 26, 89, 238, 325, 348,
    351, 381, 395, 407, 423, 520n
Ciano, Count Galeazzo, 370–71, 387, 535n
Ciano, Edda, 370, 371, 535n
Cinderella (play), 5, 64
Citizen Kane (movie), 412
Clair, Helen, 323
"Clare Doesn't Care" (King), 362
Clemens, Paul Lewis, 337
Cloister, The, 228–31
Club Mirador, 132–33
Cobb, Elisabeth (Buff), 56, 57, 237, 266, 327,
    365, 494n
Cobb, Irvin S., 56–57, 184
Cobb, Mrs. Irvin, 57
Coffin, Gladys Baker, 519n
Coffin, Henry Sloane, 141
Coffin, Howard, 230–31, 285, 519n
Colette, 165
Condé Nast Publications, Inc., 161–62, 177,
    510n
"Confessions of a Trojan Horse" (Luce),
    333–34
Congress, U.S., 85, 88, 195, 196
  CBL's race for, 448, 459–73, 467, 470
  ERA and, 111, 113
Conte di Savoia, 262–65
"Contentment" (Luce), 78
Cooper, Alfred Duff, 424, 425, 427
Cooper, Lady Diana, 110–11, 424–25, 427,
    510n, 540n
Corrias, Frances Brokaw, 505n
Corvin, Geza, 543n
Covarrubias, Miguel, 165, 215, 225–26, 231,
    327, 330, 531n

INDEX

Coward, Noel, 6, 86, 165, 386–87, 399, 494n, 502n, 536n
Cowles, Edward, 520n–11n
Cowley, Malcolm, 184
Cozzens, James Gould, 539n
Craighead, Walter B., 24, 25
Crawford, Joan, 365, 367, *367*, 464, 534n
Cripps, Sir Stafford, 456–57
Crotch Island, 200–206
Crowninshield, Francis Welch (Frank), 165–67, 169, 171–74, 181, 182, 184, 194–95, 208, 211–12, 214, 237, 516n
  CBL's correspondence with, 191–92, 239
  Frida Kahlo *retablo* and, 331, 339
Cuba, 247, 252, 281–84
Cudahy, John, 379, 380
Cukor, George, 299, 365–67, 534n
Cushman, James S., 115
Cushman, Mrs. James S., 115, 141
Czechoslovakia, 317, 319, 321, 324, 325, 377, 443

Daladier, Edouard, 325, 374
Dalí, Salvador, 323
Dalrymple, Jean, 233–34
Dana, Viola, 50–51
Daniels, Josephus, 196
Davidson, Jo, 337–38, 531n
Davis, Norman H., 341
Davis, Richard Harding, 56
Dawes, Nora, *see* Boothe, Nora Dawes
Day of the Saxon (Lea), 431
Days Without End (O'Neill), 229
"Dear Divorced, The" (Luce), 172
de Chambrun, René, 226, 373–76, 386, 535n
Déclassé (play), 60
DeMille, Cecil B., 171
Democrats, Democratic party, 85, 200, 206, 218
  in election of 1940, 396–406
  in election of 1942, 460, 462, 469, 470, 471, 544n
  1932 convention of, 191–92, 194–98, *197*
Dennison's Manufacturing Company, 93–94, 113
Depression, Great, 165, 166–67, 169, 170, 181, 182, 201, 257, 510n
"Destiny Crosses the Dateline" (Luce), 437
de Villers, Yves, 498n
de Wolfe, Elsie, 145, 343
diary of CBL, 85, 134, 184, 372
  abortion in, 94–96, 503n
  of 1918, 60, 61, 64
  of 1919, 70, 75–77, 500n, 501n
  of 1923, 102, 104, 105, 110, 114
  of 1926, 137, 139
  of 1930, 180, 181, 183
  of 1932, 192, 198, 199, 203, 206, 208, 209, 216–17, 220, 221, 514n, 536n, 541n
Dickens, Charles, 19, 57, 82
Dietrich, Marlene, 186, 333, 525n, 529n

Dimnet, L'Abbé, 155
divorce, 172, 510n
  adultery and, 25, 39, 147
  Reno, 153–56, 174, 178, 253, 264, 270, 274, 508n
  see also specific people
"Domestic Questionnaire" (Luce), 256–57
Donovan, Hedley, 317
"Double-Bind, The" (Luce; incomplete autobiographical novel), 23, 26–28, 496n, 499n
Downs, Leroy, 460, 462, 469, 470, 471, 544n
Draper, Dorothy, 323
Drawbridge, 61
Dreiser, Theodore, 177
Driftway (Sound Beach house), 68–74, 69, 77, 159, 198, 219, 447, 500n
Drinkwater, John, 63
Dufy, Raoul, 530
Duke, Doris, 425

Eagels, Jeanne, 510n
Eden, Anthony, 348
Edison, Thomas Alva, 4, 51
Edward, Prince of Wales, *see* Windsor, Duke of
Einstein, Albert, 182, 354, 355
Eisenstaedt, Alfred, 286, 322, 333
Elder, Ruth, 145
Elizabeth, Queen of England, 393
Elliott, Maxine, 274
Elwes, Simon, 386–87
Emerson, Ralph Waldo, 406
Entirely Irregular (Obermer and Luce), 143–44
Episcopalianism, 37, 55–56
Equal Rights Amendment (ERA), 111, 113
Esquire, 231, 494n, 498n
Europe in the Spring (Luce), 388, 389, 393, 395, 396–97, 422
Evans, Evan, 511n
"Ever Hear of Homer Lea?" (Luce), 441
"Exhale Gently" (Luce), 174
"Ex-Wives' Tale" (Luce), 174

Facts, see Time
Fadiman, Clifton, 534n
Fair, Joyce, 49
fascism, 257, 314, 337, 343, 432, 445
  Margin for Error and, 351–56, 533n
  see also specific countries
Feigenbaum, Dorian, 160
feminism, 111–14, 120–21, 222, 234–35
Ferber, Edna, 6
Fermoy, Lord, 101
Field, Mrs. Marshall, 196
"Fingered Octaves and Primary Extension Exercises" (W. F. Boothe), 153
Fitzgerald, F. Scott, 161, 165, 365–66, 534n
Flanner, Janet, 396
Florida, 143, 246, 247, 251, 252, 302, 309–10
Fontaine, Joan, 365, 534n
Fontanne, Lynn, 6, 397
Ford, Corey, 182

Forrestal, James, 196, 237
Fortune, 171, 241, 251, 272, 274, 283, 300, 348–49
Fosdick, Harry Emerson, 115
Four Saints in Three Acts (Thomson), 232–33
Foxcroft School, 308–9, 363, 436
France, 111, 444, 532n
  CBL in, 47, 47, 88–92, 91, 103, 105–6, 126–28, 141, 146–48, 237, 239, 265–66, 268–70, 274–75, 319, 321, 343–48, 371–77, 381–85
  fascism in, 321, 343
  Germany's relations with, 104, 105, 324–25
  World War II and, 369, 371–78, 381–87, 395, 443
Franco, Francisco, 432
Franklin, Ann Clare, *see* Austin, Ann Clare
Franklin, David, *see* Boothe, David
Franz Ferdinand, Archduke of Austria, 49
Freeman, Donald, 166–69, 167, 172–75, 177–79, 181, 233, 438
  CBL's affair with, 168, 178, 180, 185, 187–90, 200, 205–10, 227
  CBL's correspondence with, 177–78, 185–87, 189–90, 195, 198, 205–9, 510n, 511n, 524n–25n
  death of, 208–11, 516n
Freeman, Gladys, 168, 181, 208, 297, 323, 343, 349, 390
Freeman, Mrs. (Donald's mother), 168, 181, 208, 210
Freud, Sigmund, 126, 532n
Freudenberger, Herbert J., 74
Front Page, The (Hecht and MacArthur), 219
Frowert, Dorothy, 46, 52, 123
Frowert, Percival K., 46, 75
Fuller, Buckminster, 232, 237, 457
Fuller, Horace, 377, 378
Furness, Thelma, 141

Gable, Clark, 366, 525n
Gabriel, Gilbert, 278
"Gaiety of Nations" (Luce's work-in-progress), 258, 261
Gallico, Paul, 5, 207, 211, 219, 224, 226–27, 511n
Gamelin, Maurice, 372, 381, 382
Garbo, Greta, 248
Garden, Mary, 37, 39, 497n
Garner, John Nance, 196, 197, 198, 225
Garvin, J. L., 378
Gaston, Bill, 200, 202, 205, 206, 209, 237
Genthe, Arnold, 216
George V, King of England, 86
George VI, King of England, 374
Germany, Imperial, 50, 57, 65
Germany, Nazi, 317, 319–21, 324–25, 347–51, 354, 410–12, 443–44
  World War II and, 350, 351, 371, 373–87, 396, 407, 440–41, 456
Germany, Weimar, 103–5, 319
Gershwin, George, 216

Gibbons, Cedric, 366
Gibbs, Wolcott, 300, 303, 304
Gielgud, John, 6
Gilbert, Douglas, 13
Gillmore, Margalo, 8, 9, 292
Gilmore, Frank, 277
Gingold, Josef, 153
Gish, Lillian, 42
Glyn, Elinor, 171
Goddard, Paulette, 365, 367, 534n–35n
Golden, John, 219, 233, 234, 237, 516n–17n
Goldman, Sachs, 181, 510n
Gone With the Wind (movie), 299, 314, 366, 368
Good Little Devil, A (play), 42
Gordon, Max, 3, 5–6, 289–94, 317, 318, 354, 365, 468, 529n
Gordon, Ruth, 6
Gould, Jay, 145
Grandi, Count Dino, 318
Grayson, Cary, 196
Great Britain, 88–89, 98, 117, 118
  appeasement and, 324–25, 349
  CBL in, 86, 101–3, 238–39, 317–19, 340–43, 348–50, 378, 385
  World War II and, 349, 369, 371, 374–78, 381, 384–87, 396, 402, 406–7, 443, 456–57, 458, 532n
Great White Ball, 91–92
Greenbrier Hotel, 80–81, 100, 234, 260–61, 287, 288, 319, 522n
Greenwich, Conn., Luce residences in, 279, 286–87, 289, 323, 335
Greenwich Hospital, 74, 76, 94, 133
Greenwich Times, 312, 460, 470–71
Griffith, D. W., 42
Gropper, William, 184, 215
Grover, Allen, 323
Guilfoyle, Paul, 237
Gulick and Brokaw, 116, 131
Gunther, John, 343, 349

Habsburg, Otto von, 384
Hadden, Briton, 250, 251
Hale, Dorothy, 237, 240, 264
  suicide of, 326–32, 332, 339, 394, 529n–30n
Hale, Gardner, 327
Hale, William Harlan, 201, 206, 212, 228, 237, 279, 529n
  CBL's affair with, 201–2, 208, 211, 218, 221, 431, 515n
Halifax, Lord, 318, 458
Hambleton, John, 7
Hamilton, Alexander, 200
Harding, Warren G., 85, 124
Harper's Bazaar, 434
Harriman, Averell, 273, 397
Harriman, Margaret Case, 167, 174–75, 182, 407–8, 512n
Harriman, Mrs. Averell, 273
Harris, Jed, 529n

Hart, Moss, 3, 6, 336, 531n
  The Women and, 3, 5, 11, 290–95, 493n
Hart, Thomas, 426, 427–28, 440
Hawaii, 26, 305, 307–8, *307*, 420, 425, 427, 439–40
Haxton, Gerald, 265
Hayden, John, 276
Hayes, Helen, 6, 399
Hays, Ross, 18
Hazlitt, William, 393
Hearst, William Randolph, 145, 197, 395
Hearst newspapers, 238, 239
Heart of a Waif, The (movie), 51–52, *51*, 306
Hecht, Ben, 219, 250
Heifetz, Jascha, 150
Hellman, Lillian, 283
Hemingway, Ernest, 247
Henderson, Sir Nevile, 319
Hepburn, Katharine, 399
Heppe, Ramsdall and Dearborn, 19
Herbst, Josephine, 439
Hergesheimer, Joseph, 257
Herrick, Robert, 96
Higinbotham, William, 46–48, 52, 124
Hill, Isa, 19
Hill, Isabel, 323, 436
Hitler, Adolf, 105, 171, 317, 319, 320–21, 347–52, 354, 410, 431, 517n
  appeasement and, 324–25, 349
  World War II and, 371, 374, 376, 377, 379, 380, 396
Hobcaw, 223–25, *223*, 253–61, 285
Hobson, Laura, 214, 240, 242, 248–49, 253, 267, 521n
  at Hobcaw, 254, 257, 258–59
Hobson, Thayer, 203, 214, 240, 242, 248, 253
Holland, 375, 378–79, 443
Hollywood, Calif., 184–87, *187*, 305–7, *305*, 327, 365–68, 437–38
Holman, Libby, 3
Hoover, Herbert, 148, 183, 204, 206, 216–17, 230, 544n
Hoover, Lou, 216, 217
Hopkins, Harry, 272, 326–28, 394–96
Horace Liveright Inc., 188, 189, 201, 361
Horst, 333, 446, *447*, 542n
Hot Springs, Va., 144–45
Hotz, Lila Ross, *see* Luce, Lila Ross Hotz
"Hound of Heaven, The" (Thompson), 109
House, The, 323, 460–63
Hovey, Richard, 230
Howe, Louis, 226
Hudson Theatre Stock Company, 42
Hughes, Charles Evans, 226
Hull, Cordell, 354–55
Hurgronje, Snouck, 378–79
Huxley, Aldous, 170

Ickes, Harold L., 259
India, 451, 454, 455, 457, 542n

Ingersoll, Ralph, 62, 244–45, 260, 282–84, 306, 308, 526n
  Life and, 283–84, 287, 288, 291
Italy, 324, 325, 444, 518n, 535n
  World War II and, 369–71, 374, 386

Jacobs, Joel (Riggie), 52–54, *53*, 65, 77, 80, 81, 82, 90, 128, 158, 198, 220, 499n
  Ann Clare's marriage and, 100, 101, 158
  Austin compared with, 76, 247, 501n
  CBL's marriage and, 123, 124, 125
  CBL's relationship with, 52–54, 64, 67, 102, 103, 123, 247, 503n
  David Boothe's finances and, 145, 146, 159, 507n
  death of, 309–12
  Driftway purchased by, 68, 500n
  in Florida, 247, 302, 309–10, 312
  William Boothe and, 71, 72
Jacobsohn, S. E., 17
Jacobson, Ivan, 503n
Japan, 325, 413, 414, 417, 418, 420, 423, 427–30, 439–40, 443–44, 446, 450–52, 454–56
Jean (New York investor), 157, 158, 159, 508n, 509n
Johnson, Hugh, 194, 195, 518n
Johnson, Jack, 37
Johnson, Paul, 110

Kafka, Franz, 115
Kahlo, Frida, 327–32, *332*, 338, 339, *472*
Kahn, Otto, 273
Karsh, *472*, 530n
Kaufman, George S., 3, 5, 6, 289, 290, 337, 493n
Keables, Ida Boothe (aunt), 150, 158, 497n
Kellems, Vivien, 462, 463–64, 466
Kennedy, Eunice, 445
Kennedy, John Fitzgerald, 436, 445
Kennedy, Joseph P., 197, 259, 317, 318, 322, 340, 341, 364, 372, 398, 535n
Kennedy, Rose, 318, 327
Kenny, George, 377
Kerensky, Alexander, 318
Keynes, John Maynard, 236
Keystone Tire & Rubber Company, 52
Kidlodge, 53–54
Kiernan, John, 539
King, Alexander, 279, 355, 356, 360–62, 397, 463
Kipling, Rudyard, 57, 88, 449, 453
Kiss the Boys Good-bye (Luce), 313–15, 322, 333, 355, 438, 529n
  reviews of, 323–24, 336
Kiss the Boys Good-bye (movie), 324, 368
Kitchener, Lord, 89
Knickerbocker, Cholly, 132, 262, 334
Knox, Frank, 402, 403
Kommer, Rudolf, 219, 273, 361, 425
Krasna, Norman, 305, 306–7
Kreisler, Fritz, 80

Kristallnacht, 325
Krock, Arthur, 158, 237, 259
Ku Klux Klan, 320–21

La Guardia, Fiorello, 402
Lahr, Bert, 6
Larimore, Earle, 278
Larsen, Roy, 250, 325, 358–59
Laurens, Henry, 285
Laval, Pierre, 374, 376
Lawford, Betty, 10
Lawrence, D. H., 165
Lawrence, Gertrude, 6
Lawrenson, Helen Brown Norden, 215–16,
    244, 276, 315, 335, 515n, 522n, 528n
Lea, Homer, 430–31, 441–42
League of Nations, 64, 85
Leech, George A., 15
LeHand, "Missy," 394, 395
Lehár, Franz, 30
Leigh, Vivien, 366
Leland Hayward Agency, 219, 237, 289, 516n
Leonard, Sheldon, 323
Leopold III, King of Belgium, 379, 381
Leopoldskron, 273
Levant, Oscar, 324
Levene, Sam, 354, 356
Lewis, Sinclair, 86, 178, 398, 399, 502n
Life (humor periodical), 283, 288
Life (Luce publication), 324, 347, 361, 410,
    416, 418, 441, 463, 526n
    CBL as war correspondent for, 357, 363–64,
        368–88, 423–33, 429, 436–37, 439, 446,
        449–58, 453, 454, 460
    CBL refused job at, 5, 287, 288
    first issue of, 291
    planning of, 283–84, 287–88
"Life Among the Snobs" (Luce), 173
Lillie, Beatrice, 6, 399
"Lily Maid, The" (Luce), 65–66
Lincoln, Abraham, 20, 217
Lindbergh, Charles, 230, 402
Lin Yutang, 439
Lippmann, Walter, 165, 184, 194, 198, 211,
    226, 264, 396, 402
Lisbon, 382, 385, 386–87
Lloyd George, David, 378
Lockridge, Richard, 11
Loesser, Frank, 324
Loftus, Cecilia, 278
London, 86, 89, 101–3, 106–8, 340–43,
    348–50, 376, 378, 385, 410
Long, Huey P., 171, 196, 259
Long Island, 55–57, 77, 133, 134, 162, 162,
    228, 515n
Longwell, Daniel, 261, 283, 287, 288, 325,
    358–59, 517n, 522n
Longworth, Alice Roosevelt, 217, 259, 399
Longworth, Nicholas, 217
Loos, Anita, 366, 368, 534n
Lorentz, Pare, 226, 522n
"Love Is a Gift" (Luce), 235

Love Is a Verb (Luce), 463, 464
Lovell, Malcolm, 506n
Lowen, Alexander, 43
Luce, Clare Boothe:
    acid wit of, 61, 133, 179, 315, 361, 436,
        457, 522n
    acting of, 4–5, 42, 49–52, 51, 60, 99–100,
        120, 136, 144, 305, 306
    alimony of, 153, 155, 158, 266
    ambitions of, 4, 5, 6, 52, 56, 60, 61, 65–66,
        77–79, 82–83, 92–93, 102–3, 109, 111,
        143, 175, 176, 177, 181, 183, 189, 191,
        198, 224, 225, 229, 231, 255, 264–65,
        287, 297, 304, 305, 314, 342, 361,
        469–70, 500n, 519n
    art collection of, 153, 328, 329, 330, 472,
        530n
    as artistic subject, iv, 133, 216, 226, 333,
        337–39, 338, 446, 447, 531n, 542n
    Asian travels of, 412–33, 415, 429, 446,
        539n
    athleticism of, 26, 33, 81, 82, 84, 93, 101,
        102, 103, 105, 116, 120, 128, 144, 177,
        230, 266, 268, 282, 284, 307, 307, 315,
        316, 337, 496n
    autobiographical elements in writing of, 11,
        12, 154–55, 172–74, 203, 276–77, 295
    "baptism" of, 33
    beauty and glamour of, 5, 34, 42, 60, 67, 76,
        79, 82, 90, 96, 102, 106, 128, 132, 137,
        165–66, 173, 180–81, 215, 216, 234, 237,
        240, 245, 254, 255, 280, 299, 315, 335,
        337–39, 338, 347, 399, 424, 425, 446,
        466
    birthdays of, 15–16, 48, 376, 456
    birth of, 4, 15–16, 24, 407, 495n, 538n
    charm and poise of, 45, 47, 57, 77, 90, 141,
        181, 192, 193, 207, 230, 234, 238, 240,
        290, 301, 372, 390
    as child-adult, 186, 260, 270, 301, 311
    childhood of, 4, 24–48, 27, 35, 47, 101,
        160, 198, 255, 285
    clothes of, 64, 67, 76, 86, 90, 96, 102, 116,
        123, 132, 137, 143, 147, 158, 167, 216,
        221, 240, 275, 290–91, 299, 304, 322,
        333, 343, 388, 399, 425, 446, 466,
        468–69, 471, 503n, 512n, 527n
    coldness of, 216, 255, 330
    competitiveness of, 38, 160, 173–74, 216,
        272, 319
    confidence of, 14–43, 174–75, 177–78, 211
    creative imagination of, 144, 246, 251, 283,
        436; *see also specific works*
    cruelty of, 118, 172, 198, 275, 315–16
    dating and flirtations of, 61–64, 79, 81,
        90–92, 96–99, 101–2, 104–9, 114, 118,
        315, 421–23, 536n
    daughter of, *see* Brokaw, Ann Clare
    as Democrat, 200, 206, 218
    at Democratic National Convention,
        191–92, 194–98, 197
    drinking of, 90, 132, 181, 199, 223, 254

INDEX

drug use of, 80, 181, 234, 281, 358, 510n
education of, 30, 33–34, 35, 36, 37–38, 43,
  55–61, 57, 59, 64–67, 66, 77, 82,
  99–100, 220, 499n–500n
in election of 1942, 448, 459–73, 467, 470,
  472, 543n–44n
European travels of, 46–48, 47, 85–92, 91,
  101–9, 126–28, 130, 145–48, 228,
  236–39, 262–66, 268–76, 317–22, 322,
  340–50, 345
evasiveness of, 100, 101, 255–56, 277,
  501n, 504n
fame of, 4, 57, 99, 112, 132, 189, 229, 305,
  342–43, 365, 368, 424
family background of, 15–23, 219
fantasies of, 94, 102, 123, 199, 200, 304,
  319, 421, 422
feminism and, 111–14, 120–21, 121, 222,
  234–35
foreign language skills of, 65, 102, 103, 128,
  155, 167–68, 182, 510n
health problems of, 45, 143, 156, 208, 220,
  271–72, 274, 290, 336, 439, 510n
in Hollywood, 185–87, 187, 305–7, 305
humor of, 7, 79, 182–83, 237, 251, 314, 329
ideal man of, 63, 82, 94, 185, 248
illegitimacy of, 4, 15, 25, 39–40, 72, 495n,
  504n
income of, 93, 112, 113, 120, 154, 155,
  158, 163, 166–67, 178, 181, 189, 207,
  276, 289, 293, 305, 322, 391, 423, 510n,
  513n
insecurity of, 251, 270, 272, 274, 275–76
intelligence of, 5, 34, 38, 49, 55, 58, 75–76,
  79, 166, 207, 216, 237, 251, 260, 297–98,
  302, 315, 425
last will and testament of, 313
lectures of, 397, 438, 446
loneliness of, 56, 57, 94, 104, 144, 159,
  183, 220, 228, 272, 274, 363, 364,
  503n
love affairs of, 88–98, 116–18, 153, 157, 159,
  168, 178, 180, 185, 187–90, 192–93, 195,
  198–211, 223–27, 238–39, 254, 255,
  276–77, 431–32, 524n
manipulativeness of, 4, 15–16, 168,
  174–75, 216, 234, 247, 255–56, 390,
  460–63
manufacturing job of, 93–94, 503n
marriage considerations and marriages of,
  58, 99, 101, 103, 105, 109, 155, 185, 253,
  262, 488n; see also Brokaw, George
  Tuttle; Luce, Henry Robinson
masculine side of, 104, 179, 226, 315, 461
melancholia of, 16, 26–28, 30, 56, 57,
  93–96, 104, 125, 160, 220–21, 228, 239,
  255, 308–11, 329, 358, 411, 456, 494n,
  496n
modern taste of, 232–33, 251, 273, 296,
  303
as mother, 181, 184, 220, 245, 251, 349–50,
  363, 434, 436, 523n

narcissism of, 56, 57, 61, 67, 73, 156–57,
  255, 260, 274, 277, 301, 397, 436, 438
as newspaper columnist, 5, 234–39, 475–78,
  519n
noms de plume of, 174, 177, 183, 463, 501n,
  543n
old age of, 16, 26, 38, 46, 63, 94, 118, 126,
  209, 510n
painting hobby of, 26, 38, 518n
as playwright, 65–66, 100, 102, 103, 189,
  207, 219, 227, 228, 236, 308, 321–24,
  333–34, 336, 337, 340–43, 351–58,
  360–63, 437, 518n; see also specific
  works
poetry of, 77–78, 84–85, 112, 184, 501n,
  543n
pregnancies and childbirth of, 94–96,
  131–35, 206, 290, 503n, 525n
psychoanalysis of, 160, 358
radio broadcasts of, 410, 439, 471
rejections of, 219, 238, 239, 520n
religious training and experience of, 55–56,
  79–80, 261, 500n
as Republican, 183, 198, 200, 397–405,
  402, 410, 448, 459–73, 467, 470
rumors about, 125, 132, 141, 155, 199, 207,
  262, 267
satirical nature of, 171–74, 182–83,
  237–38, 323–24, 333–34
sexual frustration of, 93, 127, 136–37, 157,
  358
sexuality of, 26–28, 50, 62–63, 65–66,
  126, 135, 157, 200–206, 226, 247,
  252, 308, 431, 436, 463, 496n, 499n,
  515n
short stories of, 173–74, 178, 183, 186,
  188–89
social pretensions of, 163, 176–77, 219,
  299, 304, 316, 358
son desired by, 248, 262, 271, 290
speeches of, 64–65, 85, 399–404, 402,
  406–7, 411, 448, 460, 465, 466, 471
translation work of, 167–68, 178
trust fund of, 145–46
at Vogue and Vanity Fair, 5, 161–75,
  177–78, 180–87, 211–16, 218, 221, 222,
  225–29, 231, 238, 241, 259, 272, 283–84,
  288, 516n, 518n
as war correspondent, 357, 363–64, 368–88,
  423–33, 429, 436–37, 439, 446, 449–58,
  453, 454
weight of, 60, 76, 102, 103, 155, 203, 342,
  348
in Willkie campaign, 397–405, 402, 448
writing problems of, 335, 436–38, 460,
  531n

see also specific people and topics
Luce, Elisabeth, see Moore, Elisabeth Luce
Luce, Elizabeth Middleton Root (mother-in-
  law), 249, 401
Luce, Henry, III (Hank; stepson), 245, 251,
  253, 260, 270, 292, 301, 357, 527n

Luce, Henry Robinson (Harry; second
    husband), 240–76, 278–88, 292–309,
    315–17, 336, 377–84, 387–96, 408–20,
    439, 460, 527n–28n, 536n, 538n
  background of, 171, 249–50
  CBL compared with, 251, 254–55, 282,
    284
  CBL's campaign and, 461, 465, 468, 471,
    543n, 544n
  CBL's clandestine meetings with, 251–52
  CBL's correspondence with, 245–48, 252,
    254–58, 265, 269–72, 305, 306, 309, 313,
    342, 359–60, 364, 372–73, 376–77, 382,
    386, 424, 437, 522n
  CBL's marriage to, 5, 267–68, 272, 275,
    279, 522n
  CBL's meetings with, 240–44, 520n
  CBL's plays and, 278, 279, 292–95, 334,
    526n, 533n
  CBL's problems with, 251, 282, 306, 307–8,
    315–16, 322, 322, 334, 340, 357–64,
    424, 465, 527n, 539n, 543n
  CBL's writing on, 170–71
  in China, 171, 249, 413–20
  David Boothe and, 259, 389–92, 408–10
  divorce of, 244, 248, 253–54, 259–60,
    264–65, 267–68, 270, 273–74, 279
  education of, 250, 251
  European travels of, 266, 269–70, 317–22,
    322, 343–50, 345, 377–82
  events leading to World War II and, 317,
    319–21, 324–25, 348–51
  financial problems of, 273–74, 275
  honeymoons of, 252, 281–85, 282, 287
  lawsuits of, 343, 525n, 535n
  loneliness of, 262–63, 267, 315–16, 342
  at Mepkin, 285, 296–99, 301, 316, 358–59,
    361–62
  New Yorker parody of, 300–301, 304
  passion and romanticism of, 244–46, 249,
    267, 274, 306–9, 372, 521n
  photographs of, 2, 243, 282, 286, 322, 345
  physical appearance of, 240, 304, 520n
  religious beliefs of, 249, 251, 306
  sculpture of, 337–38, 531n
  sexuality of, 252, 268, 270, 284–85, 357–60
  stutter of, 2, 50, 249, 270
  wealth of, 251, 262, 304
  workaholism of, 170–71, 251, 287
  see also Time, Inc.; specific magazines
Luce, Henry Winters (father-in-law), 249,
    262, 304, 541n
Luce, Lila Ross Hotz (Henry's first wife), 242,
    245, 251, 252, 301
  divorce of, 244, 248, 253–54, 259–60,
    264–65, 267–68, 270, 273–74
  in Europe, 270, 271, 274
Luce, Peter Paul (stepson), 245, 251, 253,
    260, 270, 272, 301
Luce, Sheldon (brother-in-law), 279, 288
"Luce Forecast for a Luce Lifetime, A" (Luce),
    442–45

Lunt, Alfred, 6, 397
Lupas, Doris, 337

McAdoo, William, 196
MacArthur, Charles, 219
MacArthur, Douglas, 421, 423, 426–30, 429,
    432, 434, 436–37, 440, 455, 540n
"MacArthur of the Far East" (Luce), 436–37,
    439
McCaffrey, Dominick, 18
McCormack, John, 101
McCormick, Robert, 196
MacDonald, Dwight, 268
Macfadden, Bernarr, 171, 511n
McGinnis, Mae, 520n
MacKay, Clarence, 506n
MacLeish, Archibald, 244, 250, 272
McPherson, Aimee Semple, 171
McReynolds, James, 217
Maginot Line, 372–75, 377, 381, 382, 398,
    400
Main Street (Lewis), 86, 502n
Majestic, 55, 101, 109, 110–11, 126–27
Major, Clare Tree, 99
Malraux, André, 296
Mandalay, 452, 453
Manhattan, 55, 364
Manila, 421–23, 426–33, 429
Mann, Thomas, 84, 178, 354
Manners, Lady Diana, see Cooper, Lady Diana
Mannes, Marya, 240
Mao Tse-tung, 417
March of Time, The (newsreel), 251, 253,
    257–58, 274, 393, 412
Marden, Adrienne, 8, 9
Margin for Error (Luce), 351–57, 386, 533n
Margin for Error (movie), 368
Marie, Dowager Empress of Russia, 88, 502n
Marie, Grand Duchess of Romania, 513n
Marie, Queen of Romania, 171
Marine Corps, U.S., 70, 72, 146, 158
Marlowe, Hugh, 323
Marriott, "Momo," 457
Marriott, Sir John, 457
Martin, Florence, 502n
Martin, John, 241, 283, 284, 288, 518n
Martin, Mary, 324
Mary, Queen of England, 86
Mason, Cassity, 59, 65, 67, 500n
Mason, Grant, 247, 281
Mason, Jane, 247
Maugham, Somerset, 57, 177, 265, 266, 269,
    272, 465
Maugham, Syrie, 164
Mauretania, 47–48
Maurois, André, 166, 183, 321, 396
Maxwell, Elsa, 111, 174, 242, 264, 352, 401,
    522n
Mayer, Louis B., 441
Maymyo, 451–56, 453
Mei-ling Soong, 415, 415, 416, 453, 456
Melinda and Her Sisters (operetta), 111

Melinowski, Marta, 495n
Memphis, Tenn., 28–31
Mencken, H. L., 196, 361, 404
"Mephistophelean Curl, The" (Luce), 65
Mepkin, 296–99, 304, 310, 315–16, 316,
    361–63
  architecture of, 296–97, 298
  guests at, 297–98, 301–2, 309, 315, 316,
    334–36, 358–59, 361–62, 441, 445
  purchase of, 285, 296
Meredith, Burgess, 337
Mesta, Perle, 44, 45
Metro-Goldwyn-Mayer (MGM), 290, 305, 365
Meyer, Agnes, 217
Meyer, Eugene, 217
Mielziner, Jo, 7
Milholland, Inez, 111, 112
Millay, Edna St. Vincent, 165
Miller, Gilbert, 6, 219, 288, 363
Miller, Kitty, 219
Miller, Lloyd D., 62, 99
Milton Piano Company, 20, 24
Miracle, The (morality play), 110–11, 202,
    424
Mistler, Jean, 376
Modigliani, Amedeo, 165
Moley, Raymond, 240
Monte Carlo, 91–92, 93
Montgomery, Bernard, 458
Moore, Elisabeth Luce (sister-in-law), 249,
    265, 297–98, 526n, 544n
Moore, George Gordon, 510n, 511n
Moore, Grace, 221
Moore, Maurice, 297–98, 544n
Moore, Victor, 243
Morand, Paul, 168
Morano, Albert P., 448, 459, 460–63, 468,
    470, 471, 544n
Morgan, J. P., 226, 274
Morgan, Margaret Case, see Harriman,
    Margaret Case
movies, 42, 189, 207, 253, 327
  CBL in, 4, 51–52, 51, 120
  see also specific movies
M. Tecla, 44, 64
Munich, 320–21
Munich conference (1938), 324–25, 353
Muray, Nikolas, 330–32
Murfin, Jane, 366
Museum of Modern Art, 52, 331
music, 17–21, 41, 46, 53, 60, 65, 111, 144,
    153, 242, 436, 498n
  William Boothe's interest and ambitions in,
    17–21, 26, 29, 32–33, 32, 36–37, 71,
    72, 149–50, 151, 152–53, 436, 495n,
    497n
Mussolini, Benito, 183, 318, 321, 324, 325,
    518n
  World War II and, 369–70, 371, 374, 386
My Birth (Kahlo), 328
Myers, Richard, 354, 355, 533n
Myron T. Scudder School, 43

Nash, Ogden, 172
Nashville, Tenn., 31–35, 497n
Nast, Condé, 161, 163, 164, 165, 171, 175,
    181, 182, 192, 207, 237, 242, 267, 294,
    335, 510n, 514n
  CBL as managing editor and, 211–13, 218,
    221, 227–28, 231, 283–84, 288, 518n
  CBL's attractiveness to, 203, 207, 208, 212,
    227, 515n, 518n
  CBL's picture weekly plans and, 241,
    283–84, 524n–25n
Nast, Leslie, 192, 197, 203, 207, 208, 227,
    515n
Nathan, George Jean, 168, 208, 209, 229,
    293, 356
National Woman's Party (NWP), 111–14,
    120–21, 222
Nehru, Jawaharlal, 457, 539n
New Deal, 195, 198, 352, 396, 397–98, 469,
    518n
"New Era, The" (Luce), 77
New Jersey, Schneider family in, 39, 41–42,
    496n
New Masses, 396–97
New National Party (NNP), 191, 194–96, 198
Newport, R.I., 136, 141, 144, 173, 333
New York, N.Y., 20–28, 30, 40, 42–46, 49–53,
    55, 82–83, 129–43, 145, 148, 155,
    179–85, 188, 206–22, 225–28, 233–46,
    253, 262–63, 285–96, 308, 387–88
  CBL's apartments in, 163, 166, 179–80,
    228, 239–40, 245, 253, 259, 266–67, 286,
    287, 302–4
  CBL's childhood in, 4, 24–28, 43–46
  CBL's jobs in, 93–94, 161–75, 180–85, 206,
    222
  CBL's visits to, 64, 65, 69, 70, 80, 114–18,
    125, 126, 363
  slums in, 22–23, 27–28, 39, 43–45, 496n
  theater in, 2, 3–13, 9, 42, 49, 80, 99–100,
    110–11, 113, 276–79, 290–91, 293–95,
    314, 323–24, 355–56
  W. Boothe in, 20–21, 24–26, 28
New York American, 262, 267, 278
New York Daily News, 219, 323
New Yorker, 203, 212, 300–301, 337, 361,
    407–8, 460, 512n, 517n
New York Herald Tribune, 13, 194, 278, 324,
    355, 396, 398, 401, 466–68, 493n
New York Herald Tribune Forum, 402–3
New York Military Academy, 55, 62, 70
New York Mirror, 188–89, 323, 355
New York Post, 324, 494n
New York Times, 113, 120, 173, 278, 314, 329,
    368, 396, 397, 402, 493n
  theater reviews in, 49, 324, 356, 529n
New York Times Book Review, 188
New York World-Telegram, 13, 323–24,
    355–56, 463
Nice, 90–92, 91
Nicholas, Czar of Russia, 88
Nicolson, Harold, 273, 317

Noguchi, Isamu, 232, 327, 328, 331, 338–39, 338, 530n
Non-Aggression Pact, Soviet-Nazi, 351
Norden, Helen Brown, see Lawrenson, Helen Brown Norden
Normandie, 55, 340
North Africa, 449, 456–57
Norway, 375–79
Nugent, Frank, 368

"O, Pyramids!" (Luce's unproduced play), 518n
Obermer, Nesta, 144
Obermer, Seymour, 143–44
Odets, Clifford, 6, 276–77, 351, 533n
Oenslager, Donald, 354
Of Human Bondage (Maugham), 57, 177, 265
Oliver Place Studio, 50–51
Olympic, SS, 92
Olympic Games (1920), 26, 84, 116
O'Neill, Carlotta Monterey, 229
O'Neill, Eugene, 6, 229, 335, 518n–19n
Orbita, RMS, 116
Our Times (Sullivan), 194
Ouspenskaya, Maria, 278

Paddock, Ruth, 152
Paley, William, 273
Pandora's Box (Wedekind), 104
Paramount Pictures, 189, 437
Paris, 47, 47, 88–90, 92, 103, 105–6, 127, 141, 146–47, 183, 239, 269, 274, 275, 319, 321, 343, 371–72, 376–77, 381–85, 503n
Parker, Dorothy, 165, 397, 408, 510n
Patterson, Cissy, 217
Patterson, Morehead, 253–54
Paul, Alice, 111, 113–14, 120, 121
Paul Block syndicate, 234, 238, 239, 520n
Pawleys Island, see Hobcaw
Pearl Harbor, bombing of, 439–40, 541n
Pearson, Drew, 214
Pearson, Malcolm, 276
Pell, Herbert, 386, 398
Pemberton, Brock, 322, 529n
"Perfect Panhandler, The" (Luce), 475–78, 519n
Perry, Antoinette, 322
Pershing, John, 226
Pétain, Philippe, 374, 382
Peters, Edith, 51, 52
Philadelphia, Pa., 6, 19–20, 291–92, 389, 495n
Philadelphia Evening Bulletin, 291–92
Philippines, 420–24, 426–33, 440, 446, 455
Phoenix Art Museum, 339, 530n
Picasso, Pablo, 165, 346
Pickford, Mary, 4, 42, 49
picture magazines, 241, 283–84, 524n–25n; see also Life
Pierlot, Baronne, 347
Pinchot, Rosamond, 111, 202, 237, 326–27, 529n
Pius XII, Pope, 370
Plymouth, Lady, 502

PM, 397, 401
Poland, 348, 350–51, 353, 358, 371, 376, 377, 379, 443, 444, 532n
Poligny, Count de, 384
Porchester, Lord, 108
Porter, Cole, 145, 242
Porter, Katherine Anne, 29, 201
Povah, Phyllis, 7, 9
Powell, Dawn, 513n
Pozzano, Giacomo, 153
Preminger, Otto, 354
Presbyterianism, 249, 262, 265
Priestley, J. B., 96
Princeton, N.J., 323, 354, 355
Princeton Packet, 533n
Prohibition, 132, 182, 194, 227
Pryor, Samuel F., 460
Purdue University, 17

Queen Mary, 322, 322
Quezon, Manuel, 427

Rachmaninoff, Sergey, 60
Racine College, 37, 39, 497n
Radio Corporation of America, 199, 514n
Ray, Man, 165
Red Cross, 64
Reed, David A., 195
Reflected Glory (Kelly), 6
Reinhardt, Max, 110–11, 114, 143, 202, 219, 273, 354
Rennie, James, 278
Reno, Nev., 153–56
Repton Military School, 39, 43
Republicans, Republican party, 85, 148, 183, 191, 194, 198, 200, 218, 344, 448
in election of 1940, 397–406, 402
in election of 1942, 448, 459–73, 467, 470
"Return, The" (Austin), 40–41
Reynaud, Paul, 376, 381, 382, 386
Ribbentrop, Joachim von, 371
Ritchie, Albert C., 196
Ritchie, General, 458
Ritz, 371, 376, 381, 383, 384
"Ritz Racketeer, The" (Luce), 174
Rivera, Diego, 327, 328, 330, 530n
River House, 286, 287, 302
Robbins, Barbara, 278
Roberts, Frank, 450–55, 454, 462
Robinson, Edward G., 530n
Robinson, Henry Morton, 215
Robinson, Joseph, 225
Robinson, Selma, 513n
Rodeheaver, Homer, 46
Rodgers, Richard, 6, 336, 531n
Rogers, Will, 196
Rome, 369–71
Rommel, Erwin, 382, 384
Roosevelt, Eleanor, 225, 226, 294–95, 336, 394, 402, 403, 531n
Roosevelt, Franklin D., 194–99, 206, 218, 221, 269, 298–99, 460

in election of 1940, 396–405
inauguration of, 225–26
Stein's views on, 344–45
World War II and, 325, 369, 372, 377, 379,
    386, 393–96, 398, 401–3, 406–7, 423,
    427, 443, 451, 529n
Roosevelt, Theodore, 204, 351
Root, Elizabeth Middleton, 209, 241
Root, John, 323
Rose, Billy, 3, 10
Rosemary Hall, 251–52, 308
Rosenbluth, Milton, 234, 239, 247, 267, 281,
    290, 358, 390, 392, 521n, 525n
Ross, Harold, 300
Rothschild, Baron Henri de, 529n
Rubens, Alma, 120
Rumania, 350, 351, 377
Russell, Rosalind, 365, 367, 534n–35n
Russia, in World War I, 64–65
Russian Revolution, 88–89
Ryan School of Aeronautics, 408–10, 409

Sackville-West, Vita, 273
Sacred Cow, The (Luce and Gallico), 219,
    233, 516n–17n
St. Joan (Shaw), 341
St. Thomas Episcopal Church, 209, 210,
    222
Salomons, Sir Julian, 505n
Salzburg, 270–73
Sand, George, 238
Sandino, Augusto, 146
Sands Point, N.Y., 134, 135–36, 141, 507n
Sapelo Island, 230–31, 285
Sarnoff, David, 199, 200
Saturday Evening Post, 203, 441
Savely-Sorine, 133
Savonarola (Goethe), 104
Sayre, Francis, 426–27
Scarborough-on-Hudson, N.Y., 237
Schiaparelli, Elsa, 529n
Schneider, Anna Clara, see Austin, Ann
    Clare
Schneider, Arthur (uncle), 23, 496n
Schneider, Charles (uncle), 23, 496n
Schneider, John (grandfather), 21–23, 39,
    41–42, 496n
Schneider, Louisa (aunt), 23, 496n
Schneider, Louisa Weber (grandmother),
    22–23, 41–42, 74, 124, 150, 496n
Scribner's, 188
Sea Island, Ga., 228–31
Seay, Charles, 51
Selznick, David O., 437–39, 446, 468
Selznick, Irene, 424
Seneca Falls, N.Y., 120–21, 121
Seymour, Frances, 184, 186
Seymour, Jane, 7, 9
Shangri-La, 425
Shaw, George Bernard, 341–42
Shaw, Irwin, 315, 528n
Shearer, Norma, 365, 367

Sheean, Jimmy, 439
Shermund, Barbara, 188
Sherry-Netherland, 239–40, 245, 253, 259,
    266–67
Sherwood, Robert, 6, 335
Shurtleff's ranch, 17–18
Simpson, Julian Hamilton Cassan, 107–9,
    108, 116–18, 133, 172, 343, 422,
    507n
  CBL's correspondence with, 118, 127, 128,
    200, 511n
  CBL's investitation of, 128–29
Simpson, Wallis Warfield, 300, 319
Sinclair, Robert B., 5
Sinclair, Upton, 36
Skerrett, Kerry, 100, 105, 112–13, 114, 124,
    205
Smith, Al, 196, 518n
Snow, Carmel, 164
Snyder, Ann Clare, see Austin, Ann Clare
Snyder, Louisa, see Schneider, Louisa Weber
Sobol, Louis, 13
Sound Beach (now Old Greenwich), Conn.,
    5, 68–80, 82, 84, 92–93, 158, 159, 162,
    198, 220, 302
  CBL's fundraiser in, 64–65
  Kidlodge in, 53–54
  Simpson in, 116–17
  William Boothe in, 71–74, 100
South Carolina, 252–61
  see also Hobcaw; Mepkin
Soviet Union, 184, 321, 351, 358, 374, 414,
    443, 444, 456, 512n
speakeasies, 132–33, 211, 257, 506n
Sphinx brothel, 384
Stage, 333–34
Stalin, Joseph, 184, 350, 351, 374, 377, 414,
    512n
Stamford, Conn., Luce residence in, 289, 304,
    323, 460–63
Stamford Advocate, 84–85
Stanley, Oliver, 318, 341, 351, 385
Stanton, Elizabeth Cady, 121
Steichen, Edward, 165, 185–86, 187, 193,
    207, 229, 243
Stein, Gertrude, 232–33, 344–48, 345, 350,
    413, 532n
Stern, G. B., 266, 272
Sternberg, Josef von, 186
Stettheimer, Florine, 233
Steward, Samuel, 346–47
Stilwell, Joseph (Vinegar Joe), 449–53, 453,
    455, 456
Stimson, Henry, 226
Stone, Edward Durell, 296–97
Stopford, Mary Craig, 107
Strachey, Lytton, 155
Strange Interlude (O'Neill), 6
Streicher, Julius, 320
Stromberg, Hunt, 365, 366
Stuffed Shirts (Luce), 188–89, 237–38, 513n
Sudetenland, 321, 325

Index

Suicide of Dorothy Hale, The (Kahlo), 330–32, 332, 338, 339, 530n
suicides, 209, 221, 233, 310, 326–32, 464, 510n, 519n, 529n–30n
Sullavan, Margaret, 6
Sullivan, John L., 18
Sullivan, Mark, 194, 197, 199, 203–4, 204, 207, 216, 217, 234, 239–40, 279, 364, 518n
  CBL as romantic interest of, 204, 515n
  CBL's correspondence with, 223–25, 268–69, 515n, 524n, 531n
  The Women and, 3, 11, 12
Sullivan, Sydney, 216–17
Sun Yat-sen, 416, 430
Supreme Court, New York State, 136
Swanson, Gloria, 3
Swarthout, Gladys, 243
Swope, Herbert Bayard, 198

"Talking Up and Thinking Down" (Luce), 168–69
Talmey, Allene, 404
Tanner, John J., 91–94, 124, 137, 139
Tarkington, Booth, 136
Tarrytown-on-Hudson, N.Y., 58–61, 64
Tartini, Giuseppe, 33
Taylor, Laurette, 216
Tedder, Sir Arthur, 457
Temple, Shirley, 305
Thackeray, William Makepeace, 57, 211
Thaw, Benjamin, 141
theater, 42, 320
  avant-garde, 232–33
  in China, 419–20
  in Germany, 104
  in London, 86, 317–19, 340, 341, 386
  in New York City, 2, 3–13, 9, 42, 49, 80, 99–100, 110–11, 113, 276–79, 290–91, 293–95, 314, 323–24, 355–56
  in Philadelphia, 6, 291–92
  see also specific plays
"This My Hand" (Luce's autobiographical novel fragment), 203, 515n, 530n
"This World of Ours" column, 234–39, 475–78, 519n
Thomas, Gaillard, 327
Thomas, Norman, 206
Thompson, Dorothy, 398–401, 404, 405, 462, 470, 544n
Thompson, Francis, 109
Thompson, Lilian, 117, 118, 122, 505n
Thomson, Virgil, 232–33
Thornburg, Max, 369–70, 386, 464
Thus Spake Zarathustra (Nietzsche), 112
Till the Day I Die (Odets), 533n
Time, 8, 164–65, 171, 212, 240, 244, 274, 279–80, 288, 300, 319, 324–25, 343, 351
  CBL's criticism of, 272
  theater reviews in, 4, 278, 324, 526n
Time Inc., 248, 282–84, 291, 306, 317, 341, 376, 461, 522n, 535n, 539n
  HRL's divorce and, 267–68

male bias at, 5, 8, 287, 300
salaries paid by, 282, 524n
see also specific magazines
Toklas, Alice B., 344, 346–48
Town Topics, 129, 144
Tree, Iris, 361
Trotsky, Leon, 329, 530n
Trudoviki Labor Group, 88
Truex, Ernest, 42, 49
Tscheppe-Weidenbach, Baron T. von, 432
"Turnover" (Krasna), 305, 306–7
Turtle Lake, Wis., 38
Tweedles (Tarkington), 136
Twentieth Century–Fox, 305, 306
"Two on the Aisle" (Luce), 173
Tyrell, Sir William, 502n

Under the Red Robe (movie), 120
Union City, N.J., 41–42
United States, 410–11
  League of Nations and, 64, 85
  in World War I, 50, 57
  World War II and, 325, 349, 379, 386, 393–96, 401–3, 410, 423, 439–44, 468–69, 471, 529n
"U.S. General Stilwell Commands Chinese on Burma Front" (Luce), 450, 456

Valentino, Rudolph, 63
Valéry, Paul, 166
Valor of Ignorance, The (Lea), 430–31, 441
Vanderbilt, Gloria, 141
Vanderbilt, Mrs. William, II, 141
Vanderbilt, William, 111
Vanity Fair, 164–75, 180–86, 201, 204, 237–38, 279, 288, 318, 510n, 511n
  advertising and, 170, 181, 227, 518n
  CBL as managing editor of, 5, 175, 211–16, 218, 221, 222, 225–29, 231, 238, 241, 259, 272, 283–84, 288, 516n, 518n
  CBL's editorial innovations at, 181–83, 227, 511n
  CBL's writing for, 168–73, 177, 188, 189, 227, 240, 248, 512n, 518n, 543n
Van Vechten, Carl, 233, 334
Venuta, Benay, 323
Veterans' Bureau, U.S., 71
Vienna, 105, 321
Vile Bodies (Waugh), 188
Villa Margharita, 252, 257
Villa Mauresque, 265
Villa San Gustin, 266, 268–70, 274, 523n
Villa Thalassa, 127–28
Vogue, 161–67, 207, 288, 329, 362, 404, 434, 510n, 517n
  CBL as caption writer at, 5, 161–65
  CBL's photographs in, 333, 446, 447, 542n
Vreeland, Diana, 530n

Waiting for Lefty (Odets), 6
Wake Island, 425–26
Waldo, George, 463, 543n

INDEX

Waldorf-Astoria, 64, 242–44, 402–3
Waldorf Towers, 228, 302–3
Walker, Jimmie, 145, 196, 207
"Wanted: A Dictator" (Carter), 195
"Wanted: A Post-War Party" (Carter), 194
Ward Seminary (later Ward Belmont
   College), 33–34, 35
Warwick, Earl of, 168
Washington, D.C., 100, 111–14, 216–18, 357
   CBL in, 26, 56, 85, 112–14, 217, 225–26,
     252–53, 259, 323, 393–96, 446
   theater in, 323, 354–55
Washington Post, 217, 218, 228
Watts, Richard, 13, 324, 355
Waugh, Evelyn, 188
"Wealth of Nations, The" (Luce's incomplete
   playscript), 230
Webb, Clifton, 3
Weber, Louisa, *see* Schneider, Louisa Weber
"Wedding Day, The" (Luce playscript), 336,
   531n
Wedekind, Frank, 104, 515n
Weidenbach, Adolf August, 540n
Welles, Orson, 412
Welles, Sumner, 369, 376
Wells, H. G., 25
West, Rebecca, 272
West Point, 61, 62, 65, 66
Weygand, Maxime, 374, 382, 386
"What Price the Philippines?" (Luce),
   446
Whipple, Sidney, 13, 355–56
White, Pearl, 101
White, Theodore, 539n
White, William Allen, 194
White Sulphur Springs, W.Va., 80–82, 148,
   260–61
Whitney, John Hay, 314
Wickett, Walton, 434, 445
Wilde, Oscar, 277, 421
Wilder, Thornton, 250, 335, 344, 532n
Wilhelm II, Kaiser of Germany, 65, 374
Williams, Mrs. Harrison, 194–95
Willkie, Wendell Lewis, 397–405, 402, 410,
   460, 544n
Willoughby, Charles Andrew, 421–24, 422,
   426, 430–32, 436, 440, 441, 442, 463,
   540n
Wilson, Edith, 85, 196
Wilson, Edmund, 165
Wilson, Woodrow, 84–85, 196
Winchell, Walter, 262, 293–94, 323, 355
Windsor, Duchess of (formerly Wallis
   Warfield Simpson), 300, 319
Windsor, Duke of (formerly Edward, Prince of
   Wales), 80–81, 86, 135, 319

"Wings over China" (Luce), 418–19, 423
Wiseman, Sir William, 226, 229–30, 240,
   262, 265, 335
Wister, Owen, 232
Wodehouse, P. G., 56, 172, 189
Wolcot, John ("Peter Pindar"), 499n
Wolfe, Bertram, 329
Wolfe, Thomas, 173
Wolff, Marjorie, 123
"Woman, The" (Lawrenson), 498n, 515n
Women, The (Luce), 3–13, 9, 143, 178,
   287–96, 299, 314, 322, 324, 329, 346,
   355, 438, 497n, 511n, 529n
   autobiographical elements in, 11, 12,
     154–55, 295
   bubble bath in, 7, 11–12, 494n
   description of scenes in, 7–12, 289, 292–93,
     318
   European productions of, 317–19, 321, 340,
     341
   Hart-Kaufman contributions to, 3, 292–94,
     493n
   opening night of, 3–4, 7–13, 293
   reviews of, 11, 12, 13, 291–92, 340, 494n,
     526n
   revisions of, 289, 292–94, 494n
   royalties from, 153, 289
Women, The (movie), 290, 293, 365–68,
   367
"Women in War" (Luce), 235
Women's Political Union, 112
women's rights, 111–14, 120–21
Woods, Al, 276
Woods, Katherine, 396
Woolf, Virginia, 242
Woollcott, Alexander, 49, 173
World War I, 49–50, 57, 64–65, 82, 89, 117,
   166, 183
World War II, 182, 344, 347, 363, 368–88,
   393–98, 412–33, 439–46, 449–58, 453,
   454, 468–69, 497n
   events leading to, 317, 319–21, 324–25
   see also specific countries
Wrangel, Peter, 88
Wray, Fay, 186

Yale University, 250, 411
Yohimbe Tree, The (King and Luce), 361, 362,
   363, 397, 463
You Can't Take It With You (Kaufman and
   Hart), 6
Younger, Maud, 113
Ysaÿe, Eugène, 18
Yuill, Walter, 75, 81, 124

Zanuck, Darryl, 305

Grateful acknowledgment is made to the following for permission to reprint previously published material:

The Baltimore Sun: Excerpt from an article by H. L. Mencken from the November 3, 1940, issue of *The Baltimore Evening Sun.* Reprinted by permission.

Curtis Brown, Ltd: Excerpts from *Dear Sammy: Letters from Gertrude Stein and Alice B. Toklas,* edited by Samuel Steward (Houghton Mifflin, 1977). Copyright © 1977 by Samuel M. Steward. Reprinted by permission of Curtis Brown, Ltd.

Alfred A. Knopf, Inc.: Excerpts from *Europe in the Spring,* by Clare Boothe. Copyright © 1940 by Alfred A. Knopf, Inc. Copyright renewed 1968 by Clare Boothe Luce. Reprinted by permission of Alfred A. Knopf, Inc.

Life magazine: Excerpt from "Wings over China," by Clare Boothe Luce (*Life,* September 8, 1941). Copyright © 1941 by Time, Inc. Excerpt from "Burma Mission II," by Clare Boothe Luce (*Life,* June 22, 1942). Copyright © 1942 by Time, Inc. Excerpt from "Battle for Egypt," by Clare Boothe Luce (*Life,* July 13, 1942). Copyright © 1942 by Time, Inc. All material reprinted by permission of *Life* magazine.

The New York Times: Excerpt from the March 29, 1939, "Off the Record" column by Dorothy Thompson from *The New York Herald Tribune.* Copyright © 1939 by The New York Herald Tribune, Inc. All rights reserved. Reproduced by permission.

The New Yorker: Excerpt from "The Candor Kid, Part I," from *Take Them Up Tenderly,* by Margaret Case Harriman (Alfred A. Knopf, Inc.). Copyright © 1941 by Margaret Case Harriman. Originally in *The New Yorker.* All rights reserved. Reprinted by permission.

Walt and Nora Odets: Excerpt from a letter from Clifford Odets. Reprinted courtesy of Walt and Nora Odets.

ABOUT THE AUTHOR

SYLVIA JUKES MORRIS was born and educated in England, where she taught English literature before emigrating to America. She is the author of *Edith Kermit Roosevelt: Portrait of a First Lady*, and is married to the writer Edmund Morris. They live in New York and Washington, D.C.

ABOUT THE TYPE

This book was set in Goudy, a typeface designed by Frederic William Goudy (1865–1947). Goudy began his career as a bookkeeper, but devoted the rest of his life to the pursuit of "recognized quality" in a printing type.

Goudy was produced in 1914 and was an instant bestseller for the foundry. It has generous curves and smooth, even color. It is regarded as one of Goudy's finest achievements.